Encyclopedia of North American Railroading

150 Years of Railroading in the United States and Canada

Freeman Hubbard

McGraw-Hill Book Company

New York St. Louis San Francisco Auckland Bogotá Hamburg Johannesburg London Madrid Mexico Montreal New Delhi Panama Paris São Paulo Singapore Sydney Tokyo Toronto

Library of Congress Cataloging in Publication Data

Hubbard, Freeman H.
Encylopedia of North American railroading.

Includes index.
1. Railroads—United States—History. 2. Railroads—
Canada—History. I. Title.
HE2751.H8 385'.0973 81-1975
AACR2

ISBN 0-07-030828-4

1234567890 HDHD 8987654321

The editors for this book were Thomas H. Quinn and Beatrice E. Eckes, the designer was Naomi Auerbach, and the production supervisor was Thomas G. Kowalczyk. It was set in Souvenir Light by University Graphics, Inc.

Printed and bound by Halliday Lithograph.

What This Book Is All About

"Most men who have really lived have had, in some shape, their great adventure. The railway is mine." JAMES JEROME HILL

It is mine too, as author of the *Encyclopedia of North American Railroading*. By dramatizing this industry instead of sticking too closely to the nuts and bolts, I show you, the reader, how the railroads came into the United States and Canada in the 1830s and were gradually, painfully modernized over a period of 150 years. I deal mostly in history and biography and anecdotes, re-creating personalities and the excitement, achievements, disasters, and other newsworthy events in the "big parade."

No other single book covers in detail that long span of rail transportation throughout English-speaking North America. There are, of course, technical cyclopedias of motive power, cars, maintenance-of-way equipment, and even model railroading, as well as acres of volumes, many excellent ones, on every phase of railroad history, biography, technology, economics, etc.; also *Offical Guides*, who's whos, catalogs, directories, handbooks, pamphlets, and periodicals.

But in all that literature there was not, until now, an *Encyclopedia of North American Railroading* or its equivalent. There was no liberal education, you might say, in North America's railroad industry for so many years compressed into one big reference book designed to be informative, comprehensive, readable, and accurate enough to settle arguments. I wrote this book to meet a need long felt by myself as an editor-writer, by railroaders, hobbyists, authors, historians, researchers, fellow editors, librarians, lecturers, and radio and TV personnel. Before it went to press, I had railroad public relations personnel, colleagues, and other experts in the field check if for accuracy.

Here, in addition to personalities, drama, and technology, you can find the histories of many individual railroad companies, locomotive and car builders, rail labor unions, railfan clubs, etc.; also such subjects as the opening of the West and Southwest, the invention and development of safety devices and larger, more powerful, and more sophisticated equipment; circus trains, pay cars, railroad boarding houses, trainferries, electrification, trackside graves, the creation of motive power capable of hauling more and more tonnage at higher speeds, the rise and decline of the steam locomotive and rail passenger traffic, and so on.

Space limitation has hampered just about every book author since the days of Johann Gutenberg. As for encyclopedias, there is always a *plus ultra*, a vast reservoir of additional data that could not be packed into a single volume or set of volumes. The authors, compilers, and editors decide what is to be put in or left out. My own judgment was sharpened by my 36 years as the editor of *Railroad Magazine*, a nationally circulated monthly, and by writing during that time hundreds of articles for *Railroad* and other periodicals as well as several books. My first book, which I entitled *Railroad Avenue* to symbolize a way of life, was published by the McGraw-Hill Book Company but is now out of print.

In 1979 the magazine I was editing was merged into the bimonthly *Railfan & Railroad*, with me as editor emeritus. In writing the *Encyclopedia of North American Railroading*, I took more than a little material from *Railroad Magazine* and from my first book and another book of mine, *Great Trains of All Time,* now out of print. I thank *Railfan & Railroad's* publisher, Harold H. Carstens, owner of the old *Railroad Magazine* copyrights, for permission to use such material here.

I wrote (in some cases rewrote) all of the *Encyclopedia* myself, except for six items: "Model Railroading," by William C. Schaumburg, associate editor of *Railroad Model Craftsman*, a Carstens publication; "Diesel-Electric Locomotives," "Diesel-Hydraulic Locomotives," and "Neuhart, David E.," all three by James R. Edmonston, a former *Railroad Magazine* columnist; and "Subway and Elevated Railways" and "Streetcars," both by Roger Arcara, also of the old *Railroad Magazine* staff.

To credit everyone who supplied facts, illustrations, or other material that appears in this *Encyclopedia* would be a task equal to one of the seven labors of Hercules. I would have to mention thousands of *Railroad Magazine* contributors of articles, photographs, letters to the editor, etc., and the public relations personnel of hundreds of railroad companies, the Interstate Commerce Commission, locomotive and car builders, the Association of American Railroads, rail labor organizations, the National Association of Railroad Passengers, railfan clubs, the American Short Line Railroad Association, and a long list of other organizations and individuals.

To this army should be added countless books, periodicals, etc., from which I gleaned some data, and particularly I must credit the source material in my own collection of railroadiana, assembled over two-thirds of a lifetime. I am indebted also to editorial colleagues and railroad friends. Finally, I must thank my schoolteacher wife, Naomi Critchett Hubbard, who assisted me in research, by copyreading each page of manuscript, and with the compilation of the *Encyclopedia* index; and Robert A. Rosenbaum, former editor of general reference books, McGraw-Hill Book Company, who gave me this assignment on the recommendation of author-editor-publisher Oliver Jensen, and whose suggestions, patience, and encouragement helped to keep up my enthusiasm during the 2½ years that it took me to write the *Encyclopedia*.

FREEMAN HUBBARD

A

A&MR *See* ARCATA & MAD RIVER RAILROAD.

AAR *See* ASSOCIATION OF AMERICAN RAILROADS.

AAR-100 *See* LAB-ON-WHEELS.

AE *See* ALGOMA EASTERN RAILWAY.

AFT *See* FREEDOM TRAIN, AMERICAN.

Air Conditioning For more than a century, summer rail travel almost invariably meant open windows through which dust and steam-locomotive soot and cinders poured in to blacken the faces and hands of passengers. Whether the coaches were ventilated or not, the riders often suffered from summer heat. Various air-cooling experiments helped a little, but the history of air conditioning as we know it today did not start on the railroads until the years 1927–1929, when the Pullman Co. began to test the mechanical air conditioning of sleeping cars. In 1929 the Baltimore & Ohio inaugurated one air-conditioned coach, and in 1931 it put into operation the first fully air-conditioned passenger train. Today, most intercity passenger trains and many commuter locals boast air conditioning, and Amtrak is deluged with complaints whenever that equipment breaks down.

Alaska Railroad (ARR) America's northernmost rail line, owned and operated by the U.S. Department of Transportation. It runs from Seward on the Gulf of Alaska and Whittier on Prince William Sound northward through Anchorage and Mount McKinley National Park to Fairbanks and eastward to Eielson Air Force Base,

Harsh weather is an indefatigable enemy of the Alaska Railroad. Here a track has been washed out by a heavy storm and floods. [***The Alaska Railroad***]

with branches to Palmer and Suntrana. The total route length, with branches, is 522 miles.

This standard-gauge line was started in 1912 by an act of Congress calling for a commission to examine the possibilities of rail transportation in Alaska, particularly as to harbors, navigable waters, coalfields, agricultural land, and national defense. Construction began in 1915. Eight years later, a gold spike signifying completion was driven at Nenana by Warren G. Harding, the first President to visit Alaska, who died in San Francisco on his return trip. The line was lengthened by purchase of the 71-mile Alaska Northern and 39-mile Tanana Valley roads. Rehabilitation of the ARR in 1947 eliminated dangerous curves, replaced wooden bridges with steel, laid heavier rail, and improved freight depots, warehouses, and shop facilities.

After the earthquake of March 27, 1964, the worst quake ever recorded in the Western Hemisphere, had wiped out the railroad's yard and port facilities at Seward, with damage estimated at $26 million, additional rehabilitation was undertaken in a frantic race against time and frost. Within a week, trains were running again between Anchorage and Fairbanks; and service to Whittier, the ARR's second port, was restored within a month.

The *AuRoRa* dome train, an outlet from the interior wilderness, runs daily both ways between Anchorage and Fairbanks from Memorial Day through Labor Day, but only biweekly the rest of the year, and often stops to pick up hitchhikers. In 1971, when the Union Pacific turned over its passenger service to Amtrak, it sold the ARR 30 cars, including four dome cars and a business car (private car), at bargain prices. One of the world's largest single-span bridges, 700 feet long and built of steel, takes trains over the Tanana River. Another major ARR bridge, almost 900 feet long, spans Hurricane Gulch.

Railroaders in Alaska, often called the Icebox State, cope with temperatures that sometimes drop to 70°F (57°C) below zero and, at the northern end of the line, frequently undergo variations of 60 to 70°F (33 to 39°C) within a 24-hour period. Between Seward and Portage snowfalls often pile up 15 to 20 feet. Maintenance crews are kept busy all winter using bulldozers, Jordan spreaders, Snow-gos, carryalls, and rotary plows, each plow being propelled by two or more locomotives. Chinook winds often bring warm breezes, causing slides and avalanches which periodically bury hundreds of feet of track. But the line is kept open; rarely is freight delayed more than 3 hours on the road.

At Whittier the average precipitation, mostly snow, is 194 inches a year, as compared with the highest average in other states, 150.75 inches at Wynoochee Oxbow, Washington. More dangerous than snowfalls, drifts, or slides is the ice formed from seepage where the railroad follows a bench cut along the toe of a mountain. Overnight after a quick thaw, ice covers the track level with the top of the rails. Between Mileposts 209 and 350 the ARR crosses the Continental Divide through Broad Pass, 2363 feet elevation, which is claimed to be the lowest pass in the entire Rocky Mountain chain.

A unique ARR problem, which not even the old-timers have been able to solve, is keeping the large moose population off the right-of-way. In winter, with snow piled high on both sides of the track, it is impossible for these beasts to climb the high snow embankments even when a train is coming behind them; so the engineer has to adjust speed to follow the moose until they come to relatively shallow snow. As long as it can keep moving on a narrow winter trail, a moose is more or less safe, but once caught in deep soft snow it falls an easy prey to its deadly enemy, the wolf pack. Sometimes a large bull will turn around, lower its antlers, and charge the train head-on. Or one might break a leg between the ties on a bridge, and the crew kills it. In such cases, track workers dress the meat and donate it to Eskimos or a fishing village.

BIBLIOGRAPHY: Edwin M. Fitch, *The Alaska Railroad,* Praeger, New York, 1967; William H. Wilson, *Railroad in the Clouds: The Alaska Railroad in the Age of Steam, 1914–1945,* Pruitt Publishing Co., Boulder, Colorado, 1977.

Alco *See* AMERICAN LOCOMOTIVE CO.

Algoma Eastern Railway (AE) Originally the Manitoulin & North Shore Railway, it ran 87 miles between Sudbury, Ontario, center of the world's largest nickel-mining region, and Little Current on Manitoulin Island in Lake Superior. Chartered in 1888 and 1900, it was built and operated as part of the industrial empire of American financier Francis H. Clergue, whose Lake Superior Corporation and its subsidiaries made iron and steel, generated hydroelectric power, and ran an international ferry service, two streetcar systems, and a fleet of Great Lakes ships. They also mined iron ore in Ontario and West Virginia, quarried limestone in Michigan, and operated almost 400 miles of railways. The AE had both passenger and freight service, but the Canadian Pacific took it over in 1929 and uses it for freight only.

BIBLIOGRAPHY: Dale Wilson, *Algoma Eastern Railway,* Nickel Plate Rails, 1977.

Allegheny Portage Railway (AP) Quaint and novel transportation system of alternate inclined planes and graded levels over the mountains between Hollidaysburg and Johnstown, Pennsylvania, that opened in October 1834. In its 36 miles of length, power had to be changed no less than 33 times. A dozen stationary engines, as many teams of sturdy horses, nine steam locomotives, and 54 men were required to get a train over the hills, although the line was not equipped with steam until 1851.

There were five levels and five inclined planes on both slopes, with a 1½-mile level at the crest. The line included the first railroad tunnel built in the United States (there were two previous nonrail tunnels in the country): Staple Bend Tunnel, 4 miles east of Johnstown, 901 feet long, 20 feet wide, and 19 feet high. Completed in 1833, it has not been used since 1852. The railway's sleepers (ties) were large stone blocks; on sharp curves and embankments, every third sleeper extended across the track.

An odd feature of the AP was that passengers could, if they wanted to, travel the entire 36 miles by boat. Canalboats, pulled out of Philadelphia on Columbia Railroad cars and moved by rail to Columbia, were towed up the long canal to Hollidaysburg. From there they were carried over the Portage Railway on cars to Johnstown.

The first boat carried by rail over the Allegheny crest was named *Hit or Miss.* It bore westbound emigrant Jesse Chrisman, his family, and possessions. Upon reaching Hollidaysburg it was lifted onto a railway car, waited overnight on the mountain summit, and at Johnstown was put back into canal waters.

At that time the AP was part of the Pennsylvania State Public Works System, but in 1857 the young Pennsylvania Railroad bought it for $7.5 million. Although the Allegheny Portage was never a paying proposition, the Pennsy continued to operate it until November 1857, shortly after completing its own railroad division between Johnstown and Altoona.

Altitudes *See* SUMMITS.

Ambler, Pennsylvania Philadelphia suburb on the old Reading Railroad, originally called Wissahickon and renamed to honor Mrs. Mary Benjamin Ambler because of her Florence Nightingale role immediately after a head-on collision in front of her home on July 17, 1856. A Sunday school picnic train in two sections was to carry 1200 people, mostly children, to a wooded area in the Whitemarsh Valley near Fort Washington. The first 11-car section left Master Street Station 9 minutes late, and at 5:18 a.m. rammed into a mixed train on the single-track line. The boiler on the latter's engine, the *Aramingo,* exploded, setting the coaches afire. With 62 persons killed and more than 100 others seriously injured, it was at that time America's worst train disaster.

Mrs. Ambler ran over to the scene with lint, bandages, and other surgical supplies. All day, under a broiling sun, she cared for the wreck victims, and later nursed many in her home. So officials of the North Pennsylvania Railroad, as the line was called then, gave the local station her name. It still has that name.

On the same day as the Wissahickon train wreck a Lake Erie steamship burned with a death toll of 40. But maritime accidents were regarded as acts of God, while rail disasters were attributed to human errors.

BIBLIOGRAPHY: Wesley S. Griswold, *Train Wreck!,* Stephen Greene, Brattleboro, Vt., 1969; Robert C. Reed, *Train Wrecks: A Pictorial History of Accidents on the Main Line,* Superior Publishing, Seattle, 1968.

American Freedom Train *See* FREEDOM TRAIN, AMERICAN.

American Locomotive Co. (Alco) Company that, with its predecessors, built about 75,000 steam locomotives, including historic ones like the *Jupiter,* which carried into Utah the golden spike that linked East and West with transcontinental rails in 1869. But in June 1948 Alco stopped producing steam power and concentrated mostly on diesel-electrics. At that time 7652 of its diesel locos were already in global service. Its main plant in Schenectady, New York, covered 112 acres, and it had eight other plants, besides being affiliated with Montreal Locomotive Works in Canada.

In April 1955 it dropped the time-honored name American Locomotive Co. and became Alco Products, Inc., because, in addition to locomotives, it was manufacturing many other industrial items such as oil-drilling rigs, stationary and marine diesel engines, atomic power plants, and nuclear components. Then came higher costs, increasing competition, labor problems, and managerial mistakes, and in 1969 Alco got out of the locomotive business altogether, although its locos were still hauling trains throughout the United States and in more than 50 foreign countries.

American Locomotive Co. was formed at Schenectady in 1901 with Samuel Galloway, president of New York Central, as its first president. It was a combination of eight previously unrelated locomotive works: Brooks of Dunkirk, New York; Cooke of Paterson, New Jersey; Pittsburg of Allegheny, Pennsylvania; Richmond of Rich-

Alco built the first United States diesel-electric passenger train and was for years a major manufacturer of the unit for passenger and heavy-duty freight service. Pictured is a 1947 scene from its Schenectady, New York, plant. [American Locomotive Co.]

mond, Virginia; Rhode Island of Providence, Rhode Island; Schenectady of that city; Dickson of Scranton, Pennsylvania; and Manchester of Manchester, New Hampshire. Later, the ninth and oldest company, Rogers of Paterson, joined them. American Locomotive's biggest competitors, Baldwin and Lima, are chronicled separately. *See* BALDWIN LOCOMOTIVE WORKS; LIMA LOCOMOTIVE WORKS; PATERSON, NEW JERSEY.

Alco sprang from the Schenectady Locomotive Engine Manufactory, known as the Big Shop, which began production on September 27, 1848, shortly before the merger that formed the New York Central & Hudson River Railroad (NYC&HR), the components of which were among its best customers. Tall smokestacks blackened the sky at the plant beside the Erie Canal. Alco's first iron horse was the *Lightning,* a single-drivered, high-wheeled Crampton type designed by the famous Norris brothers, Edward and Septimus, of Philadelphia. It weighed 15 tons, as compared with the 450 tons of a modern diesel-electric passenger hauler, and pulled an eight-car train 82 miles in 81 minutes on the Utica & Schenectady, an antecedent of the NYC&HR, but failed otherwise because it was weak in starting power and tractive effort. With this flop, the anticipated bright future of the plant under the Norrises faded, and in 1850 the Philadelphians went back home.

For nearly a year the manufactory stood idle. In 1851 four local men reactivated it, and in 2 years it built 23 engines. Then Walter McQueen of Albany, New York, was hired as master mechanic and general superintendent; later he was made vice president. McQueen became one of the nation's leading designers and builders of iron horses. Under him, Schenectady set a high standard with very few, if any, freak designs. Hundreds of McQueens, as the 4-4-0 engines themselves were called, rolled out of the erecting shops. One was the elegant *Commodore Vanderbilt,* with Vanderbilt's portrait painted on the huge box headlight. Incidentally, Walter McQueen helped to set up in Schenectady what is now the General Electric Co., which was to collaborate for many years with Alco in producing diesel-electric locomotives.

In 1864 McQueen became part owner of the Schenectady works upon the death of its president, John Ellis. Ellis's four sons successively served as president until 1901, when the American Locomotive Co. was created and took over the Big Shop. Also in 1901, fire destroyed much of the plant, but new machine, boiler, and erecting shops were built. The works then had nine huge buildings filled with activity. Its employment peak was 6200 in 1907 and again in World War II.

The first of 10 streamlined Hudson-type steam locomotives that Alco built for New York Central's 20th Century Limited. Henry Dreyfuss designed the streamlining. [New York Central Railroad]

By 1900 the average weight of an American engine was 4 times that of the original *Lightning.* Arthur J. Pitkin had joined the works as chief draftsman and was influencing it to build increasingly heavy locomotives. Pitkin advocated large boilers and bigger grate areas. He introduced the cross-compound engine, which had a high-pressure cylinder and a low-pressure cylinder, using the steam twice and saving coal and water. Technical progess up to 1935 was due largely to greater boiler pressure. From 1905 to 1920 horsepower remained standard at about 200 pounds per square inch. In 1935, however, 300 pounds was not uncommon.

In 1904 the company built America's first Mallet compound, which had a 0-6-6-0 wheel arrangement and was sold to the Baltimore & Ohio. By using the compounding principle, the locomotive, with its two driving axles from a single boiler, developed additional power and could haul loads previously thought impossible. The trend to Mallets for heavy freight work lasted until the steam era ended.

Francis J. Cole built the company's first four-cylinder compound. The compounds saved fuel and water but lost favor when the superheater was perfected. Cole was one of America's foremost designers of simple locomotives up until World War I. His most publicized creation was Alco's 50,000th locomotive, outshopped in 1910 and delivered to the Erie. This was the first engine in the United States to use cast-steel cylinders and the first of the big Pacifics, which dominated passenger service for many years.

The Mohawk (2-8-2) type came into being in 1916, followed 11 years later by the Hudson (4-6-4), in 1935 by the *Hiawatha,* the country's first streamlined loco, for the Milwaukee Road, and in 1945 by the Niagara type (4-8-4). In 1941 Schenectady built the first Big Boy, the world's biggest loco, for Union Pacific (UP). Weighing 1,200,000 pounds, this 4-8-8-4 Mallet had sixteen drive wheels packing a 7000-horsepower wallop. Other Big Boys followed, all for UP.

Despite the technological advances in steam power, Alco faced growing competition from the more economical performance of internal combustion. So in 1924 it teamed up with General Electric and Ingersoll-Rand to create the nation's first commercially successful diesel-electric, a 300-horsepower switcher, shaped like a box, for Jersey Central's Bronx yards in New York City. Application of "juice" power was not new to Alco. In the same year, a straight all-electric loco was produced. But since electrification alone was considered too costly, experts began turning to electric power with diesel engines.

In 1929 Alco delivered American's first passenger diesel-electric to the New York Central. Two years later the first diesel-electric with an Alco diesel engine went to the Jay Street Terminal Railroad in Brooklyn. For years afterward, about 80 percent of all diesel-electric switchers serving United States railroads were built in Schenectady. By 1941, 62 percent of the company's orders were for Alco diesels. Traditional resistance to the use of such power was dwindling.

World War II temporarily halted this trend. The federal government called on Alco to build steam locos and great quantities of combat weapons and marine diesel engines. During that war the Big Shop produced more than 2000 steam locomotives on military orders. Afterward, Alco spent over $20 million on conversion to the manufacture of diesel-electrics. In 1962 Alco Products, as the company was then called, got more than 50 percent of the world's export orders for mainline diesel-electric power. But by 1969 the corporation was in serious financial difficulty.

E. G. Forbes, president of Alco Products, blamed the situation on a 1952 decision to sever Alco's ties with General Electric. "Alco vowed it would buy its electrical equipment elsewhere," he said, "and GE went into the locomotive business on its own. This put us in the untenable position of buying some 30 percent of every locomotive we make from one of our competitors." For that reason, in 1969 the Big Shop finally stopped building locomotives, thus ending a great era that had begun in 1848.

See also KUHLER, OTTO; MALLET.

BIBLIOGRAPHY: Angus Sinclair, *Development of the Locomotive Engine,* annotated ed. by John H. White, Jr., M.I.T., Cambridge, Mass., 1970; John H. White, Jr., *American Locomotives: An Engineering History, 1830–1880,* Johns Hopkins, Baltimore, 1968.

American Short Line Railroad Association (ASLRA) Organization that describes itself as "a nonprofit, unincorporated association comprised of Class I and II line-haul, switching, and terminal companies . . . with a Board of Directors elected regionally. The action of the Association is advisory and not binding on any of its members." Headquarters is 2000 Massachusetts Avenue, Washington, D.C. 20036, with other offices in Chicago and Atlanta. Regional groups founded in New York City, the South, the Southeast, and the Pacific Coast in 1910, 1911, and later years led in March 1917 to the present ASLRA, which maintains regular contact with federal departments and boards, particularly the Interstate Commerce Commission, and friendly relations with the Association of American Railroads (AAR).

Its objectives are "to provide cooperative action in the consideration and solution of problems of management and policy affecting the operation or welfare of short-line railroads" and "to promote federal legislation of benefit and resist the enactment of legislation that would be detrimental to the railroad industry." In those respects, ASLRA basically does for small railroads what the AAR does for big ones. *See* ASSOCIATION OF AMERICAN RAILROADS.

BIBLIOGRAPHY: Edward A. Lewis, *American Short Line Railway Guide,* The Baggage Car, 1978.

Ames Monument Plot A pyramid of rough-hewn granite, 60 feet square at the base, on the Union Pacific (UP) mainline in the Wyoming badlands, honors the memories of Oliver and Oakes Ames, the shovel and tool manufacturers who helped to finance the construction of the transcontinental line in the late 1860s. UP erected this landmark at a cost of $75,000. Huge medallions of the two brothers, carved in sandstone from their native Massachusetts, adorn its eastern and western faces. The monument stands 8300 feet above sea level on the Omaha-Ogden line. An airport is now located nearby. For a brief period the monument was not UP property, the explanation for which is unparalleled in railroad history.

When an act of Congress dated July 1, 1862, signed by President Abraham Lincoln, authorized the building of this line, UP became a land-grant railroad. That is, the federal government parceled out the land between Omaha and Ogden into strips each 20 miles wide on both sides of the track. Each strip was numbered. The company was given the odd-numbered sections to retain or sell as it chose, as an inducement for capitalists to back the construction of the transcontinental railroad. The government held the even-numbered sections. To encourage colonization along the route, it allowed anyone to claim 40 acres anywhere in the even-numbered sections as long as the land supply lasted. Each claimant was entitled to everything on the land: oil, gold, vegetation, buildings, and so on.

The Ames pyramid was constructed by the Union Pacific Railroad in Wyoming to honor Oliver and Oakes Ames, the shovel and tool manufacturers who helped finance the construction of that transcontinental line in the 1860s. [Union Pacific Railroad Museum Collection]

The Union Pacific was confident that it had erected its monument on one of its own odd-numbered strips. Everyone else thought so, too, until Billy Murphy, justice of the peace at Laramie, Wyoming, looked into the matter in the mid-1880s and was elated to find otherwise. Upon learning that the pyramid was located on Section 6, he quickly filed a claim, with a lawyer's help, for the 40 acres on which it stood.

Then, with a legal deed to the land actually in his pocket, he acquired a list of men engaged in outdoor advertising such as painting huge signs on big old buildings, rocks, and cliffs and let it be known that as owner of the renowned Ames Monument he was ready to receive bids for advertising space on it. The bids he received were munificent. One offer was $25,000 for the entire side of the pyramid that faced the railroad tracks, plus an additional $2000 annual royalty for as long as the proposed sign or signs remained.

Murphy wrote to the Union Pacific general offices in Omaha, announcing that he owned the land and telling what he planned to do with it, hoping that UP would buy him out at a higher price than advertisers would pay. The railroad officials were amazed and chagrined. They checked on Murphy's deed, found it was genuine, and looked into the character of the law officer himself to see if they could get anything on him. But Murphy's reputation was good. They would have to deal with him directly. So they sent three shrewd representatives to adjust this very embarrassing situation. The trio had instructions to buy the land even if they had to pay a staggering sum, up to $30,000. They resorted to threats, charging Murphy with conspiracy and other crimes. Although he had a clear title, he lost his nerve under the browbeating and finally gave up his dreams of wealth for a paltry $300. Even at that, the representatives repaid him not in cash but with other land. Thus the Union Pacific repossessed its famed Ames pyramid.

Gleaming new turbine trains imported from France added a streamlined look to Amtrak's revitalized intercity rail passenger network. [*Atlantic Container Line—USA*]

Amtrak (National Railroad Passenger Corp.; NRPC) Headquartered in Washington, D.C., Amtrak is basically a contractor buying service from the 19 railroads over which it runs passenger trains. It was created on October 30, 1970, by the Rail Passenger Service Act and actuated in May 1971, originally for a 2-year experimental stage, and was given expanded authority by congressional acts of 1973, 1974, 1975, 1976, and 1978. Prior to incorporation, the preliminary details were handled by an eight-man board, which decided, among other things, which specific rail routes should connect the 22 pairs of cities (only 22 pairs, although the country's rail mileage totaled 209,000), designated by the Secretary of Transportation, and with which trains, frequencies, and types of service. It is significant of the times that Amtrak was created in the same year as the gigantic merger of the Burlington Northern. *See* BURLINGTON NORTHERN INC.

Amtrak's formation was proposed as it became more evident that the United States could not rely solely upon further massive construction of highways and airports to meet its domestic travel needs. Highway traffic involves congestion, noise, and air pollution, excessive land use for which further dislocation of people makes space for still more road building, and appalling casualty lists. Railroads, on the other hand, already have rights-of-way and tracks (not used to full capacity) into the major population centers; and the number of human beings killed or injured by trains is but a small fraction of the highway casualties. Another good reason for mass transportation is the energy crisis. As for airlines, it is estimated that 25 million Americans fear to travel by plane.

From another viewpoint, you might call Amtrak a last-ditch effort to keep intercity passenger trains from total oblivion. Back in 1929, the nation's railroads, operating some 20,000 passenger trains, had proudly carried 77 percent of all intercity mass transportation, and it looked as if they always would. Buses ran a very poor second, 15.4 percent. The airlines' share in those days was negligible. But even then the widely prevalent private automobile was a fast-multiplying competitor.

Then the dam broke. By 1970 all but 450 intercity passenger trains had vanished, and 100 of those were doomed. The once-luxurious dining service on rails had begun to use paper napkins and slot machines. In that year the railroads' share of intercity mass transportation was a feeble 7.2 percent. Buses held onto barely 16 percent. Airlines had captured 73 percent of the intercity mass transportation. Most intercity travel, however, was and is in private autos. Motorists were classing the passenger train with the horse and buggy.

So Amtrak was created to manage the remnants of the intercity rail passenger network, modernize it, revive public interest in train travel, and operate it as far as possible on a for-profit basis. Nearly all of the big railroads, the Southern being one exception, were quite willing to let the new Amtrak operate their unprofitable passenger service.

Almost with Amtrak's inception, rail ridership, which had been dwindling for many years, reversed the trend and began to climb upward. In 1972, Amtrak's first full year of operation, ridership gained about 11 percent, with a total of 15,600,000 passengers. In 1977 the figure rose to 19,200,000, thanks to all Amtrak had done to modernize and publicize its equipment and service.

The corporation had been forced to start with a leased fleet of 1275 old cars inherited from the railroads. By 1977 more than three out of every four passenger cars on relatively short runs were handsome new Amfleet or Turboliner equipment bought by Amtrak in the previous 3½ years. Almost half of all Amtrak's nationwide passengers were using new equipment. By 1979 gleaming new Superliner cars were handling long-distance travel in the West.

Over $658 million had been spent or committed to buy new cars, turbine trains, and new diesel and electric locomotives. Also, compared with 1971, there were more places served by Amtrak, a modern reservation system, new and improved city stations, additional suburban stops, and more comfortable conditions on the trains. By law, Amtrak is permitted to experiment with routes or service frequencies at any time and often does so. It makes considerable use of name trains and of package excursions in connection with other forms of transportation, travel agencies, hotels, and so on, all over the United States, including Alaska, and to some extent in Canada and Mexico.

NRPC is financed by a combination of earned revenues from passenger service operations and federal government aid, also by a $197 million entry fee paid by the railroads over a 3-year period as compensation for Amtrak's assumption of their rail passenger service. This fee was equivalent to one-half of the participating roads' passenger service operating losses for 1969.

Far from being independent, Amtrak is subject to varying degrees of oversight, review, regulation, auditing, etc., by a long list of federal, state, and local government agencies. Its board of directors has 17 members: 8 appointed by the President of the United States, 2 ex officio members, and 7 representing the stockholders. It has servicing and repair shops in 20 cities.

Although Amtrak eliminated 5000 route miles and six long-distance trains in the fiscal year ended November 1, 1980, on the orders of Congress, during that year it hauled an increasing number of passengers, to a total of 21,200,000. This gain was due to a larger number of reliable railcars available and the rising price of gasoline. But in early 1981 the federal budget cuts requested by President Ronald Reagan threatened to reduce considerably Amtrak's services to the traveling public.

VIA, the Canadian equivalent of Amtrak, was formed in 1976 to take over most of Canada's intercity rail passenger service. *See* VIA RAIL CANADA, INC.

BIBLIOGRAPHY: Lucius Beebe and Charles Clegg, *The Trains We Rode,* 2 vols., Howell-North, Berkeley, Calif., 1965-1966; Arthur D. Dubin, *Some Classic Trains,* Kalmbach, Milwaukee, 1964; Harold A. Edmonson (ed.), *Journey to Amtrak,* Kalmbach, Milwaukee, 1972; Robert J. Wayner, *Amtrak Car Spotter,* Wayner Publications, New York, 1972.

Andrews Railroad Raid A Georgia newspaper, *The Atlanta Confederacy,* on April 25, 1862, described this raid as "the most thrilling railroad adventure that has ever occurred on the American continent." It was possibly the most dramatic piece of rail lore of the Civil War. The raid was brilliantly planned and boldly carried out on April 12, 1862, by 22 Union saboteurs—20 Ohio soldiers and two Kentucky civilians. Their aim was to seize a Western & Atlantic Railroad (W&A) train in Georgia and steam northward, destroying the tracks behind them, cutting telegraph wires, and setting fire to wooden bridges to sever rail connections between Chattanooga and Atlanta, thus crippling the single-tracked line and isolating a big Confederate supply base.

"Had they succeeded in burning the bridges," said *The Atlanta Confederacy,* "the enemy at Huntsville [Alabama] would have occupied Chattanooga before Sunday night. Yesterday they would have been in Knoxville, and thus in possession of all East Tennessee. . . . It was by no means improbable that our army in Virginia would have been defeated, captured, or driven out of the state this week." Had the Andrews men won their gamble, the Civil War might well have been shortened by 2 years.

James J. Andrews (1829-1862), born in Virginia (now West Virginia) and residing at Flemingsburg, Kentucky, led the raid. A six-footer, slender and bearded, he was dressed that day like a Southern gentleman in high silk hat, long frock coat, white shirt and collar, small bow tie, gray striped trousers, and boots under the trousers. Andrews had leadership qualities but no railroad or military experience. He had tried a similar foray before, penetrating as far south as Atlanta, but failed then because nobody in his band was familiar with locomotives. This time he took no such chances. His party included two experienced engineers: Pvt. William Knight of the Pittsburgh & Fort Wayne Railroad and Corp. Wilson W. Brown of the Mobile & Ohio (on which Casey Jones would get his first railroad job in 1880).

Knight wrote: "I was introduced to Andrews, who at once unfolded to me his daring plan to capture a train at Big Shanty, Georgia, and run for the Union lines, leaving a trail of blazing bridges behind him. There were 15 bridges between Big Shanty and Chattanooga."

On the rainy night of April 11 the saboteurs stayed at hotels in Marietta; and at about 5:30 the next morning 20 of them took a northbound train to Big Shanty, the 2 others being inadvertently left behind. Normal running time for the 137 miles between Atlanta and Chattanooga—11 hours and 40 minutes, including stops—gives you an idea of train speeds in those days. Shortly after 6 o'clock on a misty, drizzling morning the conductor's voice rang out: "Big Shanty! Twenty minutes for breakfast!"

There was no station, just the two-story frame Lacy Hotel, a little freight shed, and, across the track, a Confederate army camp. The Unionists were not going to eat with the passengers and crew but unloaded with them. Andrews spoke in an undertone: "If anybody interferes, shoot him! But don't fire unless it is necessary."

The Yankees looked around with anxious curiosity. Mostly they gazed at Camp McDonald, where, they had been told, some 3000 recruits were being trained to fight under the Stars and Bars. Andrews and engineer Knight, followed by Pvt. John (Alf) Wilson, who would act as fireman, strolled over to the engine. It was an eight-wheeled woodburner, built in 1855 at the Rogers Locomotive and Machine Works in Paterson, New Jersey, and named the *General.* All the engine and train crew men had gone to breakfast.

Without arousing the camp sentry's suspicion, Knight yanked out the coupling pin from between the third boxcar and the mail-baggage car, so that when the train pulled out, the heavier combination car and coaches would be left behind. Then Andrews directed: "Let's go now, boys! Get in! Get in!" He climbed into the wooden cab with his two engineers and Wilson. The other Yankees hid in the boxcars. Knight released the brakes and opened the throttle. The four cast-iron driving wheels, each 5 feet in diameter, gripped the slippery rails and began to revolve.

One of the men, Sgt. William Pittenger, who later became a clergyman and wrote books about the raid, revealed how he had felt then: "It was a moment of triumphant joy that will never return. Not a dream of failure shadowed my rapture. All had told us that the greatest difficulty was to reach and take possession of the engine, and after that success was certain."

The Confederate engine General, shown here, and three cars were seized by Union raiders, led by James J. Andrews, in 1862, in a bold but futile attempt to sever rail connections between Atlanta and Chattanooga. [Collection of James G. Bogle]

But one force was still to be reckoned with: conductor William A. Fuller (1836–1905), young, bearded, and robust. Fuller had been put in charge of the mixed (freight and passenger) train to bring commissary stores from Chattanooga to Atlanta; so the boxcars seized by the raiders were empty. He was eating at a table in the hotel dining room with his engineer, Jeff Cain, and Anthony Murphy, the foreman of machinery and motive power on the Western & Atlantic, a railroad owned by the state of Georgia, when the sudden chug-chug of a locomotive interrupted the meal.

Fuller hurried over to the nearest window with his companions and looked out. "Somebody's running off with our train!" he exclaimed. He did not suspect then that Federal spies had stolen it, but thought deserters from Camp McDonald had done so to avoid military service. Big Shanty having no telegraph facilities, the three railroad men set out afoot in pursuit of the *General* and three cars, expecting to find them abandoned a few miles up the line.

Meanwhile, the saboteurs had ridden the stolen train for about 2 miles to Moons Station, where they saw a section gang engaged in trackwork. They persuaded the laborers to surrender their implements on the ground that General Beauregard's army needed them. They took up a section of rail and lifted it into one of the boxcars. "Only two southbound trains to pass," Andrews exulted, "and then we'll put our engine at full speed, burn the bridges after us, and dash through Chattanooga."

But such was not the case. They had to pass more freights on sidings than they had expected, because the Confederates were moving equipment southward to get it beyond the reach of advancing Federals. This slowed the raiders considerably. When he was challenged, Andrews bluffed it out. "I've taken this train by government authority to run ammunition through to Corinth for Beauregard, who must have it at once. Fuller is coming behind with a passenger train."

After crossing the Etowah River, the saboteurs made two fatal mistakes, both due to overconfidence. They saw an old ironworks engine, the *Yonah,* under steam on the turntable, but did not disable it to prevent pursuit, and they failed to burn the bridge.

Meanwhile, Fuller, Cain, and Murphy had been running to Moons as fast as their legs could carry them. No horse was available there, but they borrowed a rail push car (not to be confused with a lever-operated handcar) and resumed the chase. By this time they were convinced that Damyankees, and not Confederate deserters, had stolen their train. Four trackmen, seated on corners of the push car, propelled it by kicking at the ties for 17 miles, mostly downgrade. They lifted the vehicle over the gap from which Andrews's men had removed a rail. At the Etowah River they boarded the *Yonah.*

Reaching Kingston in the *Yonah*'s cab, they found the yards so blocked by southbound freights that they could not get through. Abandoning the *Yonah,* they resumed the chase with another engine, the *William R. Smith* of the Rome Branch Railroad. Soon they were halted by the absence of two rails which the Northerners had removed. Then they ran afoot again, this time for 2 miles, flagged a southbound freight, and resumed the chase in its engine, the *Texas,* which Danforth, Cooke & Co. had built at Paterson, New Jersey.

Farther up the line, Andrews ordered a stop north of Calhoun to cut wires and rip up a rail; but before the rail could be loosened, they heard the shrill whistle of the *Texas* and quickly reboarded their train. The chase was so hot now that there was no time to lift rails or burn bridges, but they kept dropping ties on the track behind them to impede the pursuers. Then they vacated the rear boxcar, set it afire, and left it on a trestle, hoping the Confederates would run into it. But the pursuing engineer managed to shove it onto a sidetrack. Once more the Unionists released a boxcar, but with the same result.

The *General*'s fuel and water were fast dwindling. Knight wrote: "There is little more to tell. Wilson had thrown the last stick of wood into the fire, and water was not showing in the gauge. Soon we were running only 25 miles an hour, then 20, then 15; and then came Andrews's last command: 'Stop her, Knight! Scatter, boys! It's every man for himself now.' "

The chase had lasted about 8¼ hours, beginning at Big Shanty and ending at Ringgold, not far from the Tennessee state line. The *Texas* was less than 400 yards away when the *General* panted to a halt at the summit of a grade. Those few raiders who had remained on the train until the last fled precipitately to the woods. Within about a week all 22 Unionists had been rounded up, including the 2 who had been left behind at Big Shanty (later renamed Marietta).

Andrews was hanged in Atlanta on June 7, 1862, on almost the same day which had been set for his wedding. He died gallantly. "Boys," he said, "I have often thought I would like to see what lies on the other side of the river Jordan." Eleven days later, 7 of his followers met the same fate. Their 14 surviving comrades were thrown into Southern dungeons, from which 8 escaped to the Federal lines. In 1863 the remaining 6, gaunt and emaciated, were exchanged for prisoners held by the Yankees.

The Georgia Legislature voted a gold medal to William A. Fuller, but gold being so scarce in the South in those days, it was never minted. Fuller was fired by carpetbaggers who took over the Western & Atlantic, and he got a job with the Georgia-Pacific. Walt Disney produced a feature film on the Andrews raid, called *The Great Locomotive Chase.*

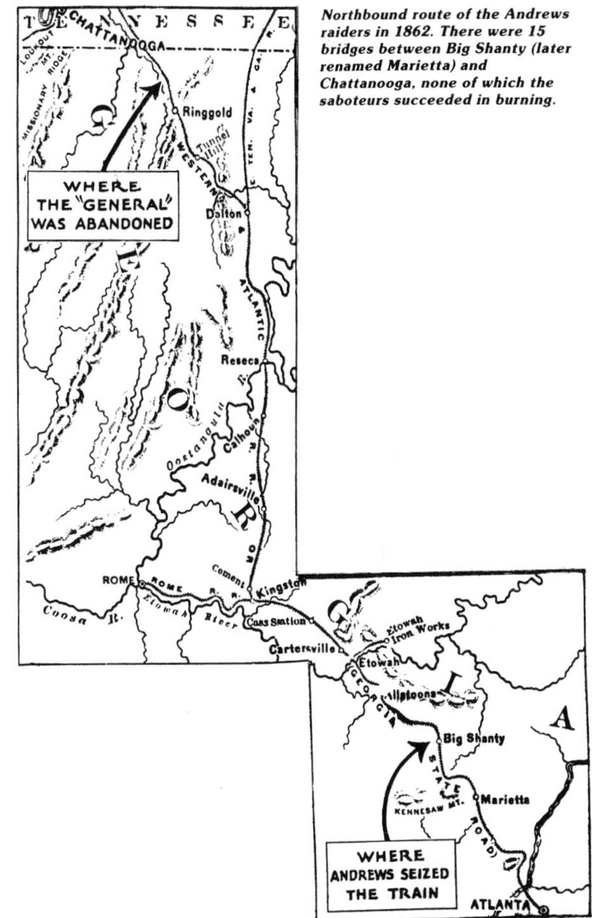

Northbound route of the Andrews raiders in 1862. There were 15 bridges between Big Shanty (later renamed Marietta) and Chattanooga, none of which the saboteurs succeeded in burning.

Both the *General* and the *Texas* continued to serve the South for many years. You can see them today in Chattanooga and Atlanta respectively. The *Yonah* ended its days ignominiously as a stationary engine at the W&A shops in Atlanta. The purported remains of the only other engine involved in the chase, the *William R. Smith,* are displayed in Birmingham, Alabama.

The National Cemetery at Chattanooga contains a monument which the state of Ohio erected to its seven sons and James J. Andrews who were hanged for their part in the raid. The eight headstones range in a semicircle, with a small replica of the *General* surmounting the shaft. In addition, bronze-and-granite markers at Kennesaw, the present name of Big Shanty, and Ringgold designate the beginning and end of the chase.

BIBLIOGRAPHY: Roberta S. Feuerlicht, *Andrews' Raiders,* Crowell-Collier, New York, 1967; Freeman Hubbard, *Railroad Avenue,* McGraw-Hill, New York, 1945, William Pittenger, *In Pursuit of the General,* reprint, Golden West Books, San Marino, Calif., 1965.

Angola Wreck "The winter massacre of travelers begins," *Harper's Weekly* commented on the Angola bridge disaster on the night of December 19, 1867. That wreck was like the one at Prospect, Pennsylvania,

5 years later, in that the engine and tender were safe across an old wooden bridge when two cars derailed, plunging into a snow-covered gully and burning many persons to death.

Angola was on the Lake Shore & Michigan Southern mainline 22 miles west of Buffalo. Near its station a truss bridge 40 feet high and 100 feet long spanned the shallow Big Sisters Creek. The eastern shore was low and flat; the western bank rose abruptly to the level of the surrounding country. Trains approached eastbound down a sharp grade.

The *New York Express,* due in Buffalo at 1:30 p.m., was 2 hours behind schedule. Engineer Charles Cascadin denied later that he had tried to make up lost time at Angola. He passed the tiny frame depot without stopping. Several hundred yards farther on, the last coach of his six-car train loosened an axle as it crossed a switch frog, throwing the wheels 1½ inches off normal position.

Cascadin did not immediately discover anything wrong. He dragged the crippled car along to the bridge, ¼ mile from the station. By that time it had left the rails, pulling off the coach just in front of it. Both derailed cars made a frightful racket that terrified the passengers. Then the rear car broke loose and fell down to the bank of the frozen creek on the north side. The second car from the end had almost reached the far side of the wooden span when it, too, plunged down to the south bank.

The train stopped. Passengers and crew, peering downward in the darkness, saw a horrid scene. Forty feet below, about 50 persons were trapped in wreckage, some still alive and struggling to escape. Piteous cries and groans rent the cold air. The car's cast-iron seat supports had been screwed down to the floor, but the sudden jolt hurled the seats, loaded with their jagged iron supports, from one end of the coach to the other, probably disabling all the passengers who were not immediately killed. "A death more horrible can hardly be conceived," editorialized *Harper's Weekly,* "but if the present plans of building cars continues, these horrors will be repeated." (They were, actually, in the Prospect wreck.)

In one fallen car, two red-hot stoves were upset into the imprisoned screaming passengers, igniting the splintered wreckage. The dry wood burned rapidly. Horrified spectators on the bridge above could not clamber down the steep, icy embankment to render aid. Before a bucket brigade could be formed, hardly a vestige was left of the car or its occupants. Fifty persons died in that firetrap. Only three passengers, all badly hurt, crawled out alive.

Luckily, the other fallen car had broken in two near the middle as it plummeted off the bridge, so its wounded survivors had a better chance of fighting their way out. This coach also caught fire, but nearly 40 persons escaped from it. The only fatality there was a man crushed between the broken halves of the car as they came partly together after the breakage.

Twenty unidentified bodies were buried in a public funeral at the railroad company's expense. Some witnesses attributed the accident to the use of double-gauge cars, known as *compromise cars.* This equipment ran interchangeably on the New York Central & Hudson River Railroad (NYC&HR; gauge, 4 feet 8½ inches) and the Lake Shore road (4 feet 10 inches).

Their wheels were designed to run on the narrower tracks of connecting roads or on track 1½ inches wider. Each wheel was made ⅜ inch wider than those of ordinary cars, so that, with the axletree, it spanned 9¼ inches. Thus, while the flange could run inside the NYC&HR track, the tread—that part of the wheel resting on the rail—would roll on the Lake Shore track but would not cover it by ¾ inch and would allow ¾-inch lateral motion to the wheels. It is not hard to believe that such an arrangement caused the Angola disaster.

See also PROSPECT WRECK.

BIBLIOGRAPHY: Charles Francis Adams, Jr., *Notes on Railroad Accidents,* Putnam, New York, 1879; Wesley S. Griswold, *Train Wreck!,* Stephen Greene, Brattleboro, Vt., 1969; Robert C. Reed, *Train Wrecks: A Pictorial History of Accidents on the Main Line,* Superior Publishing, Seattle, 1968.

Animals, Wild The Railway Express Agency (REA) accepted almost all kinds of healthy animals except skunks (unless a veterinarian's certificate showed that the smelly odor sac had been removed). Shippers had to provide food for the animals and utensils for feeding. They could either send food along with directions, accompany the animals themselves, or simply send directions and pay the bill. REA agents recalled such incidents as a ferret grabbing a fountain pen, two unclaimed armadillos hiding under an express-office floor where nobody thought of looking for them, and a raccoon received by express but left to its own devices and wrecking the darkened interior of a station.

REA rules called for crating elephants weighing up to 1000 pounds. Building such a container was a task equivalent to erecting a barn. An especially heavy elephant had to be given a whole car, with an attendant. Such beasts usually rode crosswise, and at least one circus train was wrecked by elephants shifting their weight while it was rounding a curve on a downgrade. Circuses traveling by rail almost invariably ship their large animals in their own cars of great length.

When Dr. Raymond Ditmars had charge of the New York Zoological Park in the Bronx, he shipped most of his hoofed animals—deer, buffalo, rhinoceros, etc.—by Railway Express. To avoid food that might cause indigestion, he allowed them only hay en route and water a half hour before eating. On the rare occasions when he moved such animals by freight train he'd send a man along in the railroad car. He shipped giraffes in cages set on open flatcars, with movable brackets built into the cage roofs. When the train ran in open plains country, the lids were up. and the tall creatures stuck their long necks out into the air, but when the train approached tunnels, they were more closely confined.

Even under normal conditions, travel is a hardship for most wild animals. For example, it gives nervous fits to some small members of the cat family. Dr. Ditmars shipped animals in two kinds of containers: the excitable species such as cats and deer in *turn crates,* in which the creatures could turn around, and the larger, more phlegmatic beasts in *no-turn crates.* Each container was built for the animal's comfort and safety, according to its measurement, and, of course, to conserve space.

Seals riding the rails through hot desert country must be kept wet lest their hides get dry and hard, causing them pain. A 1300-pound baby hippopotamus sent by train from Memphis, Tennessee, to Des Moines, Iowa, was enclosed in a strong crate and given repeated shower baths at St. Louis to keep its hide from cracking.

Canadian National Express men had a problem when a large shipment including a huge Bengal tiger, a leopard, and two sloths arrived at Montreal from India for the Toronto Zoological Gardens. The shipment reached Montreal at 7:50 p.m. and had to be fed at once, but the animals had used up their supply of fresh meat en route and all butcher shops were shut at that hour. Expressmen have to be resourceful. They got fresh meat from a large hotel. An especially big shipment, in 1925, transported 2000 buffalo from the national reservation at Wainwright, Alberta, to La Butte at the eastern edge of Wood Buffalo National Park, west of Fort Smith. On the 700-mile journey 400 miles were covered by rail, the rest being undertaken on river barges.

A shipment of rare monkeys and apes arrived at the Philadelphia Zoo from Havana, Cuba, via boat and the Atlantic Coast Line crack train *Havana Special.* Although it was late spring, blankets swathed the crates to keep the animals from being chilled by a change in climate. At Miami, Florida, a curious spectator edging too close to the animal car was caught in a leg by an orangutan and had to be rescued by an attendant. Apparently the news hadn't reached Savannah, Georgia, for when the train stopped there, a woman made a similar mistake. The same orangutan ripped off her dress before the eyes of astonished spectators.

One day a motion-picture company in Hollywood, California, asked the Railway Express Agency's New York office to find a chimpanzee about 4 years old, 33 inches tall, tame, and female which could wear clothes and walk upright. Animal importer Henry Bartels had such an animal named Susie. It being winter, Susie was packed in a box wrapped in burlap, with air holes on top. Directions for feeding were pasted on the outside. REA messengers all along the route followed them, inserting the food on a sliding shelf at the bottom of the cage: bananas, apples, oranges, and raisin bread, but no water. Susie reached Hollywood in excellent condition.

See also CIRCUS TRAINS.

AP *See* ALLEGHENY PORTAGE RAILWAY.

Arcata & Mad River Railroad (A&MR) Incorporated in 1881 in California but actually operated before 1860 as the Union Plank Walk & Railroad, the A&MR is probably the only railroad that started out with timbered (nonmetal) rails, 45½-inch gauge, and horse-drawn four-wheel cars without brakes but with canvas tops and straw-covered floors. In those days, several lumber railroads had wooden rails. This one added strap iron and later switched to T rails of increasingly heavy weight as the years went by.

The A&MR, an extension of the Arcata Transportation Company road, was built on a trestle to the deepwater channel in Humboldt Bay to provide the town of Arcata, originally named Union, with a major water outlet. Passengers wishing to go to Eureka rode the A&MR train to dockside, then completed their journey across the bay in an old side-wheeler ferryboat, the *Gussie McAlpine.* This sounds rather primitive, which it was; but time brought homemade little locomotives, then steam power bearing the famous names of Baldwin, Shay, and Heisler, even a mighty Mallet, and more modern cars, and finally, like all other steam common carriers in the United States, the A&MR became fully dieselized.

BIBLIOGRAPHY: W. W. Elliot, *A History of Humboldt County,* 1882.

Armored Cars The use of armored cars in the United States dates back to Civil War days. An inventor, Rufus A. Wilder, was testifying in a court case being tried by Judge George Sharswood at the critical period in the war when communications were cut between Philadelphia and Washington by the destruction of bridges

***The nation's first armored car, built during the Civil War to protect the Union engineering corps as it rebuilt a bridge on the Philadelphia, Wilmington and Baltimore Railroad.* [*William C. Russell*]**

on the Philadelphia, Wilmington and Baltimore Railroad (PW&B; later part of the Pennsylvania). A Confederate general who had once been the PW&B's chief engineer razed the bridge across the Susquehanna River. The judge said it could not be rebuilt because of Confederate sharpshooters.

That gave Wilder an idea. He conferred privately with the judge, who thereupon postponed the court case until the witness could visit Baldwin Locomotive Works in Philadelphia and put the scheme into effect. Then Wilder directed the secret building of the nation's first armored car. It was merely a lumber truck with a steel-plated cover protecting one howitzer, and it had loopholes for riflemen. The strange contraption was moved along the Susquehanna's eastern bank at Havre de Grace, Maryland, attacking the Confederates so effectively that the Union engineering corps was soon able to rebuild the bridge safely. Wilder died at Cressona, Pennsylvania, in 1908. Adaptations of his car have been used on many railroads, in many countries, and in many wars.

ARR *See* ALASKA RAILROAD.

Ashtabula Wreck On December 29, 1876, Lake Shore & Michigan Southern's *Pacific Express*—11 wooden-bodied coaches double-headed by the eight-wheeled engines *Socrates* and *Columbia*—was running from Erie, Pennsylvania, to Chicago in a blinding snowstorm whipped by a stiff gale. After a brief stop at Ashtabula, Ohio, it edged cautiously over Ashtabula Creek on a 165-foot Howe truss bridge of wrought iron with stone abutments, built 11 years before and tested at the time with the weight of six locomotives. As the *Socrates* neared the western end, engineer Dan McGuire felt the bridge sagging. As he put it, "The engine ran uphill." Widening his throttle, he reached solid land just as the span collapsed, snapping the drawbar that linked the two engines. The *Columbia* and all 11 cars fell 72 feet into the icy creek, drowning some passengers.

"The train lay in the water in a steep-walled valley," a survivor said later. "Our car was tilted on its side, with both ends smashed. The wreckage lay in every direction, maybe 40 feet high. Stoves in the cars upset, igniting the debris. Screams of imprisoned victims mingled with the roaring flames and whistling gale."

Both engineers survived, but 80 persons were killed, including evangelist-songwriter Charles P. Bliss, best remembered for his hymn "Hold the Fort, for I Am Coming." Bliss died in a vain attempt to save his wife from being burned to death. At least 35 persons were seriously injured. This was at that time America's worst train wreck.

BIBLIOGRAPHY: *Railroad Magazine,* October 1949.

ASLRA *See* AMERICAN SHORT LINE RAILROAD ASSOCIATION.

Association of American Railroads (AAR) Central coordination and research agency of North America's railway industry. The association deals with matters of common concern, such as operations, maintenance, engineering research, safety, accounting, finance, valuation, taxation, legislation, transportation, economics, and public relations. All Class I railroads in the United States, Canada, and Mexico are participating members. Railroads in many other countries are associ-

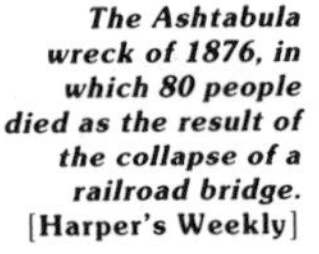

The Ashtabula wreck of 1876, in which 80 people died as the result of the collapse of a railroad bridge. [Harper's Weekly]

ate members, receiving the benefits of the association's technical and research committees.

The AAR was organized in 1934 by the consolidation of the American Railway Association, the Association of Railway Executives, the Railway Accounting Officers Association, the Railway Treasury Officers Association, and the Bureau of Railway Economics. Eight other groups were brought into the AAR by the end of 1939.

Its work is carried on in these departments: Law, including a Patent Division and a Central Claims Division; Legislative Relations; Research; Finance and Accounting; Public Relations; Bureau of Railway Economics; Office of Vice President - Assistant to the President, which has divisions relating to Purchases and Stores, Competitive Transportation, and Mail Transportation; Operations and Maintenance, which includes Operating-Transportation, Engineering, Freight Claim, Car Service, and Data Systems Divisions. Located at the AAR headquarters, 1920 L Street, N.W., Washington, D.C. 20036, is the world's largest railway library, maintained by the Bureau of Railway Economics.

Much research is being done not only by the AAR but also by individual railroads in conjunction with universities, technological institutions, industrial research laboratories, and the laboratories of companies which supply the railways with equipment. A railroad laboratory and research center is located on the Illinois Institute of Technology campus in Chicago.

One example of the AAR's efficiency is the large amount of dependable modern data that it supplied to the author for this encyclopedia. Another example is the ability of its Car Service Division to find promptly the location of any railroad freight car in the United States and Canada.

See also LAB-ON-WHEELS (AAR-100); POLICE, RAILROAD; ROMPS; STANDARD TIME.

ATC *See* AUTOMATIC TRAIN CONTROL.

Atchison, Topeka and Santa Fe Railway *See* SANTA FE RAILWAY.

Atlanta & St. Andrews Bay Railway (Bay Line) Railway line conceived by A. B. Steele, a Georgia lumberman, as a link between Atlanta and the Gulf of Mexico, which it reached at Panama City in 1905, but it never came near Atlanta. Its northern terminal is Dothan, Alabama, near which Steele had considerable forest land. When he died, Asa G. Chandler, founder of Coca-Cola, took over the 81-mile road. Then Steele's son bought the Bay Line and sold it to the United Fruit Co., intending to make Panama City a great banana terminal. Competitive roads killed that project by slashing rates. In 1931 the line was sold to its present owner, SAB Holding Co., a subsidiary of the International Paper Co., which has a large mill in Panama City.

ATSF *See* SANTA FE RAILWAY.

Auto-Train Corp. Privately owned transportation company that hauls passengers and their automobiles by rail overnight between Virginia and Florida and on a few other tourist routes. Like Ringling Bros.-Barnum & Bailey, it owns and maintains all its rolling stock but depends upon the railroads for locomotives, train and engine crews, and trackage rights. Its cars consist of enclosed bi-level and tri-level automobile transporters, refurbished coaches, diners, sleepers, and mostly double-decked lounge cars. To some extent, Auto-Train is a competitor of Amtrak (National Railroad Passenger Corp.). Although some of its consists are attached to regular Amtrak trains, it is not affiliated with Amtrak. In 1978 Auto-Train extended its service into Mexico. In September 1980 it filed a court petition for protection under the federal bankruptcy laws.

Automatic Fare Collection System installed on the Illinois Central's (IC's) Chicago suburban lines in 1965, for the first time on any railroad, and later used on the Bay Area Rapid Transit District in San Francisco and other commuter roads. It employs automatic gates interlocked with automatic ticket readers at certain stations and exits. Prior to adoption by the IC, these machines were tested on the transit system in London, England, and the Long Island Rail Road. The principal saving in operating costs is the elimination of on-train ticket collection.

Automatic Train Control (ATC) Self-regulating system or installation that applies the brakes either to stop a train when the engineer should have done so but didn't or to reduce excessive speed when the train is running too fast. Its speed-control factor restricts the speed to each of one, two, or three predetermined rates.

In 1889 S. H. Harrington patented the first recorded attempt at ATC and installed his gallowslike device on the Northern Railroad of New Jersey (part of the Erie Railroad, now Conrail) in the marshland near Bergen Hill, Jersey City. A semaphore blade jutted horizontally over the rails. From it dangled a sort of plumbline, a sash weight suspended from a chain in such a way as to clear an ordinary engine-cab roof by a scant 6 inches, but for the test one winter morning in 1889 a transverse rod set up on the cab roof had to touch and activate the weight in passing. The train line from the main air reservoir looped over the locomotive boiler a foot away. A bleed valve on this pipe was linked to the rod by an extended bell crank.

When this contraption stopped the Erie inspection train and officials got out, Harrington explained it to them. If raised to a stop position, he said, the semaphore arm swings the sash weight out directly over the path of any approaching train. If the engineer keeps going instead of halting for the stop signal, the heavy iron casting hits the rod on the cab roof, flips the bell crank, and opens the petcock, thus releasing the air and setting the brakes. "All might have gone well," the official report said, but for the fact an eminent signal engineer carelessly let himself be hit by the sash weight, which caused the Erie Railroad to reject Harrington's device.

This and other early unsuccessful devices were based on a sound principle. Combine the airbrake with the closed track circuit, and you have the basis of today's intricate ATC system. Yet 35 more years passed before the railroads adopted a practical ATC apparatus. An inefficient train-stop device of itself could be more of a nuisance than an aid. It could, for example, tie up a busy road. The kind of mechanism needed should deal with various operating conditions and be able to take charge when an engineer has overlooked indications and is jeopardizing his train.

In 1891 the narrow-gauge Boston, Revere Beach & Lynn installed ATC track trips of Rowell-Potter manufacture. So did three Chicago Elevated lines, and later four Midwestern roads tested them. The consensus was that ATC worked well except in icy weather, during which constant vigil was required. In 1906 Congress set up a Block Signal and Train Control Board, under the Interstate Commerce Commission (ICC), to investigate safety devices, including ATC. The Board accomplished relatively little and was dissolved in 1912. Later, the ICC and the Federal Railroad Administration considered more than 400 train-stop devices but found none of them satisfactory.

Meanwhile, New York Central (NYC) and several other big roads had been experimenting on their own. In 1920 they submitted five ATC mechanisms to an Association of American Railroads committee. Unlike most of the previous gadgets, all five actuated train brakes with electrical energy. All were what has since become known as intermittent types; i.e., they used special ramps or rail lengths to transmit current to passing locomotives at fixed locations (usually just in advance of a semaphore). Three of these devices involved direct contact between trains and trackside (ramp and pickup-shoe arrangements), while the others used induction or nonphysical transmission of energy.

After testing them, the ICC issued its landmark Train Control Order No. 1 on June 13, 1922, requiring each of 49 large railroads to install such equipment on one of its passenger-engine divisions. In 1924 this mandate was made more comprehensive. There were many types of ATC at that time. The inductor type proved itself superior to physical-contact devices but was costlier to install.

Simplest of all was the NYC's intermittent setup, characterized by stubby inductors (powerful electromagnetic units bolted to the ties at fixed locations). Such an inductor is energized when a corresponding wayside signal shows red, and it transmits its energy to a locomotive's overpassing receiver. Then relays (located behind the coal bunker of a steam loco) send a heavier surge of power racing forward to motivate the brake valve.

This stops the train. The fact of stoppage is recorded on a tape tracing the engine's performance throughout the run. Before starting again, the engineer must drop to the ground and actuate a reset conductor permitting the engineer to kick off the brakes. A refinement of this device was a *forestaller,* a little pressed-steel container mounted against the cab wall. A flip of the lever permitted an engineer approaching a "Stop and proceed" or "Call-on" signal to delay automatic action for 16 seconds—long enough to permit the engineer to go through.

The Pennsylvania Railroad's (PRR's) concept of train control was quite different. From the first, PRR had fought the automatic-stop idea on the ground that it was inefficient to start a heavy load again after an arbitrary air-reduction stop on a mountain grade. The Pennsy favored, instead, cab signals; its position was: Give our enginemen a clear picture of conditions ahead, regardless of weather, and advise them in advance of changing indications, and they'll take care of air-pipe reductions themselves.

So Union Switch & Signal Co. installed such signals in engine cabs of what then regarded itself as the "Standard Railroad of the World." Basically the signals were operated by interrupted or "coded" alternating current, originally fed by intermittent control. Under this setup, the ICC insisted on a supplementary train-stop mechanism, but when the Keystone Road switched over to continuous control, this requirement was relaxed.

Pennsy cabs had four position-light signals ranging from "Caution—slow speed" to "Clear." Each signal, except the most restrictive warning, imparted 100-Hertz alternating current to the running rails of the automatic signal block at a different frequency, or rate of interruption. Picked up by a receiver bar, the current passed through two amplifier tubes similar to those used in an ordinary radio but sturdier. Powerful impulses of the secondary circuit, led by the locomotive generator, were then decoded and made to illuminate the cabside roundels, giving indication of the corresponding wayside target.

BIBLIOGRAPHY: John H. Armstrong, *The Railroad—What It Is, What It Does,* Simmons-Boardman, New York, 1978; Robert S. Henry, *This Fascinating Railroad Business,* 3d ed., rev., Bobbs-Merrill, Indianapolis, 1946.

Automatic Train-Recording System The world's first railroad to use and operate such a system was not a common carrier but is believed to have been the midget Badger Central, with only 8 feet of track laid out on a table in the Spaulding family home in Pulaski, Wisconsin. It was built and installed by Erwin A. Spaulding, a teenager who later became a Soo Line telegraph operator. On January 4, 1921, he was issued a United States patent covering "a train-recording and registering apparatus." The patent explains:

> This invention relates to . . . that type of machine which is used to register and record, at a home station, the distance away from said home station a train is, as it proceeds. An object of the invention is to provide suitable means whereby a train will open or close an electric circuit, thereby operating a machine located at the home station to indicate its position. Another object is to provide changeable means, operated by an electric magnet or other suitable device, for registering and recording the position of any of many trains relative to home.

This patent is the base of every device that has been made and installed on railroads everywhere to register and record the position of trains in a central or home station. Each is a copy or improvement of Spaulding's original invention. Practically every railroad thus pays indirect tribute to Erwin A. Spaulding.

Automobile-Train Crash, First Probably the crash which occurred on a Westbury, New York, grade crossing in 1901. The driver was Henri Fournier, champion automobile driver of Europe and winner of the Paris-Bordeaux and Paris-Berlin races in 1901. He was demonstrating an $8000 Mors motorcar to five companions when an eastbound Long Island Rail Road train hit it, reducing the costly vehicle to twisted scrap and splinters. Two of its occupants were injured; two others were bruised. Fournier, unhurt, claimed that but for his quick manipulation of the controls a split second before the collision the entire party might have met instant death. "We didn't hear any bell or whistle," he said.

Avalanche *See* WELLINGTON AVALANCHE.

B

B&M *See* BOSTON & MAINE RAILROAD.

B&ML *See* BELFAST & MOOSEHEAD LAKE RAILROAD.

B&O *See* BALTIMORE & OHIO RAILROAD.

Baldwin Locomotive Works World's largest plant of its kind, with access to the Philadelphia & Reading tracks, that filled a vast acreage in Philadelphia almost adjacent to the high school the author attended. (In 1928 it was moved to suburban Eddystone, Pennsylvania.) I shall never forget the life-size bronze statue of Matthias William Baldwin (1795–1866) that faced my school on the opposite side of Broad Street at Spring Garden Street or my visits into the smoky, thunderous, high-roofed caverns that produced steam power for hundreds of railroads. I remember, too, the dramatic day when Baldwin workers, on strike, marched shoulder to shoulder southward on Broad, the city's widest thoroughfare, from curb to curb in solidarity to to meet a closely knit line of blue-coated city police, also from curb to curb, advancing toward them. A clash seemed inevitable, and I had a "ringside street," but within inches of an actual meeting the strikers' phalanx broke and scattered. Nobody fought; no arrests were made.

An estimated 100,000 or so steam locomotives were built in the United States from 1830 to 1950, mostly in the Northeast, notably Philadelphia and Eddystone; Schenectady, New York; Paterson, New Jersey; and Taunton, Massachusetts, among other places; and after 1870 Baldwin led the pack. Many units were outshopped by certain railroads, especially the Pennsylvania, Norfolk & Western, Baltimore & Ohio, Southern, Chesapeake and Ohio, Union Pacific, and Southern Pacific, but the vast majority of locos came from outside builders. *See* MASON, WILLIAM; PATERSON, NEW JERSEY.

After 1930 relatively few locos were built in New England, previously a stronghold of the industry. After 1870 Baldwin cornered about 40 percent of the market

Old Ironsides, ***Baldwin's first full-size locomotive, built in 1832.***

and ran so far ahead of its individual competitors that several of them merged to form the American Locomotive Co. Meanwhile, in 1880, Lima Locomotive Works had entered the field and become a powerful challenger. But in the 1940s diesel-electrics were supplanting steamers so rapidly that Alco bowed out of steam production altogether in 1948. Baldwin and Lima did likewise in 1949. Thus ended America's 120 years of steam-locomotive production, which had not only civilized the Far West but also greatly influenced the course of history. *See* AMERICAN LOCOMOTIVE CO.; LIMA LOCOMOTIVE WORKS.

Born in Elizabethtown, New Jersey, Matthias Baldwin learned the jeweler's trade in Philadelphia. (Several other famous loco builders also began their careers as jewelers' or watchmakers' apprentices.) He opened a small shop of his own and in 1825, in partnership with David Mason, manufactured bookbinders' tools and cylinders for calico printing. Needing steam power for this business, he designed, built, and used an effective stationary engine.

A little working model of a steam locomotive that he produced in 1830 was put into operation April 15, 1831, pulling two four-seated cars around a circular track at Franklin Peale's Philadelphia Museum. It was the master builder's first iron horse. In 1832 Baldwin and Peale went to Bordentown, New Jersey, to study and sketch the pieces of the Stephenson locomotive *John Bull,* which the Camden & Amboy Railroad had just imported from England but not yet reassembled. With these data, Baldwin built his first road locomotive, *Old Ironsides,* for the Philadelphia, Germantown & Norristown Railroad (later in the Reading system, now Conrail). It was a cabless four-wheeler with a very tall stack, 9- by 18-inch cylinders, 54-inch driving wheels, and a boiler 30 inches in diameter containing 72 copper flues; in working order it weighed about 11,000 pounds.

Baldwin's second road engine, built in 1834, was the somewhat heavier *E. L. Miller,* also a cabless four-wheeler but with a shorter, wider stack. It was named for the Southerner who had supervised the construction of the *Best Friend of Charleston* and who had ordered the Baldwin unit bearing his own name for the South Carolina Canal & Railroad Company. It became, wrote locomotive historian Angus Sinclair, "one of the most famous locomotives of its day. Its form was standard with Baldwin until the necessity for heavier power gradually led to radical change of design." *See* SOUTHERN RAILWAY SYSTEM.

Unlike some other builders, Baldwin put the drivers of his early engines behind, rather than in front of, the firebox. In about 1838 he began standardizing his loco parts, making them interchangeable to simplify repairs—a common automotive practice today. The company which Baldwin founded had built, at the time of his death, over 1500 locomotives. In addition, he gave much time and money to religious and philanthropical institutions, among them the Franklin Institute in Philadelphia, which today has among its mechanical and scientific exhibits a full-size steam locomotive.

Samuel M. Vauclain (1856–1940), one of the ablest men ever engaged in the locomotive industry, was a worthy successor to Baldwin at the Philadelphia plant. At 16 Sam was apprenticed to the Pennsylvania's Altoona shops, which probably did more to develop steam power than did any other railroad shops. He left the Pennsy to work for Baldwin, first as a departmental foreman and eventually as general superintendent of the plant, and finally as a partner in the company and chairman of the board. In 1889 he patented and the plant began building the first four-cylinder compound locomotive, a revolutionary advance in railroading. It had two cylinders on each side of the firebox, both pistons connecting with the crosshead. As years passed,

The arrival of a shipment of Forney-type Baldwin locomotives in Chicago, for the Chicago and South Side Rapid Transit Company, in 1892. The large engine in the foregound was Baldwin's exhibit at the World's Columbian Exposition of 1893. [Baldwin Locomotive Company]

thousands of Vauclain compounds went into service in the United States and other countries.

In 1931 the Baldwin Works bought the successful George C. Whitcomb Co., which had been manufacturing coal-mining equipment since 1878 and in 1906 had begun building the first effective gasoline locomotive used in coal mines. Whitcomb also had produced trolley locomotives as early as 1921, and in 1929 it had designed and constructed the nation's largest gas-electric loco. As a Baldwin subsidiary, it turned out many diesel-electrics for standard- and narrow-gauge roads.

Also in 1931, the Baldwin-Southwark Corp. was formed to handle Baldwin's heavy-machinery business. Its products included scale cars for calibrating railroad-track scales. The steam loco business dwindled. By 1940, the year Vauclain died, Baldwin was following the trend of the times by building diesel-electric switchers. After World War II its diesel output increased. But in 1949 Baldwin outshopped Pennsy's uniquely contoured T-1 steam-turbine locos, one of which was operated at the New York World's Fair.

Baldwin was the first to design and build a 6000-horsepower diesel road unit and to design and build a 2000-horsepower unit; the latter went to the Seaboard Coast Line. In 1947–1948 the giant plant built three huge steam-turbine-electrics for the Chesapeake and Ohio. Before it quit locomotive building of any kind, it made one last effort in that direction by merging with the Lima-Hamilton Corp., the new company being named the Baldwin-Lima-Hamilton Corp. (BLH).

Today BLH is still manufacturing heavy machinery, but not locomotives, and surprisingly is a subsidiary of meat-packing Armour and Company, itself a subsidiary of Greyhound Corp. Part of the old erecting shop of Rogers Locomotive Works remains in Paterson, where it is used as a railroad museum. But no known relic is left in Philadelphia of the once-vast acreage of Baldwin Locomotive Works. Even the bronze statue of Matthias Baldwin has, like the author's high school building itself, vanished.

BIBLIOGRAPHY: Baldwin-Lima-Hamilton Corp., *The Story of Eddystone,* Glenwood Pubs., Felton, Calif., 1974; Joseph Harrison, Jr., *The Locomotive Engine and Philadelphia's Share in Its Early Improvements,* G. Gebbie, Philadelphia, 1872; Angus Sinclair, *Development of the Locomotive Engine,* annotated ed. by John H. White, Jr., M.I.T., Cambridge, Mass., 1970; Frederick Westing, *The Locomotives That Baldwin Built,* Superior Publishing, Seattle, 1966; John H. White, Jr., *American Locomotives: An Engineering History, 1830–1880,* Johns Hopkins, Baltimore, 1968.

Ball, Webb C. ***(1847–1922)*** Watchmaker who helped to make train operation safe by his crusade to standardize and improve railroad watches. Born on an Ohio farm, Ball became a watchmaker. His prominence in the railroad world dated from a head-on collision near Tipton, Ohio, in 1891, which killed both engineers and several trainmen. An engineer's watch stopping unexpectedly for 5 minutes had caused the wreck. As a watch expert, Ball testified at the investigation.

Engine No. 650, built by Baldwin in 1889, is often used in Hollywood Westerns.

Later he was hired to set up a watch-inspection system on the same road. While checking employees' timepieces, Ball was surprised to learn that even alarm clocks were used sometimes in engine cabs. He founded the Ball Railway Time Service, which many roads adopted. In 1918 he organized the Official Bureau of Railway Time Service and for the rest of his life was its general time inspector. Ball repeatedly stressed the need for good watches rigidly inspected, insisting that they be compared at least twice a month, inspected at set intervals, cleaned and oiled once a month, adjusted to heat and cold, and, if used on trains, be of standard size and construction.

Prior to 1961 the use of wristwatches was forbidden in train operation because it was not believed that they could be made accurate enough. But after John W. Barriger 3d (1899–1976), then president of the Pittsburgh & Lake Erie, learned that the U.S. Air Force and commercial airlines were using wristwatches, he authorized their adoption on the P&LE, saying: "They are far more convenient, since railroaders seldom wear vests any more, and trousers often come without watch pockets." After checking with experts, Barriger laid down these requirements for approval of any wristwatch for railroad use:

> A 23-jewel movement. The new balance wheel, Dura balance. Special stainless-steel case, indented top, easy to wind. Shockproof. Waterproof. Non-magnetic shield around the movement, inside case. Non-magnetic steel dial. Six adjustments, 3 of which are for position. Movement stops when stem is pushed out for setting.

Other roads gradually followed Barriger's example. Today the use of wristwatches by train and engine crews, dispatchers, etc., is a common practice.

Ballads of the Rails Railroad ballads stem mostly from the so-called golden age of railroading, between the late 1860s and World War I, when the iron trail hummed with expansive energy and strong men worked for it proudly. These songs and poems recreate the clang of spike mauls, flanged wheels rolling, the haunting engine whistles and bells, heady, pungent coal smoke climbing to the stars, telegraph keys chattering, lights gleaming from a string of open-vestibuled coaches rushing by in the darkness, the lord of the engine cab, and his naive little daughter who just *knows* that the endangered train is safe because "My Daddy's the engineer."

The ballads, many of which can be heard on phonograph records, have a primitive quality: a crazy quilt of wanderlust, loneliness, toil and fun, pathos, heroism, disaster, and the universal love hunger. The three best-known American railsongs are "Casey Jones," "The Big Rock Candy Mountain," and "The Wreck of the Old 97." *See* CASEY JONES; MCCLINTOCK, HARRY KIRBY; "WRECK OF THE OLD 97, THE."

Possibly No. 4 is the lugubrious *In the Baggage-Coach Ahead,* written by Gussie L. Davis of Cincinnati, the first American black songwriter to become popular, and ending with:

But the father's heart was broken,
And this was all he said—
"Their mother is in a casket
In the baggage coach ahead."

Or the fourth choice might be McClintock's "Hallelujah, I'm a Bum," which says gleefully, "We'll throw up our jobs and we'll go on the bum," or the anonymous "John Henry," "There lies a steel-drivin' man," or the rollicking old folk song, "The Wabash Cannonball," especially its last eight lines:

Now listen to the rumble, now listen to the roar
As she echoes down the valley and tears along the shore.
Now hear the engine's whistling and her mighty hoboes' call
As we ride the rods and brake-beams on the Wabash Cannonball.

Now here's to Long Slim Perkins, may his name forever stand;
He'll be honored and revered by the 'boes throughout the land;
And when his days are over and the curtains round him fall
We'll ship him off to Heaven on the Wabash Cannonball.

One of the most popular ballads of the 1890s was the mournful "In the Baggage-Coach Ahead." The train on the cover of the sheet music is the New York Central Empire State Express. [Collection of Freeman Hubbard]

Long Slim Perkins must have been a freight conductor with a warm spot in his heart for vagrants. In "Paddy Works on the Erie," the leading character was one of the thousands of immigrants driven from the "auld sod" by the Irish potato famine of the 1840s. Paddy is quoted as saying:

In eighteen hundred and forty-eight
I learned to take my whiskey straight.
'Tis an ilygant drink and can't be beat
For workin' on the railway.

"Drill, Ye Tarriers, Drill," credited to Tom Casey, tells about building the first transcontinental railroad, *tarriers* meaning "loafers" (men who tarry). Tracklayers chanted such songs in unison as they worked. The work songs included "I've Been Workin' on the Railroad" and "Where Do You Work-a, John?" the answer being "On the Delaware Lackawann." Other once-popular favorites are "The Little Red Caboose behind the Train," "When That Midnight Choo-Choo Leaves for Alabam," "Please, Mister Conductor, Don't Put Me off the Train," "Jerry, Go Ile [Oil] That Car," "Life's Railway to Heaven," "If I Die a Railroad Man," "Way Out in Idaho," "I Went Down to the Depot," "The Wreck on the C&O," "The Gambler," "Still on the Hog Train," "I've Said My Last Farewell," "Toot, Toot, Good-bye," "The Gospel Train," "The Dying Hogger," "The Man in Upper 4," "When the Arkansas Express Raced Old Black Bess," "Punkin Center Line," "New River Train," "There's a Red Light on the Tracks for Parson Brown," "Asleep at the Switch," "Rock Island Line," "You Wake Up in the Morning in Chicago," "This Train is Bound for Glory," and "Railroad Bill."

Among the love ballads are "A Railroader's Bride I'll Be," the girl being convinced that nobody, not even a sailor or a banker, could equal a railfaring man as a husband; "O Lulu," in which a gandy dancer misses female companionship "so bad" that he suddenly decides to lay down his spike maul and ride a freight "cross the country" to see his "long-haired gal"; and "Cannonball Blues," which says:

Yonder comes the train, comin' down the track,
Carry me away but ain't gonna carry me back,
My honey babe, my blue-eyed babe.

Also sentimental is "The Red and the Green," about a locomotive engineer leaving home to go on his run while his only child is critically ill and near death's door. He tells his wife, "I'll leave two lanterns trimmed," and adds:

Just set a light when I pass tonight;
  Set it where it can be seen.
If our darling's dead, then show the red;
  If she's better, show the green.

Suspense ends with the last line: "Thank God, the light is green!" Typical of the blues songs is "900 Miles," which says:

'Cause I'm nine hundred miles from home
An' I hate to hear that lonesome whistle blow.

BIBLIOGRAPHY: Benjamin A. Botkin and Alvin F. Harlow, *A Treasury of Railroad Folklore,* Crown, New York, 1953; Norman Cohen, *Railroad Folksongs on Record: A Survey,* booklet reprinted from *New York Folklore Quarterly,* June 1970; Stewart H. Holbrook, *The Story of American Railroads,* Crown, New York, 1947; Freeman Hubbard, *Railroad Avenue,* McGraw-Hill, New York, 1945; Sterling Sherwin and Harry K. McClintock, *Railroad Songs of Yesterday,* Shapiro, Bernstein & Co., New York, 1943.

Ballast In a track structure, the gravel, crushed rock, slag, or cinders placed on the roadbed to drain water away from ties, spread the track load over softer subgrade, make an even bearing for ties, hold ties in place, and check vegetation growth. Track structure consists of ballast, crossties, rails, connections, and fastenings. By guiding the flanged car wheels, its unique surface of raised rails enables locomotives to pull trains of cars.

Balloon Car Railroad car, built in 1871 by a man named Casebolt, that had an oval outline and novel construction which enabled the upper body to turn freely on a supporting stationary truck. It was a horse-drawn vehicle with a capacity of 12 or 14 passengers, sitting in two rows. By removing a pin when the car reached the end of the line and directing the horses in a semicircle, the driver could make the return trip without using a turntable or wye or unhitching the horses. The only operation of balloon cars was on Larkin Street between Ninth and Mission and between Mission and Fourteenth Streets in San Francisco.

Baltimore & Ohio Railroad (B&O) First common-carrier railroad chartered and built in the United States. It was sparked by Phillip E. Thomas and George Brown, both of Baltimore. After investigating England's railways, they called a meeting of about 25 citizens on February 12, 1827, to consider ways of regaining the trade Baltimore had lost to steamboats; 16 days afterward they were granted a charter to build and operate a railroad from that city to the Ohio River, with Thomas as president and Brown as treasurer. The state of Maryland invested $500,000 in the project, and the city of Baltimore also subscribed heavily.

Among the engineers hired to build the road was Maj. George W. Whistler, who became the father of the painter James McNeill Whistler. B&O's cornerstone was laid by 90-year-old Charles Carroll of Carrollton, the only surviving signer of the Declaration of Independence. In 1830, 13 miles of track were opened to Ellicott's Mills (now Ellicott City). The early B&O had three types of track: strap-iron rails laid on stringers (wooden rails) resting on sleepers (wooden crossties) or directly affixed to stone blocks or laid on stringers above stone blocks. *See* WHISTLER, GEORGE WASHINGTON.

A view of the unique S-shaped covered Baltimore & Ohio bridge at Harpers Ferry, Virginia (now West Virginia), in 1857. In 1859, John Brown's raiders killed a B&O porter-stationmaster on this bridge, in the raid that helped to precipitate the Civil War. [American Steel Foundries]

The road's first "train," the *Flying Dutchman,* was a four-wheeled open car carrying a horse that operated a treadmill to revolve the wheels. Passengers seated along both sides faced away from the horse. They made the 13 miles in about an hour and a quarter—faster than any steam engine could travel in those days. This car was discarded shortly after what may have been the country's first passenger-train accident: the car, filled with newspapermen, ran into a cow, tossing the passengers down an enbankment, unhurt but disgruntled.

B&O's next motive power was a four-wheeled vehicle propelled by sails, invented by Evan Thomas. The South Carolina Canal & Railroad Company had already used such means of transportation. The Charleston *Courier* reported on March 30, 1830:

> A sail was set on a car on our railroad yesterday afternoon. . . . Fifteen gentlemen got aboard and flew off at the rate of 12 to 14 miles an hour. . . . The wind blew very fresh. . . . The mast went by the board, with the sail and rigging attached, carrying with them several of the crew [passengers?]. The wreck was descried by several friendly shipmasters, who kindly rendered assistance by rigging a jurymast, and the car was again soon under way.

Then B&O went back to horsepower, but of a different kind. Horses rented from a stage company pulled two-story stagecoach-type cars on rails. The animals were well treated and not worked for more than 6 or 7 miles at a time, but the expanding railroad needed motive power suitable for longer distances. Peter Cooper (1791–1883), a Baltimore merchant with mechanical ability who later became a New York philanthropist, told the B&O directors, "I believe I could knock together a locomotive." He did so, a small one named *Tom Thumb* for a tiny fairy-tale character (a name later used by one of P. T. Barnum's midgets). The four-wheeled, cabless engine had one upright cylinder, 3¼ by 2½ inches, and an upright boiler having tubes made from gun barrels. A revolving fan made its fire draft. On its first run the *Tom Thumb* pushed a car holding 23 passengers. Even with only about 1½ horsepower, it proved that steam power could operate the B&O. Later, the *Tom Thumb* raced a horse-drawn car. It came in second best, but only because the belt that operated the fire blower slipped off the pulley.

In January 1831 the B&O offered a purchase prize of $4000 for the best coalburning loco submitted by June in that year. It had to weigh less than 3½ tons and pull a 15-ton load at 15 miles per hour. There were only four entries. Oddly enough, three of the four men submitting engines in that contest were watchmakers. One of them, Phineas Davis, had formed a partnership with a machinist named Gartner. The firm of Davis & Gartner built a four-wheeled, upright-boilered engine named *York* from his designs at York, Pennsylvania. This they dismantled, hauled slowly by oxcart over the turnpike to Baltimore, and reassembled. The *York* won first prize. It weighed about 8000 pounds in working order, ran 30 miles per hour on straight, level track, and rounded the road's sharpest curves at 15 miles per hour. That July the company made Davis its chief engineer and inaugurated a regular passenger train powered by the *York.*

In 1832 the line was extended to Point of Rocks, on the Potomac River, with a branch to Frederick, Mary-

The B&O passenger-freight station in Baltimore, Maryland, as it looked in 1830, the year of the railroad's opening. Also shown is the* Tom Thumb, *at that time the only American-built locomotive pulling trains. [Collection of Freeman Hubbard]

land, 72 miles in all. Davis & Gartner built only two more engines, the *Atlantic* and the *Traveler,* both for the B&O. In 1833, after completing the erection of B&O's Mount Clare shops, which soon became famous, Davis met death in the cab of the *Traveler,* which hit the end of a misaligned rail. His *Atlantic* was the first of the road's popular grasshopper type (so called because its mechanism vaguely resembled the insect's folded legs).

In 1839 the mainline reached Harpers Ferry, Virginia (now West Virginia), where the Shenandoah River joins the Potomac. There the railroad built a unique S-shaped bridge. (There too, in 1859, a B&O Negro porter and stationmaster was shot dead in the raid by John Brown that helped to precipitate the Civil War.) In 1835 the road opened a branch line to Washington, D.C., that included a long granite bridge (still in use) with eight superb arches, built on a curve and named the Thomas Viaduct for the company's first president. Four grasshoppers wheeled excursion trains from Baltimore into the nation's capital.

Other extensions raised the mileage above 500 and eventually opened a through route to St. Louis via two connecting railroads which the B&O took over. Between Cumberland, Maryland, and Wheeling, West Virginia, 11 tunnels had to be rock-drilled, 113 bridges built, and hundreds of cuts and fills made. While some tunnels were being bored, temporary bypass tracks known as shooflies were zigzagged up the steep hills, or long roundabout detours were created.

In 1843 Samuel F. B. Morse (1791-1872) set up an experimental line for his Magnetic Telegraph Company along the B&O right-of-way between Baltimore and Washington. He installed two sets of telegraph instruments, one in the Supreme Court chamber in Washington, the other in the B&O's Pratt Street Station in Baltimore. On May 24, 1844, he sent over this line the world's first telegram, "What hath God wought," written by Anne Ellsworth, daughter of the United States Commissioner of Patents. It started the global use of telegraphy for messages of all kinds, train dispatching in particular.

B&O spent over $15.6 million to complete its mainline to the Ohio River, thrice the original estimate. By 1857 the B&O had spent an additional $11 million for branches, the Northwestern Virginia Railroad, which it absorbed, other tunnels, equipment, etc. Then came the Civil War. Much railroad property was destroyed in the fighting and much rebuilt. Many troops were moved over B&O rails.

With the return of peace, the line was extended to Pittsburgh, Sandusky, and Chicago. The B&O acquired steamboats, docks, and grain elevators, built a great Baltimore dry dock and vacation hotels in the mountains, and organized express, telegraph, and sleeping-car companies. It spent millions on terminal properties in Baltimore, Chicago, St. Louis, and Philadelphia.

The original B&O emblem, adopted in the 1880s, pictured the Capitol dome with the road's name and a slogan, "All Trains via Washington with Stopover Privilege." After B&O got control of the Jersey Central and the Philadelphia & Reading (P&R), it eliminated the slogan to make space for the names of those two subsidiaries. In 1937 it had Otto Kuhler simplify the design to show only the Capitol dome and the initials B&O within a circle. *See* Kuhler, Otto.

Meanwhile, competition had brought costly rate wars. B&O wanted to buy control of the Wilmington, Baltimore & Washington, but the Pennsylvania Railroad took it and refused to carry any more B&O cars on its line to New York. B&O retaliated by obtaining entry to Philadelphia through control of the Schuylkill East Side Terminal Railway and setting up traffic interchange with the P&R. The staggering cost of these deals threw the B&O into receivership in 1896. Two years later, after the B&O borrowed money to improve the road, the courts released the property in good shape.

Gradually the Pennsy and Edward H. Harriman's Union Pacific worked into strong positions on the B&O Board of Directors and made pool arrangements in which William K. Vanderbilt's Lake Shore & Michigan Southern also became involved. But a Supreme Court decision that the roads were violating the Sherman Antitrust Act forced the Pennsy to sell most of its B&O stock. In 1913, four years after Harriman's death, the UP liquidated its B&O holdings by distributing them to its individual stockholders as a special dividend, thus making the B&O independent again.

From 1910 to 1941 Daniel Willard (1861-1942) was president of the B&O. He had begun railroading as a track laborer and served as a locomotive engineer, among other jobs on various roads. Willard borrowed $62 million to regrade and double-track the right-of-way, eliminate traffic bottlenecks, strengthen the locomotive and car fleets, and build a new terminal and new shops. During his first 18 years as chief executive he spent nearly $150 million.

In 1927 the B&O celebrated its 100th anniversary with a mammoth Fair of the Iron Horse at Halethorpe, Maryland. In 1932 Columbia Broadcasting System made the first nationwide broadcast from a moving train on a B&O limited running from Baltimore to Washington. The B&O claimed a long list of firsts, possibly the longest list of any American railroad, such as first to earn passenger revenue, use car wheels that revolved with their axles, publish a timetable, operate an eight-wheel passenger coach, use iron wheels on passenger cars, use iron boxcars (forerunner of the present all-steel cars), use an electrically operated locomotive, operate a streamlined passenger train, operate an air-conditioned car and a fully air-conditioned train, provide door-to-door carload freight service, and many others.

In 1973, when B&O was merged into the Chessie System, it was one of the four main trunk lines between the Midwest and the Atlantic Ocean, operating 5874 miles of road, of which 4625 miles were owned outright and the rest operated under contract. *See* CHESSIE SYSTEM.

B&O, like all other roads in the Chessie System and like the Seaboard Coast Line roads, is now part of the gargantuan CSX Corp., the merger having become effective on November 1, 1980. *See* CSX CORP.

BIBLIOGRAPHY Benjamin A. Botkin and Alvin F. Harlow, *A Treasury of Railroad Folklore,* Crown, New York, 1953; Herbert H. Harwood, Jr., *Impossible Challenge: The Baltimore & Ohio Railroad in Maryland,* Barnard Roberts & Co., Baltimore, 1979; Angus Sinclair, *Development of the Locomotive Engine,* annotated ed. by John H. White, Jr., M.I.T., Cambridge, Mass., 1970.

Bangor & Aroostook Railroad (BAR) Railroad once famed as the Potato Road, with 508.98 miles of main and branch lines, which is now concentrating on forest products, especially pulp and paper, since most potatoes today are being shipped by truck. It has not had rail passenger service since 1961 (10 years before Amtrak) because the highways absorbed too many short-distance travelers while airlines took over the rail sleeping-car passengers. However, BAR operates a fleet of fine buses, originally begun largely as feeder service for the railroad, paralleling its rail lines.

The BAR (its official initials, to avoid confusion with the old Boston & Albany) is still solvent and has never been in receivership. It runs generally from north to south through the middle of Maine, from the Atlantic Ocean to the Canadian border, with branches chiefly in northeastern Maine.

On February 23, 1891, the BAR was incorporated by its founding father and first president, Albert Burleigh, and Franklin W. Cram, vice president. On Christmas Day, 1893, construction was so far advanced that the first train ran from Brownville to Burleigh's hometown, Houlton, the last few miles of rails and ties being laid temporarily on hard snow. For Maine has severe winters. Its snow has been known to pile up 11 feet high on the railroad tracks, sometimes drifting up to the crossbars of telephone poles. A train doesn't have to stand still very long in a Maine winter to be frozen solid onto the rails.

In 1899 the mainline reached Van Buren on the state's northern rim. And in 1915 Percy Todd, then president of the road, rejoiced in the completion of the international bridge from there to St. Leonard, New Brunswick, which gave the BAR a direct outlet to what became, in 1921, the Canadian National Railways.

Prior to the use of refrigerator cars in 1925, the BAR moved potatoes in boxcars which the individual farmers would line and insulate at their own expense. They would then accompany these cars to market, stoking the woodburning stoves along the way. It was a dramatic sight to see up to 200 boxcars rolling by with a separate smoke plume trailing from each car. Those first cars were replaced by Eastman heater cars, heated by charcoal.

In 1961, with rail earnings down, the BAR, like various other railroad companies, needed to diversify in order to get enough revenue to stay in business. So its holding company, Bangor & Aroostook Corp., started to acquire other industries and on October 1, 1964, merged with Punta Alegre Sugar Corp., whose physical assets the Castro administration in Cuba had expropriated. In 1969 the railroad's stock was sold to the Amoskeag Company of Boston. The railroad itself, under capable management, is still very much in business.

BIBLIOGRAPHY *The Bangor and Aroostook: 1891-1966,* Bangor & Aroostook Railroad, Bangor, 1966; Stewart H. Holbrook, *The Story of American Railroads,* Crown, New York, 1947.

BAR *See* BANGOR & AROOSTOOK RAILROAD.

Bass, Sam With a masked gang Sam Bass robbed a Texas & Pacific train on April 10, 1878, at Mesquite, Texas, 13 miles east of Dallas, in one of the four Western-style railroad stickups which occurred that spring within a 20-mile radius of Dallas. The gang appeared suddenly when the train stopped at the little depot that night and overpowered the crew. Conductor Julius Alford wounded one of the bandits and was shot in the left arm. After setting fire to the mail-express car to force express messenger Kerley to open the door, the gang quenched the blaze and fled on horseback with $152 in silver, three registered letters, and the railroaders' guns in a sack. What they didn't know was that Kerley had hidden $30,000 in bills in his car's potbellied wooden stove, which was not lit. None of the 25 passengers was molested. Guards on a nearby train carrying convicts to a state prison made a feeble effort to foil the gang but backed down when Bass threatened to free the convicts if the guards persisted.

A few months later, Bass was fatally shot in an attempted bank robbery at Round Rock, Texas. A posse found him dying under a tree in a flowery meadow.

Bay Line *See* ATLANTA & ST. ANDREWS BAY RAILWAY.

BC Rail *See* BRITISH COLUMBIA RAILWAY.

Beaver Control A beaver-control rail motor car operates over 500 or so miles of Hudson Bay Line track between The Pas and Churchill, Manitoba. The car's operator on this unique lonely job stops near a stream, culvert, or lakeshore, gets out, wades into the water, and sets out a harmless Bailey trap that looks like a suitcase. Canada has a law against killing beavers. The beaver is a national symbol, like the bald eagle in the United States, and for many years it adorned the Canadian Pacific Railway insigne. But it can be a nuisance to railroaders. In building its house, the beaver often plugs a culvert, which could flood tracks, weaken roadbeds, and delay, even wreck, trains.

The patrol takes every captive beaver to a settlement, from which it is carried, sometimes by airplane, to another stream or lake many miles from the railway. There a Manitoba game warden releases it. None of the other methods of driving beavers away from the rails, such as lights, noisy floating cans, or foul-smelling chemicals, has proved effective.

Bedwell, Harry (1890-1955) Boomer telegrapher and train dispatcher on half a dozen roads, for the longest time on the Southern Pacific (SP), who was second to none as a railroad fiction writer. *The Saturday Evening Post* published 13 of his stories, some of them serials; and *Railroad Magazine,* 32; there were many others. The federal government printed 250,000 paperback copies of his hardcover novel *The Boomer* for the armed forces in World War II. This novel, like most of his stories, featured Eddie Sand, a roving "op" and train dispatcher like himself. SP broadcast his nonfiction railroad scenario *Priority Special* and printed it as a booklet for general distribution. See BOOMERS.

As a boy, Harry hammed around his hometown depot at Whittier, California (near which he now lies buried), before and after school, often staying late at night to copy from the wire. At home he practiced on a dummy telegraph set. He listened eagerly to train and engine men's talk and boomers' tall tales. His first visit to a railroad pay car resulted from his working as a brass pounder for the Burlington at Andover, Missouri. Later he wrote: "I'll never forget the thrill, power, and importance which were mine when I took that job."

But Bedwell did not stay anywhere long. "I deviled the chief dispatcher into making me a relief agent. After that I worked on mainlines and branches, at busy stations and solitary tricks. Then I drifted west: Salt Lake City and the D&RG; Springville and Lehi, with the tall mountains coming down, and Green River, Utah."

Next the Santa Fe, and an SP desert trick. On and on he went: Pacific Electric train dispatcher; years of free-lance writing; the Rio Grande again; back on the SP—in California, Oregon, and California once more.

"Bertram, Calif., was a lone, yellow, telegraph office set on the sand," he wrote, "with the rails and semaphore before it and the dun-colored desert sloping down from behind. The trains slammed by, seldom stopping, and then the silence would come back and the sun shine furiously or the stars wink impudently. Nothing else—except, if you stayed long enough, there did seem to be something. Something that came in, out of the silence, that you could almost touch."

Beebe, Lucius (Morris) (1902-1966) Author and coauthor of books that occupy an impressive footage on many a library shelf. For years he was the only American railroad writer widely known to the general public. This status he attained with a colorful, almost flamboyant literary style and an ability to dramatize train photos, plus a flair for publicity as a *bon vivant* and modern Petronius, and also because growing apples on his vast Washington State domain and shipping them by rail all over the country helped to make him a millionaire.

For 21 years he was on the *New York Herald Tribune* staff, later revived and published an old weekly newspaper in Virginia City, Nevada, to which Mark Twain had often contributed, and finally became a columnist on the *San Francisco Chronicle.* In the early 1930s, a New York publishing house asked him to put together a popular book on American railroading in picture form. It was the first such undertaking on record except for Robert S. Henry's classic *Trains.* Beebe found the available photographic material so poor that he refused the commission. "In that case," suggested the company's editor, "why not take some railroad pictures yourself?" Beebe did so and borrowed others from *Railroad Magazine;* the resulting *High Iron* touched off a lot of other railroad books.

Beebe and his occasional collaborator, Charles M. Clegg, jointly owned two private railroad cars, the *Gold Coast* and the *Virginia City,* both richly decorated. The Henry M. Flagler estate paid him a fee of $1000 a day and expenses for a trip to Florida to supervise the restoration of that magnate's luxurious car for the Flagler Museum. Later he erected a monument over Casey Jones's grave at Jackson, Tennessee.

Among Beebe's books, some written in collaboration with Charles Clegg, were *Mixed Train Daily, The Age of Steam, Hear the Train Blow, Steamcars to the Comstock, Narrow Gauge in the Rockies,* and *The Saga of Wells Fargo.* He also wrote many magazine and newspaper articles.

Beggs, Eugene (1836-1924) Inventor and manufacturer who made some of the prettiest and most popular self-powered steam-type trains ever to run on miniature tracks. His engines and cars are treasured today as museum pieces and collectors' items. Beggs was born and worked for nearly all his life in Paterson, a city long famed for its many successful full-size steam locomotives built by such firms as Rogers, Danforth & Cooke, Swinburne, and Grant, beginning in 1835, the year before Eugene was born. See PATERSON, NEW JERSEY.

Also in 1835, his father, Hugh Beggs, and Alexander Paul were partners in a Paterson millwright shop in which they were building, as a sideline, an operable miniature steam locomotive when a disastrous fire destroyed it. Hugh died in 1844, leaving a widow and five children, including Eugene. Ten years later Eugene, having a mechanical mind, apprenticed himself to one of the local locomotive companies, Danforth & Cooke, and later went firing on the Marietta & Cincinnati Railroad in Ohio.

Returning to his home city, he made his first operable miniature steam locomotive, patented it in 1871, and began manufacturing these engines for the Christmas trade in his own toy shop (although he never admitted they were toys), and tenders for them and cars with tinplate roofs of simple, round-top design.

His earliest miniature locomotives were cap-stacked 4-4-0s, scaled close to ⅜ inch to 1 foot, but in the later 1870s he adopted the 2-2-0 wheel arrangement, his most popular type. His track gauge, ⅞ inch, was never changed in the 37 years of his manufacturing business, thus setting a type which none of his competitors adopted.

All Beggs engines were powered by alcohol burned in a tubular lamp having three or more wicks attached to a rectangular reservoir soldered in place. Some were equipped with such realistic details as handrails and pilot flagstaffs. One model had a whistle, operated by a lever running out of the back of the cab with two extensions down to the track. Ramps located at certain points along the track would lift the valve and blow the whistle at intervals. Many, but not all, of his engines included tenders, which in other cases were sold separately.

Beggs developed his own methods for manufacturing his products, but for some time he had on his payroll two men and, during the summer vacation season, a number of boys. One of his best employees, Jehu Garlick, left him in 1883 after devising and patenting a reversing valve, went into business for himself, and became a serious rival of Beggs.

Another employee, Henry Dawson, with Beggs's permission, created a new model 2-2-0 to compete successfully with the cheaper steam trains then being made by other companies. Between 1900 and 1905 Dawson exhibited Beggs trains in all of New York's leading department stores and at a county fair in Bangor, Maine, but in 1905 he left Beggs and went to work for the Paterson Fire Department. Shortly afterward, Beggs turned over most of his business to another employee, James P. McNair, who carried it on, with his wife's help, until 1907, completing and selling about 200 trains during that time. With McNair's withdrawal in the face of rising competition, the manufacture of Beggs trains was abandoned.

Between 1913 and 1915, Beggs himself built a larger-size midget 2-2-2 locomotive. It hauled a four-wheel trailer car in which he gave free rides to children over some 200 feet of track laid by the inventor. This experimental type failed to interest railroad companies, and in 1918 it was sold for scrap metal. Beggs died 6 years later.

The last Beggs engine ever constructed was assembled in August 1943 by the late Walter A. Lucas, railroad historian and managing editor of the *Locomotive Cyclopedia.* Lucas visited the old McNair shop in Paterson, made castings from some of the original dies, used parts of uncompleted engines, and, with the help of James P. McNair, Jr., produced an authentic Beggs self-operating miniature locomotive.

BIBLIOGRAPHY: Louis H. Hertz, *Collecting Model Trains,* Simmons-Boardman, New York, 1956; Frederic Shaw, *Little Railways of the World,* Howell-North, Berkeley, Calif., 1958.

Belfast & Moosehead Lake Railroad (B&ML) One of the few railroads (aside from city transit lines) owned by a municipality. The city of Belfast, Maine, is its majority stockholder. Headquartered in Belfast, a Maine Central connection, B&ML runs freight trains to and from Burnham Junction, 33.07 miles, hauling mostly poultry, feed, lumber, food products, chemicals, waste, and scrap. Opened for business in 1870, it was leased to and operated for about 55 years by Maine Central, which canceled the lease in 1926. Its passenger service ended in 1960.

BIBLIOGRAPHY: *Railroad Magazine,* October 1940; *Trains Magazine,* April 1944.

Bells, Locomotive Two of the earliest, if not the first, locomotives equipped with bells were the *John Bull* and the *E. L. Miller,* both cabless, but there is no proof that either of them was given a bell at the time it was built. Robert Stephenson built the *John Bull* in England in 1831 for the Camden & Amboy (later Pennsylvania Railroad) in New Jersey. The *E. L. Miller* was Matthias Baldwin's second engine, built in Philadelphia in 1834 for the South Carolina Canal & Railroad Company.

In railroading's early days more than 125 builders turned out locomotives, and most cast their own bells. When James N. Lauder, motive-power superintendent of the Old Colony Railroad, was casting bells in the road's shops at South Boston, Massachusetts, in 1834, he wondered why his bells cracked so easily. Journeying to Taunton, Massachusetts, he asked advice from William Mason, a famous locomotive builder. Mason said the cracking might be due to an excess of tin in the bell mixture. It was. By increasing his percentage of copper, Lauder succeeded in making bells of superior craftsmanship, at least 62 of them, nearly all for engines he built himself, until the New Haven road took over the Old Colony in 1893. *See* MASON, WILLIAM.

When casting a bell, Lauder invariably placed in the mold a freshly minted silver dollar. Maybe he did it for luck, but more likely to improve the bell's tone, for precious metal added to tin has a tendency to do that. The idea was not new. In 1867 Lewis Lawrence, a Lackawanna Railroad director, dropped 12 new silver dollars into the molten metal for a bell to be used on the road's One-Spot, built in Schenectady, New York, at what later became the American Locomotive Co. That engine bore his name. Its bell had a rich, mellow tone and took a high, silvery polish.

Bell-metal formulas vary. Baldwin Locomotive Works, which always did its own casting, preferred 95 percent copper, 4 percent silicon, and 1 percent iron. Norfolk & Western Railway got good results from 4 parts of copper to 1 part of tin. In about 1890 the Canadian Pacific tried out iron and steel bells, but it soon discarded them because tone and volume were unsatisfactory. Some experimenters made glass bells, which gave a clear, penetrating tone but were too brittle for practical use on locomotives.

During World War II, with copper much in demand, some locomotive builders again turned to steel bells, mostly for switchers and freight engines. Three sections of steel plate ⅜ inch thick were cut and welded together, and a die was cast to shape the bell. The product was known as a *victory bell,* but its dismal tone, "Dank, dank, dank," sounded more like defeat. After the war, more musically toned bells replaced the ugly-toned ones.

The locomotive bell had two advantages over the steam whistle: it could be used for longer periods because it consumed less energy, and it nearly always outlasted its original locomotive. The whistle was used for operating signals, for distant crossing warnings, and the like, while the bell evidently was intended to warn persons in close proximity to the right-of-way that the engine was about to start or was already coming. Bells were rung when approaching grade crossings, especially within city limits, and were tolled on the rare funeral trains.

The shape, height, curvature, and thickness in the wall of the bell as well as the metals used to produce sweet tones are governed by rules based on many years of trial and error. Upkeep is a trivial item: just occasional visits to the shops for sprucing up and fresh lacquer. From old bells came most of the metal that went into new ones.

Big steam power is, or was, usually equipped with bells about 18 inches in diameter at the mouth; smaller power, with bells of about 12½ or 13 inches in diameter. The Southern's road steam engines, for example, had 17¼-inch bells weighing 116 pounds, while the Canadian Pacific's bells measured 18 inches and weighed 127 pounds (250 pounds with the mounting). The larger a bell, the lower its tone. The average diesel locomotive bell is a 12-incher.

"It was not unusual," recalled C. H. Bilty, retired mechanical superintendent of the Milwaukee Road, "for men in daily contact with steam locomotives to recognize them by their bell tones, even in the dark. Mrs. Callahan, who lived near our Watertown, Wisconsin, depot, had an engineer son named George. She'd listen for the bell of his engine, No. 248, and as it pulled into town, she'd tell her daughter: 'Nellie, put the kettle on. Here comes 248.'"

On a clear, calm evening you could hear such a bell for at least a mile, but to detect tonal differences you had to be brought up on a road that operated locomotives from a variety of builders. In 1893 L. R. Andrews wrote a 36-line poem entitled "The Clang of the Bells" which includes this excerpt:

Oh! the Mason bell is balanced well,
But its voice is not for me,
As to and fro it sways so slow,
Like a bell-buoy of the sea.

Some Baldwin engines shown in Mathew B. Brady's collection of Civil War photos had bells and hangers of a style from which Baldwin never deviated after that time. Prior to the Civil War the bell itself was of about the same size and shape on all locomotives, but the mountings were highly ornate: fluted brass pedestals with acorn nuts, eagles, or other ornaments on top. In the early 1920s the cord which the fireman pulled was replaced by the automatic bell ringer. In about 1940 a newer type of bell ringer began to be installed in cabs. This device swings the clapper against the bell, which does not move. The clapper's speed can be controlled by the amount of air entering the cylinder. This type was more efficient than its predecessors, but together with the concealed bell of streamlined steam or diesel power it destroyed whatever glamour and music the locomotive bell had left.

The Mississippi Central (MC) had a bell-ringing device, patented in 1934, which provided automatic means of sounding the bell only while the locomotive was running. As far as the author could ascertain, MC steam locos were the only ones equipped with two bells. The engineer controlled one bell and rang it in accordance with a state law requiring either the continuous ringing of a bell or the blowing of a whistle beginning 300 yards before passing over a public highway and continuing until the train had crossed the highway. The other bell was located in the very front of the engine. It started ringing as soon as the engine was put in motion and continued as long as the motion lasted. Its purpose was to give additional warning of approaching trains. It

In a railroad repair shop a maintenance worker assembles pins and other accessories for mounting an engine bell. [*New York Central Railroad*]

also protected the railroad against damage suits in crossing accidents.

With the gradual disappearance of the steam locomotive in regular service, a few railroads donated many of their bells to churches, schools, small colleges, boys' and girls' camps, etc., nearly always in their own territories. However, the Santa Fe sold one for a nominal sum to a Seventh-Day Adventist mission in Jamaica, in the West Indies. A Lackawanna bell calls the faithful to church in East Africa. A Canadian Pacific bell is installed in a church in Cosford, England. A Boston & Maine engine bell was presented to a Catholic chapel in the Solomon Islands in 1940. In 1942 Japanese troops landed there and carried it off, probably for melting into cannon.

A Bessemer & Lake Erie railroader bought a BLE bell and shipped it to a mission at Suchow, China, paying only $25 for the bell and its transportation. Learning that Japanese forces were headed their way, the Chinese buried their gift in the ground before the enemy arrived and kept it there for years. After the Japanese left, the Chinese set up the bell again at their church, with great rejoicing, and put it back to use. But nearly all the bells from dismantled steam locomotives were sold as scrap metal. Private collectors of railroadiana bought some of them.

Well-balanced two-way freight traffic on the Bessemer & Lake Erie Railroad: a southbound ore train (left) passes a northbound coal train near Greenville, Pennsylvania. Note the finely ballasted track. [Bessemer & Lake Erie Railroad]

Bergoff, Pearl L. *See* STRIKEBREAKING CZAR.

Bessemer & Lake Erie Railroad (BLE) Though only 205 miles long, with all but 4.6 of those miles in Pennsylvania, BLE is a major factor in the status of the United States as a major steel producer. A subsidiary of United States Steel Corp., it links the industrialized Pittsburgh district with the Lake Erie ports of Conneaut, Ohio, and Erie, Pennsylvania, serving the entire nation indirectly from highly diversified western Pennsylvania. It owns about 10,000 freight cars, mostly open-top hoppers which transport its chief commodities: iron ore, bituminous coal, coke, and limestone. Its corporate headquarters is in Pittsburgh; its operating center and shops are in Greenville, Pennsylvania, 2 miles north of its very busy Shenango yard; and it has some 1400 employees.

BLE traces its ancestry to the Near Creek Railroad, chartered in 1865 but renamed Shenango & Allegheny Railroad before tracks were laid. Its first 21 miles were opened in 1869 to haul coal from Pardoe to Shenango for transfer to other railroads. Later it expanded north and south, reaching Butler in 1883, Conneaut in 1892, and Erie in 1893. Its destiny was determined by the first lake steamer unloading a cargo of 1250 tons of ore at the Conneaut docks in November 1892. Today's modern lake boats, some 1000 feet long, unload as much as 40 times that tonnage of pelletized ore in a few hours. In 1897 the road was extended about 40 miles south from Butler to the Pittsburgh district, connecting with the Union Railroad, an important switching road which serves the Monongahela Valley's steel mills and other industrial plants.

BLE, incorporated in 1900, had 13 major predecessor companies. It transports huge tonnages of coal to Conneaut for transshipment via lake vessels to utilities and industries in the United States and Canada. This coal originates in southwestern Pennsylvania and adjacent counties of Ohio, West Virginia, and Maryland. Also, the Bessemer receives at Conneaut considerable iron ore from Minnesota, Quebec, and Labrador for rail shipment to steel mills in the Monongahela and Shenango Valleys. Iron ore from various sources represents about half of its business. Limestone also is received at Conneaut by boat for subsequent rail movement south to steel mills. This ideal combination of northbound coal and southbound ore and limestone gives BLE an almost balanced two-way haul that other railroad managements could well envy.

BLE was America's first Class I road to install welded rail over its entire mainline. Its track, with crushed limestone ballast, its all-diesel locomotives, and its cars are beautifully maintained.

In 1940 the road began using two-way phone communication between loco cab and caboose. One of its first reported calls was: "Caboose 1904 calling engine 600. We have a hotbox 20 cars from rear end. Stop at

Coolspring." The system worked also from one train to another within a 7-mile distance. It enabled crews to check passing trains and warn them of dragging freight rigging or other faults which some crew member had observed, thus minimizing the possibility of wrecks.

In 1936 the Bessemer acquired its first diesel unit, No. 281, a B-B 530-horsepower Westinghouse switcher. By 1950 it still had four Pacifics for passenger work but only eight passenger cars. The road's last two passenger trains, with dozens of sentimental railfans aboard, made their farewell runs on March 15, 1955, between Greenville and Erie.

BLE was just about fully dieselized by December 1952 when ice closed Lake Erie navigation for the season. At that time, it put its steam locos into winter storage as usual, intending to bring back some of them the following spring. But, as more diesels were delivered early in 1953, the entire steam fleet was retired permanently, except apparently for the yard job at Butler, where 2-8-0 No. 156 (Baldwin Locomotive Works, 1911) was used for the last time on May 14, 1953. The final steam loco to leave Bessemer property was 2-10-4 No. 642 (Baldwin, 1943), on June 2, 1954. Greenville shopmen waved a sad farewell after preparing the loco for the graveyard run to a scrapyard.

BIBLIOGRAPHY: Roy C. Beaver, *Off with the Old, On with the New: The Story of the Steam Locomotives of the Bessemer and Lake Erie Railroad and Predecessor Companies,* Bessemer & Lake Erie Railroad, Pittsburgh, 1954; id., *The Bessemer and Lake Erie Railroad: 1869–1969,* Golden West Books, San Marino, Calif., 1969.

Bible Racks and Bibles Standard equipment in coaches and passenger stations of some United States and Canadian railroads in the nineteenth century, just as they were and still are in many hotels. Typical is a copy of the Bible, published in 1873, with these words gilt-printed on the front cover: "Lena Station, Illinois Central Railroad, from Stephenson County Bible Society." A sticker pasted on the flyleaf signed by A. Mitchell, General Superintendent, reads: "This book is to be cared for by employes of the railroad company and kept in rack when not in use."

Far left: *Bible racks like this one from the Central Vermont Railway were standard equipment on passenger cars in the nineteenth century.* [*Canadian National Railways*]

In 1885, when pious but rugged John Niblock became superintendent of the Canadian Pacific's 500-mile division between Swift Current, Saskatchewan, and Donald, British Columbia, a dangerous stretch of track with steep mountain grades, sharp curves, and many tunnels, he issued a Bible as standard equipment to every caboose under his jurisdiction. He did this, old-timers said, because he kept a wary eye on his men both as they existed here on earth and as they might exist hereafter.

Bicycle Railway The Bicycle Railway in New Jersey was quite different from a line operated by Eben M. Boynton in New England, although both were monorails based on the bicycle principle. The New Jersey line

Bicycle locomotive No. 1 (which looks larger in this illustration than it actually was) of the quaint but short-lived Bicycle Railway in New Jersey, which allowed people to travel quickly by bicycle. [*Collection of Freeman Hubbard*]

linked Smithville, where the H. B. Smith Machine Works was located, with Mount Holly, 2½ miles away, where some of the shop's employees lived, and provided cheap commutation service (fare, 10 cents) in the period 1890–1894. The average time for a one-way trip was 7 minutes. There was no other way to get between the two towns in those days except by walking, riding horseback, or pedaling an ordinary bicycle over bumpy and often muddy dirt roads.

H. B. Smith asked the Vermont inventor William Hotchkiss to solve the problem. Hotchkiss redesigned a type of bike that the Smith works manufactured, making it seem to operate upside down. The rider occupied a saddle seat between the two main wheels, almost touching the rail and resting his or her hands on handlebars while propelling the odd vehicle by foot power. Since the wheels were flanged, no steering was necessary. The pedals used a ratchet principle instead of the sprocket of ordinary bicycles. Two guide wheels, one on each side of the vehicle, kept the rider from falling off.

The monorail was built in a fairly straight line by bridging Rancocas Creek seven times. (This creek, meandering picturesquely through woodland, is today New Jersey's most popular stream for canoeing.) The rail line was single-tracked, with passing sidings located at intervals. When two riders pedaling in opposite directions met between sidings, one had to lift his or her bicycle off the rail to let the other pass. On pleasant summer evenings, tandem bicycles were available for romantic couples who desired moonlit rides or picnics. But this diversion was terminated suddenly after a rejected suitor murdered his former girl friend while she was riding tandem with another man. The railway itself was abandoned not long afterward. No trace of it is visible to present-day canoeists on Rancocas Creek.

Bidding In on a Run When a run is available, through resignation, transfer, death, retirement, etc., engine or train employees bid for it. The run is awarded to the employee with the greatest seniority. Once on a run, however, an employee may be bumped from it by anyone older in service who has been displaced or wants the job for any other reason.

Black Diamond Flagship of the Lehigh Valley's (LV's) passenger-train fleet for 63 years, during which time "black diamonds" (coal) gave the road much freight revenue. The luxury train began its fast daylight runs between New York and Buffalo on May 18, 1896. Because of its appeal to newlyweds visiting Niagara Falls, it was dubbed the Honeymoon Express, a title used for the first sustained railroad movie ever made. From the beginning, it kept abreast of modern trends in engineering and decor.

Finally, highway competition forced the Valley to abandon this once-popular service. The *Black Diamond* made its last run on May 18, 1959. In the words of Lucius Beebe, who was unsurpassed as a colorful historian of name trains, it went "down the long tangent and around the final curve into history." Its consist that day included a Railway Post Office car, a mail storage car, two coaches for Buffalo, and three cars that were cut off at Lehighton, Pennsylvania. A Pennsy GG-1 electric wheeled the *Black Diamond* from Penn Station, New York, to Newark. A Lehigh Valley diesel completed the run to the Valley's newly built Buffalo station.

Still operating at that time were the LV-Canadian National *Maple Leaf,* linking New York with Toronto, and the Valley's originally elegant *John Wilkes,* the first train to use fluorescent lighting. Both have since been pulled off. *See also* LEHIGH VALLEY RAILROAD.

BLE *See* BESSEMER & LAKE ERIE RAILROAD.

BLE *See* BROTHERHOOD OF LOCOMOTIVE ENGINEERS.

BLF&E *See* BROTHERHOOD OF LOCOMOTIVE FIREMEN AND ENGINEMEN.

BN *See* BURLINGTON NORTHERN INC.

Boarding Houses Long ago, railroad boarding houses would feed railmen, sometimes with all they could eat for 50 cents a meal, and provide a comfortable bed for a night's sleep at 4 bits extra. In such quarters, rail-weary hoggers, firemen, conductors, brakemen, and others would gather at the festive board and fill the air with shoptalk, politics, and comments on women that some boarding-house keepers censored. It was a place, too, where backslapping, whiskey-drinking, and cigar-smoking drummers (traveling salesmen) would rest for a spell before spending the next day spieling the virtues of the wares they toted around in their luggage.

Charlie Brady, his missus, and their daughter Jane ran such an establishment in Jackson, Tennessee, where in 1880 a tall, lanky, 16-year-old railroader named John Luther Jones (Casey Jones) first met Jane, whom he later fell in love with and married. Many years afterward the author asked Casey's aged widow if she remembered that first meeting. "Yes," she told me. "J. L. just sat there eating, and what impressed me most about him was his appetite." *See* CASEY JONES.

An old-time trackside boarding house on the Missouri Pacific (MP) line at Cotter, Arkansas, had a painted sign above the wide veranda reading "*The Eagle.* Rooms, Meals, Short Orders." It was named for the MP's No. 1 passenger train, *The Eagle.* Nearby stood the station and a rusty-looking roundhouse, with smoke rising now and then from the vents beneath which steam locomotives panted.

Mrs. Myrtle Thompson, whose husband had deserted her, ran the place with the help of her four young daughters. In the course of time two of the girls, like Jane Brady, became the wives of engineers. "Granny opened the Eagle in 1923 and operated it for about 30 years," recalled her grandson, Joseph A. Huddleston. "I'll never forget the many, many days when crews laying over in Cotter would loaf on our big porch waiting for another train to whistle in. Sometimes they'd tell me about a wreck or a runaway or a prairie fire of long ago. It was all very thrilling."

Three doors opened from the veranda into the main establishment: one into the long, narrow dining room; another into the lobby, where a few railroaders played slow-moving games of checkers, dominoes, or cards; and a third into a long and somewhat dreary hall bordered by six bedrooms on each side. Just behind the lobby and the dining room was the busy, immaculately clean kitchen, adjoining which were hidden the family bedrooms.

While the hungry boarders waited for a meal, they'd park their heels on the wooden porch railing and talk, smoke, and sniff the tantalizing food smells from the kitchen. A local train pulled by an old eight-wheeler would stop in front of The Eagle for the head brakeman to throw a switch. Shortly afterward, the entire five-man crew drifted in to eat. Mrs. Thompson stormed out of the kitchen to the porch, clanging an oversize cowbell and shouting: "It's ready! It's ready!" Railmen in faded pin-striped overalls or the dark blue, brass-buttoned uniforms of passenger trainmen would hurry inside and wash up at the pump, while switchmen from the yard across the street swarmed over to join them.

There were large bowls of mashed potatoes, gravy on the side, hot white biscuits and cornbread, platters heaped high with sliced roast beef, ham, or pieces of freshly killed chicken, and fresh garden vegetables, steaming-hot coffee, and generous-size pitchers of milk from the family cow. For dessert there might be a big round bowl of cherry cobbler and homemade apple pies. As soon as the railroaders finished eating, the boarding-house keeper and her daughters would start clearing tables and washing the mountains of dishes.

Another typical boarding house was located at Sargents, a small Colorado town on the Denver and Rio Grande Western at the foot of the rugged, steep Marshall Pass, about midway between Gunnison and Salida. That old structure is still standing today, or was at last report, but is now drab, empty, and lonesome.

"It wasn't lonesome when we lived there," recalled Mrs. Ruth A. Wood, who worked in it for years as a girl. "It was full of lively talk then, laughter, and the wholesome aroma of home-cooked food. I remember how thrilled I was at age 10 when we first moved there in 1925. The building was, and still is, railroad property, painted the same mustard yellow as the section house, the once-dripping water tank, and the low rambling depot. Many a young man down on his luck, sometimes a boomer, would ride into town on a 'side-door Pullman' and knock on our door, asking for some task to do to earn a meal. We managed to get quite a bit of our wood chopped that way."

Such establishments were once common along the iron trail. Many stories have been written around them, notably tales by Gilbert A. Lathrop, a Rio Grande fireman, who featured a kindly, plump boarding-house keeper called "Ma" Flannagan. But railroad boarding houses have long since vanished from the American scene because the crews have shorter working hours, because restaurants, hot-dog stands, hotels, and rooming houses for the general public have multiplied, because some railroad companies have built modern dormitories for the relatively few crew members who now have to lay overnight at the end of a run, and because so many railroaders now drive their own cars.

See also HARVEY, FREDERICK HENRY; STATION HOTELS; YMCAS, RAILROAD.

Boilers, Locomotive The principle of the steam boiler can be traced back to such a device reportedly built in about the 1st century A.D. by Hero of Alexandria, Egypt. Britain's Richard Trevithick invented the first steam locomotive to run on rails. In 1803, despite engineering opposition, he built a 6-foot barrel and subjected it to the then-unheard-of pressure of 100 pounds per square inch. His pioneer iron horse made its maiden run on February 24, 1804, and progress in boiler development was well under way.

As years sped by, rising speed meant greater power, larger boilers, higher pressure. Until 1895, in the United States, 160 pounds per square inch was considered the maximum. Then came 200, and in 1903 the Baltimore & Ohio outshopped the nation's first Mallet compound to operate at 215 pounds working pressure. Thereafter, locomotive builders designed steel barrels to withstand virtually any internal force required of them. An integral feature of boiler design, fire tubes extending from end to end in the barrel, takes care of staying the front and rear sheets. Passing through the sheets, such flues are rolled, beaded, and generally welded so as to tie the end walls together. Only the small areas above them require gussets or other stays.

The basic rules of construction are: (1) The locomotive boiler's diameter must be the simplest possible for the known capacity rating to keep the total load on the joints to a minimum. (2) The number of riveted joints should be reduced to the fewest practically possible. (3) All flat surfaces must be safely stayed. (4) The boiler must be shaped to expand and contract as temperatures and pressures vary.

Because much water is alkaline, caustic embrittlement or cracking may occur around the rivets. Chemists, metallurgists, and locomotive designers contributed to the solution of this problem. Steel companies began manufacturing seamless tubing formed by punching a hole in a hot billet and rolling the metal out to the proper size. This method, while costly, produced cylinders that did not fail. Much progress had been made toward doing the same with boiler shells when the railroad began replacing steam with diesels.

BIBLIOGRAPHY: Henry B. Comstock, *The Iron Horse,* Crowell, New York, 1971; Angus Sinclair, *Development of the Locomotive Engine,* annotated ed. by John H. White, Jr., M.I.T., Cambridge, Mass., 1970; John H. White, Jr., *American Locomotives: An Engineering History, 1830–1860,* Johns Hopkins, Baltimore, 1968.

A Santa Fe steam engine sits stripped for repairs. [*Santa Fe Railway*]

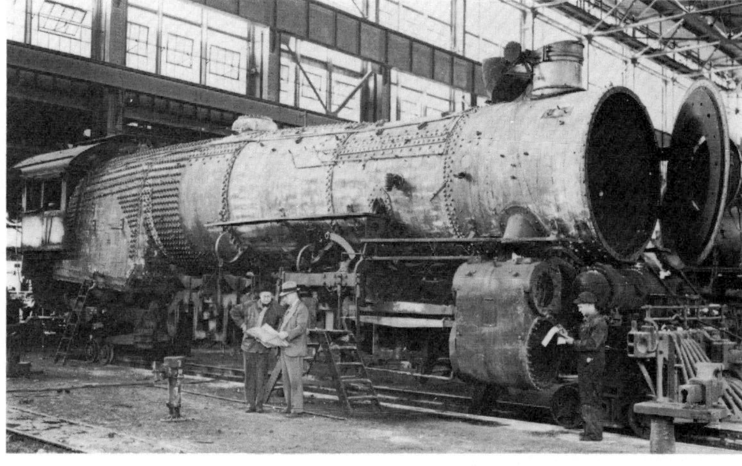

Book of Rules Often called the railroader's bible, it is based on the Standard Code adopted by the Association of American Railroads and issued, with variations, as a mandatory guide to employees of United States and Canadian roads in the performance of their duties. The variations are due to each individual road's characteristics. The book aims to ensure, insofar as possible, the safe and efficient operation of trains and other railroad facilities. It must be, and usually is, written in such a way that it can be clearly understood, with no chance for misinterpretation; and it is strictly enforced.

A typical railroad *Book of Rules* includes these sections: "General Notes," "General Rules," "Definitions," "Letter Symbols Used as Signs," "Operating Rules," and "General Regulations for Employees." The second section applies especially to employees in the transportation, maintenance of way and structures, and mechanical departments. It covers such topics as personal appearance, on-duty requirements, absence from duty, and obedience to rules. It forbids employees to delegate their duties to anyone else except as rules prescribe. The "Operating Rules" section covers operating and transportation department personnel, including certification of watches, the time comparison between conductors', enginemen's, and flagmen's watches, and signal indications and uses of flags, lanterns, fusees, torpedoes, and hand signals. Colors and positions of fixed signals receive careful notice. There are about 80 different combinations and arrangements of these signals. Also explained are the rights of trains and movement and protection of trains.

The section "General Regulations" deals specifically with employees in the transportation, maintenance of way and structures, and electrical departments. It outlines their responsibilities, duties, safety measures, and the necessity for being courteous to railroad patrons. Peter Josserand, Western Pacific chief train dispatcher and author of the classic book *Rights of Trains,* said: "The railroad man, if I may borrow a phrase from President Truman, had 'darned well better' know and obey the Book of Rules, lest he find himself knocking at St. Peter's door, or at least out of a job." But in rail lingo, anyone who is overly meticulous in this respect is known as a company man or a *Book of Rules* man.

Boomers Colorful, restless, itinerant railmen who traveled light and far, *pulling the pin* (quitting railroad jobs) at short notice for a variety of reasons. The boomer wandered from one road to another or from one division to another on the same carrier, often under a *flag* (assumed name) because his real name was blacklisted. His typical garb was a black shirt, a *thousand-miler,* so called because he was reputed to wear it on about 1000 miles of rail travel before washing it.

The boomer was bred of wanderlust, wars, strikes, depressions, seasonal rushes in the shipping of farm crops, the need to avoid shotgun weddings, or often just plain bad luck. Most boomers were activated by an insatiable urge to see what lay beyond the far horizon—a desire never fully realized because the horizon kept receding as they moved on. Many followed the wild ducks southward in the fall, northward in the spring. It was not uncommon for one to punch a foreman or a trainmaster on the jaw and then collect his pay.

Still others hit the bottle too often or carelessly let a boxcar roll off the docks. The story is told of a boomer switchman on the Lackawanna Railroad at Scranton, Pennsylvania, where the track ran down from the yard to a river's edge. The yardmen would coast a cut of freight cars down there with the boomer on top to set the brakes. One foggy night they shoved 10 cars down the grade, waited for the boomer to return, and then began yelling. Back through the murk a voice drifted faintly: "Cut off 10 more! Them 10 went into the river." Many a boomer (and *home guards,* or "company men," too) caused a wreck by misinterpreting or failing to deliver a train order. In such cases it was easy for a boomer to resign immediately and let the home guards face the music.

A million railmen were uprooted by the Civil War, the violent strikes of 1877, 1886, and especially 1894, and a succession of financial panics and business slumps. Blacklisted as strikers or furloughed when traffic fell off, they wandered to areas where work was to be had, at least temporarily. But the chief factor in creating boomers was the seasonal rushes: moving the crops of farms or ranches as soon as they were harvested or cattle ready for market. Boomers worked while the rails were hot, then rambled on to rushes just starting. *See* "CRANE WITH A BROKEN NECK"; STRIKE OF 1877; STRIKES, MAJOR RAILROAD.

In modern times the periodic needs of railroad companies for additional help to wheel the berries, the melons, the wheat, or whatever are met by recruiting local workers from the *extra board,* or *spare board,* men who are laid off when the feverish activity subsides but who can be depended upon to stick around as long as it lasts. The old-time boomer did not worry about being given the gate. He'd leave town in the firm belief that some road, somewhere, was bound to hire a capable man and that while waiting for his next pay he could eat off a *pie card* (meal ticket). When he pulled the pin, he'd tell his pals he was going to the *Indian Valley Line,* that mythical *pike* (short railroad) where you could always get a good job with ideal working conditions.

A boomer's best tangible asset—aside from a *service letter* (job reference), if he could get one honestly or buy a faked one—was a paid-up membership card in a railroad brotherhood or union. During his frequent lean periods he'd show this card to a worthy brother when he wanted to eat, sleep, ride, or all three, and it usually got results. If he had neither a service letter nor a brotherhood card and was really down and out, his temporary last resort was a trackside hobo jungle, a railroad YMCA, the Salvation Army, or a mission.

For the most part, boomers were generous, worldly-wise, self-assured to the point of insolence, humorous, profane, and given to braggadocio, but withal a likable lot. They knew railroad operating techniques better than many home guards because they had worked on numerous roads and were continually picking up new kinks. They took chances and often thumbed their noses at officials. Many chewed tobacco. As they drank too much, the company liked to blame its wrecks on booze rather than on equipment failure. Still, it required plenty of nerve and guts to make some fellows even want to railroad in the rowdy "wooden-axle" days, when the industry was young, ruthless, and sprinkled with blood. Boomers had a lingo of their own that enriched our language. *See* LINGO OF THE RAILS.

Their heyday was the period of national expansion between the Civil War and World War I. As railroading lost its pioneering quality and sense of adventure and fell into the groove, as locomotives grew heavier, trains longer, traveling safer, and job competition more keen, with increased unionization and finally social security, the old independent order of boomers gradually faded away like the tented circus and the nickel glass of beer.

See also BEDWELL, HARRY; HOBOES; MCCLINTOCK, HARRY KIRBY.

BIBLIOGRAPHY: Benjamin A. Botkin and Alvin F. Harlow, *A Treasury of Railroad Folklore,* Crown, New York, 1953; Freeman Hubbard and others, *Pennsylvania Songs and Legends,* University of Pennsylvania Press, Philadelphia, 1949; William F. Knapke and Freeman Hubbard, *The Railroad Caboose,* Golden West Books, San Marino, Calif., 1968.

Boston & Maine Railroad (B&M) A 1400-mile system serving New England and providing a vital link to the South and West for industries in that area. Its first antecedent, the Andover & Wilmington (A&W), was chartered on March 13, 1833. The A&W was renamed Andover & Haverhill in 1837 and Boston & Portland (B&P) in 1839. B&P's merger with other roads created the B&M in 1842. The new road's first locomotive was an eight-wheeled woodburner, the *Andover.* Its first station in Boston, Haymarket Square, was used from 1845 until 1894, when its first North Station was completed.

B&M carries paper, food products, energy and heating fuels, building materials, and many other items. As of 1977, it also operates 344 commuter trains for the Massachusetts Bay Transportation Authority, with 17,500 passengers a day, has 3158 employees, and handles 277,200 carloads of freight for gross revenues of $82.5 million. In that year, too, it acquired from General Motors 18 new 300-horsepower, fuel-efficient turbocharger locomotives, the most powerful engines B&M had ever had, enabling it to speed up freight over the steep grades in western Massachusetts.

Although B&M is in reorganization under the Bankruptcy Act, as of 1980 it remains independent of Conrail and operates without federal subsidies or loans. It connects with the Maine Central, Bangor & Aroostook, Conrail, Delaware and Hudson, Canadian Pacific, and Central Vermont lines and with some short lines, and it has piggyback facilities in seven cities. Located on its mainline between Portland and Mechanicville, New York, is the famous Hoosac Tunnel, 5 miles long, completed in 1877. This tunnel's track has been renewed with modern all-welded rail and lowered to permit passage of high and wide freight cars.

Nonchalant trainmen pose on the Lebanon, a typical Boston & Maine 4-4-0, built in 1866 and scrapped in 1902.

BIBLIOGRAPHY: George P. Baker, *The Formation of the New England Railroad Systems,* Greenwood Press, New York, 1968; *Jane's World Railways and Rapid Transit Systems,* F. Watts, New York, 1978; Martin L. Lindahl, *The New England Railroads,* New England Economic Research Foundation, Boston, 1965.

Brake-Test Record A record for steam power was set by Canadian Pacific's (CP's) Jubilee No. 3000 on the Winchester subdivision some 38 miles west of Montreal on September 18, 1936. Highballing at 112.5 miles per hour with a fully loaded tender and four cars, No. 3000, a 4-4-4 type, was brought to an emergency stop 78 seconds and 7905 feet after the brake application. Locomotive and tender weighed 461,500 pounds in working order; the entire train, 905,660 pounds. F2 Jubilees were designed as lightweight semistreamlined engines capable of high speed. Five of them were built for CP. Twenty Jubilee F1 units also were built. They differed in design from the F2. Each F1 had a 75-inch drive, compared with the F2's 80-inch drive, and was not capable of achieving the F2's high speed.

Bridges Estimated at 275,000 or more, railroad bridges (including trestles, culverts, and viaducts) outnumber railroad tunnels by possibly 15 to 1. No exact count is available. Both bridges and tunnels are costly to maintain. Now and then a carrier replaces a bridge of light design with a sturdier span or razes one located on a branch line it is abandoning. English-speaking North

The Baltimore & Ohio's eight-arch stone viaduct over the Patapsco River at Relay, Maryland, is the world's oldest rail viaduct. Built on a 4-degree curve, it is 652 feet long, 60 feet high, and 26 feet wide. **[Baltimore & Ohio Railroad]**

America boasts slightly more than one bridge or culvert (average length, almost 100 feet) for approximately every mile of track.

Bridge lore includes 15-year-old Kate Shelley, who risked her life by walking across a flooded bridge on a stormy night in 1881 to save a Chicago & North Western train; the Pennsy seven-arch span of solid masonry which caused a heavy death toll in the Johnstown Flood of 1889; and the wooden Stillhouse Trestle on the outskirts of Danville, Virginia, from which the plunge of a Southern Railway train in 1903 gave birth to a folk song, "The Wreck of the Old 97." *See* JOHNSTOWN FLOOD; SHELLEY, KATE; "WRECK OF THE OLD 97, THE."

The world's oldest railroad bridge is the granite arch structure at Gwynn's Falls, Baltimore, known as the Carrollton Viaduct (named for a local signer of the Declaration of Independence). Built in 1829, it still carries trains over the Baltimore & Ohio (B&O; now CSX Corp.) mainline. Since a viaduct is a bridge with more than one arch, the B&O's 652-foot, eight-arch stone bridge at Relay, Maryland, is the world's oldest rail viaduct. It is still in continuous use.

The earliest bridges, trestles, and culverts were of timber. Wooden piles or log cribs supported many of them over marshy areas or inlets. The continent's first iron bridge, 42 feet long, was made by Richard R. Osborne, a Philadelphia & Reading (P&R) draftsman, mapmaker, and construction engineer, in a P&R blacksmith shop at Pottstown, Pennsylvania. It spanned a creek on the Delaware River's west bank opposite Manayunk (now part of Philadelphia). A light engine tested it on May 4, 1854, crossing safely. Copied from the Howe timber truss, it established the principle of the modern skyscraper. One of its girders is preserved today in the Smithsonian Institution in Washington. Hand-forged lugs attached to rolled-iron chords held in place cast-iron blocks on which rested fluted cast-iron braces. That summer Osborne built three similar structures elsewhere on the Reading mainline.

Laying track on a new Kansas & Missouri Railway bridge over the Missouri River in 1872. **[Frank Leslie's Illustrated Newspaper]**

In 1857, when the broad-gauge New York & Erie was being pushed over the hills toward Binghamton, New York, its chief engineer, Julien Adams, was stymied by the problem of crossing the ¼-mile Starrucca Creek Valley at an elevation of over 100 feet 3 miles east of Susquehanna, Pennsylvania. The valley was much too long for an earth fill, but the extreme slowness of work on stone piers for a planned bridge was stalling the whole project. In 1847 he hired James P. Kirkwood, a famous civil engineer, who opened stone quarries nearby and put 800 men to work on the piers. By 1848 trains were running over Starrucca Viaduct. Its seventeen 50-foot arches are 25 feet wide at track level; total length is 1040 feet. The highest point is 100 feet above the valley floor. In 1914 and from 1958 to 1961 it was much strengthened. In 1973 it was listed by the National Register of Historic Places, Pennsylvania Historical Site and Museum Commission, and American Society of Civil Engineers as a national landmark.

In 1852 the first Portage Viaduct, then America's longest wooden trestle, was built near Silver Springs, New York, by Col. Silas Seymour, the Erie's chief engineer, and Preston Lincoln, a civil engineer. It had sixteen 50-foot spans containing over 1,600,000 square board feet of pine and spruce and was 800 feet long, 202 feet wide, 235 feet high, and single-tracked. In 1875 it burned down, but it was replaced within 90 days by a wooden bridge of ten 50-foot spans, two 100-foot spans and one 118-foot span.

The present single-track steel Portage Viaduct on Conrail's Hoboken-Buffalo mainline, is 818 feet long and 235 feet high and contains over 1000 tons of steel. It spans the Genesee River Gorge in Letchworth State Park and a now-abandoned former Pennsylvania Railroad line and an abandoned canal. It was strengthened and modernized in 1903–1904 and 1943–1944. Conrail and Delaware and Hudson freight trains use it today.

The Howe truss made longer and higher bridges possible. Some, especially in New England, Pennsylvania, and the Northwest, were wooden-covered, boxed in, to protect the trusses. In 1847 and 1870 the collapse of two adjacent covered bridges, in turn, over the Millers River near Athol, Massachusetts, on the Vermont & Massachusetts (Boston & Maine) caused four and three deaths respectively. Between 1865 and 1874 the Louisville & Nashville made history by throwing a truss over the Falls of the Ohio at Louisville, Kentucky.

American bridge building's first use of steel was the big arched structure spanning the Mississippi at St.

Louis, designed and erected by James B. Eads in connection with the construction of Union Station. It was the first, and for many years the only, bridge so far south over that river. Its central 570-foot arch, flanked on each side by a 502-foot arch, was originally the world's longest bridge arch. The ribs are steel; the rest of the structure, iron. By 1947 there were about 90,000 steel bridges, with a total length of 1500 miles, on the 240,000 miles of United States railroads.

One great engineering feat was Gustav Lindenthal's Hell Gate Bridge across the East River, connecting Long Island with the New York mainland. A Pennsylvania Railroad report on the New York terminal situation mentioned the Hell Gate route in 1892, but it was not completed and opened until April 1, 1917, when the *Federal Express* ran in both directions between Boston, New York, and Washington.

Hell Gate Bridge, nearly 1000 feet long, is the main structure in a series of arched bridges including Little Hell Gate, almost 1200 feet long, which uses two small islands as stepping-stones, and the two 175-foot spans across the Bronx Kill, which separates those islands from the mainland. In the same operation a Long Island rail-bearing structure was elevated, most of it on a steel viaduct supported by concrete and the rest between retaining walls. The total project, nearly 10 miles of four-tracked mainline, cost the Pennsylvania and New Haven railroads over $27 million.

Lindenthal also bridged the Ohio River at Sciotoville, Ohio, with one continuous 1550-foot truss supported by three piers, an engineering marvel. Charles Ellet, Jr., and John A. Roebling did much to develop the cable suspension type. Ellet spanned the Schuylkill in 1843, the Niagara in 1847, and the Ohio at Wheeling, West Virginia, in 1849. Other great American bridge builders included Ralph Modjeski, O. H. Ammann, and Joseph B. Strauss.

Rolled steel was used in the spectacular suspension bridge thrown over the Niagara Gorge in 1898. Each Niagara bridge links the United States and Canada by rail. Roebling's greatest triumph was designing the Brooklyn Bridge in 1867. This traffic artery across the East River, opened in 1882, is used by New York City's subway-elevated railway system as well as by motor vehicles and pedestrians. Lindenthal's heavily used Williamsburg and Manhattan Bridges across the same river were completed in 1903 and 1909 respectively.

High Bridge, the first railway cantilever in North America, is part of the Southern's line between Lexington, Kentucky, and Danville, Virginia. It replaced a smaller bridge built in 1871 by C. Shaler Smith and is still the tallest railway bridge over a navigable stream in

This trestle, built with more than 2 million board feet of lumber, was Canadian Pacific's largest bridge in 1885; it has been replaced in turn by two bridges since then. [CP Rail]

the United States. (The first bridge was 31 feet lower than the present one but even then was the world's highest railway bridge.)

Southern Pacific's (SP's) original cantilever over the Pecos River in Texas was built in the days of Judge Roy Bean, "the only law west of the Pecos." The first one was opened in 1883; the second, a spidery structure 120 feet high, in 1892; and the present bridge in 1944. The second bridge was built with a giant traveling crane which thrust out one-half of the immense central span as far as it could go. Then the crane was dismantled, shipped by rail over a 1200-mile detour, reassembled, and used to create the other end of the bridge. *See also* PECOS RIVER BRIDGE.

In the early days, almost every major bridge replaced a ferry service. This is true also of some modern bridges. Huey Long Bridge over the Mississippi at New Orleans eliminated a ferry service. New Orleans Public Belt Railway owns it, but the Southern Pacific made its construction possible by guaranteeing a minimum of train tolls; so the 4.4-mile artery is usually referred to as an SP bridge. Another modern replacement of ferries is SP's Martinez-Benicia vertical-lift bridge over Suisun Bay, an arm of San Francisco Bay.

A double tragedy marked the construction of the bridge across the St. Lawrence 5 miles upstream from Quebec. This is one of the world's largest cantilevers. The job was begun in 1904 under the supervision of Theodore Cooper, an American consulting engineer. In 1907 the weight of a locomotive, a traveling crane, and a load of steel on the tip of the span collapsed the bridge, killing 74 men. The work was resumed, and in 1916 the approaches were completed. The central span, 600 feet long and weighing 4701 tons, was assembled on shore and lifted onto pontoons for towing into the central gap, where jacks would raise it into position. When the heavy mass was 30 feet above the water, the hoisting frame split, dumping it into the river. This time 10 workers perished. A year later the completed bridge was put into service. The Canadian National uses it continuously with no further problems.

The first recorded fatal rail bridge accident occurred on March 20, 1837, when a burned section of trestle on the South Carolina Railroad 8 miles from Charleston wrecked a passenger train, killing the engineer. Among the most disastrous rail bridge accidents in the United States were the wrecks at Chatsworth, Illinois, Ashtabula, Ohio, and Prospect, Pennsylvania, and the Kanawha & Michigan wreck in 1851 at Charleston, West Virginia, with 15 dead. *See* ASHTABULA WRECK; CHATSWORTH WRECK; PROSPECT WRECK.

Open drawbridges can be lethal. For example, a Great Western of Canada train fell into Des Jardines Canal near Toronto in 1857, killing 60 people. On the Grand Trunk in 1867 an open drawbridge at St-Hilaire, Quebec, took 86 lives. On the South Pacific Coast Railroad in 1890 at Oakland, California, there were 8 deaths. On the Jersey Central in 1958 at Newark Bay there were 48 deaths. Nearly all of the fatal wrecks on railway bridges, culverts, or trestles were due to collapses of the spans themselves.

BIBLIOGRAPHY: Freeman Hubbard, *Railroad Avenue,* McGraw-Hill, New York, 1945; Robert B. Shaw, *A History of Railroad Accidents, Safety Precautions, and Operating Practices,* Northern Press, Potsdam, N.Y., 1978.

British Columbia Railway (BC Rail) Line owned and operated by the provincial government, originally visioned as part of an international rail line running up into Alaska and through the United States down to the Mexican border. It was chartered as the Pacific Great Eastern (PGE; named for the Great Eastern Railway of Great Britain and backed by British capital) on February 27, 1912, to run from North Vancouver along Howe Sound and northeasterly for 470 miles to the Peace River area, to colonize and develop that sparsely settled region. "Construction work along the tall cliffs was extremely hazardous," said acting chief engineer Bernard Lewall, "because our greatest problem was the removal of a large amount of rock and in many spots the rock was rotten. One 30-mile stretch has five tunnels."

Construction began at Squamish, 41 miles north of North Vancouver, and was pushed northward and southward. But the winter of 1917–1918 found steel laid only 17.5 miles north of Quesnel and 18 miles south from Prince George, leaving a gap of about 45 miles between the two points, although this section had been graded; and the contractors ran out of money. Around that time, the United States government appropriated $65 million for its program of Alaska railway construction, mostly as a military measure. Encouraged by this news, the provincial government acquired Pacific Great Eastern's stock and set to work extending the line. It was then half completed, bankrupt, and had cost about $22 million. By 1921 it reached Quesnel, 348 miles north of Squamish. Again lack of funds halted construction, but in 1949 work began on an 80-mile extension from Quesnel to a connection with the transcontinental line of the Canadian National (CN). The line was opened for traffic in January 1953. Two years later an inspection train carrying rail officials from North Vancouver to Squamish rolled several miles over skeleton track to beat a deadline, the track gang not having had time to lay ballast. It rocked and jerked along at 5 miles per hour between precipitous cliffs above Howe Sound. In 1956 train service began from Squamish to Horseshoe Bay.

Today some 20 percent of the net rail freight tons loaded in British Columbia originates on the former PGE, which in 1972 was renamed British Columbia Railway, or BC Rail. Part of it, being local, is loaded and unloaded at points along the line; but most is interchanged with other railways, including the Northern

Alberta at Dawson Creek and the CN at Prince George and North Vancouver. The last-named interchange provides a link with CP Rail (Canadian Pacific), British Columbia Hydro Railway, and Burlington Northern (BN). Also, a rail barge service between North Vancouver and Seattle connects British Columbia Railway with the Milwaukee Road, Union Pacific, and BN. Daily passenger service links North Vancouver with Lillooet. Stainless-steel dayliners run between North Vancouver and Prince George thrice weekly, returning south from Prince George on alternate days.

BC Rail is roughly Y-shaped. Its eastern fork, terminating at Fort Nelson, was opened for traffic in 1971. The western fork is planned to reach northward to Dease Lake, but lack of money has halted construction 178 miles short of that objective. The railway bought its first diesel locomotive in 1949 from General Electric and was fully dieselized by 1957. One of its steam engines, No. 2, is permanently on display in a park at Squamish.

BC Rail is Canada's first railway to be run to radio transmission to locomotive engineers and conductors. Its Squamish–North Vancouver line was the first railway anywhere to be equipped with the microwave transmission system. The line has over 3000 employees and 1620 track miles, including yard tracks, sidings, and extensions. A computing center in Vancouver assists in planning grade revisions, bridge design, and track assignment, as well as information systems for management and rail operations. Freight revenue comes mostly from forest products and manufactured goods.

BIBLIOGRAPHY: *Pacific Great Eastern Railway,* Railway Department, Victoria, B.C., 1949; R. A. J. Phillips, *Canada's Railways,* McGraw-Hill, New York, 1968; Bruce Ramsey, *PGE: Railway to the North,* Mitchell Press, Vancouver, B.C., 1962.

Train gate in the Pennsylvania Railroad's old Broad Street Station, as it looked in the 1890s. It was torn down after the station closed in 1952. **[H. Pickwell]**

Broad Street Station Passenger terminal across the street from the Philadelphia City Hall. It served for 58 years as headquarters of the Pennsylvania Railroad (PRR; during 43 of those years the author's father worked in this station). From its executive offices emanated decisions which affected not only the PRR but almost every railroad in the country as well. It was a mark of grandeur that the Pennsy's president had an office nearly half a block long.

The station was opened on December 5, 1881, survived two great fires, the Depression of the 1930s, and both world wars. It was finally closed on April 26, 1952, torn down, and replaced by the present magnificent but inadequately used 30th Street Station a mile to the west, now owned by Amtrak.

During the infancy of Old Broad there were no automobiles; even streetcars were horse-drawn. American-type (4-4-0) steam engines were the main source of motive power for the 160 trains which rolled into and out of the monumental depot. The fact that all these trains were handled in a stub-end station with only eight original tracks gives some inkling of the old-timers' railroading skill. By 1910, 378 trains were using the station, a fantastic figure for that era. In 1926, at the time of the Dempsey-Tunney championship fight, Old Broad's restaurant fed, in one day alone, some 10,000 customers.

On the station's last day, the Philadelphia Orchestra boarded a Pennsy train there for a concert tour, as it had done 885 times in the preceding 51 years, but with a difference. An hour before departure time, the orchestra's 103 musicians, under the baton of Eugene Ormandy, serenaded Old Broad with a farewell performance that ended with all the people singing, many having tears in their eyes, "Auld Lang Syne." After that, in a downpour of rain, engine No. 4800 (the first GG-1 ever to arrive at Broad Street Station) pulled the last train out at 9:47 p.m. The next day, with rain still pouring, the station was consigned to the wrecking crews. But it went down in a blaze of glory.

BIBLIOGRAPHY: Harry P. Albrecht, *Broad Street Station,* pub. by himself, Clifton Heights, Pa., 1972; George H. Burgess and Miles C. Kennedy, *Centennial History of the Pennsylvania Railroad Company: 1846–1946,* Pennsylvania Railroad, Philadelphia, 1949.

Brooks Locomotive Works Company founded by Horatio G. Brooks (1828–1887), a native of Portsmouth, New Hampshire. Young Brooks worked as a machinist apprentice, became a Boston & Maine engineer, and was hired in 1850 to deliver a locomotive from the Hinkley & Drury Works in Boston to the New York & Erie Railroad (NY&E) at Dunkirk, New York. The delivery took 2 months: by boat to New York City, through the Erie Canal to Buffalo, and by schooner to Dunkirk. When the NY&E was formally opened on May 13, 1851, he served as engineer on the pilot locomotive that preceded the nation's first presidential special, a train that took President Fillmore and his Cabinet 461 miles from Piermont, New York, to Dunkirk. *See* HINKLEY LOCOMOTIVE WORKS.

In 1865 Brooks became superintendent of motive power and machinery for the entire system. In 1869, after Jay Gould had taken over the Erie and transferred its Dunkirk shops to Hornellsville (now Hornell), New York, Brooks organized the locomotive works bearing his name and took a 10-year lease on the old Dunkirk shops. Between 1870 and 1873 he built 145 engines, the most famous one being named *Jay Gould,* shining with brasswork and nickel plate, with a black-walnut cab having Gould's portrait on either side. The financial panic of 1873 cut the plant's employees from 375 to 126. Brooks himself paid the grocery bills of the men he laid off.

In the early 1880s the company was so prosperous that it bought the property from the Erie and expanded it from 9 to 20 acres. After Brooks died, his son-in-law, Edward H. Nichols, and then Marshall L. Hinman headed the company. In 1888 the works completed its 2000th engine, which with tender weighed 309,000 pounds, for the Great Northern. In June 1901, Brooks became affiliated with the American Locomotive Co. and celebrated the building of its 4000th locomotive. Its output that year, with 2613 employes, was 382 engines. For the next 26 years it continued to build units for domestic and foreign service, but diesel competition plus what the automobile was doing to railroad passenger traffic forced it to shut down in 1927. *See* AMERICAN LOCOMOTIVE CO.

BIBLIOGRAPHY: Angus Sinclair, *Development of the Locomotive Engine,* annotated ed. by John W. White, Jr., M.I.T., Cambridge, Mass., 1970.

Brotherhood of Locomotive Engineers (BLE)

Originally called the Brotherhood of the Footboard, it is the oldest rail labor union in North America. It was organized on May 8, 1863, at Marshall, Michigan, in the home (still standing) of Jared (Yankee) Thompson. Thompson and William D. Robinson, both Michigan Central (MC) engineers, spearheaded the organization. Leading up to its formation, A. S. Sweet, superintendent of machinery on the MC (which later became a Vanderbilt road), had cut engineers' pay and discharged some of the men who protested. He also dismissed top-seniority firemen, replacing them with greenhorns. The engineers, loyal to their firemen, refused to run without them.

Thirteen MC engineers formed a protective association: if Sweet discharged any of them, the rest would quit on the spot. They also decided to extend their movement to all railroads. In connection with a Detroit convention attended by 12 delegates from five Midwestern roads, the pioneer division of the future BLE was launched at Marshall, with Robinson as chief engineer. This division, No. 1 in Detroit, heads the list of over 800 present-day BLE divisions in the United States and Canada.

In 1867 the brotherhood began publication of its *Locomotive Engineers Monthly Journal* (now the *Locomotive Engineer*, possibly the oldest labor periodical) and created a life insurance service for its members (it

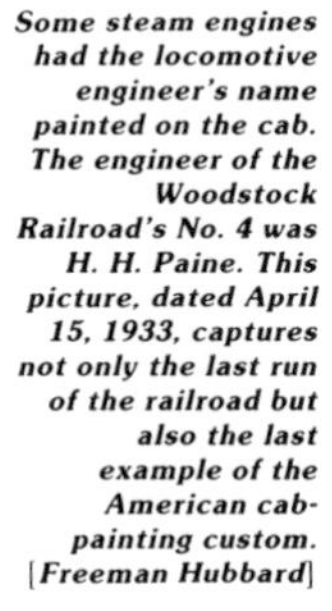
Some steam engines had the locomotive engineer's name painted on the cab. The engineer of the Woodstock Railroad's No. 4 was H. H. Paine. This picture, dated April 15, 1933, captures not only the last run of the railroad but also the last example of the American cab-painting custom. [Freeman Hubbard]

is independent of the brotherhood itself). Insurance protection was urgently needed before the adoption of modern safety devices, for railroading was considered such a hazardous occupation that many insurance companies rejected such risks. In 1887 the BLE, which then had about 25,000 members, formed a women's auxiliary for the wives of members.

BLE was involved in the major strikes of 1877 and 1888, which were accompanied by violence, but not in the American Railway Union walkout of 1894, better known as the Pullman strike. In 1915 it joined the other three transportation brotherhoods in making the first nationwide strike threat, to bring about an 8-hour day. This objective was attained by congressional passage of the Adamson Act of 1916. Not surprisingly, the carriers fought this law in the courts, but the Supreme Court upheld it.

After World War II, the BLE and the Brotherhood of Railroad Trainmen (BRT) undertook in a big way to improve working conditions for their members. Talks with railroad management got nowhere, and a nationwide strike was authorized. The 90-day breathing spell that a government emergency board ordered under provisions of the Railway Labor Act produced no agreement. The BLE and BRT members struck on May 23, 1946. Senator Robert A. Taft stalled President Truman's request for legislation to draft the strikers into military service and thus force them back to work. Finally, under White House pressure, both brotherhoods accepted Truman's terms and returned to their jobs for a pay increase of 18½ cents an hour, or $1.48 per basic day.

BLE headquarters is a 13-story office building completed and opened in 1910 at 1365 Ontario Street, Cleveland, Ohio.

BIBLIOGRAPHY: Richard J. Cook (ed.), *A Brief History of the Brotherhood of Locomotive Engineers,* Brotherhood of Locomotive Engineers, Cleveland, 1977.

Brotherhood of Locomotive Firemen and Enginemen (BLF&E) Organization founded by Joshua Leach in 1873 at Port Jervis, New York. In 1968, when it merged into the United Transportation Union and its last president, H. E. Gilbert, became an assistant president of the new organization, the BLF&E had 69,750 members, international headquarters (a grand lodge) in Cleveland, Ohio, and subordinate lodges in 49 states (all but Hawaii) and 10 provinces in Canada. It had employment contracts covering engineers on 167 railroads and firemen, hostlers, and hostler-helpers on 359 roads, as well as state and provincial legislative and education boards throughout the United States and Canada devoted to its members' welfare.

The most colorful figure in BLF&E history was Eugene V. Debs, who not only became an international officer in the union and editor of its magazine but also helped to found the Brotherhood of Railroad Trainmen, organized the American Railway Union (ARU) in 1893 as the first attempt at industrywide unionism, and in five elections was the Socialist party candidate for President. Despite appeals by the influential Gene Debs, the Brotherhood of Locomotive Firemen refused to support the ARU, but over the years it made unsuccessful merger overtures to the more conservative Brotherhood of Locomotive Engineers.

***In the tradition of steam engines decorated for special occasions, this festive locomotive pulled the train for the Thirteenth Annual Convention of the Brotherhood of Locomotive Firemen of North America, held in Minneapolis in 1886.* [Frank Fullhart/Milwaukee Road]**

See also DEBS, EUGENE VICTOR; UNIONS, RAILROAD LABOR.

BIBLIOGRAPHY: David Karsner, *Debs: His Authorized Life and Letters,* Boni and Liveright, New York, 1919.

Brotherhood of Railroad Trainmen (BRT) Organization, called the Brotherhood of Railroad Brakemen until 1889, that was founded on September 13, 1883, by eight Delaware and Hudson (D&H) train and yard service employees meeting in a caboose parked in the D&H yard at Oneonta, New York. They elected as their first grand master Charles J. Woodworth, the conductor to whom that car was assigned. The car itself, a red, wooden-bodied, flat-topped four-wheeler, has since been restored and is displayed in a semisheltered spot in an Oneonta park. The colorful Eugene V. Debs also was a major factor in helping to organize the BRT. *See* DEBS, EUGENE VICTOR.

The BRT was organized because railroading was then so hazardous that it was almost impossible for a trainman to get insurance. During the first 5 years after the Civil War, according to BRT figures, 70 percent of America's train crewmen were killed or injured on the job. A cartoon of that period showed an applicant for a braking job being told there was no opening at that time but to come around next Thursday, when it was likely that a man would have been killed. Workers in those days had no legal redress from injury or death due to an employer's negligence. There was no workmen's compensation, social security, unemployment insurance, minimum wage, or Medicare, but there *was* a 7-day week.

Eventually the BRT had contracts on some 300 United States and Canadian railroads and about 135 contracts with bus companies. Its jurisdiction covered conductors, brakemen, roadmen, yardmen, baggagemen, switch tenders, and bus drivers. In December 1965 local BRT members called a strike because of the Southern Pacific's failure to keep certain caboose equipment in good condition and to operate waycars on some trains. The walkout might have tied up the entire 10,400-mile system if a federal judge hadn't gotten out of bed before a chilly dawn to issue a temporary restraining order that kept the wheels turning while the dispute was being settled.

The BRT also dealt with such controversial issues as unemployment, railroad consolidations, long freight trains, big motive power, the 6-hour day, and the competition of trucks, buses, airplanes, and pipelines. Even before it merged with the Order of Railway Conductors in 1968 and before it became part of the present United Transportation Union, the BRT was the largest of the operating rail brotherhoods, having 185,000 members, including 30,000 in Canada, a grand lodge in Cleveland, and 1100 other lodges in 49 states of the United States (not Hawaii) and 10 provinces in Canada.

See also UNIONS, RAILROAD LABOR.

BIBLIOGRAPHY: Walter F. McCaleb, *Brotherhood of Railroad Trainmen,* Albert & Charles Boni, New York, 1937.

Brotherhood of Sleeping Car Porters and Redcaps By founding Pullman's Palace Car Co. in 1867, George M. Pullman coincidentally helped to open a new occupation for Negroes, just emerging from slavery and mostly limited to farming and other manual labor. The blacks were then a cheap, plentiful source of labor. Centuries of bondage had inured them to poverty, hard work, and servility—a background suited to the work of train porters catering to the needs and whims of white travelers. *See* PULLMAN, GEORGE MORTIMER.

Neatly uniformed, with well-shined shoes, and smiling, they fitted into the stereotyped concept of "good" colored servants. Supplementing their very low monthly wages were the often-meager tips they received. Thus their income depended upon cheerful service rendered to passengers.

No sleeping-car employee ever got rich on his wages, although Diamond Jim Brady (1856–1917), genial salesman for a railroad supply house with a personality somewhat like that of Jubilee Jim Fisk of the Erie, bequeathed $2500 to his favorite Pullman porter, and a wealthy Chicagoan left $3000 to put a porter's son through a medical college. One day in 1929 another porter, named Pierson, going through his car at the end of a run, found a chamois bag holding jewelry valued at $400,000, said to have been the largest find ever made in a Pullman. The owner, a woman, was located. She gave Pierson a $100 reward.

For Pullman porters to grovel on their jobs was humiliating. On the other hand, their handsome blue uniforms, the relative splendor of the trains they worked on, the celebrities who condescendingly spoke to them, and their opportunities to visit faraway places did much to boost the morale of men accustomed to living, often barefooted, in crude shacks on "Tobacco Road." Returning home from a run, the porter aroused the envy and imagination of other blacks by telling them about his experiences, the persons he had contact with, and the distant cities and towns he had visited. This opened a whole new world to them.

Sometimes the porter's life of hard work was combined with adventure. A porter named Blair had charge of the chair car on the St. Paul & Duluth's ill-fated train No. 4 when it rode through the holocaust at Hinckley, Minnesota, in 1894. Burning woods set the train afire. Blair calmed the terrified passengers, silenced a religious fanatic who yelled "We're all going to heaven together," stood by the water tank supplying wet bandages, and sprayed passengers lying on the floor, putting out fires that were burning the hair off women's heads. For this the railroad company gave him a gold watch. *See* HINCKLEY HOLOCAUST.

The Pullman strike of 1894 involved only employees at the manufacturing plant, not porters or maids. *See* DEBS, EUGENE VICTOR; STRIKES, MAJOR RAILROAD.

By the twentieth century the Pullman Co. had acquired such a virtual monopoly of sleeping-car service through mergers and financial deals, despite the Sherman Antitrust Act of 1890, that the only way a traveler could occupy a berth on nearly all American railroads was in a Pullman car attended by a Pullman porter. The company set its own wage scales and working conditions, ignoring labor unions.

Work hours on Pullman cars ranged from 300 to 400 a month until 1931, when they dropped to less than half that time. A porter who didn't like the hours was free to quit, but where else could he find a job? The men had to buy their own uniforms, shoe polish, etc., and unless they brought lunch from home, pay for their meals in dining cars, besides providing their own board and lodging at both ends of their runs.

Sometimes, in an emergency, a porter had to work a full 24-hour day without sleep, food, or overtime pay, while maintaining a cheerful mien and respect for even the most difficult passengers. If a car with mechanical trouble was shunted to a siding, he was expected to stay aboard until officially relieved, even though there might be no food, heat, or light. Pullman's general superintendent ordered substantial cuts in paychecks on hearsay evidence of poor performance or arguments with other personnel. There was no hearing or appeal.

The porters' attempts to organize a union in 1909, 1910, and 1913 were quickly squelched by firing the men involved. But the federal takeover of United States railroads in World War I brightened their outlook. Under the War Labor Conference Board's report of March 29, 1918, Pullman employees had the right to organize and choose representatives for collective bargaining.

Two rival groups sprang up: the Brotherhood of Sleeping Car Porters Protective Union (SCPPU) and the Railway Men's Association (RMA). Each was a Negro body seeking status as the Pullman porters' representative. The United States Director General of the Railroad Administration did not recognize either of them. The RMA was relatively free of Pullman Co. control because it included station porters as well as localized groups in the Twin Cities. It managed to get hard-contested federal hearings that led to a nationwide wage increase and somewhat better working conditions. But it and the SCPPU passed out of existence in 1920 with the formation of a company-sponsored "union," the paternalistic Pullman Porters Benefit Association.

On August 25, 1925, the long-lasting but continually struggling Brotherhood of Sleeping Car Porters (BSCP) was organized in Harlem, New York City, largely by the initiative of A. Philip Randolph, editor, writer, orator, and labor organizer. Randolph was the only non-Pullman employee at the BSCP organizational meeting, which gave him the advantage of not being subject to Pullman Co. discipline. He was elected president and general organizer of the brotherhood, which as yet existed only on paper. The work of organizing a depressed minority needed his kind of courage and resourcefulness, but he was criticized sometimes even by his own followers for being extreme in his views. *See* RANDOLPH, A. PHILIP.

By sheer force of personality, Randolph induced the Executive Council of the American Federation of Labor (AFL) to grant the new union an international charter, the first to be awarded to an all-Negro unit in the 47 years of the federation's history. From its beginning, the AFL had a clause decrying racial discrimination; but that was little more than theoretical, for the constitutions of at least 22 international unions, or more than half of the AFL affiliates, barred Negro membership.

The new brotherhood received some support from the Civil Liberties Union, Associated Press, Universal News Service, other news-gathering agencies, and most of the Negro press, although Pullman is said to have subsidized two major black papers published in Chicago to oppose the BSCP.

In 1928 the Interstate Commerce Commission (ICC) voted 4 to 3 not to have jurisdiction in the BSCP-Pullman dispute, which centered on the porters' demand for higher wages instead of tips. In that year, too, the BSCP voted for a nationwide strike for higher pay and asked AFL President William Green to use his influence to help the brotherhood invoke the services of the apathetic U.S. Mediation Board. But Green opposed a strike "at this time," and it never took place. The United States then had about 9000 porters in the transportation industries, nearly half of whom lived in Chicago, on the edge of which the Pullman Co. had its headquarters in its so-called model community of Pullman, Illinois.

Meanwhile, some time between 1890 and 1900, an unnamed luggage-carrying porter in New York's Grand Central Station (predecessor of Grand Central Terminal) tied a red flannel band around his black uniform cap for quick identification in the crowd. This strategy paid off. Other porters copied it. George H. Daniels, New York Central Railroad publicist, observed the practice, coined the word *redcap,* and ordered red uniform caps for all of Grand Central's porters. That style soon became universal.

In 1936 the BSCP opened its membership to redcaps, including all who handled baggage and otherwise assisted passengers to board and leave trains, buses, and airplanes. Until 1935, most of them, both blacks and whites, depended entirely on tips, although some stations paid their porters nominal wages of from $10 to $40 a month. Yet in prosperous years an enterprising redcap who had advanced to servicing Pullman cars could average as much as $150 a month. For that reason even well-educated blacks did not scorn such jobs.

With the help of the Brotherhood of Sleeping Car Porters and after bitterly contested ICC hearings, the redcaps were awarded minimum wages and bargaining rights under the Railway Labor Act. In 1944 they were getting a basic wage of $4.56 a day. The roads began charging travelers a fixed sum for each piece of luggage handled, pooling the money and making up the difference themselves when it fell below the minimum wage.

The Chicago Red Caps began as an AFL local on a national basis. Later, both the BSCP (black) and the Union of American Railway Clerks (white) claimed jurisdiction over the new union. The Red Caps eventually broke their AFL ties, becoming an independent union for 5 years; and in 1942 the organization, with its Negro president, Willard S. Townsend, took its 12,000 members, black and white, into the CIO, and thus eventually into the present AFL-CIO.

Meanwhile, in 1935, the Brotherhood of Sleeping Car Porters voted to uphold its claim to speak for all Negroes in sleeping-car service. It persuaded the Mediation Board to order and supervise balloting to determine which group should represent the porters in negotiations for wages and working conditions. The brotherhood won, 3931 to 1411, over the Pullman Co.'s own "union." Three years later, in a Chicago meeting, the BSCP organized the maids and other female sleeping-car employees into its International Ladies Auxiliary.

But as motor vehicles and planes began cutting sharply into rail passenger traffic, including luxury travel, the number of sleeping-car porters and maids and station porters dwindled. The brotherhood, which had long been esteemed by the black community, shrank from a peak membership of about 12,000 to barely 1000. While the original membership was all black, owing to Pullman's hiring practices, the establishment of Amtrak in 1971 brought a small group of young white Amtrak employees into its ranks. Two of them were among the delegates at the final BSCP convention, which was held on February 28, 1978, at Rosemont, Illinois.

In this special convention, the remnants of the Brotherhood of Sleeping Car Porters voted unanimously to affiliate as an autonomous member of the Railway and Airline Clerks. The merger became effective at once. Winfred W. Seymour of Denver, Colorado (a nephew of the author's wife), is the system division's secretary-treasurer.

Randolph's death on May 16, 1979, at 90 drew a flood of testimonials from all over the country. Among them, President Jimmy Carter said that, in remembering the gentility and idealism of A. Philip Randolph, future Americans should not forget that "he faced down four Presidents" [Wilson] in his pursuit of peace, [Franklin Roosevelt] in his plea for fair employment practice, [Truman] in urging integration of the Armed Forces, and [Kennedy] in the March on Washington in 1963 that helped to bring about the Civil Rights Act of 1964. Another President, Johnson, presented Randolph with a Medal of Freedom.

A tax collector who visited Randolph's modest apartment shortly after his death found a financial net worth of less than $500. The labor leader's most valued possession is said to have been a battered watch once given him by Pullman car porters.

BIBLIOGRAPHY: Jervis Anderson and Peter Stone, *A. Philip Randolph: A Biographical Portrait,* Harcourt Brace Jovanovich, New York, 1973; Brailsford R. Brazeal, *The Brotherhood of Sleeping Car Porters,* Harper, New York, 1946; Herbert Hill, *Black Labor and the American Legal System,* Bureau of National Affairs, Washington, 1977; Stewart H. Holbrook, *The Story of American Railroads,* Crown, New York, 1947; Herbert R. Northrup, *Organized Labor and the Negro,* Harper, New York, 1944.

BRT *See* BROTHERHOOD OF RAILROAD TRAINMEN.

Budd Company In addition to automobiles, trucks, and other products, the Budd Company built the first diesel-powered, streamlined passenger trains, the Burlington Zephyrs, and in the 1970s delivered greater numbers of stainless-steel rail passenger cars in the United States than any other manufacturer. Currently, with about 20,000 employees, it is the foremost builder of rail passenger cars on the North American continent. Total sales of all its products, including railroad equipment, exceed $1 billion a year.

The futuristic SPV-2000, the Budd Company's self-propelled rail diesel passenger car with an optional high-speed nose.

In 1912 Edward G. Budd (1870–1946) started the company in Philadelphia with 13 employees and $100,000 capitalization, three-fourths of which he himself supplied. He challenged the wood-fabricating establishment of his day, the carriage makers and carpenters, by working for the adoption of all-steel automobile bodies. In the 1920s he began using stainless steel in manufacturing cutlery, surgical instruments, transportation vehicles, and other items. In 1931 he built a stainless-steel airplane and had it test-flown for 100 hours.

Three years later his Hunting Park Avenue plant in Philadelphia built the *Pioneer Zephyr,* an entire three-car train weighing no more than an ordinary Pullman car. It was the first train powered by a diesel engine. On its maiden run on April 9, 1934, from Broad Street Station, Philadelphia, over the Pennsylvania Railroad mainline it attained a top speed of 90 miles per hour. Later, the U.S. Department of Transportation set a global speed record of 256 miles per hour with a research vehicle moving on rail trucks designed and built at Budd Technical Center.

Prior to World War II the Hunting Park Avenue shops rolled out families of gleaming Zephyrs, Rockets, Silver Meteors, Champions, and El Capitans for various railroads as well as such individual trains as the *Super Chief, Flying Yankee, Crusader, San Diegan,* and *Chicagoan.* Budd's new SPV-2000 self-propelled, stainless-steel, diesel-powered railcar, with its optional high-speed nose, can reach 120 miles per hour.

Budd pioneered the railway disk brake just before World War II. Higher speeds of new trains had brought a need for improved braking. Disk brakes eliminated the undesirable characteristics of iron-on-iron wheel-tread brakes and provided smoother, more efficient stopping. After the war, a high percentage of the railroads adopted this major innovation for mainline passenger trains.

During the war, like Baldwin, Alco, and other great industrial plants, Budd turned out huge quantities of military equipment. Later it broadened its field to include plastics, aluminum, testing and measuring, and electronics. As the nation's rail travel was dropping sharply in the 1960s, Budd's railway division concentrated on city rapid transit and commuter business. It built subway, commuter, and other rapid transit cars for such urban centers as Philadelphia, New York, and Chicago. These included sound-insulated, high-speed Metroliner cars for the Pennsy's New York–Washington run, self-propelled high-speed cars for the Long Island Rail Road, and bi-level gallery cars for the Chicago area.

It helped, too, to revitalize the national rail passenger system by supplying Amtrak with modern Amfleet cars.

Owing to the complexity of advanced propulsion and control systems made by outside contractors, Budd decided in the early 1970s to accept orders involving self-propelled cars only as a subcontractor but to keep building locomotive-hauled cars as a prime contractor. The company has corporate headquarters in Troy, Michigan, and scores of plants and/or offices throughout the United States and Canada, with substantial holdings in six other countries.

BIBLIOGRAPHY: Freeman Hubbard, *Great Trains of All Time*, Grosset & Dunlap, New York, 1962; Gilbert F. Richards, *Budd on the Move: Innovation for a Nation on Wheels*, Newcomen Society in North America, New York, 1975.

Buffalo-Hunting Excursions *See* EXCURSION TRAINS.

Burlington *See* CHICAGO, BURLINGTON & QUINCY RAILROAD.

Burlington Northern Inc. (BN) Rail network with nearly 30,000 miles of track in 25 states and 2 Canadian provinces, British Columbia and Manitoba. Stretching from the West Coast through the Rockies to the Great Lakes and down to the Gulf of Mexico, it is America's longest rail network and the second largest in terms of revenue (as of 1979), with assets exceeding $3750 million. In early 1980 BN had 58,500 employees, almost 3000 locomotives, and about 128,500 cars.

Its headquarters is in St. Paul, Minnesota, from which the one-eyed titan, James J. Hill, ruled his Great Northern empire until his death in 1916. BN is a merger of the Great Northern Railway (GN), the Chicago, Burlington & Quincy Railroad (known as both the Burlington and the Q), the Northern Pacific Railway (NP), the Pacific Coast Railroad, and the Spokane, Portland & Seattle Railway (SP&S), to which was added in April 1980 the St. Louis–San Francisco Railway (Frisco). Also, the BN owns the Colorado & Southern, the Fort Worth and Denver, and the Oregon Electric rail lines. *See* HILL, JAMES JEROME.

In authorizing the Frisco merger, the Interstate Commerce Commission (ICC) estimated that it would produce $20 million annual net savings and increase BN's net income by $33 million a year. The merger will save time and resources and cut loss and damage to goods because trains now can move across longer distances without having to switch cars to other roads.

This gigantic system's roots go back to 1850, when the Q's earliest predecessor began operating over 6 miles of track in Illinois. Before being merged into the BN, the Great Northern (founded in 1857) and the Northern Pacific (1864) operated over roughly parallel lines between St. Paul and Seattle. These two systems jointly controlled the SP&S, which ran through Oregon, Washington, and California, and the Burlington, which linked Chicago with Billings, Montana, and Denver.

The merger of 1970 which created the BN was not a new idea. Such a consolidation had been urged by economists and rail executives since the 1890s. Jim Hill had tried to bring it about. In 1955 railroad presidents

The awesome Columbia Gorge, between Washington and Oregon, provides an appropriate backdrop for a part of America's longest rail network, the Burlington Northern Inc. Pictured here is a Burlington Northern time freight powered by three 2000-horsepower diesel locomotives. [Burlington Northern Inc.]

John M. Budd of GN and Robert S. Macfarlane of NP jointly filed a merger application with the ICC, which, however, did not approve it until November 29, 1968. The U.S. Supreme Court affirmed it on March 2, 1970. Prior to the merger, GN and NP were keen competitors, but for some time they shared the same office building in St. Paul, separated by a solid wall. The merger figuratively broke down "the walls of Jericho."

Burlington Northern's huge freight revenue comes mostly from grain, coal, forest products, food and kindred products, chemicals and allied products, primary metals, pulp, and paper. Its intercity passenger service has been operated under contract by Amtrak since 1971. In 1972 it sold all its suburban commuter equipment in the Chicago area to the West Suburban Mass Transit District, which leased it back to BN for continued operation. Funds for the sale were given to WSMTD to use, along with federal and state grants, in subsidizing the fleet of cars and buying new equipment.

BN also has highway services for freight, including Burlington Truck Lines Inc., Burlington Northern Motor Lines, and Northern Pacific Transport Co., plus various common-carrier truck lines. It also has large quantities of piggyback equipment and facilities and operates Burlington Northern Air Freight Inc.

Even before the Frisco merger it owned 2,400,000 acres of timber and farm land, plus mineral rights to 6,200,000 acres, a Northern Pacific land-grant heritage. Its Resources Department manages and develops these valuable assets, balancing its tree-harvesting and tree-planting schedules. Included in mineral rights are rich deposits of coal, oil, gas, and iron in the Western and Central United States and in Canada. In 1976 BN built in Wyoming an oil refinery which yields about one-tenth of the diesel fuel its locomotives need. The system's recoverable coal supplies, estimated at 12 million tons, are still relatively undeveloped.

Some 640 acres of Burlington Northern timberland disappeared into the crater of the Mount St. Helens volcano in Washington or drifted across the country as fine ash after the eruption of May 18, 1980. In the 1970 merger BN had acquired the Washington forests from the Northern Pacific, which had been given them as federal land grants in 1864. BN owns 40,800 acres near the mountain, much of it now strewn with volcano-felled trees. Volcanic ash up to 40 inches deep covered considerable land within 30 miles of the crater. This ash, mixed with water, became thick, hard mud that seriously hampered plans to salvage the fallen timber.

BN's merger with the Frisco created America's largest rail system, 29,226 miles of track, the second largest being CSX Corp., 27,477 miles.

BIBLIOGRAPHY: William E. Bain, *Frisco Folks,* Sage Books, Denver, 1961; Elisabeth C. Jackson and Carolyn Curtis, *Guide to the Burlington Archives in the Newberry Library, 1851–1901,* Newberry Library, Chicago, 1949; *Jane's World Railways and Rapid Transit Systems,* F. Watts, New York, 1978; Richard C. Overton, *Burlington Route,* Knopf, New York, 1965; C. R. Wood, *The Northern Pacific,* Superior Publishing, Seattle, 1968.

Main routes of the Western colossus, Burlington Northern Inc., after the Frisco merger effective November 25, 1980. Its 29,226 miles make it the largest rail network in United States history.

Burroughs, John ***(1837–1921)*** American naturalist and writer of Esopus, New York. Returning from California, he was riding a Pennsylvania Railroad train through Ohio when he died. His last words were, "How far are we from home?"

Buttons, Uniform Buttons worn by railroad passenger trainmen and transit motormen and conductors on coats, cuffs, and sometimes cap badges. They symbolize rail passenger travel and are collected by hobbyists, who organized the National Button Society of America in 1938. Many names and initials on buttons represent carriers long vanished by merger or abandonment.

Originally, trainmen did not wear uniforms. The earliest American rail buttons known to collectors were made for the Hudson River Railroad prior to 1850. The oldest ones made for transit lines can be traced back to the horsecars of the late 1860s. The United States has had three major manufacturers of uniform buttons—Scovill Mfg. Co. (now Scovill Inc.) and Waterbury Companies, Inc., both of Waterbury, Connecticut, and the former D. Evans Co., Attleboro, Massachusetts—as well as many minor ones. Nearly all American varieties have been made of brass or aluminum, while many of those in other countries, especially in wartime, may be of wood, hard rubber, glass, or plastic.

C

C&C See CARSON & COLORADO RAILROAD.

C&S See COLORADO & SOUTHERN RAILWAY.

Cabooses No longer is the "little red caboose" (many cabooses were not red) the center of dramatic or sentimental rail freight operation, nor is it the trainmen's home away from home to the extent that it was in a bygone century and a half. No longer do trainmen scramble up from the cupola (also called crow's nest and doghouse) and walk the swaying car tops to communicate with the head end or to set handbrakes on one car after another, regardless of weather, while their train is careening downgrade out of control. Wooden cabooses, or waycars, operated with handbrakes, lit by kerosine lamps, and heated by coal stoves are ancient history. So are permanently assigned cabooses that conductors treated like personal property; today's cabooses are pooled.

Formerly, trainmen lived in these cars for days at a time on long runs or while laying over at terminals between runs, cooking their own meals on the road, maybe including field-fresh ears of corn, a mess of hastily picked beans, or a chicken that their boomer flagman had "requisitioned" during a night stop on a siding adjacent to a farm. Some meals are still prepared in cabooses, and much coffee is brewed there, but the increasing number of trackside restaurants and hot-dog stands, plus shorter working hours, has made this practice minimal.

The caboose was the original house trailer. Besides the conductor's office with a desk, it had a living room, kitchen, dining room, workshop, bedroom, den, toilet, balcony, and observation tower that he shared with the rear brakemen and any other authorized personnel riding with him. It was his source of income and personal prestige, also his means of travel. Join a railroad and see the world! Many a wide-eyed farm boy or bored factory hand answered that call in a bygone era. The caboose was a daily adventure that took them far from their native cities, towns, or farms. Naturally they became fond of it. Many a conductor loved his caboose so much that when he retired he bought for a nominal sum the little old car in which he had spent the best years of his life and had it hauled to the backyard of his home and remodeled into a den for use in his old age.

Caboose was originally a nautical word, defined by some dictionaries as "a house on deck where the cooking is done; a galley" and "an open-air cooking oven," in addition to the common railroad meaning. They link it to the Dutch *kabuis* and *kombuis,* the Danish *kabys,* the Swedish *kabysa,* the German *Kabuse,* and Low German *Kabuus,* each meaning "a little room or hut." In Canada and Great Britain it is usually called a *van* or *brake van.*

The first caboose on record was merely the last boxcar of a mixed (passenger-freight) train on the Auburn

& Syracuse (now part of Conrail). From this car in the 1840s conductor Nat Williams ran his train. In it he kept flags, lanterns, chains, tools, heavy rope, etc., and wrote his reports while seated on a wooden box, using an upended barrel as his desk and meal table, and eating out of a lunch pail brought from home.

In effect, Nat's car was a caboose. But the word is not known to have been used until 1885, when it referred to conductors' cars on the Buffalo, Corning & New York (now Conrail). In 1889, according to *The New York Times* of that year, trainman Edgerton sued Commodore Vanderbilt's New York & Harlem Railway for injuries he had received on February 29, 1859, in a "caboose car." No further details are available.

Some of the earliest cabooses were flatcars on which cabins or shanties were built, but most of them were boxcars with windows and side doors, equipped with facilities for working, eating, and sleeping. (Later, regular cabooses with cupolas and side doors were not uncommon, but this type was outlawed around the turn of the twentieth century as being unsafe.)

The most widely accepted version of the origin of the caboose cupola credits its invention to T. B. Watson, a Chicago & North Western (C&NW) freight conductor running between Cedar Rapids and Clinton, Iowa. One summer day in 1863 his regularly assigned flat-topped caboose was shopped for repair, and Watson was given temporarily the use of a "bad-order" boxcar with a large hole in the roof. The ingenious conductor piled boxes on the floor just below that gap and sat on the top one, extending his head and shoulders above the roof. This odd position gave him a fine view of his train and the Iowa prairie.

Watson decided that if all cabooses had a somewhat similar outlet, but glassed in for protection against the weather, the trainmen's work would be easier and more pleasant. Upon arrival at Clinton, he persuaded the company's master mechanic to include crow's nests in the two new waycars being built at the road's shops there. The official agreed and built them that way. Thus, C&NW may have been the first railroad to operate cabooses with cupolas.

Placement of the cupola showed much diversity. It could be anywhere on the roof from an extreme end of the car, as was often the case on logging railroads, to the exact middle, as the designer wished. Throughout the early cabooses were closets and cupboards, built mostly into or around the cupola base. They made storage space for cooking utensils, food, etc. The long lockers, covered from end to end with flat pads or cushions, served not only as seats and cots but also to hold journal brasses, knuckles, knuckle pins, and other hardware.

Cutaway view of a typical New York Central caboose, circa 1945. [New York Central Railroad]

Under the wooden body of most old-time waycars was an additional locker, known as a *possum belly,* in which were kept a jack, wrecking chains, and "dope" (oil and cotton waste for cooling hotboxes, or overheated journals).

Innumerable poems and folk songs were written about old-time waycars. Here is a typical quatrain:

Oh, the brake-wheel's old and rusty, the shoes are thin and worn,
And she's loaded down with link and pin and chain,
And there's danger all around us as we try to pound our ear
In the little red caboose behind the train.

When that song was written, most cabooses were red. Others were painted just about every color of the rainbow, even white, but probably none were purple or gold. Today's cabooses match the road's standard color. The late John Johns, a New York Central conductor who managed to find time to write stories for *Railroad Magazine* in his caboose even while officially on duty, felt such an ownership of "his" car that he painted it a smart-looking silver trim and resented his division superintendent's order to restore it to its original drab standard color.

Gone is the era when conductors wired messages like this to their trainmasters: "Brakeman Horton ill. Send man to relieve him. Must be good cook." At that time an average caboose on long runs might carry one or more hams, a huge side of bacon, a bushel of potatoes, sacks of flour and sugar, salt, onions, ample coffee, and canned goods (with variations, of course)—enough to feed all five engine and train crew men. Often the fare was supplemented with delicacies bought along the way. In those days the caboose had no facility for storing fresh meat, but canned meat went mighty well mixed with vegetables in the form of baked hash. Baked beans, too, were popular and easy to prepare.

Most famous of all cabooses is Delaware and Hudson No. 10, in which the Brotherhood of Railroad Trainmen was founded and which is still preserved at Oneonta, New York. *See also* BROTHERHOOD OF RAILROAD TRAINMEN.

The caboose is still a familiar sight on nearly all railroads, but several roads have stopped using it on every freight train. Among the very few roads that have no cabooses are the Jackass & Western and the Quebec North Shore and Labrador, both run by remote control. There is little or no romance in present-day cabooses. Trains run so fast to their destinations these days that their riders are unlikely to dream of faraway places. As for pets riding in cabooses, that is forbidden. Decades ago, it was not uncommon for a conductor to take with him on his runs a dog, bird, or some other creature. Canadian Pacific conductor A. R. McDonald had a tamed wild rabbit named Sandy that lived in his van for 4 years and rode about 100,000 miles, undoubtedly setting a world record for cottontails. *See* JACKASS & WESTERN.

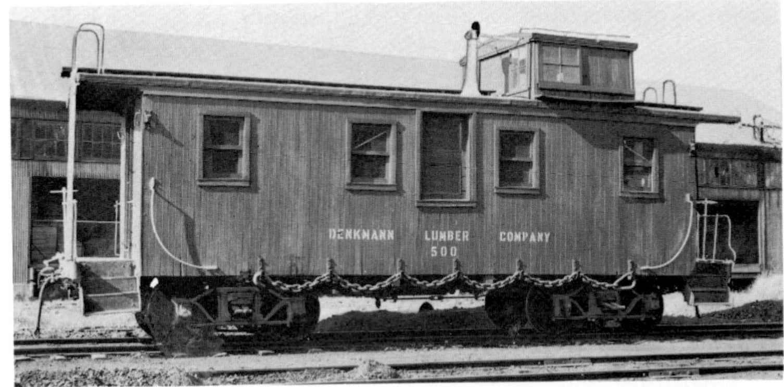

Chains for emergency use were hung outside this "crummy," shown at Canton, Mississippi, in 1940. Other cabooses carried chains in an inside locker or in a possum belly underneath. Note the cupola, or crow's nest, which has since given way to the bay window. [C. William Witbeck]

American railroads own about 15,000 cabooses. *The Pocket List of Railroad Officials* lists 13 United States and 2 Canadian manufacturers of such cars. Some railroads build their own. The time-honored cupola is beginning to disappear. As freight cars become taller and harder to look over, there is a tendency to switch to bay-window waycars. Union Pacific, which says the bay-window type affords a better view while costing less to build, put 100 such units into service in 1979. This type is roomier, since the cupola design requires a narrow walkway to the center of the car, and cupola ladders are no longer needed. Some roads retain the crow's nest but make it extra wide to extend beyond the car's side for about the same distance as the side bays and so improve observation facilities.

Most of the recently built cabooses are train-radio-equipped. The once-mandatory practice of trainmen walking the freight-car tops on moving trains is now banned. There is no need for it. Running boards have been removed from most freight-car roofs. Telltales (rows of dangling strips strung across the track a few feet above the cars near tunnels and low bridges to warn men riding the tops that they'd better duck) are no longer being installed, and nearly all the old ones have been removed.

Engineering developments in recent years have greatly improved crew comfort and safety. Most new

The most famous caboose, the Delaware and Hudson No. 10, in which the Brotherhood of Railroad Trainmen was founded in 1883, is preserved at Oneonta, New York. [H. W. Rogers]

cabooses are being equipped with axle generators, belt- or shaft-driven, to provide electric current for lighting and refrigeration. They also have electric heaters instead of coal stoves, flush toilets, permanent water tanks, and hydraulic sliding-dill or end-of-car cushioning, which corresponds to automobile shock absorbers, replacing the old accordionlike rubber gear. They also employ sound-deadening techniques.

To eliminate hazards, there are high-back seats to guard against head injuries, seat belts, grab irons, rounded corners, shatterproof windows, and nonslip floors. Some special-purpose waycars have showers, oversize refrigerators, large cookstoves, and additional bunks for track-maintenance or bridge-and-building gangs who live in them for long periods.

BIBLIOGRAPHY: *Car and Locomotive Cyclopedia,* Simmons-Boardman, New York, 1974; William F. Knapke and Freeman Hubbard, *The Railroad Caboose,* Golden West Books, San Marino, Calif., 1968.

Cabs, Locomotive The cab is the most dramatic part of a locomotive, steam, diesel, or electric—its nerve center, its human interest, where the crew meets and dominates powerful machines. The gauntleted hand at the throttle is a classic picture. Not only does the engine crew work here but railfans take great pride in being permitted to ride the cab and, on rare occasions, wield the controls for a short distance under the driver's supervision or, in the case of hand-fired steam power, toss scoops of coal into the white-hot firebox.

The earliest locos had no cabs. The driver stood on the open deck, outdoors in all kinds of weather, rocking and swaying as his iron monster sped along the rails, as wind blew swirling wood smoke and sparks into his tanned face. We do not know who rigged up the first tarpaulin awning above an engine deck. Angus Sinclair, the leading authority on early locomotives, writes that engine No. 1 of the Beaver Meadow Railroad (later Lehigh Valley, now Conrail) near Hazleton, Pennsylvania, "was noteworthy as being the first locomotive built with a deck covered to afford protection to the engineman." This engine, a four-wheeled grasshopper type, was produced at Philadelphia in 1833 by Garrett & Eastwick and named for the road's president, Samuel D. Ingham, who was Secretary of the Treasury under Andrew Jackson.

Complex machinery in the interior of a Santa Fe Railway steam locomotive cab, where the human hand will transform it into railroad magic. [Santa Fe Railway]

Another grasshopper, the *Thomas Jefferson* of the Baltimore & Ohio (B&O), was roofed, not so much for shelter from rain, snow, or sparks as to shield the crew from Maryland's blazing sun. One source credits the frst partially enclosed engine cab to Joseph Davenport of the Boston & Providence (B&P; later New Haven Railroad, now Conrail) in 1843. A B&P official scoffed at this contraption, saying it made life too easy for the drivers. "Next we'll be giving them something to sit down on, too," he added.

By the 1850s most North American railroads had enclosed cabs. Between 1846 and 1850 Ross Winans of Baltimore supplied the B&O, Pennsy, Philadelphia & Reading (P&R; now Conrail), and other lines with engines known as Camels because the cab was placed astride the middle of the boiler. During the 1860s, 1870s, and 1880s many cabs were built elaborately of such hardwoods as black walnut, mahogany, and bird's-eye maple, with upholstered seatboxes; some even had rugs on the floor. Engineers' names were painted in gold leaf on their handsome sides. *See* WINANS, ROSS.

George Hart, railway historian and curator of the Pennsylvania State Railroad Museum at Strasburg, Pennsylvania, has said:

> Changes in boiler design often brought about new cab forms. In 1877, for example, John E. Wootten, general manager of the Philadelphia & Reading, amazed visitors to an international exhibition in Paris with a curious little Ten-wheeler having an extraordinarily large firebox. In accordance with the then-current belief that a large grate was an asset in anthracite burners, this engine, P&R 408, employed a firebox seven feet six and three-quarters inches wide by eight and one-half feet long. The conventional type of cab was perched high over this abnormality.

Because the engine's clearances were too high, Hart goes on, Wootten "had the shelter, controls and all, moved to the middle of the boiler, while a running board was provided on either side of the barrel, reaching back to the floorplate on the tender. Thus was born the Mother Hubbard or Camelback type," a type having two cabs, one for the engineer midway along the boiler and a simpler one at the rear for the fireman, suggesting Mother Hubbard's cloak and the humps on a camel's back. Hundreds of Camelbacks were built and were used by a long list of railroads before the Interstate Commerce Commission finally outlawed them.

Another oddity developed for the Wootten boiler was the double-end arrangement used in many P&R

engines. This was an auxiliary shelter erected at the tender coal gates for the fireman's benefit.

As early as 1859 the era of wooden cabs had begun to come to an end, for in that year the P&R started to build cabs of sheet iron designed by its master of machinery, the famous John Milholland. These were quaintly rounded, reminding one of gazebos, with a dome-shaped roof.

Later, when New York City and Chicago built elevated railways, Matthias N. Forney designed and constructed the once-popular engine type that bore his name. Its rigid frame supported the entire locomotive, tender and all. The cab was integrated into the tank, with the fuel bin behind it. Another well-liked engine type at that time was William Mason's bogie, with a closed cab at each end so that the locomotive could run in either direction without being turned. Double-enders ran mostly in Eastern suburban service, although the Central (later Southern) Pacific had them in 1882. *See* MASON, WILLIAM.

The Lehigh Valley, in 1895, was the first road to build steel cabs. Other companies followed suit. Heavy duck canvas hung from the back roof sheltered the crew from snow, rain, and extreme cold. Among the pioneers in all-weather cabs were the Canadian railways.

Ten years before the cab-ahead articulated engines of the Southern Pacific (SP) made their first appearance, on the Overland Route, the little narrow-gauge North Pacific Coast had a rebuilt 4-4-0 with a cab in front, designed by the road's master mechanic, William J. Thomas, who had decided that a route through hilly, wooded terrain, crowded with curves and tunnels, could be safer if the engine crew had better visibility. Except for a great many on the SP, no other cab-aheads were ever built.

Since electric locomotives have no boiler or firebox, they sired a new breed of cabs such as the heavy-duty "steeple cab" on the Milwaukee Road's famous 10,000 series and the Pennsy's even more famous GG-1s. Then, in 1925, with the advent of diesel-electric switchers, other new patterns arose. Later, industrial designer Otto Kuhler, who specialized in streamlining, gave particular thought to visibility in his design of the Milwaukee Road's *Hiawatha* cab. *See* KUHLER, OTTO.

Today, thanks largely to the Brotherhood of Locomotive Engineers, refinements and conveniences such as comfortable seats, which in the boomer era would have been regarded as wildly extravagant luxuries, are being added to diesel cabs.

BIBLIOGRAPHY: Henry B. Comstock, *The Iron Horse,* Crowell, New York, 1971; S. Kip Farrington, Jr., *Railroading from the Head End,* Doubleday, Doran, New York, 1943; Angus Sinclair, *Development of the Locomotive Engine,* annotated ed. by John H. White, Jr., M.I.T., Cambridge, Mass., 1970.

Cachet Collecting Railfan hobby popular because many cachets commemorate railroad history. A cachet (pronounced ka-shā') is a picture, inscription, or both, issued for a special occasion like the inauguration of a new train, a last run, or a railroad anniversary, sometimes coincident with a new postage stamp, for example, the Casey Jones stamp issued on April 30, 1950. Cachets may be printed, painted, typewritten, rubber-stamped, or pasted on a cover. A cover, as philatelists know, is the entire envelope or wrapper sent through the mail. It includes the stamp, cancellation, postmark, address, and cachet if any. Railroad companies, railfan clubs, individuals, etc., issue cachets. On June 6, 1977, the U.S. Postal Service put out a cachet for the final runs of the last two Railway Post Office trains, between New York and Washington, D.C.

BIBLIOGRAPHY: Neil S. Utberg, *Railroad Collectibles,* pub. by author, 1973.

Campaign Trains Whistle-stop campaigning by rail, which in recent years TV has rendered obsolete, was long the traditional use of trains that stopped where crowds had gathered for political candidates to "see and be seen," as Abraham Lincoln put it, and make speeches. Nearly all of America's Presidents and major presidential nominees from Lincoln to Dwight D. Eisenhower, plus a few other aspirants for public office, adopted this practice at times.

Lincoln's rival, Stephen A. Douglas of Illinois, originated the idea in 1858 by mounting a cannon on a flatcar at the end of a train and firing it to proclaim his arrival at way stations. In 1860, as the Republican party's first nominee for the White House, Lincoln

***The armor-plated car* Ferdinand Magellan, *used by three United States presidents in their whistle-stop campaigns.* [*Association of American Railroads*]**

toured the nation in a converted day coach with hard, immovable seats, candle-lit at night, with mattresses but no sheets or blankets. Men slept without undressing, although the conductor usually made them take off their shoes or boots before lying down. As Theodore Roosevelt liked to do many years afterward, Lincoln would walk up to the locomotive to shake hands with the engine crew before starting out on a rail trip.

Lincoln's successor, Andrew Johnson, also made a rail tour, but ineffectively. In 1868, when Ulysses S. Grant ran for President, the cars still had candle lighting, but they had oil lamps 8 years later when Rutherford B. Hayes and Samuel J. Tilden whistle-stopped. In 1888 Grover Cleveland, a former New York Central policeman, took to the rails to campaign against Benjamin Harrison, traveling in a sleeper with high windows, carpets, mahogany, and upholstery.

Democratic nominee William J. Bryan spent the summer of 1896 campaigning in coaches, sleepers, even cabooses, and taking short buggy trips when his train stopped long enough. That year he set an all-time record by making 569 speeches, 24 of them in one 24-hour period. He was the first presidential hopeful to campaign in a private car, thanks to a Chesapeake and Ohio (C&O) Passenger Department official whose middle initial and last name spelled Bryan: Charles B. Ryan. He was given the free use of a C&O business car on the ground that this would be good publicity for the railroad.

Another whistle-stopper who campaigned unsuccessfully for the presidency was Socialist party nominee Eugene V. Debs, a former locomotive fireman. Instead of traveling in style like the major-party candidates, Debs used three-car trains and ate 18-cent meals as an appeal to underpaid workingmen. *See* DEBS, EUGENE VICTOR.

Whistle-stopping hit a peak in 1904, when Theodore Roosevelt, as William McKinley's running mate, covered 21,209 miles by rail and made 673 speeches. Teddy liked to ride engine cabs. His successor in the White House, William Howard Taft, made 418 whistle-stop speeches in 1908 and defeated Bryan and Debs. During his 4-year term Taft traveled 114,500 rail miles—a presidential record broken only by Franklin Roosevelt, who totaled 357,847 miles in 390 Pullman cars.

The public-address system, which later was a feature of all campaign specials, was first used on the train that carried President Warren G. Harding to Alaska in 1923. After Harding's death on his return trip, a Pennsy special took the new President, Calvin Coolidge, from Vermont to Washington, D.C. It was the only special that the frugal Coolidge ever rode; the price was too high

Democratic nominee Alfred E. Smith toured the country in 1928 in an 11-car train complete with shower and barbershop. Equipment for making advance copies of his speeches filled one entire car. Franklin Roosevelt had a standing rule that his train pull out as soon as his address ended, to avoid an anticlimax. Sometimes it left town with local politicians stranded aboard or even minus a crew member.

Wendell Willkie, a Republican nominee, paid so little attention to train schedules that he often made long speeches from the rear platform, causing his specials to lose time. Vice Presidential candidate Earl Warren, campaigning in 1952, being a railroader's son, never made that mistake. One of his aides would blow a whistle 2 minutes before the special was scheduled to pull out. This whistle told him to cut his talk short and warned staff members and reporters to be ready to leave.

The whistle-stop tour of 1948 which led to Harry S Truman's victory over Thomas E. Dewey covered 21,000 miles in 17 journeys. Occasionally a road granted a candidate's request for special equipment. For example, the Pennsy supplied an extra lounge car for Eisenhower to entertain local politicians, even repainting it to match the train's two-tone color scheme, and an open-platform observation coach, harking back to the old days, for rear-end speeches. Twice in 1952 the Pennsy handled two campaign trains simultaneously, for Eisenhower and Truman, and later specials at the same time for Adlai Stevenson and Richard M. Nixon.

For years Presidents of the United States traveled by rail, campaigning and otherwise, in an armor-plated Pullman car with bulletproof windows. If sunk under water, it would remain dry inside. Any train to which it was attached had to operate under the code word POTUS (President of the United States). Before it began to roll, all other traffic on the line was halted. Switches en route were locked and spiked in position. A pilot train ran ahead. No train could follow it by less than 15 minutes. This car, originally named *Ferdinand Magellan,* was converted for presidential use by the Association of American Railroads, which donated it to the government. It is now preserved by the Gold Coast Railroad, a Florida tourist line.

BIBLIOGRAPHY: Robert S. Henry, *This Fascinating Railroad Business,* 3d ed., rev., Bobbs-Merrill, Indianapolis, 1946; John W. Starr, *Lincoln and the Railroads,* Dodd, Mead, New York, 1927.

Canadian National Railways (CN) Entity that is not only a railway system, Canada's largest, which moves some 125 million tons of freight on its 25,000 miles of main track in all 10 of Canada's provinces and 2 territories as well as 10 states in the United States, but also comprises a vast telecommunications network, a chain of hotels, a dockyard, trucking and bus lines, a fleet of ferries and coastal vessels, and national and international consulting services. Its annual gross revenues run around $3 billion; its net profit for 1978 was $136 million. It has almost 135,000 pieces of rolling stock, including highway equipment, and 78,000 employees.

Canada is unique in having two great rail systems with contrasting ownership: the publicly owned CN and the privately owned Canadian Pacific. Back in 1915, a year when three important new railroads opened for business—the National Transcontinental, the Canadian Northern, and the Grand Trunk Pacific (GTP)—Canada had a total of 35,000 miles of railway lines. Most of these lines had been built not to make money or even to pay for themselves but primarily to unite the country and stimulate its growth. But during World War I, when emigrants stopped coming to Canada and British capital was no longer available to the Confederation's railways, three major rail lines—Canadian Northern, GTP, and Grand Trunk—among others, were close to bankruptcy.

To save them and the nation, the government stepped in, taking over the operation of many railways that were in trouble. In 1919 Parliament created a new company, the Canadian National Railway Co., owned by the people of Canada. By 1923 CN boasted 22,100 miles of track that had once belonged to 221 different railways, the most outstanding ones being the Intercolonial, the National Transcontinental, the Grand Trunk, the Canadian Northern, and the Prince Edward Island. From all these roads CN inherited 130,000 passenger and freight cars, 3200 locomotives, nine large hotels, and 100,000 employees.

The nationalized rail system also had a wide network of telegraph lines, used not only in running trains but for the public to send telegrams. Before long-distance phone calls were fast and easy to make, the telegram was the only long-distance message that could be sent quickly. In 1924 the company was experimenting with radio, and eventually it developed a nationwide network, the nucleus of today's Canadian Broadcasting Corporation.

The huge job of pulling the new CN together was given to Sir Henry Worth Thornton. He built radio broadcasting stations and placed receiving sets on passenger trains, sponsored the development of new types of motive power, increased train speeds, built new branch lines, added to the number of CN hotels, bought more modern equipment for the Canadian National Telegraph Co., and authorized installation of the world's first two-way radio station. To attract new immigrants to settle near CN lines, Thornton created a special service to help them find jobs and adjust to their new life. At about the same time, CN acquired a fleet of ships.

One of CN's most important tasks in the 1920s, as it is today, was to move grain from prairie farms to large seaports. In 1929 a new rail service was provided to the port of Churchill on Hudson Bay. Although it took less time for ships to reach Europe from Churchill, Thunder Bay remained the largest Canadian center for handling grain. *See* HUDSON BAY LINE.

But the Canadian National Railways didn't help the grain farmers only by shipping their wheat to market. Each fall, special harvest trains carried hundreds of young men from eastern Canada westward to help bring in the crops. At each stop on the prairies, farmers would be waiting to pick out the sturdiest-looking workers and offer them jobs. In those days, too, it was not uncommon for train crews to let hoboes or migrant workers ride freights headed toward the wheat fields or anywhere else in search of employment.

World War II doubled CN traffic, pulled old equipment out of retirement for rebuilding, and let women replace most of the 20,000 CN male employees who joined the armed forces. After the war CN, like other railroads, had not only to replace a lot of worn-out equipment and trackage but to tackle the even greater problem of fast-rising competition from private autos, highway trucks, and airplanes. Donald Gordon, a banker and business leader but not previously a railwayman, who was president of CN from 1950 to 1966, devoted most of his attention to these problems. He had new specialized cars built to replace the worn-out ones. Shippers liked them because they were easier to load and unload and could carry more freight. Also, over a 10-year period, CN bought an entirely new fleet of diesel locomotives, which were much cheaper than steam engines to run and maintain.

In 1949, when Newfoundland joined the Confederation, CN took over its rail lines, which were (and are) narrow-gauge, and began operating ferries between Nova Scotia and the new island province. Most of the rail lines built before the 1920s ran across the country from east to west to bind the provinces together. Now, to find new traffic, CN started building lines to the north, to transport ore from areas where minerals had been discovered. *See* BRITISH COLUMBIA RAILWAY; GREAT SLAVE LAKE RAILWAY; WHITE PASS & YUKON ROUTE.

To increase its share of the freight market, CN pioneered such developments as piggyback, containerization, unit trains, specialized quipment, and complementary trucking services. To attract passengers back to the rails, CN bought new, fast, lightweight cars for its heavily traveled lines, including the Turbo Train, first

Canadian National's seven-car Turbo Train has clamshell doors at each end to allow similar trains to be latched on for multiple-unit operations. [Canadian National Railways]

put into service between Montreal and Toronto with a streamlined contour that gave the railway a new look. Canada's rail passenger services are now operated by VIA Rail Canada. *See* VIA RAIL CANADA, INC.

Canadian National dieselization began in August 1925 with self-propelled diesel rail cars designed by C. E. Brooks, chief of motive power and rolling stock, and built in its Montreal shops. On November 1, 1925, one of these cars, No. 15820, powered by a four-cylinder, 185-horsepower Beardmore engine, left Montreal for one of the most dramatic experimental runs in rail history. It made the 2937 miles to Vancouver in slightly over 67 hours, setting a new transcontinental record. In 1928 Brooks and his associates developed Canada's first diesel-electric road loco, No. 9000.

CN found that the major operating savings of diesel locos, compared with steam, were in fuel costs, plus savings in lubrication, enginehouse expenses, and long-term repairs. Diesels were shown to have greater utilization than steam in terms of locomotive miles per day and to permit more flexible operation and to minimize the smoke nuisance. Tests proved that the cost of operating diesels on passenger runs was only one-third that of steam on the same runs. After diesels had been placed on the *Super Continental* and the *Ocean Limited* in 1955, 16 hours were cut off the transcontinental journey from Halifax to Vancouver.

The last CN steam loco in regular service was No. 6043, a Mountain type built in 1929 by Canadian Locomotive Co. at Kingston, Ontario, which completed her final run with train No. 76 from The Pas to Winnipeg on April 25, 1960, thus officially terminating 124 years of steam on CN and its predecessors. However, Northern type No. 6153, freshly painted, pulled two special steam excursions on September 3 and 4, 1960, from Montreal to Joliette and Ottawa, sponsored by the Canadian Railroad Historical Association. Among the many CN steam locos preserved and on display in museums and parks across Canada and in the United States is No. 6060 (Bullet-Nosed Betty), which as of 1979 is still operating steam excursions in Quebec and Ontario.

BIBLIOGRAPHY: Ray Corley, *Preserved Canadian Railway Equipment,* Railfare Enterprises, Montreal, 1972; Patrick C. Dorin, *The Canadian National Railways' Story,* Superior Publishing, Seattle, 1975; Freeman Hubbard, *Great Trains of All Time,* Grosset & Dunlap, New York, 1962; David P. Morgan, *Canadian Steam!,* Ryerson Press, Toronto, 1961; G. R. Stevens, *History of the Canadian National Railways,* Macmillan, New York, 1973.

Canadian Pacific Railway (CP Rail) Prosperous railway with long hauls and an excellent base of raw materials. It is also a diversified company with assets of almost $8 billion in land, sea, and air transportation, telecommunications, natural resources, hotels, real estate, and manufacturing and financial services. In 1970 it adopted new corporate designations for various components of the transportation side of its operations: CP Rail, CP Air, CP Ships, CP Transport, CP Express, CP Hotels, and CP Telecommunications. In 1971 the parent company was renamed Canadian Pacific Limited and Canadien Pacifique Limitée, but the railway is still known as CP Rail and Canadian Pacific.

As of 1979, CP Rail operated 23,518 miles of track in Canada, including yards, spurs, and sidings, and it controlled another 4600 miles in the United States. It has 1300 diesel locomotives, over 65,000 freight cars, and approximately 40 pieces of commuter passenger equipment. In 1906, by comparison, it had 1115 steam engines and a total of 37,080 cars, freight and passenger, its freight-car fleet then being much less diversified than today's. The railway has developed a sophisticated unit-train system for moving bulk commodities such as coal and sulfur and at Calgary has one of the world's most advanced automated classification yards to handle freight shipments to and from the Pacific Coast. It jointly owns Brunterm Ltd., a giant container terminal at St. John, New Brunswick, which had an annual growth of 15 percent during the 1970s. It also operates commuter passenger services, but intercity and transcontinental passenger trains are provided by a new government agency. *See* VIA RAIL CANADA, INC.

The terms of union whereby British Columbia was admitted to the Dominion of Canada in 1871 had a clause that led eventually to creation of the Canadian Pacific Railway. Predecessor lines had already done considerable tracklaying before the big company was chartered on February 16, 1881, to build a transcontinental railway linking eastern Canada with the Pacific Coast. For details of mainline construction between Montreal and Port Moody, British Columbia, completed on November 7, 1885, *see* VAN HORNE, WILLIAM CORNELIUS.

The distinctive emblem formerly used on CP rolling stock, timetables, stationery, etc., was a shield with a beaver, typical of Canada, just as the Intercolonial Railway herald had a moose head, the Great Northern a mountain goat, and the Pennsy a keystone. But the days of picturesque rail insignia are almost completely gone.

CP Rail's oldest predecessor line was the St. Andrews & Quebec Railroad, chartered in March 1836. Its oldest constituent in the United States was the Connecticut & Passumpsic River, chartered in October 1843. Its oldest still-operating constituent is La Compagnie du Chemin à Rails du Saint-Laurent et du Village d'Industrie, a 12-mile line downstream from Montreal on the St. Lawrence River, chartered in July 1847 and opened on May 1, 1850, with strap-iron rails laid on wooden crossties. The big road is still using Canada's first railway tunnel, ½ mile long, opened on December 31, 1860, under the town of Brockville, Ontario.

With CP's incorporation, it received—as railway construction was completed on the line to the Pacific Coast—grants which eventually totaled $2 million as well as 25 million acres of land, plus certain rail lines already contracted for by the Dominion government, upon their completion. On February 17, 1881, the Canadian Pacific Railway Company was organized with George Stephen as president, Duncan McIntyre as vice president, and James J. Hill on the executive committee. In 1882 it acquired the Dominion Express Company charter, enabling it to engage in local pickup and delivery services, which launched CP's widespread involvement in highway transportation. In that year, too, CP began commercial telegraph operation, using its railway telegraph lines. *See* HILL, JAMES JEROME.

Also in 1882, Hill resigned from the board as a result of CP's decision to keep its mainline completely in Canada by building around the north shore of Lake Superior instead of using Hill's lines through Sault Ste. Marie, St. Paul, and Minneapolis to Emerson, Manitoba. In the same year, CP took control of the South Eastern Railway, which became the nucleus of its lines in eastern Quebec and its route across Maine to the Maritimes. It also leased a rail network around Toronto and in eastern Ontario.

The first engine used in Manitoba and on the Canadian prairies was the 38-ton *Countess of Dufferin,* a 4-4-0 woodburner, brought in by a contractor building the line between Selkirk and Emerson. She came up in 1877 over the Great Lakes to Port Arthur, then was barged to Duluth, rolled on her own steam to St. Paul, and was transferred to another barge for the trip up the Red River to St-Boniface, Manitoba. It was a long, roundabout route, but no shorter one was available. That engine has been preserved. After being displayed for years just outside the Winnipeg station, then at several other city locations, she is now in storage at CP Rail's Weston shops. Another pioneer locomotive, the *J. C. Haggart,* was dragged over the ice of the Red River between St-Boniface and Winnipeg in December 1879 to start construction westward across the prairies in the spring.

The first transcontinental train to cross Canada pulled up at Winnipeg station on July 1, 1886, Dominion Day. From the engine front flapped a silk Union Jack, frayed by the wind and weather of half a continent. On August 10, the train reached Calgary. At a dinner there in Van Horne's official car, Father Lacombe, a Catholic missionary, was made president of CP for one unique hour because of his help to the railway as liaison with Indian tribes whose land the company wanted to cross. That December the railhead reached the Rocky Mountain summit in Kicking Horse Pass.

On November 11, 1885, the railway's last spike (of iron) was driven in Eagle Pass in the Gold Range, British Columbia, by Donald A. Smith, one of the directors; and Van Horne made his famous 15-word speech: "All I can say is that the work has been done well in every way." Next morning, a special train of CP "brass collars" reached Port Moody at Pacific tidewater, the first train to cross the country from ocean to ocean. At 8:00 p.m. the first regular train, the *Pacific Express,* with coaches, a sleeper, and a diner, left Montreal for Port Moody. After making the first scheduled rail journey across the Dominion (then the world's longest scheduled train trip), it pulled into its destination at high noon, on time.

In 1888 CP completed its short line across northern Maine to Mattawamkeag, connecting with the Maine Central Railroad, which carried traffic to the New Brunswick boundary at Vanceboro, there turning it over to the New Brunswick Railway. That railway was leased to CP in 1890.

By that time, CP had a transpacific steamship service. In 1889 the British government gave it a 10-year contract to take mail between Vancouver and Hong Kong. In 1891 three splendid CP ocean liners, the *Empress of India,* the *Empress of China,* and the *Empress of Japan,* made maiden voyages to the Orient via the Suez Canal; and the company advertised tours: "Around the World in 80 days—$610." In 1903 CP entered the North Atlantic steamer service.

The company kept acquiring rail lines and other facilities and buying or building vacation luxury hotels. In 1902 the *Imperial Limited,* a new, faster transcontinental train, was inaugurated, running at first three times a week, then on a daily basis. It supplemented the original daily *Pacific Express* (westbound) and *Atlantic Express* (eastbound). In 1905 CP acquired the Esquimalt & Nanaimo Railway on Vancouver Island.

In 1919 the *Trans Canada Limited,* an all-sleeper-diner train, made the first trip between Montreal and Toronto and Vancouver. In 1926 Dominion Express Co. was renamed Canadian Pacific Express Co., and the Prince of Wales and British Prime Minister Stanley Baldwin opened Toronto's new Union Station. Three years later the Northern Alberta Railways (857 miles) was incorporated for joint operation by CP and Canadian National Railways (CN). In 1933 some passenger-train service was pooled between CP and CN.

On a test run on September 18, 1936, a new CP

Donald A. Smith, shown bending over with a spike maul, was one of three officials who drove the last spike in the Canadian Pacific transcontinental line at Craigellachie, British Columbia, on November 11, 1885. [CP Rail]

lightweight, streamlined passenger train achieved a speed record of 112½ miles per hour near St-Télesphore, Quebec, with 4-4-4 steam loco No. 3003. It was then Canada's top officially recorded train speed and remained so until March 12, 1976, when the newer LRC (light, rapid, comfortable) diesel-powered train *FYI,* reached 129 miles per hour. Another Canadian record was set when the LRC held an average speed of 124.5 miles per hour over a 1-mile measured stretch of track.

Angus shops, CP Rail's 200-acre main repair plant for the construction and maintenance of motive power and rolling stock, built five new steam locos each month over a long period of time before the road's conversion to diesel power. In 1937 CP took delivery of its first diesel loco, switcher No. 7000, and 4 years later it acquired its first road diesels for converting motive power on the Montreal-Newport-Wells River line. In March 1949, CP accepted its last new steam engine, 2-10-0 No. 5935, built by Montreal Locomotive Works.

In 1942 Canadian Pacific Air Lines was organized through the takeover of some bush airlines in northern Canada. Seven years later, CP Air inaugurated its first route outside Canada, between Vancouver and Australia. In 1950 the railway opened its 682-acre St-Luc yard at Montreal, the Dominion's first hump-retarder freight classification yard. In 1952 it began piggyback service between Montreal and Toronto. In 1956 it installed an IBM 705 electronic computer, Canada's first integrated data processing machine, and CP-CN set up Canada's first computer-controlled message-switching service.

CP Rail, one unit of Canadian Pacific's transportation activities, operates 23,518 miles of track in Canada. Pictured here is a CP Rail freight train winding through the Rockies near Lake Louise, Alberta. [Nicholas Morant, CP Rail]

In 1955 a new stainless-steel scenic-domed passenger train, *The Canadian,* requiring the purchase of 173 new Budd Company cars, began running between Montreal and Toronto and Vancouver. It was then the world's longest dome-train run. For most of 1967 the *Expo Limited,* CP's second transcontinental train between those same points, supplemented *The Canadian* during the period of the world's fair at Montreal. In 1970 CP put into operation the country's first double-decked passenger train, with nine air-conditioned cars, in Montreal lakeshore suburban service.

In 1976 CP Rail, keen for modern ideas, harnessed solar power on an experimental basis to operate track circuits and a highway-crossing warning system near Joliette, Quebec. Also in that year, CP Rail and CN published a joint timetable whereby passenger service of both rail networks could be operated by VIA Rail Canada. In 1978, CP Rail signed a pact with the rail labor unions and VIA transferring 300 of its passenger service employees to VIA. Most of its 300 passenger cars, including those of *The Canadian,* were sold to VIA. Also in 1978, CP Rail and Union Pacific agreed to exchange motive power on run-through trains in western Canada. Instead of changing locos at border crossing points, each railway's units run through to the final destination. Crews, however, do not; they continue to change as before.

BIBLIOGRAPHY: Pierre Berton, *The Impossible Railway: The Building of the Canadian Pacific,* Knopf, New York, 1972; Freeman Hubbard, *Great Tains of All Time,* Grosset & Dunlap, New York, 1962; W. K. Lamb, *The History of the Canadian Pacific Railway,* Macmillan, New York, 1977; Omer LaValle, *Van Horne's Road,* Railfare Enterprises, Montreal, 1975; David P. Morgan, *Canadian Steam!,* Ryerson Press, Toronto, 1961.

Cannon Ball, The Train formerly operated by the Long Island Rail Road (LIRR), the largest commuter road in North America. For a short time it was America's only all-parlor-car train. In its latter years it was a "strawhat limited," meaning that it ran only in summer, with seats for all passengers. Each seat was a cozy armchair that could swivel in any direction. In the early 1960s its open-end observation car was unique; no other American railroad had one then on a regular run, although another road's *Cannon Ball,* the Wabash's, subject of a famous ballad, would couple an open-ender into a special train if you ordered it. Jersey Central also had a few open-enders, in weekday operation, but not for the general public. They were reserved for commuter clubs.

The LIRR name train was very popular. On a summer Friday afternoon, unless you had bought a ticket not later than the day before, you could not be sure of boarding it at its western terminus in Long Island City for a weekend visit to "the little world of waiting wives" at Montauk, the road's easternmost terminus, 114½ miles away, or some fashionable way stop like the Hamptons or Amagansett.

BIBLIOGRAPHY: Vincent F. Seyfried, *The Long Island Rail Road,* 5 vols., Felix F. Reifschneider, Garden City, N.Y., 1961–1972; Ron Ziel and George W. Foster, *Steel Rails to the Sunrise,* Hawthorn, New York, 1965.

Canyon War "We got here first and we're building the Cañon City & San Juan Railroad through the Grand Canyon of the Arkansas, Anyone interfering with this work is liable to stop a bullet between the eyes." This, in substance, is what W. R. Morley told a band of about 200 men whom the Denver and Rio Grande Railroad (D&RG) had hastily recruited and armed to invade the Royal Gorge on April 19, 1878. Morley was the engineer in charge of construction for the Atchison, Topeka and Santa Fe Railway (ATSF) at El Moro, California, where the D&RG line ended. The demand for laborers was so great during the crisis that hoboes told later of having been hired at $3 a day (the usual pay was $2.25), equipped with rifles, and told to "shoot any man you see across the canyon."

The Santa Fe was determined to thrust its steel northward to Leadville, Colorado, where silver had been discovered and was being mined. It wanted to add that rich area to its fast-growing system. For the same reason, the Rio Grande road was eager to push westward from Pueblo and beat out its competitor. Leadville was then the world's greatest mining camp and highest city, walled in by mountains about 10,000 feet above sea level. Working 6 days a week, 12,000 freight teams kept that camp operating and hauled away its precious metal. The only possible rail route to Leadville lay through the canyon, where for miles a sheer rock wall rises to about 3500 feet above the narrow, winding Arkansas River. Whichever railroad held this pass could serve the silver field, besides having a steel highway of rare scenic beauty for the tourist passenger business.

It was bitter rivalry from the start. In picking its route the Santa Fe had snubbed Denver, whereupon the Denverites in 1870 had organized a road of their own, the Denver and Rio Grande, to build northward and head off the Santa Fe. Their original plan was to extend a line from Denver to El Paso, Texas, 850 miles, and possibly as far south as Panama. In fact, the D&RG had already surveyed down to Mexico City and was prepared to build in a big way.

Heading this enterprise was Brig. Gen. William Jackson Palmer, then 34, who had been secretary to a Pennsylvania Railroad president and later was chief engineer of the Kansas Pacific.

While building one end of the D&RG in Colorado, General Palmer raised money to lay the first 150 miles of rail northward in Mexico, a country which until then had no rail service at all. A revolution stopped the work in Mexico. Then the panic of 1873 halted nearly all D&RG construction for the next 4 years. *See* GOULD, JAY.

This company's first clash with the Santa Fe was in February 1873 at Raton Pass, New Mexico, gateway to the south, where the D&RG had made a preliminary survey. William B. Strong, the Santa Fe's appropriately named general manager, decided that his road should take over the key pass and sent for his chief engineer, A. A. Robinson, who had made a remarkable record in building every mile of the Santa Fe that had not been acquired by purchase. He told Robinson to seize and hold Raton Pass, by force if necessary. So, with a small army, Robinson marched into the pass at 4 A.M., just ahead of the rival outfit, and stayed there without firing a shot. Thus ATSF won the first skirmish in the Canyon War.

Prior to that, the Santa Fe had leased the charter authorizing the construction of a railroad, the Cañon City & San Juan (CC&SJ), through the canyon of the Arkansas to Salida, Colorado, but did nothing about it until April 1873, when Strong decided to begin building that line. On April 18, a D&RG construction gang took a night train westward with the aim of seizing the canyon at daybreak. Apparently the Santa Fe cause was lost. But Morley, its construction engineer, rode a horse all night long in the darkness through the rough and dangerous canyon, rode it so hard that the poor animal fell dead under him, and managed to rally seven other men, all armed, and begin actual digging before the D&RG force showed up. The latter retired to avoid bloodshed.

Palmer's road then took the case to courts for a long series of litigation, but was beaten. On December 13, 1878, Santa Fe won a stranglehold lease on the whole D&RG, nearly 400 miles of narrow-gauge road. But the victor showed little evidence of giving northern Colorado the kind of rail service it needed, and so the war was on again. Both rivals kept armed forces in the canyon.

In the spring of 1879 the Rio Grande management, backed by fresh capital, forced Attorney General Wright to file a suit challenging the right of a "foreign" corporation to push its mainline through Colorado, whereupon the Colorado Supreme Court gave the Rio Grande prior right to the Leadville route and forbade the Santa Fe to operate the "paper road" it had leased. Flushed with victory, 50 D&RG men, armed with guns, blocked Santa Fe operation in the canyon "by authority of the Supreme Court and the 50 rifles you see here."

The Santa Fe retaliated by importing an armed gang under Bat Masterson. Bat is said to have had a long record of killings, most of them legally justifiable "executions," in the course of his duties as Dodge City marshal. Then, on June 10, 1879, came the news of the court decision. Fearing that the court might reverse itself, Palmer sent out a small army of his men as sheriff's deputies, each having a copy of the decision, with instructions to repossess all D&RG property in the canyon, lease or no lease.

Thus, with the aid of another Rio Grande force of deputies riding a train northward, the entire road was recaptured by its own men. They dragged Santa Fe engine crews from their cabs and forcibly evicted station agents, sometimes after gunfire. Pueblo, the last ATSF stronghold in Colorado, was held by Masterson's men, who had even stolen a cannon from the local militia and were reported ready to die hard. Santa Fe officials urged Gov. Frederick W. Pitkin to call out the state militia. Pitkin ordered the latter to wait under arms, their bayonets gleaming in the sunlight, but not to march unless local officials should lose control of the situation.

At length, R. F. Weitbree, D&RG company treasurer, waved a white flag as signal for a parley. Then they entered the Pueblo roundhouse in which Bat's gunmen were besieged. The latter agreed to lay down their arms and were permitted to leave unmolested. Embattled Santa Fe men continued to hold the Pueblo dispatchers' office until additional Rio Grande deputies arrived. They were then driven out amid a hailstorm of bullets which killed two AT&SF men and wounded two others. But still the war wasn't over.

A federal court reversed the state Supreme Court, which then threw the D&RG into a receivership. Finally, the troublemaking CC&SJ lease was canceled. The Rio Grande management agreed to pay for all construction work done by the Santa Fe in Colorado, including the landmark hanging bridge in the Royal Gorge (a world-famous engineering feat designed and built by C. Shaler Smith in 1879), and pay for the franchise (a total of $1.8 million), besides pledging itself not to extend its own operations farther south into New Mexico. In 1880 a traffic agreement let the Santa Fe run its own trains into Denver.

The Canyon War resulted in the Denver and Rio Grande's being permitted to expand locally, while the wealthier and more ambitious Santa Fe concentrated on the transcontinental field. But the D&RG had to go through three more receiverships before peace with the Santa Fe was finally won.

BIBLIOGRAPHY: George L. Anderson, *General William J. Palmer,* Colorado College, Colorado Springs, Colo., 1936; Robert G. Athearn, *Rebel of the Rockies: A History of the Denver and Rio Grande Western Railroad,* Yale, New Haven, Conn., 1962; James L. Marshall, *Santa Fe: The Railroad That Built an Empire,* Random House, New York, 1945.

***Three early types of section cars:* (above) *the push car, the most primitive construction; section workers either pushed it or sat on its rear and kicked their way along;* (center) *the four-wheeled handcar (nicknamed Buda, puddle jumper, and paddy car), which two standing riders propelled by pushing down each side of the pump handle;* (below)) *the ingenious three-wheeled velocipede, first built in 1879 by George Sheffield.* [*Railroad Magazine*]**

Car Identification Labels Automatic, light-reflecting, and color-coded labels were mandatory standard practice for 10 years on North American railroads' freight and passenger cars and highway trailer-containers in railroad service. In 1977 their use became purely optional, following an industrywide vote by members of the Association of American Railroads. A few roads still follow the old practice. The labels were designed to let optical scanners identify each rail vehicle and its order on a train, but they became outdated as some roads developed new computer and managerial systems.

Cars, Section These include push cars, track velocipedes, and rail motor cars (also called speeders and "pop" cars). Push cars originated at least as far back as the early 1500s, the date of the earliest-known railroad picture, a woodcut of a man shoving a small car along wooden rails at a mine in Germany. North America's first use of such cars is unrecorded, but it may have been on the first United States railroad, the horse-drawn line opened on October 7, 1826, to haul granite from a

Quincy, Massachusetts, quarry to build Bunker Hill Monument.

Push cars were the most primitive means of moving men and materials by rail. Most of them were board platforms mounted on flanged wheels propelled by the feet of riders or shoved over the track by human power. They differed little from the so-called flatcars of the early 1800s that carried merchandise behind steam engines, except that the more recent ones were heavier, equipped with roller bearings, and built more sturdily than their predecessors.

The four-wheeled handcar, a big improvement over the push car, was invented in about the early 1860s to carry maintenance-of-way workers and their tools, materials, and water keg to and from assigned jobs. Two standing riders in turn bent up and down to move it with a sort of pump handle. Possibly some railroad man handy with tools built himself the first mechanized handcar. Surmounting it were two big wooden wheels set close together at each end of a short axle which was supported by a beam about as high as a man's shoulder.

A crank set on the wheels' rims was turned by a sweating man on each side of the car just as an old-fashioned grindstone was turned. A chain ran from a gear or sprocket on the axle to a similar device on either the front or back axle under the car. The last-known car of this type, having a leather belt instead of a chain, is (or was) stored in the Boston & Maine's shops at Billerica, Massachusetts.

Such cars were low in initial cost and cheap to maintain, almost never broke down, and were light enough to lift onto or off the track without delaying regular traffic. A section foreman would travel all his men on one side of the car, ready to tip it over if they should suddenly have to leave the rails. Nicknamed puddle jumpers, paddy cars, and Budas (the Buda Co. of Illinois built many of them), they lasted until well past the mid-1900s, especially on short roads with few steep grades. They were often put to offbeat use, such as taking a roadmaster to church on a Sunday or a gandy dancer to a dance or tryst surreptitiously on an evening or as an ambulance.

In the early 1870s at least two handcars on the Kansas Pacific were equiped with sails used as motive power.

In 1879 George Sheffield, a mechanic, was working a 10-hour day 6 days a week at a plant in Three Rivers, Michigan, several miles from his home on the Michigan Central Railroad (MC). No train was available, so George had to walk to and from his job. This irked him. In spare time at the plant he built a three-wheeled velocipede with flanged wheels. It consisted of a seat mounted on two wheels which rode on one rail and a sort of outrigger connected with the third wheel, which traveled on the other rail, supporting the vehicle. A lever sticking up in front of the seat and connected with the wheels enabled Sheffield to propel himself along the railroad. The vehicle was so light that one man could easily lift it onto or off the track.

Without mentioning it to anyone, Sheffield began using the MC track as his private transportation system. MC officials did not learn about this use until the day he reported a break in the track which could have derailed trains. As a result, the Michigan Central decided to furnish all its track inspectors with such vehicles. But they could not be bought. So Sheffield quit his old job, set up his own Sheffield Car Co. to build such equipment, and made a good deal of money.

Within a short time, track inspectors and others all over the country were making their rounds on some version of the Sheffield invention. One type had a frame like a bicycle sitting astride four wheels, instead of three, operated by foot pedals. Another was the "bicycle built for two" type, usually with one man pedaling while the roadmaster deadheaded on the other seat.

Such vehicles carried only one or two men at a time and no heavy tools, material, or water keg. In the early 1890s some railroads installed stationary gasoline-driven engines at many of their locomotive-watering stations. This principle was soon applied to push cars and hand cars. In 1893 the Buda Co. put on the market the first ready-made rail motor car, and in 1899 the first pop car, or "put-put" car, a three-wheeler with a gas motor. Later, out of the development of the automobile came various devices which led to the building of the present-day track motor car.

At first, a section foreman could not get such a car except by paying $125 for the motor himself, although the railroad company supplied the car to mount it on and the fuel. In 1926 the International Railway Congress forced the company to pay for the motor also.

BIBLIOGRAPHY: C. Miles Burpee (ed.), *Railway Engineering and Maintenance Cyclopedia,* Simmons-Boardman, New York, 1942; Matthias N. Forney, *The Car-Builder's Dictionary,* reprinted by N. K. Gregg, Kentfield, Calif., 1971.

Carson & Colorado Railroad (C&C) Narrow-gauge line of about 300 miles, running southward from Mound House, Nevada, to Keeler, California. It may have been the only railroad named for two rivers. According to its principal stockholder, Darius Ogden Mills, grandfather of the Secretary of the Treasury in the Hoover administration, it was "300 miles too long." Keeler had a white population of about 30, plus some Indians and Chinese laborers. The other terminus was even smaller. The largest on-line town, Hawthorne, 100 miles south of Mound House, had fewer than 500 inhabitants. The train stayed there overnight. A prospector said: "It's the fust railroad I ever seen that began nowhar, ended nowhar, an' stopped all night to think it over."

C&C was started in 1880 to serve then-prosperous

gold-mining camps, but until 1900 it derived most of its revenue from soda and borax shipments. Indians rode free. In the mid-1890s the solitary train often left Mound House without a passenger in either of its two canary-yellow coaches. The train would stop anywhere, station or not, to pick up a passenger. Once it backed up 5 miles for a female passenger who had got off at Wabuska to eat lunch. Prospectors far away in the hills would leave empty barrels at trackside for the crew to refill.

In 1900 the Southern Pacific bought the C&C, and mines in that area began shipping gold and silver ore. In 1 year it took in more than the $2,750,000 it had paid for the little railroad. Later, it abandoned the line.

BIBLIOGRAPHY: George Turner, *Slim Rails through the Sand: The Classic of the Narrow-Gauge Carson & Colorado-Southern Pacific,* Trans-Anglo Books, Corona Del Mar, Calif., 1953.

Cascade Tunnel Tunnel 7.79 miles long in the Cascade Range of Washington, the hemisphere's longest railroad bore. The Great Northern built it between 1925 and 1928 to replace a shorter, less efficient tunnel at a lower altitude, just outside of which a snowslide had hurled a passenger train and other railroad property into a ravine, killing at least 101 people. *See* WELLINGTON AVALANCHE.

The Big G's St. Paul-Seattle mainline was laid through a mountain gap discovered in 1889 by John F. Stevens, who became the road's chief engineer and general manager. Originally, in 1893, it crossed what is now known as Stevens Pass by a series of switchbacks. These were eliminated by the first Cascade Tunnel, 2.63 miles long, which also shortened the distance by 9 miles, cut the maximum grade from 4 to 2.2 percent, and discarded 2.332 degrees of curvature. In 1909 that tunnel was electrified to banish the smoke and poisonous gas of steam locomotives.

Then Stevens saw the need for a second tunnel, about 500 feet lower down the same slope and thus safer, as part of a $25 million track-relocation project that would scrap 12 miles of tunnels and snowsheds and electrify the 74 miles of mainline between Wenatchee and Skykomish.

The new tunnel, driven straight as a rifle bore, double-tracked, well ventilated, and electrically operated, cost $14 million to build. Work went on without letup night and day for 3 years, in several places at once, since only a limited amount of heavy machinery could be brought into action through the two portals. The plans took advantage of Mill Creek Valley, about 2 miles from the east portal, which lent itself to opening additional working faces and served as an outlet for water pumped from the area.

Another device for increasing the points of attack was the construction of a temporary tunnel, called the pioneer tunnel, located 52 feet south of the main job and paralleling it. Through this were run huge air conduits for ventilation and the power line which operated the machinery and lighted the darkness. Trains carried workmen to and from the workings and hauled out rock and other debris.

At times, almost 2000 men were kept busy simultaneously. Dynamite blasted the solid granite. The average progress made was 1240 feet a month. (Compare this with the average advance of 8 inches a day in building the Central Pacific's Summit Tunnel without modern equipment in 1866.) So expert were the engineers' calculations that when the pioneer headings met 3000 feet underground, 4 miles from the west portal, the lines carried in from the two ends were only 7 inches apart and a distance in actual and calculated distance of barely 12 inches.

The continuous rail of 1326-foot length which in 1949-1950 replaced the 32-foot sections laid down in the tunnel in 1929 cost the Great Northern about $189,000 plus 2 months of intensive welding and polishing.

In 1956 diesel-electrics replaced the 15 General Electric (GE) and Westinghouse "juice hogs" (which uniquely had the economic advantages of both alternating and direct current) on the 74 miles of track that include Cascade Tunnel. The change was brought about by the completion of a new $650,000 tunnel-ventilation project which permits heavy diesel-powered freights to use the tunnel without seriously overheating the engines or discomforting the crews. Among the freight haulers retired then were Nos. 5018 and 5019, the world's largest single-unit all-electric locomotives. Each was a GE job boasting 24 wheels and 6000 horsepower.

Basic units of the Great Northern (now Burlington Northern) tunnel ventilation system are two 6-foot fans installed at Berne, Washington, the tunnel's east portal. Powered by 8000-horsepower electric motors and turning at 1150 revolutions per minute, the fans force fresh outside air through the bore. When a heavy-tonnage freight enters the west portal at Scenic, the operator there engages the master control, closes the east portal door, and starts a fan which forces about 220,000 cubic feet of air per minute against the oncoming train. From west to east is a 1.57 percent grade. The flow of clean air minimizes the piston effect of a diesel-powered train going through.

Lighter trains do not require aid from the cooling system, and all trains westbound downgrade can operate efficiently without it. After a train has gone through in either direction, both fans can be used to change the air completely. The fans do not function unless the doors are closed. A train clearing the tunnel automatically closes the door and starts both fans.

Casey Jones (1864-1900) Casey Jones is no myth. The author met and talked with his widow and children at his old home in Jackson, Tennessee, saw his grave there, and visited his last fireman, black Sim Webb. Born on March 14, 1864, in either Missouri or Kentucky, John Luther Jones adopted the nickname Casey because he had lived for a while in Cayce, Kentucky. After braking on the Mobile & Ohio, he went firing for the Illinois Central on March 1, 1888, and was promoted to engineer in 1890. The plaintive "moans" of his self-installed locomotive whistle told the world that "the man at the throttle was Casey Jones."

So much Casey Jones tradition is associated with the South that some readers will be surprised to learn that in the early 1890s he pulled fast freights between Chicago and Champaign, Illinois, and he shuttled pasengers between Van Buren Street Station, Chicago, and the grounds of the World's Columbian Exposition.

Casey had three railroading brothers, all of whom stood above 6 feet in their socks. He himself was a big man, 6 feet 4 inches, and lanky, with gray eyes, a ready smile, and raven-black hair. According to tradition, he could get more mileage out of a tankful of water than anyone else on the road. Seldom did he have to cut off his engine from the rest of the train and run "light" to the next water tank. Tony Hayes, one of his fellow engineers, said: "When Jones ran for water he took his train with him." He understood his "old girl," meaning his engine, as a cowboy knows his horse, how much she could perform and how to treat her to get best results.

During his 10 years at the throttle (1890–1900) Casey was never involved in a serious accident or in the death of any passenger or railroad man except his own, although he was "hauled on the carpet" nine times for infractions of rules, with suspensions of from 5 to 30 days levied against him. Casey was never a *Book of Rules* man. Some of his recklessness, such as running through switches or leaving them open behind him or negligence in handling train orders, could have led to dire consequences.

On the first day of 1900, just 4 months before he died, he was assigned two of the Illinois Central's best runs, an express popularly known as the *Cannonball,* numbered 1 when southbound from Memphis, Tennessee, to Canton, Mississippi (188 miles), and 4 when northbound. He rated these plums on a seniority basis and not because he was fearless or a teetotaler, although he happened to be both. The *Cannonball's* entire mileage extended from Memphis to New Orleans and back, but standard practice in North American railroading limits a crew to one division.

On Sunday, April 29, 1900, at 11:35 P.M., Casey left Memphis 95 minutes late but eager to make up the lost time by fast running. One of his orders told him to meet a northbound freight—the train, incidentally, that would cause his death. Its orders were to wait on a siding while the fast express thundered by.

"We'd been having rainy, foggy weather for two weeks," Sim Webb recalled years later.

> That night the clouds were mighty dark and low. But Mr. Casey seemed to be in an extra good mood. As we pulled out of Central Station he opened her up and said: "We're going to have a pretty rough time getting into Canton on the dot, but I believe we can do it, barring accidents." And I replied: "You can depend on me, Mr. Casey. I'll sure keep her hot."
>
> On south we roared, with everything working just fine. We were whittling that lost time away to nothing. At some places we got to clipping a mile off every fifty seconds, and Mr. Casey was still in high spirits. As we left Durant, he stood up and hollered over to me over the boiler head: "Oh, Sim, the old girl's got on her high-heeled slippers tonight! We ought to pass Way on time."
>
> Way was just six miles north of Canton, and he had figured out that we'd be back on time when we hit there, and we'd coast on it. Down the track we went, approaching Vaughan, which is 12 miles above Canton and at the lower end of a double-S curve. The north switch was just ahead of the middle of the first S, and as we roared down we saw two big red lights. They appeared to me as big as houses. I knew it was a train not in the clear. I could see the lights, but Mr. Casey couldn't, because there was a deep curve to the fireman's side. I yelled to Mr. Casey: "Look out! We're gonna hit something!"
>
> "Jump, Sim!" he shouted, and those were his last words. He was sitting down at the time. I heard him kick the seat out from under him and apply the brakes. I swung down as low off the engine I could, and hit the dirt. When I came to, half an hour later, Mr. Casey was dead. Our engine had plowed through the caboose of the freight and two other cars—a car of shelled corn and a car of hay.

When the engineer's body was found in the wreckage, an iron bolt was driven through his neck and a bale of hay rested on his chest, while corn lay scattered around. For years afterward, a stand of wild corn from those kernels marked the scene.

Sim added:

> The freight had pulled out some drawheads and they hadn't gotten their entire train in the clear for us. The caboose and two boxcars were still out on the mainline. The crew was chaining up the drawheads and apparently had forgotten to put out a flagman.

But the official investigation exonerated the freight crew and blamed the dead engineer. The whole countryside mourned for Casey. Wallace Saunders, a black Canton roundhouse worker, wrote a ballad about him. T. Lawrence Siebert rewrote it into a version with grossly inaccurate geography which in 1903 was listed among the nation's 10 best-sellers in sheet music. Saunders's original ballad, reprinted here, uses the term *white eye,* which meant a clear signal in the days when green indicated caution. He wrote:

> Come all you rounders, I want you to hear
> The story of a brave engineer.
> Old Casey Jones was the rounder's name;
> On a six-eight wheeler he won his fame.
>
> Caller called Casey at half-past four;
> He kissed his wife at the station door,

Climbed into the cab with his orders in his hand,
Says, "This is my trip to the Promised Land."

Through the South Memphis yards on the fly,
He heard his fireboy say, "You got a white eye."
And all the switchmen knew by the engine's moans
That the man at the throttle was Casey Jones.

It had been raining some five or six weeks;
The railroad bed looked like the bed of a creek.
They loaded him down to a thirty-mile gait
And threw the southbound Mail about eight hours late.

Fireman hollered: "Casey, you're going too fast!
You run the block-board the last station we passed."
Casey says: "Yes, but I think we'll make it through,
For she's steaming better than ever I knew."

Says Casey: "Fireman, don't you fret.
Keep knocking at that firebox, don't give up yet,
For I'm going to run her till she leaves the rail
Or make it on time with the southbound Mail!"

Around the curve and over the hump,
Two locomotives were bound to bump.
Fireman hollered: "Casey, she's just ahead!
We might jump and make it, but we'll be dead!"

Around the curve he spied a train,
Reversing his engine caused bells to ring.
Fireman jumped off, but Casey stayed on,
He's a good engineer, but he's dead and gone.

Poor Casey Jones, he was all right.
He stuck to his duty both day and night.
They loved to hear his whistle and the ring of Number 3,
And he came into Memphis on the old I.C.

Headaches and backaches and all kinds of pain
Are not apart from a railroad train.
Tales that are earnest, noble and grand
Are all in the life of a railroad man.

Unlike the above, Siebert's professionally written version became so popular that it added a new term to the dictionary, *Casey Jones,* meaning "railroad man," and caused the United State government to issue a postage stamp picturing the folk hero.

BIBLIOGRAPHY: Freeman Hubbard, *Railroad Avenue,* McGraw-Hill, New York, 1945; Fred J. Lee, *Casey Jones,* Southern Pubs., Kingsport, Tenn., 1939.

One of the ornately decorated engines used on the curved Centennial Railway for the 1876 Centennial Exposition in Philadelphia. [Collection of Donald A. Somerville]

Cassin, Dennis ***(1844–1935)*** Born at Rensselaer, New York, he fell in love with locomotives as a boy and got a job as engine wiper on the New York Central & Hudson River Railroad. At 17 he became a fireman and at 23 was promoted to the right-hand side of the cab. In May 1875, five convicts escaping from Ossining Prison seized his engine, forcing him to run her. But Cassin turned on his water pumps and flooded the boiler, stopping the engine. Two convicts were captured; one was shot dead. Prison officials gave Cassin a gold watch. Later he ran the 999, fastest engine of her day, on the *Empire State Express.*

BIBLIOGRAPHY: Edward Hungerford, *Men and Iron: The History of New York Central,* Crowell, New York, 1938.

Cat-Cracked Fuel Mixture of straight-run distillate and residue fuel for diesel locomotives that is put through a catalytic cracking process. A refinery procedure mixes the two oils, rearranging them chemically.

CB&Q *See* CHICAGO, BURLINGTON & QUINCY RAILROAD.

Centennial Narrow-Gauge Railway This 7-mile steam road in Philadelphia carried during its history more passengers than any big trunk line in the United States. It operated two eight-wheeled engines, the *Schuylkill* and the *Delaware,* named for the city's two rivers, inside the grounds of the nation's Centennial Exposition for 156 days, beginning on May 13, 1876. Two trains simultaneously made 32 round trips daily, each with up to seven eight-wheeled passenger cars, often carrying 100 people per car. The railway was nearly circular, with not an inch of straight track, and had curves of 250-foot radius on grades of 135 feet per mile and 35-pound iron T rail.

During the 156 days, each engine made 35,000 stops with the then-new Westinghouse airbrakes. The *Schuylkill* had four coupled driving wheels 3½ feet in diameter and weighed 42,560 pounds. The *Delaware* had six coupled drivers of 3-foot diameter and weighed 39,000 pounds. Neither was temporarily out of service all season because of an accident for which she was responsible. Baldwin Locomotive Works of Philadelphia built both engines.

Centralized Traffic Control (CTC) System whereby train movements are directed electrically through remote control of switches and signals from a single point where the operator sees the track in miniature on the CTC panel. Tiny lights flashing on the panel show the location and progress of all trains in the control area at all times. By pushing buttons and turning levers, the operator directs train movements over distances ranging from a few to several hundred miles.

CTC makes possible closer "meets" between opposing trains (trains running in opposite directions) and faster runarounds of slow trains by speedier ones. Controls are devised and interlocked so effectively that it is impossible to set up conflicting train movements. This system eliminated the need for telegraphers to copy train orders from dispatchers and pass them on to train and engine crews.

Chapel Cars At least 10 chapel cars, 7 Baptist and 3 Catholic, roamed the rails of the Western frontier for many years of missionary work in sparsely settled areas far from regular churches. The practice was started by the Rev. Boston W. Smith, a colporteur missionary of the American Baptist Publication Society, who observed that a certain railroad often parked a passenger coach on a siding over weekends and got permission to use it on Sundays for church and Sunday school services.

Dr. Wayland Hoyt, pastor of the First Baptist Church of Minneapolis, learned about this incident and persuaded John D. Rockefeller and other prominent Baptists to finance the building of seven chapel cars to spread the Gospel in unchurched prairie, desert, and mountain areas. The first one, named the *Evangel* and dedicated at Cincinnati in 1891, was followed shortly afterward by the *Emmanuel, Glad Tidings, Good Will, Messenger of Peace, Herald of Hope,* and *Grace.*

Each car was a combined church, parsonage, and educational building on wheels. It had an organ, pews seating up to 123 people, and living quarters, kitchen, etc., for the missionary and his wife. Wooden pews with hymnal racks attached to the back seated three people apiece on the right side of the aisle and two on the left. Brass oilburning light fixtures were suspended from the ceiling; a potbellied stove supplied heat in cold weather. Underneath each car were hung compartments for storing coal, oil, wood, ice, screens, storm windows, and a tent for summer use. For many years railroads hauled the churches-on-wheels over their lines free of charge, and some of them gave free passes to clergymen riding regular trains.

In 1904 at the Louisiana Purchase Exposition in St. Louis, Father Francis C. Kelley, founder of the Catholic Extension Society, saw one of the Baptist cars and later arranged for the building of three such cars for his society: the *St. Anthony* in 1907, the *St. Peter* in 1912, and the *St. Paul* in 1915. But after 1919 the railroads refused to haul wooden cars, so the wooden *St. Anthony* was retired. The other two, being steel, continued their travels into the 1920s.

BIBLIOGRAPHY: Edwin D. McLane, *The 7:05 and the Church Alive,* Prentice-Hall, Englewood Cliffs, N.J., 1963.

Chapman, John K. *(1836-1931)* Resident of Hornell, New York, who is said to have been the oldest man in active service in American railroading. Hiring out as an Erie brakeman on his eighteenth birthday, October 4, 1854, Chapman was continuously on the Erie payroll until his death, except for 3 years' leave of absence during the Civil War. He became a locomotive engineer in 1865, a road foreman of engines in 1875 for 14 years, went back to running, and in 1907 was given the title of yard foreman of engines, a position he held actively until his death at 95.

***A 1957 view of the Chessie System's centralized traffic control (CTC) board and signal controls in Cincinnati.* [Chessie System]**

Chatsworth Wreck On August 12, 1887, the bankrupt Toledo, Peoria & Western made up an excursion to Niagara Falls with six sleepers, two chair cars, five coaches, a baggage car, and an official business car, double-headed by locomotives numbered 2 and 15. When the train pulled out of Peoria, Illinois, at 8 P.M. it was already filled to capacity, but it picked up more people along the line. Some of the 960 passengers had to stand for the entire journey.

The train rocked and clattered over badly worn track, making the 6 miles from Forrest to Chatsworth in 7 minutes—fast going in those days, especially on poor roadbed. At 11:45 it left Chatsworth and almost immediately rolled through the prairie village of Piper City. Nearing a wooden bridge that spanned a dry gully (no rain had fallen since mid-July), Engineer Sutherland on the head engine saw a tiny blaze a short distance ahead but told his fireman: "Only a few dry leaves burning beside the track. Those section hands ought to be more careful."

But the bridge itself was on fire—the bridge they'd have to cross. Tongues of flame shot up suddenly. The engineer signaled "Down brakes," although nothing could keep the heavy train from the fiery pit. Almost miraculously, the lead engine crossed the tottering bridge, keeping to the rails. Just as she did so, the little span collapsed in a sea of flames. The second engine fell, dragging down the long string of old wooden open-platform cars. Nearly 1000 men, women, and children were flung into the wreckage.

Quick-thinking Sutherland took his engine 10 miles

east of Piper City to get help. He returned in 45 minutes with a special train bearing all the doctors, nurses, and volunteer workers he could assemble on short notice. There was no water to fight fire. Desperately, section laborers and others dug into dry, hard earth with bare hands and flung it at the advancing flames. Their only light came from the fire itself and a couple of oil lamps. Ghouls prowling in the darkness robbed dead and suffering victims of money and jewelry. An oft-printed poem ends with: "The bridge was burned at Chatsworth/And a hundred lives were lost!" The real death total was 82, plus an indeterminate number of injured persons.

BIBLIOGRAPHY: Wesley J. Griswold, *Train Wreck!*, Stephen Greene, Brattleboro, Vt., 1969; Robert C. Reed, *Train Wrecks,* Superior Publishing, Seattle, 1968; Robert B. Shaw, *A History of Railroad Accidents, Safety Precautions, and Operating Procedures,* Northern Press, Potsdam, N.Y., 1978.

Cherokee Strip Railroads assisted in the most spectacular rush of homesteaders in American history: the opening of the Cherokee Strip, comprising over 10,000 square miles of Oklahoma and Indian Territories. This area, bordering southern Kansas, was 180 miles long and 58 miles wide. Inhabited by only a few roving Indians and a few cowboys with their herds, it served as a hideout for outlaws such as the Dalton brothers.

Farmers and adventurers had tried to colonize the fertile strip, but federal cavalry razed their settlements and escorted them back to the Kansas line. Then Congress authorized the government to buy the land and open it for colonization, whereupon the railroads started building there. The first land rush occurred in 1889. The federal land office was located at the Santa Fe Railway depot and water tank at Guthrie in Indian Territory. A wild scramble marked the first trainload of homesteaders. The passengers unloaded with a rapidity which fire-drill experts would have envied. Some even climbed out of car windows, fighting one another to stake the best land claims.

The Cherokee Strip, larger than the state of Vermont, was bought from the Indians for $8.3 million (about $1.38 an acre). It was surveyed and divided into nearly 40,000 homestead sites of 160 acres each. No settler was allowed to enter the strip until noon of September 16, 1893, at which time pistol shots and a fanfare of bugles would start the race. After that, the first person to place a stake in any area would own it.

Some 100,000 or so homeseekers assembled on the border of the strip. Five trains of the Choctaw Coal & Railway Co. (later part of the Rock Island Railroad) were jammed to capacity with homesteaders. Only the lucky ones had been able to get aboard. Even the fenders and car roofs were crowded. Tense expectancy filled the air as engineers sat at their throttles waiting on the edge of the strip for the signal to go. When it finally came, a thunderous cheer arose from excited throats. Within an hour, the spot where the vast multitude had gathered was an empty wilderness, and by early the following morning every square foot of available land had been taken.

Chesapeake and Ohio Railway *See* CHESSIE SYSTEM.

Chessie System The Chesapeake and Ohio Railway (C&O), with some justification, claims George Washington as its founder. As a young surveyor, Washington visualized a transportation system for moving goods and people on flat-bottomed canalboats pulled by mules (a modern idea in those days) from Virginia to the Ohio River wilderness. But not until 1785 could he begin to carry out this project. That August the James River Co. was organized with Washington as president. He was given 100 shares of stock, which he donated to what is now Washington and Lee University.

That same river company, later renamed, continued to function in the canal business until 1880. Then a newly created railroad, the Richmond & Alleghany (R&A), took it over and used the old towpath for a 197-mile rail roadbed. Nine years later the Chesapeake and Ohio, a name born in 1868, acquired the R&A in its march to expansion.

C&O became the foremost unit of Chessie System Inc., its parent company, which was set up in June 1973. Also included in the system are the Baltimore & Ohio, the Western Maryland, the B&O Union Terminal Railroad, the Staten Island Railroad, and the Chicago South Shore & South Bend, and a group of diversified nonrail enterprises developing forest resources, coal lands, investments, etc., with a total of about 38,000 employees. Chessie roads operate 11,200 miles of track in 14 states and the District of Columbia, extending from the Atlantic Ocean to St. Louis and from the southern West Virginia coalfields into Ontario. Coal contributes roughly 40 percent of Chessie's business, with 400 active mines located on its lines and 100 others being developed or planned. This made Chessie the largest coal-hauling system in the United States, using its 78,000 hopper-car fleet mostly for this tonnage. *See* BALTIMORE & OHIO RAILROAD; WESTERN MARYLAND RAILWAY.

C&O's earliest rail predecessor was the Louise Railroad, chartered on February 15, 1836. In 1850, stretching 64½ miles from Hanover Junction (now Doswell) to Shadwell, Virginia, it was renamed the Virginia Central. With trackage rights over the state-owned Blue Ridge Railroad, it was nearing Covington, Virginia, when the Civil War broke out and badly damaged it. The Virginia and West Virginia Legislatures helped to rehabilitate it.

Both legislatures passed acts "to provide for the completion of a line or lines of railroad from the waters of the Chesapeake to the Ohio River." In 1868 the Virginia Central was given this assignment. Collis P. Huntington, one of the Central (now Southern) Pacific's Big Four, became associated with this project. *See* HUNTINGTON, COLLIS POTTER.

In 1873, a panic year, the struggling C&O became bankrupt. Five years later it was sold to a syndicate headed by Huntington and reincorporated as the Chesapeake and Ohio Railway Co. Laying steel eastward, it reached Newport News, Virginia in 1882. As it grew, it built branches and picked up lines already operating, among them the George Washington heritage. On and on the railroad builders advanced like a conquering army, northward to Washington, D.C., westward to Louisville and Dayton, up to the lower Michigan Peninsula and the Great Lakes at Toledo, then into Chicago.

By 1870 the Louise's 22 miles of 1837 had grown to only 227, but by 1920 the C&O had 2539 miles of steel. In 1945 the sun shone on its 3000 miles serving, among many other regions, some of the world's richest coalfields. Following a merger with the Pere Marquette in 1947, the system's total mileage exceeded 5000. Chesapeake and Ohio crossed Lake Michigan (by car-ferry) to Wisconsin and cut through Ontario to Buffalo, New York.

Chessie has big car-building and repair shops and a 50,000-car merchandise freight fleet. Its livery colors are yellow, vermilion, and blue. A major carrier for Michigan automobile makers, it was hurt by the severe depression of the automobile industry in the late 1970s and early 1980s. It hauls much grain and steel, using special equipment to protect valuable coated and stainless steels and specialized cars for such shipments as cable reel, wood products, wood pulp, and auto parts.

C&O acquired control of the historic B&O in 1961 and the Western Maryland in 1972. Its corporate name, Chessie System, honors C&O's much-publicized kitten mascot named Chessie. Although Amtrak now handles what is left of the system's intercity passenger service, there was a time, before motor passenger vehicles became too prolific, when the C&O was proud of its fast, handsome passenger trains, particularly the one named for George Washington, and it used the slogan "Sleep Like a Kitten" to advertise its overnight runs.

On September 24, 1980, the Interstate Commerce Commission authorized the Chessie System to merge with Seaboard Coast Line Industries. This merger, effective on November 1, 1980, formed the present CSX Corp. *See* CSX CORP.

Chicago, Burlington & Quincy Railroad (CB&Q)

Line widely known as the Burlington or the Q, now in the Burlington Northern Inc. (BN) system. It originated in the Aurora Branch Railroad (AB), which businessmen of Aurora, Illinois, built in 1848 with secondhand scrap iron spiked to 12 miles of wooden rails.

Boston investors bought the AB in 1852. By 1864 it had 400 miles of track, all in Illinois, and adopted the name Chicago, Burlington & Quincy Railroad Co., for the line stretched to Burlington, Iowa, and Quincy, Illinois, on the Mississippi River. That great name lasted 106 years, until the BN merger in 1970. Also in 1864, the Burlington completed its own line from Aurora to Chicago, and in 1865 it operated the first train into Chicago's newly opened Union Stockyards.

Among the 204 roads amalgamated into the CB&Q was the Hannibal & St. Joseph (H&SJ), one of whose promoters was Mark Twain's father, John M. Clemens. This road brought fast mail across the state of Missouri to connect with the Pony Express, relays of swift horseback riders. In 1862 it introduced the first railroad car equipped for sorting United States mail en route, thus starting the Railway Mail Service that lasted for more than a century.

During the Civil War the Burlington was often harassed by Confederate raiders. Afterward, it became an occasional target for train robbers. The Jesse James gang killed one of its conductors, William Westphal, at Winton in 1881. The Hannibal line also sparked the beginning of Kansas City as a rail center and gateway to the Southwest. In 1869, engineered by Octave Chanute, it completed the first Mississippi River bridge. In 1871, Jay Gould and his New York allies acquired control of the H&SJ. They used it during the next dozen years as a pawn in bitter rate wars and shifting alliances, but in 1883 the CB&Q took it over. *See* GOULD, JAY.

Meanwhile, in 1880, the Burlington had acquired an important feeder line, the Burlington & Missouri River Railroad, which connected with the Union Pacific at Kearney, Nebraska, and soon was extended to Denver. As CB&Q rails pushed westward, with many branches, they reached St. Louis, Lincoln, Rock Island, St. Paul, and Billings. Like other big Western systems, the Burlington promoted crop and livestock improvements, irrigation, and soil conservation. It even hired impoverished farmers for work in railroad shops during winter months until they could put their land on a full-time paying basis.

And like James J. Hill of the Great Northern, the CB&Q had many colonizing agents in the Eastern United States, England, Scotland, Sweden, and Germany to stimulate expansion and settlement. From 1870 to 1880 it sold over 2 million land-grant acres to some 20,000 people. Prior to 1886 the Burlington used two slogans: "The Cheapest, Best and Quickest" and "The Original Dining-Car Route." *See* HILL, JAMES JEROME.

Also on the CB&Q, in 1886 and 1887, George Westinghouse conducted history-making airbrake tests at West Burlington, Iowa, in connection with which he invented the triple brake valve. This device perfected the airbrake and helped to bring it into universal use. *See* WESTINGHOUSE, GEORGE.

Because farm and ranch shipments were essential to the Burlington, that line was known as a Granger road. In 1901 the Great Northern and Northern Pacific jointly bought 97.2 percent of the CB&Q stock—primarily, Hill said, because "the great provision centers are Kansas City, St. Joseph, Omaha, Chicago, and St. Louis, none of which are reached directly by the Great Northern or Northern Pacific. The Burlington lets us into all these districts and commercial centers over better lines and with better terminals than any other road."

In 1908, the Burlington purchased 70 percent of the Colorado & Southern and Fort Worth and Denver stock, partly to increase its coal freight. Two years later, it began operating the first printing telegraph, a forerunner of Teletype, and in 1915 was the first company to use train radio, although this device did not become practical until 1943. The Burlington in 1927 was one of the first roads to use centralized traffic control. In 1931, its Galesburg, Illinois, hump yard was equipped with electropneumatic retarders to slow the descent of cars from the hump. *See* CENTRALIZED TRAFFIC CONTROL.

On May 26, 1934, the Burlington staged a spectacular nonstop 1000-mile run from Denver to the World's Fair on Chicago's lakefront with the *Pioneer Zephyr,* America's first diesel-powered streamliner. This trip climaxed a "Wings of the Century" transportation pageant. Bulletins had been broadcast throughout the day as the train streaked through villages and cities. At 8:08 P.M. it completed its dramatic run by rolling onto the stage before a packed audience, and bedlam broke loose. A world's long-distance record had been set and the value of diesel-electric power firmly established. Total fuel cost for the long, fast journey was only $14.64. The highest speed attained was 112.5 miles per hour. Economy and speed formed the basis for a revolution in railroading.

In 1967, CB&Q became the first carrier to use direct-service agency vans, offices on wheels which enabled the company to discontinue station structures on many branches, yet improve service by sending agents directly to shipper offices.

See BURLINGTON NORTHERN INC.

BIBLIOGRAPHY: *Chicago, Burlington & Quincy Railroad Company: Documentary History,* 3 vols., Chicago, Burlington & Quincy Railroad, 1928–1929; Bernard G. Corbin, *The Burlington in Transition,* Corbin, Red Oak, Iowa, 1967; Freeman Hubbard, *Railroad Avenue,* McGraw-Hill, New York, 1945; Donald L. C. McMurray, *The Great Burlington Strike of 1888,* Harvard, Cambridge, Mass., 1956; David P. Morgan, *Diesels West!,* Kalmbach, Milwaukee, 1963; Richard C. Overton, *Gulf to the Rockies,* University of Texas Press, Austin, 1953; id., *Burlington Route,* Knopf, New York, 1965.

Chicago, Milwaukee, St. Paul & Pacific Railroad *See* MILWAUKEE ROAD.

Chicago, Rock Island & Pacific Railroad *See* ROCK ISLAND RAILROAD.

Chicago & North Western Transportation Co. (C&NW) America's only major railroad owned by its employees, who acquired it on June 1, 1972, by buying stock from the parent company, Northwest Industries, Inc. In 1973, its first full year under employee ownership, revenue ton-miles rose by 21 percent. C&NW was incorporated in Ohio on February 25, 1889, as successor to the foreclosed Columbus, Hocking Valley & Toledo Railway. It operates some 9990 route miles, mostly in Illinois, Wisconsin, and Iowa but also in Minnesota, South Dakota, Missouri, and Wyoming. *See also* CABOOSES; DAN PATCH LINE; GRAVES, TRACKSIDE; SHELLEY, KATE.

BIBLIOGRAPHY: Patrick C. Dorin, *Chicago and North Western Power: Modern Steam and Diesel, 1900 to 1971,* Superior, Seattle, 1972; *Jane's World Railways and Rapid Transit Systems,* F. Watts, New York, 1977; *Poor's Manual of Railroads,* any edition; George H. Williams, *Life on a Locomotive: The Story of Buddy Williams, C&NW Engineer,* Howell-North, Berkeley, Calif., 1971.

Chinese Labor A major problem in building the western end of America's first transcontinental railway through the rugged Sierra was a labor shortage. All ablebodied males who applied, both the old and the extremely young, were hired. But of the thousands signed up and sent to the mountains during 1863–1864, fewer than half reported to foremen on the job. Many took advantage of the chance to get free transportation partway to boomtowns beyond the Sierra. Booms and the Civil War siphoned off a considerable portion of the nation's labor pool. Most of the applicants who actually did go to work for the Central Pacific (CP) stayed only long enough to earn a grubstake and stage fare to the gold-mine area of Virginia City, Nevada.

This duplicity angered Leland Stanford, the railroad president. He asked the War Department for 5000 Confederate prisoners, with Union guards, to build the line, but they never came. Numerous Chinese on the West Coast were reworking abandoned placer gold mines, running a laundry or a restaurant, or peddling fruit and vegetables from their small farms. Stanford suggested hiring them. His superintendent, J. H. Strobridge, disagreed; he didn't think the Chinese had the endurance to build a mountain railroad.

Judge E. B. Crocker, head of the CP Legal Department and brother of one of the railroad's Big Four, Charles Crocker, sided with Stanford, saying he had seen Chinese toiling in gravel pits in early morning before the white workers were out of bed. He clinched his argument by asking, "Who built the Great Wall of China?"

A decision was reached when white crews threatened to strike. Strobridge retaliated by bringing 50 Chinese from Sacramento to the railhead in freight cars. Starting at dawn, the new workers used picks, shovels, and wheelbarrows vigorously for 12 hours. This astounded and pleased the superintendent and his colleagues, some of whom had predicted that the Chinese would collapse from exhaustion on the job.

Other Chinese gangs were hired. Within 2 months, 2000 pale-blue-clad, basket-hatted coolies were on the job. CP publicists hailed them as "the Asiatic contingent of the Grand Army of civilization." White workers called them "Crocker's pets," resenting the use of foreign help, which they said was a betrayal of American labor. But the complainants were mollified by being relieved of pick-and-shovel duty and promoted to jobs as teamsters, powdermen, and gang foremen, which gave them more dignity.

Even so, the controversy was widespread. It added to the company's difficulties in getting financial aid. It also led to mistreatment of many harmless pigtailed Chinese Americans who had never even seen the railroad, and it gave birth to the saying "He didn't have a Chinaman's chance."

Stanford's official reports defended the use of Chinese. "Without them," he wrote, "it would be impossible to complete the line on time. . . . They soon became as efficient as white laborers. . . . More productive and economical, they are content with less wages." (The standard rate for white laborers, and presumably Chinese also, was $40 a month, payable in gold and silver.) Stanford denied that his contractors held the coolies in serfdom.

The coolies lived peacefully in separate camps, cooking their own meals. By the end of 1865 most of Central Pacific's laborers were Chinese. Stanford wanted a total of 15,000, but no more were available on the West Coast; so he had a San Francisco firm send agents to Canton and bring back large numbers of them in boats.

There were no drilling machines, giant cranes, or bulldozers in those days. The Chinese had the exhausting task of drilling into solid rock with hammers and chisels and placing charges of black powder in the holes they dug. Others were lowered precariously by ropes from cliffs and there, high above deep canyons, slowly and painfully chipped out of sheer, hard rock a shelving on which trains would eventually run.

In building the lofty Summit Tunnel, ¼ mile long, the Chinese, crowded shoulder to shoulder, hacked through rock in 12-hour shifts, advancing at the rate of only about 8 inches a day. Besides gangs operating from both ends, a third gang worked from the middle of the tunnel by means of a shaft chipped down from above, also cutting away bits of rock. It is not easy to imagine a more difficult industrial assignment.

Before the fierce winters of 1865–1866 and 1866–1867 were half over, the cold got so extreme that thousands of shivering Chinese were sent back to Sacramento or at least down to lower levels; but as soon as spring thaws set in they were returned to work in the high altitudes, driven relentlessly by their bosses, from Crocker on down.

After the CP rails met those of the Union Pacific at Promontory, Utah, in 1869, some Chinese were retained for railroad maintenance. Others returned to China as relatively rich men or stayed in America to work small farms or open restaurants or laundries. *See* GOLDEN SPIKE CEREMONY.

Of the 25,000 workers who helped to complete the Northern Pacific Railway between 1881 and 1883 under the management of Henry Villard 15,000 were Chinese. An unknown number of Chinese railroad laborers are sleeping out eternity at Winnemucca, Nevada, in America's only known trackside Chinese graveyard.

BIBLIOGRAPHY: Oscar Lewis, *The Big Four,* Knopf, New York, 1938; James McCague, *Moguls and Iron Men,* Harper & Row, New York, 1964; Glenn C. Quiett, *They Built the West,* Appleton-Century, New York, 1934.

Cincinnati Locomotive Builders In the mid-1800s Cincinnati was the largest city west of the Alleghenies. Francis Shield is credited with having built two steam locomotives there before 1831. During the 1845–1868 period four locomotive-building companies functioned in that city: Anthony Harkness & Son, the Cincinnati Locomotive Works (also known as Moore & Richardson), Niles & Co., and G. E. Sellers.

At least 30 Harkness iron horses were built for the Little Miami Railroad between 1846 and 1856. Meanwhile, in 1853, the Cincinnati Locomotive Works took over the Harkness plant, and Anthony's son William committed suicide. By 1857 Niles & Co., operated by two brothers, Jonathan S. and James M. Niles, was in full production of locomotives, its customers including the broad-gauge Ohio & Mississippi; but in 1857 the brothers switched to the riverboat engine business, which they found more profitable. In about 1847 George Escol Sellers, in partnership with his brother Charles, won fame by developing and building grade-climbing locos.

BIBLIOGRAPHY: John H. White, *Cincinnati Locomotive Builders: 1845–1868,* Smithsonian Institution, Museum of History and Technology, Washington, 1965.

Cincinnati Southern Railway (CS) Begun in 1878, one of the few city-owned mainline railroads, the CS was the shortest rail route from Cincinnati, Ohio, to Chattanooga, Tennessee. Its 338 miles, originally all single-track, ran through the lofty Cumberland Mountains, with their deep gorges and seemingly uncrossable rivers. Included were 121 bridges and so many tunnels (27) that the road was called the Rat-Hole Division.

At first the city of Cincinnati tried to operate its railroad, but in 1881 it leased it to Baron Frederic d'Erlanger, an English capitalist who owned controlling stock in three other Southern railways. He merged the four roads into the Cincinnati, New Orleans & Pacific, (the famed Queen and Crescent Route) and installed one of America's first electric block signal systems, with banjo-faced targets. In addition, a staff system, like that of relay runners, protected four tunnels. An engineer would pick up a token designating a clear track at one station and drop it off at another depot, beyond the tunnel. If a train had several sections, the last engineer carried the staff.

Despite precautions, a succession of costly wrecks plus some management errors threw the former CS into receivership in 1893 (the other three roads remained solvent), but 16 months later it was solvent again. In 1895 it was leased to the Southern Railway, which daylighted most of the tunnels, modernized the bridges, double-tracked nearly all of the line, and installed 130-pound rail, an improved electric block system, and America's first automatic train control apparatus.

But mountain railroading was so hazardous that in one year, 1900, the line had 32 head-end collisions, not to mention rear-enders, sideswipes, and derailments. It was not uncommon for a crew to be caught in the mountains with wrecks ahead of and behind them.

CS business was so good in 1903 that 40 sections of a heavy freight train were almost daily occurrences. All trains were double-headed. Chief revenue loads were pig iron, lumber, and coal. Since 80 engines were needed to wheel 40 sections, boomers with engine experience were in big demand, and men from all over North America got jobs there. One August day in 1903 seven firemen, including students learning the road, were killed in a single wreck. Today the old CS route is finely ballasted and protected by modern safety devices.

Cinder Arrester Device, known as a cyclone front end, that was used on many Northern Pacific steam locomotives to permit the burning of subbituminous coal with a minimum of spark emission. It consisted of a sheet-metal drum with breaker strips around the interior and deflecting vanes at the intake so that exhaust gases rushed forward through the boiler tubes in a whirling motion. This delayed the passage of cinders through the smokebox, breaking them up and extinguishing them before they could be discharged through the stack. In contrast to other spark arresters, no netting was used with this design.

The Griffenfeld cinder catcher was used widely before the Civil War to snare the sparks from wood-burning engines. Unlike other devices, it functioned at the base of the stack instead of near the top, sometimes inside the smokebox. It preceded the petticoat netting inside the extended smokebox. Some early coalburners used a modified version of this device. Manufactured by Griffenfeld Metal Working Co. of Philadelphia, it was placed on the locomotives of the Baldwin Locomotive Works, which held the patent rights.

Circus Trains Early American circuses were small one-ring affairs moved by wagons over dirt roads, often mired, sometimes retracing weary miles because a rival show had blocked a road or burned a bridge. In December 1838, Bacon & Derious became the first American circus to travel by rail; details are unrecorded. Its trip must have been short, for in 1838 the entire nation had only about 2000 miles of rail lines and each railway was isolated from the others. In 1856 Dr. William A. Spaulding, a New Albany, Indiana, druggist, transported his Spaulding & Rogers (S&R) show in rented railway cars in the Midwest. The tour made history but was a nightmare. The railroads then were relatively short, and their gauge, or track width, varied on connecting lines. The S&R show people slept intermittently on planks laid across the seats. Often their slumber was broken twice or thrice a night because the train reached a junction point where the gauge changed and they had to unload the whole circus and reload it onto the cars of another railroad.

Ten years later L. B. Lentz took his New York Circus over a rail route that avoided frequent changes of gauge. He advertised this venture as the "First Summer tour per railway to a few of the principal cities and towns in the State of New York." In 1867 his ads boasted of the "Second triumphal tour by rail." The ice having been broken, other shows rode the iron trail. First to reach California was W. W. Cole's circus in 1873. Then John H. Murray's Railroad Circus delighted New England and eastern Canada, and Howe's London Circus became the first to tour Mexico by rail. Possibly the longest circus rail trip in history was 2200 miles, from Halifax to Winnipeg, by W. H. Harris's Nickel Plate outfit.

In 1870 showman William Coup persuaded the reluctant Phineas T. Barnum, then semiretired, to assemble "a great traveling attraction." Barnum did so, hiring Coup as his manager. At first the show was horse-drawn. Then Coup convinced his boss that using the "steam cars" would pay better because they could skip small towns. So in 1872 Barnum's first train, 61 cars rented from the Pennsylvania Railroad and garishly painted, rolled out of New Brunswick, New Jersey, on Pennsy rails.

The ingenious Coup, who contributed much to circus technique, devised his own system for safely and quickly loading and unloading circus trains. It was so effective that all the other big circuses eventually adopted it, and so did even the General Staff of the Imperial German Army for moving heavy artillery.

Time was when hundreds of spectators turned out at dawn, even in rainy weather, to "supervise" the unloading of a circus train. The train hardly came to a stop before it was beset by a horde of roustabouts (laborers for loading and unloading), each man with an assigned task. One crew, on the flatcars, knocked out the chocks from under the wheels of 10-ton wagons and cages, chariots, and carriages (in more modern times, trucks also) and unlocked the chains which further secured them. Others laid flat steel plates across the gaps between the flatcars so that the parade vehicles could be rolled over them from one car to another to the ground. At first elephants or horses were used for this job; later, small motor vehicles did it.

Massive horses emerged from stock cars to haul the showy wagons, etc., to waiting razorbacks (laborers who pitched and razed circus tents). These men drove them to the vacant lot on which the performances would be held.

While all this was going on, a shrill trumpeting from elsewhere on the train called attention to the elephants, which were pouring out of wide doorways and down ramps to mingle with the camels and zebras. Within an hour of arrival the long flatcars were picked clean of their cargo. Each vehicle had its number and allotted space and was placed to the best advantage for unloading and reloading later on.

Contrary to public belief, the circus did not start to reload its train at the close of the evening show. Reloading began when the noisy calliope at the rear of the morning parade returned to the lot. Equipment which could not be used again in a typical day's two performances was taken back to the train and reloaded. The cook tent was dismantled, and its tables, benches, dishes, etc., were put on the first section of the outgoing train. That section was miles out of town before the night performance ended. No meals were served on the train; a "pie car" in each section dispensed snacks.

On September 15, 1885, while the final show was still going on, Barnum's 31 elephants were being loaded onto the circus train that stood in the Grand Trunk Railway yard at St. Thomas, Ontario, where the big top was finishing a 1-day stand. The first 29 were loaded safely. But as the last 2, the world-famous Jumbo and a small clown elephant, were being led toward their car along the single track laid on a narrow fill, or embankment, an extra freight train chugged up unexpectedly behind them on the same track. There were no airbrakes in those days. The engineer yanked his reverse lever and whistled a signal for his crew to set handbrakes, but the engine, No. 88, kept steaming ahead. The elephants' keeper tried desperately to drive his charges down the embankment away from the train. The clown elephant jumped and broke a leg. But huge Jumbo was afraid to trust his ponderous weight to the shifting soil of the embankment in the semidarkness, and kept running toward his car. He had almost reached it when, at 8:18 P.M., the engine struck his hind legs, thrusting him against the car and forcing his tusks back into his skull. The poor beast died a few hours later. His skeleton stands today in the American Museum of Natural History, New York.

In the early 1870s, Bill Coup replaced the unsatisfactory cars leased from the Pennsylvania Railroad with longer new ones built to order and owned by the circus. Barnum rarely traveled on the same train with Coup because, as he said, "If we both get killed, the show will be without a head." Years later, after their train had run away down a mountain grade, Coup had all their cars equipped with the then newly invented airbrakes. Meanwhile, he organized half-rate Circus Day railroad excursions, bringing to the show grounds thousands of people from beyond the normal reach of horse and buggy. Wherever the big top went with its streaming Barnum banners, men, women, and children flocked to trackside to see the spectacular train. It was great publicity. Before its railroad era, the circus had lost much daylight time in travel; now all moves were made at night and with long jumps to skip unprofitable population centers. The new ideas paid off and eventually created the first three-ring circus, with master showman James A. Bailey as Barnum's partner and with a famous slogan, "The Greatest Show on Earth." The railroads made this triumph possible.

The show's biggest rival, Ringling Bros., did not take to the rails until 1890. The following season the Ringlings expanded their operation to a three-ring show with 130 horses and a 20-car train. In 1906, after Barnum and his partner had died, the Ringlings bought the entire Barnum & Bailey (B&B) circus and in 1907 began operating the two shows separately, each under its own name. Then in the summer of 1917, America's railroads served notice that they could not continue to handle two major circuses in wartime. That forced a decision whereby in 1919 the two shows were merged under a joint name. At first the combined aggregation had one train of 100 cars, operated in five sections, but the total soon dropped to 90 cars and much later to 20.

A long list of circuses had trains of varying lengths and for various periods of time; but after the collapse of Cole Bros. and Dailey Bros. (circuses often used the word *Bros.* in their titles even when no brothers were involved), only two trains were left with circus-owned cars (no circus ever owned a locomotive): those of Ringling Bros.-Barnum & Bailey and the Clyde Beatty show.

For many years all circus trains with their own cars had them in multiples of 5 because the railroad companies used that number as a unit in figuring transportation costs. The bill for moving 17 such cars, for example, would have been as great as for moving 20, regardless of car length or loads, which explains why circuses made a point of having extra-long cars. Circus people refer to their passenger cars as coaches, even those permanently equipped with berths. After the Beatty show folded, the Big One, meaning Ringling-B&B, became the last possessor of a circus train anywhere.

Because interstate laws restrict passenger trains to 20 cars, circus trains are classified as freight regardless of the inclusion of coaches. For years the Big One operated 80 cars, 23 of which were "home, sweet home" for its personnel. After the circus acquired reconditioned government-surplus hospital cars in 1919, each employee, but not executives or top stars, had a bunk measuring 74 by 44 inches and a locker. There was no tub or shower. During the season both men and women usually bathed in dressing tents on the lot, pouring pails of water over one another.

Before 1919, train space was so valuable that not even solo performers in the center ring were given private compartments. Every inch counted. Several circus owners had private cars on their trains; some top executives boasted private staterooms. Most of the personnel were crammed two in a bunk in three tiers. The freak fat lady, the giant, and the midgets slept in beds suitable for their sizes. There were separate cars for married couples, single men, and single women. The train accommodation for girls was known as the "glamour car" or "no-man's-land."

In 1919 Lillian Leitzel, "darling of the canvas world," an aerialist, asked and received from Ringling Bros. for her own use an entire Pullman car and a private dressing tent on the lot. No other circus performer was ever honored that way.

In the big top's heyday, the total number of railroad cars owned by a large circus usually included an advertising and publicity car (for billposting, etc.) which was used in the show's contracts with railroads but moved about 2 weeks ahead of the circus itself. In 1955, to conserve its diminished train space, Ringling Bros. dropped its advance car, replacing it with a truck and station wagons. Beatty followed suit.

The Big One often covered up to 20,000 miles in a season. Planning a route months ahead was even more complicated than graphing a railroad timetable, and it took weeks of sustained effort. A circus general agent must know about roadbed conditions, grades, mileages, yards, bridges and tunnels, distances between population centers, and railroad connections. The agent is the transportation boss of the outfit. The circus trainmaster, a lesser official, supervises loading and unloading. A sudden misfortune along the way, such as a flood or a train wreck, may cause a change in routing. Hardship-ridden communities are skipped until later in the season or until the following year.

Circus-train history includes many spectacular wrecks. The worst one occurred on June 22, 1918. It was caused by kidney pills. Alonzo E. Sargent, engineer of a westbound troop train on the Michigan Central, gulped down a few pills just before going on his run. These, doctors testified later, must have made him drowsy. Two miles east of Ivanhoe, Indiana, his train passed, without even slowing down, an automatic block signal set at caution, then a red signal, and finally a flagman on the job protecting the second section of the Hagenbeck & Wallace circus special, just ahead. Like a mighty battering ram, the troop-train engine plowed into the rear of the circus special. The latter's wooden cars crumpled like matchboxes and burst into flames. Clowns, bareback riders, and trapeze artists, many of them widely advertised veterans of the big top, perished that night in the grinding, shattering crash. Beauty, brawn, and skill—a total of 68 men, women, and children—were killed by the impact and the fire, and 128 were injured.

During the golden age of the big top there were at least 25 railroad circuses; by 1920, only 15. In 1929 only a dozen circuses, with 345 active cars, were riding the rails in the United States and Canada. The Depression of the early 1930s cut the number to three, with 165 cars. Then a brief revival set in. Six circuses owned

The advance guard of P. T. Barnum's circus was an eye-catching car filled with lithographs, placards, press releases, pastepots, slap brushes, stepladders, and other objects. [Collection of Freeman Hubbard]

and operated 305 railroad cars in 1938, but the figures dropped the following year to two with 100 cars. Great steel flatcars were given to the blowtorch. Once-gaudy coaches rotted on rusty sidings. The longtime home of three famous circuses, Peru, Indiana, became the ghost town of show business.

In 1944 came a slight rally; three circuses trouped with 152 cars, and in 1945 six of them had 150 cars. Then railroad circuses skidded again; so did the numbers of tents and street parades. The railroad companies kept piling rate increases on the dwindling canvas world. There were extra charges for moving a train in more than one section, for the use of sidetracks and crossings, and for switching. Circuses also had to pay a bonus to be hauled through certain yards and across some bridges. One railroad even assessed a circus for a series of spare locomotives spotted along the route, unused and unrequested but available in case of a breakdown of the road's first set of engines. Another railroad company billed a show for payment of its regular railroad detectives. Meanwhile, in about 1936, several circuses began traveling by rail but in leased cars, like those two pioneer ventures of long ago, and they, too, found railroad rates irksome.

And so, partly for these reasons and partly owing to such factors as radio, TV, movies, automobiles, airplanes, and cities too congested and built up for circus parades or circus lots, leading to the less colorful indoor performances, the list of circuses which own railroad cars finally dwindled to the solitary Ringling-B&B. An attempt by Dick Ringling, son of one of the five brothers, to motorize the Big One failed dismally. The more-than-a-century-old show went back to the rails, and at this writing is still there, with two separate trains operating in different parts of the country.

BIBLIOGRAPHY: George L. Chindahl, *A History of the Circus in America,* Caxton Printers, Caldwell, Idaho, 1959; Charles P. Fox, *Ticket to the Circus,* Superior Publishing, Seattle, 1959; Freeman Hubbard, *Great Trains of All Time,* Grosset & Dunlap, New York, 1962; Henry Ringling North and Alden Hatch, *The Circus Kings,* Doubleday, Garden City, N.Y., 1960; Tom Parkinson and Charles P. Fox, *The Circus Moves by Rail,* Pruett Publishing Co., Boulder, Colo., 1978; Warren A. Reeder, Jr., *No Performances Today,* North State Press, Hammond, Ind., 1972.

City of Iron Horses *See* PATERSON, NEW JERSEY.

Civil War The first comprehensive, integrated plan to construct railroads that could be used for speedy mobilization and troop movements was laid out as early as 1838 by Maj. Gen. Edmund P. Gaines, U.S. Army. He urged the War Department to build seven strategic railway lines radiating from Kentucky and Tennessee, then the nation's central areas, to the frontiers. The military did not build any of these lines, but all were built eventually for commercial use. Even at that, each one has military value.

The first strategic use of American rail transport occurred in 1846, when a regiment of Pennsylvania volunteers heading for the war with Mexico traveled partway by rail to New Orleans. But military techniques were not developed in the United States until the Civil War. The Confederates won their first big victory in 1861 by eluding Union forces assigned to watch them and by riding the Manassas Gap Railroad across the Blue Ridge Mountains to the war's first battlefield, Bull Run, where they turned the tide in their favor.

Looking at maps, the Southerners decided that too many Northern railroads ran into their territory and thus were useful to their enemy. Citizens with crowbars, backed by cavalry units, began to demolish them. It was common practice to shoot a cannon ball through a locomotive boiler or to pile dry brush around the uprights of wooden railroad bridges, pour oil on, and apply a torch.

Both sides destroyed motive power, cars, stations, and wooden water tanks. By using horses they pried up and bent the wrought-iron rails. Without too much interruption, Confederates wrecked 100 miles of the North Missouri Railway in Union territory. The Federals retaliated with raids of their own. For a start, they burned 400 Southern railway cars and numerous stations, water towers, logs held for locomotive fuel, and telegraph poles.

The rival forces found a simple way of destroying bridges. They would bore a hole into bridge timber, insert an 8-inch torpedo, and explode it with a fuse, hurling the trestle into a river or a ravine.

In 1862, for the first time in history, the Confederates moved large bodies of troops over a long distance from one theater of war to another. They transferred Gen. Braxton Bragg's Army of the Tennessee by rail from Tupelo, Mississippi, to Chattanooga, Tennessee. Although these cities are only about 27 miles apart, the rail distance in those days was very much greater. Artillery and cavalry units took the shorter route. Infantry rode the "steam cars," with a ferry transfer across 20 miles of water at Mobile, Alabama. The first infantry units reached Chattanooga in 8 days.

In September 1863, Gen. James Longstreet's corps was transferred from Gen. Robert E. Lee's command in Virginia to storm the vital rail junction of Chattanooga. The distance was 835 miles over single-track railroads of varying gauges, with no physical connection between the lines and no through trains. One unit took 7 days, 10 hours; the other, 8 to 10 days. The corps arrived in time for a decisive part in the Battle of Chickamauga.

The Union high command had learned a lesson. To assist Gen. William S. Rosecrans, two Federal corps, some 23,000 men with artillery and equipment under Gen. Joseph Hooker, traveled by rail 1200 miles from the Army of the Potomac in Virginia. A pioneer genius of military railroading, Col. D. C. McCallum, achieved this feat after insisting that he and his railroaders be given complete control of the operation. In less than 8 days the troops reached their destination, Bridgeport,

Alabama, after crossing the Ohio River twice, first by ferry and then by a pontoon bridge on coal barges.

Meanwhile, the Confederates had ripped up part of the Richmond, Fredericksburg & Potomac Railroad (RF&P) that linked the two capitals, Richmond and Washington, thus cutting communications between the Northern armies of the Potomac and the Rappahannock.

To offset these losses, the U.S. War Department sent for Herman Haupt (1817–1905). Philadelphia-born Haupt had graduated from West Point at 18 but resigned his commission to become an engineer. At 19 he was the state of Pennsylvania's principal assistant engineer in locating new railroads. Finding no text on bridge structure, he devised his own. His book, *General Theory of Bridge Construction* (1851), became the standard authority of the United States and other countries.

In April 1862, the armies of Gens. Irvin McDowell and George B. McClellan were poised north and east of Richmond in a flanking movement designed to seize the Confederate capital and end the war. McDowell planned to march south from the Potomac along the RF&P and use it as his supply line. Retreating Confederates had wrecked this vital railroad, burning all docks and buildings at Aquia Creek and destroying the first 3 miles of track. The remaining track lay in various stages of disrepair. Worse still, two key bridges had been burned. One was the Ackacreek, 150 feet long; the other, a 400-foot span over Potomac Creek.

The Union Army had no construction corps capable even of laying track, let alone building bridges. So Secretary of War Edwin M. Stanton summoned Haupt, who was then possibly the foremost railroad construction engineer on earth. Commissioned a colonel, Haupt found sufficient rail, but few tools, no bridge timber, and no workmen who had ever laid track or built bridges. Three companies of inexperienced soldiers were assigned to him.

On Tuesday, April 29, with a cold rain falling, he ordered one crew to rebuild terminal docks at Aquia Creek wharf. Another group cut crossties in nearby woods. The rest began shoveling and tamping grade on muddy soil that had been the RF&P. They laid ties and spiked rails by lantern light. In 3 days, 3000 crossties were laid on 3 miles of track, and on Friday locomotives were run over them. Soon supplies were being hauled 4 miles down the line from the wharf to Ackacreek Bridge. The bridge itself, 150 feet long and 30 feet high, was erected with green labor in 15 working hours.

Trains moved 5 miles farther to Potomac Creek. Here, amazingly, Haupt reconstructed the Potomac Creek Bridge in 9 days. Less than 3 weeks after he had agreed to build it, the line to Fredericksburg was open and 20 trains a day were crossing Potomac Creek.

A week later President Lincoln visited the bridge. He said "I have seen the most remarkable structure human eyes ever rested upon. That man Haupt has built a bridge 400 feet long and nearly 100 feet high, and upon my word, gentlemen," he added humorously, "there is nothing in it but beanpoles and cornstalks."

Despite Haupt's stroke of genius, the grand plan to end the war in 1862 was dropped abruptly. Stonewall Jackson was marching on Washington. As General McDowell's forces rushed westward along the Manassas Gap Railroad to intercept him at Bull Run, Haupt's men rebuilt five bridges, spanning from 60 to 120 feet, in one day. Before the war ended 3 years later, Bull Run Bridge had been rebuilt seven times.

In September 1862, Haupt became a brigadier general. He personally directed transportation and construction for a dozen battles. By 1864 the Union Construction Corps was so skilled that one of his assistants, E. C. Smeed, performed what Haupt called "the most extraordinary feat in military bridge building the world has ever seen." Smeed built, with trained crews, plenty of equipment, and prefabricated truss spans (invented by Haupt), a bridge 780 feet long and 90 feet wide over the Chattahoochee River in Georgia in 4½ days. The corps also played a major role in Gen. William T. Sherman's march through Georgia. Haupt's men would start fires in the fireboxes of Southern locomotives without water in their boilers and leave them to blow up. The rails they heated and twisted around trees were known as Sherman's neckties.

The Civil War's most disastrous train wrecks were probably those of July 15, 1864, at Shohola, Pennsylvania, and September 1, 1864, 2 miles above Barnesville, Georgia. An 18-car trainload of Confederate prisoners being transferred to a prison camp at Elmira, New York, over the Erie Railroad was scheduled to leave Jersey City, New Jersey, at 4:30 A.M., but was delayed by 3 prisoners who were eventually found hidden aboard the ship which had brought them to Jersey City. A 50-car coal train en route to Port Jervis, New York, was switched onto the mainline at Lackawaxen, Pennsylvania, from a branch line. The telegraph operator at Lackawaxen had notified the freight crew that the prisoners'

The roundhouse in Atlanta, Georgia, after its nearly total destruction by General Sherman's forces in the Civil War. The locomotive in the foreground was owned by the Atlanta & West Point Railroad, which was acquired by the Georgia Railroad.

extra would use the main but apparently did not tell the crew later that the train was running late and the track was not clear. The two trains met head-on on a sharp reverse curve at Shohola, killing 51 Confederates, 10 Union soldiers serving as guards, and 4 crewmen, with an unknown number of injured victims. When Gen. John B. Hood evacuated Atlanta, his retreating troops seized the Macon & Western engine *Dispatch,* filled some cars with wounded soldiers, and sent them toward Macon without informing the railway officials. Near Barnesville the unscheduled extra collided with a train rushing supplies to Hood, killing about 30 soldiers and crew members and injuring many others.

For other Civil War information, *see* ANDREWS RAILROAD RAID; ARMORED CARS; GEORGIA RAILROAD; GULF, MOBILE, & OHIO RAILROAD; HOSPITAL TRAINS; ILLINOIS CENTRAL RAILROAD; LOUISVILLE & NASHVILLE RAILROAD; NORFOLK & WESTERN RAILWAY; SOUTH CAROLINA RAILROAD; WESTERN MARYLAND RAILWAY.

BIBLIOGRAPHY: Carl R. Gray, *Railroading in Eighteen Countries,* Scribner, New York, 1955; Roy Meredith and Arthur Meredith, *Mr. Lincoln's Military Railroads,* Norton, New York, 1979; James A. Van Fleet, *Rail Transport and the Winning of Wars,* Association of American Railroads, Washington, 1956; Thomas Weber, *The Northern Railroads in the Civil War,* King's Crown, New York, 1952.

Class I Railroads According to Interstate Commerce Commission designation, railroads with annual gross revenues of $50 million or more. They operate about 95 percent of the rail mileage of the United States, employ over 90 percent of the nation's railroad workers, and handle 98 percent of the railway freight-traffic revenue ton-miles. (In addition to the 41 Class I line-haul carriers listed here, several hundred smaller companies perform line-haul and/or switching and terminal services.) The Class I roads are or were before the 1980 mergers:

Alabama Great Southern (part of Southern Railway System)
Atchinson, Topeka and Santa Fe, 80 East Jackson Boulevard, Chicago, Illinois 60604
Baltimore & Ohio (part of Chessie System and CSX)
Bessemer & Lake Erie, 600 Grant Street (also P.O. Box 536), Pittsburgh, Pennsylvania 15230
Boston & Maine, 150 Causeway Street, Boston, Massachusetts 02114
Burlington Northern, 176 East Fifth Street, St. Paul, Minnesota 55101
Central of Georgia (part of Southern Railway System)
Chesapeake and Ohio (Chessie System and CSX)
Chicago, Milwaukee, St. Paul & Pacific, Union Station, 516 West Jackson Boulevard, Chicago, Illinois 60606
Chicago, Rock Island & Pacific, 332 South Michigan Avenue, Chicago, Illinois 60604
Chessie System, Terminal Tower, Cleveland, Ohio 44101; also 100 North Charles Street, Baltimore, Maryland 21201 (part of CSX)

Union soldiers destroying Southern rails. The twisted rails were known as General Sherman's neckties. [Collection of Freeman Hubbard]

Chicago & North Western, 400 West Madison Street, Chicago, Illinois 60606
Cincinnati, New Orleans & Texas Pacific (part of Southern Railway System)
Clinchfield, 229 Nolichucky Aveune, Erwin, Tennessee 37650 (part of Family Lines System and CSX)
Colorado & Southern (part of Burlington Northern)
Consolidated Rail Corporation (Conrail), 6 Penn Center Plaza, Philadelphia, Pennsylvania 19104
Delaware and Hudson, 40 Beaver Street, Albany, New York 12207
Denver and Rio Grande Western, P.O. Box 5482, Denver, Colorado 80217
Detroit, Toledo & Ironton, 1 Parklane Boulevard, Dearborn, Michigan 48126
Duluth, Missabe & Iron Range, 500 Missabe Building, 227 West First Street, Duluth, Minnesota 55802
Elgin, Joliet & Eastern, P.O. Box 880, Joliet, Illinois 60434
Family Lines System (including the following Class I roads: Clinchfield, Louisville & Nashville, and Seaboard Coast Line), 500 Water Street, Jacksonville, Florida 32202 (all part of CSX)
Florida East Coast, 1 Malaga Street, St. Augustine, Florida 32084
Forth Worth and Denver (part of Burlington Northern)
Grand Trunk Western (part of Grand Trunk Lines), 131 West Lafayette Boulevard, Detroit, Michigan 48226
Illinois Central Gulf, 233 North Michigan Avenue, Chicago, Illinois 60601
Kansas City Southern, 114 West Eleventh Street, Kansas City, Missouri 64105
Long Island, Jamaica Station Building, Jamaica, New York 11435
Louisiana & Arkansas (part of Kansas City Southern)
Louisville & Nashville, 908 West Broadway (also P.O. Box 32290), Louisville, Kentucky 40232 (part of Family Lines System and CSX)
Missouri-Kansas-Texas, Katy Building, 701 Commerce Street, Dallas, Texas 75202

Missouri Pacific, Missouri Pacific Building, 210 North Thirteenth Street, St. Louis, Missouri 63103
Norfolk & Western, 8 North Jefferson Street, Roanoke, Virginia 24042
Pittsburgh & Lake Erie, P&LE Terminal Building, Pittsburgh, Pennsylvania 15218
St. Louis-San Francisco (part of Burlington Northern)
St. Louis Southwestern, Southern Pacific Building, 1 Market Plaza, San Francisco, California 94105
Seaboard Coast Line, 500 Water Street, Jacksonville, Florida 32202 (part of Family Lines System and CSX)
Soo Line, Soo Line Building (also P.O. Box 530), Minneapolis, Minnesota 55440
Southern, Southern Railway Building (also P.O. Box 1808), Washington, D.C. 20013
Southern Pacific, SP Building, 1 Market Plaza, San Francisco, California 94105
Union Pacific, 1416 Dodge Street, Omaha, Nebraska 68179
Western Maryland (part of Chessie System and CSX)
Western Pacific, 526 Mission Street, San Francisco, California 94105

The Canadians have four classes of railroads for accounting and statistical purposes. Class I includes Canadian National Railways and Canadian Pacific Limited and their related operations.

BIBLIOGRAPHY: For a list of United States railroads of all classes and more detailed information on specific carriers, consult *Moody's Transportation Manual*, Moody's Investors Service, Inc., 99 Church Stret, New York, N.Y. 10007, annually; *The Official Railway Guide*, National Railway Publication Company, 424 West 33d Street, New York, N.Y. 10001; *The Pocket List of Railroad Officials*, National Railway Publication Company, quarterly; *Transport Statistics in the United States*: Part I—*Railroads*, compiled annually by Interstate Commerce Commission, Government Printing Office, Washington, D.C. 20402.

Classification Yard *See* YARDS, RAILROAD.

Clinchfield Railroad Line running north and south for 277 miles in five states between Elkhorn City, Kentucky, and Spartanburg, South Carolina, with general offices and shops at Erwin, Tennessee. Besides being a mover of coal and other freight in its own right, it serves as a bridge between the Atlantic seaboard and the Great Lakes. Passenger service ended on May 2, 1955, and the line is fully dieselized except for the ownership of a lone 4-6-0 steam locomotive, with which it occasionally operates day-long excursions on weekends from late September until early November. For that reason and because of its spectacular mountain scenery and autumn foliage, the Clinchfield is sometimes referred to as a steamfan's paradise.

Its history began in 1831 with plans for building a wagon road over approximately the present rail route. No fewer than 18 companies were formed to build a railroad in that area. One of them, the Charleston, Cincinnati & Chicago (CC&C), failed like the others, but in 1908 George L. Carter reorganized it, and by 1912 it had 80 miles of track laid.

Construction of a roadbed across two mountain ranges, the Cumberland and the Blue Ridge, was a major challenge. In solving it, the engineers built 2 very long and 53 shorter tunnels and 5 miles of bridges and viaducts. By 1923 the CC&C had 97 locomotives and 7775 freight cars. Later it began using Mallets, powerful articulated engines with 2-6-6-2, 2-8-8-2, and 4-6-6-4 wheel arrangements. On January 1, 1925, after another merger, the Clinchfield began operating under its present name, was leased jointly to the Louisville & Nashville and the Atlantic Coast Line, and became part of the Family Lines System and in 1980 part of CSX Corp. *See* CSX CORP.

BIBLIOGRAPHY: Kincaid A. Herr, *The Louisville & Nashville Railroad*, Louisville & Nashville Railroad, Louisville, Ky., 1964; Maury Klein, *History of the Louisville & Nashville Railroad*, Macmillan, New York, 1972.

CM *See* COLORADO MIDLAND RAILROAD.

CMStP&P *See* MILWAUKEE ROAD.

CN *See* CANADIAN NATIONAL RAILWAYS.

Coal While coal is the No. 1 commodity hauled by American railroads as a whole, this traffic is not evenly divided. Six big rail systems account for three-quarters of the industry's total coal revenues and four-fifths of its carloadings. They are the Chessie System, Norfolk & Western, Burlington Northern (BN), Family Lines, Southern, and Conrail. These giants produce half of the rail industry's gross revenues. All six and others are investing in new equipment to handle even more coal, since the energy crisis is bringing about its wider use.

Chessie, with 17.9 percent of the rail industry's revenue from this commodity, embarked in 1973 on a $500 million program to buy many new cars and locomotives. BN's coal-related expenditures are likely to exceed $1.5 billion between 1979 and 1983. Conrail, which inherited serious track problems from its bankrupt predecessors, is carrying on a $6 billion rehabilitation program designed to move freight faster and with fewer accidents.

Seven other major railroads, all Western, were planning to haul significantly more coal in the near future: the Union Pacific, Chicago & North Western, Santa Fe, Rock Island, Rio Grande, Missouri Pacific, and Frisco Lines. (The Frisco lost its identity in the BN merger of 1980.) Even a financially distressed carrier can raise money for equipment and plant improvements that will bring in new, profitable traffic to benefit shippers using those facilities. Coal is forcing some roads to build new lines, and new short railroads are being built primarily to haul coal.

French explorers made the first discovery of bituminous coal in 1673, between the present Illinois cities of Utica and Ottawa, but no railroad capitalized on that discovery until the Illinois Central opened its first mine at Du Quoin, Illinois, in 1855. Nearly all of its initial shipment was delivered in small wooden boxcars to Cairo for use on river steamboats. Incidentally, one reason why the railroads became so coal-oriented is that in the nineteenth century the federal government granted some of them, including the Illinois Central, huge tracts of land which were later found to include rich coal deposits.

But the old Philadelphia & Reading (P&R; now part of Conrail), whose black-diamond trademark symbolized coal, was built without a land grant; yet it became America's foremost anthracite carrier. Hard coal was first brought to the attention of the civilized world in 1750 by a friendly Indian who wanted a gunsmith to repair his musket at what would later become Nazareth, Pennsylvania, in P&R territory. The smith said he could not handle the job because he had no charcoal to heat his forge. The Indian walked away, but soon came back with a buckskin bag full of hard coal. To the white man it looked like pieces of black rock, but the Indian proved it could be used as fuel, and thus the anthracite industry was born.

At first the new fuel was shipped to Philadelphia by canal, but canalboats were slow-moving and often inoperable in winter. So the Reading took over. The Reading was the first railroad to link Pennsylvania's anthracite-producing area to tidewater, an initial advantage it never relinquished in its lifetime. Figures from the Anthracite Institute proved the road's claim to the title "Greatest Anthracite Carrier." From 1929 through 1942, for example, it transported more than 70 million tons of hard coal, as compared with less than 63 million hauled by the Lehigh Valley, its closest rival in that field, and about 46 million shipped over the Lackawanna. During the Civil War the railroads used about 80 percent of the coal mined in the country.

For many years the Lackawanna advertised itself as the "Road of Anthracite" with a modern passenger service that was luxuriously clean because its engines burned hard coal instead of the softer and more grimy bituminous fuel used by most railroads. Its publicity department created a dainty young lady known as Phoebe Snow. Phoebe made her debut in 1904 in newspaper, magazine, and car-card ads, pictorially and in jingles such as "Phoebe Snow, dressed in white,/Rides the Road of Anthracite" and "Phoebe Snow was wont to go/By railroad train to Buffalo." A New York-Buffalo express train was named the *Phoebe Snow*. But the Lackawanna's finest train was the *Black Diamond*.

In 1977 President Carter called for a 75 percent jump in coal production by 1985, to 1,200,000,000 tons a year. Yet the 1979 output was only 770,000,000, and the National Coal Association estimated that only 972,000,000 would be mined in 1985. The 230,000-member United Mine Workers strike crippled United States mines for 110 days during the winter of 1977-1978.

The 1979 volume of rail coal traffic was the heaviest in more than 25 years, and the price of hauling coal by rail is rising more slowly than the cost of coal itself. In that year the U.S. Department of Energy reported that the delivered price of coal itself went up by 287 percent over the previous decade (an average of $7.62 per ton, to $28.84), while during the same period the average rate for transporting coal by rail rose by less than 145 percent. In 1967, the rail price represented 39 percent of the delivered price; in 1978 it represented only 25 percent, which was actually a drop.

A modern revolutionizing asset is the unit train, a string of freight cars moving a single commodity between fixed points on a continuous basis. When first introduced in 1960, it was known as the "train of survival," for it helped both the railroads and the coal industry to survive in the face of changed competitive circumstances. Today, unit trains haul, in addition to other products, more than half of the coal shipped by rail. These trains were developed to cut transportation costs and speed delivery. One Midwestern road which formerly used 2400 open-top hopper cars to ship 3500 tons of coal a year from eastern Kentucky to northern Illinois now does the same job with only 892 cars in unit trains. *See also* UNIT TRAINS.

A severe-winter problem in the North is coal frozen in blocks of up to 100 tons. This happened on the Chessie, for example, with coal traveling from mines during the big freeze of December 1976 and January-February 1977. At Curtis Bay in the Great Lakes region the company has a crane that looks like a torpedo. Chesapeake and Ohio employees kept ramming it down inside the cars to break up the coal. They also tried dynamite. Modern techniques include thawing sheds, probes,

Seen here waiting to move in the Norfolk & Western classification yard, coal is the chief commodity transported by American railroads and may well be the energy hope of the future. [Norfolk & Western Railway]

crushers, and chemical sprays. Each shed at Curtis Bay thawed seven cars at a time with 800 sideburners and 52 underburners, called "hot dogs" because of their long, tubular shape. The addition of 560 new burners enabled each shed to handle nine cars in one operation.

Norfolk & Western (N&W) spent nearly $1 million to increase winterizing protection of its transloading facility at Norfolk, Virginia. Its coal Pier 6 is the world's largest, fastest, and most modern coal dumper. N&W set up four new traveling hammer-mill devices known as crunchers, which split lumps of frozen coal dumped from hopper cars, letting them move easily on conveyor belts to ships.

Built in 1962, Pier 6 includes two large thawing sheds that use electric infrared heating elements to loosen frozen coal from hoppers. During the 1976-1977 winter those sheds were inadequate. Coal frozen solidly came out of the cars in huge chunks that railroad employees had to break up by hand, a time-consuming task. Despite this, N&W reports that Pier 6 dumped more coal during that winter than the combined total of all other transloading facilities on the East Coast. Now, beneath each dumper is a cruncher that slides back and forth across the grates, like a gargantuan rolling pin with hammers protruding from the rollers, and breaks apart the frozen coal lumps.

Possibly the fastest and most modern way to thaw coal that is frozen solidly in cars is used in the West Virginia-Kentucky-Ohio area. This is a relatively new chemical product, Dowell freeze-conditioning agent M-185, that is sprayed on coal as it leaves the processing plants near mines in subzero weather. Coal so treated flows right through the cars and gratings and down the chutes. Standard coal-thawing methods of using gas-fired jets or open fires fueled with diesel oil or electric heaters consume vast amounts of energy and sometimes take as long as 24 hours to thaw untreated coal, meanwhile bottling up railyards with logjams of cars needed elsewhere.

A narrow-gauge Colorado & Southern train with 2-8-0 engine No. 65 crosses the bridge on the Georgetown Loop in 1938. [Henry R. Griffiths]

BIBLIOGRAPHY: *Coal—Bridge to the Future,* M.I.T., Cambridge, Mass., 1980; Carlton J. Corliss, *Main Line of Mid-America: The Story of the Illinois Central,* Creative Age, New York, 1950; Joseph A. Fisher, *The Reading's Heritage, 1833-1958,* Newcomen Society in North America, New York, 1958; John T. Starr, *The Evolution of the Unit Train, 1960-1969,* University of Chicago, Department of Geography, Research Paper No. 158, Chicago, 1976.

Coffin, Lorenzo (1823-1915) History's most fanatical and most influential crusader for railroad safety, who drafted and was largely responsible for passage of the Safety Applicance Act by Congress on March 2, 1893. This act was vehemently opposed by many railroad managements. It made compulsory the roads' adoption of the airbrake invented by George Westinghouse and the automatic coupler invented by Eli H. Janney, which replaced the handbrake and the link-and-pin coupler. In signing it, President Benjamin Harrison said he had never before affixed his signature to anything more willingly than he did to the measure drafted by Coffin. *See* JANNEY, ELI HAMILTON; WESTINGHOUSE, GEORGE.

Born on an Iowa farm, Coffin became a farmer, a Baptist preacher, a railroad real estate agent, an army chaplain during the Civil War, and a member of the Board of Iowa Railroad Commissioners. In 1874 a freight train he was riding stopped to pick up a couple of boxcars. In doing the necessary switching and coupling, the rear brakeman lost the two remaining fingers on his right hand because of a link-and-pin coupling accident. He had lost the other fingers in a like accident the year before.

Coffin learned from the crew that relatively few brakemen of long experience possessed all their fingers because of the highly dangerous link-and-pin operation, also that many trainmen had been killed by falling from moving trains while twisting the old handbrakes. Such information turned him into a safety crusader.

BIBLIOGRAPHY: Stewart H. Holbrook, *The Story of American Railroads,* Crown, New York, 1947.

Colonist Cars Canadian equivalent of United States tourist sleepers, old Pullmans with 12 to 16 open sections for economy-minded travelers and used during both world wars for troop movements. They were called colonist because they took many westbound families to then-new frontier settlements.

Colorado & Southern Railway (C&S) Merger of several short lines, chartered in 1898 and taken over by the Chicago, Burlington & Quincy in 1908. At its peak it operated 1099 route miles, 812 of them standard-gauge and the rest 36-inch gauge. It served gold and silver mines in Colorado and extended south to Fort Worth and Houston, Texas. On one of its narrow-gauge antecedents, the broken wheel originated as a widely used funeral emblem for railroaders who died heroically.

Engine 76 made C&S's last narrow-gauge run on August 25, 1942, from Climax to Leadville, Colorado, 14 miles.

BIBLIOGRAPHY: James L. Ehernberger and Francis G. Gschwind, *Colorado & Southern, Northern Division*, E. & G. Publications, Callaway, Neb., 1968; F. Hol Wagner, Jr., *The "Colorado Road": History, Motive Power, & Equipment of the Colorado and Southern, and Fort Worth and Denver Railways*, National Railway Historical Society, Intermountain Chapter, Denver, 1970.

Colorado Midland Railroad (CM) Line known to railfans as a "glamour pike" because of its adventurous history. Incorporated on November 23, 1883, as the Colorado Midland Railway Co., it became the first standard-gauge line to pierce the Colorado Rockies. Two narrow-gauge roads, the Denver and Rio Grande and the Denver, South Park & Pacific (known as the South Park), were already hauling gold, silver, coal, and timber from those mountains, but they converged in Denver, leaving a vast triangle of mineral wealth with no rail service.

The new line was projected westward from Colorado Springs to Manitou, thence up through Ute Pass to Divide on a fairly easy grade and down to the Arkansas River Valley. From there it would run westward to Arkansas Junction, with a short branch to serve the rich, tough mining town of Leadville, about 135 miles from Colorado Springs. Then, 18 miles from Leadville, it would cross Saguache Pass by a long tunnel and drop down to Roaring Fork River, with an 18-mile branch to Aspen, a fabulous silver-mining camp, and on to Glenwood Springs.

In the spring of 1886, with the necessary surveys completed and enough money raised, the company began building the 135 miles of mainline from Colorado Springs to Leadville. Having but three engines and relatively few cars, it ordered 25 new locomotives, 35 coaches, and about 1000 freight cars. The first 15 engines, 10-wheelers built by Schenectady to haul passengers between Colorado Springs and Leadville, had very short wheelbases (12 feet) because of the many 16-degree curves in that area and at that time were probably the heaviest of their type ever built. Baldwin also built some CM 10-wheelers. All were highly decorated with brass and nickel trim, bearing the Midland's emblem, a triangle superimposed on a circle and lettered "Pike's Peak Route, Colorado Midland Railroad." Another CM herald pictured a Ute Indian.

On July 13, 1887, the road's first train from Colorado Springs to Buena Vista began a period of 31 years' continuous operation. The line was extended to Leadville 2½ months later, thrilling the miners, gamblers, saloonkeepers, and dance-hall girls there. Before 1887 ended, trains were running through the 2164-foot Hager. an Tunnel to Aspen. Thus in 21 months the CM had built 238 miles of mainline through the rugged Rockies—a mighty engineering feat.

In 1892 a new carrier, Midland Terminal Railway Co. (MT), built a branch, partly over the CM steel, from Divide to Victor via Cripple Creek, a fabulously rich gold-mining camp. Its total mileage, including the joint trackage, was 55.7. The new line shortened the Denver-Cripple Creek route by 70 miles. The first MT train entered Cripple Creek in 1895.

Two years later, mine strikes and a general business slump threw the Colorado Midland into receivership. The company reorganized after a foreclosure sale. It was further harassed by snowdrifts, slides, and train wrecks. Finally, as a casualty of World War I, the federal government took over the line, claiming it was losing about $1500 a day, and abandoned it. A major reason for the abandonment was that locomotives, cars, and equipment were needed for the railroad system that the American Expeditionary Force was building in France. On August 4, 1918, the last Colorado Midland train made its graveyard run. But the rails were not torn up until 1921.

BIBLIOGRAPHY: Morris Cafky, *Colorado Midland*, Rocky Mountain Railroad Club, Denver, 1965; Percy Hagerman, *The Colorado Midland*, Westerners' Brand Book, 1946.

Common Carrier Transportation company that is required to carry all persons or property offered, under conditions of published rates and without favoritism or discrimination. With very few exceptions, all North American railroads are common carriers. A tariff is the published price list, from which there can be no deviation. It includes transportation and miscellaneous charges such as those for refrigerating or heating cars in transit, switching, and demurrage.

Commuter Trains According to archives of the Boston & Lowell (B&L), an antecedent of the Boston & Maine (B&M), a passenger department offical named Jackson set up the nation's first commuter train. He told the B&L Board of Directors, "We are requested to stop at six places and I think it will require five minutes for each stop. If we add 20 or 30 minutes to the time it now takes our regular train to go between Boston and Lowell, my opinion is that it would injure the reputation of our road for speed. But I will try the experiment." So the directors authorized him to set up a local service with an engine and one passenger car, which he did.

Today, commutation tickets are issued at a reduced rate for a specified number of trips or a specific period over a given route. They originated in about 1840 with B&M season tickets, costing $200 each, that were good for an entire year. Later, the price was cut in half. Only 59 such tickets were sold in 1843, but sales rose to 433 in 1847.

Prior to the gasoline age, when a train was the most practical way for suburbanites to get to and from the big city, many railroads serving New York, Philadelphia, Chicago, San Francisco, Montreal, and other metropolises had a profitable commuter business. But purely suburban operation has never been efficient in the use of equipment and personnel. Fleets of passenger cars as well as trainmen must be kept available 5 days a week for the morning and evening peak traffic, but most of them are idle between rush hours and on weekends and holidays. By contrast, in expeditiously handled freight service the boxcars, flats, hoppers, and tankers are, or theoretically could be, constantly in use, depending upon prompt loading and unloading.

The automobile and the bus cut heavily into rail suburban traffic, especially for commuters who live near the city. In addition, considerable parking space must be provided at or very near suburban railroad stations, often at the railroad company's expense, for travelers who drive between the depot and their homes.

Of course, the gasoline era built up the suburbs enormously, multiplying the number of rail commuters, but this gain only compounded the railroads' inefficient use of equipment and personnel. On top of that, many commuters are notorious grumblers, often complaining of poor service. Those who normally drive their own cars to and from their city jobs overcrowd the trains when a blizzard or inability to buy gasoline prevents them from driving, and they are resentful because extra railroad coaches are not kept on hand for such rare emergencies. However, the present energy crunch has boosted rail travel, both commuter and intercity.

Amtrak's takeover of nearly all of America's intercity rail passenger service in 1971 did not include commuter traffic. The railroads continue to handle that business themselves, but only as long as its costs are subsidized by federal, state, or local funds. Some commuter lines are electrified, including much of the Long Island, the hemisphere's longest commuter railroad, owned by New York State. Several great depots such as Grand Central Terminal in New York City and La Salle Street Station in Chicago, famed for their long-distance and name trains in the palmy days of rail passenger service, would now be empty, demolished, or put to nonrailroad use if it were not for commuter runs.

The following commuter lines were operating in the United States and Canada as of 1980: Amtrak; Baltimore & Ohio; Canadian National; Canadian Pacific; Chicago & North Western; Conrail; Grand Trunk Western; Long Island; Milwaukee Road; Norfolk & Western; Pittsburgh & Lake Erie; Southern Pacific. *See also* INTERURBAN ELECTRIC RAILWAYS; LONG ISLAND RAIL ROAD.

Computer Systems Railroads were among the first users of computer systems. As in most industries, early use was limited to accounting departments, repetitive paperwork, record keeping, and making up payrolls. But as computer techniques advanced, the railroads began experimenting with ways to locate and assign their major asset, freight cars.

On an industrywide level, the experiments led to TRAIN (TeleRail Automated Information Network), a system which linked the 44 data terminals reporting for 64 United States and 2 Canadian railways to a data bank on a computer at Association of American Railroads (AAR) headquarters in Washington, D.C., and gathered data on more than 98 percent of the freight-car interchanges among railroads.

Now TRAIN II, supplementing the original TRAIN, supplies more detailed facts on a more timely basis. It provides the AAR's Car Service Division, which has access to the computer via cathode-ray tubes, with the information needed to help maintain a fair distribution of freight cars. Another major use of computers is in railroad classification yards. *See* YARDS, RAILROAD.

Conductors, Order of Railway *See* ORDER OF RAILWAY CONDUCTORS.

Conrail (Consolidated Rail Corporation) Gigantic experiment headquartered in Philadelphia and launched on April 1, 1976, to head off nationalization of America's rail system, particularly freight, in the Northeast and Midwest with a privately managed for-profit corporation. It is quite different from Amtrak, a government-subsidized company responsible for most of the nation's intercity rail passenger service. Besides freight, Conrail, under contract with local authorities, carries about 360,000 commuters each weekday to and from New York City, Philadelphia, Baltimore, and Chicago and will continue to do so only as long as state and regional agencies pay the deficits in operating costs and continue their contractual relations with Conrail. *See* AMTRAK.

Conrail comprises most rail operating facilities of six bankrupt roads: Penn Central, Reading, Central of New Jersey, Erie Lackawanna, Lehigh Valley, and Lehigh & Hudson River. These assets were conveyed to Conrail in exchange for Conrail stock. Until October 1, 1977, Conrail also operated the Ann Arbor under contract to the state of Michigan.

Conrail was created by the Regional Rail Reorganization Act of 1973, as amended in 1976 by the Railroad Revitalization and Regulatory Reform Act, and chartered by the Commonwealth of Pennsylvania. Its approximately 34,000 track miles (17,000 route miles) extend from the Atlantic Ocean to St. Louis and from the Ohio River to Montreal, an area boasting some 100 million people and 55 percent of America's manufacturing plants.

Among the problems which the bankruptcies had put up to Congress were the following: (1) Thousands of miles of freight lines were handling relatively little freight, which drained the bankrupts' revenues seriously. (2) The six roads, prior to Amtrak, also were incurring heavy losses from passenger services. (3) Especially in the Northeast, the bankrupt roads maintained highly duplicated networks of tracks and facilities. (4) Their tracks, facilities, and equipment were in a poor state of repair owing to deferred maintenance and replacement, and this greatly curtailed operations, alienated customers, and sharply decreased revenue. Congress endeavored to solve these problems by:

1. Excluding from Conrail about 6900 miles of light-density lines and setting up a program whereby on April 1, 1976, Conrail began operating about 200 track miles of those lines which the states considered essential. As of April 10, 1979, it was operating 934 miles of its system under subsidy by federal, state, and/or regional authorities.

2. Conveying to Amtrak the intercity passenger business of the Northeast corridor (Boston-Washington and Philadelphia-Harrisburg, nearly all electrified) and repaying Conrail for leases due to commuter operation and for the interstate passenger service which it handles for Amtrak outside the corridor.

3. Permitting Conrail to save many millions of dollars by consolidating operations wherever feasible.

4. Loaning money to help support physical rehabilitation and improvement programs, to provide additional working capital, and to help meet operating losses; and authorizing the Five-Year Business Plan, which specifies the need for new federal financing of $1283 million, in addition to the approximately $2 billion drawn by the end of 1978 through Conrail's financing agreement with the U.S. Railroad Administration (USRA). In October 1978, Congress voted additional funding for Conrail. These funds are not a subsidy, they are *loaned* to Conrail through the sale to USRA of 7.5 percent convertible debentures and Class A preferred stock. Total cost of the rebuilding program was originally expected to be close to $6.8 billion over a 10-year period, including additional financing of equipment needs to be sought in the private sector; but with rising inflation the original figure became unrealistic.

Conrail is managed by a board of directors consisting of 13 persons from the private sector, 6 USRA appointees, and 5 chosen by trustees of the bankrupt roads, plus the chairman and chief executive officer and Conrail's president and chief operating officer. It is privately managed and privately operated. Conrail competes with other railroads and other transportation systems and hopes eventually to earn a profit.

Instead of the system used by most other railroads, Conrail uses *depreciation accounting*, as do nearly all United States nonrail corporations. Under this method Conrail capitalizes track expenditures and depreciates the assets thus created over their useful life. (*Betterment accounting*, which most roads use in accordance with Interstate Commerce Commission regulations, requires that such capital outlays be expensed fully during the period in which they are incurred, thus creating, in a period of heavier-than-normal capital expenditures, severe distortions in the corporation's final reports.)

At the outset, Conrail was optimistically expected to start making a profit by 1980; but despite federal loans it was losing far more than the bankrupt lines had lost collectively before the consolidation, largely because so much decrepit roadbed and rolling stock had to be rebuilt, repaired, or replaced. By the end of 1978 it had laid 2769 miles of continuous welded rail.

Because of the terminal and labor-intensive type of Conrail's operations in the industrial Northeast and because of the complex of labor union agreements it inherited from the bankrupt roads preceding it, wages, fringe benefits, and railroad retirement payments absorb 63.3 cents of every revenue dollar, as compared with a 53-cent average for other railroads. After 3 years of negotiations, Conrail had signed and/or come to agreement on 20 new collective bargaining agreements, replacing 233 previous ones. The new agreements cover more than 82,000 employees, about 99 percent of Conrail's union workers. Conrail's target is about 34 single agreements to replace about 285 pacts it started with. One deal, when fully implemented, lets Conrail run trains and switchyards with a crew of two people where three crew members were formerly required. The number of trainmen in road and yard operations will, in time, be reduced by one-third overall. This phase alone could save hundreds of millions of dollars.

Early in 1981, the United States Railway Association estimated that Conrail, which had already absorbed $3.1 billion in federal subsidies, would need $2.1 billion more to operate it through 1986. But far from improving Conrail's effectiveness, the federal budget cuts proposed by President Ronald Reagan were threatening to reduce it. *The New York Times* editorialized:

> The Conrail system, jerry-built by Congress in 1976, never really had a chance of surviving on its own. Federal subsidies have been reasonably well spent in modernizing decrepit track, rolling stock, and freight yards. Some uneconomical and underused track has been abandoned. . . . [But] Conrail's cost of doing business far exceeds the industry average.

BIBLIOGRAPHY: *Jane's World Railways and Rapid Transit Systems*, F. Watts, New York, 1978; *Official Railway Equipment Register*, National Railway Publication Company, New York, bimonthly; *The Pocket List of Railroad Officials*, National Railway Publication Company, New York, quarterly; Richard Saunders, *The Railroad Mergers and the Coming of Conrail*, Greenwood Press, Westport, Conn., 1978; Robert Sobel, *The Fallen Colossus: The Great Crash of the Penn Central and the Crisis of the Corporate Giants*, Weybright & Talley, New York, 1977.

Consolidated Rail Corporation *See* CONRAIL.

Continental Divide *See* RATON MOUNTAIN SWITCHBACK.

Conventions Influential big regional railroad conventions were held in the early days of railroad promotion to demand better transportation for specific areas and to seek state and federal aid for railroad projects. Most important were those held in St. Louis and Memphis in 1849 and in Philadelphia in 1850 on behalf of building a line to the Pacific Coast; in New Orleans in 1852 to interest the state of Louisiana in a proposed Southwestern rail network; and in Sacramento in 1859 and 1860 on behalf of a central route to the Pacific and to persuade the legislatures of California, Oregon, and Washington Territory to start work on such a route. Major conventions at Memphis in 1845 and at Chicago in 1847 were concerned primarily with waterways but also insisted upon the need for more railroads.

Cooper, Peter ***(1791–1883)*** Inventor and industrialist born in New York City, the son of an unsuccessful businessman. He designed and built *Tom Thumb*, the first railway locomotive built in America. Cooper created the engine in 1830 by drawing upon knowledge and skill acquired in his boyhood apprenticeship to a coachmaker, and he built it in one of several iron foundries he had established. Before that, he had made a fortune from a glue factory. *See* BALTIMORE & OHIO RAILROAD.

Later Cooper became president of the company that enabled Cyrus W. Field to lay the first permanent transatlantic cable and president of American Telephone Co. One of his iron foundries was America's largest, at Trenton, New Jersey. The Bessemer steel process was used for the first time in this country in 1856 at his Phillipsburg, New Jersey, blast furnace. Cooper also manufactured wire, chains, and bridges, and developed iron and coal mines. A prolific inventor, he patented many small practical devices and processes.

Having had only a year's schooling himself, Cooper was determined that other New Yorkers should not be so handicapped. He led a successful fight to give the city a free public school system. His lasting monument, Cooper Union in lower Manhattan, was opened in 1858 to provide free higher education for the working classes.

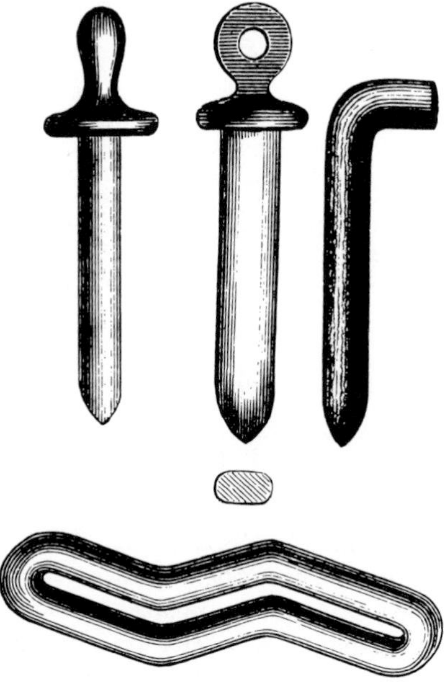

Three types of pins and a link used in link-and-pin couplers.

Copper Ore With about 300 mines, the United States produces about half of the world's copper ore. Large-scale copper mining began in 1854 at the present Keenewaw, Michigan, near Lake Superior. Until 1887 Michigan was the leading copper-producing state. Then Montana took the lead, owing chiefly to the Anaconda mine, an area of 2 square miles near Butte. Today about 20 percent of the nation's copper production comes from the Anaconda. Arizona is now the foremost copper-producing state, and since 1926 Utah has ranked second. Much copper is mined also in New Mexico, Nevada, and Alaska and in the Canadian provinces of British Columbia, Ontario, and Quebec.

The Copper River & North Western (CR&NW), once Alaska's second-longest railroad, extending 195 miles from Cordova to the copper mine at Endicott, was built, beginning in 1905, by Michael J. Heaney, who had built the White Pass & Yukon Route. The 1907 panic slowed him down, and he sold out to another Alaska railroad, the Katalla, owned by American Smelter & Refining Co. and J. P. Morgan & Co., which hired Heaney to complete the CR&NW, originally called the Copper River Railroad.

In 1911 the first copper from that mine was delivered by a combination of rail route and dogsled. The road's abandonment in November 1938 coincided with closing of the mine, except for a 13-mile section out of Cordova, which the U.S. Army used during World War II.

One important copper-hauling railroad, the Mineral Range, chartered in 1871 and serving the Keenewaw section of Michigan, was robbed in 1893 of the Calumet & Copper mine's $50,000 payroll. Three men boarded the train as passengers at Hancock, Michigan, and pulled a typical Western-style holdup, taking the money from the express car.

BIBLIOGRAPHY: Gordon S. Chappell, *Rails to Carry Copper: A History of the Magma Arizona Railroad*, Pruett Publishing Co., Boulder, Colo., 1973; Olin T. Mouzon, *Resources and Industries of the United States*, Appleton, New York, 1967; Frank J. Tuck, *Stories of Arizona Copper Mines*, Arizona Department of Mineral Resources, Phoenix, 1957.

Couplers The first automatic coupler of railroad cars was patented in 1848, another was patented in 1856, and the Erie tried out a third in 1856. The Burlington and the Philadelphia, Wilmington and Baltimore had one type in use by 1867. Three years later such couplers were in fairly general use throughout the West. The need for discarding the dangerous old link-and-pin type was obvious. Countless numbers of railroad men had lost fingers, hands, arms, and even lives from what they called the "Lincoln pin."

In 1868 Eli Hamilton Janney invented—and in 1873 patented—the device that, with further developments, became the ancestor of all automatic couplers used today by common carriers in the United States and Canada. *See* Janney, Eli Hamilton.

There were then at least 45 different couplers, no 2 of which would work together. In about 1882 Connecticut was the first state to enact a law requiring the use of automatic couplers. Other states soon followed. In 1887 the Master Car Builders Association conducted trials and accepted the Janney as standard. On March 3, 1893, President Benjamin Harrison signed the Safety Appliance Act, making the use of automatic couplers mandatory on all roads engaged in interstate commerce, but for many years some short lines and industrial roads continued to use the link and pin. *See* Coffin, Lorenzo; Safety Laws.

Cowcatcher Popular term for the steam locomotive pilot, which was invented in the early 1830s by Isaac L. Dripps, a young mechanical engineer employed by the Camden & Amboy Railroad in New Jersey (which became part of the Pennsylvania Railroad, now Conrail). So many cows trespassed on the right-of-way that he decided to install on the locomotive's front end a small truck supporting two iron spears. This device was effective but fatal to the cows. To avoid damage suits, he substituted a crosswise bar somewhat like the present-day automobile bumper, from which the once-familiar V-shaped pilot evolved. *See also* Pilots, Steam Locomotive.

CP Rail *See* Canadian Pacific Railway.

"Crane with a Broken Neck" According to old-timers who took part in the American Railway Union (ARU) strike of 1894, known as the Pullman strike (which started it), the railroads' General Managers Association (GMA) used a vicious blackball system described as the "crane with a broken neck" to keep strikers from returning to railroad work. At first GMA members refused to issue service letters, proving railroad experience, to strikers. Without such letters it was almost impossible for ARU men to get rail jobs. One victim solved the problem by suing a railroad company. He won his case and was awarded damages as well as the letter.

Thereupon the GMA saw the light. Any erstwhile employee requesting a clearance could get it. The letter set forth his record, ending with "Left the service of his own accord." But the clearances, written on stationery of a well-known paper manufacturer (Crane Bros.), had a choice of two secret watermarks which could be detected only by holding the sheet up to the light.

One showed a crane with head erect; this was given to nonstrikers. The other, used with ARU men, had the bird's neck hanging down as if to feed. It secretly warned potential employers that the applicant had been a striker. It is easy to understand how boomers, when they finally caught on to the trick, could have misinterpreted the second watermark as the crane with a broken neck, thus giving rise to the legend.

Not all roads belonging to the GMA used the blacklist. Among the few exceptions was the Chicago, Rock Island & Pacific, which, to its lasting credit, rehired more than 4000 of its 4500 striking employees.

BIBLIOGRAPHY: Freeman Hubbard, *Railroad Avenue*, McGraw-Hill, New York, 1945.

***Crocker, Charles* (1822–1888)** One of the Big Four merchants who pooled their wealth, time, and capabilities to build and operate the Central Pacific (CP) and Southern Pacific Railroads. Born in 1822 at Troy, New York, he was the son of Isaac Crocker, who failed in the liquor business, Charles quit school at 12, shortly afterward went $200 in debt to buy a newspaper agency, and helped to support his parents.

In 1836 he cleared and planted virgin soil in Indiana and worked in a sawmill owned by a man whose daughter, Mary Donnelly, he later married. Later he set up an iron foundry and smithy in Maryland. In 1850 he migrated to California and, with one of his brothers, opened a store in a gold-mining camp, then one in Sacramento. Business boomed.

Joining the new Republican party, Charles Crocker was elected an alderman and met the other three future members of the Big Four: Mark Hopkins, Collis P. Huntington, and Leland Stanford. By 1862 the four men controlled the company that would build the western end of the first transcontinental railway. His firm, Crocker & Co., with Huntington and Hopkins as silent partners, contracted to build the first 18 miles of line. He lacked railroad experience but assembled men and equipment, set up road camps and commissaries, and kept learning as the rails extended eastward. Headquartered in an old coach, he traveled back and forth over the line, rarely sleeping more than 3 consecutive nights in his Sacramento bed over a period of 6 years. *See* Hopkins, Mark; Huntington, Collis Potter; Stanford, Leland.

Crocker & Co. was paid $275,000 in cash and $150,000 in Central Pacific bonds for building the first section. Its superintendent, burly, hard-driving J. H. Strobridge, said of the men he hired and bossed that they were "as near brutes as they can get." At first Strobridge opposed Crocker's desire to use Chinese labor but soon was glad he did so. *See* Chinese Labor; Golden Spike Ceremony; Southern Pacific Lines.

Stubby-bearded Crocker patrolled the line constantly on a big sorrel mare, often bundled up in furs like an Eskimo, issuing orders and often criticizing. Only once a month did the men genuinely welcome him. That was when his two saddlebags bulged respectively with gold and silver coins, a total weight of about 150 pounds, and he personally paid each laborer.

In 1871, after his older brother, Judge E. B. Crocker,

head of the CP Legal Department, had suffered a paralytic stroke, falling at Stanford's feet, Charles Crocker retired and his partners bought him out. He died on August 14, 1888, at Monterey, California.

BIBLIOGRAPHY: Oscar Lewis, *The Big Four*, Knopf, New York, 1938; Gustavus Myers, *History of the Great American Fortunes*, 3 vols., Charles H. Kerr & Company, Chicago, 1910.

Crossties *See* TIES.

Crownsheet In a steam locomotive, heavy sheeting above the firebox and forward beyond the juncture of the brick arch that is used to keep a water level on the widest heating surface above the fire. It is held in place by hollow angular stay bolts and sloped slightly upward to the forward end. The crownsheet must be covered with at least 1 inch of water under pressure. A lesser amount causes scorching, burning, or a fatal explosion.

CS *See* CINCINNATI SOUTHERN RAILWAY.

CSX Corp. These cryptic initials, unparalleled as a corporate name in railroad history, mean "Chessie, Seaboard, much more," *X* being the multiplication sign. CSX is a merger of two great conglomerates, Chessie System Inc., and Seaboard Coast Line Industries, Inc. (SCLI). In addition to various nonrail businesses and industries, it controls 17 railroads with a total of 27,477 route miles of track in 22 states, the District of Columbia, and the Canadian province of Ontario, with $7.4 billion in assets.

The merger, approved by the Interstate Commerce Commission (ICC) on September 24, 1980, became effective on November 1, 1980, creating what was then America's largest rail network. However, a Burlington Northern-Frisco merger involving about 1800 more miles than CSX controls was cleared by the courts shortly afterward, making BN the nation's largest rail network.

Chessie System is a holding company that controls six railroads extending from the Atlantic Ocean to St. Louis and from West Virginia, rich in coalfields, into Canada. These six are the Chesapeake and Ohio (C&O), Baltimore & Ohio, Western Maryland, B&O Chicago Terminal Railroad, Staten Island, and Chicago South Shore and South Bend.

SCLI holding company controls the Family Lines System of 10 Southeastern railroads: Seaboard Coast Line, Louisville & Nashville (L&N), Clinchfield, Georgia, Western Railway of Alabama, Atlanta & West Point, Durham and Southern, Gainesville Midland, Carrollton, and Columbia, Newberry and Laurens. In addition, CSX controls the Richmond, Fredericksburg & Potomac Railroad, a *bridge line* linking North and South.

Under CSX, the 17 railroad companies remain separate operating entities, yet now offer coordinated single-system transportation as well as new, improved services, more North-South piggyback trains, and a time-saving route for coal shipments from Kentucky to the Southeast, among other advantages.

Hays T. Watkins, president and chairman of Chessie, became the first president of CSX, while Prime F. Osborn III, chairman of SCLI, became chairman of CSX. The new colossus is much more than railroads. It includes companies engaged in newspaper publishing, coal-land and forest-resources development, corporate-aircraft management and fixed-base services, oil and gas exploration, real estate development, data processing, and resort-hotel operations.

The merger application was filed on January 12, 1979. The ICC authorized it, in the extraordinarily short time of less than 2 years, because, the Commission said, the new system promised to improve public service without reducing rail competition. The ICC added that CSX, as the first rail line to link the industrial Northeast, the Great Lakes region, and the Southeast, would provide shippers with single-system service.

At the ICC hearings Chessie and Seaboard witnesses testified that the proposed new system's operational benefits would save over 14,600,000 gallons of fuel oil annually, attract new business estimated at more than $96 million a year, increase the number of run-through trains, improve the efficiency of utilization and classification of cars, permit C&O's shops to build at least 5000 new freight cars for L&N, and with additional car supply would recapture much coal volume that had been lost to truckers.

CSX is the world's largest transporter of coal, which makes up about 40 percent of Chessie's business and 20 percent of Seaboard's. Its railroads haul freight only. Amtrak handles all passenger trains that move over its lines.

See BALTIMORE & OHIO RAILROAD; CLINCHFIELD RAILROAD; FAMILY LINES SYSTEM; GEORGIA RAILROAD; LOUISVILLE & NASHVILLE RAILROAD; WESTERN MARYLAND RAILWAY.

CTC *See* CENTRALIZED TRAFFIC CONTROL.

Currency Issued by Railroads Early-day railroads cost so much to build that hundreds were never completed or operated. They took what gifts of land or money they could get; they sold stock, borrowed, and in many cases resorted to the device of printing their own currency, ranging in value from 2 cents to $1000. Some notes were fine engravings illustrated with train pictures, curlicues, etc.; others were crude scrip made on cheap little presses. But money printing came too easily. At first a convenience, it often became so inflationary that it wrecked railways as surely as floods or prairie fires. Who would accept, for example, a $5 bill issued by a short line which only moved a little coal from a mine to a wharf?

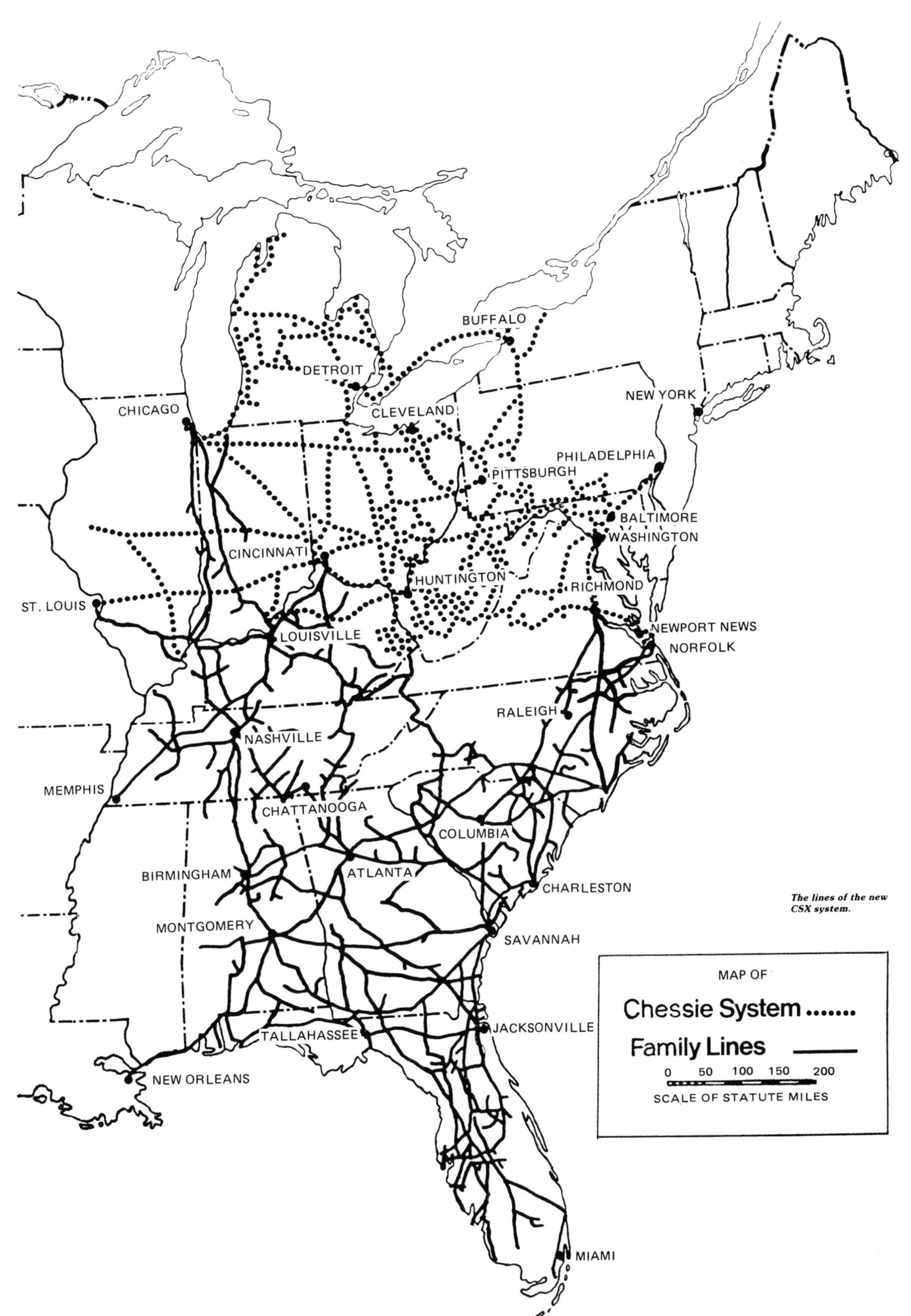

The lines of the new CSX system.

In about 1830, when railroads began printing scrip, there was no national United States currency and hadn't been since the Continental Congress of 1776 issued money that evoked the phrase "not worth a continental." Many Americans of those days, especially down South, never saw a dollar. In some areas the only availale silver coins were old Spanish doubloons, which men often chiseled into halves, quarters, "bits," and picayunes. Banks, business firms, and counterfeiters issued a variety of paper money. In 1834 about 500 state banks were putting out "folding money" which was accepted wherever the banks were known but sold elsewhere at discounts of 10 to 80 percent.

Many people felt that because railroads reached more towns they were better circulating media than banks. Even turnpike and canal companies printed currency as an easy way to pay wages and bills. In 1824 the Delaware and Hudson Canal Co., which later became a railway, opened a Wall Street bank in New York and began issuing money.

In 1835 the Erie & Kalamazoo (E&K) in Michigan, the first railroad built west of the Alleghenies, was granted rights to print money and carry on banking. It paid its workmen in 25- and 50-cent scrip; many samples still survive. Later, when too many bearers tried to swap their E&K notes for other bank money, the railroad was in trouble. Its directors leased their track, but not their bank, to the Michigan Southern (later part of the New York Central System, now Conrail). That lease is still in effect. *See* ERIE & KALAMAZOO RAILROAD.

The Central Rail Road & Banking Co. of Georgia, founded in 1833, was more than a railway with banking powers; it was a railway united to a real bank. Careful management kept both the road and the bank solvent even during the Civil War. In 1870 the two businesses were separated; both still thrive. The railway joined the Family Lines System and eventually CSX Corp.

The pioneer Champlain & St. Lawrence, which began issuing currency in 1837, was the first and almost the only Canadian railway to do so. Its notes, printed in New York, were for 7½ pence, 15 pence, and 2 shillings sixpence. Each pictured a crudely drawn train.

Certain railway scrip was exchangeable only for merchandise at company stores or for railway tickets. The New York & New Haven issued 10-cent bills "good for the payment of Fares or Freight."

If you had chosen to convert Baltimore & Ohio 12½-cent notes of 1841 to City of Baltimore stock, you would have had to present $100 worth (800 pieces of paper) at one time. By 1847 the printing of rail money had tapered off, but it shot up again around 1860. The Virginia Central issued a train view copied from a $100 Confederate note of 1861, with these words: "Six months after the ratification of a treaty of peace between the Confederate States and the United States, the Confederate States of America will pay One Hundred Dollars to bearer, with interest of two cents per day."

By December 30, 1861, coins had become so scarce and bills worth so little that the banks stopped payment in specie. In 1862 the United States government began to issue greenbacks for general use and outlawed notes for less than $1. People used postage stamps for pocket change. The National Bank Act of 1863 (with amendments in 1864) virtually stopped the private printing of money. But in 1873, during a financial panic, the Philadelphia, Newtown & New York (later part of the Reading system, now Conrail), issued a $1 note, red and black, picturing surveyors at work. And in Canada at least one line, the narrow-gauge Newfoundland North-

A particularly elaborate example of railroad currency commonly accepted as legal tender, this dollar bill** (actual size) **features a picture of a steam-powered train. It dates from about 1837.

ern & Western (now part of Canadian National), put out currency in amounts of 50 cents, $1, and $2 as recently as 1897.

Many roads also issued wooden or copper tokens, each good for a half cord or so of wood, in the days of woodburning locomotives.

Curves, Longest The three longest American rail curves are in Louisiana, probably because the state has so many lake and bayous. They are on the Illinois Central, between Ruddock and Trinity, skirting with slight variations in degree the western shore of Lake Pontchartrain, 9.42 miles; the Southern Railway System (New Orleans & Northeastern), almost 9 miles; and the Texas & Pacific, between Alexandria and Cheneyville, 5.7 miles.

D

D&H *See* DELAWARE AND HUDSON RAILWAY.

D&RGW *See* DENVER AND RIO GRANDE WESTERN RAILROAD.

Dan Patch Line In 1906 the harness racehorse Dan Patch trotted a mile in 1:55, setting a world record that stood for over 50 years. In 1907 his owner, Marion W. Savage, a horse breeder and stock-food dealer, went into the railroad business by incorporating the Minneapolis, St. Paul, Rochester & Dubuque Electric Traction Co., with himself as president and William P. Mason as vice president. In 1908 they began building the line southward from a connection with the Minneapolis streetcar system.

Savage already owned two private railroad cars; he and his family used one. The other was a Chicago & North Western (C&NW) baggage car converted to a horse's luxurious palace car, painted white with gilt lettering. It carried Dan Patch, accompanied by four white-uniformed grooms, on the racing circuit from 1900 to 1910, when he was retired to stud. During all that time the great stallion was never beaten. He set 14 global records, each time breaking his own previous record.

The railway his owner built became known as the Dan Patch Line. It used gas-electric cars. Its letterheads boasted "The First Gas-Electric Railroad in the World," with a herald that showed a lightning bolt streaking diagonally across a horseshoe. It began operating with two secondhand cars. The larger of the two, named *Irene*, built by Brill, had an all-steel body, an open-end observation platform, and elegant appurtenances. The other car was the *Augerita*. Eventually, when Savage set up an amusement park on his estate at Lakeville, Minnesota, it was put on a siding there to generate electricity for the resort, and the company bought several fine new gas-electric cars. At first the line hauled only passengers, including Dan Patch.

The inaugural run was made on July 4, 1910, from the Minneapolis terminal to Lakeville, where passengers watched the grooming and training of prize stallions and gazed wide-eyed at the owner's palatial white-columned mansion on a bluff. That December the line was extended to Northfield, Minnesota. This was as far south as the Dan Patch Line ever got. In 1913 the company bought trackage rights over the Chicago Great Western, ran gas-electrics to Faribault and Mankato, Minnesota, acquired some General Electric freight locomotives, and added freight to its passenger repertoire. It also connected with the C&NW, Rock Island, Milwaukee Road, Great Northern, and Minneapolis & St. Louis. In 1915 it modified its gas-electric policy by buying three Porter-built Mogul-type steam locos for its heavier trains.

Then disaster struck. While Savage was hospitalized on July 11, 1916, his beloved Dan Patch died at age 20. This shock killed the old horse breeder shortly afterward. With the champion racer gone, the public lost interest in the Dan Patch Line, which was thrown into receivership in August 1918. Savage's elder son, Earl, sold it to the newly formed Minneapolis, Northfield & Southern, which today is a diesel-powered freight-only line.

Date Nails Maintenance-of-way markers, with raised or sunken letters or numbers, used to determine when it was time to rework or replace crossties. For most railroads this practice ended in the early 1960s. Besides trackage, the nails were used in pilings, bridges, switches, and telegraph and ordinary street poles. Collectors estimate there are over 2200 kinds and types of date nails. Many hobbyists have sets of these items going back many years. Some antique dealers regard them as choice relics of a phase of railroading that has all but disappeared but warn that counterfeit specimens are hard to detect. The Texas Date Nail Collector's Association, founded in 1970, has about 600 members.

BIBLIOGRAPHY: Kenneth B. Shaw, *And Now It's Nail Time*, Shaw, Benche, 1971.

Death Valley Railroad Twenty-mile narrow-gauge line running between Death Valley Junction, on the Tonopah & Tidewater Railroad, and Ryan, California, that replaced the once-famous double line of mules which plodded through the hot desert hauling a huge, boxlike load of 20-Mule Team Borax, a popular grocery item in the early 1900s. The borax works at Ryan shut down in 1928; the hotel there did likewise, leaving the town deserted, and the railroad folded in 1931.

Death Valley Scotty Walter Scott, in cowboy boots, thick blue woolen shirt, red tie, and 10-gallon Stetson hat, entered the office of John J. Byrne, the Santa Fe's general passenger agent in Los Angeles, on July 1, 1905. He had won a fortune in gold mining in Death Valley, a California desert that dips 280 feet below sea level, the lowest point in the Western Hemisphere, and wanted to celebrate his good luck by riding a special train to Chicago in 46 hours—almost 12 hours faster than such a run had ever been made.

"I'm buying speed," Scotty boasted. He paid the agreed-upon price of $5500 for a mad dash across the country; and at 1 p.m. the next day a train named *Death Valley Coyote* pulled out of Los Angeles. It consisted of a baggage car, a diner, and a standard Pullman, headed by engine No. 442, a Baldwin 10-wheeler. On board with Scotty were his wife, two journalists, and the crew. Thousands of people at the station cheered, shouted, and waved good-bye.

The speedometer rose to 84 miles per hour. At San Bernardino the train picked up a helper engine to attack the steep Cajon Pass grade. Instead of stopping at the summit, the pusher was uncoupled on the fly and spurted ahead into a sidetrack. Downgrade, the train hit 96 miles per hour even while rounding curves.

"Our hogger doesn't know a curve when he sees one," the conductor apologized. "The whole road looks straight to him."

"I'm satisfied with him," said Scotty.

At Barstow, they dropped their engine and highballed across the desert with No. 1005, a Baldwin Prairie type. Then at Needles, still in California, it took them only 80 seconds to change to No. 1010, another Baldwin Prairie. As they crossed the Colorado River bridge at 65 miles per hour, the Scotts ate their first meal of the trip while salt and pepper shakers danced a jig on the table.

Three hours more of hard mountain railroading took them into Seligman, Arizona, at 10:40 p.m. After a sleepless night, they coupled onto a Pacific-type engine at Albuquerque in the morning and said good-bye to Division Superintendent Gibson, who had ridden the entire length of the Albuquerque division with them. Then they climbed Glorieta, a grade that rose 158 feet to the mile. They reached Las Vegas, New Mexico, at 12:38 p.m.

All that day they bucked the mountains, setting records that would last for years. At 5:15 p.m. they reached La Junta, Colorado, behind Baldwin Prairie No. 1215, with the worst part of the journey behind them. It took just 2 minutes to change to a new Atlantic balanced compound. There was straight track now, a level roadbed across the Kansas prairie. Elated, Scotty rode the engine cab at high speed into Dodge City on the old Santa Fe Trail, where the cattle drives used to end.

Dodge City was reached at 8:29 p.m. During a change of engines exuberant Scotty sent a telegram to President Roosevelt: "An American cowboy is coming east in a special train faster than any cowpuncher ever rode before. How much shall I break the transcontinental record?"

That night they averaged a mile every 50 seconds. Four hours after leaving Kansas City they raced across Missouri and a corner of Iowa, touching 90 miles per hour. Roaring out of Fort Madison, Iowa, the *Coyote* cut loose for the home stretch across Illinois. The Associated Press had kept the wires hot with news of the train, and the big dailies in all cities gave it front-page headlines.

Every switch was spiked shut, and the entire operating department was on its toes. "That's the way to roll 'em!" Scotty exclaimed as he helped the fireman to feed the firebox. Between Cameron and Surrey, Illinois, they bounced along at 106 miles per hour. Finally, they came into Chicago at 11:54 a.m. They had covered 2265 exciting miles in 44 hours and 54 minutes, which nobody had ever done before.

"Why did you do it?" a reporter asked Scotty. He'd been on a bender, he said. He was just telling the world that he was happy.

BIBLIOGRAPHY: Hank Johnston, *Death Valley Scotty*, Trans-Anglo Books, Corona Del Mar, Calif., 1974; James Marshall, *Santa Fe: The Railroad That Built an Empire*, Random House, New York, 1945.

De Autremont Brothers Many of the most notorious train robbers, like many great circus owners, were brothers: the Renos, Jameses, Youngers, Daltons, and De Autremonts, the last-named being Hugh and his twin brothers, Ray and Roy. It took a costly, 4-year, worldwide search to bring all three De Autremonts to justice.

Southern Pacific train No. 1-13, en route from Portland to San Francisco with a rich shipment of gold in the mail car, left the station at Siskiyou, Oregon, a few minutes past midnight on October 11, 1923, and moved slowly toward the entrance to a 3017-foot tunnel in the Sierras, 4113 feet above sea level. Two men darted from behind some boxcars as the engine passed them, boarded the tender, and forced the engineer to stop his locomotive just outside the west portal of the tunnel. Then a terrific blast put out all train lights, piled up rubble, and fouled the air with poisonous gas.

The train crew thought the locomotive boiler had exploded. They sought help. An extra engine sent into the tunnel pulled the passenger cars back to the station. When rescuers succeeded in reaching the western portal—either by climbing the mountain or by penetrating the tunnel after the air had cleared somewhat—they discovered that instead of a locomotive accident, bandits trying to blast open the steel mail car had set off the explosion. The engineer and fireman had been shot dead, the head brakeman was dying, and a mail clerk's body, horribly mangled, lay inside his car.

Dan O'Connell, SP's chief special agent (police chief), hurried to the scene with 30 of his own men to help the postal inspectors and local police already there. They learned that three desperados had been involved in the crime. Two had boarded the train. When it stopped, a third man appeared with the detonating machine. But all that the explosives did was to kill the mail clerk, set the inside of his car afire, and batter the door so effectively that the gunmen could not open it. Balked in their robbery plot, they murdered all eyewitnesses, namely, the engine and train crews, and fled. Bloodhounds rushed to the area from Seattle, 542 miles away, failed to pick up the scent.

But many clues turned up along or near the right-of-way, such as the detonating machine, creosoted foot pads, 163 feet of lead wire, a Colt automatic revolver with its numbers obliterated, and, most important of all, a pair of discarded overalls in the pencil pocket of which was found a registered mail receipt issued at Eugene, Oregon, for a letter sent by Roy De Autremont to an address in New Mexico.

The lawmen spent days patiently sifting the ashes of fires in which the bandits had burned various articles used in their camps prior to the holdup, digging bullets from trees, and searching in every direction. Two mail planes soared over the mountains in a vain effort to locate the fugitives, who were thought to be hidden there. Several clues involved all three De Autremonts. Their past history was investigated. That November a grand jury indicted the brothers for murder and other crimes. A $15,900 reward in gold was offered for their capture. More than 2,500,000 circulars with mug shots, printed in six languages, were distributed throughout North and South America, Europe, and Australia.

The first big break came on July 1, 1926, when a U.S. Army corporal returning from the Philippine Islands told Chief O'Connell that he recognized the portrait of Hugh De Autremont as that of a private stationed at Manila in Company D, 31st Infantry, under the name James Carl Price. Hugh was brought back to America and put on trial at Jacksonville, Oregon, on May 7, 1927. Meanwhile, a national newspaper syndicate had published a feature story including photos of the twins, Ray and Roy, in 500 United States newspapers. An Ohio man read the story on April 10, 1927, and recognized the pictures of the brothers as those of two men he had worked with at Hanging Rock, Ohio, and whom he had known as Clarence and Elmer Goodwin. This led to their arrest at Steubenville, Ohio, on July 8. Hugh was convicted of murder in the first degree. His brothers confessed. All three were were sentenced to life imprisonment in a state penitentiary at Salem, Oregon.

Hugh was released on parole in 1958 but died a few months later. Ray was paroled in 1961. Roy, leader of the gang, became hopelessly insane and was transferred to the criminal ward of a state hospital, where he died.

BIBLIOGRAPHY: Don DeNevi, *Western Train Robberies*, Celestial Arts, Millbrae, Calif., 1976.

Debs, Eugene Victor *(1855–1926)* Rail labor leader, nominated five times for the Presidency of the United States. Debs was born at Terre Haute, Indiana, and went to work in 1870 scraping paint off Vandalia Railroad cars at 50 cents a day. Before age 15, he got a job firing a switcher for the Terre Haute & Indianapolis at $1 a night; later he was assigned to road freight engines. In 1873 he became secretary of the Terre Haute lodge of the newly organized Brotherhood of Locomotive Firemen (BLF), and in 1878 associate editor of its *Locomotive Firemen's Magazine*. In 1880 he was promoted to editor in chief and was elected secretary-treasurer of the national organization. On top of that he had recently been elected city clerk of Terre Haute. For the next 6 years he worked 7 days a week.

BLF membership climbed from 3160 to 28,681 in 12 years, and Debs tripled the size of the magazine he edited. He married Kate Metzel and began organizing not merely the firemen but also brakemen, switchmen, telegraphers, shopmen, and trackmen. In 1893 he resigned his BLF office to form "one big union," the American Railway Union (ARU), which he felt was needed to prevent railroad managements from playing one labor organization against another.

In the spring of 1894, when the ARU was still new and untried, James J. Hill cut the wages of his Great Northern laborers. As head of the ARU, Debs called a strike that tied up 4000 miles of that road. Except for mail trains, not a wheel turned. A week later an ARU victory ended the walkout. *See* HILL, JAMES JEROME.

The following June the Pullman plant employees struck in protest against deep pay cuts but no cut in rentals of the company-owned houses they occupied. Many of those houses were wooden shanties built at a cost of only $100 each but rented for $96 a year. In some of them, it was said, five families had to share a single water faucet.

Much as Debs sympathized with the Pullman workers, he did not think the ARU was strong enough to warrant calling a general strike to support them. But the ARU delegates in convention at Chicago, flushed with their Great Northern victory, overruled their chief and decreed the strike. On 20 Midwestern roads 125,000 railroad workers joined in the walkout. If only the men would stand together and refrain from disorder, Debs said, victory was certain.

But a sweeping series of federal court injunctions against the ARU, backed by federal troops which President Grover Cleveland sent to Chicago despite protests by the Governor of Illinois, turned the tide against the strikers. Debs and other labor leaders were jailed. Railroad management crushed the strike and set up a nationwide blacklisting system against the defeated ARU men. *See also* "CRANE WITH A BROKEN NECK."

In 1900, 1904, 1908, 1912, and 1920 the Socialist party (including its predecessor) nominated Debs for the Presidency, on the last occasion while he was serving a federal prison term in Atlanta for opposing wartime conscription. Pardoned by President Warren G. Harding in 1921 and restored to citizenship, Debs died 5 years later. His old home at Terre Haute has been restored and is now a national shrine.

BIBLIOGRAPHY: David Karsner, *Debs: His Authorized Life and Letters*, Boni and Liveright, New York, 1919; Almont Lindsey, *The Pullman Strike*, University of Chicago Press, Chicago, 1942; Jean Y. Tussey (ed.), *Eugene V. Debs Speaks*, Pathfinder Press, New York, 1970.

Delano (Railroad Town) For years the Lehigh Valley Railroad (LV) wholly owned this 255-acre community, which it built in 1861 atop Mahanoy Mountain in eastern Pennsylvania's Lower Anthracite Fields. The company leased the land in 1861 and bought it outright in 1891. A little world in itself, surrounded by mountains and maintained by the railroad, the community had a peak population of about 1200. Railroad Town bore the family name of the coal-baron Delano brothers, Warren and Franklin. By marrying James Roosevelt, Warren's daughter Sara became the mother of a President, Franklin Delano Roosevelt.

A narrow pass through the Alleghenies suitable for rail traffic was a deciding factor in the choice of a site for the village. Delano, both literally and figuratively, was built upon coal. Not many miles distant from it, anthracite was discovered for the first time anywhere. The acreage never outgrew its original limits because nearby mining operations caused cave-ins that made additional construction unwise.

On June 18, 1865, the first passenger train chugged from the new town to Mahanoy City, 5 miles distant. At that time coal was being hauled by rail to tidewater for transportation to market by canalboats; but in 1867 the rails reached Mount Carmel, Pennsylvania, connecting with the Northern Central, which later joined the Pennsylvania Railroad, and this cut off much of the canal traffic. With the completion of its shops and first enginehouse, Delano became a vital division point. Earle Franklin Baker described it as follows:

> In Railroad Town the yard goats toil
> And powder up the rails with sand;
> While journals get the waste and oil,
> The crummy silently does stand.
> The hotshot's clamor fills the air;
> The drill crew men, all lean and brown,
> Go dancing nightly to the blare
> Of herding cars in Railroad Town.

With Lehigh Valley wages, Delano railroaders paid rent to the company for their homes, which valley coal heated in cold weather, and bought most of their necessities from the general store and the drugstore, both run by company officials. They vacationed on LV passes. Their local band practiced in the rear of the freighthouse. Their public library in the station building was well stocked with books on railroading and mechanics, among other subjects, supplied by the company and by townspeople.

For illness or childbirth, the company rushed a doctor into town from the outside world on an extra train. The LV even served as a handmaiden to religion. On Sundays worshipers pumped a railroad handcar to and from the nearest church at Mahanoy City. Once a week housewives were taken to "the city" on a special train consisting of an engine pulling a flatcar on which railroad ties were laid for seats.

In early days, locomotive firemen working out of Delano usually labored 12 days out of every 24, Sundays included. Besides cracking huge coal lumps, raking down the coal, and scraping it into hungry fireboxes that needed a lot of fuel for climbing mountain grades, the men were equipped with oil, lampblack, and brass polish and had to use plenty of all three. Before the invention of spark arresters, streams of pyrotechnics from engine stacks, comparable to miniature volcanic eruptions, often landed sparks on the hands, faces, and necks of trainmen.

Delano's shops were famous. Alexander A. Mitchell was the first master mechanic of the Lehigh & Mahanoy, a Lehigh Valley predecessor, and had charge of the Delano shops. While supervising the construction of those shops in 1864, he conceived the brilliant idea of installing a deep pit, a previously unknown device for taking wheels out from underneath locomotives in repair jobs.

The first entirely new locomotive turned out in Railroad Town was No. 341, built by John Campbell, who succeeded Mitchell as master mechanic, and was named the *Alexander Mitchell.* The first Delano-built Camelback, or two-cabber, was No. 170, designed by Campbell to provide an unusually large firebox and greater steam capacity. It proved so effective on the Mahanoy division's steep grades that the Delano shops converted many old Consolidations into this type.

The worst blow to Railroad Town's pride and prestige occurred on February 11, 1892, when the Lehigh Valley management leased its entire railroad to the rival Philadelphia & Reading to solve a financial crisis. This deal was intended to last 999 years but was terminated on August 8, 1893. The Reading management took away some of Delano's best engines, returning them for overhaul after they had been rather badly battered by lack of care and mishandling. A protest strike tied up the division for a day but had no other effect. Then the Reading stopped all building of engines at Delano. The last engine, No. 617, was outshopped in 1892.

Delano's importance as a railroad center was further diminished by the shifting of division headquarters to Hazleton. At that time, however, there was no letdown in the volume of freight flowing through the Delano yards. In 1926 the Lehigh Valley management made a radical change in property ownership by selling to employees the houses they occupied with their families. The total number of buildings in town was then 91. Today, there is no longer a Lehigh Valley Railroad, the line having been merged into Conrail, and railroading plays a lesser role in what is left of Delano.

See also LEHIGH VALLEY RAILROAD.

BIBLIOGRAPHY: H. O. Moser, *History of Delano, Pennsylvania,* Williamsport, Pa., 1931; Angus Sinclair, *Development of the Locomotive Engine,* annotated ed. by John H. White, Jr., M.I.T., Cambridge, Mass., 1970.

Delaware and Hudson Railway (D&H) This line, which has been part of the Norfolk & Western System (NW) since 1968, is often referred to as a bridge linking New England and eastern Canada with the South and West. Its 734 miles of road are operated in New York, Pennsylvania, and, to a minor extent, Vermont. Its mainline runs generally northeast from Wilkes-Barre, Pennsylvania, and Oswego and Binghamton, New York, east to Albany, Schenectady, Troy, and Mechanicville, and north to the Canadian border to connect with a subsidiary, the Napierville Junction Railway, which extends to Delson Junction, near Montreal. *See* NORFOLK & WESTERN RAILWAY.

The D&H began as a canal company formed by the brothers William and Maurice Wurtz to haul coal by sled and raft from Pennsylvania's Lackawanna Valley to Philadelphia and New York. A 16-mile gravity railroad built by the company from Carbondale to Honesdale, Pennylvania, was the scene on August 8, 1829, of the first run of a common-carrier locomotive in the Western Hemisphere. The rails were wrought strap iron screwed into hemlock stringers held together by crossties set at intervals of 10 and 15 feet and supported on posts set in broken stone or stone piers. The engine, a tall-stacked four-wheeler imported from England, was named the *Stourbridge Lion;* a red lion decorated her boiler front. She had no cab or cowcatcher. Above her boiler were "walking beams" described as "pumping up and down like a hurrying grasshopper."

On October 9, 1829, horses moved the first load of

Replica of the Stourbridge Lion, which made the first run of a common-carrier locomotive in North America, in 1829. It is easy to see how her "walking beams" pumping up and down above the boiler would resemble a scurrying grasshopper. [Delaware and Hudson Railway]

A Delaware and Hudson train roars under the famous Starrucca Viaduct in Lanesboro, Pennsylvania, in 1973. [R. E. Allen]

anthracite over the railroad. But the D&H soon began using locomotives in regular service. In 1836, two handsome engines, the *Erie* and the *Champlain*, pulled passenger cars so lavish that one traveler described them as "more like a moveable gallery of fine arts than a train of railroad cars." At the time of the NW merger, the D&H had 2500 employees, 125 diesel locomotives, and some 7000 freight cars, work cars, and equipment.

BIBLIOGRAPHY: Jim Shaughnessy, *Delaware & Hudson*, Howell-North, Berkeley, Calif., 1967.

Demurrage Charge made when a consignor or consignee holds a freight car overtime. The customer is allowed 1 free day to unload, excluding weekends and certain national holidays. After that, the charge is made. If the car is held for a specified period, usually 4 days after the free time, the demurrage charge per day rises.

Rio Grande the ACTION road

Denver and Rio Grande Western Railroad (D&RGW) Line that in 1980 was operating about 276 locomotives, almost 10,400 freight cars, and 19 passenger cars on 1868 miles of track between Denver and Pueblo in the east and Salt Lake City and Ogden in the west, plus lines to other points in Colorado and Utah. The system is shaped somewhat like the Great Dipper. A plaque in Denver Union Station says of its founder:

> William Jackson Palmer (1836–1909). Union cavalry general. Pioneer railroad builer, prophet of Colorado's greatness. He mapped the routes of three transcontinental railways, supervised the building of the first road to Denver, organized and constructed the state's industries, cherished its beauties, founded Colorado Springs, fostered Colorado College, and served our sister republic of Mexico with sympathy and vision in developing its national railways.

Scene on the Denver and Rio Grande Western's last 3-foot-gauge line and last steam operation, which is a popular Colorado tourist attraction. [Joseph A. Mannix]

Palmer was a Philadelphia-born Quaker. During the Civil War he commanded the 15th Pennsylvania Cavalry, which after Appomattox pursued Jefferson Davis and captured the Confederate President's treasure train.

In 1871, having served on the Union Pacific, Palmer began building a north-south narrow-gauge road, the Denver and Rio Grande (D&RG), which he had long planned. For 12 years he pushed it down the Rockies' eastern face to El Moro despite national panics, Wall Street opposition, and railroad wars. It crossed the Continental Divide to the Utah border and went down into northern New Mexico. *See also* CANYON WAR.

In 1883 Eastern financiers forced Palmer out of the presidency of his beloved D&RG, which then went into receivership. Palmer turned to building another railroad, the Denver and Rio Grande Western, as an extension of the D&RG westward from the Colorado-Utah border to Salt Lake City. At the turn of the century he sold this new road to the D&RG, making a $1 million profit. This money he distributed proportionally to all his employees, from section hands to top executives. Many laborers, for example, got $5000 each; passenger agents, $35,000.

Prior to the automobile age the D&RGW attracted a great many passengers with its slogan, "Through the Rockies, Not around Them." In 1885 it adopted a herald shaped like a steam locomotive. It pictured Curecanti Needle, a landmark mountain peak on the Marshall Pass route. Underneath, on a tasseled banner, was the legend "Scenic Line of the World." The system's present emblem is a parallelogram with the words "Rio Grande, the Action Road." Over 99 percent of the line's gross revenue comes from freight, especially autos and auto parts, steel, lumber, food products, and coal.

Today nearly all of the D&RGW is standard-gauge. For years it has been operating its last historic 3-foot-gauge trackage between Durango and Silverton, Colorado, as a summer tourist line, a "steamfans' paradise," with Alco 2-8-2 steam locomotives, old-style coaches, and open-side observation cars.

BIBLIOGRAPHY: Robert C. Athearn, *Rebel of the Rockies: A History of the Denver and Rio Grande Western Railroad*, Yale, New Haven, Conn., 1962; Cornelius W. Hauck and Robert W. Richardson, *Steam in the Rockies*, Colorado Railroad Museum, Golden, Colo., 1963; *Jane's World Railways and Rapid Transit Systems*, F. Watts, New York, 1977; Dell McCoy and Russ Colman, *The Rio Grande Pictorial*, Sundance, Denver, 1971.

Depots *See* STATIONS, RAILROAD PASSENGER.

Derail (Derailer) Combination of switch and very short section of track designed to guide runaway cars, locomotives, and other rolling stock off the rails at a selected location to avoid collisions or other accidents. Derails are used mostly on spur tracks or sidings to prevent cars from fouling the mainline. You rarely find them on a mainline except at drawbridges or in connection with interlocking plants at railroad crossings.

Deregulation of Railroads The Staggers Rail Act, enacted by Congress and signed by President Jimmy Carter on October 14, 1980, while short of complete deregulation, gave the railroads considerable freedom in rate making, car control, and other areas of the industry that had long been rigidly supervised by the Interstate Commerce Commission. According to William H. Dempsey, president of the Association of American Railroads, "Deregulation lays the foundation for a new era of railroad growth by granting railroads greater opportunity to respond to the discipline and opportunities of the marketplace."

Diesel-Electric Locomotives America's first industrial electric loco, a tiny steeple-cab switcher, was built in 1893 by General Electric Co. (GE) at Erie, Pennsylvania, for the Manufacturers Railway, a private line serving a textile complex in Berlin, New Hampshire. Its traction motors and frame were destined for greatness; their basic principle was embodied in the earliest internal-combustion locomotives.

In 1895, the first mainline electrics went to work in the Baltimore & Ohio's (B&O's) tunnels at Baltimore, eliminating the hazard of using steam locomotives underground. The power of these new small units amazed operating men. B&O used them to pull entire road trains, steam engines and all, through the tunnels. Thus began the electric age in railroad motive power, the first challenge to steam, working quietly beneath Baltimore streets. In the next two decades both GE and Westinghouse Electric Corp. built much equipment that made railroad history.

Electric railroading, though powerful and efficient, has two major hurdles that most North American roads would not or could not negotiate:

1. High initial cost of power generation and transmission and the locos themselves with their servicing needs. At first, electrified roads generated their own "juice," a huge capital investment, but soon they began buying power from existing state and municipal power agencies. This was still a high fixed cost, but it did help, although electric roads had to get their lifeblood from outside sources.

2. Inflexibility. Unless wires were strung over every foot of track, including yards and sidings, the road would still need other types of locos. Big electric installations became mainlines over mountainous territory, crowded corridors, and special-problem operating districts. Mainline installations were fed by branches and yards and worked by steam locomotives.

The time soon became ripe for power incorporating the flexibility of steam, which provided its own energy, and the electric's efficiency and ease of operation plus low maintenance costs. In 1905, W. R. McKeen, Jr., Union Pacific's superintendent of motive power and machinery, designed a kind of rail vehicle which would make a profit on short branch lines and marginal passenger runs that had been wasting the power of the typical steam loco and two or three cars in such service. McKeen's masterpiece was a coach equipped with 100-horsepower gasoline engine and mechanical transmission (a clutch, as in a modern automobile), which he put to work. The success of this invention launched the McKeen Motor Car Co. and induced General Electric to enter the motor-car field. McKeen's company also built at least one small gas-mechanical switch engine, a four-wheeler that bore the Union Pacific name in 1909 and was the first-known internal-combustion locomotive.

But 1909 was not an auspicious time to market a tiny gas-mechanical switcher. It marked the dawn of the drag era, whose goal was to move huge tonnages regardless of other considerations. Freight rarely left a yard unless the utmost tonnage was coupled behind available locomotives. Steam locos kept getting bigger and bigger, with each new wheel arrangement proclaimed "the world's largest." This period gave us the mighty Mallets and simple articulateds—behemoths which soon proved to be too much for the wooden-bodied cars they hauled. As rolling stock improved to meet motive power's challenge, bigger and more powerful locos coped with the cars. *See* MALLET.

Effect of World War I At the onset of World War I, American railroads had an incredibly mixed stable of equipment. This, plus the need of most roads for federal money to modernize their plants for national defense, led to the U.S. Railroad Administration's standard steam designs. These engines gave each receiving road a shot in the arm but at the same time slowed the quest for new and better motive power. However, World War I, particularly the early tanks, cars, trucks, and planes used in this first mechanized war, forced America to learn about internal combustion.

As the reliability of internal-combustion engines slowly improved, it became more and more obvious that a fresh utilizable source of energy had been found. Even Baldwin Locomotive Works, an old-line steam builder in Philadelphia, built over 2000 gas-mechanical "dinkies" intended for use in the war's western front and regarded as expendable. Little is known of the history and disposition of these "iron mules," whose parts littered the fields of France and Germany. *See* BALDWIN LOCOMOTIVE WORKS.

Europe had seen a number of trial locomotives using

the principles of Dr. Rudolf Diesel, the German scientist and inventor who mysteriously disappeared while crossing the English Channel in 1913, presumably having been thrown overboard by German military agents who suspected he was planning to sell his invention to the British government. But for his untimely death, more serious efforts might have been made sooner to build such locos. Diesel's internal-combustion engine burned a cheaper fuel of much lower grade and could produce more horsepower with less maintenance than the gasoline engine. His invention was successful, but at that time the railroads were preoccupied with steam.

In 1913 a short electrified railroad with a long name, the Minneapolis, St. Paul, Rochester & Dubuque Electric Traction Co. (later known as the Dan Patch Line, named for a famous racehorse), took delivery of No. 100, a boxcab locomotive with a gasoline engine driving a generator that fed power to electric traction motors. Number 100 was, in effect, an electric loco which developed its own power and was the first gas-electric. She was important because her unique use of traction motors unlocked the secret of how best to transmit power from an internal-combustion engine to driving wheels. The 100 was a success. Shortly afterward, GE delivered three improved gas-electrics to the Dan Patch Line. Thus a new locomotive type was born. It used proven electrical components and the emerging gasoline engine. Gas-electrics replaced the old gas-mechanical motor cars. *See* DAN PATCH LINE.

Inevitably, the lighter gasoline engines in these locos prompted a trial of Diesel's invention. In 1916, GE built a small, 200-horsepower V-8 diesel engine it called the GM-50. It was installed in a steeple-cab car body with a B-B wheel arrangement and sold to the Jay Street Terminal Railroad, a 5-mile dockside switching line in Brooklyn, New York. This short line was familiar with General Electric. Its No. 3 was the second gas-electric switcher built by GE, succeeding the Dan Patch 100.

Number 4, the first diesel loco in the United States, was joined by two similar units in 1918, one built for the city of Baltimore, the other for the U.S. Army Corps of Engineers. The Army unit was heavily armored for use in trench warfare in France but likely was never shipped overseas, as the armistice was signed just 2 weeks after she was built. Jay Street No. 4 was a failure, largely because of the poor operation of the GM-50 prime mover, and was returned to GE in April 1919. Both the Baltimore and the Army units had similar problems. The former was sent back to GE, equipped with a gasoline engine, and worked as a gas-electric switcher on the East Erie Commercial Railroad, the plant road serving the GE's Erie works.

Developments of the 1920s and 1930s The failure of the GM-50 diesel engine was a setback, but in 1924 General Electric and Ingersoll-Rand of Phillipsburg, New Jersey, built a demonstrator locomotive with an IR diesel engine having a 10-inch bore and 12-inch stroke. This was a 60-ton, 300-horsepower B-B unit of boxcab design, with a single cab on a rounded nose. She demonstrated in the East on major roads and industrial short lines, pulling freight and passenger trains, for a total of over 2200 hours on 14 roads. Most of her time was spent on the New York Central's West Side line in New York City (where a city smoke ordinance was causing trouble for steam switchers), but she was returned to Phillipsburg.

American Locomotive Co. (Alco) built the car bodies. After the demonstrations in 1924, the consortium of Alco-GE-IR produced the first standardized line of diesels ever offered: twenty-six 60-ton and seven 100-ton units, all in boxcab style and all with the Ingersoll-Rand engine with a 10-inch bore and a 12-inch stroke. The 100-ton models had two six-cylinder engines rated at 600 horsepower, twice that of the 60-ton units. One such 100-tonner, Long Island No. 401, made the first road freight run by any North American diesel, hauling a 379-ton train 537 miles on December 12, 1922.

The Baldwin Locomotive Works, whose fame was built almost entirely on steam locos, produced a 1000-horsepower boxcab with an A1A-A1A wheel arrangement on an articulated frame, using two Knudsen two-cycle inverted V-6 diesels. Built in June 1925, No. 58501 demonstrated on the Reading and Jersey Central roads, pulling freights between Reading and Tamaqua, Pennsylvania, over a 0.7 percent grade. Being unsuccessful, she was scrapped. In May 1929, Baldwin again fielded a demonstrator, a boxcab B-B of 1000 horsepower with a six-cylinder Krupp four-cycle engine. Billed as a switcher, No. 61000 was scrapped after testing. Baldwin did not try diesels again until 1937.

In 1928, General Electric took over the construction of car bodies from Alco, and the Alco-GE-IR consortium split. GE and Ingersoll-Rand continued as a team until the mid-1930s, when GE went to a new supplier of prime movers, Cooper-Bessemer Co. (CB). GE produced an extensive line of switching locos in this period with a variety of prime movers, particularly CB.

Meanwhile, Alco acquired the McIntosh & Seymour engine plant in 1929 and began to market locos with M&S engines. In 1928, Alco and the New York Central Railroad joined in producing a successful road diesel. Three units were built. No. 1500 was an M&S loco with a 14-inch bore and 12-inch stroke, and No. 1525 was an Ingersoll-Rand loco with a 14-inch bore and a 16-inch stroke. Both functioned well. Then came the 1550, delivered in October 1928, which became the first truly successful road diesel in the United States. She worked until 1946, when she was converted to a slug unit for hump-yard service. She was a boxcab with a 2-D-2 wheel arrangement.

Number 1525, a boxcab with a B-B arrangement, was the prototype for New York Central's three-power units: diesel-electric, storage-battery electric, and third-rail straight electric. She switched the New York City electrified zone until 1945. The 1500 was a boxcab meant for Putnam division passenger service, but failed and was stored until February 1936, when she was returned to Alco. Then Alco introduced a standardized line of switchers, using the M&S 531 engine, whereupon the GE-IR and Alco switcher lines entered competition. The battle was on. General Electric's main rival was the Lemp control, first applied with the old GM-50 engine. Alco's units still carried GE's electrical parts, traction motors, etc. Except for New York Central's 1500 and 1550, all these early diesels were switchers.

In 1930, General Motors Corp. bought the Electro-Motive Corp. (EMC), which had been building and selling gas-electric motor cars. The engines used in them came from Winton Engine Co., which also had a small line of diesel power plants. In April 1934, a Winton 210-A diesel plant was installed in Chicago, Burlington & Quincy loco No. 9900, the first power car for the first *Zephyr* streamlined train. She had been exhibited at the 1933 World's Fair in Chicago.

In the next 4 years, EMC built memorable lightweight streamliners for the Burlington, Illinois Central (IC), Boston & Maine-Maine Central, Union Pacific, and Rock Island. Two 600-horsepower motor cars with Winton 201-As went to the Seaboard Air Line in 1936. The B&O and Santa Fe took boxcab-styled passenger units in 1935. The success of these "glamour trains" firmly entrenched EMC's status in the passenger field. In 1935, EMC turned out two endcab, low-hood B-B, 600-horsepower switchers with eight-cylinder 201-A plants. Both of these units were still operating in the late 1970s. EMC followed with a successful line of 600- and 900-horsepower switchers, all using the Winton 201-A.

The greatest period of railroad diesel development was the decade 1930-1940. Firms such as Cummins, Cooper-Bessemer, Ingersoll-Rand, Baldwin, Alco, Electro-Motive, and GE had power plants within railroad units. During those years, all but Electro-Motive's and Alco's special streamliners were built for switching service.

In 1938, Electro-Motive took a giant step forward with a new power plant, the 567 (cubic inches in its displacement per cylinder). The Winton 201-A, which had started EMC on its popularity road in a line of switchers and sleek streamliners, did not have the potential for power that EMC needed. The company realized that the true breakthrough would be in freight power. However, the 567 was first featured in passenger units E-3, E-4, E-5, and E-6.

Seaboard E-4A No. 3000 was the first unit, in October 1938, to use the engine. All E units used two 567s, which gave them 2000 horsepower per unit. The 567 engines used in the E's were 12-cylinder machines.

In September 1939, a mortal blow struck North America's vast steam fleet: introduction of the FT, a "locomotive set" consisting of four units, each with a single 16-cylinder 567 and rated at 1350 horsepower per unit. This loco, numbered 103, barnstormed America, proving to all road foremen of engines that the diesel was here to stay. FT signified *F* for freight and *T* for 1350 horsepower. She went into full production in 1941, with the Santa Fe Railway (ATSF) the first and largest buyer. On January 1, 1943, subsidiaries Electro-Motive and Winton Engine Co. were merged into the giant General Motors Corp., becoming known as the Electro-Motive Division (EMD). After that, the locomotive business would never be the same again.

In 1937, while EMC was realizing the potential of its new engine, the old-line Baldwin Locomotive Works had another fling. We have seen Baldwin's failure with the Knudsen and Krupp engines in the early 1930s. Baldwin had stuck to steam (in addition to Pennsylvania Railroad electrics) until 1937, when it applied a version of the De la Vergne marine diesel engine to a switching locomotive of surprisingly modern design. She was rated at 660 horsepower, demonstrated as No. 62000, sold to the Santa Fe, and repurchased by Baldwin after "dogs" developed on the ATSF. She carried a six-cylinder De la Vergne.

Three similar locos with eight-cylinder plants were sold to the New Orleans Public Belt Railway in 1937; these continued in service for over 30 years. In 1939, Baldwin decided that the slow-running (625 revolutions per minute) De la Vergne plant was for them. With Westinghouse electrical gear, the combination of big power and heavy-duty traction motors made a fine switcher. A line of standard switchers, both six- and eight-cylinder models, came out in 1939. This committed Baldwin to the diesel.

Westinghouse Electric itself had built diesels between 1928 and 1936, using Beardmore-design power plants under license plus its own electrical gear and car-body

Early diesel switchers at the New York Central roundhouse, North White Plains, New York. [New York Central Railroad]

designs, although it farmed out most of the final assembly. The units were created as heavy switchers, usable also on the road. With Baldwin's entrance into the diesel market, Westinghouse became content to supply electrical gear and let Baldwin build the locos. After World War II, Westinghouse produced a gas-turbine electric, ostensibly as a forerunner of a line of such turbines for both passenger and freight service, but the 4000-horsepower B-B-B-B *Blue Goose*, built entirely by Westinghouse in April 1950, was not repeated.

Effect of World War II The attack on Pearl Harbor found Alco-GE, EMC, and Baldwin-Westinghouse at the threshold of the biggest motive-power boom the nation had ever known. "Diesel fever" was growing daily. It lasted through 1942, when the War Production Board clamped the lid on materials needed in the war effort. The Board treated diesel locos as experimental, preferring that roads needing power buy steam.

Restrictions put on the builders shaped the future of North American diesels. EMC, flush with the success of its FT model, was ordered to produce only road-service units (FTs and E's), while Alco and Baldwin (which had competing road units on their drawing boards) had to build only switchers. As a result, EMC, with its fine FT, became the premier builder after 1945. Alco and Baldwin flooded the switcher market. Alco had one road-passenger model, the DL-109, in production in 1940; units were produced during the war years but were not good sellers.

The war set diesel production back much more than the 4-year span of restrictions. It also taught a few lessons, mainly that the diesel locomotive could, and would, stand up to the best steam power. At war's end, virtually every railroad in the United States and Canada was lined up at the builders' doors wanting whatever production was possible and at whatever price. The once-mighty steam locomotives were fed to the blast furnaces to provide steel.

Fairbanks-Morse (F-M) entered the diesel field in 1944. A well-known supplier of railroad hardware such as scales, track cars, and standpipes, it had developed an opposed-piston firing (instead of a piston firing against a head, a piston firing against an opposing piston), which had been placed in about half of the U.S. Navy submarines used in World War II. A scaled-down version of this plant used in repowering early gas-electric motor cars was not highly successful. F-M enlarged it and in 1944 offered a 1000-horsepower switcher using a six-cylinder opposed-piston engine. The unit featured distinctive Raymond Loewy styling, a tall hood to contain the height of the opposed-piston plant, and clean lines. It was a success. An even more successful line of 1200-horsepower switchers followed. F-M was eventually to build road freight and passenger units, road switchers, and straight switchers; its last design, the 2400-horsepower *Trainmaster*, set off an unprecedented horsepower race. *See* LOEWY, RAYMOND.

Developments of the 1950s and 1960s The diesel year was definitely 1950. Railroads across the land were proclaiming in print how many steamers they had scrapped and how many new diesels their rosters had. The major diesel builders were EMD, Alco-GE, Baldwin, and Fairbanks-Morse, in that order. Locomotives were of three distinct styles. Road freight and passenger models were streamlined rectangles with rounded, pointed, slightly curved or almost flat noses, with cabs high up on one end. Switchers were simply boxes on wheels, with cabs perched on the rear.

The diesel road switcher was born of necessity. Jobs that called for road-freight power did not need streamlining, so the switcher style was lengthened and given a bigger power plant, with the cab set three-fourths back. There were hundreds of variations. As a rule, the little industrial units still favored the centered cab. These were built by GE, Fate-Root-Heath, Davenport, Whitcomb, Porter, Vulcan, etc. Some of them found their way onto common carriers, while some larger units also worked in industry.

The mighty trend in diesels which began in 1950 still continues. Back in October 1949, EMD produced its GP-7 model, another road switcher (GP stands for "general purpose"). Its 1500-horsepower rating was the same as that of EMD's road-freight units, but GP-7's design was strictly functional, with just enough car body to cover the 567 power plant, a cab hung saddlewise on the unit at the three-fourths mark, and all the footboards, walkways, and railings of a switcher. GP-7 was an immediate success, although both Alco and Baldwin had fielded road switchers of equal horsepower a few years earlier. By now EMD was the acknowledged leader.

Lima Locomotive Works, the last steam builder, threw in the towel in 1949, but not until it had put on a furious advertising campaign and had completed such handsome steamers as the Chesapeake and Ohio's (C&O's) Alleghenies and the Nickel Plate's Berkshires as late as 1948. Lima bought the Hamilton Engine Co. and built a line of switchers and road switchers, using six- and eight-cylinder Hamilton turbocharged engines and Westinghouse gear, 174 units in all, during the period 1949–1951. Its 750-horsepower switcher was the smallest, while its huge centercab 2500-horsepower Transfer model was the largest. Lima locos resembled Alco's, but there was no connection. High-end cabs and squared-off low hoods with prominent number-boards were virtually a Lima trademark. But Lima's designs were dropped when Baldwin and Lima merged in 1950. *See* LIMA LOCOMOTIVE WORKS.

The 1950–1960 decade saw road after road going 100 percent diesel and the EMD GP-7 and GP-9 models replacing steam. A switch to the more functional and less streamlined diesels led to the last of the cab units in 1959, although EMD was still building E-9s in 1963. Total replacement of steam was the aim.

A few roads (C&O, Norfolk & Western, Nickel Plate,

IC, and Virginian) were still resisting, but these were either largely coal roads or had modern steam shops or almost new steam fleets. They didn't resist very long. N&W, the last to fall, bought its first diesel in 1955.

In 1953, Fairbanks-Morse's great *Trainmaster* started a horsepower race. At 2400 horsepower, this model was the king of road switchers. Alco countered with the 2400 horsepower DL-600, and Baldwin with its big RT-624 centercab at 2400 horsepower. But EMD, the leader, had nothing close to them until a major decision was made to turbocharge the 567 engine.

Turbocharging is the art of blowing an air-fuel mixture into the combustion chamber at high pressure, thus increasing the horsepower output of an engine without adding to its size or weight. All other major builders had been doing this for years, but the turbocharger unit itself was often a prime cause of breakdowns. After Union Pacific tests, EMD accepted UP's results; and building its first turbocharged unit, the 2400-horsepower SD-24, launched a new power race.

The race accelerated between 1960 and 1970. EMD fielded the very successful 2250-horsepower turbocharged GP-30, then the 2500-horsepower GP-35. Alco refined its DL-600 and fielded the 2400-horsepower RS-37. Then came a fresh blow for functional design: one industrial buyer saw no good reason for the high short end of the car body ahead of the cab, so he cut the hood in half and thus lowered the nose of his GP-9 for better visibility. EMD began offering the low-nosed design as an alternative on its GP-18. So many buyers requested this version that it soon became standard.

Meanwhile, in 1960, General Electric resurged in the big power field. Until then it had been content to build industrial designs and export units, besides supplying other builders with electrical gear. GE now marketed its Universal line of locos, at first for export only; but in 1960 its U-25B, at 2500 horsepower, made its mark on United States dieseldom.

Alco countered with the C-425, also 2500-horsepower, and EMD replied with the GP-35 at 2500 horsepower. Both Baldwin and Fairbanks-Morse quit the market, Baldwin in 1956 and F-M with a Mexican order in 1963. Then EMD, GE, and for a while Alco controlled the market, particularly EMD, which in some years captured 89 percent of it. The horsepower race continued, with all three big builders (until Alco quit) peaking at 3600 horsepower. Each of the trio built special twin-engined models for the Union Pacific and Southern Pacific, but these were not considered catalog models. Mightiest of the UP specials is EMD's 6600-horsepower DDA-40X.

Alco Products (formerly Alco), plagued with crankshaft problems and overshadowed by EMD's more liberal service policies, quit the new loco business in 1969, with a 4000-horsepower unit still on the drawing boards. Montreal Locomotive Works, which had been building Alco designs in Canada since 1904, bought Alco's engineering designs in 1969 and continued the Alco line.

EMD and General Electric thus became the two locomotive builders in the United States which produce railroad-size diesels. Other firms produce small industrial units. The horsepower race of the 1960s has ended; more is being done to perfect existing power plants. In 1966, EMD went to the new 645 power plant, offering a line of both turbocharged high-horsepower models and normally aspirated mid-range models. The GP and the SD, or six-motor, special-duty designs, are standard. EMD also markets one true switcher model and one multipurpose heavy switcher. General Electric persists with the FDL power plant in both 12- and 16-cylinder sizes. All GE units are turbocharged; their general styling has not changed since the U-25B.

Recent Developments With the coming of Amtrak and the need for new passenger locomotives, both EMD and GE have built what amount to modified cab units, with full-width front cabs and streamlined noses—not quite a throwback to the E units but not road-switcher designs either. The growing fuel crisis is bringing about greater efficiency. Computer techniques are being applied to diesels, as are more radio control, quicker starting, modular electrical components, and even a switch by which the engineer at any time can shut down units of the locomotive which aren't needed. *See* AMTRAK.

Rebuilding older units and leasing locos to power-short roads are effective modern developments. Upgrading of existing power plants, perfecting successful models, and replacing older models have been the goals instead of a rash of new models.

The predictable future will see greater horsepower being squeezed out of smaller prime movers with less appetite for fuel. More specialty units (such as EMD's new GP-15 and GE's U-18B) will be used in situations in which high-horsepower units are wasted. The new "crew comfort," or full-width, cab will see increasing acceptance, especially because railroad companies are cutting crew size and eliminating cabooses on mainline runs. In many cases the entire three-man crew occupies the locomotive cab.

Canadian Diesels Canadian dieselization closely followed that of the United States, except that the first diesel in Canada was a huge two-unit road loco, not a switcher. She appeared in 1929. Each unit had a 12-cylinder Beardmore 12- by 12-foot plant rated at 1330 horsepower, with a 2-D-1 (4-8-2) wheel arrangement. Canadian Locomotive Co. of Kingston, Ontario, built her; Westinghouse supplied the electrical gear. The coupled units represented, in 1929, the world's largest diesel and the world's first large diesel road unit. Canadian National (CN) numbered them 9000-9001.

CN also assembled at its Montreal shops a 300-horsepower 60-ton boxcab switcher using the GE-Ingersoll-Rand designs of 1932. Canadian divisions of United States companies supplied the parts to avoid import duty. And in 1937 Canadian Pacific took delivery of its first diesel, No. 7000, a big, boxy endcab switcher built by National Steel Car Corp. of Hamilton, Ontario, with an Irish-built Harland & Wolff prime mover rated at 550 horsepower. This locomotive worked until 1964, when it was donated to the Canadian Railroad Historical Museum.

Electro-Motive has a GM diesel division in London, Ontario. Both Baldwin and Fairbanks-Morse used the Canadian Locomotive Co., which also built its own line of small centercab switchers. Montreal Locomotive Works built Alco designs. General Electric has never sold a road locomotive in Canada, although Canadian GE has sold electrical gear and industrial switchers.

At this writing, GM Ltd. of London, Ontario, and Montreal Locomotive Works (which has recently been acquired by Bombardier Ltd.) are the two main Canadian builders. GM has the lion's share, as it has in the United States. The Montreal Locomotive Works acquired Alco's designs in 1969 and does a good domestic and export business. Its own designs have now taken over. The firm has even placed two units of its own design in the United States, as well as many locally and overseas.

Conclusion Diesel displaced steam because it is more efficient. Except for certain experimentals, steam's best efficiency was 10 percent or less. Modern diesels are regarded as 30 percent efficient and are getting better each year. Men in engine service resented them at first because they were new and unfamiliar. Die-hard steam aficionados still resent them. Even so, there is little doubt that the diesel saved American railroads from ruin after World War II. One drop of diesel fuel oil can pull a 100-ton freight car 8 inches. But the diesel faces a grave challenge because oil supplies are dwindling. Will the diesel, for that reason, go the same way as the steam power it replaced? Will the railroads of the future be run eventually be electricity generated by nuclear plants?

JAMES EDMONSTON

BIBLIOGRAPHY: Departments of the Army and Air Force, *Operation and Maintenance of Diesel-Electric Locomotives*, GPO, Washington, 1965; *Diesel-Electrics and How to Keep 'Em Rolling*, Simmons-Boardman, New York, 1954; E. C. Eck, *The Modern Locomotive Handbook; Extra 2200 South*, 1968——; *The Locomotive Cyclopedia of American Practice*, ed. by Roy V. Wright, Simmons-Boardman, New York, 1941; id., ed. by C. B. Peck, Simmons-Boardman, New York, 1950–1952; George F. McGowan, *Diesel-Electric Locomotive Handbook*, New York, Chicago, 1951; Robert P. Olmsted, *The Diesel Years*, Golden West Books, San Marino, Calif., 1975; Jerry A. Pinkepank, *The Second Diesel Spotter's Guide*, Kalmbach, Milwaukee, 1940; *Railroad Magazine*, 1940——; *Trains Magazine*, 1941——.

Diesel-Hydraulic Locomotives The United States had a brief spate of interest in the diesel-hydraulic loco, in which a diesel power plant was coupled with a hydraulic transmission, thus negating the need for generators, traction motors, or related electrical gear. In 1954, Electro-Motive Corp. applied a hydraulic transmission to a standard 800-horsepower SW-8 switcher, and in 1955 it demonstrated the unit at the Railroad Equipment Exhibition in Atlantic City, New Jersey. However, it was not a success and was refitted with standard electrical gear for use as the plant switcher at La Grange, Illinois.

Then, in 1961, the Southern Pacific (SP) and the Denver and Rio Grande Western (D&RGW) astounded United States builders by each importing three diesel-hydraulic road-freight units from Krauss-Maffei of Munich, Germany. These strange-looking locos had Maybach engines and Voith transmissions. The Rio Grande wasn't impressed, but the SP saw something it liked, and in 1963 it ordered 15 additional units, although in a road-switching (hood-unit) configuration. SP also bought Rio Grande's three units. However, within 5 years all six units had been scrapped.

Alco Products, evidently impressed by the Germans, built three big diesel-hydraulics with 4300 horsepower but the same Voith transmissions. SP took delivery of all three in September 1964. These became the last large diesel-hydraulics to run on American rails, the last being scrapped in 1973.

The underlying problem of diesel-hydraulics seems to be that no transmission yet developed will stand up under the terrific torque required to move freight over American rails. The companies that build industrial-size diesels of 52 tons or less have successfully offered hydraulic transmissions and even straight mechanical (clutch) transmissions. Perhaps if the Voith transmissions

The first diesel in Canada was a two-unit road loco, not a switcher as in the United States. The coupled units pictured below represented, in 1929, the world's largest diesel and first large diesel road unit. *[Canadian National Railways]*

had been used on the old water-level New York Central (where the D&RGW units did demonstrate) or down in Florida on passenger expresses, they would have had better maintenance records. Certainly, the diesel-hydraulic has won more favor in Europe, where trains are much lighter. The issue isn't dead. Many economies could be realized if a transmission could be built to stand the mainline strain. JAMES EDMONSTON

BIBLIOGRAPHY: C. B. Peck (ed.), *The Locomotive Cyclopedia of American Practice*, Simmons-Boardman, New York, 1950–1952.

Diesel Operation Theoretically, one engineman in the controlling unit can handle any number of diesel locomotive units in a multiple-unit train. Pneumatic connections allow him to control the airbrakes on the other units independently of the rest of the train, applying and releasing locomotive brakes while the train brakes are set or released. Pneumatic pressure also lets him operate the sanders on all units. Electrical jumpers relay back to the engineman information on overload, wheel slip, hot engine, etc., from the other locomotive units.

The strength of the couplers and draft gear governs the practical limit on the number of head-end operable units. Excessive tractive effort at one end of the train could pull knuckles or do other damage. The maximum starting tractive effort exerted by five GP- or F-type diesel units is the maximum safe limit for draft gear. But to start heavy trains or move them over grades more than five units can be used, supplying maximum tractive effort, if they are placed in the middle or at the rear of the train. A system devised by Union Switch & Signal Co. allows the engineman in the lead engine to control the throttle and brakes of the helper engine more than a mile away. Either radio or inductive communications are used to bridge the gap between the two engines.

Diesel versus Steam For at least 125 years, North American steam did a great job of hauling trains through snow, sleet, and ice. But today's diesel locomotive is conquering weather conditions even more efficiently. Extreme cold has relatively little effect on its mobile power plant. Another reason for diesel superiority over steam in terms of weather is the way in which its driving wheels are spaced out beneath the locomotive. A four-unit, 6000-horsepower diesel, for example, has wheels located at intervals over about 190 feet of track. Furthermore, unlike the automobile, diesel road power needs only slight winterizing to prepare it for long cold spells. Usually, the only precaution needed is shutting off some air intakes along the engine-room walls to keep out the swirling snow.

Each diesel unit has a streamlined nose designed, among other reasons, to plow through all but huge snowdrifts, tossing aside the snow onto both sides of the track. Even on slippery rails, its four front wheels find enough traction to keep them revolving, and behind them as many as 28 powerful driving wheels grip the rails tenaciously. Such units nearly always can push through a severe blizzard of fast-accumulating snow that would stop everything else. However, diesel-powered trains have been snowbound for various lengths of time. A Union Pacific streamliner was buried in the snow for about a week at Donner Pass in the Sierra Nevada, where in 1840 the Donner emigrant party had been forced to spend the winter without adequate food, supplies, or shelter and 34 of its members perished. There were no casualties on the streamliners.

The average diesel loco can be counted upon for operating up to 6000 miles without any maintenance other than fuel oil, lubrication, cooling water, sand supplies, and signal appliances, plus occasional inspection trips to engine terminals. Only on rare occasions could a steam engine equal that common diesel record.

Diesel units on very heavy freight duty need fuel-oil service about every 350 miles. Canadian National Railways (CN) changes the lube after each 2500 miles. Also, by taking at such times tests of lubricating-oil samples for quality control, it can often extend lube service life to mileages even above 100,000. CN has running shops at Montreal, Moncton, and Winnipeg, where diesel power nearing the 6000-mile mark is given a complete inspection. Other big rail systems have comparable facilities.

BIBLIOGRAPHY: *The Locomotive Cyclopedia of American Practice*, ed. by Roy V. Wright, Simmons-Boardman, New York, 1941; id., ed. by C. B. Peck, Simmons-Boardman, New York, 1950–1952.

Dining Car, All-Electric The first such car on any railroad was designed and built by Edison–General Electric Appliance Co. in the mid-1940s for the Illinois Central. It was modeled after an electric galley developed for use on submarines in World War II. Generators placed beneath the car floor produced adequate power.

Dining Cars The first food sold to passengers on trains probably came from members of farm families standing beside the track at station stops—a practice followed today in many other countries. In early-day rail travel such items as candy, cookies, and soft drinks were peddled by train boys (later called news butchers) up and down the aisles of coaches, in addition to magazines, booklets, playing cards, cigars, souvenirs, and sometimes water. *See* NEWS BUTCHER.

In 1848 the Baltimore & Ohio experimented with serving simple meals like oyster stew, crullers, and hot coffee in two converted coaches, the stew being featured because Chesapeake Bay in B&O territory has long been famous for its prolific oyster beds.

In 1867 George M. Pullman designed and built a hotel car and tried it out on the Great Western. It was a combination diner and sleeper with berths, a kitchen, and removable tables set between the seats at mealtimes. This car was widely ballyhooed when inaugurated between New York and Chicago. Typical prices on the menu were sugar-cured ham, 40 cents; beefsteak and potatoes, 60 cents; and Welsh rabbit, 50 cents. In 1868 Pullman produced his first all-dining car and named it *Delmonico* for a New York restaurateur. Tried out on the Chicago & Alton, it became so popular that Pullman began building diners for other roads also. But for years some roads continued to make meal stops at certain points along the line where they had trackside restaurants geared to serve many travelers quickly. From this practice evolved the chain of Harvey depot restaurants on the Santa Fe. *See* HARVEY, FREDERICK HENRY; PULLMAN, GEORGE MORTIMER.

In 1882 the Pennsylvania Railroad announced that it was introducing the finest dining cars yet seen in America. Four of these cars were operated. Each contained eight tables, a silver-adorned sideboard of carved mahogany, plate glass, and wine closets. The chairs, upholstered in deep carmine velvet plush, folded back for easy access to the tables. Carved mahogany abounded, with a clerestory of stained glass, magnificent big chandeliers, and silver sconces holding red candles. The cars had thick Wilton carpet on the floor, carmine and gold-olive velvet plush window curtains on silver rods, and partitions inlaid with heavy plate glass. Attached to each dining car was an equally luxurious lounge-smoking car with a comfortable sofa, large plush armchairs, a baggage compartment, a writing desk, and a well-stocked bookcase.

Thereafter, the major railroads competed by offering gourmet food in handsome diners on their first-class trains. It is doubtful if any of them ever made money on any kind of dining-car service, although at one time the New Haven claimed to be an exception in that respect. The roads boosted rail passenger travel by absorbing the dining-car losses.

But when motor vehicles and planes cut too sharply into this business, the railroads economized increasingly on diner service by serving less varied and lower-grade meals without frills, using, for example, paper napkins instead of fine linen, serving compressed airplane-style meals on trays to passengers in day-coach seats, adopting cafeteria-type service, and on some trains even using slot machines for sandwiches, soup, coffee, etc.

A far cry from today's railroad snack cars, the Turquoise Room of the Santa Fe's Super Chief was one of the first private dining rooms on an American train. [Santa Fe Railway]

BIBLIOGRAPHY: Lucius Beebe and Charles Clegg, *The Trains We Rode*, 2 vols., Howell-North, Berkeley, Calif., 1965–1966; Will C. Hollister, *Dinner on the Diner: Great Railroad Recipes of All Time*, Trans-Anglo Books, Corona Del Mar, Calif., 1965.

Direct Steaming Technique whereby a locomotive was run out of the enginehouse without fire in her grates to save time and fuel and reduce smoke and gas nearby. Her boiler was connected to a stationary steam and hot-water plant, which built up a working pressure in the boiler in less than half the time. Under her own steam, the loco was run to a special firing-up track, where an employee lit her fire and brought the engine up to working condition very quickly, even for heavy freight and fast passenger trains. Incoming locomotives reversed the process. One direct-steaming substation reported a 20 percent saving in the cost of bringing an engine's steam up to working pressure plus a marked reduction in smoke and gas around the enginehouse.

Discovery Train The fully bilingual *La Découverte*, comparable to the American Freedom Train (AFT) of 1975–1976, set out in mid-1978 on a 5-year tour of the Dominion under auspices of the National Museums of Canada (NMC), four Canadian foundations, and four venerable Canadian commercial corporations. It is a mobile museum on a grand scale, ¼ mile long. Powered by diesel locomotives, it consists of 15 railway cars externally painted red, white, and silver, with streamers flying and with generalized portraits of historical figures, circuslike, adorning the car sides. Inside, it displays more than 1200 historical items, loaned by the country's museums, and has audiovisual and electronic equipment dramatizing Canada's natural, economic, and political aspects. *See* FREEDOM TRAIN, AMERICAN.

The train's purpose, according to NMC's Brian Segal, is to "generate a sense of excitement about our history and to improve our sense of mutual understanding in a country so geographically and culturally diverse." He adds: "The train says that with all this diversity we can still have a strong national character."

Its crew of 62 includes enginemen and trainmen, technicians, security guards, guides, and public relations and liaison officers. The itinerary serves both large and small population centers; 9 million people are expected to view its exhibits during the 5 years. The train is open between 7 and 12 hours a day for nearly 100 days each year. Since Newfoundland's narrow-gauge Canadian National rails could not hold the standard-gauge train, the public in that area was permitted to visit it in 1979 aboard a large CN ferry. For Prince Edward Island and Vancouver the entire caravan was ferried from the mainland and reassembled on the islands' railway lines.

You can enter the train for a colorful 35-minute tour of Canada. Boarding the rear car, you walk through a three-car "Discover Canada" series of exhibits that starts with a sandy cove in one of the Atlantic provinces and leads into a simulated Arctic blizzard, then through a darkened tunnel shaped like a giant Douglas fir, in which tree rings check off events in Canada's past back to approximately the year 1000 B.C.

In the fourth car from the rear you step onto a sidewalk moving at the rate of 30 feet a minute and extending continuously through 10 cars. You view prehistoric man, aboriginal Inuits and Indians, Jacques Cartier's exploring voyage and New France (1534–1689), British North America (1689–1885), a fur-trading post, animated Confederation scenes with life-size historical figures, immigration, the Klondike gold rush, the industrial boom, both world wars, the Depression of the 1930s, and scenes of the present. Included are 13 film shows, 30 slide shows, 30 videotape shows, 80 sound tracks, 80 animated figures in 10 cars, 2 audioanimatronic manikins, 19 animated manikins, 60 sound scenes, 37 special effects, and 80 lighting scenes. Car No. 14 is devoted to folk art, humor, and fantasy.

The germ of the Discovery Train was the six-car Centennial Train that toured the country in 1967 under federal auspices. In considering the possibility of the later venture, NMC officials decided at first that its cost was prohibitive. Then the American Freedom Train Foundation, having completed its own tour south of the Canadian border, sold the Canadians its equipment at a bargain price of $575,000, including about $6 million worth of rolling stock, moving walkways, audiovisual and fire-fighting apparatus, and the generators of the 15 cars.

Nine provinces combined to finance the deal, each paying in proportion to its population. In August 1977 a locomotive hauled the 15 former AFT cars (originally New York Central equipment of the late 1940s) from Washington, D.C., to Fort Erie, Ontario. Then the Canadian National Railways wheeled them to Ottawa for refitting, for which eight Canadian foundations and commercial corporations donated $2,387,000.

CN and CP Rail agreed to operate the train for nothing with their own crews. Ottawa financed the staffing and running. The project progressed from the designers' drawing boards to scale models of each display car. CN shops repainted the cars. Artisans, designers, engineers, filmmakers, and technicians from across Canada went to work inside the cars. Special lighting effects and other electronic devices were installed. The completed caravan, called the Discovery Train, officially began its seasonal 5-year tour on July 22, 1978, from Kingston, Ontario, with a historic old steam locomotive from the National Museum of Science and Technology in Ottawa. Soon, however, diesel-electrics replaced steam power.

Disney, Walt ***(1901–1966)*** Probably America's most distinguished railfan. "I have always loved trains," he once said. Born in Chicago as Walter Elias Disney, he created Mickey Mouse and many other animated-cartoon characters; built Disneyland, a 300-acre amusement park at Anaheim, California, and its steam-powered Disneyland & Santa Fe Railway; produced a long list of movies, including *The Great Locomotive Chase*, in 1956, telling the story of the Andrews railroad raid; and won 30 Academy Awards before he died at Los Angeles. *See* ANDREWS RAILROAD RAID.

At 15 he worked as a news butcher on passenger trains of the Santa Fe, Missouri Pacific, Kansas City Southern, and Katy, selling magazines, soft drinks, fruit, peanuts, candy, cigars, etc. *See* NEWS BUTCHER.

"I felt very important wearing a neat blue serge uniform with brass buttons, a peaked cap, and a shiny badge," he wrote in *Railroad Magazine:*

> As the train rolled into one station after another, I stood beside the conductor on the car steps to enjoy the envious stares of youngsters waiting on the platform. . . . My railroad career was brief, exciting, and unprofitable. Too many people were eager to take advantage of a young business man like myself. The suppliers, for example, would fill my hamper with rotten fruit. This drew so many flies that the conductor would make me dump it out, and I was stuck with the cost. Besides, I was only 15 and I ate up most of my profits. So I quit at the end of that summer with losses that absorbed the $30 bond I had posted when I took the job.

His next experience with trains, except as a passenger, occurred after he married and was living in Beverly Hills and drawing cartoons for a studio. He decided to build a midget railroad:

> I went about it systematically. After serving an apprenticeship in a machine shop, I studied metalwork and carpentry before I figured I was ready to start building. Then I built a train to ⅛ scale. The engine and tender combined was 7 feet long and operated on coal and water, like the ones I had known as a news butcher.
>
> The boxcars were big enough for a person to straddle, and the flatcars could seat two. My special pride was the caboose, which I finished entirely in miniature, right down to the pot-bellied stove. The engine was designed after one that had run on the old Central Pacific, so I named my little railroad the CP, for Carolwood Pacific, the street I lived on.
>
> All my planning worked out perfectly except for one factor, my wife. She didn't take kindly to the idea of having a railroad run around the house, and told me so in no uncertain terms. . . . I went to my lawyer and had him draw up a right-of-way agreement giving me permission to operate the railroad on the property. My wife signed it and my daughter witnessed the agreement. I figured out a route around the place, but it required a six-foot cut in one of the slopes. This time my wife put her foot down. So I compromised by building a tunnel 90 feet long and covering it with dirt.

One day the engine was wrecked just after leaving the tunnel:

> She rolled over, her stack and pilot cracking off. Then she lay there, hissing and belching steam like a dying monster. Mrs. Disney was sympathetic. Thus I had finally succeeded in getting her on my side in the railroad operation—though I had to wreck a train to do it.
>
> Then Disneyland Park came along. I had the excitement of creating an honest-to-goodness railroad—well, ⅝ scale, anyway—the Disneyland & Santa Fe. We built the two larger engines, Nos. 1 and 2, at the studio from the same plans I had used for the midget train. Later, in Southern lumber mills, we found two old chassis, with wheels, on which we built two more locomotives, Nos. 3 and 4. The latter was made to look as much as possible like the old *Montezuma*, No. 1, of the Denver & Rio Grande.

Dodge, Grenville Mellen ***(1831–1916)*** A native of Danvers, Massachusetts, at 14 he helped to build a spur line from the Eastern Railroad of Massachusetts to an abandoned church being converted into an icehouse. In 1851 he went west to join an Illinois Central (IC) surveying party. Later, he helped to make Iowa's first railroad survey, for the Rock Island, in a spectacular rail-laying race with the IC and the Chicago & North Western for the frontier hamlet of Council Bluffs. In 1859 Abraham Lincoln visited Council Bluffs and had a talk with Dodge that was destined to make rail history.

"Dodge," the future President asked, "what's the best route to the West for a Pacific railroad?"

Dodge's face brightened. "Right out from Council Bluffs through the Platte River valley," he said.

"What makes you think so?"

"Because of the railroads now building to this town from Chicago," answered Dodge. But before such a project could be started, the Civil War intervened. Dodge was commissioned a colonel of the 4th Iowa Infantry, later becoming a major general, and was wounded in two battles. His skill in building and repairing bridges and railroads increased his value to the Union Army.

Laying the Union Pacific track in Nebraska Territory in 1866 with expensive wooden ties. The completion of the UP track was General Dodge's greatest engineering achievement. [Collection of Freeman Hubbard]

In 1866 he resigned from the Army to become chief engineer for the Union Pacific Railroad Company (UP), which an act of Congress had created in 1862. He was well qualified for this post. UP promoters also figured shrewdly on Dodge's influence with Generals Grant and Sherman, who were then the nation's popular idols. Most of the construction workers were war veterans, both Northern and Southern. They worked with weapons nearby to repel Indian raids. Dodge often called for protective help from the Army post at Fort Kearney, Nebraska. From that point to Bitter Creek, Wyoming, every mile of railroad had to be surveyed, graded, tracklaid, and bridged under military protection.

One of Dodge's major problems was to find a route through the Black Hills or Laramie Mountains of Wyoming. This he solved in a peculiar manner. While he was reconnoitering with only six men in southeastern Wyoming, the Indians ambushed him. In escaping, the party came upon Frazer Pass, which proved to be the very outlet the road needed. This chance discovery saved the company considerable money that otherwise would have been spent on building over the mountains, besides lessening the grades for future trains to climb. In general, skillful engineering kept the grades within a maximum of 90 feet to the mile (less than 2 percent). Dodge's sturdy trailblazers erected a bridge over Dale Creek about 700 feet long and more than 130 feet high. Another arduous task was thrusting steel from Dale Creek down to the Laramie plains in Wyoming, with much cutting through solid rock.

Completion of Chicago & North Western trackage to Omaha in 1867 had supplied a channel for the steady flow of material for the new UP line pushing westward. Omaha was a busy terminal on civilization's frontier, and plenty of railroad jobs were available to all boomers who drifted out that way. Whenever possible, ties were hewn from nearby timber, but when hardwood could not be had, cottonwood was burnettized, i.e., submerged in zinc chloride to make it more durable. At times, loads of ties had to be hauled so far that they cost $6 apiece. More than once extreme cold forced the shivering, exhausted men to make great bonfires from the high-priced lumber in order to stay alive. Dodge reported grimly that building over the Wasatch Range added about $10 million to the cost of the gigantic enterprise.

But the Central Pacific (CP), battling eastward from Sacramento at the same time, had even greater expense for hauling supplies. Aside from such items as ties, timber, and masonry, most CP material had to be brought from the Eastern seaboard, not cross-country, but on ships sailing all the way around Cape Horn, the southern tip of South America.

Tension grew as the two transcontinental railroads approached each other because federal money was being paid for each mile of track. Probably the most exciting railroad construction race in history was the tracklaying rivalry which began when the Union Pacific was 57 miles east of Promontory, Utah, and the Central Pacific 54 miles west of that point. Each side had about 2500 workmen. The fastest tracklaying month was April 1869, with each road pushing ahead at the amazing rate of 5 miles a day. On May 10 they jointly laid the last tie—one of California laurel, finely polished and bearing a silver-plated inscription. With the triumphant driving of the golden spike by officials of both roads that day the twin bands of steel united the two oceans. General Dodge's greatest job was finished. *See also* GOLDEN SPIKE CEREMONY.

In March 1871, Dodge was elected to the Union Pacific board of directors with Andrew Carnegie, George M. Pullman, and other celebrities. Col. Thomas Scott, then president of the UP and also vice president (and a future president) of the rapidly growing Pennsylvania Railroad, offered Dodge the post of chief engineer of the incipient Texas & Pacific Railway (T&P), which the Pennsy controlled. Nothing pleased the general more than to build a new rail line.

T&P had bought the property and franchises of two other roads, the Southern Pacific and the Southern Transcontinental, besides securing a charter and land grants of more than 31 million acres (most of it then worth about 35 cents an acre), and also the property of the old San Diego & Eastern. So Dodge became a heavy stockholder in T&P, along with three Pennsy executives and locomotive builder Matthew Baird. The embryo road was to be as long as the UP and CP combined, running from Marshall, Texas, to San Diego, California. When Dodge took over, the line had been built as far as Longview, Texas. Under his driving power, it was completed to Dallas in the spring of 1873.

Yellow fever killed the workers like flies. Shotgun quarantines enforced at Shreveport, Louisiana, and Dallas made it very hard for Dodge to get men or supplies, but the chief engineer, using convict labor, stuck to his post. Then, in 1873, the collapse of Jay Cooke & Co., Wall Street bankers, brought on a national panic that ruined Colonel Scott and halted the Texas & Pacific's onward march. Jay Gould and Russell Sage took over the bankrupt T&P, and by 1876 Dodge had completed its line as far west as Fort Worth. At the same time he was pushing the International & Great Northern from San Antonio to Laredo and began building the New Orleans & Pacific from Shreveport. *See* GOULD, JAY.

After that, Dodge became president of the Missouri-Kansas-Texas, better known as the Katy, and vice president of the Mexican & Southern, of which General Grant was president. With Gould's money, they built a railroad from Laredo to Mexico City.

During most of his life Dodge handled railroad problems in a big way. A cholera epidemic kept him from building the Trans-Siberian Railway, but he served as president of the Union Pacific, Denver & Gulf until the panic of 1873 threw it into receivership. Later, in association with William Van Horne, president of the Canadian Pacific, he built a railway in Cuba. Dodge wrote *Battle of Atlanta and Other Campaigns, How We Built the Union Pacific Railroad,* and *Personal Recollections of Lincoln, Grant, and Sherman.*

BIBLIOGRAPHY: J. R. Perkins, *Trails, Rails and War,* Bobbs-Merrill, Indianapolis, 1929; Robert E. Riegel, *The Story of the Western Railroads,* University of Nebraska Press, Lincoln, 1944; Edwin L. Sabin, *Building the Pacific Railway,* Lippincott, Philadelphia, 1919; Nelson Trottman, *History of the Union Pacific,* Ronald, New York, 1973.

Dogs Railroaders' favorite mascots have always been dogs. Before the days of diesel locomotives and automation, you could have found many of them in and around depots, switch shanties, crew rooms, roundhouses, signal towers, freight yards, warehouses, and repair shops. The average railroad mutt was a stray of doubtful antecedents who wandered onto company property, was adopted by one or more workers, and made himself or herself useful as well as companionable. Even today, more than a few canine mascots claim the right-of-way as their home, but their number is dwindling.

A typical case was Jack. One hot summer night a bleeding, exhausted shepherd pup, with sore foot pads indicating that he had journeyed a long way, dragged himself into Peach Springs, Arizona, a desert town. The Santa Fe station agent there, A. M. Browning, bandaged his paws and named him Jack. It was nearly a month before the animal could walk normally again. The agent taught him tricks.

Besides chasing occasional burros and horses from his master's yard, Jack retrieved train-order hoops or forks. These are lightweight loops with a handle, shaped somewhat like large, hollow tennis rackets, in the crotch of which tissue-paper train orders are inserted. The agent or telegraph operator delivered orders to trains that did not stop at his station by passing up the orders, one set to the engine crew and another to the train crew. Three sets of orders were needed for a doubleheader train. A station signal warned the men in advance to reach for them, pretty much as carousel riders snatch at the brass ring. The trainmen quickly removed the orders and threw back the empty hoops or forks for the agent to pick up and reuse. A train rolling 40 or more miles per hour travels quite a distance before this happens, so Jack saved his master many miles of hiking in a month's time.

When Browning died, H. W. Hutchinson took his job, and the bereft dog was given to a state policeman. "He refused to stay with his new owner," Hutchinson said:

> Every morning when I opened the station I'd find Jack waiting patiently to get in, and I'd have to put him out at closing time. During the day he retrieved train-order hoops for me. You just couldn't get rid of such a dog, so I decided to keep

him. Sometimes it took him as long as 30 minutes to find hoops dropped into weeds, but he invariably brought them back. If one fell under a train and was broken, he'd return with the pieces, one or two at a time.

Each morning train No. 8 would toss off a small roll of newspapers. Jack would catch it, rarely missing, although the train didn't slow up when the baggageman threw it. The dog's reputation spread far and wide. Twice, Hollywood movie scouts stopped off at my depot and offered me a good price for Jack, to take him to the movie capital, but I refused to sell him. Today that dog lies buried beside the track.

The best known of all raildogs, a Scotch-Irish terrier of dubious pedigree, took up his abode in the Albany, New York, Post Office one night in 1892. The night clerks adopted him as "our own" dog, naming him Owney. A few weeks later, a Railway Mail clerk took him on a round trip to New York City. Thereafter, Owney spent most of his time traveling in Railway Post Office cars as mascot.

He accumulated a large collection of tags, medals, and other souvenirs given to him in nearly every state of the Union and several Canadian provinces, even a medal bestowed by the Emperor of Japan when he visited the Far East. In all, Owney traveled about 143,000 miles, mostly by rail. In 1907 he was shot dead for some unrecorded reason. His pelt was stuffed, widely exhibited, and at last reports stored at the General Post Office in Washington, D.C.

BIBLIOGRAPHY: Freeman Hubbard, *Railroad Avenue*, McGraw-Hill, New York, 1945.

Drew, Daniel ***(1797–1879)*** Known as the Great Bear of Wall Street, Drew was one of three major looters of the Erie Railroad through speculation in its securities. Born in Carmel, New York, he grew up on his father's farm with meager schooling. At 15 he began driving livestock to New York City from upstate and later from the Midwest. On one occasion he bought a large herd of starved cattle cheaply and arranged to sell them to wealthy fur trader John Jacob Astor's brother Henry, who was a New York butcher. Drew drove his herd to pasture, dumped sacks of salt over the grass, and would not let the thirst-maddened animals drink until just before the buyer's arrival. Then they gorged themselves on water, which made them look fat and heavy. Henry Astor paid a good price for them. When the truth came out, Wall Streeters chuckled and coined the now-common term *watered stock*.

Drew, who was gaunt, wily, and pious, got rich from one shady deal after another. His business ethics were typical of the post-Civil War era of industrial expansion. Entering the Hudson River steamboat field in 1834, he challenged Commodore Cornelius Vanderbilt's dominance of it. He established a Wall Street brokerage house and began edging his way into the Erie, a prosperous 773-mile road. *See* VANDERBILT, CORNELIUS.

The Erie directors needed money. By 1855 Drew had loaned them nearly $2 million at high interest, which they could not repay. This permitted Drew to take over the railroad himself and, signficantly, become its treasurer. Vanderbilt was then America's richest man and owner of the New York Central & Hudson River Railroad. In 1866 he bought stock control of the Erie and, to his later regret, kept Drew on the board. Vanderbilt aimed to use Drew as his right-hand man, largely because of the Great Bear's uncanny ability in juggling the market. But the farmer's son who had milked cattle as a boy milked the railroad in complicity with Jay Gould and Jubilee Jim Fisk. For details, including Vanderbilt's raid on Erie stock, *see* FISK, JAMES.

But Gould and Fisk double-crossed Drew also. After persuading him to leave the Erie management by giving him the profit on this deal, the two men staged another big-scale manipulation of stock without letting him in on their secret intentions. The Great Bear plunged heavily and lost heavily. The panic of 1873 completed his ruin, sending him into bankruptcy. He never regained his wealth. He said of Gould, "His touch is death." When Drew died in New York in 1879, he was a financial derelict. Before losing his riches, he had built and supported churches and the Drew Theological Seminary in Madison, New Jersey, and Drew Seminary for Young Ladies in his native Carmel.

BIBLIOGRAPHY: Matthew Josephson, *The Robber Barons*, Harcourt, Brace, New York, 1934; Gustavus Myers, *History of the Great American Fortunes*, 3 vols., Charles H. Kerr & Company, Chicago, 1910; Bouck White, *Book of Daniel Drew*, Doubleday, Page, New York, 1910.

Dreyfuss, Henry ***(1904–   )*** Stage and industrial designer who streamlined and otherwise helped to modernize New York Central's elite passenger train, the *20th Century Limited*, long a competitor of the Pennsylvania's *Broadway Limited*. *See* SPEED WAR.

His first major job after opening his New York office in 1929 was developing, in cooperation with Bell Telephone's engineering staff, the company's familiar phone receiver handset with plastic rather than metal housing and with the ringing apparatus in the instrument itself instead of in a box on the wall. Among the many other products Dreyfuss designed were the Big Ben alarm clock, Polaroid camera, Singer sewing machine, John Deere tractor, two ocean liners, and a jet-aircraft interior.

Drinking Cups, Individual Such cups were introduced to train passengers by the Delaware, Lackawanna & Western, according to the *American Engineer and Railroad Journal* of July 1909, which stated:

> The DL&W has installed in the cars on some of its best passenger trains, an apparatus for delivering individual paper drinking cups to the passengers. The arrangement is such that each cup used must be either destroyed or carried

away and each passenger takes a fresh cup which has been manufactured and put in the machine without being touched by the hands.

Prior to that, train riders drank faucet water from the same tin cup unless they brought along their own cups or glasses. Before the days of train faucets, a boy would lug a bucket of water and a tin cup through the cars, selling cups of water.

Dudley, Plimmon Henry ***(1843-1924)*** Author of three major inventions that caused him to be known as "the father of high-speed trains": (1) the dynamometer car to measure locomotive drawbar pull, (2) the track indicator to record irregularities in the track (not to be confused with the rail detector car, which pinpoints internal fissures in steel rails); and (3) the stremmatograph to determine stresses in rail caused by locomotives and cars. Instead of capitalizing on these devices, the inventor turned them over freely to the entire railroad industry for the public's benefit.

When Dudley was born on a farm in New Freedom, Ohio, the nation had only about 4000 miles of railroad track; 80½ years later, when he died, that figure had been multiplied nearly 100-fold. The story of this expansion is closely identified with his career. After studying engineering and metallurgy in college and marrying Lucy May Bronson, Dudley became chief engineer for the Valley Railway of Ohio. His first invention, the dynamometer car, dates from that period. This recording apparatus told motive-power officials exactly what results they were getting from the expenditure of steam power.

From 1880 to 1924 he was consulting engineer on rails, tires, and structural steel for the New York Central & Hudson River Railroad. During the period 1902-1915 he was largely responsible for the reduction from 1 in 600 to 1 in 142,000 in the number of broken rails on the Central. That means that the chances of accidents due to broken rails on this road were 24 times greater in 1902 than in 1915.

Dudley advanced the then-revolutionary theory that the T rail was designed on the same principle as that of the iron girder and, if stiff enough, would sustain the weight of passing trains on a smooth, level surface with no sag. This theory, which is generally accepted today, failed at that time to impress railroad officials and so-called steel experts. So Dudley set about to prove it with his second invention, the track indicator. If a rail were ⅛ inch or more off center, this machine squirted white or green paint on it, thus notifying trackmen of defects to be corrected. With this and other data, officials could plan track-improvement programs more intelligently.

Plimmon H. Dudley, "the father of high-speed trains," at work in his laboratory. [New York Central Railroad]

Dudley's third invention, the stremmatograph, was intended to clinch the argument regarding the action of too light rails under traffic. The instrument is placed beneath the base of a rail in such a way as to register and permanently record the stresses caused by each wheel passing over it. Stremmatograph records, readable only through a powerful microscope, furnished incontrovertible proof of the need for heavier rails.

The Central built a special private car to house these three inventions. Costing $150,000, it was the most expensive car built up to that time. This laboratory on wheels was fitted up with living quarters for Dr. and Mrs. Dudley.

Dudley designed a new, heavier, and higher rail section with a broad, flat, thin head. His design increased rail strength by 68 percent by adding only 23 percent in weight. It permitted the use of heavier rolling stock and led to the building by the Central in 1889 of the first American-type 100-ton locomotive. This, in turn, made possible the world's first heavy high-speed train, the *Empire State Express*, which ran for many years between New York and Buffalo. Later, Dudley redesigned the T rail to stand even greater stress.

E

E&K *See* ERIE & KALAMAZOO RAILROAD.

Eastman, Joseph Bartlett (1882–1944) The only Federal Coordinator of Railroads in United States history. Eastman was given that title by President Franklin D. Roosevelt in 1933 under terms of the Emergency Railroad Transportation Act. After he had served 3 years, Congress refused to renew the office. Besides drawing up plans to rehabilitate the railroads in Depression years, Eastman had the impossible job of trying to regulate them so as to eliminate waste and "unnecessary duplication of services and facilities."

Eden Wreck United States railroad catastrophe with the highest-known fatality list after the one at Nashville, Tennessee. In 1904 all railroads serving St. Louis, where the Louisiana Purchase Exposition was being held, offered special excursion rates to passengers wishing to visit that world's fair. One of the trains involved was the *Denver, Kansas City & St. Louis Express*, operated by the Denver and Rio Grande Railroad between Denver and Pueblo, Colorado, and by the Missouri Pacific on the rest of its long run. *See* NASHVILLE WRECK.

On the evening of August 7, 1904, the train leaving Denver consisted of 10-wheeled engine No. 1009, a baggage car, a chair car, a coach, two Pullman sleepers, and a diner and had 162 persons aboard, including railroad employees. It left Colorado Springs at 7:10 p.m., made a brief flag stop at Fountain, and was due in Pueblo at 8:15 p.m., but was running late.

At 8:20 it rolled onto Bridge 110-B in the hamlet of Eden, 5½ miles north of Pueblo, at about 18 miles per hour. This bridge spanned Fountain Creek in Hogan's Gulch. Recent rains had weakened it. As soon as the heavy engine was completely on the bridge, its timbers began cracking. The terrified engineer, Henry S. Hinman, speeded up in an effort to get his train across before the bridge collapsed. But the engine's pilot trucks and front drivers had barely reached the south bank when the locomotive started to slip backward. With a horrendous din the bridge broke, sending the engineer down to death in the 1009.

The fireman, David C. Mayfield, leaped out of the cab headfirst just before it fell. Landing in the 2-foot-deep creek, he was swept downstream into floodwaters, but managed to escape onto dry land. Then, looking up, he actually saw the engine fall. The first three cars followed, while passengers were screaming in terror, but the automatic action of airbrakes kept the two Pullmans and the dining car from joining them. A relief train took the Pullman and dining-car passengers to Pueblo. From there the Missouri Pacific conveyed them to their destinations.

A coroner's jury investigating the accident cleared the engine and train crew of blame for the wreck but criticized the D&RG for not having built a stronger bridge. A major cause of the disaster was a flash flood rushing down from the hills in a wall of water which destroyed a weaker wagon bridge 1000 feet farther upstream and weakened the railroad bridge. Eden's death toll has never been determined exactly. The Interstate Commerce Commission figure of 88 is probably much too low. According to the Federal Railroad Administration, Bureau of Railroad Safety, the official fatality list totaled 96 (including at least 22 known dead whose bodies were never recovered). There may have been more bodies that were not found. It is even possible that the Eden fatalities exceeded those of any other North American railroad wreck.

BIBLIOGRAPHY: Wesley S. Griswold, *Train Wreck!*, Stephen Greene, Brattleboro, Vt., 1969; Dow Helmers, *Tragedy at Eden*, Swallow Press, Chicago, 1971; Robert C. Reed, *Train Wrecks*, Superior Publishing, Seattle, 1968; Robert B. Shaw, *A History of Railroad Accidents, Safety Precautions, and Operating Practices*, Northern Press, Potsdam, N.Y., 1978.

EL *See* ERIE LACKAWANNA RAILWAY.

Electric Railways, Interurban *See* INTERURBAN ELECTRIC RAILWAYS.

Electrification Railroad electrification was sparked by Thomas Davenport's exhibition of a toy electric railway at Springfield, Massachusetts, in 1835. Twenty-two years later, Prof. Charles G. Page of the Smithsonian Institution ran a battery-powered car from Washington, D.C., to Bladensburg, Maryland, 5 miles, in 39 minutes. Then, in 1880, Thomas A. Edison toyed with electric traction at Menlo Park, New Jersey, and claimed to have invented the electric locomotive, which, however, a German, Wilhelm Siemens, had invented and demonstrated the year before by hauling three carloads of passengers at 8 miles per hour in the Berlin Exposition.

On June 27, 1895, a sturdy 34-foot electric loco, with General Electric's William Cooper at the control switch, made history by running through the 7300-foot Howard Street tunnel of the Baltimore Belt Line at Baltimore, Maryland, pulling a standard-weight steam train, locomotive and all. That "juice" loco, No. 1, developed 56,000 pounds of drawbar pull, which in those days was amazing.

Elsewhere, the need for electrification was emphasized by several collisions (one of which killed 15 people) of steam trains operated under street overpasses in the New York Central's midtown Park Avenue cut in New York City because of poor visibility from smoke and steam. Public indignation, fanned by yellow journalism, led to passage of a law prohibiting the use of steam engines in passenger service on tracks on Manhattan Island after July 1, 1908.

Forced to electrify this very important mainline, New York Central officials studied the Baltimore & Ohio's installation, which operated on 650-volt direct current, fed by a two-rail overhead catenary system to inclined pantographs atop the locomotives. By 1902, however, a well-protected third-rail setup had replaced the original B&O network.

Profiting by B&O's example, the Central built powerhouses with a total capacity of 60,000 kilowatts at Port Morris and Glenwood. Either of these two facilities could feed the entire third-rail network which the Vanderbilts installed for 32 miles from Grand Central Station (later Terminal) to Harmon (32 miles) and White Plains (22 miles). At Harmon and at White Plains trains changed from electric to steam locomotives and vice versa. Duplicate transmission lines were laid, together with a storage-battery system, further to assure an uninterrupted flow of 600-volt current in an emergency. After February 1907 all trains into and out of Grand Central were being moved by electric power.

Another great mainline electrification, that of the New York, New Haven & Hartford, was initially installed in 1906 to include through passenger service and suburban traffic in the territory between Grand Central Station and Stamford, Connecticut. At that time the road's management, having had a dozen or more years' prior experience with electrified operation on various branch lines, determined on a type of electrification capable of extension as opportunities might offer. After the initial step had demonstrated the wisdom of this choice, it broadened the scope to include freight and switching as well as passenger service. Eventually it covered electrically all branches of its railroad operation in the territory between New York and New Haven, one of the principal gateways to New England from the West and South.

An electric rail system, like all Gaul in Caesar's time, may be said to be divided into three parts: (1) power supply, (2) power transmission and distribution from the supply points to the locomtives, and (3) the motive power itself. The New Haven System (now part of Conrail) built its own juice plant at Cos Cob, Connecticut, in 1906, modernized and enlarged it from time to time, and gets additional power from Consolidated Edison and other sources. Power is transmitted and distributed to the locomotives and multiple-unit cars over a very elaborate network of feeder circuits and trolley wires at 22,000 and 11,000 volts.

Among its many experiments with various electric locomotive types, the New Haven in 1955, well into the dieselization age, had General Electric build for it 10 new Ignitron electric locomotives. These units combined the advantages of high-voltage AC distribution with low-voltage DC traction motors. GE substituted for the cumbersome motor generator set an electronic device that changed high-voltage AC to low-voltage DC without using mechanical rotation or other moving parts.

The New Haven also developed its own type of multiple-unit, self-powered cars, known as MUs, for commuter and branch-line runs, with high rates of acceleration and deceleration, in addition to ample seating (and standing) capacity for rush-hour crowds. MUs are lineal descendants of trolley and subway cars. They included open-end, arched-roof, railroad-roof, and stainless-steel cars, the last-named having a fluted washboard design. Nearly all New Haven MUs were built to run on both AC from a catenary system and DC from a third rail.

Third-rail operation at 600 volts was used by New Haven trains running over New York Central rails. The New Haven line branches off from the Central (now also part of Conrail) at Woodlawn, New York. There the third rail ends, and 11,000-volt AC overhead wires begin. As soon as a train gets entirely off third-rail trackage and while it is still running at high speed, the motorman lifts a switch in the cab of his juice loco or MU train, thus retracting the third-rail shoes and folding them up like a grasshopper's legs against the tracks. At the same time, he switches the control circuits and auxiliary equipment from DC to AC, while a third switch lifts the pantographs to contact the 11,000-volt wires. From that point on, the train is powered by New Haven catenary.

Three other big roads began considering the problem of poison gas from steam locomotive exhaust underground: the Grand Trunk, in its St. Clair Tunnel between Sarnia, Ontario, and Port Huron, Michigan; the Boston & Maine, in its Hoosac Tunnel; and the Great Northern, with its dangerously long (2½-mile) Cascade bore. All three tunnels were electrified in 1908, 1911, and 1909 respectively. *See* CASCADE TUNNEL.

Most American electric railroads were originally steam-powered. The first of the few built as electric lines from the start was the New York, Westchester & Boston (NYW&B), a commuter line serving suburbs north of New York City but never getting near Boston. Opened in 1912, it had been built with the highest techniques then available by interests identified with the New Haven Railroad. The NYW&B electric system was part of the New Haven's system but was separately managed. However, the NYW&B cost so much to build and operate that it could not pay its way in its rather sparsely populated area and was closed down at the end of 1937. Most other commuter-line electrifications were built to less costly specifications; among them were the Reading's from Philadelphia to West Trenton, the Illinois Central's out of Chicago, and the Delaware, Lackawanna & Western's, from Hoboken to Dover, New Jersey.

During Depression years, the Pennsylvania (PRR), still claiming the title "Standard Railroad of the World," was pushing a great electrification program on its Eastern lines that by 1940 would cover 2667 track miles, or 40 percent of the nation's entire rail electrification. This program really began in 1895 with an experimental operation on its Burlington-Mount Holly, New Jersey, branch. Later, two Pennsy subsidiaries, the Long Island Rail Road and the West Jersey & Seashore, installed third-rail, low-voltage DC electrification.

Since 1910 travelers on the old Pennsylvania Railroad (now Conrail) have not had to enter or leave Manhattan by ferryboat, for electric power takes them beneath the Hudson River. This electrification made possible the building of New York's Penn Station, one of the most magnificent of all railroad stations (torn down in the mid-1960s and replaced by the present smaller station underground).

The Pennsy turned to AC operation because its transmission characteristics are superior to DC and because the New York, New Haven & Hartford was doing well with it. Electrification of the 20-mile mainline to Paoli was completed in 1915. The great H-beam catenary poles, glistening with porcelain insulators, continued their march to Chestnut Hill, Whitemarsh, Wilmington, West Chester, Norristown, and Harrisburg and, in 1930, to Trenton, radiating out from Pennsy headquarters, Broad Street Station, Philadelphia, and finally to Washington after work trains had unreeled thousands of miles of copper and aluminum wire.

It was, in fact, the most extensive railroad electrification the world had ever seen. Almost miraculously, it was carried on and completed during the Depression of the 1930s. Even then, with mounting expenses and long before the Penn Central fiasco, the Pennsy never skipped a dividend. In the early days of electrification MP54 suburban multiple-unit coaches (eventually more than 500 of them) provided local service in New Jersey and in the Philadelphia area, while steam locomotives, in the development of which PRR was second to none, continued to haul mainline freight and passengers.

For years the Pennsy had been experimenting with a locomotive good enough to meet its mighty challenge of electrification, a power machine that would symbolize to the world its passenger service under wire. The builders of the GG-1, General Electric and Baldwin, delivered the prototype in August 1934. PRR tried her out on its test track at Claymont, Delaware. She was not only fast and powerful but sleek and handsome.

The Pennsylvania Railroad's Broadway Limited *operated between New York, Philadelphia, and Chicago. The Pennsy was one of the earliest and most enthusiastic lines to electrify some of its trackage.* [*Pennsylvania Railroad*]

Early in 1935, there were 57 GG-1 units on order. These locomotives, each geared for 90 miles per hour, were built variously by General Electric, Westinghouse, Baldwin, and the Pennsy's own Altoona shops, long famous for the steamers they had turned out.

A test run of GG-1 No. 4800, pulling a trainload of celebrities, was made on January 28, 1935, southbound. It took 110 minutes, with only one stop, Baltimore, at speeds up to 102 miles per hour but averaging 73. After that, the 4800 went on a week's exhibition tour. The first New York-Philadelphia-Washington regular passenger run with a GG-1 was made on February 10, 1935. The new type of engine cut running time on the *Congressional Limited* from 4¼ to 3¾ hours, later to 3 hours, 35 minutes. Eventually, some GG-1s were regeared for freight service.

Designer Raymond Loewy made his greatest contribution to the GG-1 by suggesting that her entire body be welded into a single graceful unbroken shell, with no rivets or seams between the plates. He was responsible also for the elegant pin-striping of gold on dark green and the expansion of the painted gilt lettering "Pennsylvania," which he said would "visually extend the length of the engine." *See* LOEWY, RAYMOND.

In 1973 the Chicago, Milwaukee, St. Paul & Pacific (CMStP&P) scrapped its entire electrified system, which was then 656 miles, the nation's longest, and went all-diesel. Until that time, the Milwaukee's mainline electrification was divided into two sections: 440 miles on the Rocky Mountain division between Harlowton, Montana, and Avery, Idaho, which began service in 1915, and 216 miles on the Coast division between Othello and Seattle-Tacoma, Washington, inaugurated in 1920. The latter had been fully dieselized for over a year, but in early 1973 catenary and substation were still in place.

Between the two sections was a 212-mile segment which, for several reasons, had never been electrified. The gap was operated by conventional power, which severely limited the versatility and efficiency of the overall juice system. Continuing the electrified operation would have meant not only electrifying the gap but also replacing the entire complex with a modern high-voltage system and buying new electric locos. In effect, it would almost have been like electrifying from scratch. Since the Milwaukee Road was forced into bankruptcy a few years later, it is easy to understand why this could not have been done.

The road's use of electric power had been declining over the years. In early 1973 only 3 percent of the entire 10,500-mile system was run by electric units. The Milwaukee's first juice-powered train had run 112 miles from Three Forks to Deer Lodge, Montana, on November 30, 1915. The original cost of electrification (exclusive of the 1927 Black River Junction-Seattle portion), including equipment, labor, material, locomotives, and structure, was about $23 million. In 1925, after 8½ years of operation, that investment had been recouped in savings, and an additional $12.4 million in savings realized by the railroad, compared with what steam operation in those districts would have cost.

Milwaukee's electrification aimed at economy in heavy freight and passenger service on mountain grades. While it was not the world's first railroad electrification, it was the first *long-distance* electrification and the first undertaken *solely for economic reasons.* Earlier electrifications were for such purposes as eliminating smoke in tunnels and increasing traction on certain mountain grades.

In 1915 the Milwaukee Road and General Electric Co. (GE) jointly produced the world's largest electric loco. At first 12 such locos were built, each 112 feet, 8 inches long, weighing 288 tons, and consisting of two units, back to back with a wheel arrangement of 2-2+B and B+B-2, with semipermanent coupling and 40,400 pounds of tractive effort. The first of these, delivered on September 25, made a trial run on the Butte, Anaconda & Pacific (BA&P).

The Milwaukee bought 12 mammoth electrics that GE had built for the U.S.S.R. but did not ship abroad because of World War II. They were called "Little Joes" (from the Soviet ruler Joseph Stalin). These engines, 87 feet, 10 inches long, with a 2D-D2 wheel arrangement, developed 5110 horsepower. Ten of them went into freight, and two into passenger service. In the mid-1950s, the Milwaukee developed a remote-control device for its GP-9 diesels, permitting a juice engineer also to run a diesel unit on the same train from his electric cab. Diesels could be coupled behind electrics to boost head-end horsepower. It was not rare to see two Little Joes teamed up with one or two Geeps rolling through the Rockies. *See* GEEP.

Juice locos have several advantages over steam: greater hauling capacity up stiff grades, less maintenance and fuel cost, and longer life expectancy. They are more reliable and more efficient in extremely cold weather. The elimination of the need for hauling and storing much coal and water for steamers and the increased use of electric locos and personnel likewise save money. Even so, diesels doomed not only steam but also, eventually, Milwaukee Road electrics.

Retired Milwaukee electric loco 10200 is part of the big collection of historic railroad equipment viewable today at the Lake Superior Museum of Transportation in Duluth. The 288-ton, 112-foot machine, given to the museum by the railroad, was the first engine with which, in 1915, the Milwaukee began its electrified operations across five mountain ranges in Montana, Idaho, and Washington. It was the largest electric loco in service when built by GE and the first to run on 3000 volts DC. It was also the first to use regenerative braking, in which its traction motors became generators when the train was going downhill. This expedient slowed the train by absorbing the energy created by the downgrade movement and restoring electric current to the overhead wire. (Diesel-electrics used in mountain service today can apply a contemporary version of dynamic braking.)

In 1913–1914, even before the CMStP&P went in for electrification, the neighboring Butte, Anaconda & Pacific in Montana electrified a 32-mile stretch between Butte and Anaconda and proved that three electric units could do more work than four steam engines of similar horsepower. An electric dragged a 55-car train of iron ore, the BA&P's main commodity, up a steep grade at 15 miles per hour, whereas a steamer could make only 7 miles per hour with the same train.

In its palmiest days the Anaconda line, connecting with the Milwaukee Road, Great Northern, Union Pacific, and Northern Pacific, had 26 electric units in service and a residual fleet of steam locos to serve the unelectrified track, including a quarry run west of Anaconda. It hauled ore from Butte to Anaconda, usually 32 cars at a clip, 2000 tons, using two electrics to Beaver, then doubling for the mainline trip to East Anaconda, the operating hub, from which loaded cars were taken to the smelter.

BIBLIOGRAPHY: Roger Arcara, *Westchester's Forgotten Railway*, Quadrant Press, New York, 1972; Raymond Loewy, *Never Let Well Enough Alone*, Simon & Schuster, New York, 1951; William D. Middleton, *When the Steam Roads Electrified*, Kalmbach, Milwaukee, 1951; Karl R. Zimmermann, *The Milwaukee Road under Wire*, Quadrant Press, New York, 1973.

Elevated Railways *See* SUBWAY AND ELEVATED RAILWAYS.

Empire Builder, The Train inaugurated by the Great Northern (GN) in 1929 and given the title long identified with the system's founder, James J. Hill. The GN's crack train was then the *Oriental Limited,* which had been operating under that name since 1924 but really was almost as old as the railroad itself. In the Depression year of 1932 the *Oriental* was pulled off, but the *Empire Builder* kept running between Chicago and Seattle via the Twin Cities. As the only mainline express to the Northwest directly serving a national park (in this case, Glacier), the *Empire Builder's* best revenue came from July and August vacationists. It ran through the 8-mile Cascade Tunnel, the longest tunnel in the Western Hemisphere. *See* CASCADE TUNNEL; HILL, JAMES JEROME.

In 1947 this train was thoroughly modernized and put on a 45-hour schedule, clipping 13½ hours from its previous terminal-to-terminal time. This change ushered in the duplex-roomette type of sleeping car, which until then had been available only in an experimental Pullman-Standard model tested extensively in wartime service. Its four sleepers also were given double bedroom and compartment accommodations. In addition, each train had a combination mail and baggage car, one 60-passenger coach, 3 day-night coaches (all equipped with reclining seats and retractable leg rests), a coffee-shop car for snacks, a diner seating 36, and an observation-lounge car. Today, under Amtrak, the *Empire Builder* runs between Chicago and Seattle via St. Paul and Havre, Montana, 2289 miles, and between Chicago and Duluth via Milwaukee, St. Paul, and Superior, 571 miles.

The pride of the Great Northern Railway was the **Empire Builder**, *inaugurated in 1929 and named for the man who indeed built an empire from his railroad, James J. Hill.* [*Great Northern Railway*]

Engine 999 *See* NEW YORK CENTRAL SYSTEM.

Erie & Kalamazoo Railroad (E&K) First railroad in both Michigan and Ohio. Incorporated in both, it was to have run from what is now Toledo on Lake Erie to the Kalamazoo River but never got that far, its western terminus being Adrian, Michigan Territory. Opened on October 3, 1836, it issued paper currency as other early railroads did. At first it used only wooden rails, which warped, but it soon added strap iron, which sometimes curled up as "snake heads" that tore holes in car floors, imperiling passengers and trainmen alike. After beng leased to several New York Central antecedents and then to the Central itself, the E&K is now part of Conrail.

BIBLIOGRAPHY: *Railroad Magazine*, November 1949.

Erie Lackawanna Railway (EL) Important part of the federally subsidized Consolidated Rail Corporation (Conrail) since April 1, 1976, this line was previously an independent 2800-mile merged railroad linking New York City with Chicago and serving the states of New York, New Jersey, Pennsylvania, Ohio, Indiana, and Illinois. With general offices in Cleveland, it had about 12,000 employees, some 550 diesel units, and about 22,000 owned or leased freight cars. It resulted from a merger in 1960 of the Erie and the Delaware, Lackawanna & Western (DL&W), identified in an old folk song

as "the Delaware Lackawann" but generally referred to as the Lackawanna. Those two great systems sprang from different predecessor companies, both of which dated back to 1832. *See* CONRAIL.

The Erie's first antecedent was the New York & Erie (NY&E), incorporated in New York State. It was organized in response to a demand by citizens in the southern part of the state for transportation to enable them to compete with the northern counties served by the Erie Canal.

Ground was broken on November 7, 1835, for construction of the first 40½-mile section of the road, between Deposit, New York, and the mouth of Callicoon Creek. Its first rail came from England, followed by American-made rail rolled in Scranton, Pennsylvania. To prevent competing railroads from moving traffic originating on the NY&E, the company built wide-gauge (6-foot) track. Some 40 years later it changed to standard gauge in order to interchange traffic with other roads. *See* ERIE RAILROAD WAR; GAUGE.

When opened for traffic on May 14, 1851, between Piermont, New York, and Dunkirk on Lake Erie, the NY&E was America's longest railroad, 336 miles. A special train carried Millard Fillmore, one of the earliest Presidents to travel by rail, and his Cabinet, including Daniel Webster, who was then Secretary of State. Webster rode part of the way in a rocking chair which was strapped, at his request, to a flatcar so that he could get a better view of the country.

In 1861, the NY&E was succeeded by the Erie Railway Co., and in 1878 by the New York, Lake Erie & Western. The Erie Railroad Co., formed in 1895, operated the road continuously until its merger with the DL&W in 1960. From its original route solely in one state, the Erie expanded into Pennsylvania and across Ohio via the Atlantic & Great Western and the Chicago Gateway. In the East it acquired rail lines across New Jersey to reach New York Harbor. *See* CHAPMAN, JOHN K.; DREW, DANIEL; FISK, JAMES; GOULD, JAY; OIL SHIPMENTS; SHAY, MATTHEW H.; VANDERBILT, CORNELIUS.

The DL&W's first predecessor was the Liggets Gap Railroad (LG) built by George Scranton, "father" of the DL&W, who also founded and gave his name to the Pennsylvania city in which the first American-made rail was rolled. He constructed the LG to haul coal from the Scranton area to an NY&E connection at Great Bend, Pennsylvania. Thus the DL&W was started not only in the same year as the Erie but also as a direct result of it. In 1851, the year of the Erie's formal opening at Dunkirk, the LG was renamed Lackawanna & Western. To reach markets east of Scranton, it acquired the Delaware & Cobb's Gap Railroad.

In 1882, by leasing the New York, Lackawanna & Western between Buffalo and Binghamton, N.Y., the DL&W eliminated its early dependence on the Erie and became a parallel competitor in providing rail service between the Great Lakes and the Atlantic seaboard. But the inflationary 1960s killed its independence; hence the mergers of 1960 and 1968.

BIBLIOGRAPHY: Charles F. Adams, Jr., and Henry Adams, *Chapters of Erie*, Great Seal Books, Cornell University Press, Ithaca, N.Y., 1956; Robert J. Casey and W. A. S. Douglass, *The Lackawanna Story*, McGraw-Hill, New York, 1951; Edward Hungerford, *Men of Erie*, Random House, New York, 1946; Frederick Westing, *Erie Power: Steam and Diesel Locomotives of the Erie Railroad from 1840 to 1970*, Alvin F. Staufer, Medina, Ohio, 1970.

Erie Railroad War An old ship's bell captured in the War of 1812 clanged an alarm from the courthouse cupola at Erie, Pennsylvania, on December 7, 1851. Men grabbed weapons and hurried to the public square, where Mayor Alfred King was mobilizing a company of militia to resist an Erie Railroad (ER) construction gang. It was a critical time in history. The railroad had pushed its mainline to Dunkirk, New York, 46 miles away, 2 years before and was now planning to connect with Erie.

In those days each railroad had its own gauge, varying from 2 to 7 feet. The ER's was 6 feet. This gauge was used on the first line to penetrate Erie, the Erie & North East (E&NE), running eastward from the city to the New York State line and connecting there with the standard-gauge (4 feet, 8½ inches) road that later became part of the New York Central. In the fall of 1852 the Mad River and Lake Erie (MR&LE; 4 feet, 10 inches) linked Erie with Cleveland. Thus, with several changes, you could have journeyed by rail between New York City and Chicago via Erie and Cleveland.

This was a big step forward in transportation, but the transfer at Erie irritated travelers. The E&NE and MR&LE depots were a mile apart, and train connections were poor. Whether they wanted to or not, travelers often had to spend a night in the lake port while waiting for a train, and they grumbled mightily.

Eventually the standard-gauge road got control of the 6-foot E&NE and decided to change its gauge to 4 feet, 10 inches, connect directly with the MR&LE, and combine the two stations into one so that no stopover in Erie would be necessary. But local merchants, hotelmen, cabdrivers, omnibus operators, and draymen agreed to fight for any scheme that would force the traveling public to spend as much time as possible in their city. Erie City Council forbade the E&NE to change its gauge and ordered it, on penalty of a $500-a-day fine, to remove its tracks from city streets. Moreover, the city constable was empowered to remove the rails by force as soon as an effort was made to change the gauge.

For months, public meetings kept up the tension. Mayor King declared: "Erie's destiny is to become a powerful rail and water terminal. No railroad shall make us a mere hamlet by the wayside." On his orders, men sawed through the railroad bridge timbers. E&NE laborers fought back but were outnumbered 20 to 1. Another mob attacked the railroaders at Harbor Creek, Pennsylvania, 6 miles east of Erie, ripping up the tracks. This made Harbor Creek a terminal village.

Travelers, both eastbound and westbound, found it was extremely hard to traverse that 7-mile stretch in dead of winter, with icy winds from Lake Erie. Many had feet, hands, and faces frostbitten. Local cab and omnibus drivers, hotel agents, and expressmen solicited their business at both ends of the gap, but most of the railroad passengers indignantly snubbed them, preferring to struggle through the snow afoot, dragging their luggage when possible and going hungry rather than buy anything in Erie.

Five times the E&NE relaid parts of the track, but each time the rails were torn up amid wild disorder. Armed men patrolled the right-of-way to see that no rails were laid. A fanatical mob burned the rebuilt Harbor Creek railroad bridge. Although a federal court decision upheld the railroad men, city police jailed them. A mob seized the E&NE station, cut telegraph wires, destroyed company records, and assaulted rail officials. In 1854 a mob tried to seize a train at Harbor Creek, but the crew drove them off.

At length the state of Pennsylvania took over the railroad from Erie to the Ohio line. With troops armed with bayonets and two cannons ready to march to any scene of disturbance, E&NE laborers relaid the tracks, and this time the rails stayed there.

Evans and Sontag After the Western-style stickups of Southern Pacific (SP) trains No. 17 twice and No. 19 once with the use of dynamite in 1889, 1891, and 1892 and a total of some $25,000 stolen and after a sheriff had been shot dead at the home of Chris Evans (1847–1917), one of California's greatest manhunts ensued. The chief suspects were Evans, whose livery stable at Modesto, California, had burned down with 22 horses inside, and John Sontag, a boomer from Minnesota who limped badly from injuries sustained in a coupling accident while braking for the SP.

Both men were understandably embittered. The criminal evidence against them was flimsy, and public sympathy was in their favor. They hid out in the mountains, sometimes eating at friendly logging camps. The SP and Wells, Fargo & Co. jointly offered $10,000 reward for their capture, dead or alive. The woods swarmed with so many armed deputies that 11 of them were wounded by other lawmen. Sontag died, a doctor said, weighted with more lead than he had ever before seen in a human body.

Evans was captured later, blinded in one eye and with an arm that had to be amputated, and was tried and convicted of murder. A gun smuggled into prison enabled him to escape, but he went back home in answer to a faked message saying that one of his children was seriously ill and wanted to see him. Recaptured, he was sent to Folsom Prison for life. His wife and daughter Eve earned money for the outlaw's legal battle by acting in a melodramatic play, *Evans & Sontag.*

John Sontag, a boomer from Minnesota, was one of the two suspects of three Southern Pacific train robberies totaling $25,000 between 1889 and 1892. When Sontag was finally killed, after a great California manhunt stimulated by the $10,000 reward offered for the two men dead or alive, a doctor said he was weighted with more lead than he had ever before seen in a human body. [Mrs. Eve Evans McCullough]

Paroled in 1911 by Gov. Hiram W. Johnson, Evans died at Portland, Oregon, 6 years later.

BIBLIOGRAPHY: Benjamin A. Botkin and Alvin F. Harlow, *Treasury of Railroad Folklore*, Crown, New York, 1953; Don DeNevi, *Western Train Robberies*, Celestial Arts, Millbrae, Calif., 1976; Stewart H. Holbrook, *The Story of American Railroads*, Crown, New York, 1947.

Excursion Trains Special trains popular in America even before regular passenger service was established. They began running out of Charleston, South Carolina, and Baltimore, Maryland, as early as 1830 and out of Albany, New York, and New Orleans in 1831. The first trains to enter Washington, D.C., were excursions from Baltimore, on August 25, 1835, upon completion of the Baltimore & Ohio between those cities. Four trains were drawn by upright-boilered engines bearing the names of the first four Presidents of the United States. President Andrew Jackson and his Cabinet greeted them. A day-long public celebration followed.

Excursion trains have been run for thousands of special occasions such as inaugurations, fiestas, picnics, parades, sporting events, circuses and carnivals, wildflower picking, railfan trips, real estate sales, the driving of golden spikes, Broadway shows, the unveiling of the Statue of Liberty in New York Harbor, Chautauqua lectures, autumn foliage, intercity journeys, visits to national parks and shrines, and even, in early days, public hangings. Prior to World War II it was commonplace to see a variey of flyers announcing $1 train excursions, many higher-priced, hung up for the taking in big railroad stations. Increasing highway competition wiped out most of the rail excursion business, but even today Amtrak is operating a limited number of such trains, although none in the $1 price range.

Buffalo-Hunting Excursions By 1812 the buffalo had been driven from New York and Pennsylvania. By 1865, across the Missouri River, they made their last stand in an area of about 1000 square miles. The railroads, pushing westward, needed meat to feed their construction workers. The Union Pacific paid Col. William F. (Buffalo Bill) Cody $500 per month to supply 25 buffalo hindquarters a day.

About 1870 the Santa Fe Railway was building toward Dodge City, Kansas, and within a short time there were more than 4000 buffalo hunters between Wichita and Dodge City. Some hunters killed for meat, some for hides, and others for fun. The railroads often ran excursion trains for sportsmen to assist in the slaughter of millions of bison. Union Pacific operated a 2-day excursion beginning on January 12, 1872, for Grand Duke Alexis, son of the Czar of Russia, under the direction of Lieut. Gen. Philip H. Sheridan, assisted by Brig. Gen. George A. Custer, with Buffalo Bill in charge of the roundup. Numerous thrill seekers traveled from New England for such safaris.

By the beginning of 1873 buffalo were becoming scarce, although earlier some trains had been stalled on the prairie from 1 to 3 days at a time while great herds slowly crossed the tracks. By 1880, with the Northern Pacific Railway building westward from Bismarck into the bison's last stamping ground, the final herd was wiped out, turning the native Indians into second-class citizens by depriving many tribes of their main source of food and clothing.

BIBLIOGRAPHY: Freeman Hubbard, *Great Trains of All Time,* Grosset & Dunlap, New York, 1962.

F&CC *See* FLORENCE & CRIPPLE CREEK RAILWAY.

Family Lines System System, totaling more than 16,000 miles, of 10 Southern railroads controlled by Seaboard Coast Line Industries, Inc. (SCLI), a holding company. In addition to the two principal lines, the Seaboard Coast Line and the Louisville & Nashville, the system includes the Clinchfield, Georgia, Western Railway of Alabama, Atlanta & West Point, Durham and Southern, Gainesville Midland, Carrollton, and Columbia, Newberry and Laurens. In 1980 the SCLI itself and the railroads it controlled became part of CSX Corp. *See* CSX CORP.

Fantail Engine Steam locomotive, usually a switcher, with a tender sloping downward at the rear, designed to give enginemen looking back for hand signals a clearer view while shunting freight cars. Some slopes were long; others, steep. *See also* STEAM LOCOMOTIVES.

Fast Freight Lines Shortly after the Civil War, many fast freight lines were organized in the United States and Canada, mostly by small groups of adjacent railroads or individual roads, to speed service to shippers and get competitive business. The sponsoring roads split their earnings and expenses in proportion to each road's mileage. Other fast freight lines were owned by stockholders entirely apart from the roads over which they ran their through freight service by contract. Still others, hauling special freight, were owned wholly by firms or individuals such as the dressed-beef industry and the livestock car lines. The carriers themselves had no direct interest in such cars but operated them simply for the revenue paid per mile. The long list of fast freight lines included the Traders Despatch, Continental Line, Canadian Pacific Despatch, Ontario Central Despatch, Empire Line, Star Union, Merchants Despatch, Louisville & Gulf, Cumberland Gap Despatch, National Despatch, Red, White, Blue, Green, and many others.

A typical railroad-sponsored service was the Green Line, chartered in 1868 jointly by the Louisville & Nashville, the Nashville & North Western, the Nashville & Chattanooga, the Western & Atlantic, and the Macon & Western. These five roads pooled proportionate quotas of freight cars, all painted green. Through service, started with a total of 96 cars, was very popular and expanded quickly. New roads admitted to membership added more cars. By 1873 the Green Line involved 21 roads and 2275 cars. Eight years later its 2275 cars were serving other cities as well as the original four. But shortly afterward the line was partly dissolved, owing to a misuse of cars, some of which were being diverted to local traffic in violation of the terms of the agreement.

Most of the specific fast freight lines folded in 1918 during federal wartime control of the railroads. The following railroad-owned or -controlled car lines exist today: American Refrigerator Transit Co., 210 North

Thirteenth Street, St. Louis, Missouri 63103; Fruit Growers Express Co., 1101 Vermont Avenue, N.W., Washington, D.C. 20005; Merchants Despatch Transportation Corp., 166 West Van Buren Street, Chicago, Illinois 60604; Pacific Fruit Express Co. (care of Southern Pacific Lines); and Western Fruit Express Co., 176 East Fifth Street, St. Paul, Minnesota 55101. Two allied services are American Rail Box Car Co. (Railbox), 300 South Wacker Drive, Chicago, Illinois 60606; and Trailer Train Co., at the same address.

Featherbedding (Make-Work) Labor practices or union rules, usually enforced by contracts, which require the employment of more workers than are needed. Featherbedding limits the amount of work one may do in a given time, or restricts output, for the purpose of creating more jobs and greater income security, especially for union members. It also includes pay for superfluous help, for unnecessary tasks, for work not performed, and for duplication of jobs already done by other employees. The word itself is said to have originated in the early 1900s, when a group of Rock Island train and engine men complained of mattresses stuffed with corn husks in a dormitory that the company provided for their use during overnight layovers between runs, and a trainmaster retorted, "What do you want—featherbeds?"

Make-work affects many industries, but its best-known and most bitter impact is in railroading. Tactful management spokespersons seldom say "featherbedding" at the bargaining table. They prefer the less antagonistic term "work rules dispute." The main point at issue, from their viewpoint, is the unions' alleged lack of responsibility for keeping down operating costs.

The unions argue that "full crews," as they are called, are needed for safety and efficiency. For many years this demand was upheld by the full-crew laws which numerous states had enacted. All but one of those laws were passed before 1920. Now they are gradually being repealed despite union pressure on state legislatures.

The first rail labor-management contract put into written form, in 1875, was a simple document. Since then, greatly expanded rules have brought about complex and elaborate agreements. The alterations were due to collective bargaining, court rulings, executive agencies, and arbitration boards. In 1920 the railroads held a near monopoly on passenger and freight traffic. As time passed, growing competition, more powerful locomotives, longer and heavier trains, faster speeds, longer hauls, and other technological advances sharply reduced the number of employees needed; but the brotherhoods still try to keep the old work rules that these changes have rendered obsolete. Today, the Association of American Railroads admits, featherbedding is a relatively minor issue.

BIBLIOGRAPHY: Jacob J. Kaufman, *Collective Bargaining in the Railroad Industry,* King's Crown, New York, 1954; Robert D. Leiter, *Featherbedding and Job Security,* Twayne, New York, 1964; Paul A. Weinstein (ed.), *Featherbedding and Technological Change,* Heath, Boston, 1965.

FEC *See* FLORIDA EAST COAST RAILWAY.

Fiction, Railroad Almost without exception, the best writers in this field were men who railroaded during the boomer era—"pounded brass," sold or collected fares, dispatched trains, threw switches, or shoveled coal into fireboxes. When the steam locomotive and Morse train order passed away, so did the railroad fictionist. Decades ago, many popular magazines from *The Saturday Evening Post* on down often carried rail fiction. Today they don't. Even *Railroad Magazine,* the last holdout in this respect, which published such stories every month, has been merged into *Railfan & Railroad* and no longer does so. But a new quarterly, *Railroads Illustrated,* reprints a rail-fiction classic in each issue.

Railroad novels and collections of rail-fiction stories, once fairly plentiful, are not being published anymore. Possibly the latest railroad novel, *The Big Ivy,* by James McCague, came out in the early 1960s.

The golden age of rail fiction was between about 1889 and 1940. Jasper Ewing Brady's exciting *Tales of the Telegraph* was book-printed from *McClure's Magazine* in 1889. The author, a Western boomer telegrapher, based his tales on his own career and personal observation: train wrecks, robbers, bridge and track washouts, love affairs with girl operators, etc. Cy Warman wrote some fine rail yarns in *Snow on the Headlight* (1889), *Tales of an Engineer* (1896), and *Short Rails* (1900). Stephen Smith's *Romance and Humor of the Road* appeared in 1893. *See* WARMAN, CYRUS.

In 1899 Frank H. Spearman began writing superior railroad stories for *McClure's Magazine* that came out later between hard covers: *Flamingo Jim, Nan of Music Mountain, Whispering Smith, Daughter of a Magnate, The Nerve of Foley,* and *Held for Orders.* The last-named two dealt with the Union Pacific's Mountain division and were especially popular. Spearman spread his tales from pioneer days into the twentieth century. A wide readership was familiar with his fictitious locales: Medicine Bend, Sleepy Cat, Spider Water, Crawling Stone, Falling Wall, Thief River, Calbases, and the Spanish Sinks. Also well known were his characters such as Abe Hawk, the "good" outlaw, and Abe's father, Dave Hawk, a conductor who knocked down passenger fares because he was underpaid.

Two Canadian writers, Arthur Stringer (*Stories of the Railway,* 1893) and Frank L. Packard, both brass pounders, used railroad telegraphy as part of their fiction material. Packard, born of American parents in Montreal, could well be called the most dramatic of all rail-fiction authors. His books *On the Iron at Big Cloud*

(1911), *The Night Operator* (1919), and *Running Special* (1925) are collections of short stories laid on the Canadian Pacific's Mountain division. The only one of Zane Grey's 60 books, virtually all of them Westerns, written as a first-person narrative is *The U.P. Trail*, published in 1918.

The Octopus: A Story of California, Frank Norris's indictment of the Southern Pacific (1901), is a novel that no SP public relations man would care to mention. A minor author, Leo K. Wood, a Frisco Lines telegraph operator during World War I, filled in his lonely night tricks with fiction writing, one of his characters being Jim Flynn, a young railroad detective. In 1896 the famous detective Allan Pinkerton wrote a book entitled *Dyke Darrel, the Railway Detective,* for teenagers.

Francis Lynde wrote a dozen rail-fiction books between 1899 and 1929. Courtney Riley Cooper's *End of Steel* came out in 1897, Gerald Hamilton's *General Manager's Story* in 1898, Paul Lester Ford's *The Great K&A Train Robbery* in 1901, Alvah Milton Kerr's *Diamond Key* in 1903, Ward W. Adair's *Lure of the Iron Trail* in 1912, Theodore Dreiser's *The Financier* in 1912, Rex Beach's *Iron Trail* in 1913, Lyle Harper's *Ghost Train* in 1924, J. M. Brown's *Boomer Bill, His Book,* dealing mostly with the Missouri Pacific, in 1930, and Rock Island conductor James W. Earp's *Boomer Jones,* about the kind of know-it-all conductor whom Earp himself would like to have been, in 1931.

In 1928 another boomer, machinist Don Waters, had two books published: *Call of the Shining Steel* and *Pounding the Rails.* Much later, two anthologies of railroad short stories came out: *Headlights and Markers* and *Open Throttle.* Like nearly all the other titles mentioned here, both are now out of print.

The last of the rail-fiction giants was still another rover, telegrapher Harry Bedwell, who wrote a novel, *The Boomer,* and dozens of magazine stories. His book and most of his stories featured Eddie Sand, a fictionized interpretation of the author himself. Any list of colorful rail-fiction creators should include E. S. Dellinger, who set an all-time record for the number of rail magazine stories published, as well as Gilbert A. Lathrop, who wrote both short stories and books, Harry K. McClintock, Charles W. Tyler, John Johns, Clifford Funkhouser, Harold Titus, A. W. Somerville, Charles Layng, and Ernest A. (Frog) Smith, all good railroad men. *See* BEDWELL, HARRY; MCCLINTOCK, HARRY KIRBY.

A myriad of rail-fiction books have been written for juveniles. Among them are one of Horatio Alger's best-sellers, *The Erie Train Boy* (a vendor of magazines, souvenirs, candy, etc.; 1890); Allen Chapman's *Ralph in the Switch Tower* (1907) and 10 others in the Ralph series; Victor Appleton's *Tom Swift and His Electric Locomotive* (1922); Oliver Optic's *Through by Daylight* (1897); Edward S. Ellis's *The Young Conductor* (1895) and *The PQ&C* (1908); and Freeman Hubbard's *The Roundhouse Cat* (1951) and *The Phantom Brakeman* (1952), both being collections of his own railroad tales.

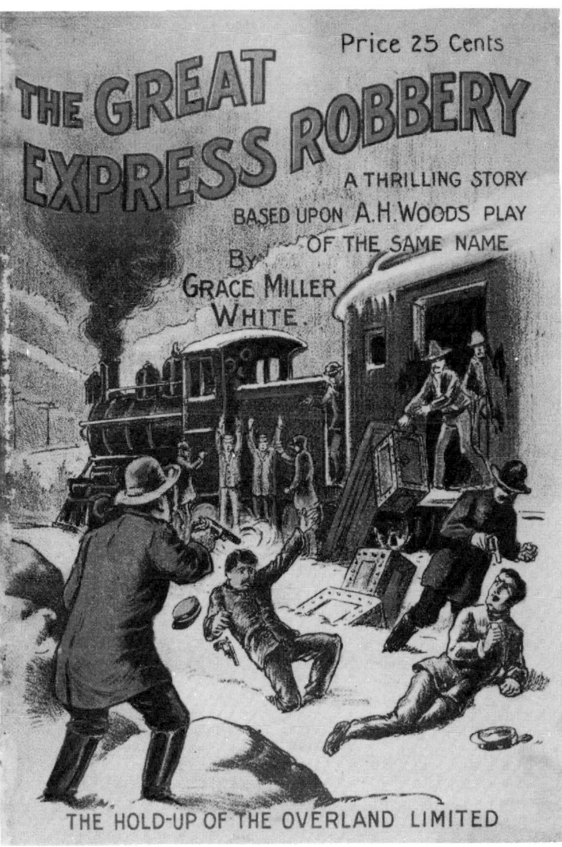

***The Broadway play* The Great Express Robbery *was the basis for the paperback novel illustrated by this sketch. It also inspired the first railroad movie,* The Great Train Robbery.**

BIBLIOGRAPHY: Frank P. Donovan, Jr., *The Railroad in Literature,* Railway & Locomotive Historical Society, Boston, 1940; id., *Harry Bedwell: Last of the Great Railroad Storytellers,* Ross & Haines, Minneapolis, 1959.

Fire Fighters Besides maintaining fire-fighting equipment for their own use and for checking forest fires along their rights-of-way, railroads have rushed many a trainload of city fire apparatus and men to burning cities, towns, etc., have often sent relief trains filled with food, medical supplies, doctors, clothing, and other necessities, and have occasionally ordered trains to haul out homeless refugees.

For example, on September 3, 1876, when flames destroyed 300 buildings at St-Hyacinthe, Quebec, with an estimated loss of $1.5 million, two Montreal fire engines accompanied by "smoke eaters" loaded onto Grand Trunk Railway flatcars helped to check the flames 34 miles away. And next morning a relief train arrived on the scene.

On July 5, 1888, when flames were gutting the village of Grafton, West Virginia, a special train sped the Parkersburg Fire Department over Baltimore & Ohio (B&O) rails to that location. It consisted of 4-4-0 engine No. 738, two flatcars holding the equipment, and a coachload of firemen and volunteers, with Patrick Flannery at the throttle. No faster ride was ever taken on that particular stretch of track—104 miles in less than 2 hours—despite many stiff grades, curves, and tunnels. Another B&O engineer, Ephraim F. Porvance, is credited with having saved Annapolis, Maryland, from destruction at a time when the U.S. Naval Academy had no fire department except a primitive hook and ladder company whose members drew their high-wheeled equipment through the streets with a long rope. That special covered 39 miles from Baltimore in 39 minutes.

One day in May 1896, the famous gold and silver mining settlement of Cripple Creek, Colorado, burned to the ground. All day long the narrow-gauge Florence & Cripple Creek shuttled trainloads of refugees to Victor and Florence.

On the night of September 4, 1927, flames were destroying Boston, Kentucky, on the Louisville & Nashville (L&N) line. The dispatcher's office heard about it and ordered Vernon Lee, night foreman at Lebanon Junction, to speed to the scene with freight locomotive No. 1773 and a carload of fire-fighting apparatus, 10,000 gallons of water, and as many volunteers as could be picked up on short notice. Boston's plight was desperate. The village had no fire department and no practical source of water nearer than ¼ mile or enough hands or buckets to bridge that wide gap.

Despair turned to hope when No. 1773 puffed out of the darkness into the fiery glare. While the imported volunteers were battling the flames, another L&N engine, racing to their aid, supplied additional water. Although the railroad station, bank, and four stores were gutted, the L&N saved the rest of the community.

See also HINCKLEY HOLOCAUST.

Fisk, James (1834-1872) Erie Railroad stock manipulator known as Jubilee Jim and Prince of Erie. He was born and buried in Bennington, Vermont. After a meager education, he became a peddler, entered the jobbing business in 1860, handled large contracts for Civil War military supplies, and bought cotton for a Boston syndicate. With the aid of Daniel Drew, for whom he was an agent, Fisk founded in 1866 a brokerage firm which made him rich. *See* DREW, DANIEL.

Two years later, Commodore Cornelius Vanderbilt, who was then America's richest citizen, acquired control of the Erie Railroad but made a strategic error by admitting Fisk, Jay Gould, and Daniel Drew to its board of directors. The trio voted a big issue of bonds, ostensibly to finance improving the road. In reality, they took over much of the bond issue on various pretexts, reissued it as shares of stock, and through their brokers sold this stock to the unsuspecting Vanderbilt. *See* GOULD, JAY; VANDERBILT, CORNELIUS.

The commodore had instructed his brokers, "Buy Erie." A flood of illegal new securities cost him millions. Learning how Drew, Fisk, and Gould had tricked him, he got a court injunction against them. With an injunction of their own, the trio worked a printing press overtime, producing new stock certificates as fast as Vanderbilt could buy them. "If this printing press don't break down," said the jovial, plump, and crude Jubilee Jim, "we'll give the commodore all he wants of Erie."

Vanderbilt responded with a court order for the arrest of the conspirators on a charge of contempt of court. Tipped off to what was happening, his opponents crammed several million dollars in cash into suitcases, together with stocks, bonds, and the Erie Railroad's books. They boarded hacks and were driven rapidly to the ferry, which carried them over to Jersey City, out of reach of Vanderbilt's influence.

There, the Erie's "executive committee" set up headquarters in a hotel and obtained a police guard of 15 men, in addition to many Erie detectives, as protection against possible kidnappers taking them back to New York. Fisk, with a flair for the bombastic, had three cannons mounted on piers near the hotel. Assuming the title and garb of an admiral, he had four lifeboats, each manned by a dozen armed men, patrol the waterfront.

Vanderbilt, desperately in need of ready cash, could not borrow from the banks by using fraudulent Erie shares as security. Gould, according to the historian Charles Francis Adams, slipped out of Jersey City with a suitcase holding half a million dollars on a secret mission to Albany, following which the New York Legislature passed a bill legalizing the fraudulent stock issues.

Then the conspirators bought back Vanderbilt's Erie stock, returned to New York, and bribed Drew to withdraw from the Erie's inner circle. This left Gould and Fisk in charge of the 773-mile railroad, of which Gould got himself elected president and Fisk vice president.

Then came what Adams called "the most extraordinary feat of financial legerdemain which history has yet recorded." It was a daring move by Gould and Fisk to pick up a few more millions by speculating with Erie stock. That autumn, as usual, the West clamored for money to move its crops. This seasonal demand was the cue for the Erie bosses to deposit $12 million in New York banks and suddenly withdraw it in the form of currency. Besides taking the money out of circulation, they increased the total amount of Erie stock from $34 million to $54 million.

To meet this artificial shortage of currency, the U.S. Treasury put an additional $50 million into circulation. But it came too late. Brokers had already felt the money pinch and demanded more margin from their customers, who then had to sell a great many shares at a loss. The Gould-Fisk scheme was to sell, at top prices, big blocks of securities for future delivery, stocks they did not own at the time but aimed to buy when the market dropped. Thus the two men deliberately forced down the market and afterward delivered, for a high price, stocks whose value they had depressed.

Not satisfied with the millions acquired by this trick,

they made another gigantic foray that brought on the gold panic of Black Friday, September 24, 1869. Meanwhile, with maintenance of the Erie's rolling stock and track being ignored, defective equipment killed or injured many railroad employees, and train wrecks were frequent.

Jubilee Jim's time was running out. At his suggestion, the Erie management had bought the New York Grand Opera House for use as company headquarters. A secret passageway connected the stage with Fisk's private office. Fisk, voluptuous and extravagant, wined, dined, and otherwise entertained ladies of the stage. One of them, Josephine Mansfield, was the mistress of a young New York businessman named Ned Stokes. Ned thirsted for revenge. On January 6, 1872, he shot Fisk on a hotel stairway. The Prince of Erie died the next day. After lying in state at the opera house, his body was given a showy funeral. *Harper's Weekly* ran a cartoon by Thomas Nast, the foremost cartoonist of his era, showing Gould and Boss Tweed standing over Fisk's grave and entitled "Dead Men Tell No Tales."

BIBLIOGRAPHY: Edward Hungerford, *Men of Erie,* Random House, New York, 1946; Matthew Josephson, *The Robber Barons,* Harcourt, Brace, New York, 1934; William A. Swanberg, *Jim Fisk: The Career of an Improbable Rascal,* Scribner, New York, 1959.

Flood Signal Devices Previously used elsewhere on rails, these devices were adapted to bridges in 1950 for the first time by the Missouri-Kansas-Texas Railroad, which installed them on two bridges at a Red River fork near Wichita Falls, Texas. The automatic signal is a float which rises with the water to break a circuit and flash a railway stop sign to trains when the water is at danger level. It warns the engineer to inspect the bridge and proceed with caution. Sudden floods and bubbling quicksand that pulls away the pilings with little warning make those two bridges particularly dangerous.

Florence & Cripple Creek Railway (F&CC) This 3-foot-gauge gold and silver ore carrier, chartered in Colorado on April 17, 1893, linked the Cripple Creek mines with a Denver and Rio Grande connection at Florence. Its first train ran in July 1894. Each of its luxurious Pullmans had three shiny brass oil lamps and coalburning Baker heaters with hot-water pipes extending along both sides of the car. In 1899 the line became part of a new railway, the Denver & Southwestern, later renamed the Cripple Creek Central, but kept its identity. By building spurs and branches and taking over the standard-gauge Colorado Springs & Cripple Creek District Railway, it expanded its mileage from 40 to 120½. But a disastrous flood and a gold-mining slump dissolved the F&CC on April 30, 1915. Remnants of it were acquired by the Cripple Creek & Colorado Springs Railway and finally by the Midland Terminal. *See* COLORADO MIDLAND RAILROAD.

BIBLIOGRAPHY: Lucius Beebe and Charles Clegg, *Narrow Gauge in the Rockies,* Howell-North, Berkeley, Calif., 1958; Morris Cafky, *Rails around Gold Hill: The Story of Narrow and Standard Gauge Railroads in the Cripple Creek District,* Rocky Mountain Railroad Club, Denver, 1955.

Florida East Coast Railway (FEC) Railroad that is unique for several reasons:

1. It built and operated for years an oversea extension from the southern tip of the Peninsula State across the Florida Keys—a line it later had to abandon.

2. More recently, it was confronted by an unprecedented period of nearly 14 years of strikes and violence.

The Florence & Cripple Creek Railway was born of the gold and silver boom in the Rockies in the 1890s but died in 1915. Its engine No. 12 is shown here in 1906 with an excursion train near Alta Vista, Colorado. [L. C. McClure, Denver Public Library Western Collection]

3. Its labor cost in the late 1970s was the lowest of any major railroad: 30 cents out of every revenue dollar, including fringe benefits and payroll taxes, whereas the United States rail industry as a whole averages around 53 percent, and Conrail in 1977 was paying out between 60 and 65 percent of its revenue in labor costs.

4. The nation's rail industry uses its freight equipment on an average of 59 miles per hour per car, but FEC exceeds that figure.

5. FEC plows back an unusually large share of its available cash into track betterment. The national maintenance-of-way ratio on Class I railroads in 1977 was 17.3 percent, while FEC's was 29 percent, making its track the envy of the chief engineers of many other roads.

Henry Morrison Flagler (1830–1913), a partner in John D. Rockefeller's Standard Oil Company, became interested in about 1883 in developing Florida as a winter playground. By buying and consolidating several local railroads, he organized the Florida East Coast Railway. He also established steampship lines, dredged Miami Harbor, and built many palatial hotels. He extended the FEC southward from Daytona through Palm Beach to Miami, then a small Indian trading post, in 1896. Ten years later the railhead reached Homestead, 28 miles farther on (today's end of track), and was being pushed out to sea southwest across the curving Florida Keys to the desolate island of Key West, from which fast, elegant steamships would bridge the 90 miles of open sea to Havana, Cuba, thus making Havana, in effect, a suburb of New York.

The Keys consist of hundreds of tiny islands of coral and rock formation, mostly bleak and uninhabited. Flagler's extension plans involved laying 37 miles of track over the water, including 20 miles of embankments and rock fills and 17 miles of bridges and viaducts. His men fought a torrid sun and hurricanes while assembling, hauling, distributing, and erecting many thousands of tons of structural steel, great masses of concrete, thousands of pine and jicara piles, and filling material for the concrete bridges.

Hurricanes leveled miles of embankments that had been laboriously built across shoals, sweeping away huge rocks like so many wood chips. Engineering plans that called for bridges spanning only 6 miles of water were revised to 17 miles of bridge and viaducts. The big blow of October 18, 1906, caught the railroaders unprepared. Hundreds of men were at work. At least 75, possibly twice as many, were killed that day. For a month afterward, wreckage was cast ashore on the mainland and on coral beaches of the treacherous Keys.

In 1909 another hurricane cut a wide swath of ruin, but this time Flagler's men were better prepared, and the loss of life and property was much less. Eventually 6 steel bridges, 4 drawbridges, and 29 concrete viaducts were built in water varying from 3 to 38 feet deep. On January 22, 1913, the oversea line was completed and put to use.

Knights Key Bridge, the route's longest structure, runs almost 7 miles across open sea. Handsome Long Key Viaduct, 2.75 miles long, consists of 180 semicircular arches of 50-foot span. It was the first large concrete bridge built anywhere and had tracks laid 30 feet above high tide.

In 1935 a hurricane wreaked appalling havoc on that extension. Besides damaging structures and washing out tracks, it overturned an entire train with heavy loss of life. So the company regretfully abandoned its famous oversea route, which today is a motor highway.

Meanwhile, the railway had been carrying the cream of society to and from winter vacations, but because summer business was slack, the FEC was thrown into

The former oversea extension of the Florida East Coast Railway, between the mainland and the Florida Keys, opened in 1913, had to be abandoned in 1935 because of hurricane damage. It is now a highway. [Florida East Coast Railway]

receivership in 1931. Its bankruptcy lasted 30 years until manufacturer Edward Ball took it over. Ball decided that 2600-plus employees were too many for a road in financial straits, and he reduced the work force by several hundred. Furthermore, he told the unions that the FEC could not afford the 10.28 cents-an-hour pay raise then being offered to the nation's railroad employees, which made his road the only one of 193 Class I carriers that rejected the proposed settlement. This knocked over a hornet's nest.

On January 21, 1963, over 1200 FEC employees walked off their jobs. The other 700 left on the payroll refused to cross picket lines. Not a wheel turned on the railroad. The management retaliated by training its nonunion office personnel and hiring men from colleges and other sources. Two-men crews began taking trains the entire 366 miles between Miami and Jacksonville, each man earning a day's pay plus any overtime worked. Previously, *three* five-man crews had received pay based upon a day's salary for each 100 miles worked, even when it took only a couple of hours to run 100 miles.

Ball's policy precipitated nearly 14 years of strikes, punctuated by sabotage and violence. Engine crews were shot at, switches and automatic warning signals at rail crossings tampered with, trains dynamited and derailed, and bridges destroyed. The federal government seemed to be siding with the strikers, even shifting the bulk of its Miami mail shipments to other carriers. FEC could not even drop its money-losing passenger business until 1968; but in 1970 the U.S. Supreme Court upheld the Florida East Coast's right to modernize its old work rules. Finally, on April 9, 1976, history's longest railroad strike ended, the United Transportation Union being the last labor organization to call off the walkout.

BIBLIOGRAPHY: Carlton J. Corliss, *Building the Overseas Railway to Key West,* reprinted from *Tequesta: The Journal of the Historical Association of Southern Florida,* No. XIII, 1953; Florida East Coast Railway Company, *The Story of a Pioneer,* St. Augustine, Fla., 1956; Freeman Hubbard, *Railroad Avenue,* McGraw-Hill, New York, 1945; Raymond K. Mason, *Confusion to the Enemy,* New York, 1976.

Fluorescent Lighting Such lighting was used for an entire train (except the locomotive) for the first time on the streamliner *General Pershing,* which the Burlington placed in service on April 30, 1939, between St. Louis and Kansas City, although the New York Central had experimented with fluorescent lighting in 1938.

Four-Train Wreck This extremely rare kind of collision occurred on a foggy, cold Friday morning, December 4, 1891, on the New York & New England Railroad (NY&NE; later New Haven System, now Conrail). The Southbridge branch local freight was being made up at East Thompson, Connecticut, from cars that mainline freights had shunted into sidings during the night. Just as its engine, No. 31, backed onto her train, the crew heard the shrill whistle of a locomotive coming from the west but did not then know that she was on the same track. They soon learned. The onrushing train, a fast freight bound for Boston, with engine No. 174, sprayed its headlight through the fog and almost immediately plowed into the branch local. The impact was heard for miles. Wreckage flew in all directions, some of it fouling the eastbound main. The local crew escaped unhurt, but the fast-freight engineer and firemen were badly injured.

Before anyone could flag the *Long Island & Eastern Express,* the pride of the NY&NE, inaugurated only 3 months before, en route to Boston, roared into the mess, throwing the momentum of its engine, No. 105, two Pullman sleepers, and two vestibuled coaches against the wreckage. Its engine fell on her right side, killing her two-man crew and breaking off her whistle and safety valve. Escaping hot water, instantly turning to steam, added to the terror and confusion. Shooting downward at a 45-degree angle, the scalding water dug a hole that looked like a small cellar excavation. Dirt and stones were flung clear across an adjoining highway.

But even that wasn't all. A boat train from Norwich, Connecticut, which had been switched onto the Boston mainline at Putnam, Connecticut, plowed into the rear of the wrecked express before a flag could be put out. The fourth locomotive did not leave the rails; its engine crew had only minor injuries. The wreckage burst into flames, which, however, city fire fighters soon had under control. There is no record of any passenger being killed in the four-train wreck, although one man could not be accounted for. He may have deliberately slipped into obscurity for reasons of his own.

BIBLIOGRAPHY: Wesley S. Griswold, *Train Wreck!,* Stephen Greene, Brattleboro, Vt., 1969; Robert C. Reed, *Train Wrecks,* Superior Publishing, Seattle, 1968.

Freedom Train, American (AFT) Special train that toured the 48 contiguous states of the United States for 21 months in 1975, 1976, and January 1977 to commemorate the nation's bicentennial. Consisting of 23 to 25 cars painted red, white, and blue, it was pulled, sometimes double-headed up grades, by steam locomotives likewise painted in patriotic colors and occasionally assisted by diesel locomotives as specified by General Motors, one of the financial sponsors. (Other big contributors were Pepsi-Cola, Prudential Insurance, and Kraft Inc.)

AFT displayed over 700 historic artifacts, including originals and copies of documents from the National Archives such as the Declaration of Independence, George Washington's copy of the Constitution, and the Emancipation Proclamation. Also exhibited were authentic historical hardware, religious, ethnic, and geographical material, inventions, labor, professions, performing arts, fine arts, sports, pioneer wagons, a small early steam locomotive, and antique automobiles.

The caravan was operated under the auspices of the nonprofit, nonpolitical Freedom Train Foundation, whose chairman, Ross Rowland, had originated the idea and served as locomotive engineer on much of the tour. Jon Foust was president and functioning manager. A walkway extending through 10 enclosed cars kept the visitors moving. With open display cars, shadowboxes, and art transparencies, all illuminated at night, the train made quite a spectacle, particularly after dark.

Besides two display cars with huge, unbreakable plastic windows and 11 former New York Central baggage cars, 2 power cars (the train carried four large diesel-powered generator sets of its own), and a dormitory car, there were 3 piggyback flatcars carrying vehicles, trailers, and containers to be set up at display sites as ticket offices, refreshment stands, sanitary facilities, etc. At each display stop power lines were hooked up, cables routed, and equipment serviced. The operation was not unlike that of a circus train. In fact, AFT's trainmaster, Paul Hudson, used to work for Ringling Bros.-Barnum & Bailey. *See* CIRCUS TRAINS.

In 1974, a four-car version of this train, the *Preamble Express,* dedicated by President Gerald Ford, had toured 48 states as a preview to gain the support of political and business leaders in 76 of the major cities AFT planned to visit.

On April 1, 1975, the complete train went on display at Wilmington, Delaware. That started the tour. Pulling it to Chicago was No. 2101, renumbered 1, a 4-8-4-type steam locomotive which the Reading Railroad had retired and left in a scrapyard. She was rebuilt and repainted in a Baltimore & Ohio roundhouse at Baltimore by paid shopmen and unpaid volunteer workers. Meanwhile, another 4-8-4 steamer, the Southern Pacific's Daylight-type No. 4449, was being readied in Portland, Oregon, to haul the train over most of its Western mileage. The 4449's restoration cost nearly $100,000.

After AFT ended its 21-month tour in January 1977 at Seattle, Washington, the foundation sold its equipment to Canadians. *See* DISCOVERY TRAIN.

BIBLIOGRAPHY: Freeman Hubbard, *Great Trains of All Time,* Grosset & Dunlap, New York, 1962.

Freight-Car Markings Besides the car number and the name or initials of the car's owner, certain abbreviations have been adopted as standard markings stenciled on car sides:

CAPY Capacity in pounds
LD LMT Load limit in pounds
LT WT Light weight in pounds
EXW Extreme width in feet
EW Eaves width in feet
IH Inside height
CU FT Cubic-foot capacity
BLT Date built

The load limit is determined by a formula based on the size of journal bearings less the unloaded weight of the car. Capacity is a nominal round figure somewhat less than the load limit. Privately owned equipment may be marked, for example, GATX, meaning "General American Transportation Corp."

Over the years railroad men, propagandists, hoboes, etc., have used boxcars, both inside and outside, as blackboards on which to write temporary messages, advertisements, political or religious appeals, or meaningless graffiti, often of a pictorial nature. Sometimes switchmen or trainmen chalk words and symbols on freight-car sides to facilitate their work. The 1920s and 1930s, for example, saw an epidemic of J. B. King jingles such as:

> Who is the fellow J. B. King?
> I see his name on everything;
> On boxcars high and boxcars low
> I see his name wherever I go.

BIBLIOGRAPHY: Benjamin A. Botkin and Alvin F. Harlow, *A Treasury of Railroad Folklore,* Crown, New York, 1953.

Freight Cars Basically freight cars consist of boxcars, flatcars (flats), gondolas, open and covered hoppers, refrigerator cars (reefers), and tank cars. But in this age of specialization each category includes many different kinds of cars. Boxcars hold a wide variety of commodities. Some have special "cushioned" undercarriages and interior load-restraining devices to protect shipments requiring special care such as automobile parts and canned food products.

The commonest flatcars are equipped with tie-down devices for hauling truck trailers or containers (known as piggybacks). Gondolas are open cars, usually with sides but sometimes with only open-end bulkheads, that carry almost anything you can load by crane, magnet, or spout. *See* PIGGYBACKING.

Open-top hoppers carry products like coal and ores, the two leading rail-haul items in the United States, and are equipped with hoppers or chutes at the bottom for easy unloading. Covered hoppers carry dry bulk goods that need protection from the elements, like grain (the third major rail-haul commodity) and flour, cement, and fertilizer. Among other important products shipped by rail are crushed stone, gravel and sand, food, primary forest products, and motor vehicles and their accessories.

The average capacity of freight cars has risen each year since record keeping began, particularly in recent years. Cars currently being built have an average capacity of about 90 tons, compared with 62 tons for those being retired. Among the new kinds of freight cars is the Big John covered hopper used to move grain. Its capacity is about 100 tons, compared with about 40 tons for an ordinary grain-hauling boxcar. Covered hoppers have a further advantage: they can be loaded in 12 minutes and unloaded in 3. Other new giants include multilevel and enclosed cars for automobiles, house-size boxcars for auto parts and canned goods, and whale-shaped tankers.

The oil that early tankers used to haul now moves within the United States largely by pipeline, a major competitor of rail freight. However, more than 1400 different materials are still being transported in rail tank cars. These range from such foods as molasses, orange juice, milk, and water to the chemicals essential to many industries.

America's freight-car fleet, according to 1977 figures, consisted of 1,722,900 cars, of which railroads owned 1,388,300 and private-car companies and shippers 334,600. The largest number of these, 353,000, were open hoppers, followed by 314,000 plain boxcars, 181,000 gondolas, 173,000 equipped boxcars, 158,000 covered hoppers, 99,000 flatcars, 73,000 refrigerator cars, 30,000 miscellaneous cars, 4300 livestock cars, and 3000 tank cars.

See also OVERSIZE SHIPMENTS.

BIBLIOGRAPHY: John H. Armstrong, *The Railroad—What It Is, What It Does,* Simmons-Boardman, New York, 1978; Matthias N. Forney, *The Car-Builder's Dictionary,* reprinted by Newton K. Gregg, Kentfield, Calif., 1971; Walter A. Lucas (ed.), *100 Years of Railroad Cars,* Simmons-Boardman, New York, 1958; Lawrence W. Sagle, *Freight Cars Rolling,* Simmons-Boardman, New York, 1960; Roy V. Wright (ed.), *The Locomotive Cyclopedia,* Simmons-Boardman, New York, 1974.

Freight Cars, Privately Owned Cars not possessed by railroad companies that are built to meet their owners' specific needs or to supply some service for which railroad-owned rolling stock is inadequate or unsuitable. Such cars, whether tankers, cagelike poultry cars, or refrigerator cars, are each marked with a cryptic symbol, the two- to four-letter designation ending in *X* to distinguish it from carrier-owned equipment.

Privately owned freight cars date back to the construction in 1865 of the first oil tank car. As the industry grew, shippers wanted the railroads to provide the rolling stock, but in those pioneer days the carriers did not want to invest money in tankers because the rapid obsolescence of earlier models had cost them dearly. They told the shippers to put up their own capital for such cars. By supporting this position in 1888, the Interstate Commerce Commission made the acquiring of tankers the shippers' concern. The roads were willing to run them into their shops for repairs when necessary—at the owners' expense, of course. *See* OIL SHIPMENTS.

By gaining control of 90 percent of the tank-car fleet between 1870 and 1880, John D. Rockefeller controlled 95 percent of America's petroleum industry. A typical Standard Oil venture was the acquisition of J. J. Vandergrift's Star Tank Line and Pipe Line and the Union Tank Line, an affiliate. In 1878 John D. created

Wheat being inspected in a Great Northern covered hopper car, one of the many types of freight cars used to transport commodities on the rails. [Great Northern Railway]

the Tank Car Trust, through which he bought cars by providing their builders with "equipment trust certificates" backed by high interest rates. In return, the manufacturers sold him their tankers at $100 each below the going rate. Soon the trust had taken over all but 200 of the 3200 cars then in the nation's tank-car fleet.

In 1880 Rockefeller transferred Union Tank from Standard Oil, chartering a "new" company to build all kinds of railway cars for itself and others, besides leasing and selling cars to railways and other corporations. Union Tank went on record as owner and lessor of all Standard Oil cars. In 1902 a major derailment at Sheridan, Pennsylvania, with the fatal explosion of tank cars, led to the adoption of a new type of car, bolted so that the tank would not shift its position on the underframe. First to build these cars was the relatively small General American Transportation Co. Its initials, GATX, eventually became recognized as identifying equipment of General American Transportation Corp., perhaps the largest private-car owner today.

BIBLIOGRAPHY: Lawrence W. Sagle, *Freight Cars Rolling,* Simmons-Boardman, New York, 1960.

Freight Lines, Fast *See* FAST FREIGHT LINES.

Freight Loss and Damage Although rail freight traffic in the United States, Canada, and Mexico reached an all-time high in 1979, the number of loss and damage claims filed against the railroads, 2,110,000, was the lowest in 43 years, according to the Association of American Railroads (AAR), while the percentage of freight revenues paid out to satisfy those claims, 1.2 percent, was the lowest in 24 years. Claim payments in 1979 totaled over $328 million. Motor vehicles continued to be the industry's chief problem, representing 28.2 percent of claims paid. Claims due to robbery, theft, and pilferage are increasing. Nearly all claims are settled within 120 days. *See* POLICE, RAILROAD.

New techniques to reduce loss and damage are constantly being developed by individual roads and collectively by an AAR division located at 59 East Van Buren Street, Chicago, which also processes customer claims and assigns responsibility to carriers at fault. Besides a full-time staff of 31, there are 472 railroad representatives to assist in its activities. It sets up rules for distributing among railroads the sums paid in freight claims. Individual roads use its *Freight Claim Investigation Directory*. The division also compiles and distributes national freight loss and damage statistics by causes and commodities and has a governmental function on federal legislative issues and proceedings of the Interstate Commerce Commission.

The division's damage prevention section, cooperating with the railroads, makes impact and over-the-road tests to evaluate new closed-car loading and bracing techniques. In addition, it conducts workshops to train railroaders and shippers in damage prevention. The AAR division is an outgrowth of the Claim Agent Association of the Middle and Southern States, founded in 1887, and the national Freight Claim Association, founded in 1892.

BIBLIOGRAPHY: Robert S. Henry, *This Fascinating Railroad Business*, 3d ed., rev., Bobbs-Merrill, Indianapolis, 1946.

Frisco Lines *See* BURLINGTON NORTHERN; ST. LOUIS–SAN FRANCISCO RAILWAY.

Frog Wars These wars weren't as funny as the name implies. In June 1871, the Pennsylvania Railroad (PRR) built a branch line in New Jersey known as the Mercer & Somerset Railroad (M&S) from Somerset Junction through Hopewell to Millstone. Four years after that, a small rival road, the Delaware & Bound Brook (D&BB, which became part of the Philadelphia & Reading in 1879), began building a 27-mile line from Yardley, Pennsylvania, to Bound Brook, New Jersey, and sought permission to cross the M&S right-of-way 1 mile west of Hopewell.

Two railroads cross at right angles in Milton Junction, Wisconsin, on a jointly used frog, the like of which caused a number of frog wars in railroad history. [Robert P. Jones/Collection of Freeman Hubbard]

The Pennsy refused and stationed engine No. 679 and a caboose on the site of the proposed crossing frog to prevent its installation. A frog is a section of two bisecting pieces of track used to permit the crossing of two railroads on the same level. Usually it is a solid piece and quite heavy. The Pennsy's M&S was a single-track line. When regular trains came along, the 679 and caboose would go into a sidetrack, returning to their vigil as soon as the train had passed.

Pretending to have given up its crossing plan, the Delaware & Bound Brook turned its attention to building eastward. But in early evening darkness of January 5, 1876, some 200 D&BB laborers and local farmers hid in a field 1 mile west of Hopewell. At 7:20 p.m. the 679 took her caboose onto the siding to let a regular train proceed eastward. After the train went by, the men ran out of ambush, blocked the 679 in front and rear with ties, and chained her to the rails, meanwhile holding a gun on the Pennsy switchman stationed there. Then they tore up a section of Mercer & Somerset track and installed the crossing frog.

Pennsy Superintendent Jackson was furious when this news was telegraphed to him. He ordered two men: "Take engine 336, run to the scene with all possible speed, burst through the obstructions, and place the guard engine on the frog."

This was done, but the 336 was inadvertently derailed. Two other Pennsy engines rushed to the spot were promptly disabled by the hostile forces, which then completed the crossing job. Thus there were four crippled PRR engines in the area. The following afternoon Jackson sent 200 reinforcements to the scene, while a special train containing himself, attorney E. T. Green, and other Pennsy officials pulled out of Trenton to collect additional help from Newark and Jersey City.

Filling three cars with grimly determined men, Jackson wired instructions to all stations along the line to assemble even more help. Eventually, nearly 1000 Pennsy employees and sympathizers were involved. At the same time, farmers and laborers from miles around gathered with muskets, pitchforks, scythes, etc., to defend the D&BB.

Hopewell's sheriff, J. B. Mount, showed up with a squad of armed deputies on January 7 but, finding the situation was out of hand, wired Gov. Joseph D. Bedle for help. The Governor dispatched four companies of state militia, who took up positions around the frog. There was no actual fighting. A court decision ended the "war" by permitting the Delaware & Bound Brook to cross the Pennsy but awarded the latter $350 damages.

Other frog wars marked railroad history. There were at least two on the Canadian Pacific (CP), for example. Winnipeg businessmen wanted CP to lay tracks from their city southward to the United States border. CP refused. So they built a railroad themselves, the Red River Valley line. In October 1888 their tracks reached the CP mainline on both sides, leaving only a 200-yard gap. One night their workmen filled the gap, pried up CP rails at that point, and spiked a crossing diamond into place. Manitoba's attorney general and 20 constables stood by to guard the precious crossing.

Next morning, a six-car train arrived with hundreds of CP shopmen, the business car of William Whyte, general manager of CP's western lines, and constables of their own. CP workmen dug up the diamond, shipped it to their local yards as a souvenir, and dumped an old engine into the mud on the Winnipegers' right-of-way. Later, three more crossing attempts failed. Finally, on December 28, 1888, the Ottawa government permitted the crossing but placated the opposition by authorizing a much-needed CP bond issue. The big system hauled away its blockading engine and soon Red River Valley trains were running to and from the United States border.

Elsewhere in Canada, James J. Hill crossed the United States border northward with his new Westminster Southern Railway, a Great Northern subsidiary, in 1891, challenging the Canadian Pacific's bid for southern British Columbia's freight business through its own subsidiary, the Kettle Valley Railway (KV). Hill tried a surprise crossing of the KV line at Grand Forks, British Columbia, but a KV engine blocked the site, and he lost the ensuing court battle. *See* HILL, JAMES JEROME.

In the late nineteenth century, a New York, New Haven & Hartford (NYNH&H) freight train pulled by engine No. 112 was used to block the area in Bridgeport, Connecticut, where the builders of a trolley line, the Connecticut Co., wanted to install a crossing frog to let their route bisect a mainline railroad track. Police arrested the locomotive engineer for blocking a city street. His fireman then took the throttle and moved the train very slowly ahead. Another locomotive occupied the site long enough for the NYNH&H to get an injunction against the streetcar company, which closed the incident.

Funeral Trains *See* LINCOLN FUNERAL TRAIN; PRESIDENTIAL FUNERAL TRAINS.

G

Gauge Distance between the rails, the gauge line being measured at a point ⅝ inch below the rail top. The railway standard gauge, 4 feet 8½ inches, is the same as that of the rutways used for chariots and carts in ancient Rome. During their occupation of Britain that began in the first century A.D., the Romans used this gauge for coal mining. Later, the Britons themselves found it convenient to retain the Roman gauge in their mine railways and then in their passenger and freight lines. George Stephenson adopted it in building the world's first practical railway and the first successful steam locomotives.

For about 60 years, American railroads had many gauges, ranging from the 2-footers in upper New England to the old New York & Erie's 6 feet. Even connecting railroads did not always have a uniform gauge. This seriously hampered travel and freight shipping, particularly the earliest circus trains. By 1887, however, every major railroad in the country, except for a large segment of the Denver and Rio Grande, was using 4 feet 8½ inches, which by that time had become standard. *See* CIRCUS TRAINS; ERIE RAILROAD WAR; MAINE TWO-FOOTERS.

BIBLIOGRAPHY: C. Miles Burpee (ed.), *Railway Engineering and Maintenance Cyclopedia*, Simmons-Boardman, New York, 1942; William J. Palmer, Lorenzo M. Johnson, and John J. Lipsey, *The War of the Gauges*, Western Books, Colorado Springs, Colo., 1961.

Geep General-purpose, all-around motive-power unit built by the General Motors Electro-Motive Division. Its name is derived from the initials of *general purpose.* Simpler and less costly than regular passenger and freight diesel-electrics, it can drop a train on the mainline, work on a sidetrack, go back and pick up the train, and get into the clear to carry out a "meet" order. Able

***Within a week, between May 26 and June 1, 1886, more than 9000 miles of rails in the United States were moved 3½ inches closer to each other to match a standard gauge of 4 feet 8½ inches, thus uniting the country more firmly than ever before. Thomas Nast celebrated the event with this drawing, entitled "Blessed Be the (Standard Gauge) Ties That Bind." Hermes, god of roads and commerce, sits astride the cowcatcher, bearing a flag exactly 4 feet 8½ inches wide.* [Harper's Weekly]**

to work its way around a station, the Geep can go easily in either direction. It can also be coupled onto a work extra or a wrecking train. *See also* SWITCHMOBILE.

BIBLIOGRAPHY: Kincaid Herr, *The Louisville & Nashville Railroad,* Louisville & Nashville Railroad, Louisville, 1964; Maury Klein, *History of the Louisville & Nashville Railroad,* Macmillan, New York, 1972.

Georgia Railroad Line with at least two distinctions. From 1836 to 1881 it was the Georgia Railroad & Banking Company, authorized to issue its own currency and handle other financial business as well as operate a railroad. And its first locomotive, the diamond-stacked 4-4-0 *Florida,* was hauled along dirt roads, without rails, by mule teams from Madison, Georgia, to Atlanta on Christmas Eve, 1834; on May 21, 1837, she pulled the first train to run in that state. *See* CURRENCY ISSUED BY RAILROADS.

Chartered on December 21, 1833, the Georgia was opened to Madison in 1842, and its 171-mile mainline was completed to Atlanta on September 18, 1845. Its builder and chief engineer, John Edgar Thompson, later became the Pennsylvania Railroad's third president. At first the Georgia prospered, but during the Civil War it had more than its share of destruction. Gen. William T. Sherman's march to the sea wrecked more than 60 miles of its track, burned depots, and destroyed bridges. Afterward, although impoverished, the line carried more than 100,000 discharged Confederate soldiers home without charge. *See* CIVIL WAR.

Besides acquiring a branch line to Macon, the road became the principal owner of the Atlanta & West Point Railroad (A&WP; West Point Route) and co-owner of the Western Railway of Alabama. In 1881 the combined roads were leased to Col. William H. Bradley for a 99-year period, and the banking company became a separate unit. Bradley leased half of his interest in the Georgia to the Louisville & Nashville, which eventually acquired the other half also and assigned it to the Atlantic Coast Line. Today the Georgia and its subsidiaries form a 400-mile part of the 16,000-plus miles of the Family Lines System and consist of a merger of three short lines running between Augusta, Georgia, and Selma, Alabama, via Atlanta and Montgomery. *See* FAMILY LINES SYSTEM; LOUISVILLE & NASHVILLE RAILROAD.

The Georgia Railroad embraces two short lines: the A&WP, which began construction in 1845 and was completed in 1854; and the Western Railway of Alabama, which had its beginning in 1832 and was completed in 1851. In 1859 the A&WP hauled over 200,000 bales of cotton, a good index of railroad prosperity in that era; and in 1863 about 200,000 of its 286,000 passengers were Confederate soldiers. Both roads suffered severe damage during the War between the States. In 1870 the Western of Alabama took over the A&WP. The merged companies went into receivership and in 1875 were sold to the Georgia, and eventually to their present owner, the Seaboard Coast Line, senior partner in the Family Lines System. *See* CSX CORP.

Ghost Train (White Train) Term commonly used to describe the *New England Limited,* which was operated over the New York, New Haven & Hartford and the New York & New England Railroads between New York and Boston via Lyman Viaduct and Putnam, Connecticut. Inaugurated on November 10, 1884, it acquired new equipment on March 16, 1891: white cars with gold trim, which made a weird appearance running through the night. Leaving New York at 3 a.m., the train reached Boston in 6 hours but was discontinued on October 18, 1895.

GM&O *See* GULF, MOBILE, & OHIO RAILROAD.

Golden Spike Ceremony Driving a golden spike into a laurel crosstie at windswept Promontory, Utah, on May 10, 1869, ended the era of the buffalo-hunting Indian, the free fur trapper, the wagon-trail pioneer, and the Pony Express. This "wedding of the rails" created the first transcontinental railroad. It materialized an idea that the press had been urging at least since 1832, when *The Emigrant,* a weekly newspaper of Ann Arbor, Michigan, pointed out the need for rails to the West Coast. Both major political parties put the idea into their national platforms in 1852, 1856, and 1860. Presidents Pierce, Buchanan, and Lincoln sent special messages to Congress strongly recommending it.

In 1851 Congress ordered a survey to find the best route. Five routes were suggested. Two of those routes were ruled out because they ran through Southern territory and two Northern ones because they did not lead directly to California. Finally, Congress accepted and subsidized the middle way in the Pacific Railroad Act, which Lincoln signed on July 1, 1862. This line roughly followed the 42d parallel up the Platte River and across southern Wyoming and Nevada into California—a route already known to the forty-niners and land-hungry immigrants. It is today the east-west route of two vast rail systems, Union Pacific and Southern Pacific.

The initial cash subsidy for laying rails was $16,000 a mile on the plains of Nebraska and Wyoming—an area which early maps designated the Great American Desert—and from $32,000 to $48,000 over the mountains. The builders also were given free use of timber, sand, and gravel from public lands and were granted alternate, odd-numbered sections of public land extending chessboard-style 20 miles deep on both sides of the track. *See* LAND GRANTS.

In the East, the Union Pacific (UP) was organized largely by Thomas Clark Durant, Oliver Ames, and Sidney Dillon. Out West, the Central Pacific (later renamed Southern Pacific) was organized by the Big Four: Leland Stanford, Collis P. Huntington, Mark Hopkins, and Charles Crocker. These men handled the financing, bossed the job, and incidentally became involved in a series of scandals that rocked the nation's capital and Wall Street. *See* CROCKER, CHARLES; HOPKINS, MARK; HUNTINGTON, COLLIS POTTER; STANFORD, LELAND.

Surveyors, engineers, graders, and tracklayers engaged in an all-out drive that began in 1866 and finished in 1869. They toiled and suffered; many died in the sultry heat above 100°F, in biting cold and deep snow, on the seemingly endless plains and in the high Sierras of California and the Wasatch Mountains of Utah. Side by side with federal troops the UP railroad builders fought the bewildered Indians, who resented the "fire horse's" invasion of their homeland and realized it meant an end to their way of life. Many were killed on both sides. By contrast, the advancing Central Pacific forces had no serious trouble with the Indians.

The logistics of the construction job were unprecedented. Rails and other manufactured supplies for the Central Pacific were shipped on windjammers around Cape Horn, the southern tip of South America, while ties for the Union Pacific had to be hauled over hundreds of miles of treeless prairies, and locomotives were dragged across hard ice before the Missouri River was bridged. Among the most modern tools available in that nonmechanized era were scrapers, hand shovels, sledgehammers, pickaxes, and black powder, plus the muscular power of men, horses, mules, and oxen.

Major Gen. Grenville M. Dodge and the Casement brothers steadily drove the UP rails westward, using crews made up mostly of Irish immigrants who had fled to America from a potato famine. Construction Superintendent J. H. Strobridge pushed and cajoled the Central Pacific's Chinese laborers in an even more difficult task of grading, tunneling, bridging, and laying rail in the Sierras and eastward across sunbaked Nevada badlands toward Promontory. *See* CHINESE LABOR; DODGE, GRENVILLE MELLEN.

As UP iron was thrust westward across Wyoming, temporary centers of vice and crime known as hell on wheels had tents that supplied liquor, gambling tables, and fancy women to the hard-worked railroad builders and occasional cowboys. In the gunfights that ensued it was not rare for men to succumb to "lead poisoning" and be buried in Boot Hill, the local graveyard. Off to the west, as the Central Pacific built tunnels and long wooden sheds to ward off record snows, the ores of newly discovered mines were sent to smelters via the new rails.

Eventually the rails converged on Promontory. Work trains carried Chinese and Irish laborers to the golden spike ceremony. A Central Pacific special from Sacramento and UP Palace cars from Omaha edged up to the 50-foot gap between the two railheads on which the nations's attention was focused. At the scene were civic

***The Golden Spike ceremony at Promontory, Utah, on May 10, 1869, celebrated the creation of the first transcontinental railroad. Two locomotives met on the newly wedded rails.* [*Union Pacific Railroad*]**

leaders, newspaper correspondents, unsavory camp followers, immigrants, and excited youngsters eager to view their first locomotives. Swelling the crowd were Mormon farmers and four companies of the 21st U.S. Infantry with their regimental band.

Every telegraph office in the country was tuned in for the event. Special wires were installed so that contact between a silver-headed spike maul and the golden spike would sound out over the wires. Thus the golden spike ceremony became the first event to be "broadcast" from coast to coast.

Two eight-wheeled engines, the Central Pacific's *Jupiter,* a balloon-stacked woodburner, and UP's No. 119, a tall-stacked coalburner, both of which had hauled the specials, reached the gap in the rail ends, each with a full head of steam but neither one decorated. Officials had brought a laurel crosstie from California, well-polished and bearing a silver plate. There was also a silver spike from Nevada's fabulous Comstock Lode, and the Governor of Arizona Territory produced a spike of gold, silver, and iron alloy. Idaho and Montana, originally far from the new railway although connected later, furnished a silver spike apiece.

Interest centered on the California spike. Fashioned from $400 worth of gold by a San Francisco jewelry firm (whose bill was only $25.24 for the work of making it, including the engraving), it bears the engraved legend: "The last Spike—the Pacific Railroad—ground broken January 8, 1863."

Just before General Dodge introduced the Rev. John Todd of Pittsfield, Massachusetts, who made a formal prayer, telegrapher W. N. Shilling tapped out: "Almost ready. Hats off. Prayer's being offered." Then the other special spikes were presented. California's Governor Stanford, who was president of the Central Pacific, and General Dodge spoke briefly, and the silver and alloy spikes were driven.

At about 12:30 Stanford swung his wired silver maul. The telegrapher sent a one-word message, "Done." Then came this official report to President Grant: "Promontory, Utah. The last rail is laid. The last spike is driven. The Pacific Railroad is completed. The point of junction is 1,088 miles west of the Missouri River and 690 miles east of Sacramento City. Leland Stanford/T. C. Durant." That touched off one of the wildest celebrations in the nation's history. People cheered, whistles sounded, 100-gun salutes were fired, and fire-alarm bells and church bells rang throughout the land. Philadelphia rang the long-silent Liberty Bell. Te Deums were sung, and special services held in churches. Festivities continued far into the night, with speeches and fireworks.

At Promontory, the two locomotives inched forward to touch pilots. Official photographs of that event show Stanford and Durant shaking hands and men standing on the pilot beams of the engines extending champagne bottles toward each other. The original golden spike may be seen today in the Stanford University Museum at Palo Alto, California. The whereabouts of the other precious-metal spikes are not known. The famous last tie was displayed at Southern Pacific headquarters in San Francisco until the 1906 earthquake and fire destroyed both the offices and the tie.

The golden spike ceremony was reenacted on its 100th anniversary, May 10, 1969, with two historic engines resembling the *Jupiter* and No. 199 at Golden Spike National Historic Site, established by the National Park Service 100 miles west of the present Brigham City, Utah. The original gold spike was borrowed for the occasion.

BIBLIOGRAPHY: Lucius Beebe, *The Central Pacific and the Southern Pacific Railroads,* Howell-North, Berkeley, Calif., 1963; Gerald M. Best, *Iron Horses to Promontory,* Golden West Books, San Marino, Calif., 1969; *Golden Spike,* National Park Service Historical Handbook No. 40, GPO, Washington, 1969; Edwin L. Sabin, *Building the Pacific Railway,* Lippincott, Philadelphia, 1919.

Gould, George Jay (1864-1923) Son of Jay Gould, who had one great ambition, to control a rail route between the Atlantic and the Pacific, which his father's wealth, power, and cunning had never succeeded in doing. The old man had died in 1892, leaving George master of nearly 6000 miles of railroad. Soon the son had five big roads under his thumb: the Missouri Pacific, the Wabash, the Texas & Pacific, the St. Louis Southwestern, and the International & Great Northern. Then came expansion. George Gould began to build the Western Pacific and gradually bought control of the Denver and Rio Grande (D&RG), the Western Maryland, the West Virginia Central, and the Wheeling & Lake Erie (W&LE). The prize, a transcontinental rail system, was then almost within his grasp. All that he still needed to achieve his goal was entry into Pittsburgh. *See* GOULD, JAY.

Until the turn of the century, the Pennsylvania Railroad (PRR) had Pittsburgh sewed up tighter than a drum. Pittsburgh's tonnage of coal, ore, and iron exceeded that of any other three American cities combined and was, perhaps, the biggest single factor in the Pennsy's greatness. Some 75 million tons of Pittsburgh freight rolled out annually on PRR rails. No wonder that the Pennsylvania had been careful to control the railroads penetrating the region, that is, all but the Pittsburgh & Lake Erie (in the Vanderbilt system) and United States Steel's Bessemer & Lake Erie. These two, however, lined up with the Pennsy against George Gould.

Alexander J. Cassatt, president of PRR, and his ally, ironmaster Henry Clay Frick, must have smiled complacently when they first heard that Gould's Wabash was planning to enter Pittsburgh. The Pennsy's virtual monopoly of that city seemed impregnable. But Gould had quietly lobbied through Congress a bill authorizing a so-called streetcar company to build a bridge over the

Monongahela River into Pittsburgh. Cassatt fought in vain in the courts to block such a bridge construction. A wave of national prosperity worked against the Pennsy by blockading its Pittsburgh yards and creating an unprecedented shortage of freight cars. By plentiful use of money, Gould brought about the election of a Pittsburgh City Council favoring his scheme.

Although backed by such financial giants as John D. Rockefeller, Andrew Carnegie, and Russell Sage, Gould took 4 years to build a 60-mile railroad from his W&LE near Jewett, Ohio, into Pittsburgh over the new bridge, one of the finest cantilever spans of its day. The line included 59 other bridges and 20 tunnels. But at last the first Wabash (Gould) train rolled into a new and expensive Pittsburgh terminal over a single-track line.

That entry into Pittsburgh had cost an estimated $35 million to $40 million, a huge chunk out of even the Gould fortune; and the line turned out to be a white elephant, a road into one of the world's busiest traffic centers but with inadequate facilities for handling freight. The combination of excessive cost plus clashes with E. H. Harriman soon led to Gould's downfall. The transcontinental dream almost but never quite materialized. Gould's ambitious structure collapsed in the panic of 1907 just as he was closing the final gap in his ocean-to-ocean scheme. *See* HARRIMAN, EDWARD HENRY.

In 1908 the Harriman interests took over most of his rail network of more than 16,000 miles, and it was split up. Long before Gould died in France in 1923 he had lost control of every unit in his rail empire except the D&RG and the Rio Grande Southern.

BIBLIOGRAPHY: Stewart H. Holbrook, *The Age of the Moguls,* Doubleday, Garden City, N.Y., 1953; Matthew Josephson, *The Robber Barons,* Harcourt, Brace, New York, 1934; John Moody, *The Masters of Capital,* Yale, New Haven, Conn., 1919; Gustavus Myers, *History of the Great American Fortunes,* 3 vols., Charles H. Kerr & Company, Chicago, 1910.

Gould, Jay (1836-1892) The "Great Manipulator" of rail stocks and the first American to amass a $100 million fortune. He was born on May 27, 1836, on a farm at Roxbury, New York, exactly 32 years after the birth of his archenemy, Commodore Cornelius Vanderbilt. After working in a rural store, Jay became a surveyor, invented a mousetrap, and wrote a 450-page *History of Delaware County.* He and a partner built what was then the nation's largest tannery, at Gouldsboro, Pennsylvania, a town named for him. The firm prospered, but Gould used more than his share of the profits to operate a bank at Stroudsburg, Pennsylvania. His second partner, whom he also cheated, shot and killed himself, making Gould an independent leather merchant.

At 24, living in New York City, he wedded Ellen Miller, whose father virtually owned the Rutland & Washington Railroad (R&W) in upstate New York and Vermont. Borrowing cash from his father-in-law, Gould took over the line himself. In an operation unlike his later railroad policy, he improved the R&W to such an extent that he sold it for about $130,000 profit to a predecessor of the present Delaware and Hudson.

Seeing big money in the railroad business, he won control of the Cleveland & Pittsburgh by speculation and sold it to the expanding Pennsylvania Railroad at thrice its cost. This transaction evoked a formula that would bring him enormous wealth and power: buy a small road when its stock is cheap, manipulate its stock to a higher level, and then sell out to a big system without having spent money to improve it.

Gould learned how to force a stock price down before buying it, how to influence legislators, judges, and political bosses by generous gifts, and how to work with money masters without letting personal friendship spoil a chance to make a big haul. As he climbed the ladder, he ruined his first two Wall Street partners.

By ingratiating himself with Daniel Drew, the Great Bear of Wall Street, Gould wormed his way into the directorate of the New York, Lake Erie & Western Railroad, commonly called the Erie. The clique then ruling the 773-mile Erie needed money. By 1855 Drew had loaned them nearly $2 million. They could not repay him, so he seized the road and, significantly, became its treasurer. Vanderbilt was then the nation's wealthiest man. He bought enough stock to control the Erie and decided to use Drew as his right-hand man. He also put two other stock manipulators on the board: Gould and the pompous voluptuary James Fisk. Vanderbilt was soon to regret this choice. *See* DREW, DANIEL; FISK, JAMES; VANDERBILT, CORNELIUS.

The Erie was a great railroad with over $16 million in reserve. Gould, Drew, and Fisk, nicknamed the Unholy Three, halted Vanderbilt's raid on its stock by printing new watered securities as fast as he could buy them. When the victim sought legal redress, the three conspirators fled across the Hudson River to Jersey City with the Erie's money and operated the railroad from a hotel there. Hearing rumors that Vanderbilt would send a gang of thugs across the river to kidnap them for trial in New York, they obtained a guard of 15 policemen and many Erie Railroad detectives. Jubilee Jim Fisk, with his usual flair for the bombastic, assumed the title of admiral and strutted around in a ridiculous uniform. At the same time, the Erie was reincorporated as a New Jersey company and opened a passenger-rate war with Commodore Vanderbilt's New York Central & Hudson River Railroad.

One day Gould quietly slipped out of Jersey City with $500,000 in greenbacks in a suitcase on a secret mission to Albany, the New York capital. There, according to historian Charles Francis Adams, who was later associated with Gould, "he assiduously cultivated a thorough understanding between himself and the Legislature," after which it passed a bill legalizing the fraudulent issue of Erie stock. The Unholy Three bought back most of the Erie stock they had sold to Vanderbilt. Thereupon

Vanderbilt and Drew pulled out of the Erie, leaving the other two plotters in full control. Gould elected himself president and Fisk vice president.

Vanderbilt wanted revenge. As head of the powerful New York Central competing with the Erie, already engaged in a passenger-rate war, he launched a costly freight-rate war. The price of hauling a carload of cattle from Buffalo to New York on both railroads had been $125. Vanderbilt cut it to $100. Thereupon Gould dropped it to $75 and Vanderbilt to $50, and finally Gould to $25. The enraged commodore cut the rate to $1 a carload. Below that Gould could not go. He restored the Erie rate to its normal level and let Vanderbilt's road handle all the cattle business, at a terrific loss.

Wily Jay Gould then bought every available head of cattle west of Buffalo, shipped them over the Central virtually free, and cleared a huge profit in Manhattan markets. The old commodore admitted defeat. "Gould is the smartest man in America," he said.

In October 1866, Gould and Fisk added two new men to the Erie board: Boss William Marcy Tweed and his chief henchman, Peter R. Sweeny. With rate wars, political contacts, and the glittering pageantry of the New York Grand Opera House on 23d Street, which served as Erie Railroad headquarters, Jay Gould found little time or inclination to improve railroad property, replace the worn-out roadbed or rolling stock, or ease the plight of underpaid employees. Exhausted crews dozed at their posts; train wrecks were commonplace. Sometimes overturning coal stoves set fire to wooden-bodied coaches with appalling casualty lists. After one such pileup a newspaper headline proclaimed, "Another Erie Massacre!"

In 1868 came what Adams called "the most extraordinary feat of financial legerdemain which history has yet recorded"—a daring move by Gould and Fisk to pick up a few more millions by Erie stock speculation. That autumn as usual the West clamored for money to move its crops. This demand cued the masters of the Erie to deposit huge sums in the New York banks and suddenly withdraw them, thus weakening the city's fiscal structure. Stockbrokers felt the money shortage first. Calling in their loans, they asked for more margin from their customers, who then had to sell their securities at heavy losses.

The Gould-Fisk scheme was to unload, at top prices, vast blocks of stock for future delivery—securities they did not own at the time but intended to buy when the market dropped. This project took $12 million in currency from circulation and raised the Erie stock total from $34 million to $54 million. Not being in on this plot, Drew plunged deeply.

To ease the money shortage and restore public confidence, the U.S. Treasury, on orders from President Ulysses S. Grant, announced that it would release $50 million in currency to the New York banks. Then without mentioning their new plans to the Great Bear, Gould and Fisk secretly swung over to the other side, bought Erie stock, and reaped huge additional wealth. Drew was cleaned out. Of Gould he said, "His touch is death."

Gould's next gigantic foray into the financial market led to Black Friday, the gold panic of September 24, 1869. Again the federal government stepped in to relieve the artificial crisis. Numerous speculators, both large and small, were ruined; several suicides resulted. But, as before, Gould not only kept his vast fortune intact but augmented it by switching again to the other side at the first hint of federal intervention. This time he did not even tip off Fisk, who lost heavily.

Encouraged by the death of Fisk in January 1872, a group of capitalists forced Gould out of the Erie. The railroad's books revealed that his mismanagement had resulted in the theft of at least $12 million of Erie money. Gould was arrested and held under heavy bonds. But pretending meekness, he promised to make restitution, and Erie stock soared. Then he disavowed his plan to disgorge. The stock slumped again, and he bought back much of his former holdings at a low price. Thus Gould made money even on his own bad reputation. He finally gave up only $200,000 of his ill-gotten gains instead of the $12 million demanded.

Between 1868 and 1873, the books showed, Gould's regime had issued $64 million of watered Erie stock. "Yet during that time," wrote his biographer, Robert I. Warshow, "not one dollar was represented by any addition to the real investment of the railroad. Though one of the most important systems in the country, and doing an enormous business, it was so crippled with its enormous security issues that for many years it was forced to remain in receiver's hands. Not until 1891 did it pay a dividend."

Expelled from the Erie, Gould turned to the Union Pacific (UP). It was already staggering under the effects of a gigantic fraud, the Crédit Mobilier scandal, and its stock had sunk to a new low. Aided by Russell Sage and other capitalists, Gould set out to seize this carrier. By 1874 he had gotten himself elected to its board of directors.

His next move was to buy the Kansas Pacific (KP), a competing road of 638 miles, then in receivership. Gould got it for a "reasonable" price. More stock buying gave him control of the Denver Pacific (DP), the Missouri Pacific (MP), and the Central Pacific (now Southern Pacific). With these properties as bait, he offered a combination of them all to amalgamate with the UP on the basis of an equal stock exchange. (Gould also held the Wabash and a large part of the Texas & Pacific.)

KP stock was then quoted at only $13 and the Union Pacific's at $66, so the big road naturally rejected Gould's proposal. But he forced acceptance. Because the bankrupt KP was unhampered by interest charges, it could and did cut both freight and passenger rates and still make a profit at the UP's expense. That anyone could so act against a company for which he was a director may seem incredible to persons unfamiliar with Gould's tactics.

Gould even threatened to open a new competitive route to the West Coast. Facing this threat, UP yielded. In May 1887, it amalgamated with the KP, DP, and MP on Gould's terms. This deal added over $10 million to Gould's bankroll. His wealth at age 45 was estimated at over $100 million; no other American had ever amassed so much riches.

Meanwhile, with Russell Sage's backing, Gould had gained control of Western Union Telegraph Co., virtually seizing it from under the nose of the late commodore's son, William H. Vanderbilt. This he did by building a rival telegraph line. Through manipulating Western Union stock he also took over the competing American Union Telegraph Co., which he had sold to the Vanderbilts some time before.

Then he and Sage, aided by Cyrus W. Field of Atlantic cable fame, acquired the New York City elevated railroads and forced Field into bankruptcy. The Gould forces added some $13 million of watered stock to the elevated lines, raised fares, and cut the wages of agents and gatemen, who already were toiling more than 12 hours a day for $1.75. Being unorganized, the el employees had to accept the cut.

But in 1885, when Gould's Missouri Pacific cut wages, the MP shopmen's union went on strike and won the strike. Gould, running true to form, ignored the shopmen's agreement. A second and more violent walkout in 1886 tied up freight traffic on more than 4500 miles of track. That time the Great Manipulator won, incidentally dealing a death blow to the Knights of Labor with its 500,000 members.

As years sped by, he aged prematurely. He had been a wolf-pack leader, and when he became ill and shaky, the pack closed in on him; the financial panic of 1884 cost Gould about $20 million. The moneyed world was stunned to see him unable to support his stocks on the market. His days of sensational plunging were over.

He spent much of his last few years quietly in his beautiful gardens in a pathetic effort to regain his health. On December 3, 1892, he died; all locomotives, steam Forney types, on his elevated lines were draped in black.

BIBLIOGRAPHY: Charles F. Adams, Jr., and Henry Adams, *Chapters of Erie,* Great Seal Books, Cornell University Press, Ithaca, N.Y., 1956; Robert H. Fuller, *Jubilee Jim,* Macmillan, New York, 1928; Julius Grodinsky, *Jay Gould: His Business Career, 1867-1892,* University of Pennsylvania Press, Phildelphia, 1957; Edward Hungerford, *Men of Erie,* Random House, New York, 1946; Matthew Josephson, *The Robber Barons,* Harcourt, Brace, New York, 1934; Edward H. Mott, *Between the Ocean and the Lakes: The Story of Erie,* J. S. Collins, New York, 1899; Bouck White, *Book of Daniel Drew,* Doubleday, Doran, New York, 1910.

Grain Traffic Cyrus McCormick's invention of the reaper in 1831 enabled farmers to grow much more wheat, but if railroads hadn't come along at about that time to haul it to market, the reaper would have been less valuable. The railroads gave the farmer a national, and later an international, market.

In 1861, during the Great Lakes navigation season, when large quantities of paper currency were in circulation and grain was the Illinois Central's (IC's) chief freight commodity, that railroad accepted millions of bushels of grain in lieu of cash, thus enabling thousands of farmers to meet their current obligations. The farmers had refused to ship their corn and wheat because they had no confidence in shinplasters, as paper currency was called. Unless they sold these crops, many of them could not make payments on land bought from the railroad. The IC agreed to take grain as legal tender, even buying it at higher prices than the local markets offered, but only in payment for land notes overdue.

The railroads' wider distribution of farm products spurred farm mechanization. More acres were cultivated with less help. That permitted farm boys to forsake the barnyard and go to Detroit, for example, to help make the automobiles and trucks that compete with the railroads.

Railroads and the farmer profit from close contact with one another. The roads' immigration departments helped to colonize the agricultural areas. Many carriers have permanent staffs of experienced agricultural agents to promote farm industry. Tillers of the soil with products to ship benefit from the technological advances made in motive power, cars, trucks, automatic classification yards, etc.

Numerous railroads were developed primarily as connecting links between the farmers and their markets. Some built feeder lines to hold and increase their grain traffic. Few American railroads could get along without the traffic originating on or destined to the nation's farms. It is also true that American agriculture could not thrive without rail transportation. The railroad is the only service at the farmers' beck and call that assures them a nationwide distribution all year around. Low grain rates made possible by unit trains led to the building of flour mills near major Eastern markets, decentralizing this activity from the Grain Belt states. Recently a unit train was introduced to haul flour from Kansas City to a new distribution center near Baltimore, making the Kansas City flour mill competitive in Eastern markets with mills located in the area. *See* UNIT TRAINS.

It seems illogical for any regulatory agency to oppose a cut in freight rates which benefits the consumer, but the Interstate Commerce Commission (ICC) did so for 4 years. This is what happened. After developing 100-ton aluminum closed-hopper cars known as Big Johns, the Southern Railway System figured that it could offer multiple-car grain shippers rates 60 percent below the prevailing level and still operate profitably. The ICC said no. Prior to its long-delayed acceptance of the rate cut, there were 7 months of ICC hearings, two appearances before lower federal courts, and two before the U.S. Supreme Court. The high court returned the case to the ICC, saying that the agency's ruling was not "supported by adequate findings." Finally, in 1965, the Commission authorized the rate cut. This was good news for the grain-surplus Midwest and saved Southern farmers, millers, and consumers an estimated $40 million a year.

The embargo on grain for the Soviet Union which President Carter imposed in January 1980 had no significant impact on America's total grain exports. In fact, during the early months of 1980 the export pace actually increased by about 2 percent over the corresponding period in 1979. Railroads moved 51.3 percent of the total volume of grain exports in the calendar year 1979, the rest being hauled to port by barges and trucks.

The improvement in rail grain service in recent years stems mainly from new types of equipment such as the Big Johns (the industry in early 1980 had some 32,000 more large covered-hopper cars in its grain fleet and 800-plus more diesel locomotives in the power fleet than it had had the previous year), new kinds of service such as unit trains and intermodal movements, more centralized and bigger elevators, and joint planning with agricultural and state interests. The use of multiple cars for grain loading produces 3 times as much car utilization as do single carloadings. Entire unit trains of grain cars can double those efficiency figures. The railroads have large sums invested in grain elevators, storage bins, warehouses, freight sidings, and loading platforms.

BIBLIOGRAPHY: Robert S. Henry, *This Fascinating Railroad Business*, 3d ed., rev., Bobbs-Merrill, Indianapolis, 1946.

Grand Central Terminal Snow began falling lightly on January 4, 1877, just as Commodore Cornelius Vanderbilt died in his Fifth Avenue mansion in New York City, but turned into a blizzard that tied up traffic and piled tons of snow on the old man's railroad station little more than a block away. So ponderous was the weight of snow that the vast glass roof curving over the trainshed fell with a mighty crash onto the eight-wheeled locomotives and wooden cars standing there.

That station was Grand Central Depot, completed about 6 years before on the present site of Grand Central Terminal. Prior to 1871, the locality was a minor 42d Street stop on the New York & Harlem Railway (later New York Central), which ran from northern Manhattan Island, through a tunnel under wide Park Avenue, to 26th Street. The roof was soon repaired. In the late 1890s the building was remodeled, enlarged, and renamed Grand Central Station.

On January 8, 1902, an express smashed into a commuter train which had stopped for a red signal in the smoke-filled tunnel, taking 17 lives. To avert similar tragedies, the State Legislature outlawed steam locomotives in the tunnel south of the Harlem River, effective in 1908. Terminal operations had to be electrified. And because the passenger load kept increasing, the edifice would have to be redesigned to handle more trains. Already it was too small and overcrowded.

The Central's chief engineer, William J. Wilgus, faced the problem of how to get more trains into and out of the station without enlarging the area. By this time midtown Manhattan land had become prohibitively expensive, and the city would not let the railroad expand its passenger-train yard. Additional tracks had to be kept within the 48 acres owned by the road. Wilgus solved the problem with a stroke of genius. He'd bring trains into the station on *two* levels. With operations electrified, the tracks could be covered over and the streets and great buildings rise above them.

So that was done. After almost a decade of complicated work, while trains continued to run normally, the present Grand Central Terminal (GCT) and right-of-way, hewn out of a rock formation, replaced the old station. Every day for nearly 10 years more than 400 carloads of rubble were taken out. The whole job cost close to $65 million.

Grand Central's real work goes on below ground level. The upper-level tracks, most of which you enter from the main concourse, lie about 20 feet below the street. Lower-level platforms are 26 feet farther down. Two even deeper levels contain a power plant, workrooms, lockers, a mail tunnel, etc. The upper level has 66 tracks totaling 18.8 miles, and the lower level 57 tracks totaling 14.9 miles, making 33.7 miles in Grand Central and its yard. There are 48 platform tracks, 11 of which are loop tracks and 37 stub-end. At 57th Street, a mile north of 42d, the four main tracks start to fan out east, west, and downward.

The yard below street level is an eerie place of gloomy caverns, heavy support columns, gleaming rails, and red and yellow signal lights. Train speed south of 57th Street must not exceed 10 miles per hour. The loop-track speed limit is 6 miles per hour. Between Grand Central and the Mott Haven yard in the Bronx, one of the world's busiest stretches of track, traffic is controlled by four signal towers. One of them, beneath the Waldorf-Astoria Hotel, is a unique two-story tower, one floor controlling train movements on the upper level and the other on the lower level, with a total of some 356 switches and 516 signal lights. At least, there were that many before Amtrak took the long-distance passenger trains out of Grand Central and moved them to Penn Station, over 1 mile away, and GCT's status sank to little more than a commuter station.

In its heyday, the big terminal served long-distance and commuter traffic on both the New York Central and the New York, New Haven & Hartford systems. The year 1946 was the high point for United States rail travel. Beginning in June of that year, passengers could board California-bound cars in Grand Central and stay on them all the way to the West Coast. At that time GCT boasted 96 long-distance trains departing and 90 arriving every day. For many years a long red carpet was rolled out across the station platform for passengers of the Central's most luxurious train, the *20th Century Limited.*

The terminal, which is only eight stories high, is dwarfed by surrounding skyscrapers, especially the giant Pan Am Building. It is 330 feet long, 280 feet wide, and 150 feet high. Below street level it is 745 feet long and 550 feet wide. Facing south on 42d Street, it sits squarely on Park Avenue. Automobiles go around it on two elevated roadways running from 41st to 45th Street. From GCT's main waiting room, which is 50 feet high, a ramp leads down to the 275-feet-long concourse.

Often, sunlight streaming down through the terminal's five high windows on the south side create a cathedral-like effect. The vaulted ceiling contains a blue-and-gold mural of the zodiac from October to March, once beautiful but now faded. It shows 2500 stars, 50 of them electrically lighted to illustrate the major constellations. The four-faced, globular gilded clock above the main information booth has been functioning since the terminal opened in January 1913 and is known to millions of people, but the booth is now used only for city and suburban traffic. "Meet me at the golden clock" has long been a favorite way of making appointments.

The green bronze statue of Vanderbilt that stands on a pedestal just outside the terminal on 42d Street, facing the upper-level motor highway on Park Avenue, was brought uptown in 1929 from the old St. John's Park freight station, where the commodore himself erected it in 1869.

Another tribute to Vanderbilt consists of three rats climbing hawsers (thick ropes that moor ships) extending upward and inward from above what used to be the marquee of a terminal newsreel theater. Each hawser includes a hollow, conelike device known as a rat guard, intended to prevent dockside rodents from entering a ship. This architectural motif is iron. It recalls the fact that the commodore began his working life as a mariner and made a fortune in the steamship business before he went into railroading.

With rail passenger revenue down enormously in recent years, owing mostly to highway competition, GCT's owner, Penn Central Transportation Company, planned to raze the old edifice and erect on its site a 53-story office building, subordinating the railroad facilities, as was done with New York's once-famous Penn Station, or at least to use the present terminal building as part of the proposed skyscraper in such a way that its distinctive character and architectural beauty would be lost forever, in addition to which the already dense traffic congestion in midtown Manhattan would be increased immensely.

Travelers stroll through Grand Central in its heyday, circling the information booth with its golden clock. **[*New York Central Railroad*]**

The gigantic Pan Am Building, which adjoins and towers high above GCT, impairing its charm, had been built before New York City's landmark preservation law went into effect in 1965, covering the terminal and other places. Now the outcry against the proposed 53-story building led the U.S. Department of the Interior to add GCT to the National Register of Historic Places, thus protecting it from destruction.

The case finally reached the U.S. Supreme Court, which rejected, 6 to 3, Penn Central's argument that prohibition of its plan would be an unconstitutional taking of its property (actually, air space above the terminal) without just compensation and that the taxpayers rather than the owners should bear the financial burden of "any restriction imposed on individual landmarks." The Trump Organization, which owns the terminal, began in 1980 to restore its interior with the aid of some city sales tax money remitted for that purpose.

BIBLIOGRAPHY: John A. Droege, *Passenger Terminals and Trains,* McGraw-Hill, New York, 1916; David Marshall, *Grand Central,* McGraw-Hill, New York, 1946; Carroll L. V. Meeks, *The Railroad Station: An Architectural History,* Yale, New Haven, Conn., 1956; William D. Middleton, *Grand Central: The World's Greatest Railway Terminal,* Golden West Books, San Marino, Calif., 1977.

Grand Trunk Railway Line that, by completing its final link in July 1853 between Montreal and Portland, Maine, became North America's first international railroad. In 1920 it joined the Canadian National System.

BIBLIOGRAPHY: George R. Stevens, *History of the Canadian National Railways,* Macmillan, New York, 1973.

Granger Laws Legislation passed in the mid-nineteenth century by Midwestern state legislatures requiring railroad rates to be cut to help depressed agriculture. At that time the states were the only authorities that regulated such rates. The laws were brought about by pressure from a widespread organization of farmers called the Patrons of Husbandry but commonly known as the Grange. The order's sudden and spectacular growth was based on the farmers' fear and hatred of the railroads, which they regarded as monopolistic and unscrupulous. For example, farmers in the region served by James J. Hill's Great Northern, harassed first by a plague of grasshoppers and then by the GN's high rates, said bitterly, "After the grasshoppers, we had Jim Hill." *See* HILL, JAMES JEROME.

Many Grange laws were both unfair and unworkable, but the "rebellion" had the effect of making railroad officials and employees in general more courteous, even conciliatory, although they did fight those laws in the courts. By 1876 the Grange itself was fast losing its influence. Congress settled the controversy by the Interstate Commerce Act of 1887, creating the Interstate Commerce Commission and later giving it power to fix rates and say yes or no to railroads' requests for abandonment of trackage.

BIBLIOGRAPHY: Stewart H. Holbrook, *The Story of American Railroads,* Crown, New York, 1947.

Graves, Trackside Thousands of trackside graves, mostly forgotten and no longer visible, dot the United States and Canada. Also there are more than a few cemeteries in which tombstones adorned with railroadish sculpture reveal the lifetime jobs of the deceased. We shall mention a few of them.

When the old Central Pacific (now Southern Pacific, or SP) was being built in the late 1860s, Chinese labor was cheap and plentiful; these men did most of the physical work. Mortality was heavy. Old-timers claimed, with some exaggeration, that one Chinese was buried for every tie laid along the route. In those days, track foremen didn't always assign men to dig graves for Chinese construction workers but sometimes heaved the bodies into the fills of earth and rock. *See* CHINESE LABOR.

Grave of an unknown boy who waved every day at Dakota Central Railway trains in the 1880s on a lonely prairie near the present town of Elrod, South Dakota. Chicago & North Western now operates the line, and each Memorial Day a train stops to let someone decorate the grave. [Chicago & North Western Transportation Company]

The only Chinese cemetery located on American railroad property is at Winnemucca, Nevada, on the Western Pacific (now part of the SP system). In years gone by, native Chinese desired, if they should die in foreign countries, to have their remains shipped back for burial in the homeland. The story is told of a special freight train, long ago, filled with Chinese bodies that had been accumulated for shipment by rail to San Francisco and thence by boat across the Pacific.

As for individual graves, some people say that "the little fellow" sleeping out eternity in a lonely spot on the South Dakota prairie near Elrod was the son of a couple who operated the cook car for a gang of laborers building the Chicago & North Western. Back in 1888 a boy, name unknown, would wave at a train which regularly hauled rock ballast for the tracklayers. Its conductor, Bill Chambers, waved back at him. One day the boy died of smallpox and was interred on the right-of-way, and the gandy dancers moved on. His death saddened Chambers, who marked the burial spot with a rectangle of stones and planted wild flowers there. For many years, even after he had been promoted to passenger service and then retired, Chambers continued to weed the tumulus occasionally and add fresh flowers. Still later, his daughter and then section foremen carried on this tradition.

On the Illinois Central Gulf (ICG) right-of-way at Gayle, Mississippi, a few miles north of New Albany, enclosed by a white picket fence, is the grave of an anonymous Frenchman who perished while helping to build the Chicago & Gulf Railroad, an antecedent of the ICG. Also down South is the tomb of an unidentified soldier, reputedly a Confedrate, who died fighting around Allatoona Pass in the mountains near Marietta, Georgia, in 1864. He was buried where he fell, near a railway track. His epitaph is "An Unkown Hero. He died for a cause he thought was right." An iron fence surrounds the site.

High on a hill blanketed with wild flowers in season near Compton, Virginia, is the sepulcher of a Norfolk & Western engineer, D. B. Menefee. Its headstone is unique in having doweled into it the actual whistle of the steam loco under which he and his fireman were crushed to death in 1906.

BIBLIOGRAPHY: Freeman Hubbard, *Railroad Avenue,* McGraw-Hill, New York, 1945.

Gravity Cars Cars that run downhill on railroad tracks with no power of their own. The best-known American examples ran on the Mount Tamalpais & Muir Woods line, called "the world's crookedest railway," near San Francisco. Shay steam locomotives pushed coaches for 8 miles to a summit ½ mile above sea level, where passengers had the option of going back on the train or coasting down the slope on one of the railway's fleet of four-wheeled gravity cars. A brakeman seated at the right front controlled each gravity car.

BIBLIOGRAPHY: Theodore G. Wurm and A. C. Graves, *The Crookedest Railroad in the World,* 2d rev. ed., Howell-North, Berkeley, Calif., 1960.

Great Lakes Trainferries "Car-ferrying can be damned monotonous or damned exciting," said Capt. Bernard Rota of the *City of Saginaw II,* the world's first turbine-electric-driven trainferry, launched in 1928. Daily for many years that flagship of the Chesapeake and Ohio (C&O) fleet crossed the 60 miles of Lake Michigan between Manitowoc, Wisconsin, and Ludington, Michigan, with a cargo of freight cars, automobiles, and passengers. Was it monotonous, really, to stand on the bridge by the moonlight, listening to the gentle slapping of waves, watching for harbor lights and changes in weather?

Exciting, yes. Wild storms arise suddenly. Many a time trainferries knifed their way through towering waves in howling gales, and not all of them made port safely. According to records kept by the United States Commissioner of Navigation, the terrible decade of 1878-1888 showed a total of 5999 vessels of all kinds wrecked on the Great Lakes, *1093 of them totally lost.*

Ice is a major problem, but along Lake Michigan there was a saying, "When C&O trainferries don't cross, nothing crosses." It was virtually true. Even in the winter of 1935, when hard, glistening ice extended from shore to shore, in some places 30 feet thick, the mighty *City of Saginaw II,* crunching ice, edged forward under full power. Somewhat more difficult was the slush ice, a mingling of sawdust from sawmills that often clogged ship's propellers in the long-gone era of Michigan's great logging industry. During heavy snowfalls, with a fierce wind blowing, dense slush often interfered with navigation so much that two or three trainferries, placed end to end and working their screws at top speed, would move ahead only a few hundred feet in several hours.

The Great Lakes' first trainferry and the first to cross an international border was the wooden *Great Western,* built in Scotland and put to work in 1866 between Detroit and Windsor, Ontario. The next two ferries, also wooden, were the *St. Ignace,* in 1888, and the *Ste. Marie,* in 1890. Both plied the straits of Mackinac, where Lake Michigan joins Lake Huron, linking two major railroads, the Michigan Central and the Duluth, South Shore & Atlantic.

One of the boats which replaced them, a steel version of the *Ste. Marie,* played a dramatic role in 1926. A blizzard which swept two big Canadian grain-shipping ports, Fort William and Port Arthur, on November 30, delayed the loading of the Dominion's grain fleet, 22 freighters, the insurance rates on which would expire at midnight. By 4 p.m. the snow had eased up; the ships were rush-loaded in 9 hours. Just before the insurance deadline, they set out to cross Lake Superior and reached the Soo Canal at 20°F below zero. There a huge ice-locked fleet, 105 other freighters, blocked their passage. News of the blockade of Canada's wheat crop nearly panicked the Chicago grain market. Something had to be done quickly. With the mercury down now to 35° below and a total of 127 cargo-laden vessels icebound in a relatively small area, the trainferry *Ste. Marie* steamed up from Lake Michigan at top speed to smash open a channel. She was the mightiest icebreaker on the lakes. For 10 weary days she bucked the ice, again and again and again, and finally broke through. Those 127 freighters headed triumphantly for open water, whistles screaming and crews cheering. Traders on the grain market slept better that night, thanks to a railroad trainferry.

James M. Ashley, builder and president of what later became the Ann Arbor Railroad, set up Lake Michigan's first trainferry service. Aware that his railroad would be locked into the Michigan Peninsula unless he conquered the water barrier, he had the trainferry *Ann Arbor I* built and induced a Pennsylvania coal operator to use her for the first time on November 21, 1892, by routing three carloads of coal through Frankfort and across the lake to Kewaunee, Michigan. Later, the Ann Arbor Railroad became the first line whose water route was longer than its land trackage.

In 1899 the *Ann Arbor I* set an all-time record for ferries stuck in ice. On February 2 she left Frankfort, bound for Menominee, but found so much ice in Green Bay that for 63 days and nights she could not move. The railroad management hired the stoutly built steamer *Algoma* to break her out, but in the process both ships smashed buckets off their wheels and lay there side by side in the frozen waste until the spring thaw. Men driving sleighs over the ice supplied the crews with fuel and other necessities.

After nearly 18 years of service, the *Ann Arbor I* was again stuck in a massive ice floe, but she got clear on March 8, 1910, and tied up at Manitowoc dock. On board were a score of freight cars loaded with lumber, charcoal, etc., and two men on duty as watchmen. Late that night while the men were sleeping, fire of unexplained origin broke out on the boat and kept up until noon the next day, burning her to the water's edge. The watchmen escaped by swimming ashore.

At first all Great Lakes ferries burned coal and were hand-fired. The overworked firemen had to stoke, dump ashes, rake out clinkers, bank fires, and clear boilers; and the turnover of boiler-room help was large. It was not very romantic to shovel dusty coal in a superheated room until your arms and back ached, your naked belly tightened into knots, and sweat and the leer of the white-hot firebox temporarily blinded you. But in time some of the coalburning ferries were equipped with mechanical stokers, and the others were converted to oil.

Long ago, trainferries starting out for a 1-day winter trip would take along enough emergency provisions to last 6 weeks. Sometimes a crew had to dynamite the almost mountain-high ice that wind piled up in their path. For years, Lake Michigan ferries maintained the only year-round navigation on open waters of the Great Lakes. Their frequent arrivals and departures rarely let surface ice get more than 4 or 5 inches thick along their routes even in the coldest weather.

The trainferry *Ashtabula,* put into service on Lake Erie in 1906, had a famous "winter bottom," so designed that she could free herself from ice jams by several methods. She had eight transverse bulkheads, the water in the compartments being controlled by ballast pumps. By filling the tanks aft and pumping out the forward ones at the same time, her bow was made to climb up onto and crush down an ice field.

For years Lake Michigan had the world's largest trainferry service, based on the amount of freight carried, the number of railroads involved, the multiplicity and size of the ferries, and the number of ports served. But in recent years the industry has petered out; most trainferries have been retired and not replaced. The C&O fleet dwindled from seven to three vessels.

In mid-1974, however, the Canadian Pacific (CP), which had had no previous trainferry line, instituted one on Lake Superior jointly with a British intermodal operator, forming Incan Ships Ltd. They put into service a bow-loading vessel of 31-freight-car capacity mainly to carry wood pulp and newsprint from Thunder Bay, on the CP, to Superior, on the Chicago & North Western. She avoids the ice problem by operating only during the navigation season.

Late in 1979 three roads, the C&O, Ann Arbor, and Grand Trunk Western, had trainferry service across Lake Michigan. That service's future is very dim. All three roads got Interstate Commerce Commission permission to abandon it and have partially done so. Trainferrying had become outmoded and profitless because the long-distance freight train of today has too many and too large cars to fit into the belly of a ferryboat. The ferries also take passengers on summer cruises across the lake. In 1978 those of the Chessie System carried 142,356 passengers at a loss. The ferries were built primarily to transport freight cars; the passenger business was only a sideline.

The Wabash Railroad ferry Windsor arrives in Windsor, Ontario, from Detroit, in 1957, through slush ice, age-old enemy of the Great Lakes trainferries. [Elmer Treloar/Collection of Freeman Hubbard]

On October 22, 1929, occurred the worst of all Great Lake ferry disasters: the Grand Trunk Western's *Milwaukee* foundered mysteriously in a Lake Michigan storm with her entire crew, between 47 and 52 men. Built at Cleveland in 1903, the *Milwaukee* left her name city at noon with 27 loaded boxcars. Not having a radio on board, she was never heard from again.

BIBLIOGRAPHY: Freeman Hubbard, *Great Trains of All Time,* Grosset & Dunlap, New York, 1962; George W. Hilton, *The Great Lakes Car Ferries,* Howell-North, Berkeley, Calif., 1962; Charles W. Turner, *Chessie's Road,* Garrett & Massie, Richmond, 1956.

Great Northern Railway *See* BURLINGTON NORTHERN INC.

Great Slave Lake Railway (GSL) Line, 432 miles long, that is really a branch of the Canadian National, which built it between 1962 and 1964. Its completion started traffic rolling for the first time into the vast northern wilderness of the Northwest Territories. The GSL runs northward for 377 miles from Roma, Alberta, the junction point with the Northern Alberta Railways, to Hay River, on the southern rim of Great Slave Lake, a desolate body of fresh water about half the size of Lake Michigan, with a 35-mile branch extending eastward to Pine Point. The railway was built mainly to develop the rich zinc and lead fields around Pine Point and to ship ore from open-pit mines to smelters about 900 miles away at Trail and Kennedy, British Columbia. Also moving over the GSL in great quantities are grain, lumber, pulp, and oil. Tall grain elevators and sawmills soon began rising beside the GSL as homesteading increased.

In 1964, for the first time rails were laid along the route in winter, when the mercury sometimes dipped to 47°F below zero. The main tracklaying equipment used was the highly automated *Pioneer,* the world's only such machine, although a few other roads have comparable monsters. Canadian National built it in 1956. The *Pioneer* served not only as a tracklayer but also as the power unit in a seven-car work train, pulling flatcars loaded with steel rails, ties, and rail fastenings. With a 50-man crew it laid track steadily, using 80- and 85-pound rail and creosoted jack-pine ties, at the rate of 1 mile or more per 10-hour day, moving forward at speeds up to 12 feet per minute.

BIBLIOGRAPHY: George R. Stevens, *History of the Canadian National Railways,* Macmillan, New York, 1973.

GSL *See* GREAT SLAVE LAKE RAILWAY.

Gulf, Mobile, & Ohio Railroad (GM&O) Like the New York Central (NYC), Great Northern, and Denver and Rio Grande, the GM&O was consistently for many years "the lengthened shadow of one man." The NYC was Commodore Vanderbilt, the Big G was James J. Hill, the Rio Grande was Gen. William J. Palmer, and the GM&O was Isaac Burton Tigrett (1879–1954), affectionately known as Ike. Those men were giants. Because major American rail systems are no longer being created from small beginnings, we will not see their like again.

Tigrett was born in Friendship, Tennessee, son of a Baptist preacher-farmer. He pyramided an $800 bequest from his father into a successful banking career after moving 42 miles to Jackson, Tennessee, where he dwelt for the rest of his life. In 1912, when the Birmingham & Northwestern Railroad (B&NW) was chartered, its promoters hired him to run it.

This was a 49½-mile, narrow-gauge, single-track link between Jackson and Dyersburg, Tennessee, many miles from Birmingham, Alabama, which it never reached. With no rail experience except a few months as B&NW treasurer, Ike became, at 33, one of the nation's youngest railroad presidents. (Before his death, he reputedly held America's all-time record for railroad presidential seniority.) In 1912 the B&NW owned two second-hand locomotives and some wooden coaches and freight cars, averaged $8000 a month in gross revenue, and was debt-ridden.

Tigrett was homespun and humorous, with friendly blue eyes behind horn-rimmed glasses, and smoked a briar pipe. He went into railroading mainly because his bank, which held B&NW bonds, needed a reliable financier to see that the road met its interest payments. His most urgent task was to find money to keep the bankrupt line operating, which he did, but it never earned enough to pay a dividend. In 1920 he became president of a much larger road, the Gulf, Mobile & Northern (GM&N), which absorbed the B&NW.

When Tigrett became president of this road, he spent a lot of time going up and down the line to learn how it was and should be operated. He talked with employees and shippers, asked questions, and solicited new business. GM&N's only future, he decided, was to offer a long-haul route. Needing money to buy additional mileage, he turned to Mobile bankers. They advanced the sum he needed; a federal loan also came through, and the rickety GM&N was on its way to expansion.

One by one, by lease or purchase, Tigrett took over various lines that of themselves were devoid of basic value. Out of them he welded a strong, coordinated rail system. Among the lines he absorbed were the Memphis & Meridian, Jackson & Eastern, and by a 99-year lease, New Orleans Great Northern. Each had undergone a dizzying succession of little mergers and name changes of its own. Soon his road had two Gulf of Mexico outlets—valuable trade links with Central American fruit steamers and Argentina's cattle industry.

Meanwhile, Tigrett had adopted Jim Hill's policy of improving the economic status of farmers in his territory. The GM&N distributed free seeds and encouraged crop diversification, dairy farming, and timber conservation and helped in pest control.

GM&O's corporate life began in 1940 with the takeover of the old bankrupt Mobile & Ohio (M&O), upon which Casey Jones had started a career that is memorialized in the best known of all railroad folk songs. The M&O, or Mobile Road, had been chartered in 1848 in a plan to connect the port of Mobile with the great river convergence near Cairo, Illinois. Its construction was financed partly by an unusual law compelling all Mobile property owners to buy stock in it. The project also had federal grants and local and state aid in Tennessee, Mississippi, Alabama, and Kentucky. In 1861 the line was opened from Mobile to Columbus, Kentucky. During the Civil War, like all other Southern and border roads, it was fought over and badly damaged. *See* CASEY JONES; CIVIL WAR.

Tigrett's next major acquisition was the Alton Railroad, which had been chartered in 1847 as the Alton & Sangamon (A&S). By 1851 the A&S had linked the Mississippi River port of Alton, Illinois, with the new state capital, Springfield. After being extended to Joliet, Illinois, it went bankrupt, had several changes of name, leased the Joliet & Chicago, and became the Chicago & Alton (C&A).

During the presidency of the highly competent Timothy V. Blackstone, from 1864 to 1899, the C&A flourished, operating almost 1000 miles, its western terminus being Kansas City. Then came disaster. An E. H. Harriman syndicate bought control of the road, watered its stock, and shifted it first to the Union Pacific and Rock Island, then to the Clover Leaf. After its third receivership, the once-great C&A was sold under foreclosure to the Baltimore & Ohio in 1929 and renamed the Alton Railroad. Finally, in 1942, it was sold for $11 million to the Tigrett system, where it helped to form the nation's second midcontinental trunk line between Chicago and the Gulf.

Tigrett gave the South its first streamlined train, *The Rebel,* and the world its first full-time train hostess, both in 1935. When *The Rebel* was in the blueprint stage, he said it needed a bit of Southern hospitality. So he hired Katherine Sullivan to make passengers comfortable. Later he engaged additional hostesses.

Other roads soon copied the idea. For such a job a woman needed good looks, vivacity, experience with people, and a knowledge of typing and first aid. On some carriers she also had to be a trained nurse. All *Rebel* hostesses were college graduates. (Today, no train hostesses are employed as such in regular service.)

The GM&O-Alton merger created a special public relations problem. One road was wholly Southern in tradition and geography, the other totally Northern. Two GM&O terminals in Alabama—Mobile and Montgomery—had served in turn as capital of the Confederate States of America. Tigrett met that challenge by changing the GM&O slogan from "The Rebel Route" to "The

Alton Route" and by operating through sleeping-car service between Chicago and Mobile on *The Rebel* and the former C&A trains *Abraham Lincoln* and *Ann Rutledge.*

GM&O was the South's first railroad to use highways paralleling its rail lines for a coordinated rail-highway service with buses and trucks, bus and train tickets being interchangeable. The buses' main purpose was to speed passenger train operation by eliminating local stops. Gulf Transport, the new service, even had the first privately owned U.S. Post Office on wheels, the postmobile. The Tigrett road's tidal wave of expansion did not cease with Tigrett's death in 1954. In 1972 the GM&O, with 2734 rail route miles in addition to its highway mileage, merged with the Illinois Central to form the present 9494-mile Illinois Central Gulf System.

BIBLIOGRAPHY: Stewart H. Holbrook, *The Story of American Railroads,* Crown, New York, 1947; Freeman Hubbard, *Railroad Avenue,* McGraw-Hill, New York, 1945; George Kennan, *The Chicago and Alton Case,* Country Life Press, New York, 1916; James H. Lemly, *The Gulf, Mobile and Ohio,* Irwin, Homewood, Ill., 1953.

H

Halifax Explosion Disaster in the harbor of Halifax, Nova Scotia, at 9 a.m. on December 6, 1917, that killed a number of Intercolonial Railway and Dominion Atlantic Railway employees in the Richmond yard and near the North Street depot and destroyed about 200 railroad cars, some being blown into the harbor and others onto the highway or over to Dartmouth. The mighty blast was caused by a collision of the French ship *Mont Blanc,* carrying 3000 tons of TNT, with the Norwegian freighter *Imo.* It was very much worse than a railroad calamity. More than 1600 people perished, thousands were severely injured, many vessels were sunk, and 20,000 people were made homeless.

First to enter the disaster area from the outside was an Intercolonial mixed train proceeding with extreme caution through the exodus of fleeing humanity. The crew converted their baggage car into a temporary first-aid depot. The train was held until 8 p.m. for refugees wishing to make a trip to any point along the line as far as Bridgewater without having to pay a fare.

From all over Nova Scotia and New Brunswick gangs of railroad workmen were rushed to Halifax to help clear up the mess and repair rail property, while trains and cars bearing medical men, nurses, food, and supplies converged on the stricken city from all Canadian provinces and some Northeastern states in the United States, especially Massachusetts.

Harriman, Edward Henry (1848–1909) Described by *The New York Times* as "the world's greatest railroad man," Harriman was born on February 28, 1848, in St. George's Episcopal rectory at Hempstead, Long Island, one of six children of the Rev. Orlando Harriman, an impoverished rector. Edward quit school at 15 to be an office boy for a New York stockbrokerage house, and did so well that 6 years later he bought a seat on the New York Stock Exchange (a rare feat for one so young) and went into business for himself as E. H. Harriman & Co. He learned stock manipulation from experts such as Commodore Vanderbilt, Jay Gould, Daniel Drew, and Jubilee Jim Fisk. Harriman was a small man, with a walrus mustache and large eyes peering through big spectacles.

More and more the young broker became convinced that control of railroads was a sure path to wealth and power. He watched the money masters grab one carrier after another, milk it dry, and then fling it into receivership. Seeing so many roads mismanaged convinced him that one well-managed road would, in the long run, yield even more revenue to its owners. Unlike Gould, he had a constructive railroad philosophy; he was a builder, not a destroyer.

Harriman's first rail venture was buying and selling a Florida short line; but he did not show a serious interest in the twin ribbons of steel until he married, as Jay

Gould had done, a railroad owner's daughter, in his case Mary Averell, on September 10, 1879. Her father, William J. Averell, was president of the Ogdensburg & Lake Champlain Railroad (O&LC) in upstate New York. The handsome dowry he gave his daughter became the nucleus of the immense Harriman fortune. He also gave O&LC directorships to Edward and Edward's friend Stuyvesant Fish. The bride was a railfan herself.

Soon Harriman was practicing on small roads the tactics he would use later on big ones. In 1881, with a few associates, he bought cheaply the Sodus Point & Southern (SP&S), a 34-mile line in New York State. He modernized it, built a grain elevator for it, and set the Pennsylvania and the New York Central bidding for the SP&S as a coal-traffic outlet. The Pennsy bought it, at Harriman's price.

Harriman's brokerage firm had allied itself with the Vanderbilts and other financial and social barons. The Illinois Central (IC) was then one of America's most profitable rail systems. Situated at the gateway to the fast-growing West, with its granaries and mines, the IC lacked extreme competition and debt, two factors which ruined many good roads. Fish became secretary to the IC's president in 1872, a director soon afterward, and then a vice president. Harriman bought 15,000 shares of IC stock and in 1883 wormed his way into a directorship. Thus began his lust for control of rail mileage. He and Fish reached out in all directions with the financial backing of Kuhn, Loeb & Co. and the influential August Belmont, who said Harriman could draw on him to the tune of $1 million at any time.

In 1884 they grabbed the worn-down Wabash, St. Louis & Pacific, next the Mississippi Railroad, and then, frustrating the wily Collis P. Huntington, the Dubuque & Sioux City, which Huntington had hoped to use to link his Southern Pacific (SP) to the Eastern seaboard. After that, Harriman and Fish built the Chicago, Madison & Northern (which later became part of the IC and ultimately part of the Illinois Central Gulf). It was almost the only new line that Harriman ever built. He liked to pounce upon bargain roads at panic prices, just as he had bought securities on Wall Street.

By 1885 this game had so fascinated Harriman he quit his brokerage firm. Two years later he blossomed forth as an Illinois Central vice president, while Fish moved up to the presidency. Harriman asserted his new authority by urging expansion that added 1000 miles of trackage within 5 years. The Central's credit was so good that it financed its growth by selling 4 percent bonds. Less fortunate companies had to pay 7 or 8 percent interest and sell at a discount. Borrowing cheaply was another secret of Harriman's success.

Under his aegis, the IC also improved its roadbed and rolling stock and more than doubled its earnings. Galled by the price that Illinois Central had paid for the unprofitable Dubuque & Sioux City, Harriman took over the short line "to make a real thing of it," as he said. This led to his first clash with the beetle-browed J. P. Morgan, who controlled a clear majority of D&SC stock but, because of Harriman, had to sell it below par. The deal glorified Harriman in Wall Street's eyes but made him an enemy of Morgan.

In 1889, sensing the approach of a depression, Harriman scrapped his expansionist policy and urged the directors to retrench. This advice proved to be wise. The Central weathered the panic of 1893 that bankrupted even the Union Pacific (UP), Santa Fe, Northern Pacific (NP), Reading, and other major carriers.

The panic found the UP hit hard by its previous overexpansion, shady financing, and mismanagement by Jay Gould. Even so, Harriman coveted the road. He envisioned vast crops on Western prairies giving it a huge tonnage. The UP had borrowed $53 million from the federal government, to be paid back in 1895, which it could not do, and had to go into receivership. Jacob Schiff wanted the UP for his Kuhn, Loeb & Co., but Harriman refused to permit this.

They compromised in January 1898. After being in federal receivership for 5 years, the UP was taken over by a syndicate which Harriman had formed through Kuhn, Loeb & Co. and which included the Vanderbilts, Goulds, banker James Stillman, and some of the road's old owners. Two years later the Rockefeller forces and Frick steel interests joined them. For the UP itself the consortium, headed by Harriman, paid $58 million in cash, plus an additional $27 million credited to old holders of first-mortgage bonds. Within 3 years the financial giants had gotten back the entire $85 million out of profits on the 1800-mile rail system. Within 2 years after Harriman took the throttle, the carrier's earnings were doubled, although freight rates had been cut 15 percent, and the company was in excellent condition.

Among the roads Harriman garnered about that time were the Oregon Railway & Navigation Co., the Oregon Short Line, the Kansas City Southern (which he lost later after a bitter fight), and the Chicago & Alton (C&A). Harriman had contributed to one Theodore Roosevelt campaign, but not to another one, because he disapproved of Teddy's policies. This enraged the trust-busting President, who thereupon prodded the Interstate Commerce Commission to investigate the methods used by the Harriman interests in taking over the Alton, which brought out the fact that they had watered its stock from $30 million to $94 million.

For this the Commission and Roosevelt sharply criticized Harriman. But the financial wizard kept his poker face and continued to reach out for more profits. The C&A had been in a bad way before that, and it must be said to Harriman's credit that he did a good job of administering the Alton, even reducing its freight and passenger rates.

In 1901, after Collis P. Huntington had died, Harriman bought the 9000-mile Southern Pacific, and later the Central Pacific, with its entrance to the West Coast at San Francisco. He visualized a transcontinental rail system under his control.

Harriman wisely left detailed work to his subordinates. When he saw a man of unusual ability wasted on clerical work, he would say: "Never do what a clerk can do for you. Save your time for better things."

Thanks to Harriman, the opulent Union Pacific aided its poor relation, the SP, by extending credit for needed improvements. From 1901 to 1907, under his regime, SP's annual revenue rose from $78 million to $128 million. Among the major engineering feats pushed through by Harriman's magic wand were the San Francisco Bay Shore Cutoff and the Lucin Cutoff across Great Salt Lake. The latter saved 44 miles of travel and shot trains farther from land than they had ever dared to run before. See LUCIN CUTOFF.

At one time Harriman controlled more millions of capital than any other person on earth. He dominated huge transportation systems with billions of invested capital (the equivalent of several times that much buying power today). He was powerful on the executive committee of America's largest national bank, virtually owned a huge trust company, and had a finger in the pie of many other corporations. Panics invariably found him with enough gilt-edged securities to weather any storm. "Two factors work against prosperity," he said. "Idle men and idle capital."

In 1903 he challenged the Santa Fe Railway, which, with a subsidiary, was trying to build a connecting line in New Mexico and Arizona. Harriman's men won that skirmish by filing their intention in a land office just 20 minutes ahead of their rivals. As a result, the Harriman-controlled SP took over the subsidiary at cost, and the little giant captured a seat on the Santa Fe board.

Five years later, he saved the long-abused Erie from bankruptcy, defying Morgan face to face, by advancing $5.5 million. He thus included the Erie in his rail network, which extended from coast to coast and from the Great Lakes to the Gulf of Mexico. This action did much to allay the panic of 1907. Had he lived long enough, he almost certainly would have added the Santa Fe, the Pennsylvania, and the Baltimore & Ohio to his empire.

Meanwhile, in May 1901, Harriman locked horns with grizzled old James J. Hill of the Great Northern, who had just won leading control of the Northern Pacific and the Chicago, Burlington & Quincy. The rector's son squirmed. He had sought to buy the Burlington himself. Abetted by Kuhn, Loeb & Co., he then tried to snatch Jim's darling NP from under his nose. His forces bought 170,000 shares of NP common stock and 420,000 shares of preferred—more than a majority. It looked as if Jim Hill was trapped.

This move brought on the panic of May 1901. In 2 days of feverish trading, NP stock rose from $58 to $300, and then to $1000. Many stockholders of other roads were caught and ruined, because their securities dropped abruptly as NP quotations soared to dizzying heights. It was one of the worst panics in Wall Street's history.

The Hill-Morgan group, with a majority of NP's common stock but only a minority of the whole, felt safe because they knew that preferred shares could be retired. Public opinion of Harriman, never very friendly, soured more than ever. It was felt that the bespectacled wizard had deliberately forced the panic for selfish reasons.

A compromise ended the fight. Hill kept his pet road, Harriman edged into the Burlington directorate, and the UP was given a director's seat on the NP board. This deal was embodied in the titanic Northern Securities Corporation, controlled jointly by the UP, Burlington, and NP. But the U.S. Supreme Court decided it was an illegal corporation and ordered it to be dissolved. After the smoke of battle had cleared away, the little giant with the Midas touch sold his NP and GN stock for a profit of nearly $40 million, with which he bought more roads for the Union Pacific system.

July 1, 1909, marked the completion of an 800-mile railroad which Harriman built in Mexico, backed by President Porfirio Díaz, from the Gulf of California alongside the Yaqui River and up the coast through Guadalajara. Harriman's inspection trip over that line was his last business trip. Shortly after erecting a $2 million mansion at Arden, New York, on the highest of the Ramapo Mountains, he died in it on September 9, 1909.

BIBLIOGRAPHY: H. J. Eckenrode and P. W. Wight, *E. H. Harriman: The Little Giant of Wall Street,* Greenberg, New York, 1933; Matthew Josephson, *The Robber Barons,* Harcourt, Brace, New York, 1934; George Kennan, *E. H. Harriman: A Biography,* Houghton Mifflin, Boston, 1922; John Moody, *The Masters of Capital,* Yale, New Haven, Conn., 1919; Gustavus Myers, *History of the Great American Fortunes,* 3 vols., Charles H. Kerr & Company, Chicago, 1910.

Harvey, Frederick Henry (1835-1901) Creator of a chain of railroad-station lunch counters, restaurants, and hotels and dining-car service on the Atchison, Topeka and Santa Fe (ATSF) system with such high standards that "Meals by Fred Harvey" became a company slogan and novelist Edna Ferber wrote, "My father used to say that those Western railroad brakemen and the Harvey lunchroom waitresses were the future aristocracy of the West."

English-born Fred Harvey emigrated to the United States at 15, got a job as busboy in a New York café at $2 a week, worked on a packet boat, then as a mail clerk on the first mail-sorting run of the Hannibal & St. Joseph (H&StJ; the first railroad to have mail cars) in 1862, and became general Western freight agent for Chicago, Burlington & Quincy (CB&Q). A tall, wiry, high-strung man with side whiskers and a small beard, he lived in Leavenworth, Kansas, with his wife and five children.

Business trips throughout the West aroused his ire over the indigestible food and poor service he found at trackside lunch counters and the miserable lodgings he endured. Meals were prepared by cooks with no finesse at all—men from logging and mining camps and cattle drives. Poor grub with bitter coffee was dished up by slovenly "hash slingers" who often did not get around to serving it until the engine whistle announced that the train was ready to depart. Many passengers and crewmen had to bring cold lunches from home or eat the junk food peddled by news butchers. In that era few Western roads had dining cars. On some lines meal stops survived into the twentieth century.

In 1875, Harvey offered his ideas on first-class lunchroom service to the CB&Q management, which rejected them. That was its big mistake. Then Thomas Nickerson, the ATSF president, leased the Topeka station lunch counter to Harvey, who ran it so capably that he was soon put in charge of the Santa Fe's restaurant and hotel in Florence, Kansas. Taking up the challenge in a big way, Harvey hired the former chef of Chicago's famous Palmer House to run it for him. As business boomed, he left the CB&Q to become a full-time restaurateur headquartered in the H&StJ depot at Leavenworth and set up a rapidly growing chain of eating houses along the Santa Fe line. Later he moved his offices to Chicago.

The legend that his dying words were "Tell the girls to slice the ham thin" probably has no basis in truth. Harvey planned generously. He ordered that pies be cut into quarters instead of the traditional six pieces, and instead of taking water for coffee from alkali-laden creeks he had it brought to his restaurants by rail in tank cars.

While inspecting his restaurants, Harvey would use his pocket handkerchief to check for dust. If a plate, saucer, or cup was chipped, he'd smash it on the floor, and he angrily overturned improperly set tables. Working for Fred Harvey was not quite the rollicking fun that Judy Garland portrayed in an MGM movie, *The Harvey Girls,* released in 1945. But the girls did have dances and other social affairs under Harvey auspices.

Waitresses at the Harvey restaurant in the Santa Fe station in Syracuse, Kansas, about 1890. Many of these women married railroad boomers, who called the Harvey chain the "Cupid of the Rails," and thus helped to settle the West. [Santa Fe Railway]

On frequent trips to Europe he ordered high-grade china, cutlery, and linen for his restaurants. His original Dodge City eating house was two old boxcars on stilts, tastefully decorated inside. In time, he operated large, sumptuous hotels. One of them, the Montezuma, in a mineral-springs resort near Las Vegas, had 270 rooms; the hotel boasted pianos, great mirrors, electric generators, and gas and water systems. Refusing to serve canned food there even in winter, he had fresh produce brought up regularly on Santa Fe trains from Guaymas, Mexico.

Most Harvey eating places adjoined ATSF stations. Before a passenger train arrived, a conductor or brakeman would go through the cars asking the riders whether they preferred the lunch counter or the restaurant. This information was telegraphed ahead to alert the manager, and a gong was sounded as the train pulled in. Passengers pouring out of the cars were met by smiling Harvey girls, neatly, almost puritanically, uniformed in black and white. Two of Fred Harvey's many rules were "No passenger shall be rushed" and "None shall be left behind when the train departs."

Waitresses were recruited mostly from the East by ads in newspapers and young women's magazines. Each woman had to be between 18 and 30, good-looking, intelligent, and reputable. All were well-trained before going to work. One of them, Laura White, recalled having to serve 16 full meals in 25 minutes. The women lived in pleasant dormitories supervised by matrons who were strict about hours of going to bed and dates with male friends and set a high moral tone, contrasting sharply with the style of the painted women in nearby saloons and dance halls. When a young woman was hired, she had to agree not to get married for at least a year. This promise was often broken.

Harvey girls helped to civilize the West. The excellent food and lodgings their employer provided for crewmen away from home (something that other carriers lacked) improved labor relations immensely. In 1893 a contract put Harvey in charge of Santa Fe dining-car service also. Such service always lost money (except indirectly by selling fares), but ATSF reimbursed Harvey for his deficits because of what he did for the passenger business.

When the old pioneer died, his chain included 15 hotels, 47 restaurants, 30 dining cars, food service on the San Francisco carferries, and even a restaurant in the giant St. Louis Union Station, not on the Santa Fe line. For years his sons, Byron and Ford, carried on the business. Today it is extinct.

BIBLIOGRAPHY: Keith L. Bryant, Jr., *History of the Atchison, Topeka and Santa Fe Railway,* Macmillan, New York, 1974; Stewart H. Holbrook, *The Story of American Railroads,* Crown, New York, 1947.

HB&T *See* HOUSTON BELT & TERMINAL RAILWAY.

Head-End Engines Why does a long freight train, especially in hilly terrain, often have a locomotive in the middle and possibly a pusher in the rear, in addition to the head-end power? Why aren't all locomotives used on the head end? The reason is that their combined pulling power and heavy weight might put too much strain on couplers of the first cars as well as overtax the capacity of bridges and rights-of-way.

Headlights, Electric The first experiments aimed at replacing oilburning headlights on locomotives were made in 1883 when Leonide Wolley of Indianapolis installed an electric-lighting machine on an engine, but it was ineffective. Two years later electric headlights made by Charles J. Janney were placed on engines running between Chicago and Indianapolis on the Chicago, Cincinnati & St. Louis. These were actually the first electric headlights, although they were taken off after a few trips.

In 1887 Wolley patented a device manufactured by the newly organized American Electric Headlight Co., which demonstrated several headlights, one on the Cleveland, Akron & Columbus and another on the Panhandle. None lasted after a few weeks' service, and the firm was soon liquidated. In 1888 Robert B. F. Pierce, also in Indianapolis, bought the rights to all electric headlights, founded the National Electric Co., and produced the first electric headlight that operated without failure from one terminal to the next; but it had maintenance trouble, and the company folded when Pierce died in 1897.

Edgar A. Edwards of Cincinnati patented an electric arc headlight and organized the Edwards Electric Headlight Co., which lasted from 1890 to 1907. In 1897 George C. Pyle built a turbine which he connected directly to the armature shaft of a dynamo, creating a new, simpler, and better arc light. He sold his patents to Royal C. Vilas, who organized the Pyle National Headlight Co. Pyle's equipment was far superior to all previous headlights. In 1899 railroads ordered 72 Pyle National sets, nearly thrice the total number of electric headlights previously in use. The company's first shipments went to the Rock Island, the Flordia Central & Peninsular, and the Houston & Texas Central. By 1906 electric headlights were commonly used on freight runs all over the country. In 1915 Congress passed a law, orginally sponsored by Texas locomotive engineers, requiring their use on all locomotives running at night under Interstate Commerce Commission jurisdiction.

"Hell of a Way to Run a Railroad" Commonly used phrase, coined by a Boston & Maine publicity manager, Herbert L. Baldwin, for a newspaper ad answering public criticism of B&M's inability to return to normal operation immediately after a blizzard.

A lovely example of the early electric locomotive headlights, advertised in 1883 by the Utica Head Light Works. [The Railroad Gazette]

Henry, John See John Henry.

Heroes Accounts of heroic actions performed by railroad employees and "civilians" enrich the lore of the rails. Here are a few documented instances of personal heroism.

Gertie Anderson, age 8, of Grand Rapids, Michigan, was picking berries beside the Duluth, Mississippi & Northern tracks near a chain of small lakes at Mahoning, Michigan, on July 14, 1895, when a special train carrying railroad officials passed her. Just behind the train about 200 feet of track suddenly sank out of sight in the muskeg, or swampy undergrowth. Gertie was terrified; but she climbed an embankment onto the track, saw a passenger train approaching about half a mile away, and ran toward it, waving her pink sunbonnet above her head. The engineer applied his emergency brake, stopped, and swung down from the cab to scold the child for playing on the track. She pointed to the long gap in the rails. Thereupon he lifted Gertie in his arms, carried her to the passengers, who were now streaming out of the coaches, and shouted, "This little girl saved our train!" When the passengers and crew realized what had happened, they took up a collection for her.

Charles S. Kreicher, 52, was suddenly stricken with paralysis while working as towerman and telegraph operator at the Delong, Indiana, crossover of the Pennsylvania and Chicago & Erie railroads. Realizing that his end was near, alone and too far gone to summon help, he made his last act setting red signals to stop all rail traffic at that point. A conductor who left his train and climbed the tower steps to discover what was wrong found the operator dying but apparently happy in the knowledge that no train would be wrecked because of his death.

Joseph Sieg, a Pennsy engineer, was speeding his passenger train through Jersey City, New Jersey, on October 22, 1882, when his cab caught fire. Sticking to his post, he stopped on the Hackensack River bridge, where the blaze swirled upward instead of being fanned back into the wooden coaches. Thus he saved the passengers. But he was a living torch when he applied the brakes and let himself down into the water tank on the tender. He died 4 days later. The Pennsylvania Railroad (PRR) honored its hero by running special trains from three cities to the funeral. He was buried near Bordentown, New Jersey.

On January 18, 1884, oil leaking from a hillside tank in a wooded section near Bradford, Pennsylvania, flooded 100 yards of track and burst into flame just as a train clattered through. The engineer, Pat Sexton, was badly burned from staying in his cab. Although the train was destroyed and three passengers perished, the death list undoubtedly would have been greater if Sexton had jumped off when he had a chance to do so.

Johnny Bartholomew showed similar heroism. He was the engineer of a Virginia & Truckee excursion train that left Virginia City, Nevada, on October 17, 1872, a few months after completion of the V&T, for the return trip to Reno. After rounding a curve beyond Gold Hill, he saw flames leaping from the mouth of the 900-foot American Flat Tunnel. He had to think fast. To keep going would risk a collision with fallen timbers, which might kill both himself and his fireman. To stop on the curve, with too little time to flag a following train, would invite a rear-end crash and almost certain death to passengers. He risked the former and luckily rolled through with no casualties.

On July 28, 1907, a Canadian Pacific passenger train was fast nearing a bridge near Rideout, Ontario, when the engineer, Ernest McAdam, saw it was burning. Telling his fireman to jump, McAdam "wiped the clock" (made an emergency application of the airbrakes) with one hand and shut off his throttle with the other. As soon as he leaped from the cab, he realized that his 163 passengers might either be burned to death or be drowned by plunging into the river. So he went back to the now-decelerated train, swung aboard the baggage car as it rumbled by, hurried through it and over the coal pile in the tender, and reseated himself in the cab. Releasing his brakes, he drove through the flames across the bridge. Although one coach caught fire, nobody was injured.

Fred Lintner was the only New York Central (NYC) engineer to get a medal from the rival Pennsylvania Railroad. On December 19, 1926, he and two Pennsy trainmen, Frank W. Geary and James B. Deegan, risked their lives to prevent an oil-plant explosion at Titusville, Pennsylvania. All three were off duty that day. Watching a fire at American Oil Works, they saw that five cars, loaded with oil and with fire already lapping at their running boards, stood directly in the path of the flames. Aware that they might be blown up, the three men boarded a nearby NYC engine, coupled it onto the smoldering cars, and hauled them away from the burning warehouse. The city fire department turned hoses on the threatened oil tanks. All three men were awarded PRR medals for heroism.

Three years later, on December 9, Ralph Toland was wheeling a Southern Pacific passenger train when a reckless driver, hauling thousands of gallons of gasoline in a truck and trailer, beat the train to a grade crossing. The truck itself cleared; the trailer didn't. Toland reached his brake valve and whistle in the same sweep. Brakes screeched, followed almost instantly by a crash and explosion. Flames enveloped the engine crew. With an agonized effort, Toland released his brakes and reopened the throttle so that the coaches would not stop beside the burning gasoline trailer with the possibility of frightful casualties. Thus he moved his train to safety. Dying in a hospital, as did the fireman and a mail clerk, he regained consciousness long enough to ask if all the passengers were safe. The doctor assured Toland that, because of his heroism, none of them were injured.

See also AMBLER, PENNSYLVANIA; ANDREWS RAILROAD RAID; KENNAR, EDWARD; POELL, GEORGE H.; POOR, JOHN ALFRED; SHELLEY, KATE.

BIBLIOGRAPHY: Freeman Hubbard, *Railroad Avenue,* McGraw-Hill, New York, 1945.

Hill, James Jerome ***(1838–1916)*** Hill said: "Most people who have really lived have had, in some shape, their great adventure. The railway is mine," meaning the Great Northern (GN), known as the Big G. He was born of Scotch-Irish farmers on September 16, 1838, at Rockwood, Ontario. (Oddly enough, Canada produced Jim Hill, America's foremost railroad builder, while Canada's foremost, William Cornelius Van Horne, was born in the States.) His father died when Jim was 15, and he went to work in a rural store for $4 a month.

As a boy, he lost sight in one eye when a playmate accidentally shot him with an arrow. At 18 he left home and roamed the East from one job to another; in 1856 he settled permanently at St. Paul, Minnesota, then a mere trading post on a Mississippi levee. Like Commodore Vanderbilt, he engaged in water transportation before his railroad career. St. Paul had no railway until 1862, when a 10-mile line linked it with the Falls of St. Anthony (now Minneapolis). Prior to that, the settlement had depended mostly on river cargoes. Jim became a shipping clerk, soliciting river traffic, appraising the value of shipments, and fixing rates. He bought grain cheaply in winter, stored it until the river was open to spring navigation, and shipped it out to meet a demand at high prices. In 1865 he took the agency for a river packet that hauled freight for three expanding railroads: the Chicago & North Western, the Illinois Central, and the St. Paul & Pacific (StP&P), the last-named being the future nucleus of his Great Northern system. He also went into the coal business, leasing 2300 acres of coal land in one Iowa county alone.

In 1867 he married Mary Mehegan, a waitress in the hotel where he lived, and got a contract to supply the StP&P with fuel. He also dealt in grain, wood, hay, feed, lime, cement, salt, and other products needed in the pioneer Northwest and accepted a fur-trading agency from his future railroad partner, Norman W. Kittson.

After working hard all day, he studied late at night: transportation, geography, geology, and economics. His first rail job, in 1866, was as local agent for the St. Paul & Pacific, handling freight by ton and carload. Cleverly, he enlarged his depot to let steamboats unload there instead of at the public levee some distance away. By 1871 he had set up through freight and passenger service between St. Paul and Winnipeg, Canada, via Duluth by rail, stagecoaches, and Red River steamboats, competing with the fur-trading magnate Kittson. A few months later the rivals joined hands in forming the Red River Transportation Line.

The panic of 1873 threw the Northern Pacific (NP) and St. Paul railroads, among others, into bankruptcy. The St. Paul road had federal and state charters and a land grant of 5 million acres, but it was overcapitalized, owing $28 million in bonds, held mostly by Dutch investors. For 5 years it wallowed in receiverships. To make matters worse, grasshoppers plagued Minnesota from 1873 to 1878. They devoured everything, it was said, except the right-of-way and even lay so thick on the rails that the eight-wheeled locomotives spun their driving wheels and had to stop. Crops were destroyed and farmers ruined.

Hill did not believe the insects would last forever, so he began building what historian Matthew Josephson called "the most perfect railroad monopoly in the country." Within a few years he had the farmers so tied up that they had to move their products over his rails to his huge lake steamers and into his grain elevators, on his terms. Thus their saying, "After the grasshoppers, we had Jim Hill."

The first step in this monopoly, or "great adventure," was to acquire the St. Paul & Pacific Railroad in conjunction with Kittson and with Donald Alexander Smith (the future Lord Strathcona), whom he had met by chance on a dogsled exploration trip, and with wealthy George Stephen (the future Lord Mount Stephen), president of the Bank of Montreal and Smith's cousin.

Hill and Kittson knew the country intimately. Kittson and Smith had political pull. Stephen was a financial wizard. Together they devised a way to buy the railroad at minimum cost. Hill knew that the road's future was bright, but the bondholders were not let in on that secret. Hill's associates closed the deal for about 25 cents on the dollar. Even at that bargain, it is said they put up only $280,000 in cash and signed a promissory note for the rest. The deal was financed on a shoestring. The company was nearly $44 million in debt, but a foreclosure suit in 1878 wiped that out. Soon afterward, Hill and his friends sold most of the railroad's land for over $13 million.

In consolidating their property, the new owners had to build extensions which the charter called for or else lose the land grants. By the end of 1878 the line was 283 miles long. Farmers returned to their abandoned land and began growing the wheat crops which made the Red River Valley famous and shipping them by rail. Hill sold his prosperous coal business and concentrated on the great adventure. Next year, with 565 miles completed and another 112 miles being built, the road was reorganized as the St. Paul, Minneapolis & Manitoba and capitalized at $31 million, each partner getting $5 million in securities.

In 1880, Canadian-born Hill became an American citizen and, with Stephen and Smith, formed a syndicate to get the incipient Canadian Pacific Railway (CP) out of politics and into construction. But the fact that the same men were jointly building competing railways in the United States and Canada evoked much criticism. So in 1883 Hill eased out of the CP and sold one-third of his $1.5 million CP stock, while the two cousins resigned as directors of the Manitoba line but retained their holdings in it. This left James J. Hill in supreme control of the future Great Northern Railway.

Three years later his far-reaching line attained its West Coast objective, Puget Sound. It made him very happy. Meanwhile, on August 21, 1882, he had become president of this road—a position he held for 25 eventful years without accepting a cent of salary—and plunged into what he called "the hardest thing I ever had to do," building a curving stone-arch bridge across the Mississippi at Minneapolis. In those days of wooden bridges this was a difficult engineering feat.

Hill's policy was to "lay the iron" in places where it was likely to create population and, of course, rail traffic. He sent many immigration agents to Europe with glowing literature about the richness of the Northwest to induce foreigners to settle in his part of the New World. "Land without population is a wilderness," he declared. "Population without land is a mob."

The rival Northern Pacific, backed by 56 million acres of public land, completed its through line in 1883. It had stolen a march on Hill's plodding road. To reach Helena, Montana, a Hill branch line would have to cross Indian and military reservations. This required federal sanction. Jay Gould kept a well-paid lobby in Washington to block other magnates. In 1886, when Congress passed a bill authorizing Hill to build the branch line, Gould's henchmen are said to have been responsible for President Grover Cleveland's vetoing the bill. Hill also had supporters in the capital. Congress repassed the bill in 1887, and this time Cleveland approved it. But Gould's lobby prevented Hill's road from getting land grants or federal money. See GOULD, JAY.

Meanwhile, the Empire Builder had organized the Montana Central with dummy incorporators to hold the field without informing the public of who was involved. When the federal government permitted his line to be built, he threw off the mask, added the new carrier to his growing system, and set a speed record for laying track: 3½ miles every working day for 7½ months. One after another, he picked up small roads for a song and coupled them into his mainline.

In time he piled up a personal fortune estimated at over $400 million, mostly holdings in the Big G and other enterprises. This sum is said to have equaled or exceeded the combined wealth of the other three top railroad barons of his day: Vanderbilt, Gould, and Harriman. See HARRIMAN, EDWARD HENRY.

In 1888 he formed the Northwestern Steamship Co. for traffic on the Great Lakes and over his rail monopoly, which was now linked to Chicago by a friendly deal with the Burlington Railroad. In that year, too, he adopted the now-famous name Great Northern for his 2770 miles of track, capitalized at $40 million. He continually plowed profits back into his company in the shape of bigger engines, better roadbed, and profitable branch lines. He kept preaching low grades, heavy power, large-capacity cars, bigger trainloads, and few empties.

With increased tractive power, his road had the mightiest locomotives and longest trains. This, of course, antagonized labor, particularly because Hill's efficient methods of hiring and firing made him a hard taskmaster; but the wave of railroad strikes in the Central and Western states in 1884, 1885, and 1886 did not even slow Hill's onward march. Like Harriman, he bought and sold shrewdly, had a retentive memory, was a stickler for detail, and hated waste.

After Gould died in 1892, the mismanaged Union Pacific was thrown into bankruptcy. Harriman took it up. This led to a titanic battle with E. H. in which Hill's empire was almost wrested from his grasp.

The one-eyed baron dominated a traffic system connecting the South's cotton fields with far-off Japan through agreements with the Illinois Central and a line of Hill-controlled steamships. This yielded a huge volume of business. With the aid of rich allies, he raised a little over $215 million, with which the Big G and Northern Pacific jointly bought control of the Burlington, thus assuring Hill's entry into Chicago. Hill closed the deal in the nick of time; Harriman was negotiating for the same road.

Quietly then, E. H. set to work on a scheme to gain a half interest in the Burlington by snatching the NP

The Northern Pacific, then a rival of James J. Hill's St. Paul, Minneapolis & Manitoba Railroad, completed its through line to the West in 1883. Former President Ulysses S. Grant helped to drive in the golden spike on September 8, 1883. [Northern Pacific Railway]

from Hill. To do this, his forces began bidding for NP stock in the open market. Hill was uneasy. Ordering a special train, he made a fast run to New York and learned face to face from Jacob Schiff of Kuhn, Loeb & Co., Harriman's bankers, that his foes already had control of the Northern Pacific.

"That isn't possible," Jim said, "I own thirty millions of Northern Pacific stock myself. Together with the holdings of my friends, we have an absolute majority."

But Schiff disillusioned him. Then Jim cabled J. P. Morgan who was on vacation in Europe. J. P. cabled back instructions for his broker to buy $15 million of NP. With his back to the wall, Hill was supported by the mighty house of Morgan. Among Harriman's backers were three of the nations's richest banking firms. Northern Pacific stock shot up to $1000 a share. After the exchange closed for the day, brokers could not deliver the stock their customers had bought. There was none to be had.

Harriman's side held a clear majority of NP's $153 million stock, but that majority lay in *preferred* shares, which Wall Street suddenly discovered could be retired before the Harriman forces could use them. The hard-pressed Hill offered a compromise: a holding corporation. Contending parties then formed the $400 million National Securities Corporation to control jointly the NP, GN, and Burlington; but the U.S. Supreme Court dissolved it. This was Hill's only major defeat. It embittered him the rest of his life.

In 1899 Hill bought some Minnesota iron-mine property for $4 million. Its market value soon rose to $135 million because it included the now-famous Mesabi Range. Instead of holding the land himself, the aging tycoon sold it to his beloved Great Northern at the same price he had paid for it. A 5-year lease on this property to the Steel Trust brought great additonal wealth to Hill and his fellow stockholders, in addition to revenue from 14 million tons of iron ore a year hauled by the railroad.

James J. Hill was now almost absolute dictator of social, political, and economic life in the Northwest. For years he had been luring thousands of immigrants into the country. He hired experts to show farmers how to earn more by diversifying crops and improving livestock. His agents combed county fairs in England and Scotland to bring back thoroughbred horses, cattle, and hogs, vast numbers of which he gave away to farmers to better their own breeds. He also distributed free thousands of tons of fertilizer. All this multiplied the Big G's freight tonnage.

On June 18, 1907, he turned the Great Northern presidency over to his second son, Louis W. Hill. On May 29, 1916, the Empire Builder died of an infection, and all Hill roads and steamship lines halted traffic for 5 minutes during the funeral.

BIBLIOGRAPHY: James J. Hill, *Highways of Progress,* Doubleday, Page, New York, 1910; Matthew Josephson, *The Robber Barons,* Harcourt, Brace, New York, 1934; Gustavus Myers, *History of the Great American Fortunes,* 3 vols., Charles H. Kerr & Company, Chicago, 1910; Joseph G. Pyle, *The Life of James J. Hill,* Doubleday, Doran, New York, 1917; *Railroad Magazine,* January 1935; February 1937; *Trains Magazine,* December 1954.

Hill, John Locomotive engineer on the narrow-gauge Denver and Rio Grande who, like Cyrus Warman, became a writer. Hill contributed to such magazines as *American Machinist* and *Locomotive Engineer* and eventually became editor and then owner of those two. In 1909 he joined James H. McGraw, Sr. (1860-1948), publisher of *Street Railway Journal,* in forming the McGraw-Hill Book Company to publish technical books, but they continued to put out their magazines separately. Hill died in 1916, leaving a string of five magazines, which were merged in 1917 with the book company and the magazines that McGraw was then publishing. *See* WARMAN, CYRUS.

Hinckley Holocaust A blue haze like a funeral pall hung over the parched, dusty woods of northern Minnesota that had not felt rain for more than 4 months. Rivers had shrunk to sluggish streams and creeks to dry gullies. A raging forest fire had not yet reached Hinckley, a lumber settlement of 1200 people, 72 miles northeast of St. Paul. Two railroads crossed this town: the St. Paul & Duluth (StP&D) and the Eastern Minnesota (both today part of the Burlington Northern). At 2 p.m. on September 1, 1894, the St. Paul road's *Duluth Limited,* northbound, stopped at Hinckley en route to Duluth. By this time the acrid haze had thickened. Fire was sweeping closer every minute. The residents were uneasy but not panicky. Only a few boarded the train.

At 2:45 p.m. the southbound Duluth-Hinckley local freight, on the Eastern Minnesota line, rumbled into town. The situation had changed alarmingly. A smoky curtain darkened the sky. Fireballs blown from the top of one tall tree to another broke into showers of sparks. Flames were closing in on the town from the west, south, and east. Hinckley's fire department was making a gallant last-ditch fight with inadequate equipment. The incoming freight had 10 loaded cars and 30 empties. The crew assembled a combination special train with two locomotives, five coaches, three boxcars, and a caboose. Residents mobbed the train. An overpowering heat wave had hit the town. Men, women, children, and animals fell dead in the streets. The smoke was suffocating, the wooden houses were collapsing, and the sky was as black as midnight.

For 45 minutes the train lingered at the depot for stragglers to get aboard. Then engineer Ed Barry, in the lead locomotive, opened his throttle and twirled the reverse lever. Running backward, pushing the train, he crossed the Grindstone River bridge and then waited 5 more precious minutes. By now the cars were blistering and smoldering. Even the ties were burning.

But Barry made a great run, traveling in reverse. He

clattered over 19 bridges, some of them afire. Even with his oil headlight on, he could see only a few yards ahead. Flames licked the engines' wooden cabs and the nine crowded cars. The train reached Sandstone, the next town, well in advance of the onrushing fire—so far ahead that the local inhabitants still felt safe. A few of them boarded the train. Blinded by smoke, Barry turned the throttle over to his fireman but later regained control and drove into West Superior, out of the danger zone. Then he collapsed and was carried to a hospital.

Meanwhile, the southbound *Duluth Limited,* on the roughly parallel St. Paul & Duluth line, had pulled into Hinckley shortly after the departure of the Eastern Minnesota train. Its engineer, James Root, said later:

> I saw people running from both sides of the track and across the bridge. They pushed their way into the cars. The depot was on fire. So was the bridge. Our crew decided to run the train back six miles to Skunk Lake. . . .
>
> Then suddenly everything seemed to let go at once. The wind rose, something sounded like an explosion, and the whole train was ignited. The heavy glass in my cab window bent over toward me and broke into many pieces. A large chunk hit the ceiling and fell down, cutting me severely. . . .
>
> Two men running toward us caught onto the pilot as we rushed by. One stayed there a short time, then fell off and was burned to death. The other managed to hold on . . . and came through all right. I must have passed out myself. Next thing I recollected was that we had reached Little Hinckley Hill. I was lying on the engine deck with one foot on the quadrant, the other on the firebox door. . . .
>
> At that moment Jack [the fireman] showed up. He'd been down in the water, almost wholly immersed in the tank! Then I got dizzy again. Jack splashed water over me. . . . I asked Jack to throw on some more coal. While he was doing this I caught sight of water in a ditch beside the track and I knew we had reached Skunk Lake. I told Jack to get the passengers out into the water.
>
> By now all the cars were blazing, inside and out. The heat had shattered every window. We had about 300 passengers aboard. Just before we got to the lake a dozen or more had gone mad and leaped off the train. Jack and another man helped me out of the engine.
>
> All of the surviving passengers were in the shallow muddy lake, also some other people, between 400 and 500 men, women, and children. . . . After crouching in the lake for four agonizing hours, we were finally rescued by volunteers who came through on handcars.

The last train to leave blazing Hinckley on September 1, 1894, after departure of the *Duluth Limited* but in the opposite direction, was driven by Aylmer Gray. His train, too, made an epic run, arriving safely in St. Paul. But 120 Hinckleyites died horribly when they sought shelter in a dry slough, near the Eastern Minnesota track, that had once been filled with water. Among the heroes killed that day was Tom Dunn, telegraph operator, who stayed at his post in the StP&D station in Hinckley to issue orders for the *Duluth Limited* to leave town. At least 476 bodies found in the burned-over area of Minnesota were buried in the scorched earth.

BIBLIOGRAPHY: Stewart H. Holbrook, *Burning an Empire,* Macmillan, New York, 1943; Freeman Hubbard, *Railroad Avenue,* McGraw-Hill, New York, 1945; William Wilkinson, *Memorials of the Minnesota Forest Fires in the Year 1894,* N. E. Wilkinson, Minneapolis, 1895.

Hinkley Locomotive Works Works founded by Isaac Hinkley, who began building steam locomotives in 1839 under the name Hinkley & Drury at Boston, Massachusetts. It turned out some superb engines, its first being the *Lion,* a four-wheel connected unit with outside cylinders, patterned after the Mohawk Valley's famous *De Witt Clinton.* One of its express types was the *Antelope,* built for the Boston & Maine in 1845, with a single pair of driving wheels 6 feet in diameter, a four-wheel leading truck, and a pair of trailing wheels under the footplate—an engine noted for fast running. (Many engines in those days bore names indicating such positive qualities as swiftness, strength, and victory.)

At Holmes Hinkley's death in 1860, the works passed out of the family's hands to Charles Williams. In 1893 it was reorganized as the Hinkley Locomotive Co., but its engine-building days were past. The property was sold to West End Railroad. In 1889 it became part of the Boston Elevated system and was used as an electric power station.

BIBLIOGRAPHY: Angus Simclair, *Development of the Locomotive Engine,* annotated ed. by John H. White, Jr., M.I.T., Cambridge, Mass., 1970.

History of North American Railroading North America's earliest railroads were wooden-railed tramways. The first was an inclined plane over which merchandise and military supplies were hauled manually up and down the Niagara escarpment in Canada, near the present New York State border, beginning in 1762. Others were built in 1795 on Beacon Hill, Boston, Massachusetts; in 1809 in Delaware County, Pennsylvania; and in about 1811 in Chesterfield County, Virginia. *See* TRAMWAY, NORTH AMERICA'S FIRST.

Early Nineteenth Century In 1815 the state of New Jersey issued to John Stevens the nation's first charter to build and operate a steam railroad. Stevens never built it, but by 1825 he had designed and constructed America's first operating steam locomotive, which he ran on a circular track on his Hoboken, New Jersey, estate. An outgrowth of the Stevens project of 1815, the New Jersey Railroad & Transportation Co. (later part of the Pennsylvania Railroad, or PRR) was chartered in 1823 and opened in 1839.

The first railway company authorized to build and operate a railroad in America that was actually built and operated was the Granite Railway Co., incorporated on March 4, 1828, by the Massachusetts Legislature. Gridley Bryant built this 5-foot-gauge line to haul huge granite blocks from a quarry in Quincy to Milton (now part of Boston) on the Neponset River for use in erecting the Bunker Hill Monument.

In early days there was much grass-roots opposition to the building of railroads, for religious reasons and for fear of the alleged danger in traveling faster than a horse could trot and of frightening horses and cattle. Henry David Thoreau, writer and naturalist, objected to trains on the ground that they disturbed the peace and beauty of the countryside. In about 1830 the Lancaster, Ohio, Board of Education was asked to permit the use of its schoolhouse for a debate on the practicability of railroads. Here is a record from the minutes of the board's meeting:

> You are welcome to use the school room to debate all proper questions in, but such things as railroads and telegraphs are impossibilities and rank infidelity. There is nothing in the word of God about them. If God had designated that His intelligent creatures should travel at the frightful speed of 15 miles an hour, He would have foretold it through his holy prophets. It is a device of Satan to lead immortal souls down to Hell.

In 1829, 8 years before he became President, Martin Van Buren used somewhat similar arguments in a letter he wrote to President Andrew Jackson denouncing railroads and defending canals.

Canal, steamboat, stagecoach, and wagon-freighting interests, including the builders of such equipment and even stablemen with horses to hire, were hostile to railroads. One of the legal cases handled by attorney Abraham Lincoln centered in Mississippi rivermen's opposition to a railroad bridge built by the Illinois Central (IC). He won his case for the IC. But steamboats and canal barges contributed to their own obsolescence by hauling railroad ties and other equipment, including locomotives and freight and passenger cars, to points along waterways where the railroads needed them. They did this even after the "steam cars" had begun to carry the passengers and goods which had previously moved on waterways.

"Sailroading" on the Kansas Pacific Railroad, now part of the Santa Fe system. Wind power was used on several of America's earliest railroads before steam power.

Canada's first railways were Nova Scotia horse-drawn coal haulers at Pictou, starting in 1827, and North Sydney, in 1828. They were reputedly the earliest railways on this continent to use iron rails and adopt the standard gauge (4 feet 8½ inches). Canada's first steam railway, the Champlain & St. Lawrence, extended 15 miles from Laprairie on the St. Lawrence River to St-Jean on the Richelieu River; it was chartered in 1832 and opened in 1836. Its first locomotive was the English-built *Dorchester.*

Upper Canada's first railway was the Erie & Ontario, originally horse-drawn, built in 1839 between Chippawa and Queenstown around Niagara Falls. Toronto Loco-

An old Nova Scotia coal hauler, on one of North America's earliest railways.

motive Works produced the first Canadian-built locomotive in 1853 for the Northern Railway. The Great Western Railway of Canada built that nation's first steam-boilered engine in 1861. Canada's first major railway collision, on the Grand Trunk Railway, killed 47 people. Its worst train wreck, near Beloeil in 1864, had at least 100 fatalities. *See* RICHELIEU RIVER WRECK.

The first United States–Canadian rail link, connecting Montreal with Portland, Maine, was completed in 1861 by the Champlain & St. Lawrence with a line extending from St-Jean, Quebec, to Rouses Point, New York. *See* INTERNATIONAL RAILROADING, UNITED STATES–CANADIAN.

The Baltimore & Ohio (B&O), chartered by the state of Maryland on February 28, 1827, was the first North American railroad incorporated as a common carrier of passengers and freight. Construction began in 1828. Its first passengers rode in single stagecoach-type railroad cars drawn by horses in January 1830. But the first locomotive to pull a train on the continent was the *Stourbridge Lion,* which the Delaware and Hudson Canal Co. imported from England to run on the rail line connecting its mines with its canal. The *Lion* made her trial run on August 8, 1829, performing well, but was too heavy for the track and was permanently retired. A year later the B&O had somewhat better success with its first locomotive, the diminutive *Tom Thumb,* built by Peter Cooper, the only engine he ever constructed.

The first engine to pull passenger cars in North America was the *Best Friend of Charleston,* built at the West Point Foundry, New York, the first locomotive built for an American railroad. She made her maiden run on December 25, 1830, on the South Carolina Canal & Railroad (later part of the Southern Railway), inaugurating service on the first 7 miles of its line. Three years later the road was extended to Hamburg, 136 miles away, across the Savannah River from Augusta, Georgia, and was then the world's longest railway.

On August 9, 1831, the engine *De Witt Clinton* inaugurated service on the Mohawk & Hudson, earliest predecessor of the New York Central System (NYC), pulling a train between Albany and Schenectady, New York. Also in 1831 the Camden & Amboy (later part of the PRR) put into service the British-built *John Bull,* the first engine with a cowcatcher, at Bordentown, New Jersey. In 1832 the Philadelphia, Germantown & Norristown (an ancestor of the Reading) began using *Old Ironsides,* Matthias Baldwin's first full-size locomotive, while the first locomotive in the southern Mississippi Valley made her initial run on the line connecting New Orleans with Lake Ponchartrain (later part of the Louisville & Nashville, or L&N). *See* BALDWIN LOCOMOTIVE WORKS.

Four years afterward, rails linked Boston with Lowell, from which the Boston & Maine sprang, with Worcester, which eventually gave birth to the Boston & Albany, and with Providence, genesis of the New York, New Haven & Hartford. Then the Petersburg (later in the Atlantic Coast Line) pushed southward from Petersburg, Virginia, into North Carolina. The big parade was well under way.

New York businessmen launched the New York & Erie, one of the roads that Jay Gould later despoiled, building it westward across New York State to Lake Erie and finally to Chicago. The Pennsylvania Railroad began as a state-owned hybrid route between Philadelphia and Pittsburgh. It included two canal trips, a railroad operated with both locomotives and horses, and a series of inclined planes to lift and lower cars over the Alleghenies.

Another state involved in railroading was North Carolina, which was a majority stockholder in corporations which built a long stretch of line that the Southern Railway is operating today under a lease. The state of Georgia built a line between Georgia and Tennessee which it leased to the L&N, and the state of Virginia acquired considerable stock in the Richmond, Fredericksburg & Potomac. Two other states, Illinois and Michigan, sponsored railroad projects that failed and were sold to private companies. A rare and successful case of public ownership is the Cincinnati Southern, built and still owned by the city of Cincinnati but operated under a lease by the Southern.

Mid-Century Expansion and the Civil War The second decade of railroad development, 1840–1850, boosted the nation's mileage from 2800 to 9000 and greatly lengthened the distances of continuous travel. The third decade, 1850–1860, more than trebled that mileage. Chicago soon became the nation's No. 1 railroad center. The Michigan Central and Michigan South-

Early opposition to the construction of railroads was sometimes vehement. Supporters of the proposed Delaware and Raritan Canal used this poster to protest against the granting of a charter to the Camden & Amboy Railroad, which later became part of the Pennsylvania Railroad.

ern entered it from the east, while roads that became the Chicago & North Western, the Missouri Pacific (MP), the Burlington, and the Rock Island headed westward. The line that operated the first locomotive west of the Mississippi River was the Pacific Railroad of Missouri (later the MP), in 1852. Four years later, the Mississippi's first bridge was built by the Rock Island, and for the first time an iron horse crossed the great river.

In that decade, too, the Illinois Central was chartered and completed its first of more than 700 miles with the aid of federal land grants. That government policy was in effect from 1850 to 1871, during which period it assisted in the building of nearly 10 percent of the country's railroad mileage. In 1850 there were about 1400 million acres of public land. Some 131 million acres of it were eventually granted to private railroad owners. *See* LAND GRANTS.

The Civil War was the first war in which railroads played a decisive role. It was marked by a slowdown in the building of new railroads, destruction of considerable railroad property, some rebuilding of that property, and the strategic movement of large bodies of troops instrumental in turning the tide of battle. *See* CIVIL WAR.

Late Nineteenth Century Congressional acts of 1862 and 1864 authorized the building of the first transcontinental rail line, which was completed in 1869. A period of considerable railroad building followed, covering the nation with an adequate network of lines. Within a decade rail mileage had doubled. Despite the panic of 1873, which threw some big systems into bankruptcy, the process of building pushed the mileage of operated lines up to 192,556 by the end of the century. *See* GOLDEN SPIKE CEREMONY.

This progress covered just about every section of the country. The area once designated on maps as the Great American Desert was crossed by five (later seven) east-west lines. This was the era of empire builders such as James J. Hill of the Great Northern, Cyrus K. Holliday of the Santa Fe; Otto Mears, Colorado tycoon; George Jay Gould, who came very close to assembling a coast-to-coast rail empire; Arthur E. Stillwell, largely responsible for creating two rail empires; and Edward H. Harriman, wizard of Wall Street. It was also the era of great inventors, crusaders, and other colorful figures in railroading such as William Mason, George Westinghouse, Lorenzo Coffin, Fred Harvey, Matthias W. Baldwin, John Henry, Kate Shelley, George M. Pullman, Death Valley Scotty, Eugene V. Debs, and A. Philip Randolph.

During the 1800s the roads were often harassed by accidents, especially prior to safety-device inventions, that killed or maimed many thousands of employees on duty; train wrecks and other disasters such as fires, floods, blizzards, and explosions; stock manipulation and financial panics that led to bankruptcies; labor strikes, two of which were bloody and destructive, in 1877 and 1894; the Civil War; and train stickups by men like the Reno brothers, Jesse and Frank James, the Younger gang, the Daltons, Sam Bass, Newton Watt and Henry Schwartz, the Hole-in-the-Wall gang, and Oliver C. Perry.

Twentieth Century Developments But the railroads kept growing. Their mileage and prestige had reached a peak when the United States entered World War I. At that time the company executives' Railroad War Board was inadequate to meet the acute problems of wartime transportation; so President Woodrow Wilson issued a proclamation taking over the railroads for federal operation during the war. He appointed his son-in-law, William G. McAdoo, Director General of Railroads. In 1920 the roads were returned to private ownership. *See* WORLD WAR I.

Long before that, the standard railroad unions had been organized. The 8-hour day was established, the Railway Labor Executives Association was formed, and in 1934 the Railroad Retirement Act was passed as one of President Franklin D. Roosevelt's New Deal measures. Rail mileage and the number of company employees was shrinking. They never did get back to the World War I level, largely because of increasing highway competition. *See* UNIONS, RAILROAD LABOR.

Management introduced many technological improvements, some of them revolutionary, in plants, equipment, methods, and services. Steel cars (in a relatively few cases, aluminum) replaced wooden cars. Diesel-electric locomotives began to replace steam in passenger service in 1934 and in freight service in 1941. Passenger trains were being streamlined, speeded up, and air-conditioned. Overnight freight runs for 400-plus miles, mechanical refrigeration, all-electric dining cars, piggybacking, and eventually unit trains were inaugurated. Also new were centralized traffic control, computerization, continuous welded rail, two-way radio service for train and engine crews, and automated freight classification yards.

In World War II the government again took over the railroads. And in May 1946 President Harry S Truman, acting under his wartime powers, seized the railroads to deal with a nationwide strike of enginemen and trainmen. Other strike threats led to additional federal seizures of the roads in 1948 and 1950. The latter lasted nearly 2 years. In 1951, an amendment to the Railway Labor Act lifted the ban on compulsory union membership as a requisite for holding a railroad job. This led to setting up union shops by negotiation, and almost universal management-labor agreements resulted. *See* WORLD WAR II.

The 1960s and 1970s produced some major consolidations. Norfolk & Western took over the Virginian, the Wabash, and the Nickel Plate. Chesapeake & Ohio acquired the larger B&O and the Western Maryland. Atlantic Coast Line and Seaboard Air Line merged to form the Seaboard Coast Line. New York Central and the Pennsy were consolidated into a 21,000-mile system, the Penn Central Transportation Company, which eventually included the New Haven.

The even larger Burlington Northern, 25,000 miles, was formed by merging the Great Northern, the Northern Pacific, the Chicago, Burlington & Quincy, and the Spokane, Portland & Seattle. As of late 1980, the Union Pacific and the Missouri Pacific had agreed to merge, but the stockholders and the Interstate Commerce Commission would have the final say. The Milwaukee Road, long famous for its electrified stretches, de-electrified. Some big rail systems, taking over other industries, reorganized themselves as conglomerates.

In 1980 BN grew still larger by absorbing the Frisco. Another colossus, CSX Corp., was formed by a merger of Chessie and Seaboard Coast Line Industries, including the Family Lines System, a group of Southeastern roads spearheaded by Seaboard Coast Line.

Gigantic Penn Central became bankrupt in 1970, ending an uneasy truce between rival officials of its two components, the PRR and the NYC. In 1976 the Penn Central, together with the Reading, the Jersey Central, the Erie Lackawanna, the Lehigh Valley, and the Lehigh & Hudson River, all bankrupt, were conveyed to the new federally created Conrail (Consolidated Rail Corporation) in exchange for Conrail stock. Later the Ann Arbor was added to Conrail. Conrail is a privately managed corporation, ostensibly run for profit but continually getting into financial difficulties. It was designed to rehabilitate rail service, especially freight service, mostly in the Northeast. *See* CONRAIL.

Rail passenger service could not meet the competition of motor vehicles and airplanes. The situation became so bad that in 1971 nearly all of the intercity rail passenger service in United States was turned over to the quasi-governmental Amtrak, one major exception being the Southern Railway System. *See* AMTRAK.

Canadian Railways The Canadian equivalent of Amtrak is VIA Rail Canada, which became a crown corporation independent of rail systems in 1978 and gradually assumed full responsibility for managing all the Dominion's rail passenger services except commuter lines. *See* VIA RAIL CANADA, INC.

Much of Canada's railway development parallels that of the United States. In early days, trains of both countries were indispensable in linking isolated populations. Until after World War II, when highway vehicles and planes began crowding them out, trains were the most popular way to travel and ship goods.

The primitive tracks of Canada's first steam railway, the Champlain & St. Lawrence, consisted of strap-iron rail resting on a wooden superstructure, with no ballast. The even earlier Nova Scotia railways served only coal mines which, in the 1820s, King George IV had given to his brother, who, in turn, had deeded them to a London jeweler to pay a debt.

Canada's rail mileage grew from 22 in 1848 to 66 in 1850 and 2065 in 1860. On July 1, 1867, date of the union of the Canadian provinces, there were 15 railways with 2495 route miles, 485 steam locomotives, 674 passenger cars, 4214 freight cars, and 9391 employees. In 1873, Prince Edward Island, with 218 railway miles being built, joined the Federation. The federal government completed the line and opened it in 1875. Six years later the Grand Trunk and Great Western railways were merged with 473 other miles of line in western Ontario.

In 1887 Canada's rail mileage was 11,891, including the Canadian Pacific's 4175 and the Grand Trunk's 2598. There were 1633 locomotives and 1350 passenger cars, ranging from second-class cars to sleeping and parlor cars, a few of which were electrically lit by 1888. Newfoundland's railway, between St. John's and Port-aux-Basques, 547 miles, 3½-foot-gauge, was completed in 1896. By the turn of the century the Dominion had 17,481 rail miles, including Canadian Pacific's 6873, Grand Trunk's 3138, and Intercolonial's 1511.

Today Canada is unique in having two great rail systems: the Canadian National (CN), government-owned and -operated, and the Canadian Pacific (CP), or CP Rail, privately owned and operated.

Canadian National, with about 25,000 miles of track in all 10 provinces and 2 territories as well as in 10 states of the United States, is one of the world's greatest rail systems. It also comprises a vast communications network, a chain of hotels, a dockyard, trucking and bus lines, and a fleet of ferries and coastal vessels. It dates back to 1919, when Parliament created a new company, the Canadian National Railway Co., which the Canadian people own. By 1923 the new company boasted 22,100 miles of track that had once belonged to 221 different railways, particularly the Intercolonial, the National Transcontinental, the Grand Trunk, the Grand Trunk Pacific, the Canadian Northern, and the Prince Edward Island, all of which CN had taken over to save them from bankruptcy.

In 1929 the CN opened rail service to the Hudson Bay port of Churchill to assist farmers in shipping wheat to European markets. In 1949, when Newfoundland joined the Confederation, CN took over its rail line, which is narrow-gauge. Between 1962 and 1964 CN built the 432-mile Great Slave Lake Railway northward through the bleak wilderness of the Northwest Territories to develop rich lead and zinc fields, to ship ores from open-pit mines to smelters, and to move grain, lumber, pulp, and oil.

The Canadian Pacific is a diversified company with almost $8 billion in assets in land, sea, and air transportation, telecommunications, natural resources, hotels, real estate, and manufacturing and financial services. It operates about 23,500 miles of track in Canada, including yards, spurs, and sidings, and controls another 4600 miles in the United States.

CP traces its origin to the St. Andrews & Quebec,

chartered in 1836. The big company was incorporated in 1881 to build a transcontinental railway from eastern Canada to the Pacific Coast and was granted $25 million, 25 million acres of land, and certain rail lines previously contracted for by the Dominion government. With William C. Van Horne supervising, the line was completed on November 11, 1885. For many years its emblem was a beaver, typical of Canada, perched on a shield. This was replaced by a simple but apparently meaningless geometrical design.

Also important is Canada's British Columbia Railway, chartered in 1912 as the Pacific Great Eastern to run from North Vancouver for 470 miles to the Peace River area, to colonize and develop that sparsely settled region. The 110.7-mile White Pass & Yukon Route was completed in 1898 into Yukon Territory, in northwestern Canada, and part of Alaska. Originally a by-product of the 1890s gold rush, it makes Yukon mineral resources competitive in world markets. Among other Canadian railways are the Ontario Northland, Algoma Central, Northern Alberta Railways (owned jointly by CN and CP), Greater Winnipeg Water District Railway, and Quebec North Shore and Labrador.

Mexico, Central America, and the Caribbean Mexico's principal rail lines are the National Railways of Mexico, the Chihuahua-Pacific, the Pacific, the Sonora-Baja California, and the United South Eastern. Cuba's 5053-kilometer rail system, nationalized in 1960, is an outgrowth of the island's first railway, built by William Van Horne. Cuba also has 9441 kilometers of railway connected with the sugar industry.

Costa Rica has four railways: the National Atlantic, the Pacific, the United Brands Company Railways, and the Southern Cra. The Dominican Republic has the Dominican Government Railway, the Central Romana, and the Central Río Hana. Guatemala has the International Railways of Central America and the Desarrollo Bananero de Guatemala. Honduras has the Honduras National, the Standard Fruit Company, and the Tela. Jamaica has the Jamaica Railway, the Alpart, and the Kaiser Bauxite. Nicaragua has the Pacific Railway.

The Panama Railroad, 1524 kilometers, was surveyed as long ago as 1828 and was built later through malarial jungles at a frightful cost of human life. The first train crossed the continent on January 28, 1855. Later the railroad was rehabilitated and double-tracked to provide for building the old (unfinished) Isthmian Canal. The rehabilitation was completed in 1907. In 1912 the line was relocated and elevated for construction by the United States of the Panama Canal. Also in Panama is the United Brands Company Railways.

Puerto Rico has the Ponce & Guayama Railway, St. Christopher the St. Kitts Sugar Railway, and El Salvador the National Railways of El Salvador.

See also the many articles on individual railroads of the United States and Canada.

BIBLIOGRAPHY: Alfred D. Chandler, *The Railroads: The Nation's First Big Business; Sources and Readings,* Harcourt, Brace, New York, 1965; Patrick C. Dorin, *The Canadian National Railways' Story,* Superior Publishing, Seattle, 1975; G. P. de T. Glazebrook, *A History of Transportation in Canada,* McClelland & Stewart, Toronto, 1964; Carter Goodrich, *Government Promotion of American Canals and Railroads, 1800-1890,* Columbia, New York, 1960; Stewart H. Holbrook, *The Story of American Railroads,* Crown, New York, 1947; Oliver Jensen, *The American Heritage History of Railroads in America,* American Heritage, New York, 1975; Omer LaValle, *Van Horne's Road,* Railfare Enterprises, Montreal, 1975; R. A. J. Phillips, *Canada's Railways,* McGraw-Hill, New York, 1968.

Hoboes Between the Civil War's end and World War II (also to a lesser extent before and since then) American railroads were plagued by hoboes, tramps, and bums, usually nonworkers, who rode freight and sometimes passenger trains without paying fares to the company but often, under threat of being thrown off moving freight cars, giving the train crews money to put into their own pockets. Prior to the 1900s an overnight ride might cost about 20 cents, but eventually the rate was standardized at $1 a division (approximately 100 miles).

A hobo toting a blanket for use wherever night overtook him was called a *blanket stiff* or *bindle stiff, bindle* being a corruption of *bundle.* The categories of hobo, tramp, and bum overlap. Ben L. Reitman, himself a drifter for years and coauthor of the book *Sister of the Road* (1937), oversimplified the distinction by stating that a hobo works and wanders, a tramp dreams and wanders, and a bum drinks and wanders. He thus confused hoboes with boomers. The latter were experienced railmen who alternately worked and loafed as whim dictated. Reitman also overlooked the pugnacity of some tramps, their fights with train crews, their thefts of and damage to freight, and their use of unscrupulous lawyers to sue the railroads for injuries incurred during free rides. *See* BOOMERS.

Peaceful hoboes were called *Weary Willies.* Empty boxcars, when available, were their choice of transportation. Often a group of them would travel in the same

In the 1890s, when hoboes and tramps were frequent nonpaying clients of the rails, they often came to blows with the freight crew and could cause considerable damage to freight. [A. B. Frost]

car, with or without paying hush money. In good weather they liked to ride the car tops, a perilous place with nothing to hold onto. The tiniest bit of shut-eye might send you off the roof of the swaying, windswept car. Even more dangerous was riding the *rods,* the iron pipes that extended horizontally about 18 inches below the wooden car body. If you were lean and had strong nerves, you could lie prone on those rods, as many tramps did and even a few women in the Great Depression. You'd have been pelted with gravel from the roadbed, blown by fierce, dusty winds, nearly deafened by the noise, and exposed to almost certain death if you moved to right or left or dozed briefly.

Another Russian-roulette form of free transportation was on the constantly shifting bumpers or couplers, especially in the days before automatic airbrakes. But riding the *blinds,* meaning the space between the baggage car and tender, was fairly safe if you held on tight. The baggage car was usually the first car on a passenger train. As a protection against train robbers, it did not have a forward door; the area was "blind." Only on rare occasions did a fireman catch sight of a vagrant in this locality and throw hunks of coal at him.

For understandable reasons, the railroad *bulls,* meaning special agents or policemen, are perpetually at war with hoboes. A few of them, like some prison guards, are downright sadistic. Federal Judge Bernard Decker of Chicago sentenced two such Penn Central (PC) employees for violating the civil rights of seven hoboes whom they had caught in the road's Chicago yards in 1972–1973. While giving each of the two railroad guards 2-year prison terms, he said that "were it in my power to do so," he would let the vagrants who had been tortured and beaten by the PC men reverse the process.

From about 1906 until 1923, when the Industrial Workers of the World, or Wobblies, were influential, red IWW membership cards ensured special privileges to many of the payless train riders. In that era, the fires of hobo jungles burned brightly at night beside the railroad tracks. An unemployed boomer who was broke, dirty, and hungry was not too proud to stop there to wash up, eat, sleep, or merely stick around between trains.

The most widely publicized train-riding hobo, identified only as A-No. 1, wrote several little paperback books about hoboing that the American News Co. peddled on passenger trains; in them he claimed to have traveled 500,000 miles by rail for only $7.61, a disputable boast. Innumerable poems and ballads have been written about vagrants. They include "Hallelujah, I'm a Bum," by Harry K. McClintock; the rollicking folk song "The Wabash Cannonball," author unknown; and the following old bit of melancholia, "The Dying Hobo," likewise anonymous:

Beside a Western water tank one cold December day,
Inside an empty boxcar, a dying hobo lay.
His pardner stood beside him with low and drooping head,
Listening to the last words the luckless floater said:

"I'm going to a better land where everything is bright,
Where handouts grow on bushes and you can camp out every night,
Where you do not have to work at all or even change your socks,
And little streams of whiskey come trickling down the rocks.

"Tell my hasher back in Denver that her face no more I'll view;
Tell her that I've jumped the fast freight and I'm going through.
Ask her not to weep for me, no tears her eyes must lurk,
For I'm going to a land where I'll not have to work.

"Hark, the train is coming! I must catch it on the fly.
Farewell, pardner, I must leave you. It ain't so hard to die."
The hobo stopped. His head fell back; he'd sung his last refrain.
His pardner swiped his hat and shoes and jumped the eastbound train.

Lines 5 to 8 of this ballad are so similar to parts of McClintock's "The Big Rock Candy Mountain" that one author must have borrowed from the other, but at this late date there is no way of telling who wrote the lines originally. *See* McCLINTOCK, HARRY KIRBY.

Nobody knows how many freeloading hoboes the railroads have carried. In 1 month alone, October 1921, on a single road, the Southern Pacific, its chief special agent, Dan O'Connell, supervised the removal of 20,643 "undesirable persons" from SP "trains and property." Possibly well over 1 million freeloaders used America's railroads during the Depression of the 1930s. The author saw some of them riding the car tops in that era.

A woman hobo, Boxcar Bertha, estimated that in those days about 0.5 percent of the nation's hoboes were female. Because of the widespread unemployment and hardship in Depression years, a few railroads tolerated their free passengers, just as the Western carriers had done with boxcar riders en route to seek jobs as harvest hands in times of labor shortages on farms and ranches in the 1880s and 1890s. Today the number of train-riding hoboes is at its lowest ebb, owing to social security, other welfare benefits, the streamlining and modernization of rolling stock, and the greatly accelerated speed of trains.

BIBLIOGRAPHY: Benjamin A. Botkin and Alvin F. Harlow, *A Treasury of Railroad Folklore,* Crown, New York, 1953; Roger A. Bruns, *Knights of the Road: A Hobo History,* Methuen, New York, 1980; Thomas C. Clarke and others, *The American Railway,* Scribner, New York, 1897; Loren C. Eiseley, *All the Strange Hours,* Scribner, New York, 1975; Stewart H. Holbrook, *The Story of American Railroads,* Crown, New York, 1947.

Hopkins, Mark ***(1813?–1878)*** One of the Big Four tycoons who built and controlled the first transcontinental railroad, the Central Pacific [(CP) later renamed Southern Pacific], the other three being Collis P. Huntington, Charles Crocker, and Leland Stanford. Reaching California shortly after the gold rush of 1849, Hopkins ran a Sacramento hardware store in partnership with Huntington. In 1861 the four men met in an office and listened to a young engineer, Theodore D. Judah, expound the possibilities of a transcontinental railroad. Eight men, including the future Big Four, agreed to finance the proposed rail line.

On January 8, 1863, construction of the CP was started, and on May 10, 1869, its tracks joined those of the Union Pacific at Promontory, Utah. After that, the Big Four, not satisfied with only the CP, manipulated to gain control of other railroads in the West as well as other forms of transportation: steamship companies, cargo boats, interurban transit lines, cable cars, docks, and so on.

Peculiarly, less is known of Hopkins than any of his close associates. After his death, many biographical documents about him, especially legal papers involving his large estate, either vanished or were deliberately destroyed or mutilated, for reasons hard to explain.

There is reason to believe that this was done because the Central Pacific, despite its apparent affluence and continuing expansion, was heavily in debt, and at the time of Hopkins's death Congress was investigating its monopolistic practices. His estate was not divided among his heirs. If it had been, this could have weakened the railroad's financial structure and might have opened the floodgates to investigation and a rising tide of public wrath against the CP. But with Hopkins's valuable holdings controlled by the other three members of the Big Four and used to buttress the railroad's shaky economy, the three survivors would have felt more secure.

This, at least, is one possible explanation of the mystery surrounding the vanished and mutilated documents. Furthermore, the manuscripts, letters, newspaper interviews, etc., of Huntington, Crocker, and Stanford are very evasive with regard to Hopkins's part in building and controlling the railroad but do admit that he was treasurer of the company and a member of the board of directors.

See also CROCKER, CHARLES; HUNTINGTON, COLLIS POTTER; JUDAH, THEODORE D.; STANFORD, LELAND.

BIBLIOGRAPHY: Stuart Daggett, *Chapters on the History of the Southern Pacific,* Ronald, New York, 1922; Estelle Latta and M. L. Allison, *Controversial Mark Hopkins,* Greenberg, New York, 1953; Oscar Lewis, *The Big Four,* Knopf, New York, 1938.

Horse Names Names of famous horses were given to 23 Frisco Lines diesel-electric locomotives, although the railroad industry as a whole has had relatively few diesels with individual names. The racetrack was represented by *Seabiscuit, Twenty Grand,* and *Dan Patch,* whose owner built the Minneapolis, St. Paul, Rochester & Dubuque Electric Traction Co. and named it the Dan Patch Line. Movies and TV were represented by *Champion,* the white steed of Gene Autry, a former Frisco employee whose theme song was "I'm Back in the Saddle Again." Among other diesel names were Robert E. Lee's *Traveler,* Andrew Jackson's *Truxton,* and buckskin pony *Comanche,* the only living thing found on the battlefield at Little Big Horn after the massacre of the Custer forces in 1876. But no locomotive was named for Jesse James's *Skyrocket,* the horse whose framed picture the train robber was dusting when he was fatally shot through the back of the head in 1882. *See* DAN PATCH LINE.

In 1893 the Central of Georgia inaugurated what is said to have been the country's first name train, called *Nancy Hanks* after a famous racehorse (which was also the name of Abraham Lincoln's mother). This elegant royal blue, gold-striped speedster made the 294-mile run between Atlanta and Savannah in 6 hours (fast running in those days), but it did not last 8 months. In 1947 the same road launched two other fast passenger trains named for racehorses, *Nancy Hanks II* and *Man o' War.* Both have since disappeared.

Hospital Trains Such trains date back to the Civil War. At first moderately wounded soldiers rode in ordinary passenger coaches. Those who could not sit up were lifted on stretchers or mattresses into boxcars and laid on hay, straw, leaves, or pine boughs. Holes cut in the car admitted daylight and ventilation. In 1862 a car equipped for 51 patients began running on the Philadelphia, Baltimore & Washington (later part of the Pennsy). Besides tiers of bunks on each side, it had a stove, lockers, and seats for attendants. Other roads soon had similar equipment. These units were coupled onto regular trains.

In 1863 a complete Union hospital train with a capacity for 500 to 600 patients was put into service on the Orange & Alexandria Railroad. It had 10 ward cars, each designed for 30 patients in bunks and as many others seated. On both sides of each car two windows were replaced by a sliding door through which stretchers were carried. There were coaches for the surgical staff, a dispensary, a storeroom, and a kitchen.

Similar Union trains ran between Atlanta and Louisville, 474 miles, on regular schedules. Their engine stacks, cabs, and tenders were painted bright red, with three red lights hung at night under the headlight, to identify them as hospital specials. Confederate troops never fired on them, even giving such trains passage when they were about to tear up tracks. After the Battle of Chancellorsville, 9000 wounded Union soldiers were transported to a base at Aquia Creek between noon of June 12,1863, and the evening of June 14. In 20 days following the Battle of Gettysburg, ambulance cars distributed 15,000 wounded to hospitals in Washington, Harrisburg, Philadelphia, and New York.

A special unit was designed and built for use overseas in World War II, especially in combat areas. It included ward cars (up to 16) for patients, a kitchen, quarters for officers and men in charge of the train, and a utilities car. Its generators and oil-fired boilers provided light, heat, hot water, ventilation, and refrigeration.

The kitchen car had mess facilities, a dining section for personnel (patients were served from trays), and a well-stocked pharmacy compartment. With its service equipment, the train could operate near the front lines, also between evacuation hospitals and the larger general hospitals several hundred miles to the rear. The cars were purposely built narrower than standard cars and about half their length to allow use on sharp curves, narrow bridges, and tunnels overseas. They were used eventually by Ringling Bros.-Barnum & Bailey circus trains.

Hotels *See* BOARDING HOUSES; HARVEY, FREDERICK HENRY; STATION HOTELS; YMCAS, RAILROAD.

Houston Belt & Terminal Railway (HB&T) Road with 1300 employees that switches an average of 5500 freight cars daily over its 234 miles of track in Houston, Texas. It is owned jointly by the Santa Fe (ATSF), Missouri Pacific (MP), and Fort Worth and Denver (FW&D), the last-named being part of the Burlington Northern; and its cars are interchanged also with those of Southern Pacific and the Katy. A considerable number of these cars serve the petroleum industry and its thousands of products.

The rail network, with East Belt and North Belt subdivisions, is shaped like the letter D. Prior to Amtrak's taking over passenger service, the Belt line also served downtown Union Station. The road's seven flat freight yards are interconnected by a Computer Automation of Railroad System (CARS), which enables yardmasters and reporting clerks to check on car inventories and movements.

A total of 24 Belt switching locos and 23 leased from MP shift the cars designed for local delivery to more than 300 industrial and commercial spotting areas. HB&T's all-time roster lists 49 switchers. To avoid the city's dense daytime vehicular traffic, much of this work is done at night. The Belt line also services its own motive power and that of ATSF and FW&D (but not MP, which has its own facilities), besides repairing cars of all members of the Association of American Railroads and maintaining its right-of-way. Its radio frequencies are HB&T, 160.77; Katy, 160.59; Santa Fe, 160.65; MP, 161.41; FW&D, 161.61; and SP, 161.58.

Hudson Bay Line Building a 510-mile railway northward from The Pas to Churchill (both in Manitoba), which the Canadian government undertook in 1909, required a combination of engineering skill, big money, raw courage, and endurance. One major problem was the miles of shifting, mushy, treacherous, and seemingly bottomless muskeg. It was frustrating to labor heroically day after day building a roadbed, laying ties and rails, only to discover next morning a yawning gap over which the track stretched like a spiderweb; and much work had to be repeated at a staggering cost of energy and materials.

Once, a supply-train engine slid off the track and vanished, dragging 10 loaded boxcars into the muck in rainy, foggy darkness. Fortunately, the crew members jumped to safety, but they never saw any part of the train again. All food and supplies for the construction job came in by rail from the south and east. Derailments, bridge collapses, brushfires, epidemics, and floods slowed progress. Nobody knows how many small wooden crosses thrust into the earth marked the last resting places of construction workers in the lonely wilderness. Sometimes hungry tracklayers had long waits for grub. Enraged moose tangled with the telegraph wires; bears and lean gray wolves raided the cook tent.

It was a life without women or liquor. In those days, women were forbidden to go beyond Mile 212, less than midway between The Pas and Churchill, the only exceptions being a few nurses to help fight epidemics. Even the men who craved the stimulus of whiskey, and there were many, had no way of getting it in that bleak country.

By 1918 they had completed the rail line as far north as Pikwitonei at Mile 214, still 296 miles from their goal. Then problems resulting from World War I stopped further construction until 1926. Again the workers had to fight for every mile of ground they pushed into. Finally, in 1929, they reached Churchill, a tiny settlement on the shore of Hudson Bay, where small white whales swam in icy water and where curious Eskimos and Cree Indians greeted the weary railroad builders. Then the white men constructed port facilities and a huge grain elevator.

In 1942 the United States set up a large base 5 miles south of Churchill and stationed ground and air forces there for the rest of World War II. In 1944 this base was turned over to Canada for joint operation by the two countries as a cold-weather training center and experimental station.

Each summer Indians camp at Churchill, sell furs and handicrafts, and buy food staples, tobacco, and clothing. The Eskimos, too, are gifted craftspersons and sell souvenirs to tourists. Today, the 510-mile railway is an operating division of the Canadian National Railways. Its annual August tour to the Far North has always been sold out well in advance, so reservations must be made early.

BIBLIOGRAPHY: Howard A. Fleming, *Canada's Arctic Outlet: A History of the Hudson Bay Railway,* University of California Press, Berkeley, Calif., 1957; George R. Stevens, *History of the Canadian National Railways,* Macmillan, New York, 1973.

***Huntington, Collis Potter** (1821-1900)* One of the Big Four merchants who built and operated the Central Pacific and Southern Pacific railroads. He was born on October 20, 1821, in Harwinton, Connecticut. His first paid job was peddling clocks and watches at age 14. Later he opened a general store at Oneonta, New York, with his brother Solin and shipped goods to California gold-mining camps. In 1850 he crossed the Great Plains to Sacramento, California, and opened a lucrative business in axes, shovels, and kegs of nails with Mark Hopkins, another future member of the Big Four.

Engineer Theodore D. Judah got the partners and two other Sacramento merchants interested in building what eventually became the western end of the first transcontinental railroad. Huntington died on August 13, 1900, at Raquette Lake, New York. He bequeathed a famous collection of paintings to the Metropolitan Museum of Art in New York and aided Negro education by endowing Hampton Institute in Virginia and Tuskegee Institute in Alabama.

See also CHINESE LABOR; CROCKER, CHARLES; GOLDEN SPIKE CEREMONY; HOPKINS, MARK; JUDAH, THEODORE D.; SOUTHERN PACIFIC LINES; STANFORD, LELAND.

BIBLIOGRAPHY: Oscar Lewis, *The Big Four,* Knopf, New York, 1938; James McCague, *Moguls and Iron Men,* Harper & Row, New York, 1964.

I

IC *See* Illinois Central Railroad.

ICC *See* Interstate Commerce Commission.

ICG *See* Illinois Central Gulf Railroad.

Illinois Central Railroad (IC) On September 17, 1850, Congress authorized the first United States government land grant to a railroad. Although the grant involved only Illinois, it set a national policy for public land and stimulated railway growth so much that the development of the West was unmatched in world history. At that time the nation owned 1,400,000,000 acres of wild land, almost half of the country's total area. Nearly 3,600,000 acres of it, in Illinois, went to the Illinois Central Railroad Co., which was chartered on February 10, 1851, and organized about 5 weeks later; but the railroad was not allowed to sell any land until the government had sold all its land in the alternate sections, each section averaging 640 acres. This took 2 years, during which time no money from IC land was available for railway construction. *See* Land Grants.

Under its original charter, the company could build only in Illinois "from the southern terminus of the Illinois-and-Michigan Canal" to "the junction of the Ohio and Mississippi rivers," plus branches to Chicago and Dubuque, Iowa, which would make it the West's first railroad. The total mileage contemplated, 705, exceeded that of the New York & Erie, then the world's longest railway. But until the Mississippi was bridged at Dubuque on January 1, 1869, the only connections with that city were by ferry during the navigation season and by rails laid temporarily on the ice each winter.

By 1852 the company had floated $9 million in bonds and ordered 80,000 tons of rail and other items—at the time the largest quantity of railroad iron ever bought by one road. But its unsettled state is shown by the fact that it had four presidents in its first 4 years. The chief engineer was Col. Roswell B. Mason, who had helped to

This old locomotive, built in 1834 for a predecessor of the Illinois Central, was given to the Chicago Museum of Science and Industry by the IC in 1938. [Illinois Central Railroad]

build the Erie Canal and several railroads and was mayor of Chicago during the conflagration of 1871. His staff included such notables as Henry B. Plant, who later founded the Plant system of railroads, hotels, and steamship lines; Grenville M. Dodge; and Timothy R. Blackstone, who did much to make Chicago the world's foremost meat-packing center. *See* DODGE, GRENVILLE MELLEN.

The company sent employment agents to the Eastern United States and overseas for men to build the railroad. Over a 5-year period some 100,000 railroad workers swarmed into Illinois. One agent brought 1000 directly from Ireland. A New York concern supplied 1500 Germans. As many as 10,000 men at a time were on the job. They used picks, shovels, axes, sledgehammers, and horse-drawn equipment, there being no bulldozers or cranes in those days.

Thousands of wagons pulled by oxen or horses crossed the open prairie, transporting rails, ties, lumber, tools, stone, and food for construction sites. It was not unusual for six or eight ships loaded with iron for the railroad to be on the high seas at the same time. One brig sank with 729 tons aboard; her crew escaped in lifeboats. Another disappeared in 1856. It took rugged, violent men to build railroads in the 1850s.

Groggeries and brothels followed the grading crews. These led to fights, crime, accidents, and lost work hours. Colonel Mason angrily banned the transportation of whiskey on the Illinois Central and enforced this rule.

Under terms of the grant, all federal land would revert to the government unless the company began construction within 2 years after passage of the act and completed it by 1856. To do this Mason's men had to lay temporary tracks so shaky that some engine and train crews balked at running over them. Cholera epidemics slowed progress. In one town 130 people died. In 1854 Chicago had 40,000 inhabitants, unpaved streets, plank sidewalks, and 1184 cholera deaths.

As the railhead moved on, trackside communities celebrated. On July 4, 1854, when the first train entered Carbondale, Illinois, that small town supplied free dinners to 2000 people. Women baked bread and cakes, cooked poultry, and brewed coffee and tea. The men barbecued meat. The company never forgot this fiesta. Long afterward, it picked the Carbondale area to launch a long-range agricultural program by giving 24 purebred bulls to help the farmers improve their livestock. And in 1943 the IC established at Carbondale the first of its several training schools to fit teenage boys for train and switching jobs.

Meanwhile, Chicago's lakefront was being swept occasionally by furious storms. In 1858 the Illinois Central completed a 4½-mile breakwater, 2 years after opening its Great Central Passenger Station, reputedly the nation's best in those days. The station lasted until 1902. Prior to the big fire of 1871 it was the Chicago terminal of the IC, the Michigan Central, and the Burlington. The Chicago & Galena and Alton roads also used it. Out of it ran the first sleeping cars ever seen in the West.

Laborers, mostly immigrants from Ireland and Norway, used picks and shovels to help build the right-of-way of the Illinois Central Railroad in the 1850s. [Illinois Central Gulf Railroad]

The earliest engines were woodburners. The first few built especially for the IC were outshopped by Rogers, Ketchum & Grosvenor at Paterson, New Jersey, and reached Chicago in ships in 1852. All cars in those days were wooden-bodied. Whale-oil lamps and tallow candles lit the passenger cars at night. Many coaches were unheated in winter; others had woodburning stoves which added to the hazards of train wrecks. There were no dining cars, but IC trains stopped for 20 minutes at certain stations to let passengers eat meals.

In 1855, just 3 years before George M. Pullman's first experimental sleeping car, the IC's *Lightning Express* was operating "Gothic" cars which had staterooms and berths. Also in 1855, the company introduced double-decked stock cars for sheep and hogs and began using coke and coal as locomotive fuel. By 1865 all but five of its engines were coalburners.

George B. McClellan, a West Point graduate, was chief engineer and vice president of the IC from 1857 to 1860, when he became president of the Ohio & Mississippi Railroad (now in the new CSX Corp.). While he was with the IC, Little Mac, as he was called, came in contact with Abraham Lincoln, who was then an Illinois Central attorney. This relationship led eventually to his appointment as commander in chief of the Union Army in the Civil War.

The IC was involved in major shipments of Chicago meat products by rail to Cairo, Illinois, and thence by water to New Orleans. In 1857 it began operating a Mississippi steamship line.

In the 1850s the IC's destiny was being determined by a few independent railways that would later form a continuous line between New Orleans and Jackson, Tennessee, and become the IC's north-south trunk line south of the Ohio River. One of these, the Jackson Road, was built from New Orleans to Canton, Mississippi, to link with the north-south Mississippi Central (MC). The MC had been chartered to build from Canton to the Mississippi-Tennessee state line, but in 1858 lack of money forced it to seek aid from William H. Osborn, IC president, to complete its line.

Osborn had McClellan tour the MC route. Little Mac inspected by rail the part already built. Then afoot, on horseback, and in a buggy he traversed the 86 miles of uncompleted road and extolled "the finest inland cotton region in Mississippi, if not in the whole South." Osborn was impressed. With the backing of George Peabody, a partner of John Pierpont Morgan's father, the Mississippi Central was completed in 1860. By 1873, for the first time, one could travel by rail from Bangor, Maine, all the way to New Orleans. Closing of the gap cut about 20 hours off travel and mail time between Chicago and New Orleans.

Immediately after the attack on Fort Sumter, Union soldiers boarded three IC troop trains at Chicago's Great Central Passenger Station on secret orders to take possession of Cairo; this was the war's first troop movement west of the Atlantic seaboard. During the next 4 years the IC was largely a military railroad, transporting men, equipment, hospital trains, and northbound funeral trains. Although as a land-grant railroad it was required by law to carry free of charge "any property or troops of the United States," the government paid for the use of rolling stock and experienced crews; however, the company had difficulty in collecting the money.

In 1865 the Confederate Gen. Pierre G. T. de Beauregard became the general superintendent and chief engineer of the New Orleans, Jackson & Great Northern Railroad (as it was then called), part of the Chicago–New Orleans setup. Under his supervision the war-ravaged line was restored, and trains resumed operation on a daily schedule. But in 1876 that road and the Mississippi Central went into receivership. The IC bought them both and operated them as the Chicago, St. Louis & New Orleans (CSL&NO), but it dropped that name in 1882 and changed the CSL&NO gauge from 5 feet to its own standard 4 feet 8½ inches. (Prior to the change, through cars had been designed and built for dual-gauge track.)

Meanwhile, the one-state Illinois Central had adopted an expansionist policy that in 25 years would stretch its 705 miles to 3700 miles in 10 states. Its first extrastate extension consisted of leasing, in 1867, the Dubuque & Sioux City, whose branches would eventually penetrate Minnesota, South Dakota, and Nebraska. The IC also renewed its prewar contract with a Mississippi River steamboat line. In 1870 two of that line's palatial packets, the *Natchez* and the *Robert E. Lee,* engaged in the most exciting race the great river has ever known: 1270 miles from New Orleans to St. Louis. The *Robert E. Lee* won.

By acquiring control of the West Feliciana Railroad (WF) in Mississippi and Louisiana in 1888 and consolidating it with the Yazoo & Mississippi Valley under the latter name, the Louisville, New Orleans & Texas brought the West Feliciana into the Illinois Central family in 1892. The WF, first proposed in 1828 and completed in 1840, was the oldest railway in the Mississippi Valley and the oldest of the more than 100 roads that went into the makeup of the IC system.

Disaster struck on the night of October 8–9, 1871. Fire starting in a Chicago barn and fanned by a high wind quickly spread to the city's mostly wooden houses and plank sidewalks. The beautiful stone-walled Great Central Passenger Station was gutted, with only the walls left standing. Tracks, a freight depot, a huge grain elevator, and some smaller railroad buildings also were destroyed. So were the homes of many IC employees and officials, including the mansion of a former president, John M. Douglas, with its valuable library.

But the IC's South Water Street yard was cleared of engines and cars before flames could reach them; the equipment was shunted to yards and sidings south of the city. A grain elevator was saved by the discovery of a fire engine on a flatcar consigned to a Wisconsin town. Railmen used it to pour water onto the elevator, which afterward was the only building left standing in the charred ruins on the south side of the Chicago River.

The Illinois Central observed the twenty-second anniversary of that holocaust by setting an all-time 1-day record for the number of passengers carried by a trunk-line railroad: 263,282 in World's Fair specials and 241,832 in regular suburban trains, plus many thousands of others on long-distance trains. Among the engineers who pulled specials that day was John Luther Jones. *See* CASEY JONES.

In 1880 the Illinois Central placed in service its first locomotives designed and built especially for suburban passenger service. Known as double-enders, they could run forward or backward with equal facility, not needing a turntable or a wye to reverse their direction. In 1889 the road installed at Rockford, Illinois, its first interlocking plant, a modern system whereby a track or crossing is "locked" for a train movement that excludes all other trains. Eleven years later, with over 5000 route miles, the Illinois Central had become one of America's 10 largest rail systems, and by 1967 it had 6458 miles in 14 states.

Its passenger name trains were famous. The deluxe Chicago-New Orleans *Diamond Special* and *Daylight Special* were launched in 1900, and the proud *Green Diamond* to St. Louis in 1936. (The word *diamond* was used to glorify the road's heavy coal traffic, *black diamonds* being a common term for coal. For many years the IC emblem, like those of the Reading and the Lehigh Valley roads, was diamond-shaped.) Another great train, the all-Pullman *Panama Limited* (named in honor of the Panama Canal completion), linked Chicago and New Orleans on an 18-hour schedule. A newer edition of the *Panama* was the last dieselized streamliner put into service on any road before the building of passenger equipment was halted for the duration of World War II. After the war, an ultramodern coach train, the *City of New Orleans,* cut the running time between those two cities to 15 hours 55 minutes.

But those great names faded with the enormous rise of highway travel. In 1971 the IC turned over its once-popular but long-unprofitable passenger business to Amtrak. The following year the 6760-mile IC and the 2734-mile Gulf, Mobile, & Ohio were merged into the Illinois Central Gulf. Aside from that, the IC never had a reorganization or merger in its entire history. Another IC distinction is that it never defaulted a dollar of its bonded debt. *See* ILLINOIS CENTRAL GULF RAILROAD.

The IC was also the first road anywhere to originate shipments of fresh fruit under refrigeration. Rent-A-Train was one of its innovations in marketing methods based on volume service to shippers. Its management-union officers' team seeking ways to create new rail business and more jobs for employees was a landmark in labor relations. Its interchange tracks connected with over 100 other railroads at about 500 junction points. Nearly every ton of rail freight moving between the Atlantic and the Pacific passed over those tracks.

The Illinois Central used to be a 14-state railroad. At that time it operated a ferryboat from Trotters Point, Mississippi, across the Mississippi to Helena, Arkansas. The cross-river service was abandoned several years ago. The Missouri Pacific took over the former Illinois Central trackage in Arkansas, making the IC a 13-state system.

BIBLIOGRAPHY: *Abraham Lincoln as Attorney of the Illinois Central Railroad Company,* Illinois Central Railroad, Chicago, 1905; Association of American Railroads, Bureau of Railway Economics, *Illinois Central Railroad Company, 1851-1951,* Washington, 1950; Carlton J. Corliss, *Main Line of Mid-America,* Creative Age, New York, 1950; Carolyn C. Mohr (comp.), *Guide to the Illinois Central Archives in the Newberry Library, 1851-1906,* Newberry Library, Chicago, 1951; John F. Stover, *History of the Illinois Central Railroad,* Macmillan, New York, 1975.

Illinois Central Gulf Railroad (ICG) An 8800-mile rail system formed in 1972 by merging the Illinois Central and the Gulf, Mobile, & Ohio (GM&O) roads. It is owned by IC Industries Inc. The ICG also operates the Chicago & Illinois Western switching line, owns the Waterloo Railroad, controls the Peoria & Pekin Union Railroad, and owns Gulf Transport Co., which operates bus service and has trucking rights along the old GM&O lines. The ICG is a strong, solvent carrier operating in 13 states from the Great Lakes to the Gulf of Mexico, with rail connections between the highly industrialized Chicago area and some 2000 other communities. Its territory includes great urban and industrial areas as well as vast coal reserves, coal being one of ICG's top traffic producers.

Under an unusual intermodal labor-management concept known as Slingshot, set up in 1975, the ICG operates truck-competitive short piggyback runs between Chicago and East St. Louis with two-man crews and no caboose. In 1976 it set up a new computerized car-control system which handles more efficiently the distribution of its empty car fleet, rejecting certain cars from other carriers, providing home-route data, and checking up on shippers' car orders.

See also GULF, MOBILE, & OHIO RAILROAD; ILLINOIS CENTRAL RAILROAD.

BIBLIOGRAPHY: *Jane's World Railways and Rapid Transit Systems,* F. Watts, New York, 1977.

Insects Caterpillars, grasshoppers, bees, and ants on rare occasions interfere with train operation. For example, in 1949 an eastbound Canadian National passenger train of 16 cars was stalled for 2 hours and 20 minutes by caterpillars about 13 miles west of Smithers, British Columbia. Slippery rails necessitated the calling of a helper engine from Smithers to move the train over the infested area.

In the 1830s stiff brooms were attached to the front of a few locomotives to brush caterpillars and grasshoppers off the track. In that decade, too, railroads began to sand their rails, mostly because of such insects. *See* SANDING THE RAILS.

"In the summer of 1893," recalled F. E. Chipman of Somerville, Massachusetts, "when I was riding a Rock Island train through Missouri, the engine ran into swarms of grasshoppers, alive, dying, or dead, which covered the pilot and deck. For some distance the track was a wriggly mess of reddish-brown slime. Shovels and brooms were put to work, the track was sanded, and after some slipping we were on our way again."

About 50 years later, thousands of bees invaded the Milwaukee Road freight yard at Hoquiam, Washington, routing a section gang and switching crews. For half an hour work in that yard was at a standstill until a locomotive engineer drove off the insects with jets of live steam.

In at least two instances red ants stopped trains by crawling into the mechanism of automatic block signals, one at Unadilla, Georgia, on the Southern Railway and the other on the Louisville & Nashville. One of the Frisco's best passenger trains was called *The Firefly.*

Inspection Cars For the use of short-line railroad officials inspection cars were made occasionally by converting ordinary automobiles built for highways into vehicles that run on steel rails. Possibly the first of these was a 1930 seven-passenger sedan which, with a few basic changes, became a comfortable inspection car on the Minneapolis, Northfield & Southern and the Minnesota Southern railways. Its regular axles were removed and replaced by especially built steel-alloy axles 3 inches in diameter and wheels equipped with a 1½-inch rubber cushion between the felly and the rail tire. This minimized noise, although its main advantage was preventing crystallization. The newly installed front wheels and axles weighed 1500 pounds, which enabled men to travel safely over the rails at speeds up to 60 miles per hour, over frogs and switches and around curves, and gave the necessary adhesion between wheel and rail. Having wheels and axles with large roller bearings, the converted car was easily propelled. In addition, the car even carried its own easily adjustable turntable. The occupants could, at any point, reverse direction within 3 minutes without having to drive to a wye.

Since then, some ingeniously devised patented vehicles have been built to run on both rails and highways at will, with an easy changeover, one of these having the commercial name Ro-Railer.

Interlocking System used to ensure the safety of train movements at terminals, junction points, grade crossings, and drawbridges. Technically, it is "an arrangement of signals and signal appliances so interconnected that their movements must succeed each other in proper sequence and for which interlocking rules are in effect." There are various interlocking methods, mechanical, electromechanical, and relay. *See also* SIGNALS.

International Boundary Line The boundary between the United States and Canada at one time had as many as 50 railroad crossings, far more than any other frontier, while the United States-Mexican border had only 11. These figures do not include trainferries or different railroads using the same tracks.

***The Pennsylvania Railroad inspection car drawn here rolling through the Allegheny Mountains around 1875 was not as unusual as some newer cars, like the Ro-Railer, which can run on both rails and highways.* [Harper's Weekly]**

International Railroading, United States–Canadian Not only are the thousands of miles of border between these two countries undefended but ever since July 16, 1851, trains have been routinely crossing the boundary line with no formality except short delays for customs and immigration inspection. This situation, from the viewpoint of people familiar with global history and geography, must be one of the wonders of the world. But that isn't all. Each nation's trains run for hundreds of miles on the other's rails. Stranger still, American railroads own thousands of track miles in Canada, while the Dominion's railways hold title to even more mileage in the States.

Hundreds of United States citizens, male and female, employed by such roads as the Central Vermont (CV); the Grand Trunk Western; the Grand Trunk lines in Maine, New Hampshire, Vermont, and New York; and the Duluth, Winnipeg & Pacific, indirectly work for the Canadian government, since these lines belong to the Canadian National (CN) trackage in the United States. Also, CP Rail [the Canadian Pacific (CP)] controls and separately operates the Soo Line, in the American Midwest, and other subsidiaries, including a mainline cutting across northern Maine, with considerably more United States track miles than CN. Many employees of Canadian-owned or -controlled lines in the States are Canadian citizens. *See* CANADIAN NATIONAL RAILWAYS; CANADIAN PACIFIC RAILWAY; SOO LINE.

The largest United States owner of Canadian trackage was the former New York Central (NYC), now part of Conrail. One of its New York–Chicago mainlines, linking Buffalo with Detroit, runs through Canada on the northern shore of Lake Erie. At one time the Great Northern, now part of Burlington Northern (BN), topped the list of United States owners of Canadian trackage, reaching up into the Dominion at several points, but subsequent track abandonment reduced this mileage. The old Pere Marquette (PM) possessed some important mileage connecting at St. Thomas, Ontario, with what is now Conrail. The Wabash, which was absorbed by the Norfolk & Western, had more than 200 miles of trackage rights over CN. *See* CONRAIL.

The PM and the Wabash also navigated carferries, or trainferries, between United States and Canadian points. In the past, many such ferries united the two countries. The first one linked NYC and CP by crossing the St. Lawrence River between Ogdensburg, New York, and Prescott, Ontario. The CN and Baltimore & Ohio jointly owned a similar service on Lake Ontario between Cobourg, Ontario, and Charlotte (Rochester), New York. Additional trainferries connected the Pennsy at Ashtabula, Ohio, with the CP at Port Burwell, Ontario. Among many others were those operated by the CN, PM, and Wabash across the Detroit River between Windsor, Ontario, and Detroit. *See* GREAT LAKES TRAINFERRIES.

Two United States roads, the Delaware and Hudson (D&H) and the Rutland, once had passenger trackage rights into Canada. The D&H also owned considerable trackage in Ontario but sold most of it in 1929 to CN. Its Canadian subsidiary was the Quebec, Montreal & Southern, including trackage left over from an abortive effort to reach Quebec city, part of which survives today as the 28.4-mile Napierville Junction Railway, a freight-only line linking Rouses Point with Delson, Quebec. D&H freight trains now use 27 miles of this short line.

In Manitoba, the Burlington Northern has running rights over the 61-mile north-south line it owns between Emerson and Winnipeg—trackage which a CN predecessor leased in 1901 from the Northern Pacific (NP). At that time the NP, now part of BN, was in financial trouble and glad to get the long-term lease money. Today, CN crews handle the BN trains that run between Emerson and Winnipeg. Among the other United States–Canadian rail links is the White Pass & Yukon Route, a 110.7-mile narrow-gauge railway, about 20 miles of which is located in Alaska and the rest in British Columbia and Yukon Territory.

The NYC had a large locomotive and car shop near St. Thomas, where Class I repairs were made on its Canadian division motive power and rolling stock and where it built some of its steam locos. The Canadian government insisted that this division's cars be relettered "Canada Southern" and definitely assigned use in the Dominion. The Pere Marquette also had a major locomotive and car repair shop at St. Thomas. Some engines on PM's Canadian division never did run in the States. For years the Wabash locos used in Canada were repaired at the Montreal Locomotive Works, 150 miles from the Wabash leased lines, and still later at the PM's St. Thomas shops. Many Wabash locos operating in Canada had the numeral 1 preceding their three-digit numbers. For example, No. 681 entering Canada was renumbered 1681, which complicated the road's numbering system.

At one time CP had shops at Lyndonville, Vermont, where its motive power operating south of the border was repaired. The power used on CN's subsidiary Grand Trunk Railway in Maine was repaired in the old Central Vermont shops at St. Albans, Vermont.

Canadian authorities regarded locos of the Northern Pacific, Great Northern, D&H, CV, and NYC's Adirondack and Ottawa divisions as international units and admitted them duty-free, provided they did not remain north of the border more than 48 hours on a single trip. In a few cases, United States railroad companies with Canadian subsidiaries were indicted on charges of smuggling rolling stock into the Dominion. One Canadian road bought a secondhand engine in the States for international service but eventually began using her between Canadian points only, whereupon a Canadian customs officer chained her to the rails, with an official seal. She was not released until the company paid a fine.

In addition to steam- and electric-powered roads operated across the border, several electric lines had international trackage. One of them, the Calais Street Railway, running between Calais, Maine, and St. Stephen, New Brunswick, in Maine's northeastern corner, was the most easterly electric railway on the continent. Another, which folded in 1932, was the International Railway (IR), of Buffalo, with a Canadian division extending from Queenstown, Ontario, through Niagara Falls to Chippawa, Ontario. This line was connected with the rest of the IR system by the so-called Honeymoon Bridge over the falls, which collapsed in an ice jam on January 27, 1938.

The IR and the Niagara Gorge Railroad until 1932 had reciprocal running rights on both the United States and Canadian sides of Niagara Gorge over a circular belt line that offered spectacular scenery. This trip was advertised so widely that you could have bought tickets for it in London, Berlin, and Paris. The Thomas Cook & Sons travel service featured it. At one time, too, the Niagara, St. Catharines & Toronto Railway, a CN electric affiliate, had running rights over that line.

Another electric line that crossed the border was the Detroit United Railways, owned by Montreal businessmen but acquired by the city of Detroit in 1923 and later abandoned. In 1932 the CP gained a majority stock ownership of the Canadian-controlled Aroostook Valley Railroad, a trolley company in Maine. The Toronto, Hamilton & Buffalo, controlled by the New York Central, with CP holding a minority stock interest, provided through passenger service between its three namesake cities. Long ago, the Canadian Pacific had an interest in the Spokane International Railway, based at Seattle, Washington, 140 miles south of the border, which terminated at the adjoining towns of Eastport, Idaho, and Kingsgate, British Columbia.

Two rail-roadway tunnels serve the border: the CN-Grand Trunk Western "subway" under the St. Clair River linking Sarnia, Ontario, with Port Huron, Michigan, opened in 1891; and the old NYC's Detroit-Windsor tunnel, put into service in 1910. As for international bridges, the CN suspension bridge between Niagara Falls, Ontario, and Niagara Falls, New York, was originally opened in 1854 and later rebuilt. A few yards south of it is the former New York Central's Niagara Bridge over the falls. The CN has an international bridge over the swift Niagara River, built in 1873, linking Black Rock, New York, with Fort Erie, Ontario.

The only violence which involved railroading on the United States-Canadian border occurred in 1866, the year after the Civil War ended and the year before Canada attained Dominion status. Irish-American malcontents crossed the border, raiding Canada, but were repulsed by militia and railroad men with the help of a locomotive loaned to the Welland Railway.

BIBLIOGRAPHY: George W. Hilton, *The Great Lakes Car Ferries,* Howell-North, Berkeley, Calif., 1962; W. K. Lamb, *The History of the Canadian Pacific Railway,* Macmillan, New York, 1977; George R. Stevens, *History of the Canadian National Railways,* Macmillan, New York, 1973.

Interstate Commerce Commission (ICC) Federal government agency created by the Act to Regulate Commerce (now Interstate Commerce Act), effective April 5, 1887, to carry out the provisions of that act and other federal laws regulating railroads, motor bus and motor truck lines, inland waterways, pipelines, freight forwarders, and certain other surface-transportation agencies engaged in interstate commerce. It consists of 11 members, including a chairman. The ICC is a subject of controversy; many railroad officials resent its restrictions.

The railroads are, or were, regulated as to freight rates, passenger fares, charges for switching and other services, publication of tariffs, and issuance of stock, bonds, and other securities. Other subjects of regulation include extension of lines, abandonments, consolidations, sales, leases, and purchases of other properties, accounting rules and practices, pooling services, interlocking directorships, safety appliances, supply of equipment, standards of equipment, and hours of service for labor. As new problems arise or old ones become acute, amendments are made to the Interstate Commerce Act.

Effective October 11, 1980, the ICC annulled the American railroads' power to meet and set freight rates collectively. That practice, conducted informally since the mid-1800s, had been specifically authorized by Congress since 1948.

See also DEREGULATION OF RAILROADS.

Interurban Electric Railways Unlike the old steam roads, these lines not only connected the streets of two or more relatively nearby cities by means of fast trolley service but made frequent local stops, not necessarily at stations, for passengers and/or goods in the communities they served and speeded up in open-country running between well-populated areas. By contrast, aside from rural short lines in the early days, steam trains made pickup stops only at regular stations, usually one or two in each city. (Even today, however, laws in some Southwestern states require all trains to stop for occasional travelers stranded in a desert or desolate area.)

The interurban was a direct outgrowth of city transit operation in the late nineteenth century. It came about through the realization that trolley cars could be built for higher speeds than those feasible in local service and could run on steel rails extending far beyond city limits—usually on private rights-of-way or at the sides of country roads—to the next city's local trolley tracks. In some cases a passenger had to ride a local streetcar out to the end of the line for a connection with an interurban. Usually, however, big interurban cars started from

Summer car of the Atlantic Highlands, Red Bank & Long Branch Electric Railway, which ran along the New Jersey coast. It was built by J. G. Brill Company of Philadelphia. [J. G. Brill Company]

a downtown terminal and rolled on local trolley tracks, picking up intercity passengers as they went along. Instead of turning back at city limits, they continued on the right-of-way at increased speed, sometimes even up to 80 or 90 miles per hour, though more commonly at 40 or 50.

Stops were made at rural stations and crossroads. When an interurban car moved onto the streetcar tracks of the next city, it would stop now and then at street corners to let off or pick up passengers before reaching its terminal. Such convenient service soon became popular. An Oregon line began operation in February 1893; another, in Ohio, about 10 months later. Within a few years vast networks of busy interurban lines appeared, some connected to others, changing the pattern of American life.

The greatest concentration of such lines radiated out of Indianapolis, Indiana, which boasted the nation's largest interurban terminal. Interurban cars were usually bigger, more powerful, and more luxuriously furnished than city trolleys. Many had baggage compartments; some carried express goods and United States mail in addition to passengers. Numerous lines operated freight trolleys for less-than-carload shipments. Some even used electric locomotives to haul freight cars interchanged with the steam roads. Freight revenues kept many an interurban company alive after its passenger traffic had ceased to be profitable.

A Chicago South Shore and South Bend freight train passes through Michigan City, Michigan, in this 1971 photograph. [Karl R. Zimmerman]

Since electric railway cars could negotiate steeper grades and sharper curves than steam trains could, the interurban lines were generally cheaper to construct and could compete with steam roads by offering cheaper fares as well as more frequent and more convenient service. Steam roads suffered from such competition. A variation of the interurban was the suburban electric line, which was similar in format but operated from the city streets (or connected with streetcar lines near the municipality's limits) out to rural towns on the outskirts instead of running to the next city. In Canada, such lines were called *radials,* since they radiated from urban areas.

Both kinds of electric railways developed rapidly during the first decade of the 1900s and for a short time thereafter. Their peak years, with about 18,000 miles of track in operation, came around World War I. Some companies operated only one or two interurban routes apiece; others had both interurban and suburban networks like giant spiderwebs, as well as local streetcars. In southern California the Pacific Electric, which the Southern Pacific eventually absorbed, had a far-reaching empire of all three types of trolley lines. Its classic big red cars are now memories. Another famous conglomerate, Public Service of New Jersey, operated in and between many areas of the heavily populated Garden State. The Midwest, too, had an impressive network of interconnected lines, especially in Ohio, Indiana, Illinois, and Iowa.

The decline of interurbans was brought about inexorably by mass-produced automobiles. Whereas the interurbans had been more accessible for many passengers than the steam railways, motor vehicles became an even greater convenience than intercity trolleys, and gradually the interurbans were doomed. The increasing spread of paved highways permitted both private automobiles and intercity buses to compete effectively with them.

The Depression of the 1930s forced the abandonment of still more interurbans. The strong ones survived for additional years by economies that included the adoption of lightweight cars and shrinking schedules. Some interurbans temporarily fared better when the demands of World War II curtailed the use of automobiles. Afterward, the proliferation of autos, buses, and highways killed off most of the remaining trolley lines, including interurbans and suburbans.

See also STREETCARS.

BIBLIOGRAPHY: George W. Hilton and John F. Due, *The Electric Interurban Railways in America,* Stanford University Press, Stanford, Calif., 1960; William D. Middleton, *The Interurban Era,* Kalmbach, Milwaukee, 1961; *Streetcars and Interurbans of Yesterday,* illustrations selected by Owen Davies from Rodney Hitt, *Electric Railway Dictionary,* McGraw-Hill, New York, 1911, partially reprinted by Davies, 1960.

Iron Ore Michigan and Minnesota have America's most important iron-ore deposits. Surveyor William A. Burt discovered the ore in the Lake Superior region in 1844. Long before the Soo Canal was dug, this ore was being mined in Michigan's upper peninsula and wagon-freighted to the lake for boat shipment to markets. In 1857 Sam and Herman Ely completed the first railway in that area, the Iron Mountain line, with strap-iron rails and a 25-ton brass-trimmed locomotive named *Sutherland.* That year it hauled 1000 tons of ore daily from the mines to Marquette. In 1863, owing to the Civil War, iron prices spurted suddenly. Within 3 years the railway was handling an annual ore tonnage of 240,000.

In the early 1890s, when Michigan's iron-ore boom had some of the aspects of a California gold rush, Samuel Beck built a new railway, the Huron Bay & Iron Range (HB&IR), through 15 miles of forested woodland from Champion and Arvon to Huron Bay, near L'Anse. The job took 5 years and cost $2 million. The HB&IR had two 100-ton locomotives and 21 flatcars. While it was being built, a longer carrier, the Duluth, South Shore & Atlantic, incorporated in 1887, extended a branch westward from Marquette to L'Anse and grabbed the rich ore freight business without which the short line could not exist. The HB&IR was "all dressed up with nowhere to go." Beck rode with the engineer on the only journey ever made over the completed line. He called that trip a "two-million-dollar ride."

Leonidas Merritt, who wrote a poem about a railroad he wanted to build, but never did, and died in 1880, bequeathed to his seven sons a seemingly worthless bag of iron dust he had picked up in 1865 at Vermilion Lake, Minnesota. The sons investigated. Tested samples were 65 percent pure iron. They named their claim Iron Mountain. When the news got out, Duluth went mad with excitement.

The Merritts made two more big strikes, including the greatest of all, Mesabi Range, and began building a railway, the Duluth, Missabe & Northern, as an outlet for the ore. Duluth City Council would not let tracks be laid through their town, so the Merritts connected their railway with the Duluth & Winnipeg Railway, which terminated at Superior, Wisconsin, just across the river from Duluth.

The first trainload of a future gigantic volume of Mesabi ore rolled over the new road. The Merritts rejected an $8 million offer for their interest in the Mesabi mines and their railway, but John D. Rockefeller took over the railway in the national panic year of 1893.

About 90 percent of United States crude ore comes from open pits. The world's largest open-pit operation is the Hull-Rust-Mahoning Mine near Hibbing, Minnesota. It is about 4 miles long, 2 miles wide, and over 500 feet deep and is laid with its own system of railroad tracks on shelving grades. The Duluth, Missabe and Iron Range and the Burlington Northern serve this area.

American steelmaster Andrew Carnegie (1835–1919), born in Scotland, at 24 became superintendent of the Pennsylvania Railroad's busy Pittsburgh division. After the Civil War he went into the iron and steel business and helped to make Pittsburgh a great steel center. The city is near huge coal deposits of western Pennsylvania and West Virginia and not far by rail from the Mesabi Range's iron-ore supply. America's railroad expansion created an immense market for steel, since locomotives are largely steel and track has millions of tons of it. As steel output grew, areas around Gary, Indiana; Chicago; and Birmingham, Alabama, assumed more importance. During World War II, mines in California, Utah, and Texas also were developed.

Carnegie's vast iron and steel holdings eventually became the nucleus of United States Steel Corp., the world's largest steel company. Other big corporate names in American industrial history include Armco, Bethlehem Steel, National Steel, and Republic Steel. Some steel companies operate their own railroads and iron-ore boats. Among the many subsidiaries of United States Steel are these railroads: Bessemer & Lake Erie; Birmingham Southern; Duluth, Missabe and Iron Range; Elgin, Joliet and Eastern; Tennessee Coal, Iron & Railroad; and Union, in the Pittsburgh area.

In Canada, the Quebec North Shore and Labrador Railway, extending 360 miles from Sept-Îles, Quebec, on the north shore of the St. Lawrence estuary, to one of the world's richest deposits of iron ore, near Knob Lake in northern Quebec, was chartered by the Dominion Parliament in 1948. Built in the mid-1950s, it hauls iron ore with crewless trains and this is one of the few partly automated railroads. It also has diesel-powered passenger service.

BIBLIOGRAPHY: Leonard Hal Bridges, *Iron Millionaire: The Life of Charlemagne Tower,* University of Pennsylvania Press, Philadelphia, 1952; Stewart H. Holbrook, *Iron Brew,* Macmillan, New York, 1939; Frank A. King, *The Missabe Road: The Duluth, Missabe and Iron Range Railway,* Golden West Books, San Marino, Calif., 1972.

J

Jackass & Western (J&W) Employees' affectionate term for a fully automated, nameless, supermodern standard-gauge short line. This road handles no interchange traffic, not being connected to any other railway, and carries no passengers or crew, not even an engineer. Built in 1957, it is a major mode of transportation at the Nuclear Rocket Development in the desert at Jackass Flat, Nevada. Its sole purpose is to aid in testing nuclear rocket reactors. There are 8⅓ miles of track serving various buildings at the plant. The train moves very slowly, usually about 1 mile an hour, so as not to jar the reactors.

At first the J&W's only motive power was a 40-horsepower, four-wheel, battery-powered locomotive, the L-1, built by Greensburg Machine Co. (since merged with National Mine Co.). Later it acquired a small former U.S. Air Force four-wheel engine built by General Electric. Other rolling stock includes a diesel-powered (not self-propelled) railroad crane with a 25-ton rating, three dump cars, six flatcars, and seven test cars. ACF Industries Incorporated operates all the rolling stock. Pan American World Airways handles the track maintenance.

Jackson, Tom (d. 1934) Man who held the all-time record for writing railroad jokes. He authored *A Slow Train through Arkansas* and other funny booklets that news butchers (train vendors of newspapers, cigars, candy, etc.) sold to passengers. He wrote, for example, of a train taking so long to make its run that a clean-shaven passenger grew a lengthy beard before reaching his destination and complained of the slow service.

"If you don't like it," snapped the conductor, "why don't you get out and walk?"

"I can't," was the reply. "My family's waiting for me. They don't expect me until the train comes in."

And this one: "The train stopped once and I asked the conductor the reason. He said, 'There are some cattle on the track.' The train proceeded and presently stopped again. I asked the conductor the reason, and he replied, 'We caught up with the cattle again.'"

James, Jesse Woodson (1847-1882) Most colorful of all train robbers, James had a dual personality. Born near Kearney, Missouri, on September 6, 1847, the second son of a Baptist minister, he was baptized and admitted to church membership. Years later, while riding in quest of booty he carried a Bible with him and often read it. The evil influence in the lives of Jesse and his brother Frank (Alexander Franklin James) may be traced to William C. Quantrill, a Confederate guerrilla chief known as "the bloodiest man in the Civil War."

Frank joined Quantrill's band when Jesse was only 15. Federal militia punished the family by lashing the boy viciously and nearly killing his stepfather. Thereupon Jesse joined the irregulars and fought under their banner until the war ended. When he tried to surrender, he was shot twice in the chest—deep wounds that never fully healed.

In 1870 the James brothers formed a gang of six or eight desperadoes, mostly Quantrill veterans, to rob stagecoaches, banks, and railroad trains. Their forays were shrewdly set up and nearly always successful. They operated largely in Missouri and Kansas, at least once in Minnesota, and probably elsewhere, living in the shadow of the gallows and within earshot of whistling lead.

Like the other Quantrill alumni, Jesse, on a fine horse, could gallop fearlessly through underbrush and woods even at night; usually his pursuers could not. He was a dead shot, carried around an arsenal, and was know as a desperate character. Few lawmen cared to tangle with him at close range. Jesse and Frank had numerous friends and kin in Missouri, a clannish lot, generally hostile to the law and bank and railroad corporations and willing to shield fugitives from justice. After each haul, Jesse would hide in his home territory behind a smoke screen of anonymity. He was kind to women, was never a horse thief, and was regarded by Missourians as a sort of benign Robin Hood.

The first train stickup definitely traced to him occurred on December 12, 1874, on the Kansas Pacific Railroad near Muncie, Kansas, a flag stop 10 miles from Kansas City, Missouri. His gang had six men. One of them, Bud McDaniels, a renegade switchman, had learned that a train leaving Denver with a gold-dust shipment would pass Muncie at 4:46 p.m. The six horsemen, armed with carbines and heavy revolvers and masked with red bandannas, piled ties on the track and set out a red flag in front of the station to make doubly sure the train would stop. It did.

While one bandit covered the engine crew, the others cowed the trainmen and passengers. They forced the crew to uncouple the express car and pull it a short distance away from the train. Then the gang looted it of $30,000 in gold dust, $20,000 in currency, and jewelry valued at about $5000—a lot of wealth in those days. This they dumped into a wheat sack (the usual receptacle carried by the James gang) and galloped away, disappearing into Missouri. Later McDaniels got drunk, talked too much, and was slain while resisting arrest.

Jesse married a first cousin, pretty Zerelda Mimms, but kept up his criminal career. From an Iron Mountain (later Missouri Pacific) train near Otterville, Missouri, in 1876, the gang of eight men took about $2000 apiece. Two months later they met disaster in a bank stickup at Northfield, Minnesota. Two gangsters "bit the dust." Three others—the Younger brothers, Bob, Jim, and Cole—were seriously wounded, seized, tried, and sentenced to life imprisonment.

Jesse recruited fresh men. In 1879 five of them, not Frank, stuck up a Chicago & Alton train border-bandit-fashion at Glendale, Missouri, grabbing considerable booty. Two years later the James brothers and two others quietly boarded a fast passenger train on the Chicago, Rock Island & Pacific, sat in the smoker, and paid their fares like ordinary passengers. At Winston, Missouri, that night on a prearranged signal they shot and killed the conductor. He had earned their enmity by working on a special train that carried lawmen in search of the elusive James brothers. Two other Rock Island railroaders also died in the stickup. The gang got away with only about $600 in currency and a nonnegotiable $1000 bond taken from the safe in the express car.

Incidentally, the Jameses never robbed a Chicago, Burlington & Quincy train, because the management, which had a line running through Kearney, was said to have given their mother an annual pass over their system as a safety-first measure. In those days, railroads commonly handed out free transportation to politicians, journalists, and other influential persons; today federal law forbids this practice.

Jesse's last train robbery occurred at Blue Cut, Missouri, in 1881. This time a Chicago & Alton express was stuck up by the same men who had pulled the Winston affair, with the addition of Bob Ford.

Meanwhile, Jesse, with his wife and their two small children, a boy and a girl, had been living under the name Thomas Howard and posing as a railroad man seeking work. They occupied a one-story frame house on the outskirts of St. Joseph, Missouri, situated on top of a small hill with no next-door neighbors. The hunted man chose this hideout so that no stranger could sneak up on him in the daytime. Outside the dwelling were a yard and a stable in which Jesse kept two fleet horses. On April 3, 1882, two relatively new members of his gang, the Ford brothers, Bob, 20, and Charles, 24, visited him. They had come at his invitation to plot another train robbery. The gang leader put them in his spare bedroom, on a wall of which hung a framed picture of his pet horse, Skyrocket.

"It's an awfully hot day," he told them, removing his coat and vest and tossing them on the bed. "I guess I'll take off my pistols, too, for fear somebody might see them if I walk in the yard."

Famous last words! Jesse unbuckled his belt containing his two .45-caliber revolvers, one a Colt, the other a Smith & Wesson, and laid them also on the bed. Then he picked up a cloth, stood on a chair with his back to the visitors, and began dusting Skyrocket's picture. Bob and Charles drew their guns. Jesse must have heard the shooting irons click, for he turned his head slightly, but it was too late. Bob fired. A bullet entered the bearded head of the outlaw chief and came out of his left eye. He died a moment later in his wife's arms, as the assassins scurried off to collect blood money.

Frank was acquitted after a sensational trial. The jurors were understandably reluctant to find him guilty. Thereafter he went straight, traveled with a Wild West Show, and died peacefully in 1915.

BIBLIOGRAPHY: Harry S. Drago, *Road Agents and Train Robbers: Half a Century of Western Banditry,* Dodd, Mead, New York, 1973; Freeman Hubbard, *Railroad Avenue,* McGraw-Hill, New York, 1945; Robertus Love, *The Rise and Fall of Jesse James,* Putnam, New York, 1926.

Janney, Eli Hamilton ***(1831–1912)*** Man who invented in 1868 and patented in 1873 the ancestor of all automatic couplers used today in the United States, Canada, and many other countries. He was born on a Virginia farm. During the Civil War he was a field quartermaster in the Confederate Army and a major on Gen. Robert E. Lee's staff. After the war, while working as a grocery clerk, he hit upon the coupler idea by clasping his hands vertically with knuckles bent. Like the hands, his coupler is unclasped by opening the knuckles.

This was the first such device to use the vertical-plane principle for its working parts and to make those parts simple, strong, and reliable. It was also the first to couple cars automatically and hold them together until released by a lever which trainmen could work without risking death or injury by having to go upon or between the cars.

McConway & Torley Corp. bought the patents and began making Janney couplers. These were first applied, in 1877, to passenger cars on the Pittsburgh, Fort Wayne & Chicago line of the Pennsylvania Railroad and soon afterward were made standard for all Pennsy freight and passenger cars. Janney used the money from his patents to buy a farm at Alexandria, Virginia, which he worked until his death on June 16, 1912.

Prior to 1889, railroads tried out 39 varieties of non-Janney automatic couplers on 80,510 cars. Each of the 39 failed to couple with any of the other 38. Under the auspices of the Master Car Builders Association (MCBA), 42 different couplers, automatic and otherwise, were tested on September 15–17, 1887, in the New York, Lake Erie & Western yard at Buffalo. These tests eliminated all but 12 of the competing couplers. In 1888 the MCBA adopted and standardized the Janney type. Not all roads adopted it until after the crusade of Lorenzo Coffin had induced Congress into passing the Safety Appliance Act, which President Benjamin Harrison signed on March 3, 1893. Today's version is much larger and stronger than Janney's original.

See also COFFIN, LORENZO; COUPLERS; SAFETY LAWS.

BIBLIOGRAPHY: Charles F. Carter, *When Railroads Were New,* 4th rev. ed., Simmons-Boardman, New York, 1926.

Jarrett and Palmer Special One day in May 1876, a man from the Jarrett and Palmer theatrical agency called on A. J. Cassatt, then a vice president, later president, of the Pennsylvania Railroad (PRR), and said, in effect: "We represent Lawrence Barrett, who has been costarring with Edwin Booth in *Julius Caesar.* One of our competitors will open a play in San Francisco on Tuesday, June sixth. We want to beat them to it. But Mr. Barrett must appear in New York City on Wednesday night, May 31st, and he'd have to be on the Pacific Coast for a rehearsal the following Sunday so we could open on June fifth. We'd like to hire a special train to get him there."

Cassatt replied that it couldn't be done; the fastest trains took more than 5 days to cover that distance. But the theatrical agent persisted. He said they'd pay heavily, of course, and that James Gordon Bennett of *The New York Herald* would give such a run tremendous publicity, which would help the Pennsy as well as the Shakespearean actor.

So Cassatt agreed. He knew that the first transcontinental railroad had been opened only a few years before and that pioneer settlers were still jogging their weary way across the country in covered wagons drawn by oxen. But he promised a special train that would leave New York (actually Jersey City, New Jersey) about midnight of June 1 and reach San Francisco not later than noon of June 4.

On May 31, engine No. 373, named *Samuel J. Tilden,* a handsome 4-4-0 of the United Railroad of New Jersey (later part of the PRR), backed into the Jersey City trainshed with a special train of three cars: the *Yosemite,* a Pullman; the *Government,* a hotel car; and a baggage coach which carried eight mailbags, some 30,000 letters, each uniquely stamped, and many sacks of coal for the engine. The latter were needed because the train would run nonstop to Pittsburgh.

At 11 p.m. the special was ready, but Barrett was still at a publicity party in New York's Hotel Astor. Already on board were Cassatt himself, other rail officials, journalists, theatrical people, Gen. Horace Porter of Civil War fame who was vice president of Pullman Palace Car Co., and engine crews for each division between Jersey City and Pittsburgh.

At 12:50 p.m. on June 1 the ferry carrying Barrett's troupe docked at the New Jersey side of the Hudson River, and a few minutes later the train began highballing. The engine would not have to stop for water or coal but would slow down to scoop up a drink from track pans, and when fuel was needed, daring firemen would crawl over the tender into the baggage car and toss back bags of coal. There were no automatic signals in those days, or perfected airbrakes, or heavy rail (only 50-pound rail, as compared with today's 100-plus).

Reaching Pittsburgh at 10:58 a.m., Barrett's theatrical agents got off, engines and crews were changed, and the train was on its way again. Despite a couple of hotboxes and another short delay, they rolled proudly into Chicago at 10:50 p.m., to be met by a brass band, brief speeches, fireworks, and free beer. Cassatt got off. Twenty minutes after arrival, a Chicago & North Western (C&NW) eight-wheeler took over. But thereafter they had to make water stops, for the C&NW had no track pans. *See* TRACK PANS.

Three hours later they reached Clinton, Iowa. Then

there was another hotbox, a 20-minute delay; but the engineer had made up the lost time when they pulled into Cedar Rapids. At 11 a.m. Friday in Council Bluffs the Union Pacific took over. Kearney, Cheyenne, Laramie, and Green River followed in quick succession. Next was Ogden, a little after noon by New York clocks, or 2 p.m. mountain time. From there, it was 876 miles to San Francisco over the Central (now Southern) Pacific with engine No. 147, the *Black Fox.* There was no Salt Lake Cutoff in those days; the special had to run around the big pond.

They climbed the Sierras, 7042 feet above sea level, a steady rise of 2 feet in every 100, followed by an equally steep drop, with sharp curves. Car brake shoes were worn so badly that between Ogden and Truckee the train had to be controlled by handbrakes. This slowed the time on descending grades, for the trainmen feared a runaway. At Truckee a coach with airbrakes in good order was coupled on, and at Summit another was added for extra safety.

By this time the whole country and much of Europe were following the news of the great run. Finally, at 9:29 a.m. Sunday the train reached the San Francisco ferryhouse in Oakland, California. It had covered 3305 miles in 83 hours and 37 minutes, or 81 hours and 36 minutes of actual running time, averaging well over 40 miles per hour between the main stops. Lawrence Barrett's scheduled appearance in Shakespeare's *Henry V* had been sold out weeks in advance. For 30 years thereafter the record time for a coast-to-coast dash was unbroken. Not until 1906, when E. H. Harriman made it in 71 hours and 27 minutes, had another train run so far at such high speed. *See* HARRIMAN, EDWARD HENRY.

BIBLIOGRAPHY: *Trains Magazine,* December 1942; April 1955.

Jim Crow *See* NEGROES AND TRAINS.

John Henry Next to Casey Jones, this black construction worker is the most popular figure in rail songs and lore. Like Casey, he was a real person but became a legend veiled in heroic myths. Reputedly he was a "steel-drivin'" man with the strength of an ox, towering 6 feet 4 inches in his socks, a banjo player with a rich bass voice, working when he felt like it but more given to fooling around with women or just plain loafing.

Like Ajax defying the lightning, John (Jawn) Henry challenged a force greater than mere man: the drill which had just been invented to split rocks by steam power as he did with a big hammer. The effort was too much. He died, a symbol of man versus machine, leaving a trail of broken hearts along the Central of Georgia Railway. His dramatic exploit is variously located in several states but it most likely occurred in 1888 near Leeds, Alabama, at the eastern portal of Oak Mountain Tunnel, where a statue of him stands today. Ditties about him were improvised and sung in rolling boxcars, by campfires in hobo jungles, and to the rhythm of gandy dancers (trackmen) tamping ties or husky riveters building steel bridges. Here are a few of the hundreds of quatrains:

Jawn Henry hammered in th' mountains,
  And blows from his shoulder did rain.
Hung his hammer on a little blue point,
  Sayin': "Lord, I'se a steel-drivin' man."

Cap'n said to Jawn Henry:
  "Gonna bring me a steam drill 'roun';
Take that steam drill out on the job,
  Gonna whop that steel on down."

Jawn Henry said to de Captin:
  "A man ain't nothin' but a man,
'Fore I let yore steam drill beat me down
  I'll die with th' hammer in m'han'."

Jawn Henry said to de Captin:
  "Send me a twelve-poun' hammer aroun,'
Er twelve-poun' hammer wid a four-poun' handle
  An' I'll beat yore steam drill down."

Jawn Henry went down d' railroad
  Wid er twelve-poun' hammer by his side.
He walked down d' track but he never came back,
  'Cause he laid down his hammer an' he died.

Jawn Henry had er little woman,
  Dress she wore wuz red;
Las' word I heard de poor gal say,
  "I'm goin' whur my man drapt dead."

BIBLIOGRAPHY: Benjamin A. Botkin and Alvin F. Harlow, *A Treasury of Railroad Folklore,* Crown, New York, 1953; Freeman Hubbard, *The Train That Never Came Back and Other Railroad Stories,* McGraw-Hill, New York, 1952.

Johnson Bar Steam locomotive reverse lever, possibly named for an official of Baldwin Locomotive Works. Its normal, or neutral, position is straight up, so that no steam will enter either end of the cylinder if the throttle should leak and let the engine run away, out of control. To drop her "down in the corner" of the cab means that you are going to start a heavy train or climb a hill, which requires all the steam you can get into the cylinders at each revolution of the wheels. "Back in the corner in reverse motion" means that as the speed accelerates, you hook her up to shorten the valve travel and keep on hooking her up until you reach the speed limit for the load you are pulling and the grade over which you are traveling.

When the Johnson bar is in the corner, the engine is running her hardest. This was known as "the company notch" because the engine presumably was making the most money by pulling "everything in the yard." An engineer who ran with the Johnson bar was called a hog mauler and had difficulty in keeping a steady fireman, for the heavy exhaust constantly kept the fire torn up, burning a lot of coal.

The old type of Johnson bar was a heavy lever, about chest high to a man standing, with a grip and latch lever at the top large enough to operate with two hands while standing. About three-fourths of it extended up into the cab and the rest below the floor, with a notched quadrant for holding it at the position wanted. You had to know how to handle this massive type, for if it got away from you, it might break an arm or a leg or cave in your chest. Another type, the *screw-reverse,* used the worm or nut and screw. It had a notched disk on the handwheel, with a pull on the housing to hold it in place. A third type, the *air-reverse,* was a timesaving, more modern version of the screw-reverse. It relieved the engineer of the hard job of reversing by hand and, more important, of the danger of changing the valve travel while the loco was running. After the roads became more fuel-conscious, many engineers were given layoffs or *brownies* (demerits) for running with the bar down in the corner.

Johnstown Flood Disaster of 1889 that caused the most spectacular railroad flood damage in American history. Near the end of May, Johnstown, in the Allegheny Mountains of Pennsylvania, was inundated by torrential rain; and on May 30 its business center was covered by 5 feet of water. Nearby, Conemaugh Lake was rising 10 inches an hour. That lake, about 700 acres to a depth of 70 feet, held more water than any other reservoir in the country at that time, although the Conemaugh River, which fed it, was normally a gentle stream no deeper than one's knee. The Pennsylvania Railroad mainline roughly paralleled this river for nearly 25 miles through the narrow valley, crossing it on a substantial bridge at Johnstown near the point where Stony Creek poured into the river.

South Fork Dam, above Johnstown, looked like a mighty bastion. Extending almost 1000 feet from shore to shore, it was 25 feet thick at the top and 90 feet at the base. Despite its huge volume of water, the entire dam was built of earth except for stones riprapping its sides. It should have been solid masonry for the job it had to do.

On the fateful morning of May 30, horseback riders galloped through the valley at intervals shouting to the inhabitants that the dam might break and urging them to flee to the hills, but relatively few people did so. At 2 p.m. part of the city was 10 feet under water. Just before 3 o'clock came a hoarse cry, "The dam is broken!"

With a thunderous roar audible for miles, a cataract as mighty as Niagara tumbled down the valley faster than express-train speed. The wall of water was nearly 40 feet high and half a mile wide. It hurled into the air giant oak trees, houses, livestock, locomotives and freight cars and miles of the world's best railroad track, huge boulders that had probably stood fast since the Ice Age, and many hundreds of screaming human beings. It demolished the railroad yards and a huge brick roundhouse at East Conemaugh, sucking locomotives and loaded boxcars into its downward thrust or bearing them along on its surface like maple leaves.

Thousands of tons of wreckage swept through the valley. From Conemaugh Lake to Johnstown, about 12 miles, the irresistible force stampeded in about 7 min-

Over 2000 people perished in the spectacular flood and fire of 1889 in Johnstown, Pennsylvania, where the Pennsylvania Railroad yards, stock, roundhouse, and rails were demolished. Pictured here is the Pennsylvania Railroad bridge, against which the flood hurled victims and debris after the weak South Fork Dam broke on May 30.

utes. Unlike South Fork Dam, the Pennsy bridge was built of solid masonry and formed a gruesome dam of its own. Debris and human bodies were barricaded there to the height of a three-story house, wrapped around by miles of barbed wire which the onrushing wave had picked up at a steel mill en route. Adding to the horror, the wreckage caught fire, burning with a lurid glow for 3 days and nights. No wonder most of the fatalities occurred at this point. On June 1 a railroad embankment gave way, water broke through the jam at the bridge, and at that moment the flood began to subside.

The Baltimore & Ohio (B&O), which entered Johnstown from the south, escaped the worst of the damage. Mark Ridenour, a B&O engineer, had just pulled an accommodation train into Connellsville with engine No. 610 and was going off duty when he received orders to make the 88.4-mile run to Johnstown by way of Rockwood with two coaches carrying doctors, nurses, and medical supplies. After a fast, desperate ride with "just one curve after another, with a rather stiff grade to boot," he said: "We were among the first rescuers to reach Johnstown, My fireboy was in a lather of sweat. The old 610 was smoking from every journal box and her side-rods were in deplorable shape, although—thank God!—they had brought us to Johnstown."

Since then, the city has had several bad floods, none of which reached the tidal-wave proportions of 1889. The estimated loss of life, over 2000, was the most appalling of any American flood except for the one of 1900 at Galveston, Texas.

BIBLIOGRAPHY: Freeman Hubbard, *Railroad Avenue,* McGraw-Hill, New York, 1945.

Jones, Casey *See* CASEY JONES.

Judah, Theodore D. ***(1820–1863)*** Construction engineer who planned and built bridges, canals, and the Niagara Gorge Railroad, all in the East. Then he planned and built the Far West's first railroad, the Sacramento Valley Railroad. Begun in February 1855 and opened a year later, this 23-mile line between Sacramento and Folsom, California, was laid in the Mother Lode country, scene of the 1849 gold rush. Grading gangs occasionally picked up bits of gold ore. Judah had a ring engraved with the words: "First gold ever taken from earth used in making a railroad bank [roadbed]."

He played a major role in building what is now the Southern Pacific Railroad (SP), surveying, with the aid of Daniel Strong, a route for it eastward over the Sierra Nevada. As pioneer promoter of that road, he persuaded Leland Stanford, Collis P. Huntington, and others to help finance it, obtained federal support, and actually began construction in 1855. But all this was largely forgotten. Others received credit for Judah's achievements, although a granite monument to him stands today facing the SP passenger station in Sacramento.

BIBLIOGRAPHY: Lucius Beebe, *The Central Pacific and the Southern Pacific Railroads,* Howell-North, Berkeley, Calif., 1963; Helen H. Jones, *Rails from the West: A Biography of Theodore D. Judah,* Golden West Books, San Marino, Calif., 1969; Oscar Lewis, *The Big Four,* Knopf, New York, 1938; Edwin J. Sabin, *Building the Pacific Railway,* Lippincott, Philadelphia, 1919.

Jumbo Circus elephant killed in a train wreck. *See* CIRCUS TRAINS.

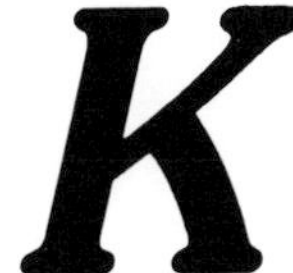

Katy *See* MISSOURI-KANSAS-TEXAS RAILROAD.

Kennar, Edward ***(d. 1887)*** New York Central engineer who was wheeling a freight train at night on April 18, 1887. Near St. Johnsville, New York, the oil headlight of his engine, No. 238, picked out a landslide just ahead. His fireman jumped to safety, but Ed stayed in his cab. Slamming on his engine brake, he yanked the whistle cord in a frantic call of "Down brakes!"—the signal for trainmen to climb the tops of swaying cars and twirl the hand brakes.

Even if those brakes had been set instantly, the momentum would have shot the train into the slide. Old 238 fell down the embankment and turned over, trapping Ed Kennar in his cab, still clutching the throttle. The trainmen found him there, with death's hand on his brow, but just before he died, Ed called out, "Flag No. 5!"

Number 5 was the westbound passenger train that usually met Ed's freight near Batavia. His dying words aroused the dazed crew to a sense of reality. A brakeman ran back with a red lantern and barely made it. Number 5's pilot halted only a few feet from the wreckage, thus averting a second tragedy. Members of Ed Kennar's lodge of the Brotherhood of Locomotive Engineers at Albany, New York, reverently removed his throttle, silver-plated it, and kept it in the lodge room as a precious relic. One of them wrote a poem ending with these words:

Farewell, ye best loved, farewell!
  I've died not all in vain,
Thank God, the other lives are saved!
  Thank God, they've flagged the train!

BIBLIOGRAPHY: Freeman Hubbard, *Railroad Avenue,* McGraw-Hill, New York, 1945.

Kuhler, Otto ***(1894-1977)*** Industrial designer, employed by American Locomotive Co. and American Car and Foundry, who won fame in the 1930s and 1940s as a streamline designer and modernizer of steam locomotives and passenger trains for the Milwaukee Road, Baltimore & Ohio, and Lehigh Valley (LV). He also stream-styled cars for New York's subway-el network, trolley cars, station interiors, and even the B&O's first air-cooled bus. The Atlantic-type engine he streamlined for the Milwaukee Road's new *Hiawatha* train was described by *The New York Times* in 1935 as the world's fastest locomotive, capable of speeds up to 2 miles a minute.

Locos streamlined in those days were shrouded with hoods that usually hid most of the running gear. Kuhler said of the *Hiawatha* Atlantic: "I reduced shrouds to a minimum so that the huge driving wheels as well as the valve gear were exposed. A radically new design of the enginemen's cab increased visibility," meaning the enginemen's view of the track ahead. In the *John Wilkes,* one of the two LV streamliners he designed, Kuhler replaced electric-bulb illumination with the then-new experimental fluorescent lighting.

Later in life, his many etchings and many oil and watercolor paintings dramatized steam power, especially in the Southwest. He sold these pictures to museums and private collectors. His autobiography, *My Iron Journey,* published in 1967 by the National Railway Historical Society, Intermountain Chapter, is handsomely illustrated.

L

L&N *See* LOUISVILLE & NASHVILLE RAILROAD.

L&S *See* LUDLOW & SOUTHERN RAILWAY.

Lab-on-Wheels (AAR-100) The Technical Center of the Association of American Railroads in Chicago is home base for a sleek 85-foot mobile laboratory. This unit, AAR-100, measures the interactions of rolling stock and its components with the environment in which they function. It is placed near the car or locomotive being studied. Measuring devices attached to the equipment being tested send electrical signals through multiwire cables to a minicomputer in the research car. This converts the signals into digital data recorded on magnetic tape. Later, the tape is played back and analyzed. The AAR-100 can accommodate a crew of up to seven persons. Besides the lab, it is equipped with sleeping quarters, lavatory facilities, a shower, a kitchen, a potable water supply, and its own heating and air-conditioning system. The car has a 50-kilowatt diesel-driven generator, but it relies for motive power on the train in which it travels.

Labor Unions *See* UNIONS, RAILROAD LABOR.

Land Grants A common misapprehension is that the federal land grants to railroads between 1850 and about 1880 were a mere giveaway. Actually, they turned out to be a good business deal by and for the United States government. A few trail-blazing railroads received a total of 131,250,534 acres, specifically for the purpose of providing them with the necessary security for borrowing money needed to finance construction. Developers of wagon roads and canals were granted 10,007,687 acres of federal land.

More than 92 percent of all railroad mileage in the country was built entirely by private enterprise, without benefit of such grants. Far from being gifts, the land grants ultimately resulted in the carriers' paying the government more than 10 times the value of the land involved. The railroad companies benefited, of course, but the greatest beneficiaries were the public and the government.

Under the first railroad land grants, the fledgling companies were awarded alternate sections of land, each section averaging 640 acres, on either side of the proposed rail route. The federal government retained title to the remaining alternate sections. Prior to that, it had offered the land for sale at $2.50 an acre. There were few takers. But when the first legislation was passed, the government doubled the price of its retained land, which, with a railroad assured, settlers bought eagerly. Thus the government followed a sound business practice of using part of its domain to enhance the value of the immense whole. The railroads converted vast areas yielding no taxes into taxable properties for the benefit of the states, the federal government, and the municipalities which sprang up along the rights-of-way. Even more important, the grants that made transcontinental rail service feasible helped to unite the nation at a critical period. *See* ILLINOIS CENTRAL RAILROAD.

Railroads were not given the land. They had to pay for it and keep on paying. Most roads receiving the grants were required by law to haul government freight and personnel at cut rates averaging 50 percent and mail at a 20 percent reduction. For competitive reasons, other roads, including those which had no land grants, made equalization agreements granting similar reductions on government business.

In 1945, when Congress finally repealed the cut-rate requirements, a congressional committee reported: "It is probable that the railroads have contributed over $900 million in payment of the lands which were transferred to them. . . . Former ICC Commissioner [J. B.] Eastman estimated the value of the lands at the time they were granted was not more than $125 million."

Reduced rates applied to the vast federal traffic during World War II, which remained in effect until October 1, 1946, raised the total estimated value of the railroads' contributions to the nation to $1250 million, or about 10 times the value of lands received. On this basis, the government's profit on the land grants was about $1,124,000.

BIBLIOGRAPHY: Robert S. Henry, *This Fascinating Railroad Business,* 3d ed., rev., Bobbs-Merrill, Indianapolis, 1946; David F. Merrick, *Land Grants; Aids and Benefits to the Government and Railroads and to the Southern Pacific Company,* pub. by author, 1969.

Landmarks *See* WATER TANKS; WATER TOWERS.

Lanterns, Trainmen's and Switchmen's These lanterns speak a language all their own. Without them, night operation would be impossible. The first glims (in railroad lingo) undoubtedly burned whale oil, because the earliest American railroads were built along the Atlantic seaboard, where whale oil was commonly used for illumination. Later came the adoption of lard oil, vile stuff which stayed liquid until a degree or two below freezing. To resist its solidifying, a copper hairpin-shaped wire was run through the lantern burner. The hairpin's closed end was immersed in oil. The open ends, heated by flame, usually kept the oil from congealing.

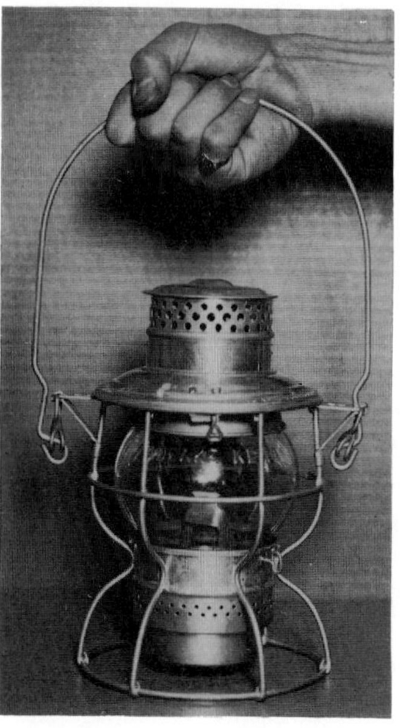

***This kind of oilburning lantern, called a glim, was commonly used for signaling trains for years, until electric hand lanterns replaced them.* [Railroad Magazine]**

In time, petroleum replaced lard oil, while flat wicks replaced the original tubular ones. Then came the woven wick and flanged oil cup, invented by Winfield S. Rogers in 1880. The lanterns kept being improved, with a bewildering variety of types. The earlier ones were poorly drafted. A swift movement, such as occurs in giving a fast hand signal, often extinguished the flame. The Fort Scott copper top was a good lantern.

Probably the most famous lantern of all time was the one carried by Kate Shelley on the night of July 16, 1881, when she saved a passenger train from destruction. More than one glim has been hurled desperately by a flagman into the cab of a locomotive whose engineer should have stopped his train short of a collision but who (in the years before the 16-hour law) had fallen asleep at the throttle, exhausted by 40 or 50 hours of continuous duty. *See* SAFETY LAWS; SHELLEY, KATE.

A little trick with a kerosine lamp to prevent smoky globes is to nip a bit from a corner of the wick and cut a V in its center. That keeps the flame from spreading too widely and concentrates it into a straight column that works well. Another trick: never wash the globe with soapy water. That takes the temper out of the glass; the globe will probably break the first time a flame touches it. Besides, soap leaves a thin film that makes the globe smoke up more quickly. One way to clean a lantern globe is with a piece of chamois or a soft leather glove.

When electric hand lanterns were introduced, railroad employees had to pay for them. Now, however, the lanterns are issued free, like red and green flags, fusees, and switch keys.

BIBLIOGRAPHY: C. Miles Burpee (ed.), *Railway Engineering and Maintenance Cyclopedia,* Simmons-Boardman, New York, 1942; William F. Knapke and Freeman Hubbard, *The Railroad Caboose,* Golden West Books, San Marino, Calif., 1968.

Lap Order Order which overlaps another order issued to a train running in the opposite direction on the same track. Thus, if train No. 2 were instructed to run from *A* to *B* to meet No. 1, while at the same time and on the same track No. 1 was under orders to go from *A* to meet No. 2, those trains could have a head-on collision. Lap orders were very rare except in fiction stories. A dispatcher who actually issued such an order while a previous order contradicting it was still valid would be discharged.

La Salle Street Station Railroad station in Chicago, opened on July 12, 1903, by the Chicago, Rock Island & Pacific and the Lake Shore & Michigan Southern. For years the Nickel Plate Road and the Chicago & Eastern Illinois also used it. The Lake Shore was part of the old New York Central System. On October 27, 1968, Penn Central operated a train out of that building for the last time. Today, only Rock Island commuter service remains.

La Salle Street Station replaced a depot opened in 1872, which in turn had replaced one destroyed in the great fire of 1871. Old stone from the Van Buren Street edifice was broken up and used for the present station's foundation. In addition, 14,000 tons of structural steel (then the largest amount ever used in any Chicago building) went into the railroads' office building, trainshed, and track elevation.

In early days the station's interior was magnificent with marble, mosaic, all-mahogany woodwork, over 6100 electric lights, a grand staircase, and two huge passenger elevators (later, esalators). An interlocking tower handled 172 switches controlling up to 1500 train movements a day into and out of the station. Willie Lewis, who worked there from 1912 to 1962, was the first and possibly the only redcap to hold such a job for half a century.

BIBLIOGRAPHY: William E. Hayes, *Iron Road to Empire: The History of 100 Years of the Progress and Achievements of the Rock Island Lines,* Simmons-Boardman, New York, 1953.

Laws Affecting Railroads *See* FEATHERBEDDING; GRANGER LAWS; INTERSTATE COMMERCE COMMISSION; MERGERS; SAFETY LAWS.

Lehigh Valley Railroad (LV) Basically a coal road, one of the three picturing a black diamond, symbolizing coal, on their insignia, the other two being the Philadelphia & Reading (P&R) and the Illinois Central. For the same reason, its greatest train, hailed as "the world's handsomest streak of varnish," running between Jersey City and Buffalo (inaugurated in 1896, discontinued in 1959), was called the *Black Diamond. See* BLACK DIAMOND.

Incorporated in Pennsylvania on April 21, 1846, as the Delaware, Lehigh, Schuylkill & Susquehanna, the railroad began laying track in 1851 and changed its name to Lehigh Valley on January 7, 1853. After completing a line from Easton to Mauch Chunk, it acquired in 1857 a junction with the North Pennsylvania Railroad (later P&R), which provided rail access to Philadelphia and New York. Then it obtained by merger a series of other roads in Pennsylvania and New Jersey and even laid a third rail on the 6-foot-gauge Erie to extend its mainline to the Great Lakes. Eventually its length exceeded 1100 miles.

Although it hauled mostly freight such as coal, slate, cement, milk, silk, and steel products and mail, it was also carrying 2 million passengers a year in first-class trains by 1945, but only 120,000 in 1950, owing to highway competition. After losing money steadily after 1966, LV took over the Pennsylvania lines which the Central Railroad of New Jersey abandoned in 1972, hoping to recoup its losses. But a year later it went into bankruptcy and is today part of the Conrail system.

Two Lehigh Valley locomotives in Auburn, New York, in 1904, just after an encounter with a blizzard. [***Donald W. Furler***]

BIBLIOGRAPHY: Robert F. Archer, *History of the Lehigh Valley Railroad,* Howell-North, Berkeley, Calif., 1977.

Leiper, Thomas ***(1745-1825)*** Merchant generally credited with having been America's first railroad operator. Born in Scotland, he emigrated to Maryland at 18, then moved to Philadelphia and engaged in tobacco importing. After serving as a cavalry officer in the Revolutionary War, he became Philadelphia's leading tobacco merchant and owned several mills and stone quarries. In 1806 (some historians say 1809) he built an experimental 180-foot wooden track or tramroad near Bull's Head Tavern, Philadelphia, close to the Delaware County line. It worked so well that he engaged John Thomson (father of J. Edgar Thomson, noted Quaker railroad engineer) to build a similar railway about ¾ mile long connecting Leiper's Crum Creek quarry with a boat landing on Ridley's Creek in Delaware County. This line was operated by horses. It continued in use until 1828 (3 years after Leiper's death). Meanwhile, in 1808, Silas Whitney built a wooden railway on Boston's Beacon Hill which may or may not have been America's earliest railroad.

Liberty Bell Bell cast in England for the city of Philadelphia and brought to America in 1752 by ship; 25 years later, when the British captured Philadelphia, a horse-drawn wagon took it to Allentown, Pennsylvania, temporary capital of the new nation. Beginning in 1855, it made trips by special trains to expositions in New Orleans, Chicago, Atlanta, Charleston, and Boston. Each time it rode a flatcar, guarded by some of Philadelphia's tallest and handsomest policemen. But by mid-

The original Liberty Bell, guarded by four proud Philadelphia policemen, traveled to various national exhibitions on special Pennsylvania Railroad flatcars like this one, from 1855 to 1903, when it was deemed too cracked for further travel.

1903 travel had enlarged its crack so much that the venerable relic was never again permitted to leave Independence Hall in Philadelphia.

On January 7, 1902, a Liberty Bell special train headed for South Carolina. Shortly after midnight it crashed into the rear of a freight at a lonely spot in a Virginia fog, instantly killing its engineer and fireman. Its two baggage cars burst into flames. Fearing for the bell's safety, railroad men uncoupled the flatcar holding the famous relic and rolled it slowly downgrade into a nearby siding. Charles Rosenberg, a Pennsylvania Railroad official in charge of the train, walked along the track through murky darkness for 3 miles without seeing a house. He broke into a tiny way station and telegraphed for help. By 7 a.m. the special was again on its way south, with a fresh engine.

After that, with some trepidation, the bell's custodians permitted it to take just one more railroad trip—to the Bunker Hill celebration at Boston in 1903. The American Freedom Trains that toured the nation in 1947–1948 and 1975–1976 carried not the Liberty Bell itself but an accurate replica. *See* FREEDOM TRAIN, AMERICAN.

Lima Locomotive Works Firm in Lima, Ohio, first organized as Carnes, Harper & Co. and then renamed Carnes, Agerter & Co., that began manufacturing mill machinery, particularly for sawmills. Reorganized as the Lima Machine Works in 1877, it built its first locomotive, a minor production, in 1879. Early in 1880 one of its customers, Ephraim Shay, an ingenious northern Michigan lumberman with a large square beard, who had been using a Lima direct-acting circular saw, approached the company with plans he had worked out for a geared locomotive. This machine, he said, could be run effectively and economically on the heavy grades and sharp curves of the crudely built logging railroads in the big woods and on mine railroads as well.

Switcher built by the Lima Locomotive Works for the New York, Chicago & St. Louis Railroad. [Nickel Plate Road]

Lima officials were favorably impressed. That year they constructed the first of very many patented Shay geared locomotives and sold it to a lumberman at Clam Lake, Michigan. It had a wood frame, a 44-inch upright stationary boiler which supplied steam power, two center bearing trucks, and a short, rigid wheelbase which enabled it to navigate sharp curves. Total weight was distributed so well that it could run on light iron or steel rails or even on the wooden-railed track that was not uncommon on early logging railroads.

Each year Lima kept improving this type slightly as it became increasingly popular, but it built all Shays on the same principle. The company enlarged its facilities by buying a 15-acre car-building plant, also in Lima, and in 1892 reincorporated itself as the Lima Locomotive & Machine Co. For a few years it built railroad cars as well as other products, but soon it devoted itself entirely to locomotives for America and foreign countries.

The building of Shays was only the start of Lima's greatness in the motive-power field, a greatness which, under the leadership of its chief engineer, William E. Woodard (1873–1942), a motive-power giant, seriously challenged the long-established Baldwin Locomotive Works. Before going to Lima, Woodard had been assistant chief engineer at the American Locomotive Co. plant in Schenectady, New York. His fame lay mostly in the creation of superpower steam locos. *See* AMERICAN LOCOMOTIVE CO.; BALDWIN LOCOMOTIVE WORKS.

At Woodard's solicitation, the New York Central (NYC) ordered the plant to build what became known as the Lima A-1, a mighty 2-8-2, for its Boston & Albany division. Because this superpower type was used first on that division in the Berkshire Hills, it was called the Berkshire type. Two additional feet of firebox length gave it a large area, 100 square feet, for improved firing capacity, as well as 284 square feet of firebox heating space, not counting the arch tube areas of 58 square feet, to expand the heating capacity. Its boiler pressure was 240 pounds per square inch. Although this behemoth weighed only 2 percent more than a comparable NYC 2-8-2, it yielded 17 percent more power, assisted by the standby power engendered by the booster attached to its trailing truck.

After completion of the A-1 in 1925, many features of its design were embodied in subsequent orders, for example, in the 2-10-4s which Lima built for the Texas & Pacific in 1927. A year later the works turned out 25 more units for the B&A division, but without the limited cutoff that the first unit had. These were followed in the 1930s, Lima's glory years, by a parade of superpowers that included 2-8-4s for the Missouri Pacific, the Detroit, Toledo & Ironton (DT&I), the Pere Marquette, the Nickel Plate, and the Richmond, Fredericksburg &

Potomac. The works also built 2-8-2s for the DT&I, 4-8-4s for the Chesapeake and Ohio and Southern Pacific, 2-10-4s for the Kansas City Southern, and Lima's biggest product, 2-6-6-6s (Allegheny type), for the C&O and the Virginian. Not all these locos had all the Woodard features, but most of them had at least enough to meet the "super" classification.

Even so, supersteam could not prevail against the rising tide of diesel-electrics. In 1948 Baldwin stopped building steam locomotives, and in 1949 so did Alco and Lima.

BIBLIOGRAPHY: Angus Sinclair, *Development of the Locomotive Engine*, annotated ed. by John H. White, Jr., M.I.T., Cambridge, Mass., 1970.

Lincoln Funeral Train An armor-plated car bearing the Great Seal of the President of the United States had been built in the military railroad shops at Alexandria, Virginia, for Abraham Lincoln. Arrangements were made for him to try it out on April 15, 1865. But on the night of April 14 he went to Ford's Theater in Washington to see a play. Next morning, a rainy morning, the tall, gaunt man lay dead in a little house across the street from the theater.

At Mrs. Lincoln's request, the body was taken in the armored car to his home city of Springfield, Illinois, for burial after being embalmed with special care for the long tour. The same car bore the remains of the Lincolns' 12-year-old son Willie, dead 3 years, which had been kept in a Washington cemetery vault until the family could take the small coffin back home with them when they left the White House.

The entire train was draped in mourning, especially the second car from the rear, the catafalque car, with its 12 windows framed by crape rosettes. A sentry wearing a black armband and white gloves stood in each of the car's open vestibules. The car's interior, swathed voluminously with black cloth, looked macabre. The large glass-windowed coffin rested on a dais, covered by a black-bordered, fringed American flag that was folded back whenever the corpse was exposed to public view. A three-man guard of honor inside the car represented the Army, Navy, and Marine Corps.

Lincoln's last journey followed in reverse almost the identical route of his preinaugural trip, but it covered less than 1700 miles (instead of 1900) over the tracks of 13 (instead of 22) railroads, and it took 13 days (instead of 12) because it moved more slowly and made longer stops. All seven cars were painted black. The armor-plated car with the catafalque rolled all the way to Springfield, but the other six cars and the engines were changed whenever the train reached a different railroad. A pilot engine ran 10 minutes ahead of the funeral special to make sure the rails were clear. A total of 26 engines were used on the trip.

With President Andrew Johnson, Gen. Ulysses S. Grant, the Cabinet, and other dignitaries standing stiffly at attention, the black train steamed slowly out of the Washington depot at six o'clock on Friday, April 21, heading for Baltimore. A densely packed crowd

Artist's rendering of the Lincoln funeral train, draped in mourning, leaving New York on its way from Washington to Lincoln's old home in Springfield, Illinois. Lincoln's last journey took 13 days. [New York Central Railroad]

watched with heads bared while the bronze bells of engines tolled a requiem.

In the coaches sat the heavily veiled widow and her two sons, Robert and Tad, five of Lincoln's friends who had accompanied him on the preinauguration trip, many notables, and journalists. Along the route possibly 1,500,000 people gazed upon the haggard face, still discolored by the effects of the assassin's bullet; and maybe 7 million more looked at the casket or hearse car, as compared with the estimated 1,000,000 or so who had seen the President-elect on his preinaugural journey to the capital 4 years earlier.

The cortege on rails reached Philadelphia on Saturday, April 22. To a muffled drumbeat, the long coffin was borne into Independence Hall, where the Declaration of Independence had been signed in 1776, and was displayed beside the Liberty Bell. A line of mourners 3 miles long moved past the bier.

At Lancaster, the crowd parted silently as a venerable man drove up in a carriage and got out to pay his respects. He was Lincoln's predecessor in the White House, James Buchanan. In Newark and Jersey City there were more acres of people. A sable-hued boat ferried the casket across the Hudson River to New York, where it was set up on view in City Hall.

Afterward, an engine fittingly named *Union* wheeled the seven black coaches northward on Commodore Vanderbilt's Hudson River Railroad. Opposite West Point Military Academy 1000 precise and caped cadets saluted their dead commander in chief. At Albany, the much-traveled body was displayed in the New York State Assembly chamber. At Syracuse, some 30,000 men, women, and children met the black train in a midnight downpour. Then, on April 26, it reached Buffalo and more crowds.

It was still raining when the train rolled into Cleveland. There a gleaming white temple with a silver-starred ceiling, draped in black, had been erected for the bier. Not to be outdone, the grieving citizens of Columbus had built a Chinese pagoda and laid a carpet of fresh hothouse roses on the planking of High Street. Over these flowers a dozen fine black horses with nodding plumes drew the glass-walled hearse from the railroad depot to the pagoda for public viewing and back later to the station.

Some 100,000 people showed up in Indianapolis despite steady rain. At Alton, yardmen of the Chicago & Alton Railroad coupled the magnificent new car *Pioneer* onto the train for the exclusive use of Mrs. Lincoln's party on the last leg of the trip, over the C&A, with compliments of George M. Pullman. The *Pioneer* was the first sleeper that Pullman had built new. It boasted the novelty of hot-air heating, was lighted by candles and loaded with mirrors, and, in fact, started a new trend in sleeping-car design. The widow thanked Pullman personally. *See* PULLMAN, GEORGE MORTIMER.

On May 3 at 9:00 a.m., one of the hottest days Illinois had ever known, the black train reached the end of its 13-day run. Lincoln's old Springfield home, like the railroad depot and public buildings, was heavily draped in mourning. The long coffin was displayed for the last time in the State Capitol. All that night, church bells tolled continuously.

Next morning, a slow cortege escorted the remains of the wartime President to a cemetery vault, there to lie until the present memorial could be built.

BIBLIOGRAPHY: Freeman Hubbard, *Great Trains of All Time,* Grosset & Dunlap, New York, 1962.

Lincoln's Trip to Inauguration On this cold, rainy morning of February 11, 1861, Abraham Lincoln departed from the Great Western Railway depot at Springfield, Illinois, on a special train consisting of a coach and a baggage car, both wooden, painted yellow, and the Hinkley-built 4-4-0 woodburner *L. M. Wiley,* to be sworn in as the sixteenth President of the United States.

Lincoln traveled with his oldest son, Robert, also bodyguards, political associates, railway officials, and newspapermen, leaving behind his wife and two other sons to join him later in Washington. The 1900-mile journey lasted 12 days. It took Lincoln over 22 different railroads, with many changes of trains, through 7 states and the District of Columbia, 12 major cities, and hundreds of towns. A century later, a train could have been routed over *one* road, the Baltimore & Ohio (B&O), in 18 hours. No such route existed in 1861.

The President-elect stopped overnight in 10 cities and made many speeches. One place where he spoke was Jersey City, New Jersey. Some of his hearers had come into town by excursion train from nearby communities in the first iron car ever built, the La Mothe patent iron passenger car, predecessor of the modern steel coach.

A plot by Southern sympathizers to murder the President-elect in Baltimore, even before he could reach Washington for his first inauguration, was foiled by railroad men. On February 22, Lincoln was dining in a Harrisburg, Pennsylvania, hotel, which he left suddenly, his meal unfinished, escorted by Gov. Andrew G. Curtin of Pennsylvania and Ward H. Lamon, an attorney who was to be his bodyguard for the night.

The three men took a closed carriage to the Pennsylvania Railroad (PRR) tracks on the edge of town. There Lincoln and Lamon boarded a darkened one-car train. The need for secrecy was due to the fact that the Philadelphia, Wilmington and Baltimore [(PW&B) later part of the PRR] had hired Allan Pinkerton, head of a famous detective agency, to investigate rumors of the murder plot and he had verified them.

Meanwhile, in Harrisburg Thomas B. Scott, vice president of the PW&B, who later became president of the PRR, had given the special train a clear board to Philadelphia and had even ordered the telegraph wires disconnected to keep news from the conspirators. The train reached the Pennsy's West Philadelphia station at 10 p.m.

There it was met by Pinkerton and H. F. Kenney, the PW&B superintendent. An hour later Lincoln, Pinkerton, and Lamon boarded the last car of the express, the three men sharing a compartment with the shades drawn. Armed Pinkerton operatives, including a woman, occupied the adjoining compartments.

At Havre de Grace, Maryland, the cars were ferried across the Susquehanna River. They reached Baltimore's President Street Station at 3:30 a.m. There, according to routine practice, they were detached, and teams of horses hauled them along Pratt Street to the B&O's Camden Street Station, where they were coupled onto the waiting Washington train and pulled into the capital at dawn—in Lincoln's words, "like a thief in the night."

BIBLIOGRAPHY: Frederick L. Holmes, *Abraham Lincoln Traveled This Way,* Page, Boston, 1930; Ida M. Tarbell, *The Life of Abraham Lincoln,* Doubleday & McClure, New York, 1900.

Lingo of the Rails One night a man went to the ticket window in the Rock Island passenger station in Topeka, Kansas, and asked, "How are trains 36 and 39?" Glancing outside, the agent said, "Number 39 is showing, and No. 16 is in the color." The customer looked dazed and muttered something about not being able to get information from a railroad; so the agent explained that train 39 was backing off the wye and 36 was standing at the block signal waiting for orders.

That is a true incident. Railroaders of long ago, especially boomers—like cowboys, circus troupers, actors, journalists, and people in other occupations, even the underworld—developed a slang of their own and used it freely, although you won't hear very much of it today. Slang in general enriches our language (sometimes it weakens it), blending with the mother tongue to such an extent that even a lexicographer would be hard put to tell which terms are acceptable and which are not. Today's slang may become academic English 10 years hence. Even purists use it sometimes, possibly without being aware of it.

Here is an exaggerated version of an old-time boomer explaining colorfully how he got injured in a railroad accident:

> It was like this: I was making up a manifest in the garden, and I had only one snake working with me. He was standing on the goat's back porch ready to cut off a battleship, and she was a heavy one. I was giving the eagle eye a washout and yelling to the stinger, "That'll do," but he gave the jack's boss a quick come-along, and the hogger threw a kick into the drag. Then one of my brogans got caught in the target where I had the points half bent, so the reefer took to the ground on top of me, and here I am.

The following thesaurus has come from thousands of old-time railroaders, men in actual service and retirees, over a period of 50 years, being compiled from words they spoke and letters they wrote. Most of it was published in 1945 in *Railroad Avenue,* by Freeman Hubbard, and is now supplemented by additional entries.

AGE: Seniority; length of railroad service.

AIR MONKEY: Airbrake repairer.

ALLEY: Clear track in a railroad yard.

AMPUTATE: Uncouple the engine or one or more cars from a train.

ANCHOR THEM: Set handbrakes on standing cars. The opposite term is *release anchors.*

APE WAGON: Derogatory term for caboose.

ARMSTRONG: Old-style turntables, handbrakes, and engines without mechanical stokers, operated by muscular effort.

ARTIST: Person adept at any phase of railroad operation, used with a prefix, as in *throttle artist* (locomotive engineer).

ASHCAT: Fireman on a coalburning locomotive.

ASHPIT ENGINEER: *See* HOSTLER.

B&B CARPENTER: *See* BRIDGE HOG.

BABY CARRIAGE: Centercab Pennsy electric locomotive.

BACK TO THE FARM: Laid off on account of slack business.

BAD ORDER: Crippled car or engine, often called *cripple.* It must be marked by a blue light at night and a blue flag by day if men are working around it.

BAIL IT IN: Feed the locomotive firebox.

BAILING-WIRE MECHANIC: Man of little mechanical ability.

BAKEHEAD: Steam locomotive fireman.

BALL OF FIRE: Fast run; also called *balling the jack. See also* RED BALL.

BALL THE JACK: *See* JACK.

BALLAST SCORCHER: Speedy engineer like Casey Jones.

BALLING THE JACK: *See* BALL OF FIRE.

BANDWAGON: Pay car or pay train, from which wages were handed out to railroad employees.

BANJO: Fireman's shovel; old-style banjo-shaped signal.

BAT THE STACK OFF OF HER: Make fast time; work a steam engine at full stroke.

BATTING 'EM OUT: Switchman's term for a yard engine switching a *string* of cars.

BATTLESHIP: Large freight engine, interurban car, or coal car; also a formidable female, landlady, etc.

BEANERY: Railroad eating house; *beanery queen,* waitress.

BEEHIVE: Railroad yard office.

BELL RINGER: Steam locomotive fireman.

BIG BOYS: Special trains for officials; the Union Pacific's largest and most powerful steam locomotives.

The old-time railroad station telegrapher of the days of oil-wick lamps was known as a brass pounder. [Frederic Shaw]

BIG E: Engineer, so called from the big initial on the membership button of the Brotherhood of Locomotive Engineers.

BIG FOUR: Former four operating brotherhoods: Brotherhood of Railroad Trainmen, Order of Railway Conductors, Brotherhood of Locomotive Firemen and Enginemen, and Brotherhood of Locomotive Engineers. It also means the Cleveland, Cincinnati, Chicago & St. Louis Railway. In addition, it refers to the Big Four who built and ran what eventually became the Southern Pacific Railroad: Leland Stanford, Collis P. Huntington, Mark Hopkins, and Charles Crocker.

BIG HOLE: Emergency airbrake application; quick stop. *Big-holing her* is making an emergency stop. *See also* WIPE THE CLOCK.

BIG HOOK: Wrecking crane, hauled on a special train.

BIG O or BIG OX: Train conductor, named for the first initial in the Order of Railway Conductors.

BIG ROCK CANDY MOUNTAIN: Hoboes' paradise as described in the song of that name written and originally sung by Harry K. McClintock. *See also* INDIAN VALLEY LINE.

BINDERS: Handbrakes on railroad cars.

BINDLE STIFF or BLANKET STIFF: Hobo who totes a *bindle* (bundle) or blanket to use wherever night finds him.

BIRDCAGE: Brakemen's or switchmen's lantern.

BISCUITS HANG HIGH, THE: Food handouts are scarce in that area.

BLACK DIAMONDS: Coal. *See also* DIAMOND CRACKER.

BLACK HOLE: Tunnel.

BLACK ONES: Railway Express refrigerator cars; any boxcars without interior illumination that are pressed into mail service during the Christmas rush.

BLACK SNAKE: Solid train of loaded coal cars.

BLACKBALLED: Blacklisted or boycotted, especially after a railroad strike. *See also* "CRANE WITH A BROKEN NECK."

BLACKJACKS: Fifty-ton Santa Fe coal cars painted black.

BLANKET STIFF: *See* BINDLE STIFF.

BLASTING: Hard, sharp exhaust of a steam locomotive.

BLAZER: Hot axle journal with its packing afire.

BLEED: Drain air from. A *bleeder* is a valve by which air is bled from a car's auxiliary reservoir.

BLIND BAGGAGE: Hobo riding the head end of a baggage car next to the tender; there is no door, or it is kept locked. This is known as *riding the blinds.* It is usually cold, especially in winter, always dangerous, and sometimes fatal. *Compare with* RIDING THE RODS.

BLIND TRANSMISSION: One-way telegraphic communication.

BLINDING IT: *See* RIDING THE BLINDS.

BLIZZARD LIGHTS: Lights on either side of a locomotive headlight that served in an emergency when the oilburning headlight blew out; also nonscheduled, or extra, train.

BLOOD: Steam locomotive built by Aretas Blood at the Manchester (New Hampshire) Locomotive Works.

BLOW 'ER DOWN: Reduce water in a steam locomotive boiler that is carrying too much.

BLOW SMOKE: Brag.

BLOW UP: Use the blower to increase the draft in a locomotive firebox, thus raising boiler steam pressure; also quit a job suddenly.

BLUE FLAG or BLUE LIGHT: Equipment placed to notify all persons that men are working on a *crippled* car or engine, which must not be coupled into or moved.

BLUE STRIP: Inaccurate telegraph message handed back to the operator to be corrected.

'BO: Hobo. A *'bo chaser* is a freight brakeman or railroad policeman.

BOARD: Fixed signal regulating rail traffic, usually referred to as *slow board, order board, clear board* (for clear track), or *red board* (stop). It should not be confused with another kind of *slow board,* or *starvation list,* meaning *extra board* or *spare board,* that usually lists qualified crewmen or telegraph operators not in active service but called to work in emergencies. Names appear in order of seniority, the man hired most recently being the last man to be given an assignment.

BOBTAIL: Switch engine; short trolley car.

BOILER ASCENSION: Locomotive boiler explosion.

BOILER HEADER: Brakeman riding in the engine cab.

BOOK OF RULES: Examination based on facts in the rule book, given before anyone is hired or promoted in train, engine, or telegraph service.

BOOTLEGGER: Train that runs over more than one railroad.

BOOMER: Drifter who went from one railroad job to another, usually staying but a short time on any job or road. The term dates back to pioneer days, when men followed boom camps or towns. The opposite is the *home guard,* a one-road man. *Boomers* should not be confused with tramps, who refused to work. Boomers were railroad workers, often in big demand because of their wide experience. A common practice was to follow the "rushes," i.e., apply for seasonal jobs when and where available; for example, when the movement of grain, melon crops, strawberry crops, etc., made the railroads temporarily shorthanded. Virtually no boomers are left in North America today. Men needed for seasonal jobs or other emergencies are called from the *extra board.*

BOOMER PIKE: Railroad on which the personnel changes often.

BOUNCER: Caboose.

BOWLING ALLEY: Hand-fired coalburning engine. A fireman tossing extra-heavy chunks of coal into the firebox went through motions that resembled bowling.

BRAINS or THE BRAINS: Conductor; sometimes called *brainless wonder,* a term applied also to any crewman or official who did things his fellows considered queer.

BRAKE CLUB: Three-foot hickory stick used by freight trainmen to tighten handbrakes; sometimes called *sap* or the *staff of ignorance.*

BRASS: Babbitt-lined bronze that forms the bearings upon which the car rests. To *brass* a car is to replace one of those bearings.

BRASS BUTTONS: Railroad conductor or streetcar conductor.

BRASS COLLAR or BRASS HAT: Railroad official; possibly derived from the gold-braided collar of a passenger conductor's uniform or brass-plated cap, or of military origin.

BRASS POUNDER: Telegraph operator.

BRIDGE HOG: Bridge and building (B&B) carpenter in the era antedating steel and concrete bridges.

BROKEN KNUCKLES: Railroad men's sleeping quarters.

BROWNIES: Demerits. In 1885, George R. Brown, general superintendent of the Fall River Line, thought the then-current practice of suspending or discharging men for breaking rules was unfair to their families, so he substituted demerit marks. Too many brownies in a given period led to dismissal. Eventually the railroad industry widely adopted variations of that system. *Brownie box* or *brownie wagon* means any railroad official's business car.

BUCK THE BOARD: Work the *extra board. See* BOARD.

BUCKLE THE RUBBERS: Connect train hose or steam hose.

BUG: Telegraph instrument; trainman's or switchman's light, also called *bug torch*; three-wheeled electric-powered truck carrying mail and baggage around terminals.

BUG LINE: Phone connection between the enginehouse and the yard or the telegraph office.

BUG TORCH: *See* BUG.

BUGGY: Caboose. The term is rarely applied to other cars.

BULGINE: Steam locomotive.

BULL, FLATFOOT, or GUMSHOE: Railroad policeman or detective. Distinctively rail terms are *cinder dick, bo chaser,* and *car-seal hawk.*

BULL PEN: Crew room.

BUMP: Get another man's job by exercising seniority. When a crew loses its assignment, as when a train is taken off the schedule, its members pick the jobs they wish from those held by men with less *whiskers* (seniority).

BUNCH OF THIEVES: Wrecking-train crew.

BUNCHING: Accumulation of freight cars for loading and unloading in excess of those needed.

BUST UP A CUT: Separate cars in a train, removing some that have reached their destination and assigning other cars to through trains, etc.

BUTTERFLY: Note thrown or handed down from a train by an official to a section boss or other employee, so called because it may flutter along the track, although if tossed from a car it is usually weighted down.

BUZZARD'S ROOST: Yard office.

CABOOSE BOUNCE or CABOOSE HOP: Train consisting of only the engine and a caboose.

CAGE: Caboose.

CALLBOY or CALLER: One whose duty is to round up and summon train and/or engine crews; train announcer.

CALLIOPE: Steam locomotive.

CAMEL or CAMELBACK: Double-cabbed locomotive with the control cab built over the middle of the boiler, suggesting a camel's hump; also called the *Mother Hubbard* type.

CAN: Tank car. A *tin can* is a diesel locomotive.

CAP: Track torpedo, part of a flagman's equipment.

CAPTAIN: Train conductor. The term dates from the Civil War period when the U.S. Army ran some railroads.

CAR CATCHER: Rear brakeman or flagman.

CAR KNOCKER: Car inspector or repairer (wheels are tapped to detect flaws); also called *car whacker, car tink, car tonk,* and *car toad* (the inspector often squats).

CAR-SEAL HAWK: Railroad company policeman.

CAR TOAD: *See* TOAD.

CAR WITH THE TOP BLOWN OFF: *See* FLAT.

CARD: Credentials of brotherhood or union membership. *Carrying a card* means belonging to a rail labor organization.

CARRY A WHITE FEATHER: Display green (flags by day, lights by night) on the engine to indicate a second section is following closely. Prior to World War I, white, not green, was the clear signal. *Carrying white* in the same manner signifies an extra train.

CARRYING A CARD: *See* CARD.

CARRYING THE BANNER: Flagging; ostentatiously wearing brotherhood emblems, which hoboes sometimes did while working the *main stem* for handouts.

CARRYING THE MAIL: Bringing train orders.

CARRYING WHITE: *See* CARRY A WHITE FEATHER.

CASEY JONES: Any railroad man, particularly a locomotive engineer and most especially a fast runner like the real John Luther (Casey) Jones.

CATWALK: Plank walk atop boxcars; also called a *deck.*

CHAIN GANG: Engine or train crew assigned to pool service, working first in, first out.

CHAMBERMAID: Roundhouse machinist.

CHARIOT: Caboose; general manager's business car.

CHASING THE RED: (Flagman) going back with a red flag or a red light and other equipment to protect the rear of a train.

CHECKER or SPOTTER: Company spy, particularly one checking up on the loss of materials or an agent's or conductor's receipts.

CHERRY PICKER: Switchman (because of red lights on switchstands); also any railroad man who is always figuring on the best jobs and dodging tough ones (as in the old saying "Life is a bowl of cherries").

CHEWING CINDERS: Action of steam locomotives when reversed while running and while working quite a bit of steam.

CINDER CRUNCHER: Switchman or flagman. A *cinder skipper* is a yard clerk; a *cinder dick,* a railroad policeman; a *cinder snapper,* a passenger on the rear open platform of an observation car.

CIRCUS: The whole railroad; any railroad operation.

CLAW: Clinker hook used by the fireman of a coalburning locomotive.

CLEAR BOARD: *See* BOARD.

CLEARANCE CARD: Authority to use the mainline.

CLINKER BOY: Fireman on a coalburning engine.

CLOCK: Steam gauge (*see also* WIPE THE CLOCK), not to be confused with *Dutch clock,* a speed recorder; also fare register.

CLOWN: Switchman or yard brakeman. The *clown wagon* or *clown's tent* is the caboose.

CLUB: Brake club. A *club winder* is a switchman or brakeman. A brakeman's club was usually his only weapon against hoboes or other assailants.

COAL HEAVER or STOKER: Fireman on a coalburning locomotive.

COCKLOFT or CROW'S NEST: Cupola of a caboose.

COFFEE or SPOT: Respite enjoyed by the baggageman and others while awaiting the arrival of the next train.

COFFEEPOT: Little old steam locomotive.

COLLAR-AND-ELBOW JOINT: Railroad boarding house. There was not much room at the dinner table.

COLOR-BLIND: Designating an employee who can't distinguish between his own money and the company's. The term has nothing to do with eye tests for engine or train service.

COME-ALONG: Equipment used to pull a line wire taut.

COMPANY BIBLE: The standard *Book of Rules.*

COMPANY NOTCH or WALL STREET NOTCH: Forward corner of a steam locomotive's reverse lever quadrant. The engine exerts full pulling power when worked with a full stroke, thus bringing in the most revenue.

CONDUCER: One of many slang terms for a train conductor.

CONSIST: Contents or equipment of a train; report form sent ahead so that the yardmaster can make plans for switching a train. *Dropping the consist* is giving the report to an operator.

COOLING A SPINDLE: Cooling a *hotbox* (overheated journal) by replacing the brass or putting water on the bearings.

COPPERPLATE FIST: Fine, clean, fast transcription of telegraphic messages.

CORNERED: Designating a car on a sidetrack, not in the clear, that is struck by an engine or train. For example, the caboose that Casey Jones's loco hit on his last run was *cornered.*

CORNFIELD MEET: Head-on collision or one narrowly averted. Derailment sometimes sends trains into a cornfield.

COULDN'T PULL A SETTING HEN OFF HER NEST: Derogatory allusion to an inferior locomotive.

COUNTING THE TIES: Reducing speed; trackwalking. Many a freshman at Dartmouth College was hazed by being forced to hike all 14 miles of the Woodstock Railroad in Vermont and make an exact count of its crossties.

COW CAGE or COW CRATE: Cattle car.

COWCATCHER: Steam locomotive pilot. Railroad officials discarded the term as a butt for many jokes.

CRADLE: Gondola or other open-top freight car.

"CRANE WITH A BROKEN NECK": Secret blacklisting system (*see* separate article).

CRIB: Caboose. Crewmen sleep in it.

CRIPPLE: *See* BAD ORDER.

CROAKER or SAWBONES: Railroad company doctor or surgeon.

CROW'S NEST: *See* COCKLOFT.

CRUMMY: Derogatory yet affectionate word for a caboose.

CUPOLA: Observation tower on a caboose.

CUSHIONS: Passenger cars. A *cushion rider* is a passenger or a member of a passenger-train crew. *See also* VARNISH.

CUT: Several cars attached to an engine or coupled together by themselves; part of the right-of-way excavated out of a hill or mountain that is not run over or tunneled through.

CUT THE BOARD: Lay off men from the extra list who have been hired most recently.

DANCING: Spinning by wheels, usually engine driving wheels.

DANCING ON THE CARPET: Being called to an official's office for investigation or discipline.

DEADHEAD: Employee riding on a pass; nonpaying passenger; fireman's derisive term for a head brakeman who rides in the engine cab; locomotive being hauled "dead" on a train; telegraph message sent free.

DEADMAN'S BUTTON: *See* DEADMAN'S THROTTLE.

DEADMAN'S HOLE: Old-time method of righting an overturned car or engine. A 6-foot hole was dug about 40 feet from it, long and deep enough to bury a large solid-oak plank for leverage. With chains attached to the plank, a road locomotive hauled the overturned equipment upright and back onto the rails.

DEADMAN'S THROTTLE: Throttle requiring pressure by the operator's hand or foot to prevent a power shutoff and the application of brakes. An engine so equipped stops instantly if the driver loses consciousness or otherwise discontinues such pressure. An alternative term is *deadman's button.*

DECK: Floor of an engine cab; *catwalk* on a boxcar roof. To *dec(k)orate* means to get out on top of freight cars to set handbrakes or to receive or transmit signals.

DELAYER or DETAINER: Train dispatcher, designated *DS.*

DIAMOND: Diamond-patterned trackage over which one railroad or branch crosses another.

DIAMOND CRACKER or DIAMOND PUSHER: Fireman on a coalburning locomotive, *black diamonds* meaning coal.

DIE GAME: Stall on a hill.

DINGDONG: Gasoline or gas-electric self-powered coach, usually on a small railroad or branch line not important enough to support a regular train. The name is the sound of its bell. A *dinger* is a conductor who rings the bell.

DIPLOMA: Clearance; service letter; fake service letter.

A striking example from 1890 of what was known, in the lingo of the rails, as a cornfield meet because such head-on collisions sometimes sent trains into a cornfield. [Collection of C. W. Jernstrom]

DIRTY CAR: Storage car holding an assortment of mail, including parcels, that demands extra work in separating it.

DITCH: Part of right-of-way lower than the roadbed. A derailed engine or train is *ditched* or *in the ditch.*

DOGCATCHERS: Crew sent out to relieve a crew that is *outlawed,* i.e., overtaken by the Hours of Service Act that limits continuous duty to 12 hours [the limit used to be 16 hours (and may be cut to 10)], known as the *dog law, hog law,* or *pure-food law.*

DOGHOUSE: Caboose or its cupola.

DOLLY BAR: Tool for holding a rivet in place while the opposite side is being hammered to form a second head.

DONEGAN: Former railroad car, with wheels removed, used as a residence, office, etc. Around 1900, three Jersey Central employees named Donegan lived in separate shacks in the same vicinity. People were directed to the Donegans so often that the shacks themselves, and later cars set up off the rails, were given their name.

DONKEY: Small auxiliary engine; track worker; any self-operated rail passenger car.

DOODLEBUG: Rail motor car for section men, linemen, etc.

DOPE: Orders, official instructions, explanations, etc.; composition for cooling hot journals. To *dope it* means to use a compound to keep water from boiling when the engine is being worked hard. It also means to add oil, soap, or *pin dope* to an overheated journal.

DOPE MONKEY: Car inspector.

DOUBLE: Cut a train in two when going up a hill and take each section up separately.

DOUBLEHEADER: Train hauled by two locomotives.

DOUSE THE GLIM: Extinguish a lantern, often by a sudden upward movement.

DRAG: Heavy train of nonrush freight, especially coal, iron or copper ore, gravel, etc.; any slow freight train, as contrasted with the speedy *manifest, red ball,* or *hotshot;* also the time taken to move telegraph messages.

DRAWBAR FLAGGING: Action of a flagman leaning against the caboose drawbar or standing near it to protect the rear of his train, instead of walking back "a sufficient distance" as the rule requires. Such a man is taking a chance, owing maybe to laziness, exhaustion, bad weather, or fear that the train may leave him behind.

DRIFTING THROTTLE: Running of a locomotive with the throttle cracked open to keep air and dust from being sucked into the steam cylinders.

DRILL CREW: Railroad yard crew.

DRONE CAR: Official's private (business) car.

DROP: Switching movement, cars being cut off from an engine and allowed to coast to their places. *See also* HUMP.

DROP 'ER DOWN: Pull the reverse lever forward. To *drop 'er in the corner* is to make fast time with a steam locomotive, dropping the *Johnson bar* into the corner of the cab.

DROPPING: Burning off an overheated car journal.

DROWNING IT OUT: Cooling an overheated journal.

DRUMMER: Yard conductor; traveling salesman.

DRUNKARD: Late Saturday-night passenger train.

DS: *See* DELAYER.

DUCATS: Passenger conductor's hat checks.

DUMMY: Employees' train; switcher-type locomotive with the boiler and running gear entirely housed, used occasionally for service in public streets.

DUST RAISER: Fireman shoveling coal into the firebox.

DUSTING HER OUT: Putting sand into the firebox of an oilburning locomotive to cut out soot in the flues while the engine is working hard and thus to keep up steam; also known as *giving the old girl a dose of salts.*

DUTCH CLOCK: *See* CLOCK.

DUTCH DROP: Risky, obsolete way to bring a car into the mainline from a spur. A locomotive headed into the spur, coupled head-on to the car, and backed out. When the car was moving fast, the engine was cut off and speeded up to get back onto the mainline before the car, then moved forward ahead of the junction between the mainline and the spur so that the car could roll out behind her.

DYNAMITE: Emergency application of an airbrake. A *dynamiter* is a car on which a defective mechanism sends the brakes into full emergency; also a quick-action triple valve.

EAGLE EYE: Steam locomotive engineer.

EASY SIGN: Signal ordering a train to move slowly.

ELECTRIC OWL: Night operator.

ELEPHANT CAR: Tall circus car to hold elephants; special car just behind the engine accommodating the head brakeman.

END MAN: Rear brakeman on a freight train.

EXTRA BOARD: *See* BOARD.

EYE: Trackside signal.

EYES-AND-EARS GUY: Company physician who gives tests for colors, sight, hearing, etc.

FAMILY DISTURBER: Pay car or pay train.

FIELD or GARDEN: Railroad-car classification yard.

FIELDER or FIELD MAN: Yard brakeman.

FIGUREHEAD: Yard brakeman.

FIREBOY: Fireman on a steam locomotive.

FIRST READER: Conductor's train book.

FISH WAGON: Gas-electric or other motor car equipped with an air horn, which sounds like an old-time fishmonger's horn.

FISHTAIL: Semaphore blade.

FIST or MITT: Often preceded by *Op,* a telegraph operator's handwriting. This script, especially in the days before telephones, typewriters, and teletypes, was characterized by its swiftness, its legibility, and the bold, flowing curves which connected one word with another. *Ops* were proud of their penmanship.

FIXED MAN: Switchman in a *hump* yard assigned to one certain post from which he rides cars being humped.

FIXED SIGNAL: Derisive term for a student brakeman standing on a boxcar with his lantern out and a cinder in his eye.

FLAG: Flagman; assumed name. Many a boomer worked *under a flag* when his own name was blacklisted.

FLAG STOP: Small station where a train must be flagged to stop for occasional passengers.

FLAT: Flatcar; also called *car with the top blown off.*

FLAT WHEEL: Car wheel with flat spots on the tread; employee who limps.

FLATFOOT: *See* BULL.

FLATTOP: Boxcab type of Pennsy electric locomotive.

FLEW UP AN' LOST 'ER FEET: Locomotive driving wheels lost their traction and slipped or spun.

FLIMSY: Train order. Standard practice calls for the use of tissue paper to facilitate making carbon copies.

FLOATER: Alternative name for a *boomer.*

FLY LIGHT: Miss a meal. Boomers and hoboes often did that.

FLYING SWITCH: Switching technique whereby a steam locomotive pulled away from a car or cars immediately after she had started them rolling. This permitted the car or cars to be switched onto a track other than the one the engine used. The switch was thrown instantly after the engine passed it and just before the car or cars reached it. This practice, common in bygone days, is outlawed today.

FOG or PUTTY: Steam.

FOOTBOARD: Low single step on the front end of a switch or freight engine; a similar step was on the rear. Many casualties were due to switchmen's missing these steps, especially on dark, icy nights.

FOOTBOARD YARDMASTER: Conductor who acts as yardmaster in a small yard.

FOREIGN CAR: Car running over any railroad other than the one which owns it.

FOUNTAIN: That part of a steam locomotive where steam issues from the boiler and flows into pipes for lubrication, injection, and so on.

FREEZE A HOB or FREEZE A BLAZER: Cool an overheated journal.

FREEZER: Refrigerator car; also called *reefer* or *riff.*

FROG: Steel implement for rerailing cars or engines; X-shaped plate where two tracks cross. A *frog war* occurred when one railroad refused to let another railroad cross its tracks. In such cases, the crossing was often done by force, by stealth, or by court decision.

FUSEE: Red flare used for flagging purposes. Its sharp end is driven into the right-of-way. No following train may legally pass as long as it is burning except in cases where some railroads permit a train to stop, extinguish the *fusee,* and proceed with caution in automatic block signal limits.

GANDY DANCER: Track laborer. The name may have originated from the old Gandy Manufacturing Co. of Chicago, which made tamping bars, claw spikes, picks, and shovels.

GANGWAY: Space between the rear cab post of a steam locomotive and her tender.

GARBAGE: Food sold at cheap lunch counters.

GARDEN: *See* FIELD.

GASHOUSE: Yard office, where men talk or *gas.*

GATE: Switch. To open or close a *gate* is throw the switch.

GAY CAT: Tramp held in contempt by fellow vagrants because he is willing to work if a job comes along.

GENERAL: Yardmaster, often abbreviated YM.

GET THE IRON: Throw a switch.

GET THE ROCKING CHAIR: Retire on a pension.

GET UP: Get off the telegraph wire now; you're no good. Ask for a relief operator.

GET YOUR HEAD CUT IN: Boomer slang for "wise up," learn by experience.

GIN POLE: Guyed pole with a block and tackle for lifting loads.

GIRL or OLD GIRL: Affectionate and common term for a steam engine. The locomotive, like the sailing ship, was often called *she* instead of *it.*

GIVE HER THE GRIT: Pour sand on the rails.

GIVING THE OLD GIRL A DOSE OF SALTS: *See* DUSTING HER OUT.

GLASS ARM or GLASS HAND: Paralytic condition of the wrist not uncommon among veteran telegraphers.

GLIM: Switchman's or trainman's lantern.

GLIMMER: Locomotive headlight.

GLORY HOLE: A fireman just promoted to engineer was said to be *in the glory hole.*

GLORY HUNTER: Reckless, fast-running steam loco engineer.

GLORY ROAD: Sentimental term for railroad.

GM: General manager.

GO HIGH: Alternative term for *dec(k)orate. See* DECK.

GO-TO-HELL SIGNAL: Gesture given with a violent motion of the hand or lantern.

GOAT: Yard engine. *See* YARD.

GODS OF IRON: Huge, powerful steam locomotives.

GON: Gondola, or steel-sided, flat-bottomed freight car.

GONE FISHING: Laid off.

GONE TO GLORY: Killed, especially in a train collision.

GOO-GOO EYE: Steam locomotive with two firedoors.

GOOSE: Make an emergency stop. *Goose her* is to reverse a locomotive under headway.

GRAB IRON: Steel bar attached to cars and engines as a handhold.

GRABBER: Passenger conductor (he grabs tickets).

GRASS WAGON: Tourist car; tourists like scenery.

GRASSHOPPER: Early type of steam locomotive with a vertical boiler and vertical cylinders.

GRAVEDIGGER: Section man; track worker.

GRAVEYARD: Sidetrack or part of yard occupied by obsolete and disused engines and cars; scrap pile.

GRAVEYARD WATCH: Period from 12:01 a.m. to 8 a.m. or any midnight shift, so called because it includes the quietest hours.

GRAZING TICKET: *See* PIE CARD.

GREASE MONKEY: Car oiler.

GREASE THE PIG: Oil the engine. *See* HOG.

GREASY SPOON: Railroad eating house. The bill of fare was colloquially the *switch list,* a fork was a *hook,* butter was the *grease pot,* hotcakes were *blind gaskets,* and beans were *torpedoes.*

Highball ***signal at the north end of the Portland, Maine, terminal yards in 1954.*** **[*Lucius Beebe*]**

GREEN EYE: Clear signal. When Cy Warman wrote his famous poem "Will the Lights Be White?" white was the clear signal; green meant "Proceed cautiously." This was changed in the early 1900s because when a green or red roundel fell out, the signal showed white, thus erroneously giving a *clear board* to engineers even though the signal itself was set to "Stop" or "Go slow."

GREENBACKS: Frogs for rerailing engines and cars.

GREENBALL FREIGHT: Fruit or vegetables.

GREETINGS FROM THE DS: Train orders from the dispatcher.

GRIEVER: Union spokesman on a grievance committee; union representative at an official investigation.

GROUNDHOG: Brakeman; yardmaster; switch engine.

GRUNT: Locomotive engineer. A *traveling grunt* was a road foreman of engines *(hogs).* A *grunt* also was a lineman's ground helper. *Grunting* was working as a lineman's helper.

GUMSHOE: *See* BULL.

GUN: Track torpedo, in trainman's standard equipment, attached to a rail to signal the engineer to stop; steam locomotive injector that forces water from the tank to the boiler. To gun means to control the airbrake system from the rear of the train.

GUNBOAT: Large steel freight car.

GUT: Air hose. *Guts* is a drawbar, a locomotive's "internals."

GYM: General yardmaster.

HACK: Caboose.

HAM: Incompetent telegrapher; student telegraph operator.

HAND BOMBER or HAND GRENADE: Steam locomotive without a mechanical stoker that must be hand-fired.

HAND-ON: Train order or company mail that a crewman catches from a hoop or fork without stopping the train.

HANGING UP THE CLOCK: Boomer term for hocking a watch.

HARNESS: Passenger trainman's uniform.

HASH HOUSE: Railroad restaurant or lunch stand.

HAS WHISKERS ON IT: Designating a delayed telegraph message.

HAY: Sleep, especially on the job. A caboose was sometimes called a *hay wagon.*

HAYBURNER: Hand oil lantern; inspection torch; any live horse in streetcar or railroad service.

HEAD-END REVENUE: Money paid to railroads for hauling mail, express, baggage, newspapers, and milk in huge cans on passenger trains, usually on cars nearest to the locomotive, such shipments being *head-end traffic.*

HEAD IN: Take a sidetrack to meet an opposing train.

HEAD MAN or HEAD PIN: Freight brakeman riding the engine.

HEARSE: Caboose, which is vulnerable to fatal wrecks.

HEEL: Cars standing at end of tracks with brakes applied.

HERDER or HOSTLER: Worker who couples and uncouples engines of departing and arriving trains.

HIGH DADDY: Flying switch.

HIGH IRON: Mainline or high-speed track, laid with heavier and taller rail than is used on branch lines.

HIGH WHEELER: Passenger engine with driving wheels of large diameter; fast passenger train. One version of the Casey Jones song mentions "a right high-wheeler."

HIGHBALL: Signal given by waving an arm or a lantern in a high, wide semicircle, meaning "Come ahead," "Leave town," or "Pick up speed." It is derived from the old-time ball signal on a post, raised aloft when the track was clear. A very few such ball signals are still used in New England. To *highball* or to *ball the jack* means to make a fast run. A *highball artist* is a locomotive engineer noted for fast running.

HIGHLINER: Fast passenger train on the mainline.
HIT 'ER: Work a locomotive harder.
HIT THE DECK: Mount the top of a freight train; *dec(k)orate.*
HIT THE GRAVEL: Fall or jump off a car or locomotive or be kicked off; also called *hit the grit.*
HOBO: Tramp or migratory worker. The word may have been a corruption of "Hello, boy!" with which workers on the Burlington Route used to greet one another.
HOG: Any large steam locomotive, usually in freight service. *Hogger, hoghead, hogmaster, hogineer, hog jockey, grunt,* and *pig mauler* are terms for locomotive engineer. Some men resented these terms as disrespectful, which they rarely were intended to be. *Hoghead* is said to have originated on the Denver and Rio Grande Railroad, being used to label a brakeman's caricature of an engineer.
HOG LAW: *See* DOGCATCHERS.
HOLD HER AGAINST THE BRASS: Run an electric car at speed.
HOLE: Passing track where a train pulls in to meet another.
HOME GUARD: Railroad employee who stayed with one company, unlike the *boomer.* A *homesteader* was a boomer who got married, settled down, and became a home guard.
HOOK or BIG HOOK: Wrecking crane or auxiliary; the wrecking train itself.
HOOK 'ER UP AND PULL HER TAIL: Get a steam locomotive's reverse lever *(Johnson bar)* up on the quadrant and pull the throttle well out for high speed.
HOPPER: Steel-sided freight car that opens at the bottom to unload coal, gravel, ore, etc.
HORSE 'ER OVER: Reverse the engine. On the more modern steam locomotives this was done with compressed air, but in early days manually operated reversing equipment required much jockeying to reverse an engine while it was in motion.
HOSE COUPLER: Brakeman who handles trains by himself with a road engine around a big passenger terminal.
HOSTLER or ASHPIT ENGINEER: Any employee (usually a fireman) who services steam locomotives at division points and terminals. *See also* HERDER.
HOT: Designating a locomotive with plenty of steam pressure.
HOT JEWEL: *See* HOTBOX.
"HOT RAIL!": Lineman's shout when a train is coming.
HOT WORKER: Boilermaker repairing leaks in a locomotive firebox or flue sheet while boiler pressure is on.
HOTBOX or HOT JEWEL: Overheated journal or bearing, a frequent cause of delay and wrecks in the old days but now less common on trains equipped with ball bearings or one of several devices used to control that situation. Trainmen are sometimes called *hotbox detectors.*
HOTFOOTER: Yard engineer or conductor always in a hurry.
HOTSHOT, MANIFEST, or RED BALL: Fast train, often carrying perishables or urgently needed merchandise.
HOUSE TRACK: Line on which an engine returns to the roundhouse.
HOW MANY MS HAVE YOU GOT?: How many thousand pounds is your engine pulling? (*M* stands for 1000.)
HUMP: Artificially built knoll at the end of a freight classification yard over which cars are pushed so that they can roll on their own momentum to separate tracks to be coupled into trains; summit of a hill division at top of a major grade. *Boomers* called the Continental Divide the *Big Hump.*
HUMPBACK JOB: Local freight job. A conductor often bends over the wheel reports he writes in his caboose.
HUMPING: What an experienced telegrapher does to a mediocre receiving operator.
HUT: Brakeman's shelter built onto the rear of coal bunkers on the tenders of steam locomotives that ran through Moffat Tunnel; caboose, engine cab, switchman's shanty, or crossing watchman's shelter.
IDLER: Unloaded flatcar that is coupled just ahead of or just behind a car from which projects oversize machinery, a pipe, a log, or other very long shipment.
IN: A trainman at the home terminal and off duty is *in.*
IN THE CLEAR: Designating a train that has passed over a switch and frog so far that another train can pass it safely.
IN THE COLOR: Designating a train in a signal block waiting for a go-ahead.
IN THE DITCH: Wrecked or derailed.
IN THE HOLE: Designating a train on a sidetrack; also a lower Pullman berth, as contrasted with an upper berth, said to be *on the top.*
IN THE MUD: Designating a telegraph wire too sluggish to function.
INDIAN VALLEY LINE: Imaginary railroad at the rainbow's end, on which you can always find a good job and ideal working conditions. *Boomers* quitting a job or being fired said they were "going to the Indian Valley." Sometimes the term meant death or a railroad in the sky. *See also* BIG ROCK CANDY MOUNTAIN.
INGERSOLL: Any open-faced watch used by a railroad man.
INWARD or OUTWARD: Designating the direction in which a Boston & Maine train is moving, either toward or away from Boston.
IRON or RAIL: Track. A *single iron* is a single track.
IRON HORSE: Academic slang for a steam locomotive, not used by railroad men; telegraph transmitter.
JACK: Steam locomotive. To *ball the jack* is to make a fast run.
JACKPOT: Miscellaneous mail piled in a baggage car aisle for removal before clerks can work mail in the stalls.
JAILHOUSE SPUDS: Waffled potatoes.
JAM BUSTER: Assistant yardmaster.
JANNEY: Uncouple, derived from the automatic coupler invented by Eli H. Janney to replace the old link and pin.
JAWBONE SHACK: Switch shanty. Men chatter there.
JAY ROD: Clinker hook used for the locomotive firebox.
JERK A DRINK: Take water from a track pan, centered between the rails, without stopping a train. *Jerkwater* describes a locality serving only to supply water to steam locomotives on passing trains, a place other than a regular stop and of minor importance, such as a *jerkwater town.*
JEWEL: Journal brass. *See also* HOTBOX.
JIB: Derrick or boom.
JIGGER: Full tonnage of "dead" freight.
JIM CROW CAR: Coach formerly reserved for blacks regardless of how few passengers rode in it and of how overcrowded the rest of the train was. Laws today forbid such segregation.
JIMMIES: Four-wheel coal or ore cars.
JITNEY: Four-wheel electric truck that carries baggage inside a terminal; unregulated private automobile that cost passengers a 5-cent fare on public highways in direct competition with tax-paying trolley lines.
JOHNSON BAR: Reverse lever on a steam engine. The term's origin is unknown.
JOIN THE BIRDS: Jump from a moving engine or car, usually when a wreck seems to be imminent.
JOINT: Length of rail, generally 33 or 39 feet. *Riding to a joint* means bringing cars together so that they will couple.
JOKER: Independent or locomotive brake, part of engine-train (E-T) equipment.
JUGGLER: Member of a way-freight crew which loads and unloads less-than-carload (LCL) lots at station stops.
JUGGLING THE CIRCLE: Missing a train-order hoop.

JUICE: Electricity. A *juice fan* is an electric railway hobbyist.
JUNK: Hodgepodge of letters in a telegraph message.
JUNK PILE: Old, worn-out steam locomotive still in service.
KANGAROO COURT: Official hearing or investigation which may be held wherever most convenient, anywhere along the line, jumping around like a kangaroo, to act on mainline mix-ups or other urgent problems.
KEELEY: Water can for hot journals or bearings, derived from the Keeley cure for alcoholism.
KETTLE: Any small steam locomotive, especially a leaky old one; also called a *teakettle* or a *coffeepot.*
KEY: Part of the telegraph instrument.
KICKER: Locomotive triple valve in defective order, which throws airbrakes into emergency when only a service application is intended or sometimes by train bumping.
KING: Freight conductor or yardmaster. A *kingpin* is a conductor; a *king snipe,* the foreman of a track gang.
KISSING 'EM: Colliding.
KITCHEN: Caboose; engine cab. The firebox is the *kitchen stove.*
KNOCK OUT: Alternative term for *bump.*
KNOWLEDGE BOX: Yardmaster's office; president of the road.
LADDER: Main track of a yard from which individual tracks lead off; also called a *lead. See also* YARD.
LAP ORDER: Train-order mistake made by a dispatcher, sometimes causing a wreck because of an overlap of train meeting points.
LAPLANDER: Passenger jostled into someone else's lap in a crowded coach, subway car, or trolley car.
LAST CALL or LAST TERMINAL: Death.
LAY-BY: Passing track; sidetrack. *Laid out* means delayed.
LAYOVER: Time spent waiting for a connection with another train.
LCL: Less-than-carload lot of freight.
LEAD: Track from which yard tracks diverge.
LEANED AGAINST 'EM: Pulled gently on train.
LEFT-HAND SIDE: *See* RIGHT-HAND SIDE.
LETTERS: Service letters or references given to railroaders who resign or are discharged. Railroad job applicants often submit *letters* proving previous employment. In the old days, when these were unfavorable, *boomers* used faked letters or worked *under a flag* on someone else's certificates. *See also* separate article "CRANE WITH A BROKEN NECK."
LEVER JERKER: Operator of an interlocking tower.
LIBRARY: Caboose cupola. The trainman occupying it was sometimes called the *librarian.*
LIE-BY: Sidetrack or siding.
LIFT TRANSPORTATION: Collect fares.
LIGHT ENGINE: Road engine moving without cars attached.
LIGHTNING SLINGER: Telegraph operator.
LIKE A BELL: Descriptive phrase for perfect sending or transcribing of a Morse telegraph message.
LINCOLN PIN: *See* PINHEAD.
LINER: Mainline passenger train.
LINK AND PIN: Old-time type of coupler. The term is used to denote old-fashioned methods of railroading.
LIZARD SCORCHER: Dining-car chef or cook.
LOADS: Loaded freight cars.
LOCAL LOAD: Truckload of mail in sacks and parcels sent from a storage car directly to a car on a local train, containing mail for towns along the train's route.
LONE WOLF: *See* WOLF.
LOOKOUT: Cupola of a caboose.
LOUSE CAGE: Caboose.
LUNAR WHITE: Color of white used on some switches (except those on the mainline).
LUNCH HOOKS: A person's two hands.
LUNG: Drawbar or air hose. A *lung doctor* or *lung specialist* is a locomotive engineer who pulls out drawbars.
MAIN IRON or MAIN STEM: Main track.
MAIN PIN: Railroad company official.
MAKE A CUT: Take one or more cars from a train.
MAKE A JOINT: Couple cars.
MAKING HAY: *See* POUNDING THEIR EARS.
MANIFEST: *See* HOTSHOT.
MARKERS: Signals on the rear of all trains, flags by day and lamps by night.
MASTER MANIAC: Master mechanic, often abbreviated MM. Oil was called *master mechanic's blood* because storekeepers often doled it out sparingly.
MASTERMIND: Any railroad company official.
MAUL: Work a locomotive with full stroke and full throttle.
MEAT RUN: Fast run of perishable freight, especially livestock.
MEET ORDER: Train order specifying a definite spot where two or more trains will meet, one on a siding and the other on the *high iron.*
MERRY-GO-ROUND: Turntable, usually located just outside the roundhouse and with tracks leading into and out of it.
MIDDLE MAN or MIDDLE SWING: Second brakeman on a freight train.
MIKE: Mikado-type engine (with 2-8-2 wheel arrangement). Built originally for the Imperial Railways of Japan, it was renamed the *MacArthur* type by some United States roads during World War II.
MILEAGE HOG: Engineer or conductor, paid on a mileage basis, who uses seniority to the limit in getting good runs.
MILL: Steam locomotive; typewriter.
MITT: *See* FIST.
MIXED LOAD: Truckload of mailbags and parcels for many destinations sent from a storage car to an outside platform of the yard for further separation before forwarding.
MONKEY: When a train crew remains for too long a time on continuous duty and is caught out on the road, *the monkey gets them.* Interstate Commerce Commission rules require the crew to *tie up* until a new crew comes to relieve them. *See also* DOGCATCHERS.
MONKEY HOUSE: Caboose.
MONKEY MOTION: Walschaert or Baker valve gear on a locomotive.
MONKEY SUIT: Passenger trainman's uniform or any smart-looking garb.
MONKEY TAIL: Backup hose.
MOONLIGHT MECHANIC: Night roundhouse foreman.
MOPPING OFF: Escaping of steam.
MORSE CODE NUMBERS: 3—What time is it? 4—Where shall I go ahead? 5—Have you any business for me? 6—I am ready. 7—Are you ready? 12—Do you understand? 13—I understand. 25—Busy. 30—The end. 73—My compliments; Best regards. WIRE—Signal that preempts a circuit and takes precedence over everything except 95, the president's signal. 9—Peremptory signal meaning "Close your key for priority business from wire chief, dispatcher, etc." 27—Signal also signifying priority—very important message.
MOTHER HUBBARD: *See* CAMEL.
MOTION: Signal with a lantern to direct train movement.
MOTOR: Electric locomotive.
MOUNTIES: Messengers or *callboys* using bicycles.
MOVING SPIRIT: Train dispatcher, more often called *DS.*
MTYS: Empty freight cars.
MUCKERS: Excavators in construction work.

MUD CHICKEN: Surveyor.
MUD HEN: Saturated steam locomotive; one not superheated.
MUDHOP: Yard clerk. The *mudshop* is his or her office.
MUDSUCKER: Nonlifting locomotive injector.
MULE: Small car pusher operated by cable on narrow-gauge trackage laid between standard-gauge track to lift cars, usually coal cars, up an incline for unloading at a dump.
MUSIC MASTER: Paymaster.
MUTT-AND-JEFF PUMP: Denver and Rio Grande steam locomotive with a big air pump on the right and a small one on the left.
MUZZLE-LOADER: Hand-fired locomotive.
NEWS BUTCHER: Peddler who sells magazines, candy, souvenirs, etc., on passenger trains, usually employed today by Union News Co.
NICKEL GRABBER: Streetcar conductor in the days of the 5-cent fare.
NIGGERHEAD: Turret at the top of a locomotive boiler, over the crownsheet, from which saturated steam is taken to operate pumps, stoker, injector, and headlight turbine.
19 ORDER: Train order that need not be signed for. The operator hands it up to crew member on a hoop or delivery fork as the train slows down but does not stop. *See also* 31 ORDER.
99: Rule covering failure to protect or flag one's train.
NO-BILL or NONAIR: Nonunion railroad worker.
NOSE BAG: Lunch carried to work (like a bag of oats for a horse). To *put on the nosebag* is to eat a meal.
NOSE ON: Couple onto the head end of a locomotive.
NUMBER DUMMY or NUMBER GRABBER: Yard clerk or car clerk.
NUT BUSTER or NUT SPLITTER: Railroad machinist.
OFFICE: Any railroad job (a common *boomer* term).
OILCAN: Railroad tank car.
OLD GIRL: *See* GIRL.
OLD HAND or OLD HEAD: Experienced railroader.
OLD MAN: Superintendent or general manager.
OLE HOSS: Salvage warehouse; freight on hand.
ON CLOSED KEY: Working as a telegrapher without interruption.
ON THE ADVERTISED or ON THE CARD: According to schedule, right on time (the card is the time card).
ON THE (SLAVE) BLOCK: Out of work; unemployed.
ON THE CARPET: Short form of *dancing on the carpet.*
ON THE GROUND: On the ties, as a derailed train.
ON THE SPOT: *See* SPOT.
ON THE TOP: *See* IN THE HOLE.
OP: Telegraph operator.
OPEN or CLOSE THE GATE: Throw the switch.
OPEN-AIR NAVIGATOR: Hobo riding on top of a boxcar.
ORC: Conductor. *See also* BIG O.
ORDER BOARD: *See* BOARD.
OS: On (train) sheet, to report a train to dispatcher.
OUT: Designating a trainman at a point other than his home terminal.
OUTBOUND OPERATOR: Telegrapher capable of fast sending but not so good at receiving.
OUTLAWED: *See* DOGCATCHERS.
OUTWARD: *See* INWARD.
OVER THE KNOLL: (Getting a train) up a hill.
OVERLAP: Situation in which two block signals control the same stretch of track.
OWL: Streetcar or train that runs late at night; almost anything having to do with night.
PADDLE: Semaphore signal.
PADDLE WHEEL: Narrow-gauge steam locomotive with driving boxes outside the wheels.
PAIR OF PLIERS: Conductor's ticket punch.
PALACE: Caboose; drawing-room car built by Webster Wagner.
PAPER CAR: Baggage car carrying only newspapers.
PAPERWEIGHT or PENCIL PUSHER: Railroad clerk; office worker.
PARLOR: Caboose. A *parlor man* or *parlormaid* is the hind brakeman or flagman on a freight train.
PASSING THE CROAKER: Being examined by a company physician.
PEAKED END, POINTED END, or SHARP END: Head end of a steam-powered train.
PEANUT ROASTER: Any small steam locomotive.
PECK: Twenty minutes allowed for lunch.
PEDDLE: Set out freight cars. A *peddler* is a local freight train.
PELICAN POND: Place outside a Southern roundhouse with ooze and slime owing to the running of many steam engines 30 days without a boiler wash. Boilers were kept clean by blowing them out with blowoff cocks.
PENCIL PUSHER: *See* PAPERWEIGHT.
PERSUADER: Blower for a steam locomotive fire.
PETTICOAT: Portion of the exhaust stack that guides exhausted steam into the engine stack proper. When this is displaced, spent steam goes back through the flues, cutting off the draft from the fire.
PIE CARD or GRAZING TICKET: Meal ticket.
PIG: Steam locomotive. A *pig mauler* is an engineer; a *pigpen,* a locomotive roundhouse. *See also* HOG.
PIKE: Any railroad, but usually a short line.
PIN AHEAD AND PICK UP TWO BEHIND ONE: Cut off the engine, pick up three cars from siding, put two on the train, and set the first car back on the siding.
PIN DOPE: *See* DOPE.
PIN FOR HOME or WASH UP: Go home for the day.
PINHEAD: Brakeman. A *pin lifter* is a yard brakeman; a *pinner,* a switchman; a *pin puller,* a switchman who cuts off cars from a train; and a *Lincoln pin,* an old-style link-and-pin coupler.
PINK: Caution card; rush telegram.
PINNER: *See* PINHEAD.
PLANT: Interlocking signal system.
PLUG: "One-horse" passenger train; throttle of old-style steam locomotive. A *plug puller* is an engineer; *plugging her,* using the reverse lever as a brake instead of the air; and *plug run,* some passenger trains.
PLUSH RUN: Passenger train, especially on the mainline.
POCATELLO YARDMASTER: Derisive term for *boomers,* all of whom presumably claimed to have held, at some time, the tough job of night yardmaster at Pocatello, Idaho.
POINTED END: *See* PEAKED END.
POLE PIN: Superintendent of telegraph.
POP: Release safety valve on a locomotive boiler, wasting steam, making a loud noise, and, when engine is working hard, raising water in the boiler, thus causing the locomotive to operate less efficiently.
POP CAR: Gasoline car or *speeder,* used by section men, linemen, etc.; named for the put-put noise of a motor exhaust.
POSITIVE BLOCK: Steam locomotive engineer.
POSSUM BELLY: Toolbox built under a caboose or working car.
POUND HER: Work a steam locomotive to full capacity.
POUNDING THEIR EARS or MAKING HAY: Sleeping.
PR: Telegrapher's personnel record.
PUD: Pickup and delivery service.
PULL FREIGHT: Leave or give up a job.
PULL THE AIR: Set brakes by opening the conductor's valve or angle cock, done only in an emergency.
PULL THE CALF'S TAIL: Yank the whistle cord.
PULL THE PIN: Uncouple a car by pulling up the coupling pin; resign or quit a job.
PULLER: Switch engine hauling cars from one yard to another

at the same terminal; operator of an electric truck that transfers baggage and mail around a terminal.

PURE-FOOD LAW: Hours of Service Act. *See also* DOGCATCHERS.

PUSHER: Extra engine on the rear that assists a train in climbing a grade. When a train is very long or a grade is steep, other pushers may be used on the head end or in the middle of the train.

PUSSYFOOTER: Railroad policeman, known as a special agent.

PUT 'ER ON: Reduce air in a train's braking system. *Put 'er all on* or *big-hole her* means to apply the emergency brake.

PUTTY: *See* FOG.

QUILL: Whistle (term used especially in the South). *Quilling* is a personalized technique of blowing a steam locomotive whistle, applicable only before whistles were standardized.

RABBIT: Derail or derailer, an arrangement for preventing serious wrecks by sidetracking a runaway train, cars, or locomotive on a downgrade. Unlike regular sidetracks, the derail ends rather abruptly on flat, trackless land instead of curving back onto the mainline. *Rabbit* is a name suggesting timidity.

RACETRACK: Straight, flat stretch of track on which an engineer can safely make unusually high speed; parallel stretches of track of two competing railroads upon which rival trains race one another (despite company rules but to the delight of enginemen, trainmen, and passengers and perhaps to the secret joy of some officials).

RAG WAVER: Flagman.

RAIL: Any railroad employee. *See also* IRON.

RAILFAN or RAILROAD BUFF: Railroad hobbyist.

RAP THE STACK: Give your steam locomotive a wide-open throttle; increase speed. A *rapper* is one who works a loco too hard.

RATTLE HER HOCKS: Get speed out of a locomotive.

RATTLER: Freight train.

RAWHIDER or SLAVE DRIVER: Railroad company official or any employee who is especially hard on men and/or equipment, causing some men to do more than their share of work. He may run an engine too fast when picking up a crewman on the footboard or make a quick stop just short of the fellow who is expecting to step on but has to walk back. There are many other ways of *rawhiding.*

REAL ESTATE: Poor coal mixed with dirt or slag. When mixed with sand, it is called *seashore.*

RED BALL or BALL OF FIRE: Fast freight train; *hotshot.*

RED BOARD: Peremptory stop signal. *See also* BOARD.

RED EYE: Alternative term for *red board;* also alcoholic liquor.

RED ONION: Eating and/or sleeping quarters for railroaders.

REDCAP: Station porter, term coined in about 1900 by New York Central publicist George H. Daniels.

REEFER or RIFF: Refrigerator car.

RELEASE ANCHORS: *See* ANCHOR THEM.

REPTILE: *See* SNAKE.

A rare illustration of hoboes riding the rods in the days of wooden-bodied railroad cars. This dangerous method of free travel has long been abandoned. [Collection of Oliver Jensen]

RETAINER: Small valve located near the brake wheel for drawing off and holding air on cars' airbrake equipment.

RIDING 'EM HIGH: Traveling on the tops of boxcars.

RIDING THE BLINDS or BLINDING IT: Riding between *blind baggage* cars on a passenger train. It was uncomfortable, dangerous, often very cold, but faster than freight.

RIDING THE POINT: Riding a steam locomotive, *point* referring to the shape of the pilot (cowcatcher).

RIDING THE RODS: Obsolete hobo practice. A tramp placed a board across the truss rods under a car and rode on it. This was very hazardous even in good weather. Pelted by cinders and gravel, the tramp might doze, get careless, become too cramped, or lose his nerve and roll under the wheels.

RIDING TO A JOINT: *See* JOINT.

RIFF: *See* REEFER.

RIGHT-HAND SIDE: Engineer's side of the cab on all North American roads but the Chicago & North Western. The *left-hand side* is the fireman's side. A promoted fireman is *set up to the right-hand side.*

RINGMASTER: Yardmaster.

RIPRAP: Loose pieces of heavy stone or masonry used in some places to protect roadbeds from water erosion.

RIVET BUSTER: Steam locomotive boilermaker.

RJ: Relief telegraph operator.

ROAD HOG: Big highway vehicle that cuts railroad revenue.

ROOFED: Caught in a close clearance.

ROUGHNECK: Freight brakeman.

RUBBERNECK CAR: Observation car favored by tourists.

RULE G: "The use of intoxicants or narcotics is prohibited," a rule in the standard code adopted by the Association of American Railroads. Countless thousands of railroad men, especially *boomers,* were fired for violating Rule G, but only if they did so while on duty or about to go on duty.

RUN: The train to which a man is assigned is his *run.*

RUN LIGHT: Run an engine without any cars.

RUNAROUND: If it is your turn to work but you are not called, you have been given the *runaround* and may claim pay for the work you missed.

RUNNER: Locomotive engineer.

RUNT: Dwarf signal, installed near the ground.

RUST or STREAK OF RUST: Any railroad, especially a short line.

RUST PILE: Aged steam locomotive.

RUSTLING THE BUMS: Searching a freight train for hoboes. In bygone days, crew often collected money from freight-riding tramps at the rate of a dollar a division (a division was usually about 100 miles).

SADDLE: First step on a freight car, under the lowest *grab iron.*

SANDHOG: Laborer who works in a caisson under a river boring a tunnel for a railroad, subway, or highway.

SAP: *See* BRAKE CLUB. To *sap up binders* is to set handbrakes.

SAW BY: Perform a slow, complicated operation permitting one train to pass another on a single track when the siding is too short to hold an entire train. *Saw by* is applied to any complex move through switches that is necessitated by one train passing another.

SAWBONES: *See* CROAKER.

SAY WHEN: In Morse telegraphy, this phrase has nothing to do with whiskey in a glass but means "Report when the order has been carried out."

SCAB: Strikebreaker; any nonunion worker; car without an automatic airbrake system.

SCISSORBILL: Derisive term for an incompetent yard or road brakeman or a student in train service.

SCOOP: Fireman's shovel; step on the front and rear ends of switch engines.

SCOOT: Shuttle train.
SCRAP PILE: Worn-out locomotive still in service.
SEASHORE: Coal mixed with sand; sand in an engine sand dome.
SEAT HOG: Passenger who monopolizes more than one seat in a car or station waiting room while others are standing. He or she may spread luggage, lunch, etc., over adjacent seats.
SECRET WORKS: Automatic airbrake application; draft timbers and drawbar of a car when extracted by force. If only a drawbar is pulled out, you say, "We got a lung," but if draft timbers come out with it, you say, "We got the whole damned secret works."
SENIORITY GRABBER: Railroad man who is glad when someone above him dies, resigns, is killed, or is fired so that he can move up the seniority list to a better job.
SEPARATION: Sorting Railway Mail sacks and parcels within a storage car before transferring them to trucks.
SERPENT: *See* SNAKE.
SERVICE APPLICATION: Gradual speed reduction, as contrasted with an emergency stop caused by *wiping the clock.*
SETTING UP: Loading a baggage car with mail and parcels according to a prearranged plan to facilitate rapid unloading at various stations along the line.
SETUP: Four to six hand trucks placed in formation beside a storage-car door to facilitate the separation of mail and parcels being unloaded. Each truck is loaded with matter to be transferred to other trains or to the Railway Post Office terminal office.
SHACK: Brakeman; occupant of a caboose. A *shack's master* is the conductor of a freight train.
SHAKE 'EM UP: Switch.
SHAKING THE TRAIN: Putting on airbrakes in an emergency.
SHANTY: Caboose.
SHARP END: *See* PEAKED END.
SHINER: Brakeman's or switchman's lantern.
SHOOFLY: Temporary track, usually built around a flooded area, a wreck, or other obstacle but sometimes merely to facilitate a rerailing.
SHORT FLAGGING: Alternative term for *drawbar flagging.*
SHORT LOADS: Cars consigned to points between division points and set out on sidings at their destinations.
SHORT ONES: Freight cars to be set out en route.
SHORT-TIME CREW: Crew working overtime but not yet affected by the Hours of Service Act. *See also* DOGCATCHERS.
SHUFFLE THE DECK: Switch cars onto a *house track* at every station you pass on your run.
SHUNTING BOILER: Switch engine.
SIDE-DOOR PULLMAN: Boxcar in which hoboes steal rides.
SIDING: Passing track with a switch at both ends.
SINE: Symbol (one, two, or three letters) assigned to a telegrapher by the *old man* for use on the wire.
SINGLE IRON: *See* IRON.
SKATE: Shoe placed on a rail in a hump yard to stop freight cars with defective brakes.
SKIN YOUR EYE: Engineer's warning to the man on the opposite side of locomotive cab when approaching a curve.
SKIPPER: Train conductor.
SKYROCKETS: Red-hot cinders from a locomotive smokestack.
SLAP ON GUNS: Put an injector to work supplying boiler water.
SLAVE DRIVER: *See* RAWHIDER.
SLING MORSE: Work as a telegraph operator.
SLIPS: Bananas shipped by railroad.
SLOW BOARD: Signal to proceed at slow speed. *See also* BOARD.
SLUG: Heavy fire in a locomotive firebox.
SLUGS: Shipment of magazines, catalogs, automobile license plates, etc., in sacks weighing about 100 pounds each.
SMART ALECK: Passenger conductor.
SMOKE or SMOKE AGENT: Steam locomotive fireman. A *smoker* is an engine or a firebox. *Smoking 'em,* or *running on smoke orders,* is a dangerous, obsolete method of taking a train from one station or siding to another on a single-track line without a dispatcher's orders. You moved cautiously, continually watching for the smoke of any train that might be approaching on the same track.
SNAKE, REPTILE, or SERPENT: Switchman, named for the initial letter in Switchmen's Union of North America.
SNAKE HEAD: Rail coming loose from the ties that pierced the floor of a car. This was a fairly common accident with the strap-iron rails of the early 1800s.
SNAP: Push or pull with another engine. A *snapper* is the engine that does the pushing or pulling.
SNIPE: Track laborer. A *king snipe* is his boss.
SNOOZER: Sleeping car.
SNUFF DIPPERS: Coalburning engines that burn lignite, which on some roads was the color of snuff.
SOAK: Saturated steam locomotive.
SODA JERKER: Locomotive fireman.
SOFT BELLIES: Cars with wooden frames.
SOFT-DIAMOND SPECIAL: Bituminous-coal train.
SOFT PLUG: Fusible plug in the crownsheet of a locomotive that is supposed to drop when water gets below the top of the sheet.
SOLID CAR: Completely filled mail storage car.
SOLID TRACK: Track full of cars.
SOW BELLY: *See* WHALE BELLY.
SPAR: Pole used to shove cars into the clear when switching. *See also* STAKE.
SPARE BOARD: *See* BOARD.
SPEED GAUGER: Locomotive engineer.
SPEEDER: *See* POP CAR.
SPEEDY: Callboy; crew caller. Some callboys used bicycles.
SPIKE A TORCH: Throw a fusee.
SPOT: Place a car in a designated position; also rest, sleep, or lunch period on company time. *On the spot* means an opportunity for railroad men to take what is now known as a coffee break, chew the rag, or swap experiences.
SPOT BOARD: Guide used by section men in surfacing or ballasting track in order to obtain an even roadbed.
SPOTTER: Spy; company man assigned to snoop around and check up on employees, especially when strikes are threatened. *See also* CHECKER.
SQUAWKER: Steam locomotive whistle.
SQUEEZERS: Car-retarding system used in some railroad yards.
SQUIRRELING: Climbing up the side of a car.
STAFF OF IGNORANCE: *See* BRAKE CLUB.
STAKE: Pole used in a perilous, now-extinct method of switching. A *cut* of cars was shoved by a *stake* to the car immediately in front of the engine. This method was supposed to be superior to the ordinary method of *batting 'em out* because of less wear and tear on drawbars and less damage to freight, but the human casualties gave more than one yard the nickname "slaughterhouse." Another meaning of *stake* was the money a *boomer* saved on a job so that he could quit and eat regularly while seeking another job.
STAKE DRIVER: Any engineering department man.
STALL: Space inside a mail or baggage car containing mail or parcels consigned to a certain destination and separated from other shipments by removable steel posts.
STARGAZER: Brakeman who fails to see signals.
STARVATION LIST: *See* BOARD.
STEM: Track or right-of-way. The *main stem* is the mainline.

STEM-WINDER: Climax type of geared locomotive; trolley car without brakes.

STICK: Staff formerly used on certain stretches of track to control the block (engine crews took it from one station to another); pen or stylus used to transcribe telegraph messages.

STINGER: Brakeman, derived from the initial letter B(ee) in Brotherhood of Railroad Trainmen.

STINK BUGGY or STINKER: Bus. A *stinker* is also a *hotbox.*

STIRRUP: First step of a freight car, under the lowest *grab iron.*

STOCK PEN: Railroad yard office.

STOCKHOLDER: Any zealous employee always looking out for the company's interests.

STORAGE CAR: Baggage car or (during rush periods) Railway Express car containing a mixed shipment of parcels and mail sacks consigned to certain terminals for sorting and rerouting to various destinations via other trains.

STRAW BOSS: Foreman of a small gang; acting foreman.

STRAWBERRY PATCH: Railroad yard studded with red lights as seen from the rear door of a caboose.

STREAK OF RUST: *See* RUST.

STRETCH: Railroad terminal located between divisions.

STRETCH 'EM OUT: Take up slack in couplings and drawbars.

STRING: Several cars coupled together; telegraph wire.

STRING OF VARNISH: *See* VARNISH.

STRUGGLE FOR LIFE: Existence in a railroad boarding house.

STUDE TALLOW: Student fireman. *See also* TALLOWPOT.

STUDENT: Learner in telegraph, train, or engine service.

SUCK IT BY: Make a *flying switch.*

SWELLHEAD: Conductor or locomotive engineer.

SWING A BUG: Make a good job of braking. *See* BUG.

SWING MAN: Alternative term for *middle man.*

SWITCH LIST: Bill of fare at a railroad eating house.

SWITCH MONKEY: Switchman.

TAIL OVER HER BACK: Designating an engine with a full head of steam, with a plume resembling a squirrel's tail from the safety valve.

TAKE THE RUBBER OUT OF THEM: Disconnect the air hoses on a train.

TAKING YOUR MINUTES: Stopping for lunch.

TALLOWPOT: Steam locomotive fireman, so called from the melted tallow used to lubricate valves and shine the engine.

TANK: Steam locomotive tender. A *tanker* is a tank car used in hauling oil, water, milk, chemicals, or other liquids.

TAP LINE: Short railroad usually owned or controlled by the industry it serves, *tapping* (connecting with) a trunk line.

TEAKETTLE: *See* KETTLE.

TEAM TRACK: Track where wagons or trucks could unload cars.

TELLTALES: Any device that serves as a warning; specifically, the row of strips hanging down a short distance in front of a tunnel or low bridge to inform trainmen riding the car tops that they'd better duck.

TERMINAL LOAD: Shipment of mail consigned to a certain Railway Post Office terminal office for sorting and reshipment in other sacks.

TEST: Conditions created by an official to learn whether a train crew obeys rules.

30: Telegraph term meaning "the end" or "no more." It originated when a telegraph operator on an Eastern road suddenly died of heart failure before completing a message he was sending, his last word being "30."

31 ORDER: Train order that must be signed for. The train must stop to pick it up. *See also* 19 ORDER.

THOUSAND-MILER: Black satin or blue percale shirt worn by *boomer* crewmen, expected to last for 1000 miles between washings. The usual basis of a day's work was 100 miles, so two shirts could last from one payday to the next.

THREE-BAGGER: Train pushed or pulled by three engines (a baseball derivative).

THROTTLE JERKER: Steam locomotive engineer.

THROWING AWAY THE DIAMONDS: Missing the firedoor with a scoop of coal and spilling some of it.

TIE 'EM DOWN: Set handbrakes on cars.

TIE ON: Couple on. To *tie 'em together* is to couple cars.

TIE UP: Stop the train for a meal or for rest.

TIER: Pile of mailbags or parcels occupying the full width of each end of a car.

TIMKENIZED: Equipped with Timken roller bearings.

TIN CAN: *See* CAN.

TIN LIZARD: Streamlined or diesel-powered train.

TING-A-LING: Small engine with a tinny bell.

TISSUE: Train order. *See also* FLIMSY.

TOAD: Derail (*see also* RABBIT). A *car toad* is a car inspector.

TOEPATH or TOWPATH: Running board of a steam locomotive; *catwalk* on top of boxcars; part of a railroad embankment lying between the ends of ties and the shoulders of fill.

TONK or WHEEL BEATER: Car repairer.

TONNAGE HOUND: Trainmaster or other official who insists on longer or heavier trains than the crew and/or the motive power can handle efficiently.

TOP BLOWN OFF: Term designating a flatcar.

TOP DRESSER DRAWER: Upper bunk in a caboose.

TOWER BUFF: *Railfan* so avid that he ignores signs such as "Private," "No admittance," and "Stay out" in interlocking towers and other railroad structures.

TOWPATH: *See* TOEPATH.

TRAFFIC: Aggregation of telegraph messages to be moved or transmitted.

TRAIN LINE: Pipe carrying compressed air for airbrakes.

TRAMPIFIED: The way a boomer looked when long out of work. His clothes were "ragged as a barrel of sauerkraut," and he needed "a dime's worth of decency" (shave).

TRAVELING CARD: Membership card given by a railroad brotherhood to a man seeking a job; empty slip bill.

TRAVELING GRUNT: Road foreman of engines; traveling engineer; sometimes called a *traveling man.*

TRICK: Shift; hours of duty.

TRIMMER: Engine working in a hump yard that picks out misdirected cars and shoves them to clear. *See* HUMP.

TWO-WHEELER: Two-wheeled hand truck for transferring baggage and mail around a station.

TURN IN WIND: Admit compressed air from engine to train.

TURNAROUND: Usual name for a train that leaves a point, proceeds to another point, and returns to the original spot, with the same crew, in one operation.

TWIST 'ER TAIL: Open the locomotive throttle wider.

UNCLE SAM: Any Railway Post Office clerk.

UNDER THE TABLE: Just as a man who "can't take his liquor" is sometimes actually *under the table,* so figuratively is a telegraph operator when messages are being sent to him faster than he can receive them.

UNDERGROUND HOG: Chief engineer.

UNLOAD: Get off a train hurriedly.

VARNISH: Passenger train; also called *varnished job, varnished shot, string of varnish, varnished wagons,* etc. The terms are not applied to modern streamliners.

WABASH: Hit cars going into adjacent tracks (*see* CORNERED); also the officially frowned-upon practice of slowing, instead of stopping, for a stop signal at a crossing of another railroad. The engineer looked up and down to make sure everything was safe; then he resumed speed, having saved a little time by not stopping entirely. *Wabash* also means a heavy fire in the firebox.

WAGON: Railroad car (English term).

WALK THE DOG: Wheel a freight train so fast that the cars sway from side to side.

WALK UP AGAINST THE GUN: Ascend a steep grade with the injector on.

WALL STREET NOTCH: Forward corner of the reverse lever quadrant of a steam engine (more often called *company notch*). A locomotive worked that way because of the heaviness of the train pays maximum dividends.

WASH UP: *See* PIN FOR HOME.

WASHOUT: Stop signal, waved violently by using both arms swung in downward arc by day or by swinging a lamp in low, wide circle across the tracks at night.

WATCH YOUR PINS: Be careful when walking around stacks of ties, rails, or other obstacles.

WAYCAR: Caboose; car of local freight.

WEARING THE BLUE: A blue flag or blue light placed on a car indicates that it is being worked on and must not be moved or coupled into.

WEED BENDER: Railroaders' derisive term for a cowboy, other such epithets being *hay shaker, clover picker,* and *plow jockey.* The common term for cowboy, *cowpuncher,* has a railroad origin; cowboys prod the cattle into and out of stock trains.

WENT FOR THE AIR: Pulled the airbrake valve. Conductors do this in an emergency when the engineer ignores their stop signal.

WESTINGHOUSE or WINDJAMMER: Airbrake, invented by George Westinghouse.

WET MULE IN THE FIREBOX: Bad job of firing a locomotive.

WHALE BELLY or SOW BELLY: Coal car with a drop bottom.

WHEEL BEATER: *See* TONK.

WHEEL 'EM: Let a train run without braking. You say *wheeling the berries* when you mean hauling a berry crop at high speed, or *highballing* them.

WHEEL MONKEY: Car inspector.

WHEN DO YOU SHINE?: What time were you called for?

WHISKERS: Seniority. *See also* BUMP.

WHISTLE-STOP: Term for a small locality, which originated from the fact that a passenger-train engineer whistles an acknowledgment of his conductor's signal to stop at the next station, a place where he normally doesn't stop.

WHISTLES OUT A FLAG: (Engine) blows one long and three short blasts for the brakeman to protect the rear of the train. One form of ending a letter to a friend is "Yours till the last flag is whistled in."

WHITE FEATHER: Steam plume over a safety valve, indicating high boiler pressure.

WHITE RIBBONS: White flags denoting an extra train.

WHITE SHIRT: Railroad company official.

WHITEWASH CAR: Milk car.

WIDEN ON HER: Open the throttle more; increase speed.

WIGWAG: One type of grade-crossing signal.

WILLIE: Waybill for a loaded car; *weary Willie,* hobo.

WIND: Airbrakes.

WINDJAMMER: *See* WESTINGHOUSE.

WING HER: Set brakes on a moving train.

WIPE THE CLOCK: Make an emergency application of the airbrake. *See also* BIG HOLE.

WISE GUY: Station agent; anyone who seems to know it all.

WOLF or LONE WOLF: Nonunion worker.

WOODEN-AXLE PIKE: Short railroad in very poor condition.

WORK WATER: Some steam locomotive engineers preferred to *work the water* (operate the injector and watch the water glass or gauge cocks), normally a fireman's job.

WORKING A CAR: Unloading a storage mail car.

WORKING MAIL: Mail in sacks and pouches consigned to Railway Post Office cars to be *worked,* or sorted, in transit.

WOUND HER UP: Finished a work shift; got speed quickly.

WRECKING CREW: Relief crew; derogatory term derived from the difficulty that regular men sometimes experience in rearranging the contents of a car used by relief men.

WRONG IRON: Main track on which the current of traffic is in the opposite direction.

WYE: Tracks running off the mainline or *lead,* forming a letter *Y,* used for reversing cars and engines when no turntable is available.

X: Empty car. *XXX* is an empty car in bad order.

YARD: System of tracks for making up trains or storing cars (*boomers'* version: "System of *rust* surrounded by a fence and inhabited by a dumb bunch of natives who will not let a train in or out"); also called *garden* and *field. Yard geese* are yard switchmen; *yard goat,* a switching engine.

YM: Yardmaster.

YOUR EIGHT: Eight hours of rest required by the Hours of Service Act.

ZULU: Boxcar used exclusively by an emigrant family with its household goods, farm equipment, and sometimes livestock in moving to new location. *Zulu* had two meanings: the car itself and the car plus all its contents. This method of travel was not uncommon in homesteading days on Western United States and Canadian prairies, although Canadian homesteaders usually rode in colonist cars, shipping their possessions by freight. At that time colonist cars were the cheapest and crudest form of rail passenger travel. The term *Zulu cars* has a British origin. After the British had conquered the African Zulu tribes, they hired some of the warriors, with their wives, children, and possessions, to make an exhibition tour of England by rail in special cars. Later, a modified version of this idea spread to the New World.

BIBLIOGRAPHY: Benjamin A. Botkin and Alvin F. Harlow, *A Treasury of Railroad Folklore,* Crown, New York, 1953; Freeman Hubbard, *Railroad Avenue,* McGraw-Hill, New York, 1945.

LIRR *See* LONG ISLAND RAIL ROAD.

Livestock

Most of America's agricultural land is used partly or wholly to produce cattle, sheep, and hogs. This vast meat production would be practically worthless without quick, efficient, and economical transportation of the animals to points with a cash demand for them.

The earliest shipment of cattle by rail was in 1852, when a herd of 150 head was moved by a roundabout route from Lexington, Kentucky, to New York City. First they were driven overland to Cincinnati, which took about a week. There they were loaded into boxcars and shipped to Cleveland, where they were transferred to a Lake Erie steamboat and sent to Buffalo. After several days' rest, they were driven on foot again, this time to Canandaigua, New York, from which they were hauled by rail in immigrant cars to Albany. Here they were unloaded again and rested for 2 days in a feedlot. Finally they were taken down the Hudson River by steamboat to New York, after being en route for nearly a month.

Improvements followed rapidly. Stock cars were roofed, and in 1860 the first double-decked car for small animals was put into use. Today, railroads have fleets of stock cars of standardized dimensions built under specifications for animal comfort and safety in transit. Railroads also provide expedited service for such shipments. Probably no other commodity is more perishable. The roads recognize this by running regular livestock trains whose schedules are worked out to ensure the quickest possible delivery.

The wider distribution, or movement, of livestock creates problems. While the animals are being moved from place to place, inhumane treatment may depreciate their value. Furthermore, there is a hazard of infectious diseases that could spread to human beings unless the shipments are properly regulated and policed by authorities trained for that purpose. In 1884 Congress gave the Secretary of Agriculture power to regulate the interstate shipment of livestock, to which it later added amendments as additional needs arose. Individual states legislated rules of their own. Most of these regulations were designed to guard against the spread of such animal diseases as tuberculosis, hog cholera, foot-and-mouth disease, scabies, anthrax, and Bang's disease.

The 28-hour law, as amended, prescribes the maximum length of time during which livestock in interstate movement can be confined in railroad cars without being unloaded for feed, water, and rest. Besides being a humane act, the provisions of this law prevent an undue shrinkage in weight, which most shippers probably regard as far more important.

Shippers must sign a uniform livestock contract. In addition to stating the terms under which the carrier accepts a shipment, information is required on the number and kind of animals, their origin, the shipper's name, the consignee, destination, and route. The railroad keeps a copy of this contract, the shipper gets the original, and a third copy may be mailed to the consignee. The shipper may or may not sign a 36-hour release authorizing the carrier to extend from 28 to 36 hours the time of confinement in cars without unloading for feed, water, and rest, 36 hours now being the legal maximum. Finally, the shipper must present health certificates or other affidavits, if required, before the road accepts the animals.

The local freight agent then fills in waybills, which are given to the train conductor and must accompany each car to its final destination. These waybills include all pertinent details of the shipment. If government certificates also are required, they are attached to the waybills. The railroads cooperate with livestock markets, meat packers, the National Livestock Loss Prevention Board, humane societies, and other agencies interested in the safe shipment of animals.

BIBLIOGRAPHY: Frank Benton, *Cowboy Life on the Sidetrack,* Western Stories Syndicate, Denver, 1903; Robert S. Henry, *This Fascinating Railroad Business,* 3d ed., rev., Bobbs-Merrill, Indianapolis, 1946; James A. Michener, *Centennial,* Random House, New York, 1974.

Locomotive Drifting This is not a passive act like, for instance, lying back on your oars in a rowboat on a quiet stream. When a steam locomotive engineer "drifts," he doesn't just shut off the throttle and give the boiler and cylinders a well-earned rest. It takes as much careful handling for him to go down a grade as to adjust the throttle and reverse the lever while climbing a back-breaking mountain. Some of the greatest damage may be done when the steam supply is shut off and the locomotive allowed to drift leisurely. The reasons for this, while too technical and complicated to explore here, have to do with lubrication and the action of the pistons drawing pumplike back and forth through the cylinders, building up compression on one side and creating a partial vacuum on the other.

Locomotive Obstacle Course Course at Erie, Pennsylvania, less than ½ mile long. It may present the roughest track conditions any locomotive will have to face in actual service. This is General Electric's (GE's) riding-quality test track, located on an East Erie Commercial Railroad spur. This line enables the company's locomotive and car equipment department to study locomotive reaction to various types of abnormal track conditions. One set of rails 819 feet long simulates low rail joints with ¾ inch between the high and low joints. Another section has a 1½-inch difference between high and low rail joints. A third set has a ¾-inch lateral wave in rail length for a total distance of 819 feet, followed, after a space of 936 feet of straight, level track, by a last section where the lateral wave amplitude is increased to 1½ inches. The effects noted in GE tests result in corrective measures for units that are not to be operated on particularly rough track.

Locomotives, Bicentennial Painted In 1976 at least two dozen railroads in United States each repainted one of their diesel locomotives red, white, and blue, some with big stars, flags, eagles, and other patriotic symbols, for the nation's bicentennial year. Some locomotives were renumbered 1776. All were kept in regular service as rolling advertisements of the roads' patriotism. Many caboose and some passenger cars, also bedecked in that manner, continued to run in trains as usual.

Possibly only three steam locomotives were repainted red, white, and blue. Only one of them wore that livery in regular service: No. 1, an 0-6-0 *fireless cooker* (steam engine without a firebox) on an industrial road, Beaunit Corp. of Elizabethtown, Tennessee. Because of her type and her coloring, No. 1 attracted so much attention that on October 11 and 12 Beaunit had her pull three Southern Railway sight-seeing cars on seven 4-mile round trips between Elizabethtown and Sycamore Shoals. Such large overflow crowds showed up that many prospective passengers could not ride the limited-capacity train.

The other two bicentennial-hued steam locos hauled the *American Freedom Train* (AFT) in special service. One was an ex-Reading T-1 type, No. 2102, which had the first turn at wheeling the AFT. The other was an ex-Southern Pacific Daylight type, No. 4440, which pulled that train west of the Mississippi but was temporarily taken out of service and replaced by a diesel while the Union Pacific's Omaha shops repaired her excessive flange wear. *See* FREEDOM TRAIN, AMERICAN.

New cars on the Chicago Elevated were painted red, white and blue for the United States bicentennial of 1976. **[Chicago Transit Authority]**

Locomotives, Decorated For over a century steam engines were draped with flags, streamers, bunting, evergreens, flowers, etc., for railroad employees' Fourth of July picnics, first and last runs, presidential specials, the homecoming of national heroes, golden spike ceremonies, and anniversaries. Some passenger cars and cabooses also were festooned, but the engine was the favorite. Crew members, often assisted by fellow employees, used ingenuity in placing the ornaments.

That practice was in addition to the personal decoration of locos applied by hoggers to suit their own tastes prior to about the 1880s. Among such items were elk antlers, an Indian figure with bow and arrow, the Masonic emblem, and the Brotherhood of Locomotive Engineers insigne. These were so common as to attract little or no attention.

David Fant, a Southern Railway engineer and evangelist, kept on the pilot of No. 1456 a replica of an open Bible with the legend "Thy word is truth." A Michigan engineer mounted on his pilot beam a brightly painted cast-iron image of a Negro servant in livery, originally used as a hitching post. Each morning before he started on his run his wife would place a bouquet of fresh flowers in the figure's outstretched hand.

In 1944 a "war of the roses" occurred on the Boston & Maine (B&M). Several commuters brought big bunches of fresh-cut flowers to Boston's North Station to decorate engine No. 2386. Rivalry ensued. Other B&M passengers raided their own gardens, and for weeks the smoky ends of suburban trains looked and smelled like rolling floral shows.

Prior to World War I, whenever Presidents of the United States traveled by rail, engine crews vied in their efforts to adorn the locos that pulled their special trains. Some were quite elaborate. A Southern Pacific cap-stacked 10-wheeler drawing President Benjamin Harrison's special was profuse with wreaths, streamers, drapery, floral emblems, shields, flags, and on the pilot, beause of his military record, two small cannons, two swords, and a drum. Almost as impressive was Pennsy engine No. 142, behind which President Grover Cleveland rode on his honeymoon trip from Washington to St. Louis in 1886. Commodore George Dewey's homecoming by rail after the Battle of Manila Bay likewise had a gala engine display.

In 1860, when the Prince of Wales (later King Edward VII) toured Canada, locomotive No. 12 of the European & North American Railway (since divided among the Canadian Pacific, Canadian National, and Maine Central) was named *Prince of Wales* for him and given a large cast-iron plate on which the royal coat-of-arms was painted in bas-relief, in front of her smokebox. Two colorful cast-iron statuettes of Scottish Highlanders about 3 feet tall were attached to the pilot beam where flag brackets normally stood, their right arms extended aloft to hold signal flags.

The year 1883 saw the Northern Pacific opened from St. Paul to Portland, and a special train was pulled by engine No. 154, flaunting flags and cheesecloth, to a spike-driving ceremony. Aboard were former President Ulysses S. Grant, Henry Villard, president of the road, and other notables. Seventy years later Congress passed a law against displaying the Stars and Stripes on the top, back, or sides of a locomotive or car.

Locomotives, Diesel *See* DIESEL-ELECTRIC LOCOMOTIVES; DIESEL-HYDRAULIC LOCOMOTIVES.

Locomotives, Double-Ended While locomotives of this type were popular in the British Isles and continental Europe and operated in South America, India, New Zealand, Australia, and elsewhere, relatively few ran in the United States, possibly only one in Canada, and three in Mexico. Nearly all were narrow-gauge woodburners; all could run in either direction without being turned, and, with more power than single-unit engines, were generally effective in dragging trains up steep mountain grades, which was the main reason they were designed and built.

The many Forney engines which ran on New York and Chicago city elevated railways and various suburban lines in the late 1800s superficially resembled double-enders in that they were rigid-wheelbased and could go in either direction. But they were not true double-enders, each being a single locomotive, not Siamese twins drawing steam from the same firebox and not twin-stacked.

Horatio Allen (1802–1890), the leading United States railroad authority of the early 1800s, designed the first double-enders used in the United States. At that time he was chief engineer of the pioneer South Carolina Canal & Railroad Company (SCC&R). He had spent months in England studying its railways and had made history by piloting the first locomotive that pulled a train in the New World, the British-built *Stourbridge Lion* on the Delaware and Hudson Canal Co. at Honesdale, Pennsylvania.

In 1829 Allen built the SCC&R rail line, a fairly level track stretching from Charleston to Hamburg, South Carolina. He designed its third, fourth, fifth, and sixth engines, all double-enders built at the West Point Foundry in New York City and based on the concept that more axles under a locomotive not only distribute its weight better but also add to its tractive effort. Those four were of radical design, beginning with the world's first double-ender, the *South Carolina,* delivered with a gala ceremony in January 1832 and put to work a month later.

The other three were the *Charleston* and *Barnwell* (1833) and the *Edisto* (1834). Each of the four consisted of two 2-2-0 locomotives connected back to back, but with only one firebox for both, one throttle valve, one escape valve, and one reversing mechanism, but, as in all other locomotives of its day, no cab.

This bold experiment did not work out quite as well as Allen had hoped. It kept his mechanics busy on repair jobs. Pipes and axles got broken. The wheels, of cast iron and wood, had to be replaced by cast-iron wheels with wrought-iron tires. After 11 months' service the *South Carolina*'s boiler failed, idling her for 4 months; shortly thereafter she had to be shopped again, for boiler alterations and new frames. A sister engine, the *Charleston,* had valve-gear trouble.

An SCC&R committee reported that the problems caused by these engines had nothing to do with their basic design but were due to unsound materials, imperfect workmanship, and, especially, the inadequate proportion of the working gear to the stress they endured. Other difficulties, according to the committee, were the engines' velocity, their relatively heavy trains, and the mishaps caused by lack of experienced help. But no more double-enders were built for the South Carolina road. Even so, Horatio Allen was years ahead of his time. Given better materials, tools, and track and more expert employees, his design might have succeeded.

Not until 1866 were additional double-enders built. Then Robert F. Fairlie, superintendent of an Irish railway, revived Allen's idea by building a double-ender for a narrow-gauge railway in Wales. One of the double-enders built in America under Fairlie's patents, by William Mason in 1871, was the 0-6-6-0 type *Janus,* named for the two-faced Roman god. It was really two engines atached back to back, each having its own frames, driving wheels, cylinders, smokebox, and wood-fuel bunker. Unlike the Allen type, which hauled wood and water on a tender at the rear, this one's fuel bunker was carried on her side. Both *Janus* engines had a common boiler and a single throttle. The firebox, with a middle door, was located longitudinally instead of transversely. *See also* MASON, WILLIAM.

The driving wheels, 42 inches in diameter, were pivotally mounted, turning on a truck, and there were four 15- by 22-inch cylinders. Total weight was 163,520 pounds. This design permitted the use of a larger boiler than would otherwise have been possible and a more even distribution of weight with a lighter axle load.

The *Janus* served as a helper engine up steep hills on the Boston & Providence, then the Boston & Albany, and finally the Lehigh Valley, where she was eventually painted white with gold stripes and assigned to the pay train. Finally, she was cut into two separate 0-6-0s, one being used for switching service at Sayre, Pennsylvania, and the other for heating service at Perth Amboy, New Jersey.

In 1873, the Duke of Sutherland had a Fairlie double-ender built at the Vulcan Foundry and gave her to the Denver and Rio Grande Railroad, then being built. She was an 0-4-4-0 with four 10- by 12-inch cylinders and 30-inch drivers, weighing 162,000 pounds. The narrow-gauge road named her *Mountaineer,* numbered her 101, and put her to work as a helper on La Veta Pass in the charge of John Moulton. Moulton, representing her English builder, had come to Denver with the engine to assist in assembling her and had liked Colorado so much that he never returned to England. In 1883, for a reason unknown today, the *Janus* was cut up for scrap.

Meanwhile, Canada's only chronicled double-ender, the *Caledon,* was put to work in freight service on the narrow-gauge Toronto, Grey & Bruce Railway (TG&B) between Toronto and Owen Sound. Built originally for use on Caledon Mountain, a very stiff grade, she had trouble in rounding a horseshoe curve there; in addition, it was difficult to balance her on a turntable. Her engineer had to handle two engines under one roof. He sat on one side, with two firemen on the left. Those firemen had uniquely unpleasant duties. They had to go up and get the fuel wood from what they called "the baskets," above the boiler, toss it down to the deck, then scramble down and fire. Every time the main valve needed tallow, regardless of weather conditions, one of them had to walk over the tank and down to the front of the engine. The *Caledon* was an 0-6-6-0 type with copper fireboxes and 145 pounds steam pressure. In 1881, the Canadian Pacific (now CP Rail) took over the TG&B, standardized it, and scrapped the *Caledon.*

Mexico's three double-enders were designed by the Mexican Central's mechanical superintendent, built in the United States at the Rhode Island Locomotive Works, delivered in 1892 and 1893, and numbered 150, 151, and 152. Each was a 2-6-6-2, fastened back to back, with a cab in the middle. After a few years of service, the Mexican Central rebuilt all three of its double-enders along conventional lines.

In 1897 Baldwin built a double-ender for the standard-gauge McCloud River Railroad, which extended 125 miles between Upton and Alturas, California, with sharp curves and many switchbacks, and carried mostly lumber. The locomotive, No. 6, joined cab to cab, was designed so that each engine could, if desired, be operated as a separate unit. Each unit had its own throttle lever, but the reverse levers were connected. Either lever could control both sets of link motion. The units were equipped with Vauclain compound cylinders and had fuel-wood racks and tanks alongside the boiler. Total weight of the double-ender was 161,400 pounds. It could haul 125 tons up a 7 percent grade.

After acquiring control of the McCloud River Railroad, the Southern Pacific assigned No. 6 to a lumber company and cut it into separate units for switching chores around the mill. One of the twins was bought by a construction company and used in building a dam for a water supply company. Later she helped to create the Pageant of the Pacific on Exposition Island.

Another double-ender was the Raub Central Power locomotive, an oddity built by the Grant Locomotive Works in Paterson, New Jersey. She had two small boilers, each with firedoors on both sides, and a smoke flue going back to a stack in the cab. Vertical cylinders transmitted the power through a central shaft. Christian Raub himself had sold stock to pay for building his novelty and have her shipped to his home city, St. Louis, where she was given a test run pulling several coaches. She rocked so violently that she was considered unsafe. Raub sent her back to the Grant works, where she rusted away on a weed-grown track and was finally scrapped.

Although double-enders as a whole found little favor in North America, the type was instrumental in developing the massive and tremendously popular Mallets, which were used successfully for many years in hauling long, heavy freight trains. See MALLET.

BIBLIOGRAPHY: Angus Sinclair, *Development of the Locomotive Engine,* annotated ed. by John H. White, Jr., M.I.T., Cambridge, Mass., 1970; John H. White, Jr., *American Locomotives: An Engineering History, 1830–1880,* Johns Hopkins, Baltimore, 1968.

Locomotives, Experimental

Locomotives, Experimental An experimental locomotive was the woodburning *Vixen,* which William Mason built for the Dubuque & Iowa City Railroad in 1861. According to locomotive historian Charles E. Fisher, she was a 2-2-0 with a woodshed tender and an attached baggage car but looked like an eight-wheeler with the front pair of drivers and rear pilot wheels missing. There is no record of how long or how effectively she operated. See MASON, WILLIAM.

Somewhat like both the *Vixen* and the more modern gas-electric "doodlebugs" was the *Shakopee* (named for a Sioux Indian chief), a combined locomotive and passenger-baggage car, one of the relatively few successful motive-power oddities. W. Romans, master mechanic of the Columbus & Indianapolis Central, built this "dummy" type for the Minnesota Valley (MV) line in his own railroad's Columbus, Ohio, shops. With 10- by 18-inch cylinders, 57-inch driving wheels, and 160 pounds of steam pressure, she used to make four trips daily between Minneapolis and West St. Paul, starting slowly but attaining a high speed. Later, the MV used her as a pay car and still later leased her to the Northern Pacific for official inspection trips while that road was being built. She went to the scrap pile in the late 1870s.

Unlike almost everything else was the Raub Central Power engine, which resembled a small electric loco of later date. Built in 1886 by Grant Locomotive Works at Paterson, New Jersey, she had cylinders set upright in the center and connected with her eight wheels (all of them drivers) at right angles by means of a revolving disk on an axle between the center drivers. See PATERSON, NEW JERSEY.

Another freak built in Paterson was designed by Eugene Fontaine of Detroit and built by the Grant Locomotive Works in 1881. Her driving wheels were located in the very rare position of above the boiler, placed in

Two experimental locomotives: **(above)** *Raub Central Power engine, built in 1886 with her cylinders set upright in the center; and* **(below)** *the Fontaine freak of 1881, whose driving wheels were located above the boiler, a very rare position. [Collection of Freeman Hubbard]*

such a way that frictional contact caused their tread to press upon and transmit motion to the carrier wheels. She was tried out in service on several railroads on many kinds of trains and received much publicity but remained little more than a curiosity. After a few years she was converted to an ordinary eight-wheeler.

Engines with more than two cylinders were not rare, but Henry F. Shaw's four-cylinder type was unlike just about everything else before or after his time. She resembled an average 4-4-0, but instead of a single cylinder on each side of her front end she carried two cylinders alongside each other. Thus it was necessary to counterbalance the drivers. Hinkley built the Shaw engine in about 1881. The Boston & Providence, Camden & Atlantic, and Reading tried her out, but the rest of her history is unrecorded.

One engine, widely criticized as the Holman absurdity, built by Baldwin about 1897, was actually less absurd, according to Fisher, than were many other freak contraptions. W. J. Holman designed her to make high speeds with her driving wheels contacting small wheels between them and the rails. The principle was not without merit. She actually hauled trains on the Jersey Central. "But," says Fisher, "she rocked like a canoe in mid-ocean, and her crew were ready to jump whenever she took a curve. Moreover, she often broke down and spent much of her life in the shops."

There were many other experimental locos, some worthless, others with good ideas inadequately adapted, and still others that played a major role in steam locomotive development.

BIBLIOGRAPHY: Henry B. Comstock, *The Iron Horse,* Crowell, New York, 1971; Angus Sinclair, *Development of the Locomotive Engine,* annotated ed. by John H. White, Jr., M.I.T., Cambridge, Mass., 1970; John H. White, Jr., *American Locomotives: An Engineering History, 1830–1880,* Johns Hopkins, Baltimore, 1968.

Locomotives, Gas-Turbine-Electric First developed in Switzerland in 1941, these locomotives never took hold in America except for the Union Pacific's (UP's) fleet of 30, built by General Electric at Erie, Pennsylvania. The world's only fleet of its kind, it challenged for slightly more than 10 years the universally accepted diesel-electric power. The UP's first turbine was delivered in 1958 and the last one in 1961, but the bold experiment lasted until the end of 1969. No turbine locomotive has been operated on any mainline railroad in this country since then.

Designed to haul heavy tonnage over prairies and up and down mountain grades, these power plants on wheels while on the Union Pacific ran only between Council Bluffs, Iowa, and Salt Lake City, Utah. The performance of the 4500-horsepower machines of the early 1950s pleased the UP so much that it ordered 8500-horsepower behemoths built on the same principle, turbines that could make 12 miles per hour on straight, level track with 735 loaded cars, a ponderous train 7 miles long, or walk up the 1.53 percent grade of Utah's Echo Canyon with a 5000-ton drag.

These locomotives were the mightiest internally powered units of their day. It was routine for one of them to handle more than 4200 tons of freight in a single train from Omaha, Nebraska, to Cheyenne, Wyoming. To duplicate this achievement by highway transportation would require about 170 of the largest types of truck trailers, each hauling 25 tons of lading. The superturbines were 16 feet high and 179 feet long, with tender, had 12 axles on C-C trucks, and could make a top speed of 76 miles per hour.

The locomotive's power was compressed into a relatively small space. An 8500-horsepower giant yielded about 47 horsepower per foot of locomotive-plus-tender length, as compared with 35 horsepower for a modern diesel-electric freight hauler. The turbine delivered up to 25 percent more power in comfortably low temperatures than in midsummer heat. Altitude also affected its performance. With a full load, it used about 800 gallons of residual fuel per hour. For each pint of fuel oil consumed it could move one freight car with 50 tons of lading 1 mile on a straight, level track. Its fuel consumption rate was high, which is one reason why the UP eventually sold most of its turbines back to General Electric and the rest to Continental Leasing and Nielsen Enterprises.

BIBLIOGRAPHY: Harold Keekley, *Big Blow . . . Union Pacific's Super Turbines,* George R. Cockle & Associates, 1975; Thomas R. Lee, *Turbines Westward,* A.G. Press, Manhattan, Kans., 1975.

Locomotives, Manufacture of *See* articles on individual companies and cities, including AMERICAN LOCOMOTIVE CO.; BALDWIN LOCOMOTIVE WORKS; BROOKS LOCOMOTIVE WORKS; BUDD COMPANY; CINCINNATI LOCOMOTIVE BUILDERS; HINKLEY LOCOMOTIVE WORKS; LIMA LOCOMOTIVE WORKS; NEW YORK LOCOMOTIVE WORKS; PATERSON, NEW JERSEY; TAUNTON LOCOMOTIVE WORKS; *also* STEAM LOCOMOTIVES.

Locomotives, Military Unlike other kinds of locomotives, these almost invariably are designed for short and possibly intensive service under a wide range of conditions. The ideal military loco could operate on any railway at any time, in any country and in any climate from arctic to tropical. By contrast, the average civil motive-power unit merely has to run on one specific railway in a given country. It is far from easy to build a unit for universal use because, for one reason, gauges vary in different countries. Some progress has been made in making military locos readily convertible from one gauge to another. In that respect, diesels are more adaptable than steam power.

Also, for military purposes, detailed items, even nuts and bolts, should be standardized as much as possible. And locomotives should be designed and built for quick disassembling and reassembling for shipping purposes.

During World War II, some American 65-ton, 500-horsepower standard-gauge diesel-electrics were each shipped in three crates, one holding the chassis, tools, and parts and the other two, each weighing slightly less than 13 tons, containing a truck assembly.

In 1953, American Locomotive Co. of Schenectady, New York, began delivery of 83 diesel-electric locos adapted to worldwide use by the United States military forces on tracks of differing widths and in temperatures as low as 65°F below zero. Adjustable wheels permitted operation on wide-gauge tracks such as those in China, the Soviet Union, etc. This problem had previously required the conversion of standard locos to meet that specific need.

The idea of an all-purpose locomotive was conceived in Iran in 1942, when Alco was given the job of converting standard units for use on that country's wider-gauge and lighter tracks. The building of 83 all-purpose units resulted from designing that had been continued after that time. While this was the first large-production order of its kind, General Motors had previously built 8 similar locomotives for the Army. For subzero temperature they had electric heaters able to start on low-battery power and melt a single blob of fuel oil in a 3-gallon tank to begin a chain reaction warm-up to starting temperatures of 60°. Standard diesel units operating in subzero climates must be kept running or be housed in a heated building.

BIBLIOGRAPHY: *Operation and Maintenance of Diesel-Electric Locomotives,* Departments of the Army and Air Force, GPO, Washington, 1965; Ron Ziel, *Steel Rails to Victory,* Hawthorn, New York, 1970.

Locomotives, Steam *See* MALLET; STEAM LOCOMOTIVES.

Loewy, Raymond *(1893–)* One of America's three leading modern industrial designers who specialized in the railroad field, the others being Otto Kuhler and Henry Dreyfuss. Born in Paris, he has been an American citizen since 1938. In 1934 Loewy visited Martin W. Clement, then president of the Pennsylvania Railroad, offering to stylize a Pennsy locomotive. Instead, Clement had him design trash cans for New York's Penn Station but soon afterward accepted his design for styling the new GG-1 electric locos, which were destined for fame. *See* ELECTRIFICATION.

Loewy's chief contribution to the GG-1 was to weld the whole exterior into one sleek, unbroken shell, discarding all rivets and seams on the surface, which incidentally cut construction and maintenance costs. He changed the lettering, too, extending the classic name *Pennsylvania* all the way across the GG-1's side, and put five thin, elegant gold stripes along the entire length of the locomotive, curving over its nose to meet at the pilot.

At first 57 GG-1s were ordered. General Electric, Westinghouse, and Baldwin collaborated with the Pennsy's own Altoona shop to build them. Eventually 130 of them, with minor variations, ran on Pennsy rails. But in the late 1970s only 40 were left on the now-Amtrak roster, with indications that the type, despite its beauty and good service record, would not last far into the 1980s.

A group known as Friends of the GG-1, sponsored by the National Railway Historical Socety, succeeded in 1977 in getting one of them, No. 4935, restored to its original livery of Brunswick green with Loewy-designed stripes and lettering which had been lost over the years and revived the once-familiar red-and-gold keystone. It was unveiled at Washington Union Station, with Loewy as guest of honor, and returned to Amtrak's pool of passenger power besides being used now and then on railfan excursions.

Meanwhile, in 1936, Loewy, working for the Pennsy, added a streamlined shroud to steam locomotive No. 3768, a Pacific type in the prolific K4 class. More than 100 wind-tunnel tests influenced the contour that was the first of many somewhat similar hoods designed by Loewy. Another was on the 6100, Class S1, an experimental duplex passenger engine built by the Altoona shops and exhibited at the New York World's Fair in 1939–1940. Then Loewy streamline-designed the passenger duplex T1.

In addition to his Pennsy jobs, Loewy did significant work for Fairbanks-Morse locomotives in the mid-1940s and wrote a monograph entitled *The Locomotive: Its Esthetics,* in which he criticized then-current methods of streamlining. In 1937 he streamstyled a new lightweight version of Pennsy's *Broadway Limited,* while Henry Dreyfuss did as much for its rival, New York Central's *20th Century Limited.*

Among other trains that bore the imprint of Loewy's genius were *The General, Liberty Limited, Spirit of St. Louis, Jeffersonian*, and a New York–Chicago innovation, the overnight all-coach *Trail Blazer.* Loewy also styled passenger cars for the Delaware and Hudson, Missouri Pacific, Boston & Maine, Northern Pacific, and Monon, besides modernizing Norfolk & Western's Roanoke station.

BIBLIOGRAPHY Raymond Loewy, *Never Let Well Enough Alone,* Simon & Schuster, New York, 1951; id., *The Designs of Raymond Loewy,* Smithsonian Institution Press, Washington, 1975; Karl R. Zimmermann, *The Remarkale GG1,* Quadrant Press, New York, 1977.

Logging Railroads In the big woods of the Northwest and the South these railroads replaced oxen and mules, steam donkey cables, and transportation by mountain streams, and skid roads where no running water was available to transport logs ("Paul Bunyan's toothpicks") from cutting grounds to sawmills. The first such railroads were built without technical engineering. The woods boss had little time to plan further ahead than the section he was working in. These roads were extended from year to year until the area was logged off or until some major obstacle was encountered.

A mule-drawn car was still used in 1950 by the Grey Lumber Company in Virginia to haul finished lumber on a 3-foot-gauge track. **[H. Reid]**

Clearing the right-of-way was costly. Many miles of track were built with no power except the dynamite needed to remove stumps and logs up to 10 feet in diameter. Horses and steam donkey engines (in later years, gasoline donkeys and caterpillar-tread tractors) were used in the clearing. Howe truss bridges (later steel girders) and a few tunnels had to be built on some roads. In 1940 Weyerhaeuser Co. erected a bridge 1130 feet long, 230 feet above a canyon bottom, in Cowlitz County, Washington. All the timber in its spidery framed trestle portion, except stringers and handrails, was preframed and creosoted.

From the late 1870s to the late 1940s Shay, Heisler, and Climax locomotives did nearly all the hauling. Then internal-combustion power took over with caterpillar treads and rubber tires, and most of the steel rails were torn up.

The great success of Ephraim Shay prompted the development of rival geared steam locomotives, the Heisler and the Climax. Geared locos attained the height of their popularity in 1927, when at least 825 of them were used in West Coast logging operations. The last Lima Shay came out of the erecting shop in April 1954 and is now preserved in the Baltimore & Ohio Museum. *See* LIMA LOCOMOTIVE WORKS; MUSEUMS.

A logging train of the 64-mile McCloud River Railroad in California is ferried across the McCloud River around 1910. **[Collection of Edwin P. Alexander]**

The Heisler people argued that since a locomotive's gears were most vulnerable to wear and breakage, there should be as few of them as possible. So only one axle of each Heisler truck was geared to the main crankshaft. Power was transmitted to the other axle through side rods connecting the two pairs of wheels. Thus a Heisler could motivate 12 pairs of drivers with only 4 pairs of gears. Furthermore, Heisler gears ran in oil inside sealed housings, thus being protected from mud, water, and windblown ballast.

Built by Heisler Locomotive Works at Erie, Pennsylvania, these log haulers had only two cylinders but could drag monstrous loads. On level track the biggest Heisler could pull 3531 tons without spinning her drivers. Even on a 10 percent grade, after a shot of sand under the drivers, she could start 111 tons.

Of the three geared types of engines, the Climax, built at Corry, Pennsylvania, looked most like a conventional rod locomotive. On either side of her frame a cylinder was mounted roughly parallel to the track but inclined at about a 40-degree angle toward it. These cylinders drove a crankshaft running crosswise under the boiler. The Shay had a master gear to transmit power to a longitudinal center shaft, connected in turn by bevel gearing to each of the four or six axles, depending upon how many trucks the engine had.

The Shay was most successful because it had several advantages over the other two geared designs. All its bigger models had three cylinders, leaving two always in power for use if the engine should stop on a hill with the third cylinder at dead center. Also, with its exposed shaft and gearing, the Shay was easier to repair. Logging-camp mechanics could replace a broken coupling or a stripped gear without jacking up the loco or running her over a repair pit.

When the original Shay patents ran out, about 35 somewhat similar locomotives, most of them oilburners, were built for the logging trade by Willamette Iron & Steel Co. at Portland, Oregon. They eliminated the fireman by letting the engineer operate the oilburner. Oil fires gave off fewer sparks than wood, thus lessening the danger of forest fires.

Geared locos hauled billions of feet of logs to the mills in the Pacific Northwest from the Queen Charlotte Islands of northern British Columbia to Humboldt Bay in California and from Hoquiam, Washington, to Libby, Montana. In 1922 in Washington alone 242 logging operations owned railroads, each with from 4 to 120 miles of mainline track over which rolled Shays, Climaxes, and Heislers with surprisingly few accidents. British Columbia had at least 10 logging roads. Other such roads were in Alabama, Arizona, Arkansas, Florida, Louisiana, Mississippi, New Mexico, South Carolina, Texas, Virginia, and West Virginia.

Today, highway trucks dominate the logging industry,

although many miles of railroad continue to haul finished lumber from sawmills to lumberyards, furniture factories, etc. Some modern logging railroads in Idaho, Washington, and Oregon and on Vancouver Island still move unhewn logs from forests to saw and pulp mills. In Oregon these roads include the vast Weyerhaeuser operations at Sycan and Springfield and the Oregon & Northwestern and the Oregon, California & Eastern railroads.

***Far left:* Logging train on the Lake County Railroad in Michigan in about 1894.**

BIBLIOGRAPHY: Kramer A. Adams, *Logging Railroads of the West*, Superior Publishing, Seattle, 1961; Richard S. Allen, *Rails in the North Woods*, North Country Books, Lakemont, N.Y., 1973; Freeman Hubbard, *Great Trains of All Time,* Grosset & Dunlap, New York, 1962; Hank Johnston, *They Felled the Redwoods: A Saga of Flumes and Rails in the High Sierra*, 3d ed., rev., Trans-Anglo Books, Los Angeles, 1969; John Krause and H. Reid, *Rails through Dixie*, Golden West Books, San Marino, Calif., 1965; Robert D. Turner, *Vancouver Island Railroads*, Golden West Books, San Marino, Calif., 1973.

Long Island Rail Road (LIRR) With 321 route miles (740 single-track miles), of which 265 miles are third-rail-equipped for electric operation, the LIRR is really an elongation of New York City. But for the big, sprawling metropolis, the modern steel highway would not exist. The LIRR is unique in several respects. Besides being the continent's busiest commuter road (aside from municipal transit lines), it is state-owned and is also the continent's second-oldest railway still operating under its original name, the Georgia being older.

The LIRR was the first railroad in the world to operate a steel-car fleet (in 1905) and the first to discard all wooden passenger equipment (in 1927). Also, by electrifying a line through Brooklyn between its Flatbush Avenue Terminal and the seaside resort of Rockaway Park (in 1905), the LIRR became the first steam road to make practical use of juice as motive power.

An even greater novelty is that the LIRR is the only Class I road whose passenger revenue exceeds its freight revenue. It owns no freight cars but connects directly with Conrail via an all-land route over Hell Gate Bridge for freight trains. LIRR freight operations yield \$18 million a year; 90 percent of its freight comes *to* Long Island; the rest is moved *off* the island. (The ideal proportion would be 50–50, as in the case of the Bessemer & Lake Erie Railroad.) A large part of Long Island's economy is agricultural, but much of its vegetables, fruit, ducks, etc., is moved by highway trucks.

The carrier was chartered on April 24, 1834, as one of a chain of railroads intended to stretch between New York and Boston. The island route was chosen because engineers did not believe a rail line could be built along Connecticut's bay-indented shore. Plans called for construction of the LIRR from Brooklyn (then an independent city) eastward through Jamaica to Greenport, on the island's north fork, 94 miles away, from which point passengers could cross Long Island Sound by boat, then board other trains to Boston. The Boston service flourished for 5 years, but it ended when predecessors of the New Haven Railroad built a through line along the Connecticut shore.

In 1850 lack of business forced the LIRR into receivership. In 1854 it set itself a new goal, that of a local carrier, and began branching out to regional communities. One branch, from Jamaica to Long Island City, permitted riders to board ferryboats to East 34th Street in Manhattan. From 1876 to 1888 the LIRR merged with or bought competing rail lines. In 1895 it reached Montauk, on the island's south fork, 117 miles from Manhattan.

Two Baldwin eight-wheelers, the *Ariel*, built in 1835, and the *Post Boy*, in 1836, hauled all LIRR traffic in the earliest days. Each weighed 7 tons and had 10- by 16-inch cylinders and 56-inch drivers.

A unique monument stands on Lot 28583 in Greenwood Cemetery, Brooklyn, honoring the memory of Oscar Dietzel and his wife, two of the 15 persons killed in a foggy-night collision of two Long Island passenger trains just east of the present Haberman station on August 26, 1893. The monument includes a small replica of the disaster sculptured in granite. The LIRR could not have such a wreck today. It uses an automatic speed-control system on all high-density electric lines, restricting a segment of track to only one train at a time and alerting following trains of its presence ahead. If the second train moves closer to the first train, electrical impulses signal the second engineer to reduce speed. A bell or a whistle tells the engineer to acknowledge the new speed command. If the engineer does not acknowledge it within a few seconds, the brakes on his train are

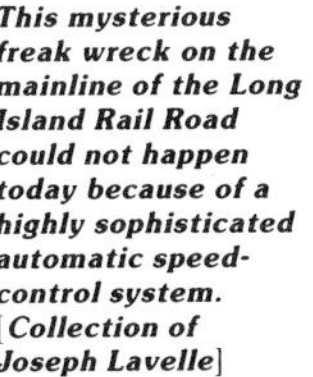

This mysterious freak wreck on the mainline of the Long Island Rail Road could not happen today because of a highly sophisticated automatic speed-control system. [Collection of Joseph Lavelle]

automatically applied, maintaining safety in operation. The LIRR also uses traffic-control systems on some lines to permit remote control of switches and bidirectional operations on all tracks. Automatic speed control works in conjunction with this.

The LIRR received legislative permission to build a midtown Manhattan terminal and a tunnel beneath the East River to approach it but lacked funds for these costly projects. The Pennsylvania Railroad wanted to tunnel under the Hudson River from New Jersey into New York City, instead of being limited to a ferry connection, and had the money to do so, but no permission. In 1900 an agreement was reached whereby the Pennsy would build both sets of tunnels and the midtown terminal, Penn Station, which it did, in exchange for a controlling interest in the LIRR. (The original terminal has since been replaced by a smaller one.)

By operating the first train underneath the East River into Penn Station in 1910, the LIRR started a fast transportation service that led to a real estate and building boom on Long Island. In 1925 the Babylon branch was electrified. Then came the Depression of the 1930s, increasing use of the automobile, new highways and bridges, and the opening of the Independent municipal subway line between Manhattan and Jamaica in 1937. Twelve years later this combination of events had taken away so many LIRR passengers, a staggering 80 percent, that the island railroad went into a bankruptcy from which the Pennsy refused to bail it out.

In 1954, the year before the road operated its last steam loco, it was rescued from bankruptcy by a New York State-based 12-year development program. In 1966 the Metropolitan Transportation Authority, founded in 1965, bought the ailing LIRR from the Pennsy for $65 million and began operating it with 764 new passenger cars, upgrading and modernizing its electrified power system, extending electrification to Huntington in 1970, rehabilitating track, installing much welded rail and rubberized crossings, and eliminating grade crossings by the costly method of elevation.

The LIRR has 6700 employees and 144 passenger stations. A temporary station built at the main entrance to the 1939-1940 New York World's Fair was used by a record 228,000 passengers in a single day. The road has 63 electrified substations converting 11,000 volts of Consolidated Edison and Long Island Lighting alternating current to 700 volts for operation of Class M-l electric cars. Maximum speed for electric trains is 80 miles per hour, for diesel passenger trains 70, and for freight trains (17 operated daily) 45.

The system had 67,364,000 passengers in 1976, 69,463,000 in 1977, and 72,434,000 in 1978. The figure could rise even more drastically if motorists continue to feel the pinch of rising gasoline prices. On an average working morning or evening rush-hour period some 89,000 passengers use the LIRR. In addition to its usual excursions, the LIRR operates fishermen's, racetrack, and other specials, and for years it ran parlor cars.

Like other Class I roads, it uses radio for instant communication between trains and crews, control towers, maintenance and supervisory personnel, etc. It also has a public-address system to keep its riders informed. Information may also be transmitted to passengers at stations from a console located in the road's operating base, Jamaica. The LIRR operates through the nation's busiest terminal, Penn Station, and busiest suburban station, Hicksville, which handles 5800 passengers during a morning rush-hour period. Amtrak owns Penn Station; the LIRR rents space in it. LIRR uses four tunnels under the East River, two of them exclusively, sharing the other two with Amtrak.

BIBLIOGRAPHY: George H. Burgess and Miles C. Kennedy, *Centennial History of the Pennsylvania Railroad Company: 1846-1946*, Pennsylvania Railroad, Philadelphia, 1949; Freeman Hubbard, *Railroad Avenue*, McGraw-Hill, New York, 1945; Frederick A. Kramer and John Krause, *Long Island Rail Road*, Carstens Publs., Newton, N.J., 1978; Vincent F. Seyfried, *The Long Island Railroad*, 5 vols., Felix F. Reifschneider, Garden City, N.Y., 1961-1972; Ron Ziel and George W. Foster, *Steel Rails to the Sunrise*, Hawthorn, New York, 1965.

The Lookout Mountain Incline Railway climbs the mountain face in a straight line for 0.9 mile to over 2100 feet above sea level. [Bridon American Corporation]

Lookout Mountain Incline Railway Line at Chattanooga, Tennessee, that may well be the world's steepest and safest passenger railway. Instead of winding around, it climbs the mountain face in a straight line for 0.9 mile to over 2100 feet above sea level. Near the top is an almost incredible 71.7 percent grade. Two steel, glass-roofed, wide-windowed cable cars operate it. Although primarily for tourists, the railway also carries commuters. Long ago it hauled coal, food, etc., for winterbound mountain families. Two 100-horsepower motors supply power. If they should fail, brakes would stop the drums around which two steel cables are wound. One cable is fastened to each car, wound twice around a drum in the control house atop the mountain, and connected to the other car. If one cable should break, the other cable would still hold. Over 500,000 persons a year ride the line, which has never had a casualty accident.

Louisville & Nashville Railroad (L&N) Nicknamed the Old Reliable, the L&N, with headquarters in Louisville, Kentucky, has 6635 route miles of track in 13 states of the central South and Midwest from the Great Lakes and the Ohio River Valley to coastal plains bordering the Gulf of Mexico. L&N is the second-ranking member of the Family Lines System, which totals more than 16,000 miles and includes the Seaboard Coast Line, the Georgia, the Clinchfield, the Western Railway of Alabama, and the Atlanta & West Point Railroad.

Over the years, L&N absorbed 57 other roads by purchase, lease, or construction. One of its major acquisitions was the Nashville, Chattanooga & St. Louis, a Class I road famed for the Andrews raid of 1862. L&N got control of this line in 1880 and consolidated its 1200 miles in 1957. Other major additions were portions of the Chicago & Eastern Illinois (C&EI) and the Tennessee Central, both in 1969, and the 541-mile Monon in 1971. The C&EI and the Monon provided entry into Chicago. *See* ANDREWS RAILROAD RAID.

L&N began as a two-state railroad chartered in Kentucky on March 5, 1850, to build from Louisville south to the Tennessee state line. At about the same time, it was chartered in Tennessee to run north from Nashville to join the Kentucky segment. Despite opposition by stagecoach and steamboat interests, construction was started in 1855, with crossties of white oak, cedar, and black locust laid 2700 to the mile.

The original 6-foot gauge was changed to 5 feet before the first train ran in 1855. It was narrowed still further in 1886 to the national standard of 4 feet 8½ inches. Tunneling mountains and bridging two rivers slowed the tracklayers. One bridge, over the Green River, 1800 feet long with its approaches, was then America's longest iron bridge. On October 27, 1859, L&N's first through train, flag-bedecked, ran from Louisville to Nashville in 10 hours.

As a vital link between the Ohio River and the Deep South this road was destructively fought over in the Civil War. It was in a difficult position because half of the line was in a neutral state (Kentucky), and the rest in a seceded state (Tennessee). During the war's early months the railroad prospered. The bulk of its traffic moved into Tennessee for the South's needs. Later, as Union armies advanced through Kentucky and Tennessee, the L&N moved men and material in support of the North. By then, the road had already lost about half of its rolling stock, and as Union troops pushed back the Confederates, they retaliated by destroying railroad facilities.

In the Reconstruction era, L&N launched a major expansion. In 1871 it reached Memphis, and a year later Montgomery and coal-and-iron-rich Birmingham. In 1880 it entered the Gulf ports of New Orleans, Mobile, and Pensacola, and in 1881 it rolled trains into St. Louis and Cincinnati and began to tap the coalfields of Kentucky and Tennessee.

Birmingham was barely a village when L&N tracks first reached it in 1872, and the L&N played a major role in its growth by building scores of spurs and branches to nearby coal and iron deposits. L&N also helped underwrite the first successful efforts (at Oxmoor in 1876) to make pig iron from Alabama ores with coke and, later, the production of steel (at Ensley, in 1899). To encourage local production of coal and pig iron, the L&N also granted attractive freight rates.

From a tonnage standpoint, L&N's most important expansion came just after 1900, when it began pushing lines into eastern and southeastern Kentucky to tap the rich coal deposits. L&N also created a low-grade (without excessive grades) double-tracked line from Harlan, Kentucky, to the Cincinnati gateway, 255 miles away, to funnel coal to major industries and utilities in the Midwest and Great Lakes region.

L&N's premier passenger train was the *Pan American*, for a time an all-Pullman express between Cincinnati and New Orleans. The run was unique in that its sounds were broadcast live daily except Sunday by the Nashville radio station WSM during the 1930s and 1940s.

In 1940 the streamlined *South Wind* and *Dixie Flagler*, originally all-coach but later coach-Pullman, began running between Chicago and Miami via L&N and other

Railroads occasionally employ divers, like this one on the Louisville & Nashville, to inspect bridges or locomotives or cars sunk in rivers or lakes. [Louisville & Nashville Railroad]

roads. The *South Wind's* heavy Pacific-type engine was coupled to a supertank with a capacity of 27½ tons of coal and 20,000 gallons of water. With this advantage, her Nashville-Birmingham run of 205 miles in 1941-1942 is believed to have been America's longest, regularly scheduled, nonstop coal-powered run.

The L&N had bought its first two engines in 1855. Ninety-five years later, in 1950, it took delivery of its first five diesel-electric units for general freight, but as a major coal carrier L&N was loath to change its motive power from steam to diesel. It became fully dieselized only in 1957, when it earmarked its last 36 steam locos for scrapping. To commemorate in 1959 the 100th anniversary of its first train service to Nashville, it had to borrow an Illinois Central steamer to pull the special. Steam returned briefly, in 1962-1966, when L&N sent the *General* of the Andrews raid on a tour over its system.

In 1950, L&N carried over 2,600,000 riders, but in the following decade highway and air competition cut that number so sharply that it dropped 74 passenger trains, besides eliminating passenger service on 34 mixed trains. In 1971, L&N turned over its remaining passenger service to Amtrak. The road is a major coal carrier, in 1979 originating over 59 million tons of coal. It also hauls much piggyback traffic, grains, chemicals, wood, and automotive products. In 1972 the Seaboard Coast Line, owner of 35 percent of L&N stock for many years, acquired the remaining stock, making L&N a wholly owned subsidiary of Seaboard Coast Line Industries, a member of the Family Lines System, and eventually part of CSX Corp. *See* CSX CORP.

BIBLIOGRAPHY: Kincaid A. Herr, *The Louisville & Nashville Railroad,* Louisville & Nashville Railroad, Louisville, Ky., 1964; Maury Klein, *History of the Louisville & Nashville Railroad,* Macmillan, New York, 1972; Richard E. Prince, *Louisville & Nashville Steam Locomotives,* rev. ed., Green River, Wyo., 1968; John E. Tilford, *L&N: Its First 100 Years,* Newcomen Society in North America, New York, 1951.

Lucin Cutoff Bridging of Great Salt Lake, Utah. Shortly before his death in 1900, Collis P. Huntington, president of the Southern Pacific-Union Pacific system (SP-UP), authorized the building of causeways and trestles for a shortcut across the lake so that the system could continue to command its share of cross-continent traffic. Among the equipment he ordered for this job were steam shovels, larger than any previous design, that could bring up 7 tons of dirt and rock at a single scoop. *See* HUNTINGTON, COLLIS POTTER.

Lucin Cutoff, bridging Great Salt Lake in Utah, took over a year to complete and was first used in 1904. A Southern Pacific train is pictured here crossing it. [Southern Pacific Railroad]

In 1902, E. H. Harriman, president of SP-UP, began work on this project—a 103-mile link between Lucin and Ogden, Utah, including trackage to the lakeshore and construction across the salty, marshy water. The system's chief engineer, William Hood, supervised the monumental undertaking. From surveys and soundings of the area, he knew that the lake depths varied from 0 to 30 feet. The lake bottom was some 15 feet of soft mud, covered by a crust of salt. *See* HARRIMAN, EDWARD HENRY.

Hood's plans called for a wooden trestle, 11 miles long, over the deepest part of the lake, between the tip of Promontory Point and the west shore, with fills bridging the gaps. A fill would also connect Promontory Point with the east shore. By midsummer of 1902 steel rails began to arrive at the lake, then trainloads of piles. Some 3000 men built the trestles, from which dirt and rock were dumped, until finally the completed roadbed was ready for laying rails. Every day, in addition to food and supplies, 1680 tons of fresh water for the workmen had to be brought by rail from 80 to 100 miles over the desert.

At times, the trestle crew rammed home the piles so fast that an average of 1140 feet of roadbed a day were completed. Giant piles, some 125 feet long, 2500 in all, many so long that they had to be hauled on three flatcars coupled together, arrived from the Oregon forests. Material for the fills was hauled by 400 steel dump cars pulled by 80 locomotives.

Operating headquarters was Lakeside, a boomtown similar to earlier railroad construction camps, with one important difference: no liquor was allowed in it. The men worked in shifts, including Sundays and holidays, for Hood's goal was at least 1000 feet of construction a day. His major problem was the soft muck on the lake bottom. Rambo Fill, at the western end of the trestle, required 75,000 carloads of rock, or approximately 4 million tons.

On Thanksgiving Day, 1903, Lucin Cutoff was officially completed, but freight traffic was not diverted over the new line until March 8, 1904, and the first passenger train ran over it the following September.

BIBLIOGRAPHY: Lucius Beebe, *The Central Pacific and the Southern Pacific Railroads,* Howell-North, Berkeley, Calif., 1963.

Ludlow & Southern Railway (L&S) This 7½-mile narrow-gauge line connected the rich Bagdad-Chase gold and silver mines with the Atchison, Topeka and Santa Fe Railway (ATSF) at Ludlow in California's Mojave Desert. Twenty-mule teams had already hauled some $60 million worth of precious ore from nearby Province Town, and a monstrous noisy steam tractor pulling three wagons had rumbled over another desert route; but in about 1900 the mine operators built the L&S for more efficient transportation. A major stockholder was Chauncey M. Depew, New York Central Railroad president.

An armored combination car from the New York Central, L&S No. 100, made regular trips across the desert, often bearing gold bullion directly to Los Angeles, then up the coast via the Southern Pacific, total value over the years being estimated at $17 million. That same car took miners and their families down to Ludlow each payday. The L&S had two locomotives. Southbound L&S trains included a flatcar loaded with a cargo more precious to desert people than their gold: water, hauled in via the ATSF. No successful wells could be sunk in that arid land. By 1927 the Bagdad- Chase mines had petered out to such an extent that the L&S was abandoned.

BIBLIOGRAPHY: David F. Myrick, *Railroads of Nevada and Eastern California*, 2 vols., Howell-North, Berkeley, Calif., 1962–1963; George B. Turner, *Narrow Gauge Nostalgia*, 2d ed., rev., Trans-Anglo Books, Corona del Mar, Calif., 1971.

LV *See* LEHIGH VALLEY RAILROAD.

M

McCallum, Daniel Craig ***(1815–1878)*** In some respects the Leonardo da Vinci of American railroading. Besides being a railroad builder, McCallum was a bridge engineer, architect, inventor, and railway operator. As military director and superintendent of United States railroads during the Civil War, he operated 2105 miles of railroad. Forces under his direction built or rebuilt 641 miles of railroad and 26 miles of bridges. One of his high wooden bridges, spanning a ravine and creek in Virginia, caused President Lincoln to remark, "McCallum's bridges are made of cornstalks and string."

In one campaign he transported supplies for 100,000 men, also 60,000 horses, over 60 miles of a single-track rail line constantly under attack. Among the valuable lessons from his notebook, ignored in World War I but heeded with great profit in World War II, was his insistence that freight cars should not be used for storage but always kept available for transportation; i.e., they should be loaded, unloaded, and moved promptly and not left standing under load.

Born in Scotland in 1815, McCallum moved with his parents to Rochester, New York, and became a successful architect. In 1851 he originated and patented an inflexible arched-truss bridge and later organized the McCallum Bridge Co. According to the *American Railroad Journal,* he was the first person to introduce conductors' uniforms on American railroads.

McClintock, Harry Kirby ***(1880–1957)*** Boomer brakeman, switchman, humorist, and minstrel, author of such ballads as "The Big Rock Candy Mountain" and "Hallelujah, I'm a Bum." McClintock was the most colorful railroad man the author ever knew. Born in Knoxville, Tennessee, he ran away from home at 14 to join a circus. "As many boomers and hoboes were drifting south for the winter," he told me, "I soon found myself riding freight trains with a choice collection of bums from all over the country. Small towns in the South, almost without exception, were hostile to tramps, but as a kid I managed to get handouts where experienced panhandlers failed. At age 16 I learned to plunk a guitar. My voice, plus the 'git-fiddle,' was good for a meal ticket in any community."

His first step on the railroad boomer trail was hiring out to the Pennsy in the highly industrialized Pittsburgh area, but he didn't stay there long. "I worked," he said, "on more railroads than I can remember. I also herded sheep in Nevada, punched cattle in Montana, and got married." In between jobs he'd write songs, singing and playing his guitar in saloons, mining camps, hash houses, dance and concert halls, and freight cars and on board ship. Essentially he was a wanderer.

Besides railroading, Haywire Mac, as he was called, won success on radio with his own cowboy band, made some phonograph records, and wrote stories and true tales in railroad vernacular, mostly for *Railroad Maga-*

zine, his last one being "Boomers and Their Women," published posthumously. "Drain your glass to the bottom," was his swan song. "I'm getting on in years now."

This great man died in poverty—gone to the Big Rock Candy Mountain. Here are two stanzas from his best-loved ballad:

One evening as the sun went down
And the jungle fires were burning,
Down the track came a hobo hiking
And he said: "Boys, I'm not turning;
I'm headed for a land that's far away,
Beside a crystal fountain.
So come with me; we'll go and see
The Big Rock Candy Mountain."

. . . .

"Oh, I'm bound to go
Where there ain't no snow,
Where the rain don't fall
And the wind don't blow—
In the Big Rock Candy Mountain."

BIBLIOGRAPHY: Freeman Hubbard, *Railroad Avenue,* McGraw-Hill, New York, 1945.

McCoy, Elijah (1844-1929) Inventor, with at least 50 patents to his name, who was best known for his lubricating devices designed to help locomotives move faster with less friction. A full-blooded Negro of African descent, he was the son of parents who had fled from slavery in Kentucky a few years earlier. His father, George McCoy, served in the Canadian Army. The Canadian government gave him a pension of land, on which Elijah was born.

The boy studied engineering at Edinburgh University, then applied for work with the Michigan Central Railroad (MC), in the Vanderbilt system, at Ypsilanti, Michigan. There he met race discrimination. White employers did not want black engineers, whatever their training or skill; so he settled for a locomotive firing job on the MC. The machinery he handled fascinated him. What interested him most was lubrication.

In the early 1870s a major cause of train delay was overheated engines. Crews had to stop now and then to lubricate them. This wasted time and cost money. After experimenting for 2 years, McCoy invented and patented in 1872 an oil cup that lubricated engines automatically while the train was running. Some contemptuous white engineers referred to this invention as "the nigger oil cup." But hardheaded Michigan Central executives, interested in dollars and cents, took a different viewpoint. They not only installed McCoy's device and rewarded him for it but had him instruct their engineers in its use.

When he wasn't teaching co-workers the use of his oil cup, he was tinkering with machinery, not only in the railroad field, and working on other inventions. In 1915 the railroads faced a new crisis. McCoy's lubricator, which had served their needs since 1872, now proved inadequate for the new-style superheater locomotives. *See* SUPERHEATERS, LOCOMOTIVE.

At 70, McCoy solved this problem with his graphite lubricator, which was generally regarded as his greatest invention. It lubricated the new superheated locomotives and saved time, valve oil, and fuel in the old-style power as well. Introduced 2 years before America entered World War I, it helped the rail industry to meet the increased demands of wartime production.

Like many previous great inventors who had brought wealth to others, McCoy died in poverty. Years later, Michigan's secretary of state affixed a plaque to the spot in a vacant lot in Detroit where the home of Elijah McCoy and his wife Mary once stood, making it a national shrine.

McKeen, William Riley, Jr. Inventor and builder of the famous cars bearing his name and holder of over 2000 railroad patents, one of which, dated as early as 1904, was for an air-conditioning system. For years his grandfather and then his father owned the Vandalia Railroad (later in the Pennsy system). He himself began railroading in 1891 as a shop apprentice, became the Union Pacific's (UP's) superintendent of motive power and machinery, and left that job to head his McKeen Motor Car Co., founded in 1908.

He built about 157 McKeen motor cars and one or several locomotives. Approximately 50 of his cars operated on the E. H. Harriman lines [UP, Southern Pacific (SP), and subsidiaries]; he was a friend of Harriman. His first car was assembled in 1905 at the UP erecting shop in Omaha. This 100-horsepower marine-type gasoline engine mounted on a four-wheeled truck was the wooden predecessor of a long line of distinctive steel cars credited with ushering in a new streamlined era in railroading.

The pioneer car measured 31 feet over sills and had four 42-inch wheels, but only the front pair was powered. All subsequent McKeens had 42-inch drivers and 33-inch trailing wheels. The type bore some resemblance to an inverted boat, with a sharp prow to cut the air and permit speeds. It had a rounded end and was heated by hot water from the motor-cooling system. Top speed was usually around 50 miles per hour, but short bursts of 75 miles per hour were recorded.

The first McKeen car was assigned to UP branches in Nebraska. The second, also in Nebraska, caught fire and was scrapped. Car No. 3 ran on SP lines in Texas, and No. 4 first on the Chicago & Alton, then on the UP. Car No. 5 burnished the rails of the San Pedro, Los Angeles & Salt Lake, then the UP. Car No. 6 operated on Nebraska branches.

Car No. 7 was the first car with the depressed center door and round windows that thereafter distinguished McKeens. A catalog in 1912 described such windows as "airtight, watertight, and dustproof, three features not heretofore attained in a single car window. The frame is made of aluminum. The sash, 21¾ inches in diameter, is hinged at the top and when raised is automatically locked to the car ceiling, thus giving a full window opening."

The eighth car was the first one with a McKeen engine, rated at 200 horsepower. McKeen cars had great pulling power and could make a 3 percent grade in high gear. The company took over UP's old Omaha shops with Harriman's approval. A solid train of seven McKeens sent out from Omaha to the SP is said to have been the first all-steel passenger train west of the Mississippi River. A few McKeen cars were sent to Australia, to the Alberta & Great Waterways Railway in Canada, and possibly also to Cuba, Mexico, and Spain.

The interior of a railway postal car in 1875. Over 100 years later, in July 1977, the last RPO cars, between New York and Washington, made their final run. [*Collection of Freeman Hubbard*]

Mail Formal opening of the Baltimore & Ohio between Washington and Baltimore on August 25, 1835, marked the beginning of regular Railway Mail Service, although the South Carolina Railroad had taken its first mail sack aboard in November 1831 and the B&O had begun hauling mail about January 1, 1832, just 8 months after it opened for regular passenger and freight business. Around that time two other pioneer roads, the Camden & Amboy and the Saratoga & Schenectady, also launched mail services. The U.S. Post Office Department dates its first rail-mail fiscal year from 1835.

During that year, trains carried mail 270,504 miles but were subordinate to their competitors: post coaches and stages, 16,874,050; sulkies and horseback riders, 7,817,075; and steamboats, 906,959 miles. In 1836 mail was carried on at least 200 miles of railway, the total annual rail transportation of mail being nearly 300,000 miles. In 1838 Congress passed a law making every American railroad a post route. In 1845 Railway Mail Service had only 43 employees; their annual pay totaled $37,513.

The Pony Express, predecessor of rail-mail transportation, wrote its most dramatic chapter in the summer of 1860 when it made its fabled dash from Sacramento, California, to St. Joseph, Missouri, 1600 miles, crossing high mountains, lonely plains, and flooded streams and rivers, through herds of stampeding buffalo and other wildlife, and despite Indian arrows and tomahawks.

In the 1860s Col. George Buchanan Armstrong, assistant postmaster in Chicago, developed plans to speed the mail. Much time could be saved, he told Congress again and again, if the mail were sorted on board speeding trains. But Congress procrastinated. Among the men impressed by his ideas was William A. Davis, assistant postmaster at St. Joseph, who experimented with such a service on the Hannibal & St. Joseph [(H&SJ) today part of the Burlington Northern], which had recently been built across Missouri and was competing with stages and the Pony Express in handling mail.

America's first mail car (except possibly one on the Philadelphia, Wilmington and Baltimore Railroad in the 1830s) was a converted baggage car fitted with an old letter case and a mail-sorting shelf put into service on the H&SJ on July 28, 1862, between West Quincy, Illinois, and St. Joseph. One of the mail clerks on its first run was Fred Harvey. Thereafter, Davis served as superintendent of overland mail on the H&SJ. *See* HARVEY, FREDERICK HENRY.

In 1864 Colonel Armstrong wrote, published, and distributed at his own expense a series of three pamphlets telling the public how faster mail delivery could be achieved. They created such a stir that Postmaster General Montgomery Blair authorized him to experiment with his ideas. Armstrong did so, on the Chicago & North Western (C&NW) between Chicago and Clinton,

Sorting letters aboard a Fast Mail train in the 1890s. [*The American Railway*, Scribner, 1897]

Iowa, 138 miles, with a remodeled baggage car somewhat like the H&SJ's. He and several newspapermen rode the car on its initial run. C&NW claims to have built, in 1867, the nation's first five full Railway Post Office (RPO) cars at its shops in Fond du Lac, Wisconsin.

The Traveling Post Office, as the new system was called, was an instant success. Armstrong's second mail-sorting run was between New York and Washington. Others followed in quick succession. In 1869, when Congress finally got around to approving Railway Mail Service, Armstrong was made its first general superintendent, a job he held until his death in 1871.

George S. Bangs, who succeeded him for 5 years, nearly doubled the nation's RPO mileage. By making promotions from the ranks regardless of politics, Bangs pioneered in civil service reform but aroused some personal enmity. He talked William H. Vanderbilt into building and operating an all-mail train, with sorting en route, between New York and Chicago. From its first trip, New York Central's *Fast Mail* was a success. So, too, was the *Limited Mail* which the Pennsylvania Railroad launched between Philadelphia and the Midwest at the same time. The running time for both, 24 hours, was high speed in those days. Both trains were discontinued after 10 months because Congress cut the appropriation for this special service. But in 1877, with new federal funds, they were resumed and later connected with the Union Pacific, which relayed mail to and from the West Coast on regular passenger-mail trains.

Fast Mail caught the public's fancy. Songs, poems, and Broadway plays were written around it. RPO clerks became adventurous figures working on trains that roared through the night and, without stopping, picked up mail pouches from the stanchions at way stations. People liked to think that the village postmaster's pretty daughter hung up the mailbag and waited around to see it being snatched into the train.

There was tragedy, too. In the 9355 accidents to mail-carrying trains from 1876 to 1905, a total of 207 clerks were killed, 1516 others seriously injured, and 3764 slightly injured. The Railway Mail Association, a sort of union and benefit society founded in 1891, joined the American Federation of Labor in 1917. *See* "WRECK OF THE OLD 97, THE."

Shortly after World War II 1500 RPO routes were crisscrossing the United States, with 30,000 men working in more than 4000 individual RPO cars. By 1961 the number of routes had dwindled to 282, as the Post Office Department kept taking mail transportation business away from the railroads and giving it to airlines and trucks. This accelerated the decline in rail passenger traffic. Many trains which had depended upon mail revenue had to be dropped.

By 1972 only one RPO route was left: one train running in each direction between New York and Washington. Those two trains made their final trips on the night of June 30–July 1, 1977, passing each other near Philadelphia at speeds better than 80 miles per hour. Both had begun operation on October 16, 1864. Philatelic cachets were issued on the graveyard runs. *See* CACHET COLLECTING.

BIBLIOGRAPHY: Wayne E. Fuller, *The American Mail,* University of Chicago Press, Chicago, 1972; Alvin F. Harlow, *Old Post Bags,* Appleton, New York, 1928; Stewart H. Holbrook, *The Story of American Railroads,* Crown, New York, 1947; Bryant A. Long and William J. Dennis, *Mail by Rail,* Simmons-Boardman, New York, 1951; David P. Morgan, *Fast Mail: The First 75 Years,* Chicago, Burlington & Quincy Railroad, Chicago, 1959.

An old-fashioned mail crane, photographed on the New Haven Railroad in 1944. A bag of mail was hung from the crane and was picked up by the RPO car as the train sped past. [New Haven Railroad]

Maine Central Railroad (MEC) One of the very few major roads in the Northeastern United States that as of 1980 are solvent and profitable. Chartered in Maine in 1856 (the year the first railroad bridge was built across the Mississippi), it was organized in 1862 with the consolidation of the Androscoggin & Kennebec. It now operates 749 route miles in Maine, 58 in New Hampshire, 22 in Vermont, and 5 in New Brunswick.

The first two of its more then 50 antecedents, the Calais Railway and the Bangor & Old Town (B&OT) both in Maine, were chartered in 1832. The Calais began as a 2-mile horse railroad. Even before the B&OT laid track, the rival Bangor & Piscataquis Canal & Railroad bought it. The rival's earliest track was 12 miles of strap iron, ¾ inch thick, spiked to timber rails. Its first engine was the English-built *Pioneer,* a Stephenson two-wheeler previously used on the Boston & Worcester.

Two of Maine Central's ancestors were built to a wide gauge (5 feet 6 inches). In 1871 the whole system was standard-gauged. For years MEC also operated two 2-foot-gauge roads, the Sandy River & Rangeley Lakes and the Bridgton & Saco River, both abandoned in the early 1930s. One MEC antecedent, the 131-mile Portland & Ogdensburg, cut through New Hampshire's forbidding White Mountains, a major engineering feat. *See* MAINE'S TWO-FOOTERS.

In 1955 Maine Central bought the European & North American Railway, projected by John A. Poor, extending from Bangor to the Canadian border at Vanceboro; and in 1974 it sold 56 miles of it to the Canadian Pacific but kept trackage rights over that segment. In 1917, when the federal government took over the operation of all United States railroads, Maine Central had 1358 track miles, the greatest mileage in its history. *See* POOR, JOHN ALFRED.

The Boston & Maine (B&M) controlled the MEC from 1933 to 1955. MEC was involved in the resort business, had two nationally famous hotels, operated coastal steamers, ferries, and buses, and in partnership with the B&M ran an airline service with aviator Amelia Earhart as a vice president.

Nearly 60 percent of MEC's present freight tonnage comes from hauling raw materials and finished products for the pulp and paper industry. In 1975 the road named 10 new diesel locomotives for persons or events in the Revolutionary War period. Relatively few of the nation's diesel units have been given individual names.

BIBLIOGRAPHY: Bradley L. Peters, *Maine Central Railroad Company*, Maine Central Railroad, Portland, Me., 1976.

Maine's Two-Footers The Sandy River & Rangeley Lakes, longest 2-foot-gauge railroad on the continent, began operation on November 20, 1870, on 18 miles of track from Farmington to Phillips, eventually becoming a Y-shaped carrier slightly over 100 miles long extending to Rangeley and Bigelow. It started with two 11-ton engines, two coaches, a baggage car, and a flatcar, all acquired from the defunct Bedford & Billerica in Massachusetts. By 1918 it had 10 locomotives, one weighing nearly 60 tons, and more than 300 cars. It even had a midget parlor car, the only one of its kind, with single seats on either side of the aisle. Lumber and pulpwood brought prosperity to the Sandy River line; and when that industry petered out, the railroad was doomed. A junk dealer bought it on May 18, 1935.

At various times Maine had other two-footers. The shortest and first to be abandoned was the 5-mile Kennebec Central. Built in 1890 between Randolph and the Soldiers' Home at Togus, it made its last run on June 30, 1929. The 6-mile Monson, built in 1882, folded in the mid-1930s. Another two-footer, the 16-mile Bridgton & Harrison, built in 1881-1882, likewise is gone. Still another, the Wiscasset, Waterville & Farmington, though chartered in 1854, did not start building until 1884. By 1898 it had reached 59 miles, and in 1933 it bought the defunct Kennebec Central, but it shut down later that year.

Hand-coaling an engine of the 2-foot-gauge Monson Railroad in Maine. This 6-mile road, like the other Maine two-footers, was rather short-lived. [Linwood Moody]

BIBLIOGRAPHY: Linwood W. Moody, *The Maine Two-Footers,* Howell-North, Berkeley, Calif., 1959; *Railroad Magazine,* May 1939; February 1942; May 1953; *Trains Magazine,* May 1947; May 1948; September 1951; May 1953; February 1959; October 1965.

Make-Work *See* FEATHERBEDDING.

Mallet America's first Mallet-type locomotive was the 2400, a 0-6-6-0 built by American Locomotive Co. (Alco) at Schenectady, New York, and weighing over 150 tons, an unheard-of figure in 1904, when she was exhibited at the Louisiana Purchase Exposition. The type was named for its inventor, Anatole Mallet, a young member of the French Academy of Sciences. He never claimed to have originated the compound-articulated principle on which the type was based, but his

The Union Pacific's famous Big Boys, 4-8-8-4 Mallets, are the world's largest steam locomotives. They were put out of service by diesels. [Union Pacific Railroad]

design so far surpassed all others that many railroads eventually adopted it.

The type had three main characteristics: (1) There were two sets of cylinders. (2) It was a compound; i.e., the high-pressure, or exhaust, steam from one set of cylinders was used to operate the other, low-pressure set. (3) The rear drivers and high-pressure cylinders were rigidly attached to the boiler, while the frame that carried the other cylinders and the front drivers turned on a pivot, in somewhat the same way as in any steam locomotive truck. This construction permitted the Mallet to get around curves as easily as an engine with half the number of driving wheels.

James E. Muhlfield, designer of America's first Mallet, the 2400, applied the principle in the United States by supplying the Baltimore & Ohio with new heavy engines of greater power but with no more weight on the individual wheels than other locomotives had. The 2400 was an amazing success.

After that, Alco and the Baldwin and Lima locomotive works built hundreds of Mallets, which were widely used for hauling ponderous freight trains up mountain grades. Many improvements were made on the Frenchman's original design. Alco, for example, perfected a valve arrangement permitting the locomotive to run as a single-expansion engine (with steam entering each cylinder directly from the boiler) by throwing a single lever. Although commonly known as Mallets, single-expansion articulated locomotives did not technically rate that name.

The word *articulated,* as applied to locomotives, meant hinging the entire forward engine unit to permit so long a locomotive to round curves. Actually, articulated engines were built as early as 1831, when Horatio Allen built his first double-ender for the South Carolina Canal & Railroad Company. She had two engine beds, placed back to back, with one pair of wheels and a set of drivers supporting each assembly, but she was not a Mallet. *See* LOCOMOTIVES, DOUBLE-ENDED.

As astounding as the 2400's drawbar pull was the fact that this radical engine had been worked out so perfectly in the blueprint stage that she exhibited none of the bugs which cursed so many experimental engines. For example, steam was made to enter the side of the cylinder forward from where the piston was moving a fraction of a second before it reached the end of the stroke, thus tempering the shock of reversal and starting it back with increased snap.

In 1910 the Santa Fe Railway produced the strangest Mallets of their day: the 2-6-6-2 wheel arrangement with a hinged boiler. Fifty rings of high-carbon steel, each 75½ inches in diameter and 10 inches wide, were riveted together alternately on their outer and inner edges to form a huge bellows containing the flues and an open feedwater course. An engine was belted rigidly to each unit, eliminating all but one flexible steam-pipe connection. This coupling joined the high-pressure cylinders with the receiving pipe.

Then, in 1913, the Santa Fe made its last articulated effort, converting 10 Santa Fe types into 2-10-10-2s at its Topeka shops. For them Baldwin built a special design of 12-wheeled turtleback tenders, as well as the forward low-pressure engines. These monsters weighed 306 tons without tank. Their tractive effort was 111,000 pounds, making them by far the largest locomotives of their day. Yet they were kept barely 4 years in service before being reconverted to 2-10-2s.

For years the world's most powerful locomotive was the Virginian Railway's 2-10-10-2 Mallet, which exerted 147,200 pounds of tractive force compound and 176,600 pounds simple. For years, too, the Northern Pacific's 5000 class 2-8-8-4, built by Alco in 1928, was the world's largest. Running a close second in size was the Western Pacific (WP's) 252 class (Baldwin, 1931). However, the WP Mallets were not as powerful as the Great Northern's 2044–2059 series. In 1909 the Canadian Pacific built a strange Mallet, No. 1950, with 23½- and 34- by 26-inch cylinders, weighing 262,000 pounds without tank, but rebuilt her in 1916 as a Decapod, No. 5760, with 23½- by 32-inch cylinders, weighing 230,000 pounds without tank.

On the Southern Pacific, plans for 15 cab-in-fronters of the 2-8-8-2 design were drawn up by Howard Stillman in 1909, and the engines themselves were completed a year later. Objections to the crew's vulnerable position in the event of a collision were met by making the rear engine bed of extremely sturdy construction. Eventually, the SP was using on steep grades more than 200 cab-in-fronters, all converted into single-expansion machines or built as such. They were unique in being tailored exclusively to the needs of one railroad.

The Union Pacific developed its famous Challenger-type Mallets, beginning with fifteen 4-6-6-4s, received from Baldwin in 1936, capable of negotiating 24-degree curves and operating on grades up to 3 percent. With 22- by 32-inch cylinders, 69-inch drivers, 250 pounds boiler pressure, and a weight of 291 tons, of which 201 tons was applied to adhesion, these machines showed a startling tractive effort of 87,400 pounds. Their four-wheeled leading trucks added greatly to their speed potential. They did so well in freight and passenger runs between Green River and Laramie, Wyoming, that additional orders soon raised their total number to 85.

Then the Union Pacific put twenty 4-8-8-4s to work, the famous Big Boys, as the world's largest steam locos. Weighing 381 tons without tank, engines of this class had an overall wheelbase of 117 feet, 135,375 pounds of tractive effort, and 68-inch drivers, with a top speed potential of 80 miles per hour. Of course, the diesel age eventually put them and all other Mallets permanently out of service, although one of the Big Boys was making rare occasional runs for railfan trips in the early 1970s.

The Chesapeake and Ohio (C&O) and the Norfolk & Western (N&W) were the last two Class 1 roads to use the big compounds in regular service. As recently as 1948 the C&O surprised the railroad world by ordering from Baldwin twenty-five 2-6-6-2s, a number subsequently cut to ten. These were the first Mallets Baldwin had built since the 1920s. Last of the ten 2-6-6-2s to be outshopped was No. 1309, which had the additional distinction of being the final steam locomotive Baldwin ever built. The last Mallet outshopped in the United States was N&W's final Y6b compound, No. 2200, equipped with everything from roller bearings to mechanical lubricators, built in the road's own Roanoke shops in 1952.

BIBLIOGRAPHY: Henry B. Comstock, *The Iron Horse,* Crowell, New York, 1971; *Railroad Magazine,* March 1944; August 1955; Angus Sinclair, *Development of the Locomotive Engine,* annotated ed. by John H. White, Jr., M.I.T., Cambridge, Mass., 1970; *Trains Magazine,* November 1957; Roy V. Wright (ed.), *The Locomotive Cyclopedia of American Practice,* Simmons-Boardman, New York, 1941.

Mammoth Cave Railroad Rail line incorporated in 1874 and opened in 1880 between Glasgow Junction and Mammoth Cave, Kentucky. The Louisville & Nashville leased and operated it for its first 25 years. The line's favorite locomotive was a quaint box-shaped Baldwin steam dummy named *Hercules.* Automobiles doomed the road to extinction in 1931, just 5 years before Mammoth Cave National Park was established. Mammoth Cave Railroad generally made money for its owners and never had a wreck or a lawsuit brought against it.

Manitou & Pike's Peak Railway Standard-gauge, 8.9-mile rail line in Colorado, North America's highest railway which is not a through line. Opened on June 1, 1891, it has an average gradient of 1 in 6 (16.66 percent), but for 2 miles on Windy Hill the gradient is 1 in 4. Its lowest terminal is 7538 feet above sea level; its summit, 14,110 feet. Swiss-built diesel-electric cars replaced its original steam locomotives in 1963. One of the latter is preserved at Manitou; another, at the Colorado Railroad Museum in Golden, near Denver. For highest railways, *see* LOOKOUT MOUNTAIN INCLINE RAILWAY; SUMMITS.

BIBLIOGRAPHY: Morris W. Abbott, *Cog Railway to Pike's Peak,* Golden West Books, San Marino, Calif., 1973; *Trains Magazine,* February 1949.

Martha's Vineyard Railroad Rail line named for the small island on which it ran, 2½ miles off Nobska Point, Massachusetts. It originated in a town meeting at Edgartown in March 1874. Prior to that, the island had had a short horsecar line, built in 1873, of which little is known. The steam road was a 9-mile, single-tracked, 3-foot-gauge line, built in 1874 by laborers hired at $1.75 a day who held out for $2, thus winning one of the earliest strikes in railroad history. It ran southward from Oaks Bluff to Katama (later it was extended slightly to South Beach).

Its first engine, a box-shaped dummy, was soon discarded because she was too rigid to take curves readily and her noisy, jerky motion frightened horses. For 21 days after that no train ran on Martha's Vineyard rails. The engine which replaced her, built by H. K. Porter and named *Active,* fell into Buzzards Bay before reaching the island but was fished out, overhauled in Boston, put to work on August 21, and renamed *Edgartown.* She could be turned on a turntable at Edgartown, on a wye at Oaks Bluff, and on a wye at Katama. Original rolling stock consisted of a red-upholstered coach with *crosswise* seats for 47 passengers, a coach with *lengthwise* seats for 56, and a boxcar with removable seats for 22.

But the route had not been chosen wisely. Most of it ran along sandy beaches; tracks were washed away, undermined, or buried by drifting sand. In 1892 fire destroyed the big Sea View House, wharf, casino, and railroad facilities at Cottage City. Four years later, closing a rather dismal season, a train pulled by the engine *South Beach* made the island's farewell run.

Meanwhile, in 1891, a new 3-mile Cottage City Electric Railway had begun operating. In 1897 the abandoned steam road was revived and electrified, eventually merging with the Cottage City line. But in 1917 the increasing use of automobiles completely wiped out this final venture.

BIBLIOGRAPHY: Walter Blackwell, *Tracing the Route of Martha's Vineyard Railroad, 1874–1896,* 2d ed., rev., Blackwell, Miami, 1973.

Mason, William *(1808–1883)* Builder at Taunton, Massachusetts, of steam locomotives with such beautiful lines that another great locomotive builder, Matthias N. Forney, described them as "melodies cast and wrought in metal." Early in life, Mason manufactured cotton and woolen textile machinery, gearing, shafting, car wheels, and other equipment; and during the Civil War he turned out 600 Springfield rifles weekly.

Competing with the already popular locomotives built by Thomas Rogers and Matthias W. Baldwin, Mason completed on October 11, 1853, his first locomotive, the eight-wheeled *James Guthrie,* for the Jeffersonville Railroad. She had outside horizontal cylinders hollowed to provide air space and polished to prevent heat radiation. Her valves had a shifting link motion of a pattern practically the same as that used nearly a century later. Mason's second iron horse, the *W. G. Armstrong,* similar to his first, went to the same railroad. *See* BALDWIN LOCOMOTIVE WORKS; PATERSON, NEW JERSEY.

Mason's sleek, handsome *Missouri* was delivered in 1858 to the Hannibal & St. Joseph Railroad. She pulled a mail train to connect with the Union Pacific's *Overland Limited,* making a run that was unbeaten for 50 years. The only freak Mason ever built was the double-ended *Janus* (named for the ancient Roman deity with two opposite faces). Completed in 1871, she went to the Lehigh Valley (LV). But because she could not carry enough coal and water, the LV rebuilt her into two separate locomotives. Her design incorporated two engines from one firebox, a characteristic of the powerful Mallet type developed in France 5 years afterward. *See* LOCOMOTIVES, DOUBLE-ENDED; MALLET.

Except in the *Janus,* Mason never used a double boiler. He built the tender on the engine frame, somewhat like the later tank-type engines, applying the pony trucks to save flange wear on his drivers. Then he arranged to have his drivers swivel on a pin, and lastly he tried the flexible steam-pipe connection. Mason called these improved engines bogies and built more than 100 of them.

Mason adopted the Walschaert valve gear because the cylinders of his Bogies were so close to the drivers that this gear was found to work best. The first of his engines using it was the *William Mason,* built in 1874 for the Boston, Clinton & Fitchburg. But his Bogies never became very popular. Bigger and heavier trains and longer runs made them impractical.

The late Charles E. Fisher, longtime president of the Railway and Locomotive Historical Society, who supplied most of the foregoing information, credited Mason with the following improvements in steam locomotives: (1) bringing the cylinders to a level, (2) making the driving wheels with hollow spokes and a hollow rim and pouring in lead for counterbalance, (3) spreading the wheel trucks, (4) introducing the conical stay bolt for the crownsheet, (5) designing the arrangement of wedges in the jaws of driving-wheel boxes, (6) improving the locomotive's appearance, and (7) popularizing and setting the style for the 4-4-0, or American, type. For many years afterward, other builders merely increased the dimensions. Mason had perfected the type's initial design.

BIBLIOGRAPHY: Angus Sinclair, *Development of the Locomotive Engine,* annotated ed. by John H. White, Jr., M.I.T., Cambridge, Mass., 1970; John H. White, Jr., *American Locomotives: An Engineering History, 1830–1880,* Johns Hopkins, Baltimore, 1968.

Mastodons *See* TWELVE-WHEELERS.

Maternity Specials Hundreds of babies have been born on trains, and dramatic stories are told of racing the stork to a hospital. One night when Max J. Moore, a Baltimore & Ohio conductor, was running a Pittsburgh-Buffalo train, his Pullman conductor rushed into the coaches and said excitedly: "Max, come back with me! There's a woman in the Buffalo sleeper who's going to have a baby."

"Good God," was the dumbfounded reply, "I'm not a doctor." But Max did what he could. He explained the predicament to a woman coach passenger, who agreed to act as midwife. Unfortunately, the baby was stillborn, but the mother made a normal recovery.

Pullman porter Lou Thomas was known as "Doctor" on the Erie run between Buffalo and Cincinnati because he had assisted at three births on his car. Another porter, Stephen L. Hopkins, had such an experience when his car was filled with Cook County male politicians returning to Chicago, and the only woman aboard gave birth to a baby. Hopkins wrapped the mother and infant in blankets and presented them to the waiting husband and father. "He gave me 10 cents," the porter said later, "but I informed him there was no charge. That night he returned the two blankets with 10 dollars."

Mauch Chunk Railroad Rail line in northeastern Pennsylvania that, when opened in 1827, was the nation's longest and most important railway. This 9-mile coal carrier, consisting of level track and steep inclines, linked mines with the Lehigh River, over which anthracite was shipped. At first its cars were pulled up by mules and descended by gravity, but in 1844–1845 the addition of a famous switchback (zigzag pattern of tracks on a steep incline) eliminated the mules. From about 1870 until its abandonment in 1931 it was a scenic passenger line in a popular vacation area.

Meadow Brook Disaster On the morning of April 19, 1873, when the Boston-Stonington boat train (so called because it met the steamboat *Stonington* daily) reached Richmond switch, Rhode Island, a broken dam suddenly flooded Meadow Brook and washed away the bridge abutments on both sides of the Boston & Providence Railroad. The train consisted of an engine, with William Gould at the throttle, a baggage car, three coaches, and a smoking car. Too late to stop, the locomotive leaped the 20-foot watery gulf and buried her nose in the opposite bank.

The impact dumped live coals into the baggage car, making it a sea of flames, while overturned lamps and hot stoves set fire to the coaches, killing seven persons. When Gould's body was found, his dead hand was still clutching the reverse lever.

BIBLIOGRAPHY: Wesley S. Griswold, *Train Wreck!* Stephen Greene, Brattleboro, Vt., 1969; Robert C. Reed, *Train Wrecks,* Superior Publishing, Seattle, 1968.

Mears, Otto *(1841–1926)* Operator of a toll road and wagon-freighting service in the Colorado Rockies who developed a one-state narrow-gauge rail empire. On the map, it formed a three-pronged pitchfork, each fork representing a railroad, with the rival Denver and Rio Grande (D&RG) as the handle. All three Mears railroads ran generally from south to north, connecting with the D&RG at Silverton (9300-foot elevation), in an area famed for its huge output of high-grade gold and silver ore.

The left prong of the pitchfork was the Silverton Railroad, the most important of the three. From a northern terminus at Albany, 9800 feet above sea level, it turned and twisted to cross Red Mountain (10,910-foot elevation) and Chattanooga (10,280 feet). To reach the top of Red Mountain Pass it rounded a sharp hairpin curve, then descended by means of fantastic loops, switchbacks, and one of the very few covered turntables in railroad history. For most of its distance it paralleled Mineral Creek down to Silverton and the Animas River.

The middle fork was the Silverton, Gladstone, and Northerly, shortest of the Mears railroads. Beginning at Gladstone (10,600-foot elevation), it paralleled Cement Creek all the way down to Silverton, where it emptied into the Animas River. This railroad was built by Cyrus W. Davis of Waterville, Maine, president of the fabulous Gold King Mine at Gladstone, and was acquired by Mears, who constructed the other two prongs of the pitchfork. The right tine was the Silverton Northern (SN), which followed the Animas River from the Forks of the Animas to Silverton.

The biggest money-maker of the three lines was the Silverton Railroad, which hauled between 20,000 and 50,000 tons a year of rich ore, in addition to miners, fancy women, coal, liquor, hardware, clothing, and other necessities. It operated the showy palace car *Animas Forks,* adorned with red plush and solid silver, with accommodations for dining, drinking, and sleeping.

Mears helped to publicize his railroads by issuing picturesque passes printed on white buckskin or silver that have since become collectors' items. To Jay Gould, George M. Pullman, David M. Moffat, and other notables he presented gold-filigreed passes. But as the mines gradually closed down, so did his three railroads. The last survivor, SN, folded as the result of a miners' strike in 1941. Today, the SN is part of the Rio Grande system.

BIBLIOGRAPHY: Lucius Beebe and Charles Clegg, *Narrow Gauge in the Rockies,* Howell-North, Berkeley, 1958; Josie M. Crum, *Three Little Lines: The Silverton Railroad, the Silverton, Gladstone & Northerly Railroad, and the Silverton Northern Railroad,* Durango *Herald-News,* 1900; Robert E. Sloan and Carl A. Skowronski, *The Rainbow Route,* Sundance, Silverton, Colo., 1975.

MEC *See* MAINE CENTRAL RAILROAD.

Mergers In America's railroad industry mergers involve such factors as talks in boardrooms, law courts, financial control by stock buying, consolidations, long-term leases, operating agreements, holding companies, and action by Congress, the Interstate Commerce Commission (ICC), and the Department of Transportation. Since 1955 alone, the ICC has received more than 70 railroad merger applications and helped to cut the number of line-haul railroads from 6000 to 332 (as of May 1980).

Possibly the nation's first rail merger was that of the Wilmington & Susquehanna and the Baltimore & Fort Deposit, which became the Philadelphia, Wilmington and Baltimore in 1838. Fifteen years later the merger of 10 short lines created the New York Central. Today those 12 roads are part of Conrail through additional mergers.

Between 1884 and 1888 a total of 425 consolidations took place. In a 16-month period in 1899–1900 one-sixth of the nation's total rail mileage was absorbed in various transactions. Creation of the ICC in 1887 slowed the merger trend. Early in the twentieth century the rail network was virtually frozen; the few consolidations allowed during that trust-busting era were relatively small and difficult to bring about.

No mergers occurred in the Depression years of the 1930s and not many in the 1940s, but in the mid-1950s they popped up all over the country. Twenty mergers were applied for between 1955 and 1960, involving 38 major roads and about 90 percent of the nation's 218,000-mile rail network. In the 1960s, 47 were proposed, but only 13 in the 1970s. The merger of the Nashville, Chattanooga & St. Louis into the Louisville & Nashville in 1957 took 31 months to eventuate.

Some merger proceedings lasted only 3 months; others took years. The longest period was a case involving several petitions seeking all or a portion of the Chicago, Rock Island & Pacific, which took 50,000 pages of testimony and 11 years and 4 months to settle. Even at that, the ICC's decision was dismissed later because of the Rock Island's bankruptcy. The second longest, a little over 9 years, was the merger in 1970 of the Great Northern, Northern Pacific, and Chicago, Burlington & Quincy into today's Burlington Northern Inc. (BN), to which the Frisco was added in 1980.

In the decade following the BN merger of 1970 the ICC received 48 merger proposals. Most of these were granted; the others were denied, withdrawn, dismissed, or stayed or are still pending.

The federal government often intervenes in merger proceedings. In 1920, for instance, Congress told the ICC to evolve a plan for consolidating the nation's railroads into a limited number of systems. The ICC, in 1929, came up with a plan for 21 independent rail networks. That plan was dropped. In 1933 the Railroad Emergency Act tightened the ICC's control over mergers. Then Congress passed the Transportation Act of 1940, relieving the ICC of its 20-year-old obligation to devise a national merger plan and leaving it up to the railroads themselves, subject to the Commission's approval.

The ICC's policy statement of 1978 states seven factors (plus legal requirements) governing its approval of merger applications. These are (1) continuation of essential rail services by some railroad affected by the merger; (2) opportunities for increased operating efficiencies; (3) elimination of redundant facilities; (4) enhanced ability of the merged system to attract new business; (5) financial viability of the merged company; (6) maintenance of effective competition, subject to economic realities, among railroads and between railroads and other modes of transportation; and (7) environmental impact on the region that is served by the merged system.

On May 15, 1980, the Southern Pacific Company and Santa Fe Industries announced a preliminary agreement to merge SP into the Santa Fe by exchanging securities and filed an application with the ICC to authorize that merger. It would have created a 25,000-mile rail system, but the Santa Fe called it off.

Previously, the Union Pacific Corp. announced plans to acquire the Missouri Pacific Corp. and the Western Pacific Railroad, which would preserve UP's status as the nation's largest railroad holding company. The 1980 merger of the Chessie System and Seaboard Coast Line Industries made Southern Pacific (SP) the largest stockholder in the new CSX Corp. SP owns 9.9 percent of Seaboard. *See* CSX CORP.

In mid-1980 the Southern and the Norfolk & Western announced a preliminary agreement to merge by exchanging stock, subject to approval by both roads' boards of directors and stockholders and by the ICC. Total assets would be $5.7 billion.

Miles of Railroad Track According to the U.S. Federal Railway Administration and other sources, mileage in North America in 1976 was 390,600. This included first, second, third, and fourth tracks, switching and terminal operations, and sidings and yard tracks operated by common carriers but not municipal rapid-transit lines. The total divides into United States, 311,500; Canada, 64,000; and Mexico, 15,100.

Ownership of these lines is: United States, 191,880 miles by private companies, 1250 miles by national bodies (government corporations), and 380 miles by state and municipal entities; Canada, 18,595 miles by private companies, 24,550 miles nationalized, 1860 miles by provincial and municipal entities, and 920 miles by a combination; Mexico, 15,100 miles, all nationalized.

The peak year for route-mile trackage in the United States was 1916, with 254,000 miles. Here are the figures by decades: 1830, 23; 1840, 2818; 1850, 9021; 1860, 30,626; 1870, 52,922; 1880, 93,267; 1890, 163,605; 1900, 140,313; 1910, 143,366; 1920, 252,865; 1930, 249,182; 1940, 234,182; 1950, 224,331; 1960, 217,551; 1970, 209,001. Since 1916, despite a more than doubling of freight ton-miles, the total line mileage has dropped by about 24 percent owing to the consolidation of traffic and the abandonment of parallel and unprofitable branch lines, brought about by competition including highways, waterways, airlines, and oil pipelines. Also, much other traffic has been downgraded from through-line to secondary status.

BIBLIOGRAPHY: John H. Armstrong, *The Railroad—What It Is, What It Does*, Simmons-Boardman, New York, 1978.

Milwaukee Road (Chicago, Milwaukee, St. Paul & Pacific Railroad; (CMStP&P) A system started in 1850 with the opening of 5 miles of Milwaukee & Mississippi Railroad (M&M) from Milwaukee to Wauwatosa, Wisconsin. The line was extended in 1851 to Waukesha and in 1857 to the Mississippi River at Prairie du Chien. In 1858 another road, the La Crosse & Milwaukee, was completed between its two name cities, and in 1866 it merged with M&M as the Milwaukee & St. Paul.

A reminder of that period is the lone trackside grave of an unknown trackman, killed accidentally while helping to build the M&M in 1858. Shaded by two great oak trees near a cut through which the line passes about 6 miles west of Portage, Wisconsin, it inspired Alfred Burrett to write a poem, "The Grave of a Section Hand," which includes this verse:

They laid him away on the brow of a hill,
Outside of the right-of-way,
And the old boss whispered: "Peace, be still
Till the call on the Final Day."
They had placed him where he wished to lie
When his turn would come, he said;
Where he'd list to the wires' mournful sigh,
To the foreman's "Joint ahead!"

In 1874 the company was renamed Chicago, Milwaukee & St. Paul (CMStP). In the 1880s routes were lengthened to Kansas City, Omaha, and Fargo, North Dakota. The CMStP became, in 1880, the first railroad to illuminate its passenger trains with electricity and, in 1887, the first road west of Chicago to equip all its passenger trains for steam heat. The extension from South Dakota to Puget Sound, completed in 1909, cost very heavily because no land grants were involved.

In 1921 the CM&StP acquired Indiana lines. In 1924 bandits staged a $3 million train stickup on the Milwaukee Road. The system was reorganized in 1925 as the Chicago, Milwaukee, St. Paul & Pacific. The year 1935 was one of triumph and disaster: the first *Hiawatha* streamlined train entered service as an immediate success, but the company plunged into a 10-year bankruptcy.

A new management built three great automated freight yards, terminated the use of steam locomotives, and began operating westward to Council Bluffs, Iowa, city-named streamliners, trains which were sped to the West Coast by the Union Pacific and Southern Pacific. In the 1960s the system was modernized on a large scale with computers and other electronic equipment but failed in its efforts to consolidate with one or more other Midwestern carriers.

In 1971, like nearly all of America's large passenger-hauling railroads, the Milwaukee turned its deficit-ridden passenger business over to Amtrak. Also in 1971 it acquired trackage rights to Portland, Oregon, and 2 years later to Louisville, Kentucky. But with the inflationary spiral in full swing and despite rigid economies, the Milwaukee Road in 1977 was forced into its third bankruptcy. *See* AMTRAK.

In 1980, still in bankruptcy and wishing to help finance its continued operation, the road shrank considerably, selling and abandoning parts of its transcontinental line, including the sale of tracks and rights-of-way in Montana, Idaho, and Washington for a total of $40 million to the Burlington Northern and the Union Pacific

(UP). Later in 1980 it sold more of its assets, mostly in Washington State, for $23 million. UP bought 91 miles of Milwaukee Road line plus yard, port, and industry-access trackage in Seattle and Tacoma. Weyerhaeuser [lumber] Co. bought 123 miles of line and 99 rail cars.

BIBLIOGRAPHY: August W. Derleth, *The Milwaukee Road,* Creative Age, New York, 1948; H. H. Field, *History of the Milwaukee Railroad,* Chicago, Milwaukee, St. Paul & Pacific Railroad, Chicago, 1941; Charles F. Martin, *Milwaukee Road Locomotives,* Normandie House, Chicago, 1972; Jim Scribbins, *The Hiawatha Story,* Kalmbach, Milwaukee, 1970; Charles R. Wood and Dorothy M. Wood, *Milwaukee Road—West,* Superior Publishing, Seattle, 1972.

Minibridge Movement of international containerized shipments that originate or terminate at a United States port and require a trip across America in addition to an ocean voyage. For instance, shipments originating in the United States and bound for the Orient are assembled at a Gulf or East Coast port, move across the country by rail, and are loaded onto ships at West Coast ports for the voyage to Asia. The same process works in reverse for cargo coming from the Orient to the East Coast. *See* SILK TRAINS. This operation is one of the fastest-growing rail services.

Allied to minibridge are *landbridge* and the new *microbridge.* The former involves railroad movement of containerized cargo across the United States bound for the Orient from Europe, or vice versa. In microbridge, initiated in 1977, import-export shipments either originate or terminate at certain designated inland United States ports such as Kansas City or Chicago. These services cut thousands of miles from international shipping by bypassing the Panama and Suez Canals and trips around the tip of Africa or South America. Railbridge is a key factor in the phenomenal increase in piggyback traffic. *See* PIGGYBACKING.

Minneapolis & St. Louis Railway *See* RECEIVERSHIP, LONGEST, IN THE UNITED STATES.

Missouri-Kansas-Texas Railroad (Katy) The first railroad to enter Texas from the north, it did much to develop the Southwest. In 1870, when the total route mileage of railroads in the United States was 52,922, a group of men who had 182 miles of line planned and partially built on Kansas soil adopted the name Missouri, Kansas & Texas Railway (MK&T) and entered the race into Indian Territory. The federal government had limited its land grant in that area to the first railroad to enter the territory below the Neosho River Valley.

On June 6, 1870, the Katy completed the necessary tracklaying and sent a diamond-stacked woodburning engine across the territorial line into the Cherokee Nation at a point a few miles south of what is now Chetopa, Kansas. This gave Katy the exclusive right to build through the vast wilderness of Indian Territory under the land grant, but only with the Indians' consent. The natives agreed reluctantly. The railroad's first emblem, a shield, carried the words "Katy" and "M-K-T Railroad" and palms indicating the territorial victory.

There is a wealth of romance and adventure in the Katy's early records: frontier chaos, wild animals, prairie fires, floods, Indians fighting in defense of their land, longhorn cattle, dust and mud and sudden riches, bandits, gamblers, prostitutes, gun-toting train and engine men armed as a requisite to continued existence, and reckless chance taking by pioneer financiers and workers.

The railroad was built largely by Civil War veterans. Its financial backers included August Belmont, J. Pierpont Morgan, Levi P. Morton (destined to become Vice President of the United States), John D. Rockefeller, Levi Parsons, and George Denison. The last two, president and vice president, respectively, of the MK&T and active builders of the new system, had cities named for them.

As the Katy grew, it brought in settlers by the hundreds of thousands and provided more accessible markets for such products as cotton and cattle. For hundreds of miles the Katy was laid on old cattle trails famed in frontier literature. As the railhead crept south, the bandit era swung into high gear. The James and Younger boys, the Dalton gang, Sam Bass, and others robbed trains and galloped away. The last armed robbery on the Katy was on August 21, 1923, when the Spencer gang rifled a mail car of $21,000 near Okesa, Oklahoma. Every member of this gang was killed or captured.

By 1970 the Katy was operating 2787 route miles that stretched from Kansas City and St. Louis to Altus in western Oklahoma and to San Antonio and Galveston, Texas. Its principal traffic is the movement south to tidewater of wheat, lumber, steel products, coal, minerals, and motor vehicles.

BIBLIOGRAPHY: Donovan L. Hofsommer, *Katy Northwest: The Story of a Branch Line Railroad,* Pruett Publishing Co., Boulder, Colo., 1976; Vincent V. Masterson, *The Katy Railroad and the Last Frontier,* University of Oklahoma Press, Norman, Okla., 1952; *Missouri-Kansas-Texas Railroad: 1870–1970,* Missouri-Kansas-Texas Railroad, Dallas, 1970; Sylvan R. Wood, *The Locomotives of the Katy,* Railway & Locomotive Historical Society Bulletin 63, Boston, 1944.

Missouri Pacific Railroad (MP) On July 4, 1851, ground was broken at St. Louis, Missouri, for construction of the first rail line west of the Mississippi River. The discovery of gold in California in 1848 had sparked the need for faster and more dependable transportation to the West. St. Louisans visualized an iron highway running all the way to the Pacific Ocean and called their project, chartered in 1849, the Pacific Railroad. Congress refused to help them financially.

Rails bought in England were shipped via New Orleans and upriver. The first locomotive, a woodburning 4-4-0 named *Pacific,* was built in Taunton, Massachusetts, in 1852. In 1855 the road reached Jefferson City,

Missouri, and transferred passengers by its own boats to Kansas City, Missouri.

Meanwhile, the St. Louis & Iron Mountain, the Hannibal & St. Joseph, and other railroads, some originating in Texas, which were eventually to become part of the future Missouri Pacific system, were being built. The Iron Mountain line managed to overcome a War Department requirement that its trains be pulled by horses or mules to avoid a fire hazard from woodburning engines.

By July 1858, the Pacific Railroad had completed 160 miles to Tipton, Missouri, the eastern terminal for a new stagecoach service to San Francisco, the Overland Mail. This took mail and passengers between St. Louis and San Francisco in nearly 25 days, or 10 days faster than the old Isthmus of Panama route.

Like many other railroads, the Pacific suffered heavily from Civil War raids, especially in 1864, when bridges, buildings, tracks, and rolling stock were destroyed all the way from Franklin to Kansas City. But on September 20, 1865, the first train was run from Kansas City to St. Louis. In 1869 the Pacific changed its wide gauge to standard to permit a free interchange of cars of standard-gauge Eastern roads.

By 1874 there was rail service between St. Louis, Dallas, and Houston. In that year, too, the famous Eads Bridge was completed over the Mississippi. Also in 1874, the Union Depot Co. in St. Louis was incorporated, and a station was built that served the railroad until 1894, when the present huge Union Station was opened.

Financial difficulties in 1872 forced the Pacific Railroad to be reorganized with a new name, Missouri Pacific Railway Company. Shortly afterward, Jay Gould bought control of the MP and other Western and Southwestern roads, welding together a mighty network of rail lines known as the Southwest System. But in 1885 Gould lost his grip on his vast rail empire. Two of his roads, the Texas & Pacific (T&P) and the International-Great Northern, but not the Iron Mountain, slipped away from MP control by 1888. *See* GOULD, JAY.

Between 1885 and 1892, however, there was a large increase in MP mileage through the building of subsidiary lines. Pueblo, Colorado, became MP's western terminus and Alexandria, Louisiana, southern terminus of the Iron Mountain. From 1892 until 1910 the MP built or purchased considerably more mileage. In 1909 many smaller subsidiaries were merged into the parent Missouri Pacific Railway. In 1917 a final merger of the MP with the St. Louis, Iron Mountain & Southern produced a new corporation, the Missouri Pacific Railroad Company, popularized as the Missouri Pacific Lines. Additional roads serving Texas and Louisiana joined the MP family in 1925. And in 1938 the system organized its own freight transport trucking company to supplement its rail service.

In 1937 MP acquired its first diesel locos, switchers. In 1940 passenger diesels were powering the company's first lightweight streamlined train, the *Missouri Pacific Eagle.* (Other famous MP passenger trains were the *Colorado Eagles* and the *Sunshine Special.*) By 1955 MP had retired all its steam engines. In 1933 the system had gone into a bankruptcy that would last 23 years. During that long period, however, it continued to expand and modernize.

In 1963 the MP and Texas & Pacific consolidated their operations, with a total mileage of nearly 12,000 in 12 states. In 1967 the system acquired control of the Chicago & Eastern Illinois (C&EI), thus forming a direct rail route between the nation's largest rail center, Chicago, and the West, bypassing the busy St. Louis gateway. But the merger of C&EI and T&P into the MP was not consummated until 1976.

In January 1980 the MP and the Union Pacific (UP) announced a preliminary agreement for a merger, valued at about $900 million, that would form the country's largest transportation-based conglomerate. The UP would be the surviving company, the nation's third largest railroad, with a revenue exceeding $5 billion and 21,200 miles of track. The proposed merger was subject to approval by stockholders of both companies and the Interstate Commerce Commission.

The MP, with 11,500 miles of track, is America's sixth-largest rail system. The UP, with 9700 miles, is the ninth-largest. The lines meet at 13 points, mostly in Kansas. A combined system would stretch from Chicago westward to Los Angeles and Portland and southward through the Midwest to the Gulf Coast. As both MP and UP are conglomerates, many other businesses would be involved.

BIBLIOGRAPHY: Thomas B. Brewer and Allen Dickes, *History of the Missouri Pacific,* Macmillan, New York; *Corporate History of the Missouri Pacific Railway Company and the St. Louis, Iron Mountain & Southern Railway Company and Their Constituent Lines,* Missouri Pacific Railroad, St. Louis, 1915; *Jane's World Railways and Rapid Transit Systems,* F. Watts, New York, 1977; John Leeds Kerr, *The Story of a Western Pioneer: The Missouri Pacific; An Outline History,* Railway Research Society, New York, 1928.

Model Railroading At its best, model railroading is a technological hobby involving handicraft, mechanical and artistic skills, small tools and small machinery, electronics, and a passion for perfection, in addition to a love of railroads. At its lowest level, it is playing with toys. Both types are model railroading, but scale modeling takes the subject seriously. The latter consists of creating or assembling accurate replicas of prototype locomotives and/or cars and/or the railroads on which they run—the track pattern, stations, signal towers, trackside installations, tunnels, bridges, etc., and the right-of-way landscape.

This sort of thing attracts men and boys (rarely women) who like to re-create railroad scenes and experiences they are familiar with or once knew or those in distant places or bygone years. A layout may be historical and/or geographical, carefully patterned after real railroads in specific localities, or it may be built in a general manner with the modeler using equipment to suit his or her fancy.

There must be 250,000 scale modelers alone in North America, representing an annual sales potential of some $90 million at the retail level, and a great many more than that number of occasional or casual modelers and adults who buy train sets for themselves or children. Numerous products are adaptable to both the owners of train sets and the avid-hobbyist market, especially in the most popular scales. This permits mass production of cars, locomotives, track, and accessories. The modelers' demand for realism and accurate detail greatly influences the manufacturers of such products. By extending their sales outside the serious-hobby field, these firms can keep their prices lower. Buyers in both areas benefit. Scale model railroading began as an offshoot of the toy industry, and toys set the standards. Today, the situation is partly reversed.

HO is by far the most popular scale. Developed around 1930, it did not achieve preeminence until after World War II. Since the early 1950s it has gained an increasing share of the total number of modelers, at least three-quarters of whom have adopted it. An HO locomotive, car, or railroad structure is built to the scale of 3.5 millimeters to the foot. The ratio is 1:87.1. An HO scale model is about 1/87 the size of its prototype. This size permits a high level of realistic detail, yet is not too large for building a relatively complete layout.

Such balance is important in creating a realistic overall effect for scenic and operating purposes. The average space available in a home can usually accommodate a model layout of railroad yards, industrial plants, and servicing facilities, or whatever, plus a reasonably long portion of mainline.

As the most widely liked scale, HO has the largest variety of commercially made products such as simple-assembly plastic kits, craft kits composed of wood and metal parts, and individual parts, for greater detail. Considerable scratch-building also occurs in this scale. Thus you can produce realism without having to build from scratch. The more extensive a layout is, the more it can reflect the patterns of real-world geography and railroading.

During the hobby's formative years, few raw materials designed for model work were available. You had to cut wood parts from full-size lumber and score and scribe cardboard for siding, besides milling, filing, brazing, soldering, and bolting everything together. But after kits from Varney, Mantua, and Future Designs came out, you did not have to be a machinist to build a miniature railroad; so the hobby attracted more participants.

Most HO enthusiasts choose to model standard-gauge railroads in one of two distinct time periods, 1940–1960 and 1960–present. The standard railroad gauge, 4 feet 8½ inches, is equivalent to 16.5 millimeters in HO. This mixture of metric and English units is due to the scale's

***This realistic ¼-inch scale model of a United Railways combine used both commercial and home-built parts. It reaches up to a copper web to draw power, just as the prototype interurban car did.* [Robert Hegge / Railroad Model Craftsman]**

history. Around 1930, British hobbyists developed the OO scale (4 millimeters = 1 foot) and 16.5-millimeter track gauge. (The correct gauge should have been 19 millimeters, but the wheel treads were oversize, so it was narrowed.) When OO crossed the Atlantic, many American modelers adopted it because it was almost half the size of the most popular scale of the time, O scale (¼ inch = 1 foot). This permitted greater operation in the same space. Both scales coexisted until World War II, when HO won out.

Modelers build narrow- as well as standard-gauge layouts. That is why the term *HO scale* is used instead of *HO gauge*. Narrow-gauge models are built to the ratio of 1:87.1. All details, structures, etc., are the same as standard-gauge HO, the only difference being the distance between the rails and the prototypes. Colorado's famous 36-inch-gauge lines form the basis of inspiration for most narrow-gauge modeling because of their colorful history and because they were ridden and photographed so often. Initially, narrow-gaugers had to scratch-build nearly all their engines and cars, and many still do, but much of that rolling stock and power is now commercially made. The only other narrow gauge that appeals to more than a few followers is the 2-foot gauge once used mostly in Maine. *See* MAINE'S TWO-FOOTERS.

Even though the final regularly scheduled mainline steam locos dropped their fires for the last time in 1960 (Grand Trunk Western's commuter runs between Detroit and Pontiac, Michigan), the steam engine is still a symbol of railroading. Many modelers remember its heyday or at least its decline. Fantrips and museum operations have kept it visible even to young modelers. Nearly half of the model railroaders, like most railfan photographers, prefer the steam era, especially the 1940–1960 period. The mixture of steam and diesel-electric equipment has a wide appeal. Nearly one-third of the active HO modelers use this period. Some others prefer electrical equipment such as juice locos, streetcars, and interurbans. *See* MUSEUMS.

Besides the common plastic-bodied engines and those either scratch-built or assembled from kits, there are imported brass locomotives. In the mid-1950s, Japanese firms began contracting to manufacture models of United States steam locos, eventually adding diesels and cars to their list of imports. Over the years, their quality has tended to improve, and they have readily been accepted despite their relatively high prices. The brass import provides an alternative to scratch-building by allowing rather short runs of specific cars and locomotives. Collectors of brass locomotives like to leave their equipment unpainted, whereas modelers usually paint, detail, and add a weather patina to theirs.

N scale, the newest common modeling scale, currently accounts for nearly one-seventh of the hobby's activity. It operates on a 9-millimeter track gauge, has a ratio of 1:160, and is scaled at 0.075 foot = 1 inch. A growing number of firms offer ready-to-run N-scale equipment, mostly with injection-molded bodies, and a variety of structure kits and accessories. In 1961, British and German companies entered the United States market with what was called OOO scale (1:160 size). The two main manufacturers of this scale initially used different couplers.

While N scale has an advantage in size (you can build a more complete railroad in a smaller space and operate more realistic-appearing trains), O is the oldest scale in continuous use among modelers. Today O's ratio is 1:48 (in the United States and Canada); the models are built to a scale of ¼ inch to the foot. The standard gauge is 1¼ inches because of the early use of wheels and locomotives derived from train sets. During the 1930s, O was the most popular scale. Initially, it was the smallest indoor model railroad size.

Possibly one-twelfth of the active modelers now work in ¼-inch scale. Proportionally fewer commercial products are made for O, and most locos and rolling stock must be built from kits or scratch. Numerous hobbyists enjoy scratch-building. An extensive line of superior-quality detailing and car parts makes the job easier and helps to get outstanding results.

This is not an aerial view of a roundhouse, turntable, and locomotives but models built to scale, at the Westchester, New York, Model Railroad Club. It is photographic proof of the skill involved in model railroading.

Z scale, with a 1:220 ratio, manufactured in Germany, has gained a following. TT scale, ⅒ inch to the foot, was popular in the 1950s but did not interest many commercial suppliers. There are also ⅜-inch and ½-inch scales. A number of scales and gauges used today focus on the construction of operating live-steam engines fueled by alcohol or coal, some of them large and powerful enough to pull midget trains on which passengers ride. Scale modeling also includes the occasional building, by mechanically skilled individuals, of painstakingly accurate locos or pieces of rolling stock for exhibition purposes only.

The most important minor scale, as measured by the number of adherents, is S, which uses an 0.875-inch gauge. It is scaled at 3⁄16 inch to the foot and has a 1:64 ratio. When first introduced around 1937, it was called CD scale. One of American Flyer's (AF's) toy trains used 3⁄16-inch scale. Many scale modelers adapted this equipment by replacing trucks and couplers and by adding details. AF ceased production long ago, but some small firms now put out scale products for that market.

Toy locomotives and trains, like wagons and fire engines, first appeared in cast iron, wood, and other materials. Carlisle & Finch of Cincinnati began making electric train sets in 1896, competing with the windup trains of Ives and others. Collectors today pay good prices for those antiques as well as for pre-World War II products of Lionel, Märklin, Howard, and Voltamp. Other collectors specialize in Lionel, AF, and early-day O and HO models: Megow, Westbrook, Varney, etc. Because so many of these toys were made from stamped steel plated with tin to prevent rust, the word *tinplate* is used to describe them. *See also* BEGGS, EUGENE.

Such items as couplers, track gauge, and wheel standards caused confusion in the early years of model railroading. Formation of the National Model Railroad Association (NMRA) in 1935 helped both hobbyists and manufacturers by setting standards for interchange of equipment. NMRA is headquartered at P.O. Box 2186, Indianapolis, Indiana 46206, and issues the *NMRA Bulletin.* Allied to this field is the Train Collectors Association, Paradise Lane, Ronko, Pennsylvania, 17572, which puts out the *Train Collectors Quarterly.* Other periodicals are the *Model Railroader, Railroad Model Craftsman, Traction & Models, Railroad Modeler, Narrow Gauge and Short Line Gazette,* and *Prototype Modeler.*

BIBLIOGRAPHY: John Armstrong, *Creative Layout Design,* Kalmbach, Milwaukee, 1978; Louis H. Hertz, *Handbook of Old American Toys,* Mark Haber & Co., Wethersfield, Conn., 1948; Paul Mallery, *Electrical Handbook for Model Railroads,* 2 vols., Carstens Publs., Newton, N.J., 1971-1973; id., *Design Handbook for Model Railroads,* Carstens Publs., Newton, N.J., 1979; Robert Schleicher, *The Model Railroading Handbook,* 2 vols., Chilton Book Company, Radnor, Pa.,

1975–1978; id., *Building Plastic Railroad Models,* Kalmbach, Milwaukee, 1979; David Sutton, *The Complete Book of Model Railroading,* Prentice-Hall, Englewood Cliffs., N.J., 1964.

WILLIAM C. SCHAUMBURG, *Associate Editor,* Railroad Model Craftsman

Moffat Tunnel Work was begun in 1923 on this 6.1-mile bore which cut 173 miles in Colorado from the rail distance between the Atlantic and the Pacific and reduced the average grade from 2 to 3 percent. Five years of day and night work and $16 million finished the job on February 27, 1928, when the first train out of Denver rolled through the new tunnel beneath James Peak. Only after completion of the Dotsero Cutoff between the Denver & Salt Lake and Denver and Rio Grande Western (D&RGW) railroads in 1934 did the tunnel get its full usefulness. The cutoff enabled D&RGW through trains to run between Denver and Salt Lake City, which they have been doing ever since.

Monon Route Since 1971 part of the Louisville & Nashville and now part of CSX Corp., the Monon Route was an independent X-shaped road terminating at Chicago, Indianapolis, Michigan City, and Louisville, but mostly a Hoosier State line. Lew Wallace, who spent most of his life in Crawfordsville, Indiana, wrote parts of *Ben Hur* while riding its trains to and from Indianapolis.

The Monon sprang from the New Albany & Salem (NA&S) in Abraham Lincoln country. The NA&S was incorporated in 1847, when New Albany, with 8181 population, was Indiana's largest city. Its charter was unique in authorizing the company to extend its lines, by tracklaying or by buying short lines, to "any other point or points" in the state.

Its earliest track consisted of ties laid 4 feet apart, connected by stringers embedded in them, and bar-iron rails secured by spikes countersunk so as not to project above the ties. Occasionally, spikes gave way, causing rail ends to break through car floors as *snake heads,* the common term for them, terrifying and sometimes injuring passengers and occasionally derailing trains. Adopting T rails eliminated this danger.

After the panic of 1857 the road was reorganized as the Chicago, New Albany & Louisville and again in 1897 as the Chicago, Indianapolis & Louisville, or Monon Route. In 1946, when John W. Barriger, one of America's most competent rail executives, took over its presidency, the system was badly run down, but he went a long way toward modernizing it. He bought new freight cars, began retiring steam locos, and announced that the Monon would be the first completely dieselized Class I road of its size. He also had Raymond Loewy redesign its passenger equipment, and he set out to eliminate all mainline grades of 5 percent or more and all curves exceeding 2 degrees.

See LOEWY, RAYMOND.

BIBLIOGRAPHY: Frank F. Hargrave, *A Pioneer Indiana Railroad,* Wm. B. Burford Printing Co., Indianapolis, 1932; Stewart H. Holbrook, *The Story of American Railroads,* Crown, New York, 1947.

Monorails Shown at the Philadelphia Centennial Exposition in 1876, among many other new ideas, was a monorail railroad with a steam locomotive moving astride an elevated single track like a train running atop a fence. The rail was fastened to a wooden stringer resting on top of upright posts, with guard rollers hanging down on both sides. This contraption was widely ridiculed as a freak. But E. W. Coddington and Col. A. I. Wilson, both from the oil boomtown of Bradford, Pennsylvania, took it seriously and built the Bradford & Foster Brook Railway (B&FB), which was nicknamed Pegleg because it embodied the monorail principle.

The first mile was completed on January 17, 1878, and put in operation with a saddle-tank engine and two coaches. That summer 5 more miles were completed to Gilmore, a thriving oil town. For a while the odd railroad prospered, making 10 round trips daily at about 20 miles per hour. But on January 29, 1878, it tried out a new engine, which exploded, killing three crewmen and two company officials and seriously injuring three others. The B&FB never ran again. In 1880 it was sold to a junk dealer.

Another unique monorail, based on a somewhat similar principle, was operated briefly in the early 1920s near Trona, California, in the Mojave Desert. It ran up through a canyon in the bleak, treeless Slate Mountains to haul out magnesium sulfate (Epsom salt) from a deeply crusted mineral deposit in Searles Lake, a body of water measuring about 14 by 7 miles.

Its motive power was a converted Fordson tractor with two double-flanged steel wheels, both driven by the gasoline engine. The track was a single steel rail attached to timber atop an A frame. Ore cars and "locomotive" carried cargo on both sides of the track simultaneously but well below the rail level so that the center of gravity was low enough for stability.

The first monorail railroad in the United States was built in 1878 and nicknamed Pegleg, but it was very short-lived. It had a steam locomotive running on an elevated single track.

Passenger-carrying monorails have been used mostly for entertainment in the United States. The 1939 New York World's Fair operated a line with seven trains, each having two cars. [American Machine and Foundry Company]

Because this machine could not develop sufficient traction up and down the canyon's 10 percent grade, its wheels slipped on the solitary rail. So the railroad's operators ordered General Electric Co. to build new equipment. But the new train never hauled ore. The enterprise went bankrupt, and the monorail line gradually disappeared beneath the shifting desert sand.

Passenger-carrying monorails got little encouragement in the United States except for entertaining rides at world's fairs, amusement parks, and zoos, beginning near the mid-1900s. Others were proposed as city transit lines, but the only one ever built as such was erected to take people to and from the Seattle World's Fair in 1962 and is still in transit service. It is true that monorails could take passenger traffic off city streets. Offsetting this advantage are the obstacles and danger that their supports would offer to motor vehicular traffic, the overhead noise, the partial darkening of streets, and depreciation of real estate values on those streets—some of the reasons why most municipal elevated railways have been dismantled and not rebuilt.

See also BICYCLE RAILWAY.

BIBLIOGRAPHY: Hermann S. D. Botzow, Jr., *Monorails*, Simmons-Boardman, New York, 1960; Derek G. T. Harvey, *Monorails*, Putnam, New York, 1965.

An armed bandit, far left, sneaks up on an unsuspecting railroad stationmaster in a scene from The Great Train Robbery, *the first railroad movie ever made (1903).*

Motion Pictures Films are no longer shown aboard trains to entertain long-distance travelers, in contrast to a common practice on airlines today. The earliest-known experiments of this kind were conducted in 1920 on the Atlanta & West Point and the Western Railway of Alabama. In 1922 the Illinois Central showed films on a Chicago–New Orleans run. Three years later, the Canadian National tried out motion pictures on Montreal-Quebec trains. In 1929 sound movies were shown aboard a train for the first time, on the Union Pacific. In 1933 the Atlantic Coast Line began showing films on New York–Florida trains.

Motion Pictures, Railroad Feature A Hollywood train, certainly the world's most versatile and most changeable train, virtually chugged its way around the world without leaving the 1000-foot track on a Metro-Goldwyn-Mayer lot in Culver City, California. It was ridden to various places by many of moviedom's all-time greats as well as by starlets and extras.

Among the actors were Irene Dunne, to Southampton, England, in *The White Cliffs of Dover;* Spencer Tracy, aboard a Wells-Fargo express car in *Sea of Grass;* Robert Walker, in New York's Penn Station (the one since torn down) in *The Clock;* Robert Taylor, to Moscow in *Song of Russia;* Robert Shannon, to Winton, England, in *The Green Years;* and Mickey Rooney, as *Young Tom Edison* working out of an exact duplicate of the Port Huron, Michigan, depot out of which the future inventor worked as a news butcher selling candy, souvenirs, etc.

That same train was involved in stickups, wrecks, bombings, speed records, and bridge washouts. It made just about every kind of run from extra-fare luxury liners to decrepit freights. Its passenger lists ranged from royalty, statesmen, concert singers, and tycoons to plain people, criminals, and animals. Innumerable changes were made in the cars and engines to fit its roles. It had a genuine Cooke-built 4-4-0 that had begun life as No. 9 on the Fort Worth, Denver & Gulf and a somewhat more modern Baldwin. Among its rolling stock were cars bought from common-carrier railroads and replicas of foreign luxury equipment built especially for Hollywood.

The very first storytelling feature movie, made in the infancy of the film industry, had a railroad subject: *The Great Train Robbery,* produced in 1903 and shown in large United States cities. Some of the earliest serial photoplays were about trains, such as *The Lost Express* in 1916. Possibly the most outstanding silent train feature, *The Iron Horse,* depicted the construction of a Western railroad. Among early sound pictures were *Silk Express, Sleepers East, Union Depot, Murder in the Private Car* (a predecessor of the relatively recent spectacular *Murder on the Orient Express*), *Western Limited, Rome Express, Shanghai Express, The Golden West,* and *Silver Streak,* dealing with the first Burlington *Zephyr* streamliner.

Of course, a great many photoplays were made on real railways, usually with interior shots of Pullmans, coaches, diners, etc., done on Hollywood stages.

The passing scenery shown outside car windows of "moving" trains is real scenery but previously shot and flashed on a screen several feet outside the car windows in the studio. The big producers have film libraries that include landscape scenes taken along many rail lines throughout the world. There is also a film library company in Hollywood that rents various scenes to the studios: stock shots of trains in action, stations, bridges, tunnel entrances, trackside installations, and so on. Sounds also are usually dubbed in: recordings of whistles screaming, the thunder of locomotive exhausts, bells, toots, the clank-clank heard on observation platforms, etc.

Steam-engine cab sequences were usually made from facsimile cabs built on the indoor stage from wood or metal or sometimes cabs from junked locomotives. A screen was rigged up outside the fireman's window. As soon as the projection machine started, telegraph poles, trackside signals, and landscape began to race past the movie viewer. Dry ice was often used to simulate steam from the boiler.

This information is in the past tense because, with the virtual vanishing of "romantic" steam locomotives, there has been almost a total stoppage in the production of railroad movies. It used to be standard practice, even in nonrail photoplays, to show brief flashes of revolving engine and train wheels to indicate that the movie characters were going to different locales. That technique is virtually never used today.

Paramount bought an old Virginia & Truckee engine and used her in, among other films, *High, Wide and Handsome,* one sequence of which shows an oil pipeline being ripped up by a heavy chain attached to an Atlantic & Great Western locomotive. Movie producers often employed railroad men as technical advisers for railroad films. Dozens of Union Pacific shopmen were hired for roundhouse repair-shop scenes in *The Power and the Glory,* one of the most authentic railroad feature movies ever made.

Sometimes the camera crew rode on the tender to shoot players in the cab. Other cameras were rigged up at various points off and on the train. Nearly all train-wreck scenes and bridge collapses were done in miniature. In the early days of filming, though, it was not rare for a producer to wreck a full-size train for a photoplay. Once a Western mainline was tied up for 22 hours until a movie wreck could be cleared up. But movies were relatively new then, and nobody seemed to mind very much.

***Jack Daugherty rescues Louise Loraine in the nick of time from an oncoming locomotive in the silent movie* The Iron Trail.**

Nobody knows how many movie heroines were rescued just barely in time from death under the wheels of the iron horse. A notable instance occurred in *The Perils of Pauline,* a silent movie serial of hair-raising thrills, when the villain tied the sweet young thing to the track. The engine which rushed toward her presumably was not equipped with an airbrake for a quick stop, but the hero rescued her in time.

Most rail movies were made in the West, particularly with tracks and equipment of the Southern Pacific (SP), the Santa Fe, and the short Sierra Railroad. Present-day steam tourist lines are used on rare occasions. A stretch of seldom-operated SP track near Chatsworth, 35 miles northeast of Hollywood, appeared in many outdoor scenes. The Warner Brothers lot boasted a trainshed, railroad cars, studio-built European coaches, a prop trolley car, and a small railway depot.

Twentieth Century-Fox, largest of California's studios, built a realistic-looking replica several blocks long of a New York City elevated railway which could be dismantled and replaced when needed. Derricks hoisted cars onto it. These sets were occasionally rented to other producers.

With rare exceptions, Hollywood has ceased making rail photoplays. The oldtime rail classics are almost never borrowed from film libraries for reshowing. Virtually the only rail movies shown in America today are safety, educational, or propaganda shorts made by the carriers, plus amateur footage of train travel or railroad operation shot by individual railfans and screened at their regular group meetings.

MP *See* MISSOURI PACIFIC RAILROAD.

Mud Run Collision October 10, 1888, was a big day for Hazelton, Pennsylvania. All morning, excursion trains from the coal regions rolled into the city for a

Among the exhibits at the Henry Ford Museum is this engine, originally the Satilla of the Atlantic & Gulf Railroad, which was built in 1860 by the Rogers Locomotive and Machine Works of Paterson, New Jersey. [Courtesy of the Henry Ford Museum, Dearborn, Michigan]

great parade for the birthday of the Rev. Theobald Matthew, an Irish champion of total abstinence. A delegation of 5500 persons from Lackawanna and Luzerne Counties arrived on a Lehigh Valley Railroad train of eight sections. Each section had from 8 to 12 coaches and was pulled by two eight-wheeled locomotives.

On the return trip, No. 452, head engine of the sixth section, with Harry E. Cook at the throttle, whistled the signal "Down brakes!" to the engine it was paired with, because Cook had spied the preceding train too closely ahead, just beyond the station at Mud Run, Pennsylvania, although all eight trains were under orders to run on a 10-minute headway.

None of the engines had airbrakes in those days and could not stop promptly. Number 452 crashed into the rear of the fifth section. The impact telescoped the last car into the one just ahead of it, and that one into the preceding car. Above the ripping of timbers and hiss of steam could be heard the screams of victims. Sixty persons were killed, and nearly as many injured. Engineer Cook denied that there had been a red signal or even a torpedo east of the Mud Run station. The accident happened in an area known as Pleasant Valley, which because of the disaster was renamed Avoca. (Railroads often renamed locations where wrecks had occurred.)

BIBLIOGRAPHY: Wesley S. Griswold, *Train Wreck!* Stephen Greene, Brattleboro, Vt., 1968; Robert C. Reed, *Trains Wrecks: A Pictorial History of Accidents on the Main Line,* Superior Publishing, Seattle, 1968; Robert B. Shaw, *A History of Railroad Accidents, Safety Precautions, and Operating Practices,* Northern Press, Potsdam, N.Y., 1978.

Museums Hundreds of railroad and trolley-car museums of various sizes, some large and impressive and others merely private collections, in the United States and Canada are open to the public. Also, many major establishments display railroad rolling stock and/or other railroadiana as well as nonrail exhibits. The latter include the Smithsonian Institution, Washington; Chicago Museum of Science and Industry; Franklin Institute, Philadelphia; Circus World Museum, Baraboo, Wisconsin; Greenfield Village (Henry Ford Museum), Dearborn, Michigan; Henry M. Flagler Museum, Palm Beach, Florida; Lake Superior Museum of Transportation and Industry, Duluth, Minnesota; National Museum of Science and Technology, Ottawa, Ontario; British Columbia Forest Museum, Duncan, British Columbia; Sherburne (Vermont) Museum; British Columbia Provincial Museum, Victoria, British Columbia; Historic Ellicott City, Maryland; Knott's Berry Farm, which operates a steam tourist railway at Buena Park, California; and Indiana Museum of Transport and Communications, Noblesville, Indiana.

The two most important museums owned by railroad companies are the Union Pacific's (UP's) in Omaha and the Baltimore & Ohio (B&O; Chessie System) Transportation Museum in Baltimore. The latter is housed and well maintained in a former locomotive roundhouse adjacent to the road's old Mount Clare shops and the world's oldest railroad station, from which the first B&O engine, *Tom Thumb,* set forth to race a horse-drawn railroad car on a parallel track and from which, many years later, the world's first telegram was sent. The major exhibits in this setup are large: historic steam engines, cars, etc. The UP Museum displays smaller but no less interesting pieces of railroadiana, for example, silver-plated hollowware from Abraham Lincoln's private car that the UP acquired in 1866 and the leg-irons used on train-robber George Parrott.

The Pennsylvania Railroad could have had an important museum, having preserved many of its locomotives and cars of long ago; but it donated this material instead to the fine new Pennsylvania State Railroad Museum at Strasburg, Pennsylvania, home area of the ancient but still-operating Strasburg Rail Road and a unique chain of authentic old red wooden cabooses now used as motels. Also state-owned is the California State Railroad Museum, located in the faithfully reproduced Sacramento terminal of the first transcontinental railroad as part of reconstructed Old Sacramento. Among its exhibits are three locomotives of the gold- and silver-hauling Virginia & Truckee Railroad, donated by the Railway & Locomotive Historical Society.

Also outstanding are the National Railroad Museum at Green Bay, Wisconsin; Travel Town, operated by the Department of Recreation and Parks, Los Angeles; National Museum of Transport, Barretts Station, St. Louis; California State Narrow Gauge Railroad Museum, Carmichael, California; Colorado Railroad Museum, Golden, Colorado; two Canadian Railway Museums, Toronto and Montreal; Forney Historic Transportation Museum, Denver; and Roanoke (Virginia) Transportation Museum.

Also worth visiting, among many others, are the Kentucky Railway Museum, Louisville; Gold Coast Railroad operating museum, Fort Lauderdale, Florida; Empire State Railway Museum, Middletown, New York; Trains of Yesterday Museum (American Railroad Equipment Association), Hilliard, Florida; Age of Steam Railroad Museum, Dallas; Cass Scenic Railroad, Cass, West Virginia; Edaville Railroad, a 2-foot-gauge operating line and museum; Valley Railroad operating museum, Essex, Connecticut; Illinois Railway Museum, Union, Illinois; New Jersey Museum of Steam, operating, Allaire State Park; Ohio Railway Museum, Worthington, Ohio; E. P. Alexander Railroad Museum, Yardley, Pennsylvania; Casey Jones Museum in Casey's last home, Jackson, Tennessee; Steamtown Foundation, Bellows Falls, Vermont; and a 12-acre museum being built near Duluth, Georgia, by the Atlanta Chapter of the National Railway Historical Society.

Electric-line museums include the New York City Transit Society's Old New York, mostly old subway, el, and trolley cars, Brooklyn; Trolleyville USA, Olmsted Falls, Ohio; Orange Empire Railway Museum, electric and steam, Perris, California; Baltimore Streetcar Museum; Arden (Pennsylvania) Trolley Museum; Seashore (operating) Trolley Museum, Kennebunkport, Maine; National Capital Trolley Museum, Wheaton, Maryland; California Railway Museum (Bay Area Electric Railroad Association), San Francisco; Connecticut Electric Railway Association, operating museum, East Hartford; and Branford Electric Railroad Association, operating trolley museum, East Haven, Connecticut.

Dozens of other short tourist lines, including the one in Disneyland at Anaheim, California, mostly steam-operated but some powered by electricity, may be found in the United States and Canada. The most dependable of these are listed in *Steam Passenger Service Directory*, published annually by Empire State Railway Museum, Middletown, New York. Another publication which covers this and a broader field is the monthly *Passenger Train Journal.*

Mystery of the 13 Most train robberies in the Old West had a similar pattern, but this one on September 18, 1877, is said to have been without a parallel. The scene: Big Spring, Nebraska, on the Union Pacific mainline, a fuel and water stop for woodburning engines. Bill Barnard, a lone telegrapher, was on duty there 7 days a week in a tiny station shack. The only other buildings in "town" were a frame house for track workers and a wooden, iron-banded water tank. Twelve miles westward across the prairie lay the nearest settlement, Julesberg, a hell-roaring vice center in railroad construction days but now little more than a ghost city.

Bill had just taken a train order over the wire for the

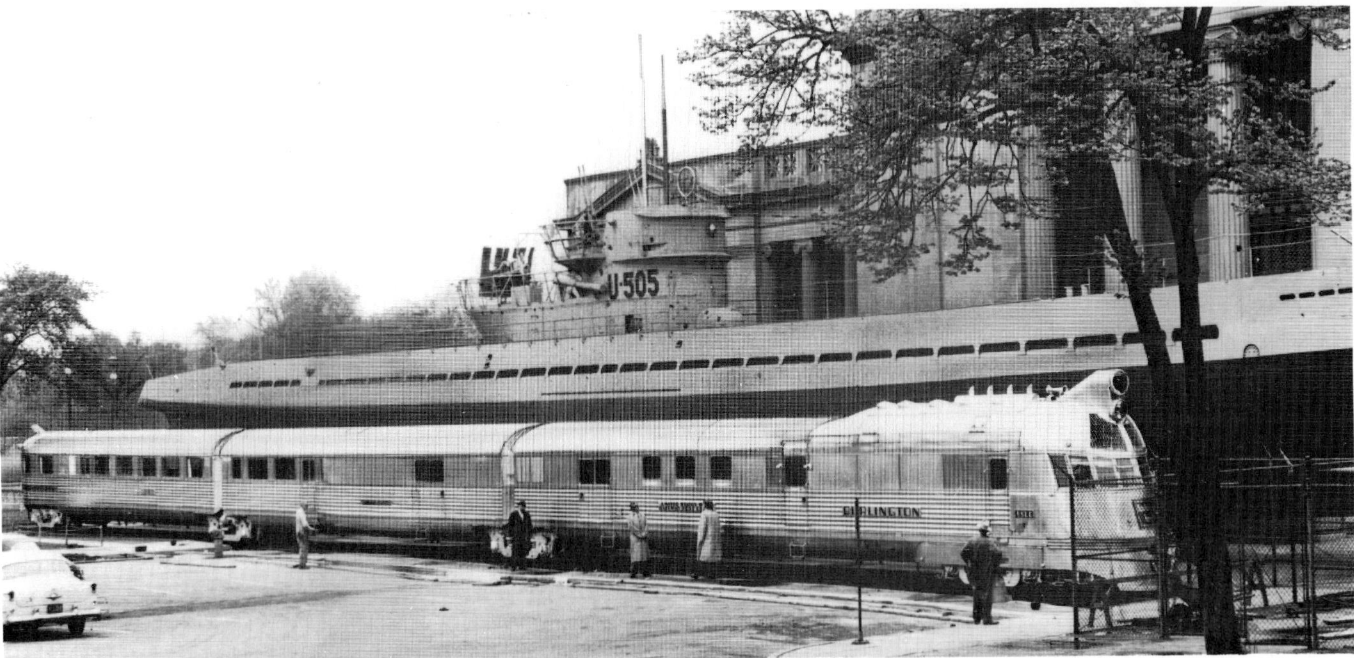

On permanent exhibition at the Museum of Science and Industry in Chicago is the Burlington's* Pioneer Zephyr, *the first diesel-powered streamlined train in the United States. It stands beside a captured German submarine. [Museum of Science and Industry, Chicago]

eastbound express which left Cheyenne, Wyoming Territory, at 3 o'clock that afternoon. It was due to reach Big Spring at 11 p.m. He glanced toward the section house. Lights were out; the gandy dancers had gone to bed. From the deep pine woods behind him came the unexpected whinny of a horse. Picking up his kerosine lamp, he cautiously peered out into the darkness.

At that moment he heard feet shuffling on the platform. The station door flew open. Whirling around, the operator faced two red-masked men with revolvers leveled at him. Bill kept a loaded pistol in his desk drawer but knew he couldn't use it against them. Besides, he heard other men outside. There were, he soon learned, 13 masked gunmen in all. One yanked the relay off his desk, so that he couldn't tap out a message for help, and tossed it onto the prairie. Then the men made the terrified railroader hang out his red light just as if everything were normal.

Promptly at 11 the express stopped for the red signal. The bandits forced Bill to knock on the door of the Wells, Fargo & Co. express car. When express messenger George Miller opened it, half a dozen desperadoes piled in. There were two safes, both loaded with money, as well as 300,000 ounces of silver bullion in bars from Colorado mines for the U.S. Treasury. One strongbox had a combination that the messenger could not open; but the other, his way safe, yielded about $60,000 in gold and $5000 in lesser currency, which the robbers dumped into burlap bags they had brought along for that purpose. The silver bars, being too heavy to carry, were left behind, and the mailbags were untouched; but the gang systematically robbed most of the passengers.

While trying to break into the locked and barricaded sleeping car, they heard the whistle of another train coming up from the rear. Fearing a trap, they galloped off into the darkness. Before leaving, one outlaw picked up a bucket of water he had left on the station platform and poured it into the locomotive firebox. This made the engine useless until a new fire could be built and might have delayed reporting the robbery. But the locomotive on the train, a freight, that came up behind was uncoupled and run around the stalled express by means of a sidetrack. Then she sped to Ogalla, 15 miles away, to announce the holdup.

Although Union Pacific management offered a $10,000 reward for capture of the gang and although the U.S. Cavalry aided other law forces in the manhunt, none of the mysterious 13 was ever found or identified.

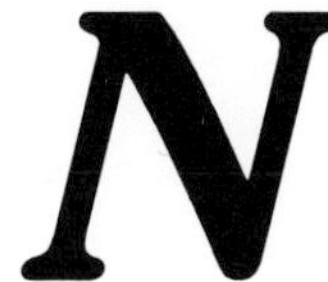

Name Trains, Passenger In 1843, when the Central of Georgia opened its mainline between Savannah and Macon, 191 miles, it was America's, if not the world's, longest railway under one management. Fifty years later it inaugurated the country's first name train, *Nancy Hanks,* which was intended to honor not Abraham Lincoln's mother but a famous racehorse named for her. This elegant blue, gold-striped passenger train covered the 294 miles between Atlanta and Savannah in 6 hours but lasted less than 8 months. Its two diesel-powered streamlined successors, both launched in 1947 but now extinct, victims of the automobile age, also were named for racehorses, *Nancy Hanks II* and *Man o' War.*

The seventy names which have survived, been revived, or, in a few cases, been adopted fairly recently, represent sets of good American trains that lack the elegance, distinctiveness, elite service, and proportion of on-time arrivals that characterized their more famous predecessors. Hundreds of name trains were permanently abandoned over a long period of years. Here is a list of those being operated as of early 1980. Many may be discontinued as a result of federal budget cuts proposed by President Ronald Reagan.

Adirondack (New York-Montreal); *Ann Rutledge* and *State House* (Chicago-St. Louis); *AuRoRa* (Anchorage-Fairbanks, Alaska); *auto-train* (suburban Washington-Florida); *Bankers, Ben Franklin, Betsy Ross, Congressional, Embassy, Liberty Express, Merchants Limited, Metroliner Service, Minute Man, Murray Hill, Night Owl, Patriot,* and *Senator* (Boston-New York-Washington); *Black Hawk* (Chicago-Rockford-Dubuque); *Blue Ridge* and *Shenandoah* (Washington-Cumberland-Cincinnati-Chicago); *Blue Water Limited, Michigan Executive, St. Clair, Twilight Limited,* and *Wolverine* (Chicago-Port Huron/Detroit); *Broadway Limited* (New York-Washington-Pittsburgh-Chicago); *Cardinal* (Washington-Cincinnati-Chicago); *Champion, Palmetto, Silver Meteor,* and *Silver Star* (New York-Washington-St. Petersburg/Miami); *Chesapeake* (Philadelphia-Wilmington-Baltimore-Washington local); *Coast Starlight, Mount Rainier,* and *Pacific International* (Vancouver-Seattle-Portland-Oakland-Los Angeles); *Colonial* and *Tidewater* (Boston-New York-Washington-Richmond-Newport News); *Crescent* (New York-Washington-Atlanta-New Orleans); *Crusader* and *Wall Street* (New York-Newark-Philadelphia); *De Witt Clinton, Empire State Express, Henry Hudson, Niagara Rainbow, Salt City Express,* and *Washington Irving* (New York-Albany-Buffalo-Niagara Falls); *Empire Builder* (Chicago-St. Paul-Havre-Seattle); *Floridian* (Chicago-Jacksonville-St. Petersburg/Miami); *Hilltopper* (Boston-New York-Washington-Richmond-Lynchburg-Tri-state); *Illini* and *Shawnee* (Chicago-Champaign-Urbana-Carbondale); *Illinois Zephyr* (Chicago-Galesburg-Quincy-Kansas City); *Inter-American* (Chicago-St. Louis-Fort Worth-Laredo); *Lake Shore Limited* (New York/Boston-Albany-Chicago); *Lone*

Star (Chicago-Fort Worth-Dallas-Temple-Houston); *Montrealer* (Montreal-New York-Washington); *National Limited* (New York-Washington-St. Louis-Kansas City); *North Coast Hiawatha* (Chicago-St. Paul-Billings-Seattle); *North Star* (Chicago-Milwaukee-St. Paul-Superior-Duluth); *Panama Limited* (Chicago-Memphis-New Orleans); *Pioneer* (Salt Lake City-Ogden-Boise-Portland-Seattle); *Rio Grande Zephyr* (Denver-Salt Lake City); *San Diegan* (Los Angeles-San Diego); *San Francisco Zephyr* (Chicago-Omaha-Denver-Ogden-Oakland); *San Joaquin* (Oakland-Bakersfield); *Silverliner Service* (New York-Philadelphia-Lancaster-Harrisburg); *Southwest Limited* (Chicago-Kansas City-Flagstaff-Los Angeles); *Sunset Limited* (New York-New Orleans-Houston-San Antonio-Phoenix-Los Angeles); *Turboliner* (Chicago-Milwaukee-St. Paul-Superior-Duluth); *Valley Forge* (New York-Philadelphia-Lancaster-Harrisburg); and *Western Hills Express* (New York-Newark-Phillipsburg).

Amtrak operates, or operated, all the foregoing except *AuRoRa* (Alaska Railroad); auto-train (Auto-Train Corp.); *Crusader, Wall Street,* and *Western Hills Express* (Conrail), and *Rio Grande Zephyr* (Denver and Rio Grande Western).

See also WOMEN, TRAINS NAMED FOR.

BIBLIOGRAPHY: *The Official Railway Guide: North American Passenger Travel Edition; United States, Canada and Mexico,* National Railway Publication Company, New York.

Nantucket Railroad Rail line named for the small island on which it ran, 15 miles east of Edgartown, Martha's Vineyard, and 11 miles south of Monomoy Point on the Massachusetts mainland. In the 1840s, with nearly 100 whaling ships, Nantucket was the world's greatest whaling port. Later it became a vacation resort. In 1879, spearheaded by Philip H. Folger, ground was broken for a 3-foot-gauge railroad, 7 miles long, between a town with the same name as the island itself and Siaconset (Sconset), to connect with steamships for Woods Hole, Massachusetts.

Its first train ran on July 4, 1881. The first locomotive, the 4-4-0 woodburner *Dionnis,* came from the Boston, Revere Beach & Lynn Railroad (BRB&L). Its second one, acquired in 1885, was the *Sconset,* a Mason-built double-truck 0-4-4. As the line had no turntable or wye, the engine ran backward on return trips.

Unlike the Martha's Vineyard Railroad, this company had several changes of management for financial reasons. In 1906 its train did not run. For a few months in 1907 a gasoline motor car, with a trailer hauling baggage and freight, was used instead of a train. The road never had a human casualty, although one of its engines turned turtle in 1908. After that, another gas motor car, this one seating 30 people, burnished the rails. Steam power returned again in 1909 with another BRB&L engine. The Nantucket was an obliging little road. Its train would stop to recover a hat which had been blown off or to let passengers pick blueberries. Finally, in 1917, automobiles forced the Nantucket out of business.

Nashville Wreck The worst rail disaster in United States history occurred at Nashville, Tennessee, on the Nashville, Chattanooga & St. Louis (NC&StL) in the early morning of July 9, 1918, just 17 days after the most tragic of all circus-train wrecks. *See* CIRCUS TRAINS.

Two trains cannot run on the same stretch of single track at the same time. NC&StL passenger trains Nos. 1 and 4 tried this impossible stunt. No. 1 was scheduled to leave Nashville at 7:00 a.m., whereas No. 4 was due to arrive 10 minutes later. Ordinarily, they met safely on the double track between the city station and Shops, 2½ miles away.

Double track ended at Shops. If No. 1 were a bit late in reaching the Nashville depot, it was up to No. 4 to wait at Shops until the other arrived. According to the rule book, No. 1 was the superior train because of the direction in which it was going. Its 4-8-0 engine No. 281 pulled a baggage car, five wooden coaches, a steel Pullman car, and a steel-under-frame Pullman. An interlocking plant was located at Shops. Operator Johnson looked out the interlocking-plant window at 7:15 a.m. and saw No. 4 pass by at moderate speed. Puzzled, he scrutinized the train order to see whether or not No. 1 had shown up yet. It hadn't. He called dispatcher Phillips. Horror-stricken, Phillips told him to try to stop it. The towerman sounded an emergency air whistle, but the crew did not hear it or, if they did, failed to heed it.

The doomed trains rushed toward each other on the single track with nothing to stop them. Because of curves, a slight grade, rather dense woodland, and an overhead bridge, it was impossible for the engineers to see each other's trains until it was too late. The dispatcher called out a wrecking-train crew and phoned for ambulances.

The trains met head-on at 7:20 a.m. on a curve 2 miles out of Shops. Engine 281 was derailed, her boiler stripped as clean as if she had been through a back shop. When the big hook finally jacked her up, 30 persons, only 1 living, were found underneath. The other engine, 282, and five cars likewise were demolished; 101 persons were killed and 171 injured. The Interstate Commerce Commission said that the wreck could have been prevented if there had been a manual block system to keep the two trains apart and that the loss of life would have been less if all-steel equipment had been used.

BIBLIOGRAPHY: Wesley S. Griswold, *Train Wreck!* Stephen Greene, Brattleboro, Vt., 1969; Robert C. Reed, *Train Wrecks,* Superior

Publishing, Seattle, 1968; Robert B. Shaw, *A History of Railroad Accidents, Safety Precautions, and Operating Practices,* Northern Press, Potsdam, N.Y., 1978.

National Railroad Passenger Corp. *See* AMTRAK.

Negroes and Trains Racial segregation on trains, railroad dining cars, buses, station waiting rooms, and station toilets all over the United States was outlawed early in 1956 by the Interstate Commerce Commission (ICC), activating a Supreme Court decision. This was a victory not only for black travelers but also for economy-minded rail and bus company officials (and some stockholders) in the South because it let them use space more efficiently in trains, buses, and stations. No longer need they cater to sectional prejudice by duplicating facilities that often were inadequately used.

A few roads in the South, like the Texas & Pacific, had ended racial separation on through trains years before the ICC ruling. Prior to 1956, stations in the South, even small rural depots larger than flag-stop shacks, routinely had separate waiting rooms for light- and dark-skinned passengers as well as four toilets apiece, for white men, white women, colored men, and colored women respectively. This setup wasted countless square miles of real estate, besides increasing plumbing and maintenance costs, while the separate cars for Negroes were inefficient and expensive to operate.

Prior to the Civil War, slave labor built considerable railway mileage in the South, but the very few black freedmen or freedwomen who could afford trainfare were restricted to shabby Jim Crow accommodations. For many years after the war, no matter where Negroes were employed, they were paid less than white workers for the same jobs and usually were limited to the hardest and dirtiest tasks. The railroads hired many blacks as strikebreakers and later kept on a large proportion of them. The Negroes who became scabs, as strikebreakers are called, did so because otherwise they could not get jobs of any kind; but that practice reinforced racial prejudice.

The worst offenders were the standard rail unions, which invariably drew the color line, excluding black workers except for sleeping-car porters and maids, from union membership. John Henry, the giant black famed in history, songs, and legends as a "steel-drivin' man," was not eligible to join a maintenance-of-way workers' union. *See* BROTHERHOOD OF SLEEPING CAR PORTERS AND REDCAPS; JOHN HENRY.

At the 1898 convention of the Brotherhood of Locomotive Firemen, Grand Master Frank P. Sargent said one of the chief purposes of the meeting was to "begin a campaign in advocacy of white supremacy in the railway service." Delegates roared approval. The most famous Negro fireman, Simeon T. Webb, who survived the Illinois Central train wreck in Mississippi that killed his engineer, Casey Jones, in 1900, quit his IC job under pressure and became a house painter, among other occupations. Wallace Saunders, the black roundhouse worker at Canton, Mississippi, who wrote the original Casey Jones ballad, was never credited with its authorship in the historically inaccurate printed versions that in 1903 were listed among America's 10 best-sellers in sheet music. See CASEY JONES.

In 1909 the Georgia Railroad laid off 10 white firemen and replaced them with blacks at lower wages. This caused a turmoil.

The firemen's union went on a strike aimed at eventually driving all Negro firemen from roads in the South. Some newspapers, like the Augusta *Herald,* supported the strikers with editorials, saying that it was "a mistaken policy to give preference to Negroes when white men would ultimately have to be put in charge of engines and trains." They had a point. The carriers all over the country were then employing many Negroes as firemen, brakemen, flagmen, and train porters as well as station porters and laborers in track gangs, shops, etc., but never promoted any of them to become engineers, conductors, or foremen. That was largely because the standard white-only rail unions signed contracts with management limiting promotions to union members.

For a week the 1909 walkout cut Atlanta-Augusta train service almost to zero, with some violence. Then an arbitration board ruled that the Georgia Railroad could hire qualified Negroes as firemen but must pay them the same as white workers. This meant, technically at least, that the union had lost its strike.

One contract signed by the Brotherhood of Locomotive Firemen and Enginemen specified, according to testimony presented to a congressional committee, that "at least 51 percent of the firemen on this line must be white," and the roads agreed "not to employ Negro firemen" and said that "in the future all vacancies will be filled by white firemen." The constitutions of at least 22 international and national unions, including rail labor, of which over half were affiliated with the American Federation of Labor (AFL), banned Negroes. The Brotherhood of Railway Carmen demanded that new "members be white and Christian." The Association of Colored Railway Trainmen and Locomotive Firemen, founded in 1913, enrolled 3000 members. In 1933, when the Congress of Industrial Organizations (CIO) was formed, it enrolled many Negroes. Finally, the merged AFL-CIO made the blacks' place in the labor movement secure.

Meanwhile, when the Railway Labor Act of 1926 was being amended in 1934, the leaders of the standard rail brotherhoods, aside from the Brotherhood of Sleeping Car Porters (BSCP), agreed that new provisions of the act need not apply to sleeping-car employees. Only after A. Philip Randolph, president of the BSCP, had harangued the House and Senate committees was the act expanded to include porters as well as other railroad workers. *See* RANDOLPH, A(SA) PHILIP.

One result of World War I was the trek from plantations, farms, cities, and towns that brought an estimated 1,200,000 Negroes from the South to the North during the 1915–1918 period. After America entered the war, an increasing number of blacks went North to replace draftees. Recruiting agents from Northern industries, armed with railroad tickets and glowing promises, begged them to fill the suddenly created holes in the labor market.

For dark-skinned workers it was a mild version of paradise. For the first time they were actually being invited, even begged, to go north. They traveled in droves, nearly all of them by train. An estimated 50,000 poured into Chicago alone, riding mostly Illinois Central trains. They found unskilled jobs plentiful, especially in the stockyards, steel mills, rail and construction industries, automobile plants, and factories. They wrote home telling friends and relatives of their newly found prosperity, which intensified the migration. When the tide slackened in 1920, with soldiers returning home from overseas, Chicago had over 100,000 Negroes among its population, an increase of 148 percent in 10 years.

This migration, plus the drafting of men for army, air, and naval service, cut heavily into the South's labor supply. Many Southerners resented this. Jacksonville required labor recruiters (presumably from the North) to get $1000 licenses. Macon raised the license fee to $25,000. At Brookhaven, Mississippi, a chartered railroad car carrying 50 men and women northward was deliberately uncoupled from its train and sidetracked for 3 days. The South, unwilling to be deprived of its low-priced labor supply, held out promises of social reforms to Negroes in hopes of keeping them at home.

The Chicago *Defender,* an influential Negro weekly edited by a native of Alabama, stimulated the migration, scoffing at the reforms that the Southerners were proposing under duress. "Turn a deaf ear to everybody," it editorialized. "You see they are not lifting their laws to help you. Are they? Have they stopped their Jim Crow cars? Can you buy space in a Pullman sleeper? . . . We'd like to oblige these unselfish (?) souls and remain in the South, but to their section of the country we have said, as the song goes, 'I hear you calling me,' and have boarded the train singing 'Good-bye, Dixie Land.'"

Streetcar Segregation Horsecars replaced omnibuses in New York in about 1852. Negroes were excluded from them until 1855, when a decision by Judge Rockwell gave them the right to enter such cars. The street railway company ignored this ruling and continued to bar dark-skinned riders.

One Sunday the Rev. James W. C. Pennington reminded his black congregation of Rockwell's decision. He urged them to stand up for their rights and to tell their friends who might visit the city that Negroes were no longer excluded from New York streetcars. He himself boarded a Sixth Avenue car, refused to leave when asked to do so, and was forcibly ejected. Thereupon he sued the company and won his case. After that, the company operated Jim Crow horsecars in addition to the service for whites. But in the mid-1860s this form of discrimination in Manhattan was ended.

See also MCCOY, ELIJAH.

BIBLIOGRAPHY: Benjamin G. Brawley, *A Short History of the American Negro,* 4th ed., rev., Macmillan, New York, 1939; St. Clair Drake and Horace R. Cayton, *Black Metropolis,* Harcourt, Brace, New York, 1945; Herbert Hill, *Black Labor and the American Legal System,* Bureau of National Affairs, Washington, 1977; James G. O'Hara, "The Negro and the Labor Movement," *Congressional Record,* July 14, 1971.

Neuhart, David E. (1901–1973) Railroader hired out to the Union Pacific as a coach cleaner in 1918, transferred in 1926 to the mechanical department, and in 1949 named general superintendent of motive power for the entire UP system. A giant among motive-power men, Neuhart was responsible for developing the world's largest and most powerful diesel locomotives. By striving for the highest possible horsepower in the least number of units he made the UP famous for its mammoth freight haulers. From the M-10000 earthworm streamliner of 1934 to the mighty *Centennial* DD-40X units of 1969, the 1948–1970 period of this road's major achievements in diesel progress coincided almost exactly with Neuhart's term of office.

UP diesel road units are painted yellow and red. The road never adopted a one-builder policy but catered to all leading suppliers. It was the first to buy the world's most powerful switcher (Fairbanks-Morse M-2-44), pioneered in low-nose power in 1959, and is credited with much of the success of General Electric's entry into the road-unit field. UP also was the biggest user of cabless hood units.

With Neuhart's policy, UP became the only road with a fleet of gas-electric-turbine locomotives. In 1969 General Motors delivered Neuhart's masterpiece, the world's largest and most powerful diesel locomotive, just in time for the golden spike ceremony in Utah which marked 100 years of the Union Pacific. Next year, Neuhart reached the mandatory retirement age. *See* LOCOMOTIVES, GAS-TURBINE-ELECTRIC.

JAMES R. EDMONSTON

BIBLIOGRAPHY: William W. Banks and Harold E. Banks, *Motive Power of the Union Pacific,* Barnhart, 1958.

New Hamburg Wreck On the night of February 6, 1871, a fast passenger train on the New York & Hudson River Railroad was involved at New Hamburg, New York, in one of history's most spectacular smashups. This is what happened. The second section of the *Pacific Express,* a balloon-stacked engine pulling a baggage car, five sleepers, and a day coach, all wooden-bodied, left New York City at 8:05 p.m., 5 minutes late, and reached Fishkill 17 minutes behind schedule. Engineer Edward Simmons could not make up the lost time.

Meanwhile, a mixed freight and oil train was thundering down the road with about 30 cars, some carrying huge tanks of kerosine; and James Stafford at the throttle likewise tried to make up lost time. Suddenly an axle on an oil car snapped. Unaware of that, the engineer did not reduce speed but dragged the car over the ties to Wappinger Creek. The shattered axle caught onto a beam of the 200-foot pileway drawbridge crossing the creek. Wrenched from the rails, the car was overturned on the adjoining track.

Just then the *Pacific Express,* northbound, rounded the curve to the bridge. Too late, Simmons threw his engine into reverse and went to his death with a tight grip on the throttle. The fireman saved himself by jumping.

Their engine hit the derailed oil car with a mighty roar. Kerosine gushing over the firebox ignited quickly. Lurid flames rose to a height of about 100 feet. The wooden drawbridge, crushed by the weight and disjointed by the impact, sank with its load into the ice-covered water below. The death list, 26, included both engineers, the sleeping-car conductor, a brakeman, and a porter. Most deaths were attributed to breathing the fiery air. As the creek in that area was less than 4 feet deep, few people were drowned.

BIBLIOGRAPHY: Charles Francis Adams, Jr., *Notes on Railroad Accidents,* Putnam, New York, 1879; Wesley S. Griswold, *Train Wreck!* Stephen Greene, Brattleboro, Vt., 1969; Robert C. Reed, *Trains Wrecks,* Superior Publishing, Seattle, 1968; Robert B. Shaw, *A History of Railroad Accidents, Safety Precautions, and Operating Practices,* Northern Press, Potsdam, N.Y., 1978.

New York, Ontario & Western Railroad (NYO&W) Originally named the New York & Oswego Midland (NY&OM), it was probably the only railroad directly involved in breaking up a religious community. Extending from Oswego, New York, on Lake Ontario, to the seaport of Jersey City, New Jersey, plus various branches, the line had about 500 route miles. It tunneled through the formidable Shawangunk Mountain barrier that hemmed in much of mideastern New York State, was opened in 1867, and lasted just 90 years. It catered to tourists, advertising summer cabins for hunting, fishing, and canoeing that rented for $6 or $7 a week, 1600 feet above sea level and only 4 to 10 hours from New York City, in an era when butter sold for 7 cents a pound.

On its line was the famous Oneida Community of Perfectionists. This cult, centered in the Big House, was widely known for its handicrafts, particularly the manufacture of some of America's first steel traps and, later, silverware. Its religion was an early type of Christian commune. It practiced polygamy because the community had a shortage of men, but what attracted tourists even more was the bloomerlike garb of its women, comparable to today's feminine pants but a scandalous novelty in those days.

The cult made a deal with the NY&OM whereby, in return for transporting its supplies and handicrafted wares, train passengers were allowed to visit the Big House. This stimulated railroad passenger business but eventually boomeranged against the cult. After satisfying their curiosity, many train riders launched a movement that drove the Perfectionists out of the country and into Canada in 1880, although the Oneida station building was not razed until 1939.

Meanwhile, in 1879, the road was sold under foreclosure and reorganized as the New York, Ontario & Western. In 1885 it bought the bankrupt New York, West Shore & Buffalo and leased it to the New York Central for 475 years, but retained trackage rights into Weehawken, New Jersey. Nicknamed the Old & Weary, the NYO&W became, in 1948, one of the first Class I roads to go all-diesel, and in 1953 it dropped its passenger service. On March 20, 1957, the line operated its last train, a motley lot of equipment for sale or scrapping, to its Middletown, New York, shops, and the tracks were torn up. Two groups currently concentrate on NYO&W history: the Ontario & Western Technical & Historical Society, Box 405, Franklin Lakes, New Jersey 07417, and the Ontario & Western chapter of the National Railway Historical Society, Box 713, Middletown, New York 10940.

BIBLIOGRAPHY: Gerald M. Best, *Minisink Valley Express,* Beverly Hills, Calif., 1956; William F. Helmer, *O.&.W.: The Long Life and Slow Death of the New York, Ontario & Western Railway,* Howell-North, Berkeley, Calif., 1959; John Krauss and Ed Crist, *The Final Years,* Carstens Publs., Inc., Newton, N.J., 1977; Manville B. Wakefield, *To the Mountains by Rail,* Wakefield Press, Grahamsville, N.Y., 1970.

New York Central System Its slogan, "The Water Level Route—You Can Sleep," catered to overnight travelers, as did the Chesapeake and Ohio's cat Chessie and "Sleep Like a Kitten." The Central, unlike its rival, the Pennsylvania, bypassed steep grades on its mostly east-west line between New York City, Chicago, and St. Louis. It operated in 11 Eastern and Midwestern states and two Canadian provinces, Quebec and Ontario. In 1904 its oval-shaped emblem was devised by Clyde S. Thompson to adorn a special timetable for the Louisiana Purchase Exposition at St. Louis. The road's publicist, George H. Daniels, who coined the word *redcap* to define the station porter, liked the oval so much that he adopted it permanently.

The Central's earliest ancestor, the Mohawk & Hudson (M&H), was New York State's first railway. George W. Featherstonehaugh and Stephen Van Rensselaer founded it. The M&H began running on August 9, 1831, between Albany and Schenectady with the *De*

Witt Clinton, a 4-ton woodburner built at the West Point Foundry in New York City and named for the Governor of the state. This engine had four small wheels, all drivers, a horizontal boiler with 30 copper tubes, and a very tall stack. Its two cylinders, slanted at the sides of the firebox, transmitted the power to inside-cranked axles on the first pair of wheels, enabling it to pull five small wooden cars on the level at about 30 miles an hour.

In 1853, the merger of 10 short railroads in the Mohawk Valley and Erie Canal area into a single corporation created the New York Central Railroad, which in those days extended only from Albany on the Hudson River to Buffalo on Lake Erie. Erastus Corning, the company's first president, and John V. L. Pruyn were prime movers in the consolidation.

In 1869 Cornelius Vanderbilt amalgamated the Central with his New York & Harlem and Hudson River roads and became president of the new system, which he named the New York Central & Hudson River Railroad. In 1915 it was merged with the Lake Shore & Michigan Southern and several shorter lines to form the New York Central of the twentieth century.

One of Lake Shore's components was the Erie & Kalamazoo (E&K), which was Michigan's and Ohio's first railroad. Incorporated in both territories, it was to have run from what is now Toledo on Lake Erie to the Kalamazoo River but never got farther west than Adrian in Michigan Territory. Opened in 1836, it issued paper money. Its first rails were of wood, which warped; strap iron replaced them. Sometimes the latter curled up as *snake heads* that tore holes in car floors, imperiling trainmen and passengers. The E&K was leased to several NYC antecedents and then to the Central itself, and is now part of Conrail. *See* CURRENCY ISSUED BY RAILROADS.

In 1891 William Buchanan, the road's superintendent of motive power, a great man in locomotive building, cooperated with Albert J. Pitkin, general manager of Schenectady Locomotive Works, in designing and constructing an express locomotive, No. 870, which led the way in a race with the Pennsy for the swift, powerful engines later put into service. In 1893 the Central built the American-type No. 999 at its West Albany shops, under Buchanan's direction, and gave her a test run on May 10 on the westbound *Empire State Express* before exhibiting her that year at the World's Columbian Exposition in Chicago, as a bid to capture New York-Chicago passenger traffic.

Charles H. Hogan was given the honor of topping the world's speed mark. He had won old Vanderbilt's confidence to such an extent that he usually pulled the trains which the commodore rode, and he was the first spokesman of an employees' committee to air grievances before the sometimes irrascible Vanderbilt. With Hogan at the throttle, the 999 picked up the *Empire* at Syracuse for the first lap of a fast run to Buffalo, 150 miles away. He didn't do badly on the early part of his trip, but when he came to the 36 miles of straight, level track between Batavia and Buffalo he opened his throttle to the last notch and held it there. The testimony of two men with stopwatches confirmed the fact that he covered 1 mile of the 36 at the rate of 112.5 miles per hour. Nothing on wheels had ever traveled so fast before.

In 1954, 6 years after the Central had bought its last steam locomotive and was rapidly being dieselized, financier Robert R. Young won a bitter proxy fight to control the system. He appointed Alfred E. Perlman as (the last) president of the Central. Perlman did much to modernize and strengthen the road, but could not stem the rising tide of highway and air competition and the dwindling of passenger service. In 1962 the Central's and Pennsy's directors and stockholders approved an agreement to merge the two big systems. Their aim was to eliminate wasteful rail competition and overlapping facilities by developing a single strong corporation instead of two financially ailing ones. Legal action on the merger was delayed until 1968. After it did come, the last-ditch effort failed.

New York Central made many notable contributions besides the 999 to the railroad industry. The list includes the first track pans, in 1869 at Montrose, New York; and the first recording dynamometer, a device to measure the drawbar pull exerted by locomotives in hauling trains, and the establishing at Elkhart, Indiana, of the first railroad apprentice school, both in 1872. The

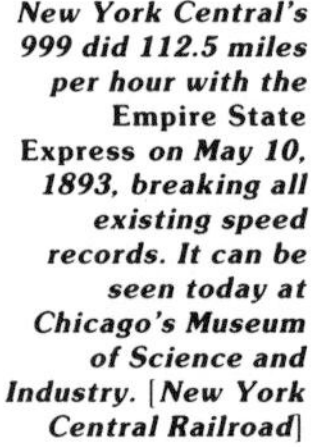

New York Central's 999 did 112.5 miles per hour with the Empire State Express on May 10, 1893, breaking all existing speed records. It can be seen today at Chicago's Museum of Science and Industry. [*New York Central Railroad*]

NYC adopted the first high-powered brakes for heavy steel passenger equipment in 1910 and the first all-steel boxcar 2 years later. *See* TRACK PANS.

In 1925 the Central used the first automatic train control and in 1927 activated the world's first ATC system, near Toledo, Ohio. In 1928 it began operating the first diesel-electric freight locomotive built in the United States. In 1958, under the Perlman management, it was the first railroad to adopt the air-flotation principle for moving freight by rail; a year later it introduced the first jet-powered snow-removal equipment, and in 1967 it formulated the world's first low-cost fuel oil specifically for use in diesel-electric locomotives.

See also ASHTABULA WRECK; CASSIN, DENNIS; CONRAIL; DUDLEY, PLIMMON HENRY; GRAND CENTRAL TERMINAL; NEW HAMBURG WRECK; PENN CENTRAL TRANSPORTATION COMPANY; PERRY, OLIVER CURTIS; SPEED WAR; VANDERBILT, CORNELIUS; WAGNER, WEBSTER.

BIBLIOGRAPHY: Lucius Beebe, *20th Century: "The Greatest Train in the World,"* Howell-North, Berkeley, Calif., 1962; Freeman Hubbard, *Railroad Avenue,* McGraw-Hill, New York, 1945, Edward Hungerford, *Men and Iron: The History of New York Central,* Crowell, New York, 1938; Robert Sobel, *The Fallen Colossus,* Weybright & Talley, New York, 1977; Alvin F. Staufer, *Steam Power of the New York Central System,* Medina, Ohio, 1961; Robert J. Wayner, *New York Central Cars,* Wayner Publications, New York, 1972.

New York Locomotive Works Misnamed locomotive plant. New York City never had such a plant. New York, however, had a successful West Point Foundry, which produced such famous machines as the *De Witt Clinton* and the *Best Friend of Charleston.* But West Point merely *assembled* engines built at Cold Spring, New York. In 1853 a Jersey City plant adopted the impressive name New York Locomotive Works and hired Encrease P. Gould, master mechanic of the Hudson River Railroad (later part of the New York Central System) as its superintendent. Gould had learned locomotive building as an apprentice of the Thomas Rogers locomotive works in Paterson, New Jersey.

The new company got its first order for engines from Gould's old road. Later it became Breese, Kneeland & Co. The financial panic of 1857 closed the plant, and Gould resigned, but it reopened in 1858 as the Jersey City Locomotive Works. In 1863 the 6-foot-gauge Atlantic & Great Western Railroad leased the shops and built 80 engines, mostly 4-4-0s, for itself and 80 Moguls for the Erie. In 1869 the plant was sold to the East Boston Locomotive Co., which renamed it the McKay & Aldus Iron & Locomotive Works. That company finally collapsed in the panic of 1873.

BIBLIOGRAPHY: Angus Sinclair, *Development of the Locomotive Engine,* annotated ed. by John H. White, Jr., M.I.T., Cambridge, Mass., 1970.

News Butcher Common term for the old-time train boy or the present-day news agent. The boys peddled such items as newspapers, magazines, candy, gum, fruit, playing cards, cigars, cigarettes, souvenirs, and even drinking water aboard trains. Among the popular books they sold were those of Tom Jackson. *See* JACKSON, TOM.

The name of the first train boy or news butcher is unknown. He may have been Billy Skelly, who held such a job on the New York & Erie in early days but in time controlled all sales on Erie trains and finally sold out at a huge profit to the Union News Co., which has carried on the business ever since, currently with agents mostly working at newsstands in stations.

Usually the train boy in the late 1800s did not get wages but worked on a commission basis for a concessionaire like Skelly of the Erie or was self-employed. He had to be a hustler, worldly-wise, shrewd, alert for any chance to earn an honest dime or quarter or maybe shortchange a buyer. Many of them aped the drummers, or traveling salesmen, their steadiest customers. They generally wore a blue uniform with brass buttons and a cap badge that said "News Agent," which gave them a semiofficial status.

Their "office" was in the baggage car, where they stored their wares. They read the *Police Gazette,* an illustrated pink-paper journal of crimes, scandals, and disasters, which they sold. Some furtively dispensed lewd pamphlets or mysteriously wrapped packages of "girlie" cards so far from pornographic that some buyers regarded themselves as having been gypped.

In 1859 at age 12 Thomas A. Edison became a train boy on a Grand Trunk accommodation train. Besides the usual sales in the cars, he would buy butter, vegetables, and berries at way-stops along the line and peddle them in Detroit and Port Huron, in each of which he had a boy working for him. Young Edison also bought a small handpress and a font of type, set them up in the baggage car, and published and sold a little newspaper, *The Weekly Herald.*

He also experimented with chemicals. One day his train bumped into a minor derailment, tipping over his chemicals and starting a fire in the baggage car. The enraged conductor, Alex Stevenson, quenched the blaze and boxed the lad's ears, an act which eventually led to total deafness. Stevenson also tossed the amateur laboratory, the printing press, and young Edison himself off the train at Mount Clemens, Michigan. Undaunted, Thomas became a railroad telegrapher and then went on to a lifetime of inventions.

Samuel R. Rosoff, who became president of a company which excavated much of New York's underground-rail land, likewise started with a train job. As a boy, Sam had won $10 by shooting dice. He used the money to stock up as a news butcher on the West Shore Railroad. In true Horatio Alger fashion a rich passenger, impressed by the lad's ambition, sent Sam to school and later to a lumber camp. Logging toughened Rosoff further and led to a lucrative building-razing contract. Eventually he received $50 million worth of subway contracts. For a time he owned the old Delaware & Northern Railroad in New York State.

Among other train boys who became celebrities were William A. Brady, Broadway theatrical producer; Tom Taggart, Democratic boss of Indiana and Democratic national chairman; and Walt Disney, movie producer and creator of Disneyland. *See* DISNEY, WALT.

BIBLIOGRAPHY: Benjamin A. Botkin and Alvin F. Harlow, *A Treasury of Railroad Folklore,* Crown, New York, 1953; Stewart H. Holbrook, *The Story of American Railroads,* Crown, New York, 1947.

Nicknames of Railroads Among such names, many based on initials, often affectionate, and widely used, are Ma and Pa (Maryland and Pennsylvania); Old and Weary (New York, Ontario & Western); Model T (Detroit, Toledo & Ironton, once owned by Henry Ford); Cheapest, Best, and Quickest (Chicago, Burlington & Quincy); Long and Narrow (Louisville & Nashville); Big Suitcase (Grand Trunk); Leave Early and Walk (Lake Erie & Western); Mud Hen (Central Indiana); May Not Arrive (Missouri & North Arkansas); All Tramps Sent Free (Atchison, Topeka and Santa Fe); Jerusalem, Mexico & Ireland (Jeffersonville, Madison & Indianapolis); To Hell and Back (Toronto, Hamilton & Buffalo); Watch Very Carefully and Proceed (West Virginia Central & Pittsburgh); Rich Folks and Pedigrees (Richmond, Fredericksburg & Potomac); Bent, Zigzag, and Crooked (Bellaire, Zanesville & Cincinnati); Cold, Hungry, and Dry (Cincinnati, Hamilton & Dayton); Bumpy, Rocky, and Peculiar (Buffalo, Rochester & Pittsburgh); Damned Small Salaries and Abuse (Duluth, South Shore & Atlantic); Slow, Tired, and Easy (Stockton Terminal & Eastern); Hoot, Toot, and Whistle (Hoosac Tunnel & Wilmington); Less Sleep and More Speed (Lake Shore & Michigan Southern); Methodist and Episcopal (Morris & Essex, which did not run on Sunday until 1899); Hoboes and Tin Cans (Houston & Texas Central); and Hell Either Way You Take It (Houston, East & West Texas).

NW

Norfolk & Western Railway (NW) Rail line, wih 15,010 track miles in 16 states and two Canadian provinces, that dates back to an 8-mile single-track predecessor line connecting Petersburg and City Point (now Hopewell), Virginia, in 1838. It reached its present size by a long series of mergers; the most recent were the following. In 1959 it took over the Virginian Railway, mostly a coal hauler. In 1964 it acquired the former Nickel Plate (NKP), the Wabash, the Akron, Canton and Youngstown (operated as a subsidiary), the Pittsburgh & West Virginia, and the Sandusky line of the former Pennsylvania Railroad. Then in 1968 an Interstate Commerce Commission mandate arising from the NKP-Wabash-NW consolidation added the Erie Lackawanna and the Delaware and Hudson to the vast NW system. But the Erie Lackawanna eventually became part of Conrail.

NW lines run chiefly east and west, linking the port of Norfolk, Virginia, with Omaha, Kansas City, and way points. Headquartered in Roanoke, Virginia, the system had 25,500 employees in 1978, 74,000 shareholders, 1575 locomotives, and 110,000 freight cars, and used about 19 million gallons of fuel oil in an average month. Its main revenue items are coal (NW is America's largest originator of bituminous coal), autos, automotive parts, primary steel products, grain, furniture, chemicals, and forest, glass, and stone products.

At about the same time that NW's first predecessor railway was being started, another 8-mile line, which eventually became the Wabash and then joined the NW, was built in Illinois as the Northern Cross Railroad (NC). On November 6, 1838, the NC operated the first locomotive in the area west of the Allegheny Mountains and north of the Ohio River. Rogers Locomotive Works built this engine, named the *Roger,* in Paterson, New Jersey. For nearly 10 years the state of Illinois operated the NC, despite opposition by rivermen and proponents of a canal system. In 1854 the little railroad was completed between Springfield and the Indiana state line, after part of it had been sold to Nicholas N. Ridgely, who renamed his part the Sangamon & Northern (S&N). Later, he took over the entire line.

While the S&N was expanding, other interests formed the Lake Erie, Wabash & St. Louis (first rail use of the name Wabash) in 1852 and the Toledo & Illinois in 1853. These two merged in 1856 as the Toledo, Wabash & Western, which eventually acquired the S&N and other roads. Another reorganization created the Wabash Railroad Co. in 1879.

Meanwhile, the North Missouri Railway, chartered to build in Missouri from St. Louis to the Iowa state line, was almost totally destroyed during the Civil War but survived to help form the Atlantic, Missouri & Ohio (AM&O), a Wabash predecessor, in 1870. Also in 1870, the Wabash's basic route had taken shape, linking Toledo, Ohio, Quincy, Indiana, and Keokuk, Iowa, along a 520-mile route, which was expanded to reach Chicago in 1880 and Detroit in 1881. The Wabash was called the Banner Railroad because its emblem showed a flag bearing its name and the slogan "Follow the Flag."

During the Depression of the 1930s, like many other railroads, the Wabash passed into and out of a receivership. But prosperity followed World War II. In 1946 the Union Pacific, Southern Pacific, and Wabash jointly began operating a luxury passenger train, the *City of St. Louis,* followed in 1947 by another new streamliner, the *City of Kansas City,* under the same auspices. Both met with immediate success. In 1950, a third great train, the Wabash *Blue Bird,* took to the rails with the first dome cars to run between St. Louis and Chicago.

The Wabash dieselized in 1954 and began piggyback service. Wabash steam power made its last run in 1955 over the line in Illinois where its first antecedent had been born 117 years before. The engine, Mogul No. 573, built by Rhode Island Locomotive Works in 1899, was then donated to the National Museum of Transport in St. Louis County. Nine years later, the Wabash was added to the Norfolk & Western Railway, which had come into being in 1896 through a reorganization of the Atlantic, Missouri & Ohio.

On February 3, 1881, 7 days after the AM&O had been sold to organizers of the NW, $13.5 million was subscribed in just 15 minutes to build another road, the New York, Chicago & St. Louis, which eventually became a segment of the NW. Twenty months later the new road was opened for business with 523 miles of track completed. Its initials, compressed to NYCL, gave it the name Nickel Plate (NKP). In 1885 it joined the New York Central System, whose president, William H. Vanderbilt, commented: "Judging from the price we paid for this line, it *ought* to be nickel-plated." Despite its name, it never reached New York and did not enter St. Louis until 1922. *See* SILVER CREEK WRECK.

In 1914, congressional passage of the Clayton Antitrust Act forced the Vanderbilts to give up the NKP, which they sold in 1916 to the brothers Oris P. and Mantis J. Van Sweringen of Cleveland, who nearly succeeded in pyramiding this and other holdings into a transcontinental railroad empire. A planned merger of the NKP with five other Van Sweringen roads, including the Chesapeake and Ohio, failed to materialize; so in 1947 the C&O relinquished control of NKP, which thus became an independent system, eventually 2170 miles long, with a total of 4000 miles of track serving five states. In 1964 NKP joined the NW system.

Meanwhile, in 1959, the NW had absorbed the Virginian Railway. At that time, this was the largest completed rail merger in history. The Virginian had the distinction of being the only relatively large railroad ever built with the capital and credit of one man. That man, Henry H. Rogers, was an associate of John D. Rockefeller.

Rogers built the railroad—actually, expanded it from a small lumber carrier dating back to 1896—at a cost of $50 million, because surveys made in 1903 had indicated that a line with a low grade from the coalfields eastward to tidewater was feasible and would save on the freight charges he had been paying to the NW and C&O for hauling coal from West Virginia mines in which he had an interest. Completed in 1909 and later electrified, the Virginian Railway was a financial success for each of the 50 years of its existence.

NW and the Southern in mid-1980 announced a preliminary agreement to merge by exchanging stock, subject to approval by both roads' boards of directors and stockholders and by the Interstate Commerce Commission. The proposed new system would have 17,500 route miles and $5.7 billion in assets. Total 1979 earnings of the two systems were nearly $100 million.

Engine storage facilities of the Norfolk & Western at Portsmouth, Ohio. [**Norfolk & Western Railway**]

See also ERIE LACKAWANNA RAILWAY; DELAWARE AND HUDSON RAILWAY.

BIBLIOGRAPHY: Taylor Hampton, *The Nickel Plate Road,* World Publishing, Cleveland, 1947; *History of the Wabash Railroad,* Wabash Railroad Company, St. Louis, 1953; John A. Rehor, *The Nickel Plate Story,* Kalmbach, Milwaukee, 1966; H. Reid, *The Virginian Railway,* Kalmbach, Milwaukee, 1961.

North America Car Corp. Company that operates 10 railroad-car repair shops in the United States and Canada.

Northern Pacific Railway *See* BURLINGTON NORTHERN INC.

NRPC *See* AMTRAK.

NW *See* NORFOLK & WESTERN RAILWAY.

NYC *See* NEW YORK CENTRAL SYSTEM.

NYO&W *See* NEW YORK, ONTARIO & WESTERN RAILROAD.

Oahu Railway On a semitropical island in the mid-Pacific, sharing the narrow beach with coconut palms and kiawe trees, were the steel rails of the Oahu Railway & Land Co. (OR&L), 3 feet apart. Prior to December 31, 1947, when the last passenger train ran over its 72-mile route between Honolulu and the sugar-mill village of Kahuku, Hawaii had more than 1000 miles of track, mostly plantation lines, several hundred locomotives, and thousands of railroad cars. Today, railroading there is nonexistent.

The OR&L made a semicircle around the western end of Oahu, Hawaii's main island. Its builder, Benjamin F. Dillingham, had intended to encircle the entire island but never got beyond Kahana village. The line was double-tracked to Waipahu, junction point for the branch to Schofield Barracks, U.S. Army post. This branch climbed from sea level on a 3 percent grade to the 1000-foot-high level plateau. During World War II it served as a supply line between Pearl Harbor and Schofield. Before double-tracking, the branch was a dispatcher's nightmare, with more than 80 train movements of 85 cars each daily in both directions.

The 36-inch gauge was important because it matched all but one of the island's plantation railways, thus permitting an interchange of freight for points otherwise inaccessible except by laborious trucking. The railway turned the island's unproductive interior into miles of sugar and pineapples. Most of its 1300-plus freight cars were flats equipped to haul crated pineapples direct from fields to canneries. The line also carried thousands of tons of molasses a year, some oil, structural steel, machinery, gravel, and other merchandise. All its steam engines burned oil. The first two were 0-4-2 saddle tanks. Later came 4-4-0s, 0-6-0s, 4-6-0s, 2-8-2s, Shay-geared 4-4-4s, and, in the 1940s, diesel power.

The first regularly scheduled passenger train left Honolulu on November 16, 1889. Originally there were two classes of travel: first-class cars painted Pullman

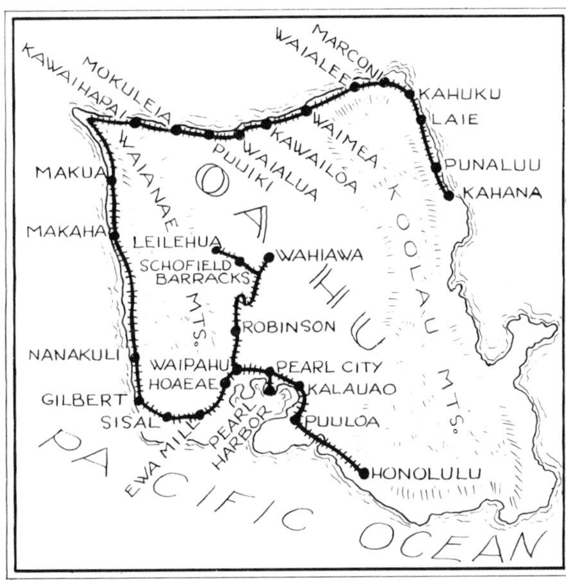

Map showing the original route of the Oahu Railway in Hawaii; it ran as a freight and passenger line from 1889 to 1947. [Railroad Magazine]

green and second-class cars in bright yellow. A single class replaced this category.

In time, motor trucks, buses, and autos supplanted rail transportation. The U.S. Navy bought the railway from Hawaii, then a territory, in 1950, for a nominal $1 fee, used it extensively during the Korean War, but did not operate more than one train every few weeks or months thereafter. Finally, despite persistent efforts of the Hawaiian Railway Society and the Historic Buildings Task Force, the former OR&L was abandoned and its tracks were torn up.

BIBLIOGRAPHY: Jesse C. Conde and Gerald M. Best, *Sugar Trains: Narrow Gauge Railroads of Hawaii,* Glenwood Pubs., Felton, Calif., 1973; John B. Hungerford, *Hawaiian Railroads: A Memoir of the Common Carriers of the Fiftieth State,* Hungerford Press, Reseda, Calif., 1963.

Official Railway Guide, The Subtitled *North American Passenger Travel Edition: United States, Canada and Mexico,* it is an updated single source of rail travel information including timetables, equipment and service data, sample fares, and connecting ferry and bus services. The schedules cover intercity trains, particularly Amtrak, VIA Rail Canada, and Mexican services; also long-haul commuter rail services for major United States and Canadian metropolitan areas. There are also a passenger-train station index, with phones and baggage checking, a rail-travel news digest, lists of common carriers and train names, travel tips, fare discounts, and national parks in the United States and Canada. In addition, there are maps and train schedules for Western Europe, Australia, Japan, and South Africa.

This edition is published 10 times a year (not in February or August), with about 250 pages, 8¼ by 11 inches, by National Railway Publication Company, 424 West 33d Street, New York, New York 10001.

The *Guide* is kept in thousands of places such as libraries, hotels, shipping offices, and government agencies. Historians, journalists, and railfans use it to check, for example, when train service began over a certain route or when a given railway station was established. Photostats from pages of the *Guide* verify employment dates of railway officials for railroad retirement benefits. Fiction writers use the *Guide* to check schedules and routes mentioned in their stories. Its evidence has been accepted in civil suits, divorce proceedings, and even murder trials.

This book was originally called *Travelers' Official Guide* and had 140 pages when it first appeared in June 1868. Before then, several railway guides had been in common use in the United States, such as Distornell's *Railroad, Steamboat and Telegraph Guide,* founded in 1846; Doggett's *Railroad Guide and Gazetteer,* 1848; Appleton's *Railroad and Steam Navigation Guide,* 1848; Dinsmore's *American Railway Guide,* 1850; and Lloyd's *American Guide,* 1857.

Probably the most extensive file of this publication extant is in the New York Public Library at 42d Street and Fifth Avenue, which lacks only five numbers from being complete. The Library of Congress file begins with January 1878. In the 1950s the *Guide* ran to about 1500 pages, but it shrank considerably as America's railways cut their passenger service and especially after Amtrak was created in 1971. Amtrak's condensed listing takes but a fraction of the previous space.

A companion piece to this classic is the same publisher's bimonthly *North American Freight Service Edition,* with about 700 pages, listing all North American railroads, standard codes and abbreviations, railroad officials, and freight services, with maps, TOFC ramp locations and schedules, government agencies, state railroad commissions, railroad associations, foreign railroad representatives in North America, water carriers, railroad stations, news digest, etc.

The same company also publishes (1) *The Pocket List of Railroad Officials,* including officials of transit systems, truck lines, and authorities, supply-company representatives, products, and services, with titles, railroad equipment owned, and miles of track operated; (2) *The Official Railway Equipment Register,* a quarterly which lists freight cars operated by North America's railroads and private-car companies, as well as junction points, connecting roads, personnel, Association of American Railroads (AAR) rules and directives, special-type flatcars, and the auditing of freight bills; (3) *The Official Intermodel Equipment Register,* a quarterly listing of containers, trailers, and chassis in intermodel service, specifications, ramp locations, port facilities, personnel, AAR service rules, etc.; and (4) the annual *Railway Line Clearances,* both horizontal and vertical, including weight limitations, for more than 250 North American railroads, and maps, instructions, and AAR diagrams.

Oil Shipments On August 27, 1859, Edwin L. Drake, a former New Haven Railroad conductor, drilled America's first oil well at Titusville, Pennsylvania. This was a major factor in ushering in the modern machine age, providing enormous and highly profitable rail shipments and enabling industry, including the railroads, to reach a high state of efficiency. Because of it, for 25 years the state of Pennsylvania overshadowed the rest of the world in oil production.

The wild boom that followed Drake's discovery of oil far exceeded in importance the California gold rush of 10 years before. At first tank wagons and flatboats hauled the crude oil to refineries. Before the Civil War began, the only railroad located near wells in the Titusville area was the Philadelphia & Erie (P&E), 60 miles of single track between Warren and Erie, Pennsylvania. Oil shipped over this line was transferred to the Lake Shore Railroad at Erie, then to New York City via the New York Central and its connections. A competitive route to the metropolis was over the New York & Erie

[(NY&E) commonly called the Erie], connecting with the Lake Shore at Dunkirk, New York.

The Philadelphia & Erie, which at first had the edge on its competitor, the NY&E, in hauling crude oil, consisted of 10 different rail lines, each of which insisted upon its own timetables and rate schedules. If you shipped via that route, you had to make a separate bargain with each of the 10. Not only that, but the P&E was standard-gauge (4 feet 8½ inches) and had to transfer its westbound shipments to a railroad of another gauge. The New York & Erie then had a 6-foot gauge, the New York Central 4 feet 8¼ inches, and the Ohio roads, including the Lake Shore, 4 feet 10 inches. The situation was frustrating, wasteful of time and money, and unnecessarily laborious. *See* ERIE RAILROAD WAR.

The Pennsylvania Railroad (PRR) partially simplified it by leasing the P&E and, in 1865, founding the Empire Transportation Co. (ETC), whose purpose was to mediate between railroads and shippers. ETC solicited freight business, supplied cars and terminal facilities, and collected payment from consignees, but did not set rates. Shippers welcomed this simplification, and ETC prospered.

Meanwhile, in 1860, British capitalists began building a new railroad, the Atlantic & Great Western (A&GW), westward from Salamanca, New York. A year later it reached Corry, Pennsylvania, 60 miles distant, where it connected with the P&E, and in 1865 one of its branches entered Oil City, Pennsylvania. The A&GW mainline, by pushing westward and leasing other roads, arrived at Cleveland, where young John D. Rockefeller was beginning to scramble to the top of the oil-refining trade.

The British-owned system was proud of being able to move petroleum over the most direct route between the oil regions and the refineries, with no change of track gauge, and boasted of its part in making Cleveland a great refining center. Handling an enormous volume of business, it could offer shippers a relatively low rate.

The oil business then was highly speculative. Nobody could foresee when or where new wells might spring up, or how prices might fluctuate, or what new uses would be found for petroleum. So until the Civil War ended, PRR moved warily. But the growth of both the AG&W and the New York & Erie prompted the Pennsy to throw caution to the winds.

Boldly taking over the Philadelphia & Erie, the Keystone Road set about making itself the leading carrier of crude oil to tidewater. At the same time, the Pennsy bought control of a new broad-gauge line, the Oil Creek Railroad, which had been serving the New York & Erie, and added a third rail to it for moving standard-gauge equipment.

The Pennsy also extended the P&E all the way to Philadelphia. Thus the road made an emphatic bid for the expanding oil trade, flinging down the gauntlet to the Erie-Atlantic & Great Western hookup. In 1865 the latter hauled 750,000 barrels of oil, more than twice the Pennsy's figure. And during the same year 700,000 barrels were poled down the Allegheny River to Pittsburgh, for in those days railmen and watermen fought each other ruthlessly for business.

From 1865 to the early 1900s, tank cars like this one, consisting of two wooden tubs bolted onto a flatcar, carried oil by rail. They also carried water to desert areas.

However, PRR offered the shortest route from wells to refineries through control of the Catawissa, Lehigh Valley, and Philadelphia & Reading roads. You can judge the Catawissa's cutoff value from the fact that oil shippers paid the P&R $12 extra for each car using the shortcut.

Meanwhile, as early as 1861 came a failed attempt to build an oil pipeline. And that same year two other projected pipelines also came to naught. Then J. L. Hutchings actually laid and used two pipelines, in 1862 and 1863 respectively, but both were leaky. Although Hutchings died in poverty and frustration, he had devised and put into execution a method that one day would revolutionize the transportation of oil and, incidentally, prove a bed of thorns to rail officials. At first the railroads favored the use of pipelines because it lowered the cost of conveying oil to their property. But before long they were singing a different tune.

By 1866 the war between Pennsy and Erie-A&GW interests to dominate oil transportation had developed

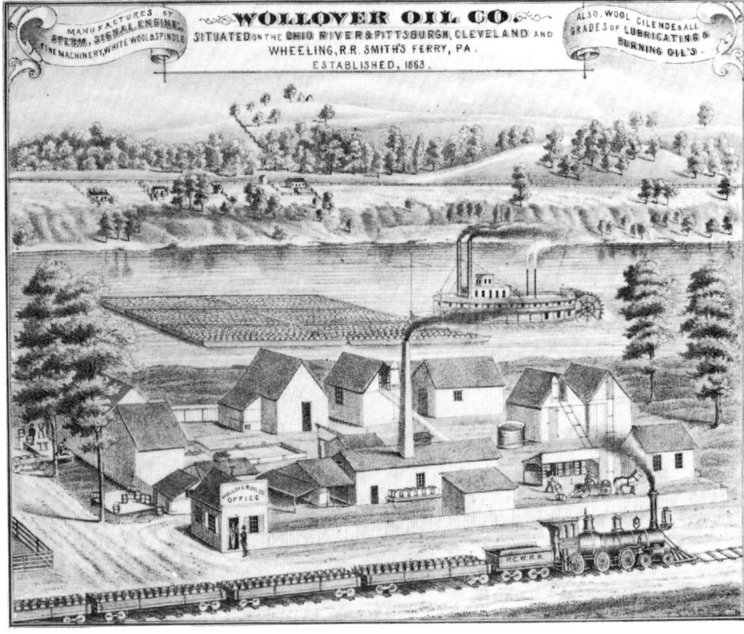

This old print shows how the Wollover Oil Co. shipped oil in the 1860s. In the foreground, barrels are being shipped by rail on flatcars; in the rear, they travel on barges, drawn by steamboat. [Collection of Freeman Hubbard]

into a mad scramble to cut railroad rates, provide cars, and lay pipelines. In 1870 the situation simmered down to this: PRR interests controlled the rail movement of most of the crude oil from the wells to shipping points and shared with the Erie-A&GW a monopoly on tank-car loads to the Eastern seacoast. Still not satisfied, the Pennsy had a monopolistic charter rushed through the Pennsylvania Legislature, blocking the efforts of all persons and companies to lay pipelines in that state without PRR permission.

Three powerful rail systems had extended branches into the oil regions: the Pennsy with the Philadelphia & Erie, the New York & Erie with the Atlantic & Great Western, and the New York Central with the Lake Shore & Michigan Southern. It was a three-cornered battle. All these roads, evidence shows, resorted to trickery to get oil traffic. They issued standard freight rates (perfectly legitimately on the surface) but secretly undercut those rates for the benefit of large shippers. Only the little fellows had to pay the regular published rates.

The rebate system tended to make the big shippers bigger and freeze out the small ones. By this and other means Rockefeller's Standard Oil Company became a gigantic monopoly the like of which had never been seen before.

In 1872 Rockefeller and his associates bought an old Pennsylvania state charter with fantastically sweeping provisions which authorized them to engage in any kind of business in any country. Armed with this grant, they organized the South Improvement Co. (SIC), with the Lake Shore's general freight agent as president. This concern with a dubious name was given control of less than 10 percent of the nation's oil-refining business, but it won very profitable concessions from the three great railroads entering the oil regions by claiming to represent the bulk of America's refineries.

The storm that followed SIC's going into business led the railroad executives to run for cover. Jay Gould of the Erie, Commodore Vanderbult of the Central, and George B. McClellan, the Civil War general who had become president of the A&GW, disavowed all part in what a congressional committee termed a "gigantic and daring conspiracy."

Modern tank cars with cupolas provide safety from leakage, fire, and theft. [*Burlington Northern Railroad*]

The Pennsylvania Legislature followed suit by revoking the South Improvement charter. Under date of March 25, 1872, rail freight rates were stabilized at the advertised figures, with no rebates and no drawbacks, or so the law stated. But shortly afterward the railroads were found to be violating this agreement in many deals. A congressional committee unearthed figures showing that for the brief period between October 11, 1878, and March 31, 1879 (about 5½ months), the four big railroad systems paid Standard Oil a total of more than $10 million in rebates.

Even after Congress in 1887 had passed the Interstate Commerce Act, which, among other provisions, forbade the giving or accepting of rebates, such discrimination was still being carried on. Finally, in 1903, the stronger Elkins Act, effectively enforced by trust-busting President Theodore Roosevelt, terminated this practice.

To the credit of the Pennsylvania Railroad, it must be said that at one time it tried to encourage independent refineries. In 1884 Rockefeller blocked this move with a contract whereby if the Pennsy persisted in such an effort he would carry virtually all PRR's eastbound oil shipments himself, via Standard Oil pipelines, collecting from the shippers and paying the railroad a 5 percent rebate for keeping its hands off the business. Thus John D. had grown powerful enough to *pay* rebates as well as to receive them.

In recent years the railroad industry has lost nearly all its crude-oil business to competing pipelines.

The first tank car, built by Amos Densmore in 1865, consisted of two large wooden tubs, each with a tight-fitting cover, bolted onto a flatcar he had borrowed from the A&GW. In addition to oil shipments, such cars were used to carry water to arid regions. They were soon replaced by shiny new cylindrical metal tank cars that introduced even greater safety from leakage, fire, and theft. Then a dome or cupola was added, permitting expansion and further eliminating leakage.

By the late 1970s there were about 170,000 tank cars on North American rails, most of them carrying liquids other than oil and all but about 3000 possessed by private-car owners. Tank cars make up 35 percent of the privately owned freight-car fleet. Railroads make money by moving them under load, paying the owners from 13.01 to 25.24 cents per loaded mile for the use of the vehicles. This profitable business developed indirectly from the oil industry but now has relatively little to do with it.

BIBLIOGRAPHY: Gustavus Myers, *History of the Great American Fortunes,* 3 vols., Charles H. Kerr & Company, Chicago, 1910; Richard O'Connor, *The Oil Barons: Men of Greed and Grandeur,* Little, Brown, Boston, 1971.

Operating Ratio Percentage which total operating costs bear to a railroad's total operating revenue. For instance, if the operating revenue for a given period is $10 million and operating expenses are $7.5 million, the road's operating ratio is 75 percent.

Order of Railway Conductors Renamed the Order of Railway Conductors and Brakemen in 1954, it was founded in the spring of 1868 at Amboy, Illinois, as the Conductors Union (CU). Thomas (Tommie) J. Wright, an Illinois Central conductor born in Benton, Wisconsin, was only 22 but had been railroading for 7 years when he spearheaded the movement to improve conductors' pay, working conditions, and job security.

Conductors were then earning $2.10 per trip, whether on the road 6 hours or 60. Overtime pay was unknown. Working on trains with link-and-pin couplers, coal stoves, and inadequate brakes was risky and often fatal. Tommie knew men with red stumps bearing mute testimony to the countless toll of limbs, fingers, and toes claimed by the link-and-pin. Daniel Elliott, who was elected the first grand secretary of the international order, was killed in 1868 while working as a conductor on the Chicago, Burlington & Quincy (CB&Q). Tommie had also seen men, honest and hardworking but pushed beyond endurance, punished for accidents they could not have prevented. So there was a real need for the group he was instrumental in founding and of which he was elected chief conductor.

At first the union had only Illinois Central members, but word soon got around. In June of that year CB&Q conductors at Galesburg, Illinois, set up Division No. 2. The original organization had a very modest program. It proposed that the members, through education, sobriety, and safety, make themselves more valuable workmen entitled to higher pay and greater respect by their associates, including railroad company management, and it used discipline to enforce a strict moral code.

At that time the engineers had already organized a union (1863); the firemen did likewise in 1873, the trainmen in 1883, craft unionism in the American Federation of Labor in 1886, the ill-fated American Railway Union in 1893, and the switchmen in 1894.

Joe Packard, one of the men discharged for ignoring a Burlington bulletin of 1868 demanding that conductors quit the CU, was elected grand secretary of the conductors' brotherhood in its first United States-Canadian convention, held at Columbus, Ohio, in November 1868. Besides electing grand officers, the delegates adopted a revised constitution and set up a mutual insurance service. A year later the CU was renamed the Order of Railway Conductors of America (ORC), and in 1884 Cedar Rapids, Iowa, became its international headquarters. An auxiliary was formed for wives of members.

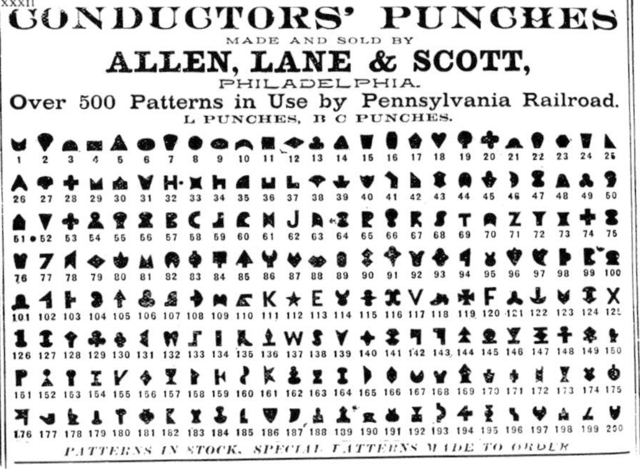

Each railway conductor's punch has an individual design in order to trace responsibility for errors on passengers' tickets. Samples are shown in this advertisement by Allen, Lane & Scott, manufacturers of conductors' punches in Philadelphia.

In 1885 the ORC directed its executives to aid in negotiating wage agreements. The year 1890 saw a strike clause adopted; the order had come a long way from its original timid program. It implemented a militant policy of fighting for the welfare of conductors in wages, hours, rules, safety, etc. As a result, thousands of new members joined up. In 1889, 65 percent of all American railroad conductors belonged to the order; in 1910, 90 percent belonged. In 1942 the Order of Sleeping Car Conductors was amalgamated with the ORC. The organization's magazine, *The Conductors' Journal,* had five different names over the years, the last one being *The Conductor & Brakeman.*

ORC, like the other brotherhoods, played a major role in wage negotiations and legislation and other matters affecting rail labor, such as the 16-hour law, the 8-hour day, the Railway Labor Act and its amendments, the Railroad Retirement Act, job protection in rail mergers, the strike date set for December 30, 1943, that led to wartime federal control of the railroads, a brief strike in 1946, two other federal seizures of the railroads, pension plans, the system for graduated rates of pay, and the work-rules controversy. The influential Railway Labor Executives Association grew out of concerted action by the rail brotherhoods during World War II.

In 1907 Congress passed a law limiting to 16 hours in 24 the period during which railroad men could stay on the job. It was called the hog law (*hog* is rail lingo for "locomotive"). An outlawed crew must wait until a fresh crew is sent to relieve it. This law lessened the number of disastrous wrecks that occurred because weary men had to stay on duty for excessively long hours. The law benefits the public as well as railroaders. *See* SAFETY LAWS.

In 1969, with 13,700 members, the ORC&B became part of the United Transportation Union.

BIBLIOGRAPHY: Gerald G. Eggert, *Railroad Labor Disputes: The Beginnings of Federal Strike Policy,* University of Michigan Press, Ann Arbor, Mich., 1967; Edwin C. Robbins, *Railway Conductors: A Study in Organized Labor,* AMS Press, New York, 1970.

Orphan Trains With the surge of railroad construction that followed the Civil War, a restless tide of humanity began flowing westward. Included were hundreds of thousands of immigrants who had fled from Europe, many of whom had settled originally in the disease- and crime-ridden slums of big American cities, where sweatshops and child labor prevailed. The West was then wide-open. Impoverished and disillusioned people of all ages and national origins needed a place to make a fresh start.

Fred Harvey set up a chain of first-class station restaurants and hotels beside the Santa Fe tracks and advertised in the East for young women of good repute to come out West and work for him. There were many other opportunities. In 1853 Charles Loring Brace, a social worker, founded the New York Children's Aid Society. Later he established orphanages and schools in the metropolis for boys and girls whom society had rejected. Then he decided that city waifs could find a more wholesome life in the West, believing that farm families would willingly adopt extra pairs of hands for the chores. *See* HARVEY, FREDERICK HENRY.

The families did. From the late 1850s until the Depression year of 1929 it is estimated that nearly 100,000 deserted or parentless children were shipped westward on so-called orphan trains. A few of the older girls qualified for Harvey House jobs. The trains consisted of wooden, open-platform coaches in which chaperoned groups of city children crossed the country in hopes of being adopted. During the peak year, 1875, more than 4000 waifs were sent out from the East, mostly to isolated towns in the prairie states.

On New Year's Eve, 1980, the Columbia Broadcasting System presented nationally a 3-hour TV dramatization of the orphan trains.

Otis Railway Picturesque, 7000-foot inclined line up a mountainside, built in 1892 from Otis Junction, New York, to the summit and the white-columned Catskill Mountain House, one of America's leading vacation resorts, which overlooked four states and the Hudson River 2200 feet below. Double steel cables passing over a huge drum at the top hauled the cars up. Ascending and descending cars moved simultaneously on the same track but passed each other on a loop switch midway between the terminals.

Passengers, often 75 to 100 on a train, sat with their backs to the mountain, gazing eastward over a vast panorama. Flatcars carried baggage and freight. This line connected with the Catskill Mountain Railway, a narrow-gauge steam-powered road built in 1880 by Charles L. Beach, stagecoach operator and owner of the famous hotel.

Finally, the multiplication of autos doomed the two railroads. Using convict labor, New York State built a concrete highway to the mountaintop, and in 1918 locomotive whistles ceased to echo through the area.

Oversize Shipments Loads exceeding the typical limits of 20 feet above the rail, 11½ feet wide, and/or 125 tons net weight. An estimated 100,000 such shipments roll over United States rails each year. To move them, railroaders specializing in this problem work with shippers in lining up routes to bypass close clearances of tunnels, bridges, etc., bridge load limits, and other bottlenecks. Some routes are almost incredably roundabout. Railroad limitations may even predetermine the size or weight of a bridge girder, pressure vessel, generator, etc., to be designed and manufactured and may even dictate whether it is shipped whole or piecemeal (and assembled at its destination).

The operating department of one or more railroads, depending upon the route, sets up in advance various restrictions such as the use of a local freight or special train, low speed, locking the uncoupling levers of flatcars on which the oversize load is carried so that the cars cannot come apart, and scheduling to avoid contact with other trains on adjacent tracks. Some big railroads move oversize or overweight loads on their own special depressed-center, wellhole, or high-capacity flatcars, for the use of which they charge an additional fee each time one is loaded. The largest power-generating machinery rides on Schnabel cars, some of which are equipped with jacking devices to shift the loads, if necessary, a few inches in any direction to clear obstacles. Maximum capacity for a 20-axle car is about 500 tons.

The heaviest single item ever shipped by rail may have been the Westinghouse Electric Corp. generator, 50 feet long and weighing over 900 tons, hauled from the company's East Pittsburgh, Pennsylvania, plant to the Duke Power Co. nuclear station about 25 miles north of Charlotte, North Carolina, in 1975. The generator stator alone weighed over 500 tons. It was designed for shipment on Westinghouse's largest railroad car, a 22-axle Schnabel car. To handle it, the consignee built a special track into its plant on Lake Norman, near Cowans Ford Dam.

P, Q

P&LE *See* PITTSBURGH & LAKE ERIE RAILROAD.

Pacific 231 Symphonic composition by Arthur Honneger, believed to have been named for locomotive No. 231 of the Northern Pacific's *North Coast Limited,* inaugurated on April 29, 1900, as the first electrically lighted train between the Midwest and northern Pacific Coast.

Paterson, New Jersey Eighteen miles northwest of New York City, Paterson was known as the City of Iron Horses because four steam locomotive works involving such great names as Rogers, Swinburne, Cooke, and Danforth, with a total output of over 13,500 locomotives, were located there. All four were situated near the Passaic River Falls, which supplied their power, but all were handicapped by being about a mile from the nearest railroad connection. Two of the firms—Rogers, Danforth & Cooke and the New Jersey Locomotive & Machinery Co.—organized and operated a street railway to solve this problem. That line, Paterson Horse Railroad, with a solitary horse-drawn passenger car, was ostensibly a passenger carrier but actually served to provide track connection with an Erie Railroad yard. Not until 1901 did the city let locomotives run on the Horse Railroad; so horses hauled not only material and equipment for the locomotive works but even the finished engines.

In 1832 a machinery manufacturing firm, Rogers, Ketchum & Grosvenor (RK&G), began making wheels and axles for the few railroads then existing in the United States. Three years later, one of those roads finished laying tracks from Paterson to Jersey City, imported a British locomotive, and hired RK&G to assemble it. The job took 4 weeks. During this time the firm's president, Thomas Rogers, studied the locomotive's mechanics.

Thereafter, Rogers concentrated on loco production. His first engine, the *Sandusky,* built in 1837, was sold to the Mad River & Lake Erie Rail Road, an Ohio project that had not yet laid a foot of track. Delivered by water, she was the first iron horse west of the Ohio River. The road's gauge, 4 feet 10 inches, became Ohio's standard gauge. Patterned in English style, the *Sandusky* had such then-new features as counterbalanced, hollow-spoked, cast-iron driving-wheel centers, outside eccentrics, and a wire-netting spark deflector in the smokebox. *See* ERIE RAILROAD WAR.

Rogers originated many improvements in engine construction such as outside cylinders and boilers of the wagontop type. After he died in 1856, the company was reorganized as the Rogers Locomotive and Machine Works, headed by his son Jacob. Rogers's most famous engine, eventually named the *General,* was built for the Western & Atlantic Railroad and was seized by Union raiders in a dramatic Civil War episode. This 4-4-0 is preserved today in Chattanooga, Tennessee. Rogers also built the first true Mogul, or 2-6-0. Because of its relatively great size and superiority over other wheel arrangements of its day, the type was called Mogul. In 1893 the company became the Rogers Locomotive Co. Eleven years later, after building 6231 engines, it was sold to American Locomotive Co. (Alco), which closed the plant in 1914, and sold most of its machinery to the Cooke works, another Paterson enterprise. *See* ANDREWS RAILROAD RAID.

Meanwhile, in 1845, William Swinburne quit as superintendent of the Rogers works. His son-in-law, John Cooke, succeeded him. Swinburne became senior partner in Swinburne, Smith & Co., which in 1848 began building locos, its first one being the New York & Erie's No. 11. Three years later, the firm was reorganized as New Jersey Locomotive & Machine Co. (NJL&M). In 1867 it became the Grant Locomotive Works, operated by Oliver D. F. Grant and his son David B. Grant. Its masterpiece, the *America,* later Chicago, Rock Island & Pacific No. 109, won first prize, a gold medal, at the Universal Exposition in Paris in 1867. Thereafter, the Grant works placed a replica of this medal on the cab of every engine it built.

Seriously damaged by fire in 1887, the Grant Locomotive Works moved to Chicago in 1890 and shut down in 1894. While located in Paterson, it constructed more than 1850 engines. *See* LOCOMOTIVES, EXPERIMENTAL.

Meanwhile, in 1867, William Swinburne founded Paterson's third engine plant, the New Jersey Locomotive & Machine Co. But after it had built 104 locos, his inability to collect money which railroads owed him for engines forced him to close. The Erie Railroad bought his shops and used them for many years.

Charles Danforth operated another Paterson engine plant, founded in 1852 in partnership with John Cooke, who had been superintendent of the Rogers works. It was located across the street from the main works of NJL&M and just around the corner from Rogers, Ketchum & Grosvenor. Its first engine, named *Vincennes,* was one of five built for the Ohio & Mississippi (later merged into the Baltimore & Ohio), but none of these was delivered because the O&M defaulted in payment. The first Danforth engine actually delivered went to Ohio, to the Junction Railroad (later part of the New York Central) in 1893. Like Rogers's first engine, she was named *Sandusky.*

The Rogers works in Paterson, New Jersey, built the first engine to run west of the Ohio River, the* Sandusky, *in 1837. It boasted such features as the first counterbalanced driving-wheel centers and a wire-netting spark deflector in the smokebox. [Republic Steel Corporation]

In 1865 the firm reorganized as Danforth Locomotive & Machine Co. After Danforth's death in 1876 and Cooke's in 1882, it became the Cooke Locomotive & Machine Co. In addition to 2675 locos outshopped at Paterson, it built many steam rotary snowplows. In 1901 International Power Co. acquired its shops and sold them to Alco, which operated them under the Cooke name until 1926, after which the plant ceased to turn out locomotives but made other products. Under Alco ownership it produced 2500 locomotives, making a total of 5175 from this Paterson plant.

NOTE: Condensed from Walter A. Lucas, "City of Iron Horses," *Railroad Stories,* June 1933.

BIBLIOGRAPHY: Edwin P. Alexander, *Iron Horses: American Locomotives, 1829–1900,* Norton, New York, 1941; John H. White, Jr., *American Locomotives: An Engineering History, 1830–1880,* Johns Hopkins, Baltimore, 1968.

Pay Car For over a century, beginning in the 1830s, the glad cry "Here comes the pay car!" thrilled railroad men. Known as the *money wagon* or *bandwagon,* it would chug seemingly out of nowhere, dispense its treasure to groups waiting eagerly along the line, and vanish around the bend.

"In between pay-days," said an ancient switchman, "it retired to some remote and fanciful region like the Big Rock Candy Mountain, there to remain until the tenth of the month rolled 'round again." Actually, it rode the rails for the first 3 weeks of every month and spent the rest of the time on a siding while the *grand lama* (rail lingo for *paymaster*) balanced his books and got ready for the next trip. It traveled only in daylight, for security reasons, putting up for the night at some wayside depot.

The pay train, especially in the old West when banks were scarce, was a famous institution. It might run as the second section of a passenger train, sometimes coupled behind a local, but mostly it ran special. Foremen and department heads were notified of its coming a day or two in advance, either by telegraph or by signal flags whipping the breeze on the locomotive of a regular train.

The car was often a remodeled Pullman with a piano-rub hardwood finish, gold-leaf striping, crystal-clear windows, and ornate rear-platform railings. The earliest versions were remodeled boxcars. Many were converted coaches. The engine, too, was often a work of art. On the Pennsy's Philadelphia division the grand lama made his rounds in a car pulled by a locomotive so elegant that she could not be stabled with ordinary iron horses but occupied a private stall in the roundhouse at Harrisburg, Pennsylvania.

One Southern Pacific (SP) paymaster told a reporter that the largest sum he ever started out with was $265,000. "We had so much gold," he said, "that I couldn't get it all into the big safe and had to stack it alongside the car walls."

Usually riding in the car with the grand lama were his clerk, the auditor's clerk, two *cinder dicks* (armed guards), a cook, and a Negro porter. Some roads added a combination sleeper-coach to the pay train and possibly a boxcar stocked with tools and supplies for section gangs along the line. Occasionally a third car doled out signal oil, kerosine, and coal to section houses and stations. A famous SP pay car had boiler plate ¼ inch thick extending from door to roof on each side of the pay window, and portholes through which a paying teller could shoot if necessary.

No matter which road he worked for, the grand lama was expected to have a memory like an elephant's. One SP paymaster claimed he could recognize about 8000 persons and call them by name.

Long ago, the problem of paying widely scattered employees was hazardous, particularly in the West but sometimes in the East as well.

In 1886 three men robbed a Louisville & Nashville pay car of $8222.85 at Bristow, Kentucky, and fled, but eventually were caught and sent to prison. That same year, three other desperadoes stole an entire Richmond & Danville pay car, supply car, and Georgia Railroad engine from the Atlanta yards. Two of them were caught and put behind bars. What finally happened to the third is obscure, except that he was involved in a wife-murder case.

A pay-car stickup around the turn of the century caused a brief strike in the Texas & Pacific yards at El Paso. The men refused to work until the frantic paymaster was able to borrow a large sum from a local bank and pay them. During the panic of 1907, when the money market was tight, many roads printed their own scrip in denominations of $10, $20, and $30 to pay wages and bills. The pay car finally became extinct because of the railroads' decision to pay by check instead of in cash. When was that? The dates vary: Southern Pacific, 1910; Delaware and Hudson, 1921; Union Pacific, 1933; National Railways of Mexico, early 1970s. *See* CURRENCY ISSUED BY RAILROADS.

BIBLIOGRAPHY: Joseph Bromley, *Clear the Tracks*, McGraw-Hill, New York, 1943; Freeman Hubbard, *Great Trains of All Time*, Grosset & Dunlap, New York, 1962; *Railroad Magazine*, February 1965.

Pecos River Bridge Spidery wrought-iron viaduct in Texas, spanning the river gorge at a height of about 300 feet. It was the world's highest bridge in 1892, when the Phoenix Bridge Co. built it for the Southern Pacific (SP). Train passengers crossing it at 12 miles per hour had a spectacular view. This famous structure was the scene of a movie thriller, a wedding high up in the air, and a daring girl's horseback ride. It was 2180 feet long. In 1909 it was reinforced and its capacity much increased, but in the mid-1940s SP decided that it required too much attention and replaced it with a somewhat shorter bridge to minimize traffic delays.

Penn Central Transportation Company Corporation formed in 1968 by what was then the largest merger in United States history: a consolidation of two giant rivals, the Pennsylvania (PRR) and the New York Central (NYC). Just 2½ years later it was plunged into the nation's biggest corporate bankruptcy and the worst fiasco in the annals of railroading.

Penn Central had two primary roots. One dates back to 1823, when Pennsylvania granted the inventor John Stevens a charter for a rail line to extend from Philadelphia to the Susquehanna River, and to 1824, when the Philadelphia & Columbia, earliest predecessor of the Pennsylvania Railroad, was opened. *See* PENNSYLVANIA RAILROAD.

The other root, the New York Central's embryo, sprouted in 1825, when George W. Featherstonehaugh, a gentleman farmer, announced on December 28 the formation of New York State's first railroad, the Mohawk & Hudson, which was chartered in 1826 to run between those two rivers (i.e., between Schenectady and Albany, the capital) and would use horse-drawn cars.

It was followed by the Utica & Schenectady, the Syracuse & Utica, the Auburn & Rochester, the Auburn & Syracuse, the Schenectady & Troy, the Rochester & Syracuse, and the Rochester, Lockport & Niagara Falls, the last-named being completed in 1852. To the western end of this chain of individual railways across New York State were added the Buffalo & Rochester, the Attica & Buffalo, and the Buffalo & Lockport, and there were some mergers. The result was rail connections between Albany and Buffalo. In 1853 this east-west chain was consolidated into one railroad named the New York Central. Also in that year, the 141-mile north-south Hudson River Railroad (HR) was opened from Manhattan to East Albany.

In 1864, Commodore Cornelius Vanderbilt, who already had the 131-mile north-south New York & Harlem (NY&H), first of the Vanderbilt roads, linking Manhattan with Chatham Four Corners, got control of the HR line, and in 1869 he merged it into the NY&H. Then he took over the New York Central, and built Grand Central Depot in New York City on the site of the present Grand Central Terminal. *See* VANDERBILT, CORNELIUS.

In 1878, the year after his death, his son William, as president of the NYC System, acquired several roads that gained him access to Chicago and St. Louis. William died suddenly in 1885, after more than doubling his $100 million or so inheritance from his father. Upon his death, the Central was run not so much by his sons as by technicians, lawyers, and bureaucrats.

Meanwhile, its major rival, the Pennsy, had been

expanding also, in a big way, and boldly adopted the slogan, "The Standard Railroad of the World."

In the Depression year of 1932, the Central, with $293 million in operating revenue, slipped behind the Keystone Road's $311 million, while its funded debt, $670 million, exceeded PRR's $626 million. In the late 1940s, like most other railroads, the two rival systems began playing down their passengers and concentrating on the more lucrative freight business, thus paving the way ultimately for Amtrak. *See* AMTRAK.

Mid-1957 was a time of inflation and a new recession. That September the Pennsy and the Central opened exploratory talks on a series of possible mergers. The talks were long and devious, partly because the two systems had duplicate facilities. The chief protagonists were James Symes, Pennsy chairman, David Bevan, chairman of the Pennsy Finance Committee, and Alfred Perlman, last president of the Central. Perlman kept delaying the final action because he knew that it would make PRR the senior partner, dictating policies and programs and holding most of the top executive positions.

Retiring prior to the merger, Symes was succeeded by Stuart Saunders. Perlman clashed repeatedly with the PRR officials on policies. He also disliked them personally, and they were antagonistic to him. But all three realized that railroading was on the decline, and they had little choice. Railroad labor lobbied against the merger because it would cause thousands of layoffs. But a Supreme Court ruling on January 15, 1968, made it effective 2 weeks later.

The new corporation was headquartered in the Pennsy stronghold of Philadelphia, where Chairman Saunders initiated policies and developed strategy, while Perlman, as president, stayed in New York, in the old New York Central headquarters, to supervise day-by-day railroad operations.

The details of mismanagement, even involving criminal charges, and conflicts of authority, the role of bankers, and trading on the New York Stock Exchange are important bits of history. The financial position of Penn Central (PC), bad as it was, was worsened by the fact that Congress and the Interstate Commerce Commission forced the new system to take over the New Haven Railroad, whose 1968 deficit was $22.3 million.

On June 21, 1972, PC's plunge into bankruptcy stunned the industrial world. Later, it was known that certain railroad officials had unloaded their Penn Central holdings before the crash, an action which had a bad smell. A trustee appointed by the U.S. District Court in Philadelphia supervised the bankrupt system's railroad operations until Consolidated Rail Corporation, instituted on April 1, 1976, took them over. Meanwhile, another part of Penn Central, the nation's most heavily traveled rail passenger route, between Boston and Washington, had been entrusted to Amtrak, which began to function in 1971. Amtrak also won major stations such as New York's Penn Station and Philadelphia's 30th Street; but Conrail, handling commuter service, acquired control of Grand Central Terminal. *See* CONRAIL.

After nearly 8 years Penn Central was released from bankruptcy on October 24, 1978, fully reorganized to do business on its own, but very little railroad business. It now operates real estate, amusement parks, hotels, a pipeline, an oil company, etc., through subsidiaries. Still in the railroad business on a tiny scale, it was trying in the late 1970s to sell 3000 miles of scattered track, as well as subsidiary railroads, tugs, barges, and bridges, for scrap or reassembly elsewhere.

BIBLIOGRAPHY: Robert B. Carson, *Main Line to Oblivion,* Kennikat Press, Port Washington, N.Y., 1971; Joseph R. Daughen and Peter Binzen, *The Wreck of the Penn Central,* New American Library, New York, 1973; *Moody's Transportation Manual,* Moody's Investors Service, New York, 1975; Robert Sobel, *The Fallen Colossus,* Weybright & Talley, New York, 1977; John F. Stover, *The Life and Decline of the American Railroad,* Oxford, New York, 1970.

Penn Station Functional monument to the golden noontide of railroading, completed and opened in 1910, it was built, like a cathedral, strongly and beautifully enough to last for a millennium. Many people were shocked because within 50 years this great edifice, though still sturdy and handsome, was razed and replaced by a smaller station, partly on the same site but hidden underground. This was done without seriously disturbing train traffic, an engineering triumph in itself.

The story began in 1871, when the Pennsylvania Railroad (PRR), while negotiating a lease with the United Railroad of New Jersey, started to plan ways of running its trains into New York City instead of depending upon ferry service for its passengers. One plan, a very long bridge across the Hudson River, was vetoed by tight money and the opposition of competitors.

The major accomplishment of the administration of Alexander J. Cassatt (1839–1906), who became seventh president of the PRR in 1897, was extending its trackage underwater from New Jersey into mid-Manhattan and onto Long Island and acquiring a controlling interest in the Long Island Rail Road (LIRR).

In 1901 the Pennsy got permission to tunnel under the Hudson and East Rivers and to erect on Manhattan Island a passenger station and a huge backup yard for train classification and servicing. Its 8-acre station site was bounded by Seventh and Eighth Avenues and 31st and 33d Streets. With William G. McAdoo (later wartime Director General of Railroads) as chief engineer of tunnel construction, digging began in 1903.

Sandhogs bored two separate single-track tunnels through New Jersey's Bergen Hill and drove tubes through mud and sand 70 feet below the surface of the Hudson River. They extended these tubes beneath and beyond the station site to Ninth Avenue and sank four other single-track tunnels eastward across Manhattan

Island, with four tubes under the East River to a connection with the Long Island Rail Road at Long Island City. The project included construction of a large coach yard and train terminal on the Long Island side to provide for the LIRR's suburban traffic and the movement of empty trains to and from the Sunnyside yard (then the world's biggest passenger yard) for storage and servicing. The line was electrified only from its point of departure from the old mainline east to Newark, a station known later as Manhattan Transfer, where all trains stopped to change engines until the line to Philadelphia was electrified in 1933.

In materializing this gigantic, costly project, the Pennsy met many difficulties, political, legal, and financial, including New York City franchises. Meanwhile, Cassatt assisted at the birth of the electrified Hudson & Manhattan Railroad, incorporated in 1902, which built the next tunnels under the Hudson and permitted abandonment of the old 23d Street ferry.

James McCrea (1848–1913), who succeeded Cassatt as Pennsy president in 1907, carried on to completion the building of the great new terminal. Its architect was Stanford White.

Its Roman Doric design was surmounted by an attic, with tall colonnades on two sides. Exterior walls were Milford pink granite, which more than 1000 flatcars had brought to the site from Massachusetts. Travertine marble imported from Italy adorned the interior. Also used were 27,000 tons of steel and 15 million bricks. The vast interior was modeled after the baths of the Roman emperor Caracalla. The main entrance reminded travelers of Berlin's Brandenburg Gate.

Fourteen majestic eagles, sculptured from sandstone by Adolph A. Weinman, were perched above the various entrances. Each bird was 6 feet tall, had a 3-foot wingspan, and weighed almost 3 tons. (Today, you can see two of these eagles grounded on Penn Plaza, where the original station once stood. The others have also found worthy resting places.)

Inside the now-gone Penn Station were numerous statues, including a full-length bronze figure of Cassatt, bas-reliefs, and other ornamental works typical of the period. Everything about the station seemed to be massive. More than 500 buildings had been torn down to make room for it. Highest of the subterranean tracks was 9 feet below sea level, 5 feet below the street. The broad canopy over the trainshed was 150 feet from floor to ceiling. The main waiting room, flanked by two smaller waiting rooms, was at that time the world's largest. Some of the station clocks measured 7 feet in diameter.

Penn Station was reputed to be the only railroad depot with a fishermen's bureau where you could charter boat sailings and find out the special bait or tackle to use and the species of fish that were running. It was also the first depot to use an electric "green to go" train signal system from ushers to train crews. It was the first one equipped with automatic train stop controls and was the site of the first public display of television.

This was one of the very few stations that ever had railroad motive power designed and built especially for it. The Keystone Road's first locos for New York Terminal service consisted of two units coupled back to back, the double unit being designated Class DD-1. Four roads—Pennsy, Lehigh Valley, Long Island, and New Haven—ran about twice as many trains through Penn Station daily as Amtrak now runs through the entire United States.

The original edifice complex boasted 57 tracks, including storage tracks, 231 signals, 45 double slips and movable frogs, and 98 single switches controlled by four interlocking stations. According to rules, trains in the station and tunnels had two blocks' headway which meant that they could run on the same track about 2 minutes apart.

The structure which replaced the old building is still commonly called Penn Station. Except for comparison with its predecessor, it is a depot to be proud of, with all modern facilities. Its main floor, below street level but accessible by moving stairs, is one of Amtrak's showplace passenger terminals: handsome, efficient, and often busy, the "home port" of *Metroliners* and the *Broadway Limited,* among other name trains. Metropolitan Transportation Authority operates the large floor beneath that level, which serves the Long Island (commuter) Rail Road and, at both eastern and western entrances, New York's gigantic subway system.

BIBLIOGRAPHY: Edwin P. Alexander, *The Pennsylvania Railroad: A Pictorial History,* Norton, New York, 1947; George H. Burgess and Miles C. Kennedy, *Centennial History of the Pennsylvania Railroad Company, 1846–1946,* Pennsylvania Railroad, Philadelphia, 1949.

Concourse of the original Penn Station in New York, now replaced by a smaller underground station. [A. F. Sozio, Pennsylvania Railroad]

Pennsylvania Railroad (PRR) In its proudest years this rail line filled twice as many pages in *The Official Guide* as did its nearest rival, the New York Central, and occasionally 4 times as many as the Southern Pacific. Its best-remembered slogan was "The Standard Railroad of the World." Traversing 13 states and the District of Columbia, it joined East with West and ran latitudinally from the land of spring wheat to the cotton fields.

Just before the 1930s' Depression it boasted "a greater volume of traffic, measured in terms of tons of freight and passengers carried per mile, than is handled by any other transportation system, not only in the United States, but in the world." Its maximum locomotive ownership was 7667 in 1920. By 1945, the year before the Pennsy's centennial, this figure had dropped to 4718, but the average starting tractive force had risen by about 43 percent over 1920. The Pennsy's investment in road, equipment, etc., at its peak was estimated at well over $2.5 billion. Its 142,600 stockholders were said to have exceeded in number those of any other railroad. Not in any year until 1946 did PRR fail to make a profit or skip a dividend—probably the longest unbroken rail-dividend record in history.

Unlike the big Western systems, the Pennsy rail network was generally compact and served the country's most closely populated areas. Its densest traffic was between New York and Washington, a showplace over which the electrified rails of its four- to six-track mainline were said always to be hot.

But in the diesel age its forward march bogged down in a financial morass, owing largely to federally subsidized highway and airline competition. In 1968 the PRR admitted defeat by merging with the weaker New York Central into the ill-fated Penn Central, which become part of Conrail in 1976. Thus the Pennsy lost its identity. Gone is its gold-on-red keystone that symbolized a great system identified with the Keystone State, in which it was born and from which it ruled at one time 11,600 miles of road, or 28,000 miles of total trackage, including double, quadruple, and sextuple tracks. *See* CONRAIL; PENN CENTRAL TRANSPORTATION COMPANY.

Number 3880, one of the Pennsy's famous powerful Class K-4 engines, on the New York & Long Branch line. Note the keystone emblem on the front of the locomotive. It identified the Pennsy with the Keystone State in which it was born. [Bud Rothaar]

The keystone emblem was used first by Thomas E. Watt, the company's Pittsburgh agent, immediately after the strike of 1877, the world's first major rail walkout, in which the Pennsy suffered heavily, especially in the burning of its Pittsburgh station. PRR was one of the very few roads which used their insignia on the locomotive front. During the many years when the Long Island Rail Road was part of the Pennsy System, its trademark also was a keystone but with its own initials interlaced. From 1881 to 1930, despite two disastrous fires in that Philadelphia edifice, the system's general offices were located in Broad Street Station. *See* BROAD STREET STATION; STRIKE OF 1877.

Chartered by a group of Philadelphians on April 14, 1846, the Pennsylvania Railroad was preceded by a unique chain of transportation facilities called the State Works. For its first 20 years it was fortunate in having as its chief engineer John Edgar Thomson (1808–1874), whom historian Stewart H. Holbrook described as "one of the greatest all-round railroad men America has ever known." Thomson had worked on railroads in his native state of Pennsylvania and in Georgia. After arranging for the decrepit state-owned Philadelphia & Columbia to carry PRR freight and passengers, he put crews to work building a line to Pittsburgh.

Then the Pennsy bought the state road and extended it to Harrisburg, the state capital. On September 1, 1848, it operated its first passenger train from Philadelphia to Pittsburgh, drawn by the *Mifflin,* a 47,000-pound Baldwin 4-4-0 woodburner with driving wheels 72 inches in diameter and with 14- by 20-inch cylinders. *See* ALLEGHENY PORTAGE RAILWAY.

The Pennsy continued to expand, leasing and later buying the Pittsburgh, Fort Wayne & Chicago. It also acquired the United Railroad & Canal Co. of New Jersey with terminal facilities across the Hudson River from New York City. Then Thomson and his associates organized the Pennsylvania Company, possibly the country's first holding company, to protect their leased or controlled properties from raids by outsiders. On behalf of the PRR, Thomson picked up the Cleveland & Pittsburgh with its important gateway to the Great Lakes, many small Ohio lines, and the Pittsburgh, Chicago & St. Louis.

Later, the Pennsylvania pushed southward to Washington. In its growing years it acquired over 600 distinct corporations, which must set a record. One of its roads, the Camden & Amboy in New Jersey, had the world's first T rails and the *John Bull,* the first locomotive with a cowcatcher or pilot.

The Pennsy is credited with being the first road to initiate smart uniforms for its passenger conductors. Even before the Civil War, it dressed them in fine cutaway coats of blue broadcloth with shiny brass buttons, buff vests, black trousers, and gilt-embroidered caps.

In 1853 the then-new railroad tried out coal as locomotive fuel, Pennsylvania being the nation's top producer of anthracite. By 1864 all PRR engines were coal-burners and remained so for nearly 100 years, except on the electrified New York-Washington mainline and westward to Harrisburg. The tests proved the advantages of the firebrick arch in the firebox. That construction, with various refinements, became standard on all Pennsy steam power. In 1861 the road developed a steam injector to feed water into the boiler. Four years later it made the Westinghouse automatic airbrake mandatory on its engines and began to standardize its freight, passenger, and switching power.

It seems certain that Pennsy did more than any other railroad to develop the steam locomotive into an efficient machine, designing locomotives for construction in its own shops and by such notable builders as Baldwin, American Locomotive Co., R. Norris & Son, and Ross Winans. The Pennsy had building and repair shops in Altoona (not far from its spectacular Horseshoe Curve), Columbia, Mifflin, Conemaugh, and Pittsburgh, all in Pennsylvania. These constructed locomotives, cars, iron bridges, and other equipment. Altoona was world-famous. In 1873 it began to build locos, producing 57 of the 155 new units acquired by the company that year.

Of the railroad's first 26 locos, Baldwin had built 23 and Norris 3. Between 1853 and 1856 Winans built 11 of his Camel types for the Pennsy. These freight and switching units with the cab placed above the boiler were not satisfactory until Altoona rebuilt them.

In 1864 the road standardized the use of locomotive drivers with cast-iron centers and wrought-iron tires, replacing its chilled-tread cast-iron drivers. Before 1861 it used pumps to force feedwater into the loco drive, but in that year the steam injector was developed and because of its simplicity was quickly adopted. In 1862 steel sheets manufactured by the Bessemer system replaced copper fireboxes. John P. Laird, master of machinery, began to standardize PRR motive power in 1862, for reasons of economy and greater efficiency, reducing the time during which engines were out of service for repairs.

In 1904 the road set up a locomotive-testing plant, first displaying it at the Louisiana Purchase Exhibition in St. Louis and subsequently installing it at Altoona. In 1945, based on the total drawbar horsepower of Pennsy locos in service, steam freight haulers represented 73 percent of the road's total power, steam passenger locos 13.5 percent, and steam switchers and electrics the remainder.

Although the number of PRR steam passenger locos dropped from 1182 in 1900 to 693 in 1945, their total tractive starting force rose by 53 percent during that time. The smaller number was due partly to the substitution of electric power on lines east of Harrisburg and a general decrease in passenger-train mileage on branch and secondary lines. In 1945 the Pennsy system was handling 16.27 percent of all passenger-miles of Class I roads in the United States. Its passenger motive power showed considerable growth up to 1914, crowned by Class K-4s, which were 7⅜ as powerful as the Class D-2s of 1882.

Prior to Pennsy's extension into New York City by underriver tunnels and the building in Manhattan in 1910 of the magnificent Penn Station (since razed), passengers from points south and west rode trains into Jersey City, where they changed to railroad-owned ferryboats that landed them in downtown Manhattan. Direct access to New York on Pennsy rails could not have been brought about at that time without the electric locomotive. By 1916 a related project, the Hell Gate Bridge route, completed that year in cooperation with the New York, New Haven & Hartford, gave PRR a direct through route between New England and the Middle Atlantic and Midwestern and Southern states. Detroit was added to the network in 1923.

For many years PRR held a controlling interest in the Norfolk & Western, the Lehigh & New England, and the Lehigh Valley and a half interest in the electrified Virginian Railway. In 1902 it adopted a direct-current third-rail system of electricity, built three experimental locos, and tried them out on the West Jersey & Seashore's electrified tracks. Two locos of this type were coupled together and used in the 8-mile run from Manhattan Transfer through the tunnel into New York with trains of up to 14 cars.

This type of power remained in service until 1933, when the 11,000-volt AC overhead-wire system replaced the 11,000-volt DC third-rail system. With the extension of electrification beyond the terminal area, high-speed locomotives were developed. In 1933, when electric operation of through passenger service went

***Engine No. 1361 of the Pennsylvania Railroad is pictured here on permanent exhibition on the Horseshoe Curve near Altoona, Pennsylvania.** [Bud Rothaar]*

into effect between New York and Philadelphia, the factor of crew safety in the event of a collision led to relocating the cab in the center of the locomotive. Later, the more powerful Class GG-1 was developed for these runs. *See* ELECTRIFICATION.

Because the Pennsy served so many coalfields, its management was reluctant to turn to the use of diesel power. In 1929, however, it designed and built three internal-combustion switchers for the New York area. In 1945 it bought a two-unit, 4000-horsepower passenger diesel-electric, which it subsequently raised to 6000 by adding a third, or booster, unit. A few years afterward the entire Pennsylvania system, except for its electric service, was dieselized.

In 1906 the Pennsy built and placed in service the first all-steel coach created and operated anywhere (although the all-*iron* Mothe coach on another road dated back to 1865), and it discontinued the construction of wooden-bodied passenger cars. It was also the first road to standardize all-steel passenger equipment and the first to stop building coaches with open platforms, using enclosed vestibules for greater protection to riders walking between the cars of a moving train, and the first to adopt an all-steel passenger train.

In 1882 the Pennsy began experimenting with electric lights on passenger runs. The world's first train to be fully equipped with such fixtures was the *Pennsylvania Limited,* predecessor of the *Broadway Limited,* the New York-Chicago flyer, which began using the new illumination in June 1887. Even before electricity was introduced generally in American homes, it was lighting trains on the Keystone Road. By 1932 the Pennsy was operating air-conditioned dining cars all over its system. From that time on, it boasted of having the world's largest fleet of air-conditioned trains. *See* SPEED WAR.

BIBLIOGRAPHY: Edwin P. Alexander, *On the Main Line: The Pennsylvania Railroad in the 19th Century,* C. N. Potter, Crown, New York, 1971; Benjamin A. Botkin and Alvin F. Harlow, *A Treasury of Railroad Folklore,* Crown, New York, 1953; George H. Burgess and Miles C. Kennedy, *Centennial History of the Pennsylvania Railroad Company; 1846-1946,* Pennsylvania Railroad, Philadelphia, 1949; Stewart H. Holbrook, *The Story of American Railroads,* Crown, New York, 1947; Angus Sinclair, *Development of the Locomotive Engine,* annotated ed. by John H. White, Jr., M.I.T., Cambridge, Mass., 1970.

Periodicals Although all rail management-type magazines are profitable now, there is a feeling in the industry that as the number of railroads continues to shrink, one or more such magazines will eventually fold up, particularly because of the trend of railroad supply companies to merge, thus reducing the potential market for advertising.

The oldest magazine in its field is *Railway Age,* inaugurated on June 17, 1876, the nation's centennial year. Its roots go back to 1832. As years passed, it absorbed four competitors: *Northwestern Railroader,* founded in 1877; *Railroad Gazette,* founded in 1856; *Railroad Review,* founded in 1875, and *Railway Locomotives & Cars,* founded in 1832 as the *American Rail-Road Journal.*

The management-oriented *Railway Age,* with about 22,000 circulation, reports on contemporary developments and trends in line-haul freight and passenger railroading and rail rapid transit. It is issued twice a month by Simmons-Boardman Publishing Corporation of New York and Chicago, which also puts out *Railway Tracks and Structures, International Railway Journal,* and two reference books, *Car and Locomotive Cyclopedia* and *Who's Who in Railroading and Rail Transit.* Years ago this company also published many other railroad books.

The monthly *Modern Railroads Rail Transit (MR)* covers the nuts-and-bolts side of the industry and emphasizes such issues as finance, labor, legislation, regulations, and railroad management. It was launched in 1945. In 1980 *MR* was being distributed to 17,175 readers, especially railroad and transit officials and supervising personnel, government agency officials, and management personnel in rail industry-related manufacturing firms. It is published in Chicago.

First appearing in 1964, *Progressive Railroading* is a small product-oriented magazine.

Railroad Man's Magazine, founded in 1906 by Frank A. Munsey and published in New York, was a monthly for railroad employees which reached a peak circulation above 167,000. Suspended in 1919, it resumed publication under its original name in 1929. Later, Freeman Hubbard, who edited it for about 36 years, renamed it *Railroad Magazine* and modified its policy to attract hobbyists as well as rank-and-file railroaders. In 1979 it was merged into the present bimonthly *Railfan & Railroad,* published at Newton, New Jersey.

Trains magazine, founded in 1940 and published monthly in Milwaukee, covers common-carrier railroading, past and present, domestic and international. It is edited from a combination of railroad management and railfan viewpoints. Circulation exceeds 69,000.

Virtually all railroads and large railroad equipment and supply manufacturers issue employee publications. Among other house organs are the monthly *NARP News,* published by the National Association of Railroad Passengers, 417 New Jersey Avenue, S.E., Washington, D.C. 20003, and the monthly *The Timetable Collector,* 1443 West Fargo Avenue, Chicago, Illinois, 60626.

Periodical reprints include the bimonthly *Traction Heritage,* facsimile articles from the former *Street Railway Journal, Electric Railway Journal,* and *Transit Journal,* published by Vane A. Jones in Indianapolis; the monthly *Brill Magazine,* facsimile reprints from the house organ of old J. B. Brill Co., Philadelphia, once the nation's largest builder of street and interurban railroad cars, published by H. F. Cox, Forty Fort, Pennsylvania. Among other magazines are *Passenger Train Journal,* monthly; *Rail Travel Newsletter,* semimonthly; *Rail Classics,* quarterly; *Extra 2200 South,* bimonthly; *Western Railroader,* monthly; and *Railroads Illustrated,* quarterly.

BIBLIOGRAPHY: Paul B. Cors, *Railroads: Spare Time Guides,* Libraries Unlimited, Littleton, Colo., 1975.

Perry, Oliver Curtis ***(1865–1930)*** Lone-wolf bandit who robbed the same express train twice, 5 months apart, and fought the most amazing gun duel in railroad history. Born in Amsterdam, New York, he was sent to a reformatory at 11 and later to a penitentiary. Then as a cowboy in Montana he acquired skill with a six-shooter and, while lassoing cattle, developed his own method of entering a car of a speeding train. Still later, at Stillwater, Minnesota, while imprisoned for robbery, he devised ways of smuggling articles, such as a tiny file hidden in a cake, into prison.

At Troy, New York, he met Amelia Haswell, a social worker, apparently fell in love with her, joined her Bible class, and got a brakeman's job on the New York Central at $2 a day. But he had not reformed. On the night of September 30, 1891, at Albany, New York, he slipped into the front vestibule of the Central's *American Express,* which was carrying U.S. Treasury specie for Western banks. The money car, in the charge of express messenger E. A. Moore, held four safes, three of them hidden under piles of merchandise at the rear.

Perry, a small, agile man, meticulously groomed and wearing glasses, toted a satchel in which he kept a mask, two six-shooters, and a few tools. Using a gimlet and a saw, he cut out a door panel large enough for him to enter the car. Moore said afterward:

> While sorting packages as usual beside an open safe, near Utica, I heard a noise, and a masked man thrust a gun into my face and pushed me down. I was unarmed and too scared to resist. "Lie still," he told me. Glancing backward, he added: "Keep him covered, Jim. If the damn fool wriggles, let him have it." I thought at first he had an accomplice, but I think now he was only bluffing. He rummaged through the open safe. I don't know how much loot he took. Maybe several thousand dollars. But he overlooked a package of $5000 in currency and the three other safes. Backing out of the car, still holding his gun, he reached down and cut the rubber hose that connected the airbrake coupling, which led me to believe he was a railroad man. This set the brakes on the entire train. As the speed slackened, he jumped off and fled in the darkness.

Perry went back to Amelia, bade her an affectionate farewell, and said he was "going out West to make good." Pinkerton's men and railroad police sought the bandit in vain. Moore's description of him was so meager that no one suspected Oliver Perry. On February 21, 1892, after his money had run out, he again robbed the same train.

Daniel T. McInerney, express messenger, had charge of the money wagon. Perry entered the train in Albany at midnight. He confessed later:

> I swung aboard the seventh car, crawled over the roofs to McInerney's car, second car from the end, and strapped my valise and derby to the railing on its roof. I took out my hooked rope ladder—a kind of fire-escape invention of mine—attached it to the car roof, and peeped in to see if the messenger was suspicious. He seemed all right, so I let down my rope ladder over the edge and hung suspended in mid-air on the side of the train speeding through the cold wintry night at maybe 50 miles an hour.
>
> I tried to hold onto the car roof, but we traveled so fast that the strong wind blew me away from the car several times. Once I nearly hit a bridge. I wore kid gloves. My hands were so numbed with cold that when I drew a revolver I couldn't cock it. I rubbed my hands and slapped my sides to get my blood circulating. While doing this, I looked through the glass-paneled door and spied the messenger. He didn't see me.
>
> When I got inside the car I leveled my pistol at him. McInerney pointed his own gun at me and I ducked as I fired. The bullet grazed his forehead. He tried to pull the bell cord. I shot him in one arm and then in a leg. He doused the lamp and hid at the rear of the car, but I found him and made him light it again.

The next stop was Lyons, New York. Perry stepped off jauntily and tried to lose himself in the small crowd gathered at the station. But a brakeman remembered having seen the debonair stranger at Syracuse before the train pulled out, and the chase began. The bandit faced his pursuers with drawn revolvers. "Not so fast!" he said. "I'm leaving here and I don't want any company."

He walked toward a coal train whose engine had steam up, ready to pull out. He yanked the link-and-pin coupler between the tender and first car, climbed over the coal pile, forced the crew out with his guns, and opened the throttle.

Armed with a shotgun, several railroad men pulled the pin on the express engine, cutting off the cars, and took up the chase on the four-tracked railroad. Both locomotives headed west on adjoining tracks. The faster engine soon overtook the lone wolf, who suddenly reversed and let the pursuers pass him, spraying bullets into the cab as they went by. Forward and reverse, again and again, the two engines briefly raced side by side, with guns blazing but no casualties. At length Perry found his steam giving out, not having had time to shovel coal into the firebox.

Abandoning the freight engine at a crossroad, he ran on foot over the snow-covered ground and "borrowed" first a horse and then a horse-drawn sleigh, scaring the owners off with a revolver. A sheriff's posse trapped him in a swampy field 5 miles south of Newark, New York. The loot from his second robbery, estimated at $27,000, was never found. The police grilled Amelia Haswell, who denied all knowledge of it.

Perry was sentenced to 49 years and 3 months in Auburn State Prison. Five months later he broke out of his cell by digging a hole with a tin spoon under a brick wall but was recaptured after a few hours. So he tried another trick. Feigning insanity, he was transferred to the Matteawan Hospital for the Criminal Insane. Amelia continued to visit him. "Oliver," she pleaded, "promise me that if you ever get out of this awful place, you will cleanse your heart of bad things and make a fresh start."

Oliver promised. Escaping from Matteawan on April 10, 1893, by means of a key made from an iron spoon, he went straight to the Jerry McAuley Mission in New York City, knowing that its founder had once been a criminal, to keep his promise. Amelia was haled into court, charged with complicity, but managed to clear herself. Four fellow inmates fled with Perry and stole clothing from a farmhouse to replace their telltale prison garb. Within a few days all four were recaptured.

After leaving the mission, Perry sought food and shelter at a hobo bonfire in the West Shore Railroad yard at Weehawken, New Jersey. There a railroad policeman found him. Back in Matteawan, he became increasingly miserable. Not even Amelia's visits could cheer him up. On September 17, 1892, his twenty-seventh birthday, he blinded himself permanently by thrusting nails hammered through a thin board into his eyes, using a powerful narcotic to deaden the pain. Seven years later, the once-debonair lone wolf, now a physical wreck, was transferred to Dannemora State Hospital for the Criminal Insane. There he lingered until death released him a week before his sixty-fifth birthday.

Piggybacking Trailer-on-flatcar service designed to expedite the movement of goods by rail at truck rates by using transportation facilities more efficiently. It is bringing back considerable highway freight to the rails. Its assets are its profitability, its power to attract new business rather than merely transfer freight from boxcar to flatcar, and effective competition with trucks. As recently as 1972, piggybacking was sixth on the carloading list, with only 5.1 percent of total loadings. In 1976 it rose to third place, behind only coal and metallic ores, and it moved up to second in 1977 by setting what were then all-time records in carloadings (1,600,000), in trailers and containers handled (2,700,000), and in revenue (over $1 billion).

Long Island Rail Road farm trains ran at least twice a week in the late 1800s, illustrating an early form of piggybacking. Each flatcar carried four produce-laden wagons; horses rode in special cars on the same train. The drivers rode free in a coach. [Long Island Rail Road]

Major factors in piggyback's growth include:

1. Response to aggressive efforts by the railroads to improve service, attract new business, and achieve a more favorable traffic balance and better car utilization.

2. Continued growth of *rail-bridge service,* first introduced in 1972. This involves the ocean-to-ocean or Gulf-to-ocean rail movement of intermodal containerized freight in international commerce at near ocean rates and on a single bill of lading.

3. A solid comeback in freight forwarder and shipper association traffic. This consists of less-than-trailerload-lot (LTL) shipments that are combined into trailer or container loads by the forwarder or association for rail shipment.

4. Spiraling fuel costs, which work to the advantage of railroads because of their established fuel-efficiency edge over highway competitors.

Experiments are under way in equipment innovations aimed at curtailing fuel consumption and operational costs by reducing car weights and by wind-resistance factors. Major innovations in the late 1970s included skeletonized, articulated low-profile piggyback cars and *stack cars* for container traffic. *Road-railer cars,* introduced in about 1955, are highway trailers equipped with flanged wheels and couplers to make them equally at home on rails and highways. New, more efficient piggyback yards are being built in strategic locations, while branch-line ramps that slow the service are being closed.

Piggybacking is divided into handling (1) rail-billed less-than-carload-lot (LCL) freight on railway-owned or leased trailers; (2) rail-solicited freight in railway-owned or leased trailers; (3) trailers owned by carriers who solicit the business; (4) trailers owned or leased by shippers on flatcars also owned or leased by shippers, at a flat charge per car; and (5) the railroads' own trailers, or common-carrier truck trailers, under joint rail-truck rates on an end-to-end basis.

A major aspect of piggybacking is containerization: handling freight in units without wheels which, in various standardized sizes, can be loaded on specially built container trucks and railroad cars. This service is used also in ocean shippng, where it is called *fishbacking.*

American Railroad Journal on September 21, 1833 (only 3 years after the first rail service began in the United States), had an illustration showing a steam engine pulling a single passenger car and a flatcar carrying a road carriage filled with passengers. That marked the beginning of piggybacking. From 1843 to 1855 sectionalized canalboats were hauled on flatcars between Philadelphia and Columbia, Pennsylvania, and between Hollidaysburg and Johnstown, Pennsylvania, in Philadelphia-Pittsburgh rail-water service on a route that eventually became part of the Pennsylvania Railroad. *See* ALLEGHENY PORTAGE RAILWAY.

In 1885 Canadian farmers began loading their teams and wagons on Halifax-Truro Railway cars to ease the long, tiresome trip to market. And in the late 1800s, similar regularly scheduled farm trains were run twice a week, then 3 times a week, by the Long Island Rail Road between Albertson and Long Island City. This service started in 1885 and was discontinued around 1893, but in 1915 it was revived and extended across the East River into Manhattan. Each flatcar held four loaded wagons, with horses riding in specially built cars on the same train. And circus trains used their own piggybacking for about a century. *See* CIRCUS TRAINS.

In May 1936 loaded motor trucks were hauled by rail for the first time, the experiment being made by the Chicago North Shore & Milwaukee line between Chicago and Milwaukee. And in the fall of 1956 highway trailers began riding the rails from coast to coast. Since 1951 Canada's two big rail systems have been operating their own piggybacks.

BIBLIOGRAPHY: John H. Armstrong, *The Railroad—What It Is, What It Does,* Simmons-Boardman, New York, 1978.

Pilots, Steam Locomotive In 1832 Isaac Dripps, the Camden & Amboy's (C&A's) first master mechanic, designed and built the antecedent of the first locomotive cowcatcher, or pilot, in Philadelphia. He built it for the engine *John Bull,* which the C&A had just received from England but in parts which Dripps assembled and to which he added also a makeshift tender of his own creation. His cowcatcher's purpose was to prevent cattle, horses, and other obstructions from derailing the engine. It consisted of a hinged extension which rode upon two wheels in advance of the driving wheels, bearing part of the engine weight and having a plowlike nose to throw impediments aside. Similar contraptions were applied to several C&A engines but found little favor elsewhere.

Some roads, like the Baltimore & Ohio, were still relying upon simple iron guards projecting downward from the loco frame just ahead of the leading drivers. Stiff brooms were attached to a few of these to brush grasshoppers and caterpillars off the track. As more railroads were built, mechanically minded men devised new designs. A Philadelphia & Reading master mechanic studded the crossbeam on engine fronts with spikes to prevent cattle from falling under the wheels. But in time the pointed pilot, first wooden, then iron, and finally steel, became standard all over the continent. Such builders as William Mason of Taunton, Massachusetts, produced long, graceful cowcatchers worthy of the handsome machines they outshopped. *See* MASON, WILLIAM.

Metal pilots generally replaced wooden ones during the period 1860–1878 because increasing speeds brought about greater impact in collisions. Some Eastern and Western roads adopted a combination of round and flat iron bars, while others were still putting their money into seasoned oak and ash with lag-screw assembly, reinforcing iron bars, and supplementary braces extending back to the engine frame. Steel pilots appeared in the latter 1890s.

An 83-foot-long trilevel car is shown piggybacking 12 full-size Chryslers in 1960.

Around that time, the *knee* and *hen-coop* types became popular. On the knee type an inverted L-shaped piece extended from its apex up and under the coupler, thence back to connect with the rest of the framework. Slats tapering from this knee formed an almost unbroken face from the point to the coupler. The hen-coop type bore some resemblance to those old barnyard pens which sheltered hens and chicks. It was designed to present a continuous surface to obstacles, but it almost totally disappeared around 1906 with the advent of the Baldwin pilot, which for years was standard on the Pennsylvania Railroad. The latter was originally made of wood and was rather long, with a round coupler pocket. The coupler stem itself was abbreviated and protruded slightly beyond the pilot proper.

As link-and-pin couplers passed out, cowcatchers shrank in size. George McCormick, a Southern Pacific general superintendent of motive power, introduced the SP's stub pilot. The long, plowlike structure jutting out in front of the loco made the automatic couplers unable to engage each other; so McCormick had the pilot recessed partly under the beam, with its point extending out not more than 20 inches beyond. Two engines so equipped could be coupled as easily as rolling stock could.

The hen-coop locomotive pilot was designed by H. J. Small to prevent small objects or animals from getting lodged between pilot and coupler and to toss aside any animal it might strike. [David L. Joslyn]

In 1910, Charles T. Wheeler gave the iron horse its first cast-iron pilot, fashioned in a single piece but still retaining the traditional row of slats. Baldwin countered in 1914 with a pressed-steel job that remained in style for virtually a half century. The year before the United States entered World War I, many railroad draftsmen saved metal by making pilot slabs from old boiler flues. Some railroads held the pilot in such low esteem that they used freight power with no more collision protection than a switcher-type footboard.

The sturdy beam to which the pilot is attached has served a multitude of purposes, chiefly to protect the cylinders in the event of a collision. Originally made of wood and finally of steel, they sometimes were an integral part of the engine bed, as, for example, on the Pennsy's streamlined S-1 passenger locomotive. The pilot beam has carried such appliances as flag holders and sockets for classification lamps, the coupler pocket, the coupler release bar, air and steam hose brackets, and grab irons.

On articulated locomotives, in which the forward engine moves independently of the boiler and more nearly in line with track curvature, most roads preferred the headlight on the pilot beam. Others, like the Chesapeake and Ohio, followed this practice on nonarticulated locos as well. Even before the diesel-electric era, the pilot had shrunk to a mere stub on most locomotives or else had entirely disappeared.

BIBLIOGRAPHY: Henry B. Comstock, *The Iron Horse,* Crowell, New York, 1971; Angus Sinclair, *Development of the Locomotive Engine,* annotated ed. by John H. White, Jr., M.I.T., Cambridge, Mass., 1970; John H. White, Jr., *American Locomotives: An Engineering History, 1830–1880,* Johns Hopkins, Baltimore, 1968.

Pittsburgh & Lake Erie Railroad (P&LE) Known as the Little Giant, with 703.69 track miles, the P&LE was the most prosperous link in the old New York Central (NYC) chain, to which it was leased, and has paid substantial dividends annually except for 3 years in the mid-1880s. Chartered on May 19, 1875, and financed partly by Cornelius Vanderbilt and Andrew Carnegie, it was completed in 1879 between Pittsburgh, Pennsylvania, and Youngstown, Ohio, a region famed for steel mills. In 1883 a connecting road, the Pittsburgh, McKeesport, & Youghiogheny (PM&Y), financed by Vanderbilt to the tune of $4.5 million, was completed and leased to P&LE, which was thus extended to Connellsville, Pennsylvania, on the Youghiogheny River, and later to Brownsville, on the Monongahela River, in the same state.

In 1965 P&LE acquired trackage rights between Youngstown and Ashtabula, Ohio, and in 1976 between Youngstown and Shenango, Pennsylvania, a total of 86.5 miles, which gave P&LE an interchange with two other prosperous roads, Norfolk & Western and Bessemer & Lake Erie.

Meanwhile, in the 1880s, NYC got control of P&LE stock. This control passed over to Penn Central in 1968 but ended in 1979, when P&LE became independent in its centennial year. The road is well-maintained and hauls primarily coal, iron ore, limestone, coke, and iron and steel products in trains longer and heavier than the national average. Today the P&LE's only passenger service is a commuter train that runs between Pittsburgh and College (Beaver Falls), Pennsylvania, 31.2 miles.

BIBLIOGRAPHY: Alvin F. Harlow, *The Road of the Century,* Creative Age, New York, 1947.

Poell, George H. Locomotive fireman on the St. Joseph & Grand Island Railway, a Union Pacific subsidiary. He was the first railroad man to receive the Interstate Commerce Commission's bronze medal of honor, exactly 110 days after Congress had authorized the ICC to issue such awards. On June 26, 1905, he saw a baby boy playing on the rails directly in front of his fast-moving train. His engineer slammed on the emergency brake. George scrambled out onto the pilot while the train was slowing down. Reaching forward, he grabbed the child and thrust him clear to safety; but in doing so George himself fell under the engine, breaking both hands and mangling his left foot so badly that it had to be amputated. For other heroic exploits, *see* HEROES.

Police, Railroad In the old West and Southwest, when the smoking six-gun was law and the railroads were very vulnerable to attacks by outlaws and thievery by freeloading hoboes, they began as early as 1850 to get help from private detective and investigating agencies, particularly Allan Pinkerton's. Early in the 1880s they started hiring their own police. In the East their lawmen were usually known as detectives; and in the West as special agents, but in boomer lingo all were *bulls, cinder dicks,* or *cinder crushers,* the latter terms referring to the cinders on the right-of-way. Especially notable was gunman Bat Masterson, who became the Santa Fe's first chief special agent. *See* CANYON WAR.

Among the most colorful rail police stories are those involving the Wild Bunch, which included such notorious desperados as Harvey Logan, also known as Kid Curry; Robert Leroy Parker, alias Butch Cassidy; and Harry Longbaugh, the Sundance Kid. On June 2, 1889, they boarded the Union Pacific's (UP's) *Overland Limited,* forced the crew to uncouple the express car from the passenger cars, and in dynamiting its safe blew up the entire car. The UP then organized its best special agents into a posse known as the Rangers, who relentlessly chased the gang on horseback. Eventually each man in the Wild Bunch met a violent death. The story is told in the Hollywood movie *Butch Cassidy and the Sundance Kid.*

Today, railroad police deal mostly with thieves and other criminals sneaking into yards to steal freight or to deface or damage railroad property. They also cope with sabotage, often due to people piling objects on the track for kicks, and train crews victimized by those who get fun out of tossing things at passing trains. Some law enforcement officers use police dogs on their rounds.

North America has about 4500 railroad police, some 3500 of them in the United States. All of the latter are fully commissioned police officers, their authority varying from state to state. Some hold statewide commissions, a fact which is helpful to the industry because many rail lines run statewide. Others are limited to city or county borders.

The Association of American Railroads (AAR) is seeking federal commissions for the industry's entire police force. Canadian railway police have held such authority since passage of the Railway Act of Canada in 1860, but in the States only United States marshals, Secret Service agents, and FBI agents enjoy such power.

The AAR has established a program to teach newly hired policemen basic railroad operation and terminology, how to search a boxcar, how to set up a command post at a derailment site, etc. This AAR section uses the facilities of the Mississippi Law Enforcement Officers Training Academy near Jackson, Mississippi. It also monitors legislation and the proceedings of government agencies affecting railroad law enforcement, issues a monthly statistical report, and acts as liaison between the rail industry and International Association of Police Chiefs.

BIBLIOGRAPHY: Don DeNevi, *Western Train Robberies,* Celestial Arts, Millbrae, Calif., 1976; Henry Stephen Dewhurst, *The Railroad Police,* Charles C Thomas, Springfield, Illinois, 1955.

Pontchartrain Railroad First railroad in the Mississippi Valley. It operated between Elysian Fields Street, New Orleans, and the shore of Lake Pontchartrain. Chartered on January 20, 1830, it was opened on April 23, 1831. Horses pulled its cars until its first steam locomotive, the *Pontchartrain,* built in England, went into service on September 17, 1832. For many years, until it was abandoned in 1935, it was part of the Louisville & Nashville Railroad.

Poor, John Alfred (1808–1871) Pioneer of Maine's railroad development. His wild trip by a one-horse sleigh from Portland to Montreal during a heavy blizzard to promote the building of a rail system radiating out of Portland and including Montreal was a saga of willpower, heroism, and suffering. Haste was necessary because Montreal's Board of Trade would vote on February 10, 1845, on a rail system expected to favor Boston, bypassing Portland.

Poor sent men ahead to hire relays of strong, spirited horses. Then, wrapped in furs and blankets and accompanied by a friend named Cheney, he set out on February 5 at 12:30 a.m. over a route buried by falling snow. Hard snow pellets cut men and horse so sharply that they bled. Over the St. Lawrence River, which Poor described later as a dark, fearsome sight with a swift current and floating ice, a dauntless ferryman landed the travelers at 5:00 a.m. on February 10.

Five hours later, after only an hour's sleep, Poor presented his case to the board of trade, extolling Portland's harbor and pointing out that it was nearer than Boston was to Canada and Europe. His eloquence and stature (6 feet 2 inches; 250 pounds) brought Montreal's acceptance of the Atlantic & St. Lawrence Railroad charter, granted on February 10 by the Maine Legislature. In 1846 this line's first rail was laid; 7 years later it connected Portland with Montreal, and in 1853 the then-new Grand Trunk Railway of Canada leased it for 999 years. In 1867 a brother of John Poor founded the annual *Poor's Manual of Railroads.*

Portage Bridge World's largest wooden bridge when it was built in 1852. It carried the Erie Railroad across Genesee River at Portage, New York. More than 246 acres of timber were used to construct it. The structure cost $175,000 and was 800 feet long and 200 feet high. A big celebration marked the first train crossing it en route from Buffalo to Hornellsville (now Hornell), New York, where the Erie's shops were located. On May 6, 1875, it was burned down, but a new wooden bridge replaced it within 90 days. Today, a steel bridge carries the rails across the river.

Portage Railway *See* ALLEGHENY PORTAGE RAILWAY.

Porters *See* BROTHERHOOD OF SLEEPING CAR PORTERS AND REDCAPS.

Portland Company America's most northern locomotive builder, chartered in Portland, Maine, in 1846. Founded largely by John A. Poor, it produced 631 locomotives between 1848 and 1906. Of these, 259 were sent to Canada, 103 to the Northern Pacific, and others to various lines, including the Panama Railroad. Actually, the company built more railroad cars than engines, in addition to other machinery, which it is still turning out today. In 1890 it completed for railroad use the country's first Russell snowplow. *See* POOR, JOHN ALFRED.

Twenty-four oxen dragged the first Portland engine, the standard-gauge *Augusta,* through the city streets to the Portland, Saco & Portsmouth track. On her trial run to Portsmouth, she made the last 20 miles at the then-amazing speed of 60 miles per hour. A total of 308 Portland engines were woodburners, built before 1883; the rest burned coal. One Portland loco, Grand Trunk No. 40, is currently displayed in Ottawa, Canada, by the National Museum of Science and Technology.

Postage Stamps *See* STAMPS, POSTAGE.

Potato Shipments Although the Bangor & Aroostook was built largely on Maine's potato industry and was known for years as "the Potato Railroad," it lost much of that traffic to trucks. Today the Union Pacific is the prime source of transportation for potato shippers in the four leading potato-growing states: Idaho, Oregon, Washington, and California. *See* BANGOR & AROOSTOOK RAILROAD.

Presidential Funeral Trains The lavish outpouring of public grief and ceremony on Abraham Lincoln's funeral train (the first of many presidential funeral trains) was followed, but to a lesser degree, by the funeral trains of other Presidents and former Presidents of the United States and of Jefferson Davis, the only President of the Confederate States of America, as well as those of many railroad officials and other celebrities. There were engines and cars draped in black, the honor guard in the catafalque car, the dense throngs of mournful and/or curious people, flowers strewn on the track, the lanterns, bonfires, and torches in rural areas at night, and so on, but with variations, of course.

President Garfield James A. Garfield was shot by a disappointed office seeker in the Pennsylvania Railroad station at Washington, D.C., on July 2, 1881. After lingering 12 weeks in the White House, wracked by pain and by the intense summer heat, he was taken by train to Elberon, New Jersey, in the hope that ocean breezes would help him to recover. Some 2000 men toiled all night to lay a temporary spur track from the Elberon depot to a beachfront cottage, but he died there on September 19. One mourning-draped train carried the corpse to Washington for a national farewell tribute in the Capitol; another later bore it to Cleveland for burial near the Cuyahoga County farm on which Garfield had been born 50 years before.

President Grant Two funeral trains swathed in black likewise were operated for Gen. Ulysses S. Grant, who died of lung cancer, attributed to his well-known habit of smoking cigars, a few days after completion of the manuscript for his two-volume *Personal Memoirs.* Death came on July 23, 1885, at the Mount McGregor vacation resort in upstate New York. A little train on a winding narrow-gauge railway trundled his body down a mountainside to Saratoga, then a fashionable vacation spot. There it was solemnly transferred to the Vanderbilts' New York Central & Hudson River Railroad for transportation to New York City, where Grant had lived for years after leaving the White House.

The train consisted of the catafalque car *Woodlawn* (the name of a cemetery in which many celebrities are buried), four coaches, a baggage car, and engine No. 210. As it passed the frowning battlements of West Point Military Academy, a cannon boomed farewell while the cadets stood beside the track at present arms and a band softly played "Sweet Spirit, Hear My Prayer." Farther south, hundreds of persons laid coins on the rails to have them flattened by the train as souvenirs. Today, Grant's Tomb, in classic white marble along Riverside Drive and above the former New York Central tracks (now Conrail), is a Manhattan landmark plainly visible from Hudson River boats.

Confederate President Davis Jefferson Davis died of bronchitis at New Orleans in 1889 after writing, as Grant did, his memoirs in two volumes. His body lay in state at City Hall for 4 days. Then a procession that included former Confederate soldiers grouped in companies escorted it to a semiunderground vault in a local cemetery, with nine governors of Southern states as pallbearers. In 1893, at his widow's request, the remains were moved to the old Confederate capital, Richmond, Virginia, for permanent burial.

The casket was lifted into a maroon glassed-in observation car draped in black on a special nine-car Louisville & Nashville (L&N) train pulled by the tall-stacked, coalburning eight-wheeler No. 17 (ex- No. 69). Among those aboard were Davis's daughters Winnie and Margaret. The special headed northward, stopping at Beauvoir, Mississippi, where Davis had spent his last 12 years on a plantation. For 300 yards children strewed flowers along the track. The train rolled on. About midnight the Alabama State Artillery, waiting at Mobile, saw the

President James A. Garfield's funeral train leaving Elberon, New Jersey, for Washington, D.C., in 1881. [Harper's Weekly]

approaching oil headlight of No. 17 and fired the traditional 21-gun salute. Mobile being an L&N division point where engines were changed, a hostler replaced the 17 with another cap-stacked 4-4-0, No. 45, and the cortege rumbled on through the rain.

Soon came a dramatic entry into Alabama's capital, Montgomery, which had been the Confederacy's first capital. All businesses and schools in Montgomery were closed for the city's final tribute to the old chieftain. The rain eased in time for a procession to and from the Capitol building as church bells tolled.

Afterward, the train proceeded to Atlanta, Georgia, over the Western Railway of Alabama and the Atlanta & West Point. There the coffin was moved in a slow procession from the depot to the Capitol and then back to the station. The last stage of the trip was over the Richmond & Danville (now part of the Southern Railway), with a long stop in Raleigh, North Carolina, for the body to lie in state in the Capitol. At Richmond, after the 1300-mile journey over four roads, Mrs. Davis joined in the final rites for her distinguished husband. No photograph of the funeral train is known to exist.

President McKinley In answer to an invitation to meet President William McKinley on September 6, 1901, at the Pan American Exposition in Buffalo, New York, Robert Todd Lincoln, son of Abraham Lincoln, arrived to see a group bending over the Chief Executive who had just been shot. It must have revived painful memories. McKinley was taken to the home of the exposition's president. Police kept the surrounding area quiet. A Lackawanna special train carrying surgeons, nurses, and medical supplies sped from Hoboken, New Jersey, to Buffalo in an effort to save the dying man. The engineer, John Draney, was given a clear track and made the 395-mile run in the record-breaking time of 405 minutes; but death occurred on September 14.

The Pennsylvania Railroad provided two funeral trains for McKinley. One took the body to Washington; the other wheeled it to Canton, Ohio, his native state. Both trains were festooned with black crepe from pilot to marker lights. McKinley's widow, riding the second train, in a daze, was aroused at Harrisburg, Pennsylvania, by hearing a choral society sing her husband's favorite hymn, "Nearer, My God, to Thee," and wept for the first time since leaving Buffalo. The new President, Theodore Roosevelt, traveled in that train with his Cabinet and, as it rolled along, transacted official business that could not be postponed.

McKinley spent his last night at the White House lying in state in the flower-banked East Room. Then the rail trip to Canton followed the Ohio River for miles. Steamboats saluted the deceased with long, mournful whistle blasts. At Pittsburgh a bold young man recklessly climbed the outside of a tall church steeple to get a good view of the train. McKinley was buried in Canton at the going down of the sun. The exact time of starting the funeral service was observed by railroads all over the country stopping their trains for 5 minutes.

President Harding President Warren G. Harding died of pneumonia and a blood clot in San Francisco on August 2, 1923, while returning from a long trip after driving the golden spike that completed the Alaska Railroad. A special train, appropriately draped, took his body in the car *Superb* to Washington over lines of the Southern Pacific (SP), Union Pacific (UP), Chicago & North Western, and Baltimore & Ohio. With 11 cars and a Pacific-type locomotive, it rolled out of SP's Third Street station in San Francisco at 7:15 p.m. on August 3 for the 840-mile run to Ogden, Utah, where the UP took over. The SP trip lasted 25 hours, 44 minutes—21 minutes faster than the crack *Overland Limited* schedule. The three other roads handling this train made equally fast time. *See* ALASKA RAILROAD.

In Washington, the corpse was laid on the identical spot under the Capitol dome where Lincoln, Garfield, McKinley, and later the Unknown Soldier were honored. Mountains of floral tributes perfumed the air. Finally, heavy Pacifics 2928 and 2833 pulled the train over the Erie Railroad to Marion in Harding's native Ohio for entombment in a vault.

President Roosevelt The Harding Pacifics were the last black-draped power to handle a funeral train in the United States. After Franklin D. Roosevelt died of a blood clot in the brain on April 12, 1945, at Warm Springs, Georgia, none of the engines or cars in either of the two Roosevelt rail corteges was decorated in any way. A 12-car train wheeled by two Southern Railway steam locos sped north with his body in a mahogany copper-lined casket covered with an American flag. The bier was in the last car, the *Magellan,* from which FDR had often directed the nation's destiny, continuing to work there even on the rare occasions when his train was delayed.

After lying in state in the East Room of the White House amid a wilderness of blossoms, the deceased was taken in the Pullman compartment-lounge car *Conneaut* by special train to Hyde Park, New York, for burial. The late President's pet, a black Scottie named Fala, rode in both trains with the Roosevelt family. In the absence of somber trimmings, the Roosevelt funeral trains looked like first-class limiteds.

Since 1945 the United States has had no presidential funeral train; the bodies of Presidents and former Presidents have been borne by airplanes and/or automobiles, except that President Eisenhower's body was borne to its final resting place on a regularly scheduled train. *See also* LINCOLN FUNERAL TRAIN.

Prineville, City of, Railway One of America's few city-owned freight railroads, it is an 18.3-mile modern short line linking an Oregon community with the Oregon

Trunk Railway at Prineville Junction. It was built in 1918 because the Union Pacific and the Great Northern had bypassed Prineville when they jointly built a central Oregon north-south cutoff in 1912. The local citizens felt lost with no rail outlet to the rest of the world. So they voted, 365 to 1, to construct a railroad, and did so. A nonpolitical three-man commission runs it. There are 26 employees and two daily trains 5 days a week. The railway brought so much prosperity to the area that until recently Prineville had no city taxes. Now it imposes only a small personal property tax. Long ago, an Alco diesel replaced the original 4-4-0 steam engine. The railway scrapped its two coaches but occasionally carries two or three bicyclists or other passengers in its caboose.

BIBLIOGRAPHY: John F. Due and Frances Juris, *Rails to the Oshoco Country,* Golden West Books, San Marino, Calif., 1968.

Prospect Wreck On Christmas Eve, 1872, a northbound two-car train on the Buffalo, Corry & Pittsburgh [(BC&P) later part of the Pennsylvania Railroad, now Conrail] consisted of the woodburning 4-4-0 engine *N. P. Bemis,* a mail-baggage car with a load of Yuletide mail and gifts, and a coach carrying 38 passengers, most of them going home for the holiday season. Nine railroad men were aboard: the engineer, fireman, conductor, brakeman, mail clerk, and baggagemaster; two deadheading BC&P officials; and a railroad machinist.

The train left Corry, Pennsylvania, at 1:30 p.m. and Mayville at 3:15. Some 50 yards south of the next scheduled stop, Prospect, the single-track line rounded a curve and crossed a deep gulch spanned by a wobbly wooden trestle about 20 feet high by 320 feet long on a downgrade. The brakes were partly set for the descending grade. Engineer Joe Haire shut off steam but gave two piercing whistle blasts as a signal to release brakes so that the train would not stop short of Prospect's tiny frame depot.

He was about to increase steam pressure when, peering back from his cab window, he saw with horror that his tender's rear truck was off the rails, while the two cars were toppling off the bridge. Both cars broke loose and fell down into the snow-filled gully, but the engine was able to make it to the far side of the trestle. The tender rocked but finally halted, partly suspended over the gulch. Coal stoves quickly set both cars afire, the coach burning at both ends at the same time. Passengers, pinned beneath the wreckage, shrieked with terror.

A few who managed to escape risked their lives in aiding entrapped victims and recovering bodies. Several persons who had been waiting at the station did what little they could to help. No water was available, the scraped-up snow had a very slight effect on the flames, and only two axes could be found. The 18 corpses, laid on an ox-drawn sleigh, were taken to the Mayville

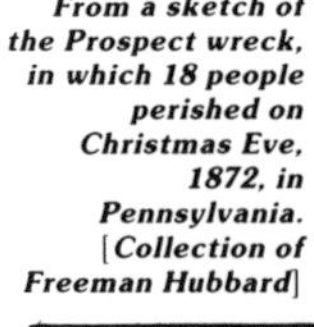

From a sketch of the Prospect wreck, in which 18 people perished on Christmas Eve, 1872, in Pennsylvania. [Collection of Freeman Hubbard]

freighthouse for identification. This spectacular accident was traced to one of the tender's wheels breaking a flange while rounding a curve.

BIBLIOGRAPHY: Wesley S. Griswold, *Train Wreck!* Stephen Greene, Brattleboro, Vt., 1969; Robert C. Reed, *Train Wrecks,* Superior Publishing, Seattle, 1968

PRR *See* PENNSYLVANIA RAILROAD.

Pueblo Test Center Facility operated by the Federal Railroad Administration for full-scale testing, evaluation, and associated development of prototype ground transportation systems. Located in Colorado prairie land near Pueblo and within sight of Pikes Peak, it has about 22 miles of railroad test track.

Three experiments there, planned by the Facility for Accelerated Service Testing (FAST), constitute one facet of the International Government-Industry Track-Train Dynamics Program, a 10-year cooperative effort by the railroads' suppliers and government to study the interaction of train with track.

The first experiment began on September 22, 1976: a train going around in circles until the track had been subjected to a minimum of 450 million gross tons. This, researchers estimate, represents a lifetime of wear on the track (a 4.8-mile loop) and extended exposure of car and locomotive components to the test conditions. For 16 hours a day, 5 days a week, a 76-car train pulled by four diesel locomotives rolled around the track at an average speed of 42 miles per hour.

During approximately its first year the train, weighing about 9500 tons, logged 72,424 miles (equivalent to going around the earth almost three times), subjecting the track to 135 million tons of wear. Between continuous runs around the track, hundreds of different kinds of data were collected on the wear and response of track, car, and locomotive components. The data were recorded on magnetic tape and sent daily to the Technical Center of the Association of American Railroads in Chicago for analysis.

This operation simulated up to 10 times the traffic that regular mainline track is exposed to. And the FAST train could accumulate up to 5 times the mileage that an average train does in regular service. The accelerated service allowed researchers to determine the behavior of track and train components within a short time. FAST bridged the gap between testing a piece of equipment in the laboratory and testing it in regular train service. A by-product of this research was improved track-maintenance techniques.

The 4.8-mile track includes 22 experimental stations. Each contains different kinds of ties, ballast, rail, joints, or spikes. Of the track components, 95 percent were donated by manufacturers. In case of a problem with a component, the manufacturer was given the opportunity to analyze and solve it. The FAST train, pulled by four-axle locomotives, consisted of loaded 100-ton hopper cars and a few flatcars loaded with trailer and tank cars. The locos and cars were donated by various railroads.

For the second experiment, 70-ton cars replaced the 100-ton cars in the train. Researchers were then able to compare the effect these two car types have on track. The third experiment, another basis of comparison, used heavier, six-axle locomotives. Transportation Test Center employees operate the FAST train and maintain the track. AAR and railroad personnel are consulted to ensure that the FAST operations parallel, as much as possible, those of a normal railroad.

Another of the various projects at Pueblo Test Center is a high-voltage AC, single-phase electrification system, including overhead catenary, substations, and transmission lines capable of testing locomotives at nominal AC voltages of 12.5 kilovolts and 52 kilovolts at speeds up to 150 miles per hour. This design was described as "the first step in developing hard answers to questions on installing, operating, and maintaining electrified track."

Puerto Rican Railways For many years Puerto Rico had several short steam railroads that hauled sugarcane from plantations to refineries, often bags of sugar also, occasionally other freight, and passengers. One ran around the island's western end between the capital, San Juan, and Ponce in the south. The engines were imported first from France, later from the United States, and were oilburners. Puerto Ricans operated the engines and cars and built some of the cars. Another line served Fajardo and Humacao on the eastern shore. There was also a standard-gauge electric trolley line, the Canadian-owned Puerto Rico Railway, Light & Power Co., which ran out of San Juan. The same company owned a 30-inch-gauge steam railroad. Its rails were light and rested on steel ties as protection from termites.

Eventually bus and truck competition put all but one of the Puerto Rican rail lines out of business. The island's only railway today is the Ponce & Guayama, about 44 miles, which has 22 locomotives (diesel-hydraulic, diesel-electric, and diesel-mechanical) and about 1280 freight cars.

Pullman, George Mortimer ***(1831-1897)*** Most outstanding of three great American pioneers who developed railroad cars for safe, comfortable, and luxurious travel, the others being Theodore T. Woodruff and Webster Wagner. All three were born in upstate New York. Pullman's birth on March 1, 1831, almost coincided with the origin of railroading in the United States. At 14 he got a job in a rural store, working nearly 3 years at $40 a year. Then in his brother Albert's cabinetmaking shop at Albion, New York, he acquired the knowledge, skill, and self-assurance that were to help him in car building. He set up his own contracting business, moving certain structures to permit widening of the Erie Canal. *See* WAGNER, WEBSTER; WOODRUFF, THEODORE T.

A Midwesterner seeing him work invited the young man to Chicago to raise some brick-and-stone buildings from their swampy foundations below street level. One was Madison Block, the city's finest store-and-office building. Pullman raised it and its sidewalk in such a way that none of the tenants had to interrupt their regular activities. This job boosted his bank account to $20,000 and financed his earliest experiments with railroad equipment.

Pullman's first ride in a sleeping car, a crude type with three tiers—upper, middle, and lower berths—from Buffalo to Westfield, New York, kept him awake most of the night thinking of how it might be improved. Later he studied sleeping-car history. Deciding that no sleeper was satisfactory, he designed one of his own and in 1858 hired Leonard G. Seibert, a woodworker at the Chicago & Alton (C&A) shops in Bloomington, Illinois, to remodel two coaches into the initial Pullman sleepers. The Alton road then had only about a dozen passenger cars. He picked Nos. 9 and 10 for the experiment. Each car was 14 feet long, flat-roofed, with small single-sash windows 14 on a side, and an inside height of 7 feet from floor to ceiling.

"Into this car," Seibert said later, "we got 10 sleeping-car sections, a linen closet, and two tiny washrooms, one at each end. Remodeling cost about $1000 a car. We had no blueprints to go by. Mr. Pullman and I personally worked out the details as we came to them. The cars were upholstered in plush, heated in cold weather by box stoves, and each was mounted on four iron-wheeled trucks."

Pullman's first conductor, J. L. Barnes, a youth of 22 with muttonchop whiskers, wore street clothes on the job, with no uniform except a badge. The C&A maiden trip from Bloomington to Chicago began at night, September 1, 1859. According to Barnes, "The people of Bloomington, little reckoning that history was being made in their midst, did not come down to the station to see the Pullman car's first run. The car, lighted by three tallow candles, moved away in solitary splendor. A berth cost only 50 cents, but that night only four were sold, including one to Mr. Pullman himself."

Shortly afterward, Pullman converted a third Alton coach into a sleeper. Then he made a similar experiment on the Galena Railroad, also in Illinois. Among the rolling stock commandeered by the Union Army during the Civil War were all of Pullman's cars as well as the sleepers which the Baltimore & Ohio had put into service.

In 1864, despite the war, Pullman had a master car builder construct a large model car after his own design and named it the *Pioneer.* Built and equipped on the site of the present Chicago Union Station at a cost of over $20,000, it had massive construction, improved trucks, and springs reinforced by solid rubber blocks. It was 1 foot wider and 2½ feet higher than any other car on standard-gauge rails, the extra height accounting for its hinged upper berths.

These dimensions caused trouble and embarrassment for Pullman. With elegance and comfort hitherto unknown in rail service, the *Pioneer* was a marvel of the age, but it was too wide for station platforms and too high to run under any railroad bridge in the United States. People scoffed at the inventor for having created a white elephant. "Change the station platforms and the bridges," Pullman urged. But that was asking too much. No railroad could operate his car. Pullman's future was tottering in the balance. Then came the assassination of President Lincoln on April 14, 1865.

Lincoln's body was taken from Washington to Springfield, Illinois, on a train of seven coaches painted black. At Chicago his widow and her party boarded the *Pioneer,* courtesy of Pullman, for the last leg of the trip, over the Chicago & Alton. This gave Pullman much-needed good publicity, as the inventor had known it would. But to make such a trip possible, the C&A had hastily to alter its bridges and station platforms along the route. *See* LINCOLN FUNERAL TRAIN.

A few months after the Civil War ended, Gen. Ulysses S. Grant rode in that same car in a triumphal return from Detroit to his home town of Galena, Illinois, for which other bridges and platforms were overhauled. This, too, was a windfall of national publicity for Pullman.

Eventually the *Pioneer,* big though it was, matched the new standard size of railroad equipment in general, and no more trackside changes had to be made for it. Until the advent of streamliners, the only change made in the dimensions of later Pullman cars was increased length.

Meanwhile, in 1864, Pullman and Ben Field jointly patented a folding upper berth, and in 1865 they invented a lower berth made by hinging the back and seat curtains. In 1867, the year Pullman married Hattie Sanger, he and Field organized the Pullman Palace Car Co., with Robert Todd Lincoln, the late President's son, as its legal adviser. Lincoln became president of the company 30 years later.

One improvement after another was made on the cars, methods, and service to the traveling public. Pre-Pullman cars had 8 wheels; Pullman gave them 12. Finding cars without springs, he gave his own cars springs. He adopted the Miller platform, the powerful steel underframe for cars which not only lessened operating hazards but blazed the trail for all-steel construction. Pullman also originated elevated roofs, elegant interior decorations, and costly woodwork.

As years rolled by, his company became the world's greatest car-building and -repairing enterprise, with plants located at Pullman, Illinois (now part of Chicago), and many other places in North and South America and even in Europe. George Pullman's brother Albert, in whose shop he had learned cabinetmaking as a youth, served the flourishing business as general superintendent.

The first hotel car used on any road was the *President,* a combined restaurant-sleeper put into service by the Pullman Co. in 1867 on the Great Western Railway. In 1868 Pullman introduced on the Alton road the first regular dining car, which he named *Delmonico* for a noted New York restaurateur.

Completion of the transcontinental railroad in 1869 was very profitable for Pullman because sleeping and dining cars were soon regarded as essential on long-distance travel. A Pullman trip from Chicago to the Pacific Coast was advertised as 6 days in a luxurious hotel on wheels. In 1875 Pullman put out a reclining-chair car named *Maritana,* which was America's first parlor car.

Soon Pullman cars were running also on half a dozen British railways in competition with cars designed and built by Col. William D'Alton Mann. In England on October 14, 1881, Pullman applied the first electric lighting to any railroad cars. Twenty-five years later the English Pullman Co. severed its ties with its American sponsor. In 1883 Pullman replaced oil lamps with brilliant Pintsch lighting on the *Erie Limited* that linked New York with Chicago. In 1930 the company introduced indirect electric lighting on passenger trains.

As the Pullman Co. grew, it absorbed competitors. In 1899 the Woodruff and Mann car-building organizations merged into the Union Palace Car Co., which Pullman soon took over, leaving no rivals in the field except the Monarch Sleeping Car Co., which served only one Ohio road and part of New England, plus Wagner's Drawing Room Car Co., which had a monopoly on the Vanderbilt lines. Pullman Co. took over those last two competitors after both Pullman and Wagner had died.

Wagner was Pullman's major competitor. They clashed on patent infringements. Unlike Woodruff, Wagner was backed by the immensely rich Cornelius Vanderbilt; but Pullman made a deal with Vanderbilt's hated rival, Jay Gould, at a time when Gould was the Erie's big boss, to cut into Wagner's monopoly of the New York-Chicago service. In 1887 Pullman, and then Wagner, put vestibule cars into service. Pullman triumphed in the litigation that followed.

In addition to car building, Pullman helped to build the Northern Pacific and West Shore railroads and New York City's first elevated railway but lost money on the ill-fated Nicaragua Canal. His great record of achievement is clouded by niggardly treatment of his approximately 14,000 employees in 1893-1894. Some 12,000 of them lived in slums on the fringe of his "model city" of Pullman, Illinois. That community's civic center was a handsome showplace occupied mostly by company officials, while many of the workers' wooden shacks did not have running water or individual toilets.

In the panic of 1893, 4000 Pullman employees were laid off, and the others took wage cuts averaging 24 percent and, in some cases, 29 percent. Piecework pay was cut even more drastically. One employee complained that his part-time wages for 12 days totaled only $9.07, from which he had to pay $9 in rent for the company-owned shack that he and his family lived in. How he squandered the other 7 cents is not recorded.

The employee felt that inasmuch as Pullman Co. was cutting wages deeply, it should also lower the rents in its model community, "the welfare of which," Pullman said, "has been my most constant source of solicitude as president of the company." He pointed out that the rents his company charged were equivalent to those in adjoining Chicago.

At that time the Pullman sleeping-car service covered 125,000 miles of railways, or about three-fourths of the nation's total, and the company was capitalized at $16 million. The workers could not understand why, under the cirumstances, wages were cut in the repair shops, which were running full blast, although orders in the Pullman manufacturing plant had slumped badly. For these and other reasons, they went on strike.

Meanwhile, the American Railway Union (ARU) had been organized in Chicago, mainly through the efforts of Eugene V. Debs. It aimed to represent all the railroad workers but was far from doing so; the standard rail labor brotherhoods held themselves aloof from it.

Pullman refused to arbitrate the grievances of his workers, despite urgent pleas by the ARU, the Governor of Illinois, Chicago's mayor, who himself was a former Pullman employee, the Chicago Board of Aldermen, and many others. "There's nothing to arbitrate," he said repeatedly. For the story of the strike, the ARU's participation in it, and what happened after it failed, *see* "CRANE WITH A BROKEN NECK"; DEBS, EUGENE VICTOR.

Pullman died of heart disease 3 years later, leaving a personal fortune of $7 million. Debs commented:

A complimentary annual pass for Pullman's Palace Car Co., signed by the sleeping-car king himself, George M. Pullman, for the year 1894.

"Death is a social democrat. The time was when Mr. Pullman had nothing to arbitrate. Now comes the time when Death had nothing to arbitrate."

The corporation Pullman founded in 1867, but under another name, is still manufacturing railroad cars, both freight and passenger; but his somewhat more recent company which supplied Pullman service to travelers and staffed its diners and sleepers has ceased to exist. So has the sleeping-car porters' brotherhood. *See* BROTHERHOOD OF SLEEPING PORTERS AND REDCAPS.

Ten years after Pullman's death his plant created the world's first all-steel sleeper. In 1926 it introduced the first single-room car. In 1927–1928 it developed the first spring mattress for sleeping cars. Then it put mechanically refrigerated, air-conditioned cars into service, the first successful such car being the *McNair*.

Other Pullman innovations, the adjustable four-position section seat and the double-decked bedroom car, came in 1931. The following year the company equipped cars with experimental dressing platforms in upper berths. In 1933 it built new-type cars with eight upper and eight lower rooms and America's first all-aluminum sleeper, named *George M. Pullman*. Many other items could to be added to this list. Undoubtedly, Pullman and his successors led the world in modernizing railway travel, but his company, like the railroads themselves, was hard hit by the serious decline in the rail passenger business.

See also SLEEPING CARS.

BIBLIOGRAPHY: Lucius Beebe, *Mansions on Rails,* Howell-North, Berkeley, Calif., 1959; id., *Mr. Pullman's Elegant Palace Car,* Doubleday, Garden City, N.Y., 1961; Carroll R. Harding, *George M. Pullman, 1831–1897, and the Pullman Company,* Newcomen Society in North America, New York, 1951; Joseph Husband, *The Story of the Pullman Car,* A. C. McClurg & Co., Chicago, 1917; Almont Lindsay, *The Pullman Strike,* University of Chicago Press, Chicago, 1942; John H. White., Jr., *The American Railroad Passenger Car,* Johns Hopkins, Baltimore, 1978.

Pullman Strike *See* "CRANE WITH A BROKEN NECK"; DEBS, EUGENE VICTOR; PULLMAN, GEORGE MORTIMER.

Quebec North Shore and Labrador Railway *See* IRON ORE.

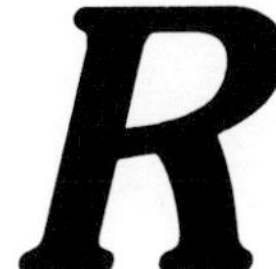

Racehorses, Special Cars for For many years the rail shipment of fine horses, especially racehorses, has been a specialized business. In the 1880s Harrison Arms bred such steeds on his Michigan farm and trained them for Eastern markets. One of his shipments, made in a freight car, was snowbound in a cut, and for nearly 3 days nobody could feed or water the poor creatures. As a result, Arms designed and had built a new type of car, probably the world's first, which provided an individual stall for each horse, also mangers, a water tank, and an aisle for feeding.

At first he used it only to transport his own property, but it became so popular that friends borrowed it to move their stock. In 1885 he launched the Arms Palace Horse Car Co., later renamed the Arms-Yager Railway Car Co., built more cars, and sold or leased them to the public. The cars were designed for use in either freight or passenger trains. Most of them were leased to trotting-horse owners for summer racing seasons.

Other horse-car companies, using Grossman, Keystone Palace, and Burton cars, sprang up. The Arms company eventually absorbed them all. Arms cars were used extensively by United States cavalry units in the Spanish-American War and World War I. Meanwhile, the establishment of now-famous racetracks had turned racehorse transportation into big business, and soon most thoroughbreds were riding in state in passenger trains. The movement between tracks became so large that by 1940 the Railway Express Agency was handling about 2000 carloads annually. In addition, an almost equal number of horses was being moved by motor truck, but the costliest animals and most frequent winners continued to travel more comfortably by rail.

The railroads developed their own types of horse cars. Thirteen major United States roads, as well as the Canadian Pacific and Canadian National, had varying numbers of such cars. A few individual breeders also had luxurious horse cars. M. W. Savage kept an especially fine car for his Dan Patch, which in 1906 set a world's trotting record that stood for 34 years. This car, white-enameled, had a full-size picture of the champion on both sides. Known from coast to coast, it usually covered from 10,000 to 12,000 miles a year. Savage also had an electric railway, the Minneapolis, St. Paul, Rochester & Dubuque Electric Traction Co., which he called the Dan Patch Line. Since the decline in rail passenger service, however, an increasingly large number of racehorses have been moved by well-padded trucks. *See* DAN PATCH LINE.

BIBLIOGRAPHY: Lawrence W. Sagle, *Freight Cars Rolling,* Simmons-Boardman, New York, 1960.

Rail Detector Cars Cars used to discover and to indicate by dropping a little white paint on the rail itself the presence of flaws in steel rails, especially transverse fissures, invisible internal cracks, so that they can be replaced to avoid derailments. This practice has nothing to do with low joints or gauge but only with the condition

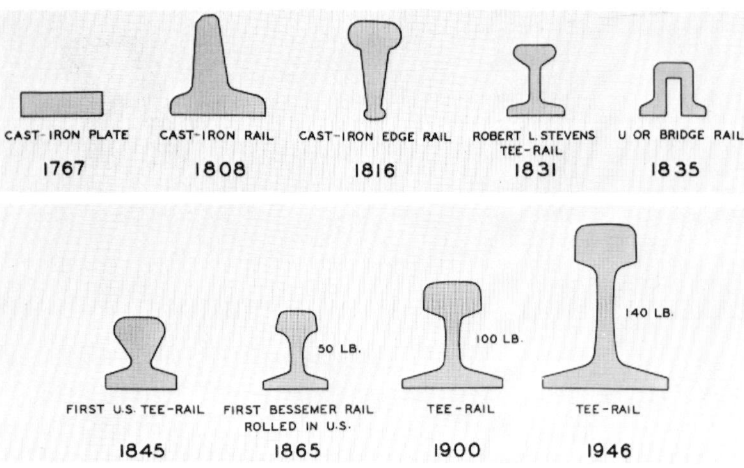

***Cross-sections of rail developed over a span of 179 years.* [*Bethlehem Steel Co.*]**

of the rails. Most but not all such cars are yellow Sperry cars. Some railroads own other detector cars. The former New York Central, for example, had car No. X-8015, with Sperry-type apparatus, which pinpointed defects with an electric current passing through the rail between brushes. A different kind of detection, developed by the Association of American Railroads, involves powerful electromagnets.

Railroads have always had defective and broken rails. An Atlantic & Great Western report said that in the 5 months ended March 11, 1867, rail breakage was "comparatively insignificant" on the third and fourth divisions (21 and 87 broken rails respectively), but the first and second divisions told a different story (1899 and 805 rails respectively).

Sperry Rail Service's first such vehicle began operation on a Wabash Railroad yard track at Monticello, Ohio, on September 14, 1928. An all-time Sperry roster lists 52 rail cars and 20 ultrasonic detector cars of various types. Currently, 25 of them are operating by assignment on North American railroads and 3 in Australia. Such famous car builders as Brill, St. Louis, Electro-Motive Corp., and Mack have contributed to the Sperry fleet, which is based at Danbury, Connecticut, and East St. Louis, Illinois.

Rail Shrinkage Canadian National Railways' engineering staff discovered in 1929 that although a train running between Vancouver, British Columbia, and Halifax, Nova Scotia, covered 3786.5 miles of transcontinental line over the same roadbed in summer and winter alike, the length of steel spanning that distance is 2.6 miles less in winter than in summer. The explanation is that the coefficient of expansion of steel rail is .0000065. This means that for every temperature change of 1°F the rail length varies by 65/10,000,000 from what it was at the original temperature. One rail, which is 33 feet long, varies that much from its original length. A mile of rail varies that much from the original mile.

Steel expands when temperature rises and contracts when it gets colder. A fair average of temperature fluctuation between the two months of January and February and the two months of July and August was found to be 53.4°F, taking 61° for the summer average and 7.6° for winter. If you multiply these figures by 53, you get 2.6 miles of variation in total Canadian National trackage between the Pacific and Atlantic terminals, which represents the miles of shrinkage between summer and winter.

The shrinkage and expansion take place between the rail joints. Therefore, in building a railway, trackmen never join the rail butts together but allow for this factor. In hot weather, tightly butted rails would buckle and wreck trains. Gaps between rails are wider in winter than in summer. Theoretically, on an ideal summer day, with the temperature just right, the rail butts would meet precisely, and the rail and railway mileage would be identical.

Railfans English-speaking North America, while less rail-minded than England, the birthplace of railways, may have at least 250,000 *railfans,* mostly unorganized. We use the word *railfan* rather loosely to define men and boys, some women also, who are seriously or casually interested in any railroad hobby. The term *railroad hobby* covers especially model railroading; photographing trains, locomotives, streetcars, and other rail subjects; and collecting railroadiana. One acid test of railfans is whether or not they often ride trains and encourage other people to do so by either personal solicitation or public appeal. *See* MODEL RAILROADING.

Collectibles include photos; train orders; timetables; picture postcards; calendars, posters, and old prints; tickets; transportation tokens; switch keys and locks; books, mostly histories of railroad companies and motive power; pamphlets; flyers; buttons and badges from trainmen's uniforms; matchboxes, pencils, pens, wallets, playing cards, tote bags, etc., issued by railroads and imprinted with their names; dining-car china, silver, glassware, linen, and menus; trolley transfers; lanterns, semaphore signals, and marker lights; detachable parts of dismantled steam locomotives and cars—all sorts of gadgets and artifacts that suggest railroading. *See* BUTTONS, UNIFORM; SWITCH KEYS; TRAIN ORDERS.

Joseph Lavelle (1892-1953) of New York City reputedly had the world's largest collection of engine pictures of any individual hobbyist: about 35,000 photographs, all different, nearly all North American steam, all locomotives with or without trains, all actual photos (no drawings, magazine clippings, etc.), nearly all both prints and negatives, classified and filed. Lavelle made a large number of these photos himself, doing his own developing, printing, and enlarging. Others he obtained by swapping with fellow collectors, borrowing and copying, or receiving gifts from railroad companies, locomotive builders, etc. His lifetime regret was a bad eye which kept him from an engine-service job. Four friends inherited his unique collection.

Most railbuff collectors buy, sell, or swap photos or other items. Many get railroadiana free by getting in touch with old-timers or the widows of railfaring men and having requests published in small magazines or weekly newspapers. Innumerable fans write, illustrate, edit, publish, and distribute or otherwise contribute to railbooks, periodicals, calendars, brochures, etc., everything from amateurish mimeographed or photocopied sheets to high-class books. A few aficionados reprint out-of-print rail classics: books, catalogs of locomotive or car builders, forgotten transit magazines, and so on. Some technically minded fans spend seemingly endless hours compiling detailed locomotive or car rosters with specifications.

In some circles, hobbyists are judged by their dues-paying memberships in regional and/or national fan-clubs, their attendance at meetings, their efforts to keep these get-togethers lively by lining up important speakers or movies and slide lecturers, and their willingness to handle thankless jobs of secretary or treasurer (without pay, of course) and to assist in planning fantrips or putting out the club's newsletter.

Aside from groups interested in model railroading, the biggest of these organizations are the National Railway Historical Society (NRHS), with nearly 10,000 members; the Railway & Locomotive Historical Society (R&LHS), Central Electric Railfans' Association (CERA), Railroad Enthusiasts (RE), and Electric Railroaders' Association (ERA), each with nearly 2000 members; Canadian Railroad Historical Society (CRHS), with 1700, only about 800 of whom are Canadians; and Michigan Railroad Club, with about 1400. The American Railroadiana Collectors Association has some 900 members; the Upper Canada Railway Society (UCRS), 700; the Railroad Station Historical Society (RSHS), 400; and the Railroadians of America and the National Association of Timetable Collectors (NATC), each a little over 300.

There was no American railfan organization until 1920, just 100 years after Col. John Stevens operated the nation's first steam railroad as a private experiment on his estate at Hoboken, New Jersey. In 1920, Charles E. Fisher of Boston, while writing the *History of the Old Colony Railroad,* felt the need of a group to assemble and preserve historical railroad documents. So, with Arthur Curran and Warren Jacobs, both railroaders like himself, he organized the R&LHS. As the membership grew, they incorporated in 1922 and began publishing a periodical devoted to railroad history and lore, originally called *The Bulletin* (currently called *Railroad History*), which Fisher edited for 50 years. The society has national headquarters in Harvard Business School, Kresge Hall, Boston, and four chapters, one in New York, one in Chicago, and two in California.

The CRHS was launched in 1932 with John Loye as president and Robert Brown as secretary, just 100 years after the birth of Canada's first steam road, the Champlain & St. Lawrence. Its purpose is "the collection, preservation, exhibition, and distribution of information, relics, documents, photographs, etc., relative to railway, locomotive, and other transportation history in Canada." The UCRS was founded in 1935 and incorporated in 1954. Its quarterly newslatter is *Rail and Transit.*

Horace W. Pontin, a Boston & Albany locomotive engineer and photographer of Allston (Boston), Mass., organized and incorporated the Railroad Enthusiasts in 1933. RE has divisions in various cities, puts out a magazine, *The Enthusiast,* and, like the other major railfan clubs, sponsors train excursions.

In 1934 the ERA was established by a group of electric railfans and railmen, sparked by electrical engineer E. Jay Quinby. It has headquarters in Grand Central Terminal, New York, and regional divisions. Its magazine is *Headlights.* The NRHS was formed in 1935 by a merger of two Lancaster, Pennsylvania, groups to collect and preserve historical data on steam and electric railways and to boost rail transportation. It issues *The National Railway Bulletin* and has chapters in 123 localities. Michigan Railroad Club, founded in 1937, issues *The Michigan Railfan* monthly.

The CERA was formed in 1948 by a small group of fans on board a private car chartered by Frank Butts on the Gary Railways. George Krambles, now executive director of Chicago Transit Authority, is credited with having sparked the organization. CERA has issued more than 120 *Bulletins,* each one an illustrated book on electric transportation. Headquartered in Chicago, it has divisions elsewhere.

The RSHS was founded in 1967 for the study of stations, signal towers, roundhouses, and other railroad structures. It issues *The Bulletin* bimonthly and an approximately annual *Monograph.* The NATC, inaugurated in 1964 by William Wagner and others, has divisions in several cities and issues a newsletter, *The First Edition.* Among many other hobby organizations are the Rocky Mountain Railroad Club and the Pacific Railway Society.

An elite group, the American Association of Private Railroad Car Owners, headquartered in Mountainside, New Jersey, issues a periodical, *The Varnish.* Founded in Chicago in 1977, it helps to solve common problems of its members. Another unique body is the National Association of Railroad Passengers, headquartered in Washington, D.C., which engages in lobbying and litigation on behalf of rail passenger service, mostly at the federal level. It issues the monthly *NARP News.*

BIBLIOGRAPHY: Edwin P. Alexander, *The Collector's Book of the Locomotive,* Clarkson N. Potter, New York, 1966; Stanley L. Baker, *The Railroadiana Collector's Price Guide,* Hawthorn, New York, 1977; Paul B. Cors, *Railroads: Spare Time Guide,* Libraries Unlimited, Littleton, Colo., 1975; Louis H. Hertz, *Handbook of Old American Toys,* Mark Haber & Co., Wethersfield, Conn., 1948.

Railroad; Railway Interchangeable words, the first being preferred in the United States and the second in Canada and the United Kingdom. Three or four American companies such as the Long Island (the country's largest commuter system, owned by New York State) and the Strasburg (one of the oldest and shortest freight and passenger lines, in Pennsylvania) use *Rail* and *Road* as two words in the corporate names.

Railroad Quiz, 16th edition (1976), issued by the Association of American Railroads, defines *railroad* as

> the right-of-way containing a double band of steel fixed to the ground on ties for the use of locomotives and cars to carry goods and people from one point to another. A railroad is also people—about half a million of them in the United States—working toward a common goal: the movement of freight and passengers in the most efficient manner possible. A railroad is also buildings and yards where people work and where rolling stock and motive power are serviced and stored.

American railroad employees once exceeded 2 million men and women, but this figure has been dropping steadily since the 1930s, owing to the declining number of passenger trains and the greater productivity of freight operations.

Railroad Operations Modular Processing System *See* ROMPS.

Railroad Terminology *See* LINGO OF THE RAILS.

Railroad Town *See* DELANO.

Railroad Yards *See* YARDS, RAILROAD.

Railvan Freight carrier invented by K. A. Browne to combine truck flexibility with train economy, first used on the Chesapeake and Ohio in 1956. It has two sets of wheels, one set rubber-tired for streets and highways and the other flanged for rails. With an adapter car, the railvan can be operated behind a regular locomotive or converted to a rubber-tired truck trailer for transportation to and from a consignee's loading platform or dock. Each unit has a compressed-air motor to raise and lower wheels. It compares with piggyback service without the expense of providing a flatcar.

Railway *See* RAILROAD; RAILWAY.

Randolph, A(sa) Philip *(1889–1979)* Labor organizer and president of the Brotherhood of Sleeping Car Porters. Born on April 15, 1889, at Crescent City, Florida, he inherited his oratorical ability from his father, an African Methodist Episcopal minister who simultaneously served three parishes, all impoverished. The family ran a small cleaning, dyeing, and tailoring shop to eke out its meager income. Philip sold newspapers and later worked in a railroad section gang that loaded flatcars with sand and laid crossties and rails.

As a high school graduate he went north and studied politics, economics, and philosophy at a New York college. Despite his education, the only jobs he found open to blacks were heavy, menial, dirty, or irksome. He was fired from a waiter's job on a Fall River Line ship for organizing a protest against miserable working conditions and became a waiter in a railroad terminal restaurant at Jersey City, New Jersey.

As a writer, lecturer, Socialist, and pacifist he rejected both Marcus Garvey's black nationalist movement and the Uncle Tom type of acquiescence. "We do not accept the doctrine that the Negro is satisfied to be himself," he said. "We desire as much contact as possible between the two races." He also said, "No race is good enough to dominate another race."

In 1915 he married. With America's declaration of war in 1917, he and Chandler Owen launched *The Messenger,* a monthly that called itself "the only radical Negro magazine in America." Its influence may be gauged from the fact that in the 1917 New York election over 25 percent of the black voters supported the Socialist ticket.

Randolph helped to unionize shipyard, laundry, and other workers. Both he and Owen became instructors at the Rand School of Social Science in New York. Randolph wrote for a variety of publications, attacking politicians and churchmen for racial prejudice, and lectured in many cities. He ran unsuccessfully as Socialist candidate for New York secretary of state, the state Assembly, and Congress.

On August 25, 1925, under Randolph's leadership, the Brotherhood of Sleeping Car Porters (BSCP) was organized in a Harlem recreation hall. He was elected president and general organizer and promptly made *The Messenger* the new union's official organ. Like the brotherhood's national secretary, Ashley T. Totten, Randolph was so deeply dedicated to the BSCP that he worked for it even at times when no funds were available for union salaries.

During the brotherhood's first 10 years the Pullman Co. refused to recognize it and dismissed more than 500 employees for union activities. It could not discipline Randolph because he never worked for the company. But its paid advertising induced some Negro newspapers to carry antilabor propaganda in their news and editorial columns, and thousands of reprints of articles hostile to the brotherhood were mailed free to the porters and maids. Eventually Randolph and his associates forced Pullman to recognize the brotherhood and the American Federation of Labor Executive Committee to grant it an international charter—the first such award to an all-Negro union in 47 years of AFL history.

Randolph received two medals: a Workers Defense League medal in 1944 for having "contributed most to the protection of the United States workers' rights during the preceding year" (an award which bypassed all other labor leaders in the country) and the nation's Medal of Freedom, presented by President Lyndon B. Johnson in 1964. The Louisiana Legislature also honored him, with a joint House-Senate resolution taking note of the Sleeping Car Porters as the first successful all-Negro union.

Randolph died on May 16, 1979, at 90, a little over a year after the brotherhood's merger into the Railway & Airline Clerks. The tax collector who visited his modest apartment in settling his estate found a net worth of less than $500. President Jimmy Carter described the deceased as a man of "integrity and dignity."

See also BROTHERHOOD OF SLEEPING CAR PORTERS AND REDCAPS.

BIBLIOGRAPHY: Brailsford R. Brazeal, *The Brotherhood of Sleeping Car Porters,* Harper, New York, 1946; Bruce Minton and John Stuart, *Men Who Led Labor,* Modern Age, New York, 1937.

Rapid City, Black Hills & Western Railroad Narrow-gauge line in western South Dakota, running through the scenic grandeur of Rapid Creek Canyon, that crossed and recrossed the turbulent creek 105 times on its 33.5-mile run between Rapid City and Mystic. Originally called the Dakota Pacific (an ambitious name for a road more than 1000 miles from the Pacific Ocean) and then the Missouri River & Northwestern, it was opened in 1904, reorganized in 1909, abandoned in 1948, revived as the Black Hills Central in 1957 by an international firm, and standard-gauged in 1965.

Currently it operates only in summer, 7 days a week, as a tourist attraction with a 20-mile round trip, from Hill City to Keystone Junction, over a 4 percent ruling grade. It uses steam power: a 2-6-2 Baldwin (1919), with a diamond-shaped smokestack installed by a movie producer, and a Cooke 2-6-0 (1880). It has open-platform wooden coaches, open observation cars, and a caboose and displays other old-time rolling stock.

BIBLIOGRAPHY: Mildred Fielder, *Railroads of the Black Hills,* Lead, S.Dak., 1961.

Rat-Hole Division *See* CINCINNATI SOUTHERN RAILWAY.

Rate Bureau Rail service charges vary with new market relationships, competition of other modes of transportation, volume of available traffic, and competition among the railroads themselves. Three regions each have their own rate bureaus to provide a forum where a railroad or a shipper seeking a freight rate change can make it known to other carriers and the public. The bureau places the case on a public docket, publicizes it in a trade journal, and authorizes a public hearing at which other roads, shippers, and the public can air their views. The Interstate Commerce Commission (ICC) makes the final decision. Typically, proposed tariffs are filed with the ICC at least 30 days before the effective date. If no interested party objects, they usually take effect. But if there are protests, the railroads can respond and support the change. The ICC may suspend a rate for up to 7 months while investigating it. Often no hearing is held, and the issues are presented in writing.

See also DEREGULATION .

Raton Mountain Switchback During construction of the big transcontinental lines the greatest obstacle to overcome, symbolic of them all, was the Continental Divide, crest of the lordly Rockies. After the Atchison, Topeka and Santa Fe had built as far west as La Junta, Colorado, it paused at the mountains. Behind lay prairies; ahead, the golden West—on the far side of the Rockies. The engineering department decided to turn left and south before assaulting the divide.

Then at Trinidad, Colorado, near the New Mexico line, surveys made in 1878 showed that the best route would be over or through Raton Mountain. But what a mountain! Seldom had construction crews faced such a job. One of two choices was open: detain traffic at the foot of the mountain or build a temporary track, a switchback, for use until the tunnel could be finished. The latter was done.

A switchback is an odd engineering feat. Ordinarily, when a rail line was laid up a steep hill, with an ascending grade of, say, 2 feet in every 100 feet of track (2 percent grade), the simple thing to do was to lengthen the route by building many curves so that trains could ascend the 2000 feet without excessive climbing. But suppose that there was no room for curves. In that case, your only alternative was a switchback, a track which "sawed" back and forth on the mountain side by means of ascending grades. A train was run up the first grade to the end of the track. A switch was thrown behind it, and the train backed up—not the way it came, of course, but up the next grade. Again it reversed and headed up another grade, until finally it reached the top.

Raton Mountain switchback just barely enabled trains to get over the crest of the Continental Divide. On the east side the grade was about 6 percent (6 feet in every 100), while on the west side it was almost 5 percent. This was a terrific climb for the Santa Fe's sturdy little eight-wheelers, but somehow they did the job. The first ones used were 37-tonners with 17- by 24-inch cylinders and driving wheels 57 inches in diameter. They could pull only 33 tons up the switchback.

But early in 1879 what was then the world's largest locomotive, a new giant Baldwin-built Consolidation, No. 204, began pulling seven 15-ton cars at a time up the forbidding slope. This was the famous *Uncle Dick,* named for Richard Wootton, a well-known early settler in the region served by the Santa Fe. Late in 1879, Raton Tunnel was completed, and the switchback was abandoned.

BIBLIOGRAPHY: James Marshall, *Santa Fe: The Railroad That Built an Empire,* Random House, New York, 1945.

Reading Railroad Originally named Philadelphia & Reading (P&R) and now in the Conrail system, the line was basically a coal road; it had a black-diamond insigne, symbolizing coal. The Reading's claim to the title of largest anthracite carrier in its heyday can easily be proved by Anthracite Institute figures showing that from 1920 through 1942, for example, it transported more than 70 million net tons of coal, as compared with less than 63 million handled by its closest rival in the field, the Lehigh Valley (whose insigne also showed a black diamond), and about 40 million shipped over the Delaware, Lackawanna & Western. (The Chesapeake and Ohio, now merged into CSX Corp., has long been the biggest hauler of *bituminous* coal.)

In 1842 the average P&R coal train en route from Pottsville, Pennsylvania, to Philadelphia, consisted of a 10-ton engine and 50 to 60 cars, each loaded with 1.75 to 4 tons, bobbing along at about 10 miles per hour, which was rather fast for coal trains in those days. A century later the average consist, with an engine weighing up to 407 tons and as many as 125 cars, covered the same route but on 130-pound instead of 45-pound rail and at the rate of 30 miles per hour.

The Reading also was distinguished by being America's biggest terminal road, i.e., a compact network. A circle of 100-mile radius drawn from Reading includes almost the entire old Reading system. The longest possible direct haul on this cobweb was about 230 miles between Shippensburg in south central Pennsylvania and Port Reading, on New York Harbor.

In 1831, the Little Schuylkill Navigation Railroad & Canal Co. was incorporated to build a railroad in the coal area at a point near the mouth of the Little Schuylkill River. It was the first of many small roads which, through construction, purchase, or lease, ultimately formed the Reading system. The P&R itself was incorporated on April 4, 1833, as the first carrier to link the great anthracite-producing land with tidewater. Including its leased, operated, and jointly controlled lines, the system's total mileage was about 6400. At one time it controlled the Jersey Central and the Communipaw Terminal at Jersey City, New Jersey, just opposite the lower tip of Manhattan.

The first trackage, from Reading to Pottsville, was opened early in 1838, and the line southward to Philadelphia went into service in late 1839. The railroad set up at Reading what became a very important machine shop which designed, built, rebuilt, and repaired locomotives, some of them famous in history. Another Reading distinction was the inclined planes in the Pennsylvania coal region. The estate of Stephen Girard, a wealthy Philadelphia merchant who died in 1831, built half a dozen of them. Each plane pulled cars up a steep hill with the aid of a rope or cable. This was regarded as the simplest and cheapest way of getting a loaded coal train up a heavy grade.

Although the road was named for a small Pennsylvania Dutch city that squats on both banks of the Schuylkill River upstate, its headquarters was in Philadelphia in Reading Terminal, an eight-story edifice with a farmers' market on the street floor at the rear. Trains came and went beneath a glass-roofed trainshed on the second floor, with business offices higher up.

BIBLIOGRAPHY: Joseph A. Fisher, *The Reading's Heritage: 1833–1958,* Newcomen Society in North America, New York, 1958.

Rebates and Rate Wars The railroads' rapid expansion after the Civil War multiplied the number of communities they served and greatly increased freight and passenger rate cutting and rebates in the competition between railroads and with some water carriers. Previously, these abuses had been only occasional, but after the big roads reached the Midwest, they were intensified, angering small shippers, reducing railroad revenue, creating a demand for government regulation, and leading to public protests such as the Granger laws. *See* GRANGER LAWS.

Conspicuous were Erie–New York Central (NYC) rate wars in the Gould-Vanderbilt era and the Pennsylvania Railroad rebating that helped to build John D. Rockefeller's monopoly of the petroleum industry. *See* GOULD, JAY; OIL SHIPMENTS; VANDERBILT, CORNELIUS.

The panic of 1873, bankrupting many roads and other companies, was due partly to the carriers' unbridled competition, including rebates and rate cutting with the attendant drop in earnings and failure to pay dividends on capital stock. Disastrous rate wars ensued, involving the Erie, NYC, Pennsy, Grand Trunk, and Baltimore & Ohio and leading to cuts in employees' wages that in 1877 brought about the most violent of all rail labor crises. *See* STRIKE OF 1877.

Mainly to correct such evils, Congress passed the Act to Regulate Commerce of 1877, setting up the Interstate Commerce Commission; the Elkins Act of 1903, primarily upon the initiative of the railroads themselves to prevent revenue losses from rebates and rate cutting; and the Hepburn Act of 1906, which strengthened the previous laws.

BIBLIOGRAPHY: Stewart H. Holbrook, *The Age of the Moguls,* Doubleday, Garden City, N.Y., 1953; Matthew Josephson, *The Robber Barons,* Harcourt, Brace, New York, 1934; Gustavus Myers, *History of the Great American Fortunes,* Charles Kerr & Company, Chicago, 1910; Guy M. Walker, *Railroad Rates and Rebates,* New York, 1917.

Receivership, Longest, in the United States The longest receivership in American railroad history was that of the Minneapolis & St. Louis (M&StL), a 1500-mile railroad dating back to 1854. This road was known as the Peoria Gateway Line but nicknamed Misery & Short Life. It went into bankruptcy in 1923. When its receiver applied for an additional loan in 1934, Jesse Jones, head of the Reconstruction Finance Corporation (RFC), shook his head. "I don't know whether you could *give* your road away," he said, "but you might be able to *throw* it away." He advised that the unprofitable line, with a mountain of debts, be cut into 43 pieces, of which 19 (totaling 507 miles) were to be abandoned at once, and the rest sold to larger roads.

Then, in January 1935, Julian C. Sprague, a veteran railroader, took over the thankless receivership. He had no intention of presiding at a funeral. By scrapping worthless equipment he raised quick money to meet payrolls and pay some of the most urgent bills. Changes in operating methods yielded large economies. Sprague persuaded at least 300 new industries to locate trackside and capitalized on Jim Hill's time-tested theory that if you labor for the prosperity of the territory you serve, you yourself will share in that prosperity. From $7,500,000 in 1934, the road's gross annual income rose to $13,550,000 in 1942. During the same period net income changed from $41,000 in the red to $2,800,000 in the black. Sprague had won. The RFC then offered to lend the M&StL up to $4 million. But now Sprague didn't need it. At the end of 1942, 86 American railroads were in the hands of receivers or trustees, but the old Peoria Gateway was not one of them.

BIBLIOGRAPHY: Frank P. Donovan, *Mileposts on the Prairie: The Story of the Minneapolis & St. Louis Railway,* Simmons-Boardman, New York, 1950.

Records, Speed *See* DEATH VALLEY SCOTTY; JARRETT AND PALMER SPECIAL; SPEED WAR.

Redcaps On Labor Day, 1890, a black porter in New York's Grand Central Station tied a bit of red flannel around his black uniform cap to be more easily identifiable in a crowd and thus get more baggage-toting jobs. Other porters copied the idea. New York Central publicist George H. Daniels noticed this device, was instrumental in getting the color of the caps changed, and coined the word *redcap.* *See also* BROTHERHOOD OF SLEEPING CAR PORTERS AND REDCAPS.

Refrigerator Cars Known as *reefers,* these cars originated with the first use of ice in shipping milk and butter, and possibly other perishable foods, by rail from upstate New York farms to cities and towns. *The Boston Traveler* of June 15, 1842, had a news item headed "Freaks in Railroad Transportation" that may have been the first printed reference to this subject:

> We understand that the Western Railroad [of Massachusetts] are about preparing refrigerator cars in which fresh beef, pork . . . and other fresh meat can, by a moderate quantity of ice, be kept in perfect order in the heat of summer and in which (in winter) they can be kept from freezing; thereby, in either case, adding much to the value of the article when carried to market. . . . These refrigerator cars will be used for the like advantageous purpose to carry eggs, butter . . . all berries and fruits.

Whether or not those cars were actually built is not recorded. The first reefer known to have been put into service began operating in June 1851 on the Northern Railroad of New York (later part of the Rutland), less than a year after the road had been opened between Ogdensburg and Rouses Point on Lake Champlain. According to a *St. Louis Republic* reprint from an unidentified New England newspaper, the "icebox on wheels" was designed by a Mr. Wilder, one of the road's employees, for the use of farmers around Ogdensburg who made butter but previously had not been able to ship it except in cold weather.

Old records of assessed valuations show that within 2 years after this experiment, dairy-farm values in that area increased by 100 percent. Evidently Wilder's cars had a lot to do with the increase. Improvements in such equipment were designed and patented in the 1860s by W. A. Chandler, head of Union Star Line, under the aegis of the Pennsylvania Railroad, and by J. B. Sutherland and D. W. Davis, both of Detroit. Gustavus Franklin Swift, Chicago packer, set up reefers for dressed meat, beginning with 10 cars in 1857. Other firms soon did also.

The mechanical reefer, which in principle is a gigantic version of a domestic electric refrigerator, was a by-product of the frozen-food trade, developed for long-distance shipments for which ice and salt cooling is inadequate. Its diesel-powered unit could keep foods cool for as long as 2 weeks unattended. Today, most reefers have mechanical air-cooling systems that can maintain various temperatures. A typical car has a 67-ton capacity.

***The Tiffany summer and winter car, a predecessor of the modern refrigerator car, pictured in the 1879* Car-Builders Dictionary.**

Specialized XF cars protect the contents additionally with seamless plastic linings and *plug* doors which the operating mechanism forces inward, when closed, to maintain a smooth interior. These elite XFs are assured of quick unloading because of special daily penalty charges.

BIBLIOGRAPHY: *Car and Locomotive Cyclopedia,* Simmons-Boardman, New York, 1974; Robert S. Henry, *This Fascinating Railroad Busi-*

Electronically controlled icing machine at the ice dock of the Santa Fe icing station in Fresno, California. [Santa Fe Railway]

ness, 3d ed., rev., Bobbs-Merrill, Indianapolis, 1946; Rodney Hitt, *The Car-Builders Dictionary,* Railroad Gazette, Chicago, 1906; Lawrence W. Sagle, *Freight Cars Rolling,* Simmons-Boardman, New York, 1960.

Reid, John (1835–1911) First of a long line of eminent railroad cameramen. Born in Scotland, he came to America at age 6, got a job at Rogers Locomotive Works, Paterson, New Jersey, and in 1857, before fighting in the Civil War, became a professional photographer. When an engine was built, the builder wanted her picture taken. There were no snapshots in those days. Portraying an engine was an event. Reid would coat an 11- by 14-inch or larger glass plate with collodion emulsion in his darkroom. Then he'd put it in a light-tight holder, trundle his huge camera down the street in a four-wheeled cart, and make the exposure. He often waited until sun glare had vanished behind the hills to minimize shadows. Then he hastened back to his studio to develop the glass plate before it dried, always making engine pictures with wet plates.

Reid also photographed railroad bridges, machinery, and buildings, traveling over America with a large yellow light-tight tent as a darkroom. His prints on thin, strong rag paper, made by a gold-toning process and distinguished by a rich brown color, won numerous medals and other awards at world's fairs. Hundreds of Reid photos are in collectors' hands today, many preserved without spot or blemish.

Remote Control System that guided a railroad passenger car for the first time in American history in 1956 on the 7½-mile stretch of New Haven track between New Rochelle and Rye, New York. One of the road's new self-propelled commuter cars was started, stopped, speeded, and slowed down from a control panel on the Larchmont station platform. Aboard were 75 journalists, railroad officials, and representatives of the Union Switch and Signal Division of Westinghouse Air Brake Co., which manufactured the equipment. The operation was merely an extension of the electronics mechanism used to control switches and signals over distances as long as 400 miles. Electrical impulses in this test, transmitted by radio and existing signal wires, operated the throttle and brakes. *See* IRON ORE; JACKASS & WESTERN.

Reno Brothers There were five brothers. John, Frank, Simeon, and William became outlaws, and Clinton remained honest. The first four, together with some accomplices, made up America's first organized gang that specialized in train robbery. The first stickup for which any Renos were arrested and indicted (but never tried) occurred on October 6, 1866, in early evening on the Ohio & Mississippi Railway. From one of the express car's two safes they took about $13,000 after "borrowing" the messenger's keys. The bandits then stopped the train by signaling the engineer with the bell cord and jumped off.

Nearly a year later a similar holdup was perpetrated on the same train near the same locality. As before, masked robbers entered the unlocked express car as the train was pulling eastward out of Seymour, Indiana. For this crime the Pinkertons caught John Reno and were responsible for having him sent to a Missouri penitentiary, from which he emerged 15 years later. He went straight thereafter. (Another train was robbed twice by Oliver Curtis Perry. *See* PERRY, OLIVER CURTIS.)

Four members of the Reno gang were imprisoned for a burglary in Iowa, but all four escaped. Later the gang held up a train while the engine was taking on wood at Marshfield, Indiana, killed the messenger, and looted the express car. Other stickups followed on the Cincinnati, Hamilton & Dayton and the Ohio & Mississippi. Lawmen were taking three alleged members of the gang to Seymour for trial when vigilantes seized the suspects and hanged them from a tree beside the track. Finally, one November night in 1868, other vigilantes broke into the jail at New Albany, Indiana, where three Reno brothers and one of their accomplices, Jack Anderson, were awaiting trail and, after a desperate fight, wiped out the gang by hanging all four inside the jail.

BIBLIOGRAPHY: Alvin F. Harlow, *Old Waybills,* Appleton-Century, New York, 1934.

Revere Wreck Possibly no other accident had such a beneficial effect on the railroad industry, because it was a major factor in bringing about the adoption by railroads all over the country, but especially in Massachusetts, of such important safety devices as the Westinghouse airbrake, the Miller platform and buffer, and the automatic block signal system. This wreck occurred on the mainline of the Eastern Railroad (now part of the Boston & Maine), which connected Boston with Portland, Maine. At that time the Eastern was carrying more passengers (3,500,000 in 1870) than it was equipped to handle. A neighboring road, the Boston & Albany, with several times as much rolling stock, carried only 200,-000 in 1870.

On Saturday night, August 26, 1871, the weekend-excursion rush was at its peak. The Eastern's trains pulled out of Boston whenever they could, with almost total disregard of schedules. Four were due to leave Boston station between 6:30 p.m. and 8 p.m.: two Saugus branch trains, an accommodation, and the through express to Portland. It was that express which later overtook the local, because of the crews' inability to stick to their schedules on an overcrowded mainline, and plowed into it at Revere, Massachusetts.

According to the timetable, two branch trains should have departed before the accommodation, but in the confusion the latter left before the second branch train. All four were late in getting started, and the night was misty. With such a setup, there was bound to be trouble. Complicating the situation, the regular signalman at Everett Junction had been laid off for illness. His replacement did not know the regular man's tricks of the trade, one of which was to relieve congestion by permitting the branch line to be used temporarily as a siding. The substitute did not do that; he railroaded by the rule book.

The *Portland Express* consisted of eight loaded heavy Pullmans and the engine *Newburyport.* The Boston stationmaster had given its engineer, Ashbel S. Brown, a *verbal* order to look out for trains ahead of him. The words were shouted up to him *after* his train had already started to pull out of the noisy depot. If Brown failed to hear or heed such a warning, you could hardly blame him.

Because all four trains were running off schedule and because the accommodation train's red taillights were not plainly visible in the foggy night, Brown, trying to make up lost time, saw for one ghastly second the headlight of the *Newburyport* illuminate the interior of the last car of the local. Then his express telescoped it with a horrendous din, shattering kerosine lamps and tearing off his engine's smokestack. Scalding hot steam burst from broken valves and live coals from the firebox, igniting the lightweight wooden-bodied cars. Out of a welter of agony and heroism came the news: 29 persons dead, 56 injured.

Headlines screamed, "Slaughter!" Indignation meetings were held. Noted orator Wendell Phillips denounced the wreck as "deliberate, cold-blooded murder." The charges were extreme and unfair, but out of them grew a mighty impetus leading to the adoption of safety devices that otherwise might have been delayed for years. Thus the catastrophe helped to make future railroading safer. In Massachusetts only two persons were killed on railroads during the 7 years that followed the Revere disaster.

Prior to that time, with the single exception of the Boston & Providence, Bay State railroads had refused to recognize the need for the Miller platform and buffer or the airbrake, the two greatest safety devices used in car construction at that time. Nor did the nation's railroads in general adopt the automatic block signal system until an enlightened public opinion, inflamed by the Revere disaster and other preventable rear-end wrecks, goaded rail officials into action. The main use of block signals is to provide a safe distance between moving trains.

Also in 1871, railroad coaches were badly built and loosely connected. At high speed they bounced and jostled dangerously. Not all the car floors were on an even level with the cars before and behind them. In a rear-end collision the telescoping of cars was almost inevitable. The Miller platform and buffer greatly minimized these hazards. It aligned the strong longitudinal floor timbers of the coaches and forced them close together with the aid of heavy spring couplers, making the train a relatively solid unit. The combined weight and semirigidity tended to hold each car steadily on the rails.

See COFFIN, LORENZO; SAFETY LAWS.

BIBLIOGRAPHY: Charles Francis Adams, Jr., *Notes on Railroad Accidents,* Putnam, New York, 1879; Robert B. Shaw, *A History of Railroad Accidents, Safety Precautions, and Operating Practices,* Northern Press, Potsdam, N.Y., 1978.

RI *See* ROCK ISLAND RAILROAD.

Richelieu River Wreck An iron bridge spanned Richelieu River between Beloeil and St-Hilaire, about 27 miles northeast of Montreal. Paralleling the river on the Beloeil side was a canal leading to Lake Champlain. Thus the iron span was a combination bridge over the river and drawbridge over the canal. On June 29, 1864, Bill Burney, an experienced engineer unfamiliar with that division, was pulling a Montreal-bound special of 11 cars with 354 immigrants from Germany who had landed at Quebec the night before.

He reached the Beloeil side of the bridge at 1:15 a.m. The draw that lay ahead had swung open to permit the passage of a steamboat loaded with grain; but owing to thick woods and a curve, Burney could not see the red light attached to the swing span itself. He thundered onto the bridge without slowing down. The locomotive fell 45 feet onto a barge, sinking it immediately, but the barge captain and his family scrambled ashore safely.

One after another, the tender, baggage cars, and coaches, all but the last one, plunged off the bridge. The last coach hung over the edge, slanting downward at a dizzying angle. Its passengers were terrified, but all of them survived. As the canal was only 10 feet deep, the combined height of the sunken barge and the locomotive kept the cars from being entirely submerged in water, thus preventing a greater loss of life by drowning.

The death list of 86 persons included the fireman, the conductor, and the brakeman. About 200 others were injured.

Canada's worst train wreck occurred on this bridge over the Richelieu River in Quebec in 1864. The engineer of a special train failed to see that the drawbridge at the far end of this bridge was open, and more than 80 recently arrived German immigrants died in the disaster. [Collection of Freeman Hubbard]

BIBLIOGRAPHY: Wesley S. Griswold, *Train Wreck!* Stephen Greene, Brattleboro, Vt., 1969; Robert S. Reed, *Train Wrecks,* Superior Publishing, Seattle, 1968.

Right-of-Way Strip of land of varying width on which railroad facilities are located. It is wide enough to provide for tracks, drainage, signals, bridges and their abutments, sidings, buildings, telegraph and telephone lines, and other railroad requirements. It also includes water rights necessary for the roadbed and its accessories.

Robberies The first train robbery by an armed gang in the United States occurred on May 5, 1865, when an Ohio & Mississippi Railway train bound from St. Louis to Cincinnati was derailed and partly overturned by a track obstruction 14 miles west of Cincinnati. Outlaws swarmed aboard and robbed the baggage-car safe and the male passengers and then fled across the Ohio River in skiffs with their loot. Presumably they were irregulars who had been ravaging Kentucky during the Civil War. For accounts of subsequent train robberies, *see* entries under individual names, including DE AUTREMONT BROTHERS; JAMES, JESSE WOODSON; PERRY, OLIVER CURTIS; RENO BROTHERS; TRUMMER, FRANK. *See also* MYSTERY OF THE 13.

BIBLIOGRAPHY: Alvin F. Harlow, *The Serene Cincinnatians,* Dutton, New York, 1950.

Rock Island Railroad (Chicago, Rock Island & Pacific Railroad; RI) As of 1979 the Rock Island (also known as the Rock) was operating 6595 route miles in the Midwest and down to the Gulf of Mexico in the face of intense competition. Since 1975 it had been in bankruptcy. In 1974 the Interstate Commerce Commission authorized the RI to merge most of its property into the Union Pacific under numerous conditions, including the sale of its Southern lines to the Southern Pacific and involving the Santa Fe and the Missouri-Kansas-Texas; but no such action had been taken by 1980.

In 1845, when Rock Island, Illinois, was not even a town but a frontier military post, a few well-to-do men meeting there gave birth to the RI's ancestor, the Rock Island & La Salle Railroad, with $300,000 worth of shares to sell. Tracklaying began on October 15, 1851, out of Chicago, then a town of 30,000. Under the leadership of Henry Farnum of New Haven, Connecticut, an experienced railroad builder, the new company built 180 miles of road from Chicago westward to Rock Island in less than 2 years and then spanned the Mississippi with its first railroad bridge, a drawbridge linking Rock Island with Davenport, Iowa.

Major General Grenville M. Dodge assisted in pushing the Rock Island line into Iowa City, the state capital. After the Civil War, and out of many separate court actions, the road was reorganized with its present name, built numerous branches, and acquired smaller roads. It also bought the sensationally beautiful engine *America,* with a nickel silver jacket plus gleaming silver trimmings. Grant Locomotive Works had built this 4-4-0 in Paterson, New Jersey, and exhibited her at the Paris Exposition of 1867. She won an important United States mail contract for her owner in a race in which she outran by hours her Chicago & North Western contender. *See* DODGE, GRENVILLE MELLEN.

The Jesse James gang robbed two Rock Island trains, one near Adair, Iowa, in 1873, the other near Winston, Missouri, in 1881, murdering a conductor. A year later, when Jesse himself was shot dead, a special Rock Island train took the bandit's body and members of his family to Kearney, Nebraska, for the funeral. *See* JAMES, JESSE WOODSON.

In the winter of 1887–1888 the road's construction crews entered Oklahoma, then Indian Territory, southward from Kansas, 5 years before the Cherokee Strip was opened to settlers. Because of a takeover by a Wall Street clique at the turn of the century, the company lost some $20 million through stock manipulation and was forced into its first receivership, from which it emerged in 1917. Meanwhile, on March 21, 1910, it suffered its worst train disaster. Two passenger trains collided while backing up to reverse their engines near Green Mountain, Iowa, killing 52 persons and seriously injuring 30 others. Most of the casualties occurred in old wooden cars. Today's cars, of course, are steel.

BIBLIOGRAPHY: Ed Gardner, *Rock Island Lines: A Pictorial Review,* 1978; William E. Hayes, *Iron Road to Empire: The History of 100 Years of the Progress and Achievements of the Rock Island Lines,* Simmons-Boardman, New York, 1953; *Jane's World Railways and Rapid Transit Systems,* F. Watts, New York, 1977; Frank J. Nevins, *A Yankee Dared,* O'Sullivan Publishing House, Chicago, 1933; id., *Great Rock Island Route,* reprinted by Ed Gardner, 1977.

ROMPS In the current age of initials and computerization, vastly different from the adventurous railroading of boomer days, ROMPS is short for Railroad Operations Modular Processing System, which fills a gap in the computerizing ability of TRAIN II. The latter could tell a Class I railroad almost everything about the movements of one of its freight cars, including location, origin, destination, waybill number, commodity carried, and whether it was loaded or empty, in storage, or being repaired. But TRAIN II didn't know what happened to a car once it rolled onto the property of any of the more than 300 short-line railroads, because the latter did not feed data into the system. Short lines by definition operate less than 100 miles of track, but they handle nearly 7 percent of United States rail traffic.

To bridge the gap in car information ROMPS was developed in December 1978 by the Association of American Railroads, the Federal Railroad Administration, and the American Short Line Railroad Association. In return for data on the movement of "foreign" cars on its line, TRAIN II provides a short line, through ROMPS, with a complete list of cars on its tracks, indicating which are loaded and which are empty.

Through ROMPS, short lines also can locate their cars on other railroads and learn how long they have been there. This saves the lines money by permitting them to prioritize the movement of outside cars off their properties, beginning with those having the most *per diem* charges. The brains of ROMPS is a minicomputer in Rockville, Maryland.

Royal Train On May 17, 1939, King George VI and Queen Elizabeth, the first ruling monarchs to set foot on North American soil, landed at Quebec from a Canadian Pacific (CP) liner for nearly a month's rail tour of more than 10,000 miles in Canada and the Eastern United States. The rail route included over 3000 miles by CP westward to Vancouver, British Columbia, 4212 miles eastward on the Canadian National, and the rest on the New York Central, Pennsylvania, New Haven, and Delaware and Hudson.

The royal train and its pilot train were the most luxurious trains which had ever been operated in Canada. Their equipment was reconditioned at CP's Angus shops and CN's Point St-Charles shops. The royal train's westward run of over 3000 miles with engine No. 2850, a 4-6-4 type, was made without change of locomotive. More than 200 CP engineers, firemen, conductors, trainmen, and baggagemen saw service on the two trains. Other hundreds guarded the switches, patrolled the track in advance of the trains, and assisted at station stops. A similar situation prevailed on the CN eastbound run from Vancouver to Niagara Falls, Ontario.

A special end-door baggage car, coupled just behind the tender, carried a self-contained power plant which furnished electric current for the 12-car train, including the refrigerated storage compartment for food supplies. A telephone switchboard in the combination sleeper and baggage car provided communication between all cars on the train. In addition, there were facilities for miscellaneous equipment, such as steel cable and pickets with sledges to be used where required in setting up a barrier around Their Majesties' cars at stops where local facilities were inadequate for protection.

Royster, William Wallace Locomotive engineer, father of the national railroad pension law. In 1929, when banks were going broke, life savings being swept away, and old people suddenly becoming destitute, Royster was a railroad labor legislative representative in Minnesota and decided to do something about it. The system he worked out and obtained support for became the basis of the Railroad Retirement Act, which Congress passed in 1934 despite the objections of certain railroad companies. That act predated the creation of social security. Congress later had to repass it because of technical details which the U.S. Supreme Court rejected in 1935.

Rules, Book of *See* BOOK OF RULES.

Run-Through Trains Unlike other freight trains, they do not stop at the end of their own railroad but halt there briefly to pick up a connecting line's crew without changing engines or cars and continue running over other lines to their destination. For example, Chessie System operates run-throughs from Chicago to Montreal and from coast to coast. Connecting railroads have the same arrangements with Chessie.

S

Safety Laws The Safety Appliance Act, passed by Congress on March 2, 1893, covered the automatic coupler, automatic airbrake, and safety handholds, or grab irons, on side ladders, rooftops, and ends on all freight cars.

Dozens of styles and shapes of link-and-pin couplers were in use until 1893. Probably the worst were the old round heads, or turtle heads, which often dodged back between the draft timbers, thus letting two cars come together closely enough to squeeze a trainman who might be between them. Another was the old Potter drawhead with three links, a dangerous finger pincher. The old hook and three-link chain couplers, with their steel-faced man crushers, were used mostly on Eastern roads.

Handholds, or grab irons, also were a menace. All old-time box and stock cars had wooden side ladders put together with lag screws instead of bolts. Rusting lag screws often rotted the wood, causing the grab iron to pull off and drop a trainman screaming between the cars or atop a switch stand. Under the Safety Appliance Act, which some railroad managements opposed at congressional committee hearings, as they did later safety measures, all side ladders and handholds had to be bolted on and the ends of the bolts riveted to keep the nuts from working off.

Installing Westinghouse airbrakes in *old* freight cars was an expensive process because the wooden brake beams then in common use had to be replaced with steel beams. (The wooden ones had been hung from the car body.) A brake-beam hanger might pull down, or the beam would snap in two and drop the brake rigging onto the center of the track or under a pair of truck wheels; and in the early days of handbrakes there were usually brakes on only one pair of car wheels. The railroad companies burned up hundreds of old, worn-out freight cars rather than go to the expense of reequipping them under the Safety Appliance Act. It took them 10 years to comply with the new law, during which time nobody knows how many train and yard men were crippled by the slow compliance. *See also* COFFIN, LORENZO; JANNEY, ELI HAMILTON; WESTINGHOUSE, GEORGE.

Under the former company employee law, the railroads gave relatively little attention to the safety of their employees. Finally the brotherhoods got that company-made law repealed so that for the first time the roads could be sued for personal injuries. Then, but not until then, safety became a keystone of management policy.

In March 1907, Congress passed the 16-hour law, known as the *hog law,* taking all engine and train crews out of service at the end of 16 hours of continuous duty and not letting the men "make hogs of themselves" by covering big mileage for more pay while working long hours with short rests. Many crewmen resented this law. Then, in May 1908, the Ashpan Act got the fireboys out from underneath the engines. This also was a badly needed law.

The fourth railroad safety law, the Electric Headlight

Act of April 1910, helped to brighten the track ahead on dark nights. Then came the Boiler Inspection Act of February 1911, which sent thousands of steam locomotives to junkyards. It is still in effect despite the shift to diesel power.

The sixth rail safety law was the Automatic Firedoor Act of April 1911, which was needed especially in cases of heavy firedoors on shallow fireboxes. Many firemen on shallow-firebox engines had worn leather aprons to keep from getting blistered by the heat thrown back from the furnace when hand-swung firedoors were used.

Seventeen years later, in November 1928, the seventh rail safety law, the Cab Curtain Act, was enacted. Why a law was necessary to compel the railroad companies to put cheap canvas curtains on their engine cabs is hard to understand. That form of protection against biting cold and stiff winds was needed so urgently that before passage of the law many crews installed such curtains at their own expense.

The eighth safety measure was the power reverse-gear ruling of 1938, which the Interstate Commerce Commission adopted for old heavy steam locomotives. The ninth dealt with the use of mechanical stokers, which the roads were willing to install on all new engines but not, at higher expense, on old engines. Another safety ruling required the use of automatic bell ringers on locomotives, thus making mandatory a practice that some Western lines had adopted as early as 1880. The main point at issue was not so much crew safety as the fact that drivers of vehicles hit by locomotives stood a better chance of collecting damages from a railroad if they could convince juries that the engine bell had not been ringing at the time of the accident.

Since 1910 American railroads have had to report, under oath, all accidents involving the death or injury of human beings or damages to equipment or track exceeding a certain sum, which for many years was $750 but since 1975 has been raised to $1750. In recent years, despite a fairly steady drop in the number of such accidents, an increasingly large proportion of them have been caused by track defects attributable to the use of larger, heavier, and faster freight cars.

More than 92 percent of all deaths in American train-service accidents, but less than 20 percent of all injuries in that category, involve grade crossings and/or trespassers on railroad property. Nontrain accidents comparable to those in other heavy industries account for over one-third of all injuries to railroad employees. The current slogan, "Safety First," is a far cry from the profits-first era of Jay Gould.

BIBLIOGRAPHY: John H. Armstrong, *The Railroad—What It Is, What It Does,* Simmons-Boardman, New York, 1978; Robert B. Shaw, *A History of Railroad Accidents, Safety Precautions, and Operating Practices,* Northern Press, Potsdam, N.Y., 1978.

FRISCO

St. Louis–San Francisco Railway (Frisco Lines) Line which lost its identity in April 1980 by merging into Burlington Northern Inc. It had 4673 miles of track in nine Central, Southeastern, and Southwestern states and about 8300 employees, and it hauled 15 million ton-miles of freight a year. In 1978 *Railway Age* described it as "a railroad with a record of profitability that extends back, unbroken, for well over three decades."

The Frisco stemmed from the Pacific Railroad charter granted by the Missouri Legislature in 1849 for a road to Missouri's western border, there to meet any line to be built eastward from the Pacific Coast. At that time no rails had been laid west of Pittsburgh. Construction of the new line began on July 4, 1851, at the river trading post of St. Louis, but it never came within 1000 miles of San Francisco. The line's first engine, an eight-wheeler built at Taunton, Massachusetts, exploded, killing the engineer and fireman.

Few railroads, if any, went through so many reorganizations as the Frisco. In 1865 its mainline reached Kansas City, Missouri. Gen. John C. Frémont bought its southwestern branch. The gold boom had made him rich. He also had a federal land grant of millions of acres, with which he aimed to extend the rails all the way to San Francisco. But in 1870 he went broke.

The St. Louis and San Francisco, organized in 1876, acquired many feeder lines. One of them, the Kansas, Fort Scott & Memphis, brought into Frisco history George H. Nettleton, a great railroad builder and developer of the Kansas City area. From 1900 to 1911 the Frisco had a phenomenally rapid growth under the presidency of Benjamin Franklin Yoakum, who was obsessed by an ambition to create the world's longest rail network. Yoakum not only extended the Frisco itself but welded it into a 17,000-mile system with the Rock Island, the Chicago & Eastern Illinois, and others, a total of 154 railroad companies having a working agreement with the Frisco. This vast empire linked Chicago with the Gulf of Mexico and connected with the Mexican National Railways, but it disintegrated in receiverships in 1913–1914.

Reorganized in 1916, the Frisco later plunged into another receivership and then a trusteeship that a new reorganization ended in 1947. The line was then modernized and has prospered ever since. That is why the Burlington Northern system was glad to take it over in 1980.

BIBLIOGRAPHY: William E. Bain, *Frisco Folks,* Sage Books, Denver, 1961; H. Craig, *The St. Louis-San Francisco Continental Railroad,* University of Kansas, Lawrence, 1973; *Jane's World Railways and Rapid Transit Systems,* F. Watts, New York, 1977; Lloyd E. Stagner, *Steam Locomotives of the Frisco Lines,* Pruett Publishing Co., Boulder, Colo., 1976.

St. Louis Southwestern Railway Railroad, popularly called the Cotton Belt, that began service on October 1, 1877, with 1 engine, 1 coach, and 16 freight cars. A century later, as a Southern Pacific affiliate, it was operating about 100 trains a day, including the *Blue Streak Merchandiser,* one of America's fastest freight runs, in connection with the SP, between East St. Louis and Los Angeles. (This train had been launched in 1931 as the *Blue Streak,* linking St. Louis with Pine Bluff, Arkansas.)

Originally the Cotton Belt was the 21.5-mile Tyler Tap Railway, a narrow-gauge line between Tyler and Big Sandy, Texas. A series of mergers made it part of the Texas & St. Louis in 1879, the St. Louis, Arkansas & Texas in 1886, and the standard-gauge St. Louis Southwestern in 1891. Its earliest locos burned wood; then the line was coal-powered. In 1890 Cotton Belt engines began using crude oil from Texas wells.

In 1890 a connection with the Chicago & Eastern Illinois meant freight and passenger service between Chicago and the Southwest, but for 5 years a paddle-wheel steamboat had to ferry Cotton Belt cars across the Mississippi. In the early 1900s the road reached Memphis, St. Louis, and Dallas. In 1932 the Southern Pacific took it over. From 1935 to 1947 the line was in bankruptcy, but eventually its trustees repaid all creditors in full and returned the line to its stockholders.

St. Thomas Wreck Exactly 22 months after a Grand Trunk (GT) engine killed Jumbo, the most highly publicized elephant in circus history, at St. Thomas, Ontario, a crossing collision in that area took a frightful toll of human lives. On July 15, 1887, the London & Port Stanley (L&PS), operated by the GT, ran a 1-day excursion for a Baptist church picnic from St. Thomas to Port Stanley, on Lake Erie's north shore, 9 miles each way. The train had seven wooden coaches, with a boxcar between them and the engine. The boxcar had no airbrake, so a dummy pipe (without an angle cock) was rigged up under the car from the locomotive tank to the first coach. *See also* CIRCUS TRAINS.

The run to the picnic ground was pleasant, but on the return trip the brakeman who turned the angle cock on the engine failed to do likewise on the first coach, which left all seven passenger cars without airbrake protection. Engineer Donnely handled his engine expertly with wheel reverse, so he did not need to use the air until he came to the point where the Michigan Central track crossed the L&PS at approximately a right angle.

Seeing a westbound Michigan Central freight head for the crossing, he tried to reverse his engine and blew frantically for brakes, but it was too late. His pilot rammed into the first gas tank, causing a fire and explosion that killed Donnely and 22 passengers in the first coach. A big crowd gathered to watch the rescue work. Unexpectedly the other tank car blew up, burning or scalding about 400 people, 3 so badly that they died in a day or two. A coroner's inquest blamed the excursion-train crew for not testing the air on all the cars before leaving Port Stanley.

Sanding the Rails The first recorded use of sand (*seashore,* in rail lingo) to halt or mitigate the slippage of driving wheels was not prompted by rain, snow, heavy grades, or excess tonnage. According to the archives of the old Philadelphia & Reading [(P&R) now part of Conrail], the incentive was a grasshopper plague in eastern Pennsylvania i 1836. Slipping wheels crushed insects by the thousands. Trackmen vainly swept the iron clear before each train. (Rails then were iron, not steel.) At length they began sanding the rails. This was so effective that soon afterward small bins full of sand stood on the pilots (cowcatchers) of all P&R engines, which led eventually to rail sanding by valve-and-gravity-control feed from the cab.

The first locomotive sandbox, a small funnel-shaped container, poured sand on slipping driving wheels. Its inventor, Jordan L. Mott, born at Manhasset, New York, in 1798, was a grocer, an ironmaster, and the inventor and manufacturer of the first anthracite-burning cookstove. The former New York Central's Mott Haven yards in the Bronx, New York City, which are still in use, were named for Mott because his foundry was located there.

An early type of sand reservoir was a square or cylindrical receptacle of sheet iron, with a cast-iron base and cap, set atop the boiler, preferably with its centerline directly above the lead edge of the forward pair of drivers. This made for vertical standpipe tangent to the driving axles' horizontal plane. From it pipes were bent down and backward to conform to the tire curves. Such reservoirs (later given rounded tops called domes) were ornately embellished from the first, with landscapes painted on their sides, flamboyant scrollwork, and brass belting and often with a sculptured metal eagle on the lid. Dome types helped to identify the various engine builders.

Some locomotives had wedge-shaped sand bins concealed beneath the running boards or behind false aprons around the upper halves of driving wheels. Small

Hostler filling the sand dome of No. 751, one of the last Camelbacks in service on the Jersey Central Railroad or any other road. [A. F. Sozio]

lids flush with the boards furnished access for refilling. Regardless of the reservoir's location, seldom was more than one set of sand pipes fed from a single dome during the era of gravity delivery to the rails.

Switchers had sand domes placed both before and behind the drivers. Early multiwheeled engines had two receptacles, one in advance of the steam dome and the other adjacent to the cab. A major problem was water thrown up from the wheels on rainy days that wet and solidified the sand. This partly or fully closed the pipe ends, which could not always be cleared by repeated rapping. It created a real hazard. Added adhesion of wheels to rails might, and often did, make the difference between a quick stop and a disastrous wreck.

To solve this problem, pneumatic sanders were developed as a logical adjunct to the airbrake. Such devices blow air jets into traps inserted into sand lines just below the reservoir. Shaped like a tilted letter S, each trap is constantly replenished from the dome. Air-jet force determines the precise quantity of sand lifted out of the trap and ejected to the rail. Nozzles may be adjusted individually to apply the same amount of sand regardless of the delivery-pipe curvature.

En route to or from its open position, the engineer's sand valve automatically sends an air jet down each pipe to clear it before and after every blast of "seashore." The valve is designed to tilt in either direction for delivery to either forward and reverse sanding, as desired. A modern sander's ability to boost its delivery over long distances, combined with the ever-increasing demand of huge locomotives that make relatively few service stops, caused the sand dome to swell into impressive proportions—a 5-ton capacity, for example, on some steam locomotives.

The old-time wooden sandhouse, with its elevator, ventilator louvers, dryer, storage elevator, and delivery pipes, was a familiar sight at railroad terminals in the days of wooden water towers. With the need for shorter servicing stops, a blending of sand and coal stations in many yards handled steam engines at a single spotting. Diesel power brought its own brand of sanding problems. Diesel locos and the cars they pull are equipped with reservoirs and sanders that cut in automatically when brake-pipe reductions are made at any but the lowest speeds.

BIBLIOGRAPHY: Henry B. Comstock, *The Iron Horse,* Crowell, New York, 1971; Roy V. Wright (ed.), *Locomotive Cyclopedia,* Simmons-Boardman, New York, 1911.

Santa Fe Railway (Atchison, Topeka and Santa Fe Railway; ATSF) Line that operates about 11,750 route miles stretching from Lake Michigan to the Gulf of Mexico and the Pacific. Its principal founder, Cyrus K. Holliday (1826–1900), born near Carbondale, Pennsylvania, began his rail career in 1852 with a firm of railroad-building contractors in that state. In 1854 he married and journeyed by rail, riverboat, and stagecoach to Kansas Territory. There he promoted Topeka village as a potential city, was active in the abolitionist movement, and engaged in politics.

By 1857 Kansas had incorporated at least a dozen paper railroads. Holliday wrote a charter for one of them, the St. Louis & Topeka, which was granted on February 11, 1859. A corporation was set up in September 1860 in a small Atchison, Kansas, law office. Soon the Civil War began. Kansas became a state. The Atchison & Topeka, one of the Kansas land-grant roads, was renamed the Atchison, Topeka and Santa Fe on November 24, 1863. Each land grant gave a railroad odd-numbered sections on both sides of the track. If settlers had already preempted railroad-designated sites, the company was entitled to other land within 20 miles of its line.

After a long, discouraging drive for money to build the ATSF, construction began in the late fall of 1868, a few months before Union Pacific and Central Pacific rails were united in Utah. A railroad bridge over the Kansas River at Topeka, connecting the new line with the Kansas Pacific Railroad (KP), one of its rivals, was completed in March 1869. Ties and 56-pound iron rail hauled over the KP were spiked into place.

The first Santa Fe locomotive, named *Cyrus K. Holliday,* was a secondhand 4-4-0 woodburner with a flaring stack which Niles Machine Works of Cincinnati had built for another railroad. On May 30, 1869, it pulled five flatcar loads of rails, the Santa Fe's first train, over the new bridge. At that time the road owned a used coach named *Holliday,* 12 flatcars, and a handcar. Later that year it acquired 24 coal cars to service the Carbondale coal mines, 12 boxcars, another coach, a baggage car, and a lightweight woodburning engine, the *General Burnside,* named for a Civil War hero and built by Rhode Island Locomotive Works. *See* RATON MOUNTAIN SWITCHBACK.

As money got scarcer, Boston financiers took over the company, stepped up its stock sales, and appointed Albert A. Robinson chief engineer. Robinson supervised the building of about 5000 miles of track, which may have set a world record. The federal land grant to ATSF was contingent on its track reaching the Colorado state line by March 3, 1873. In July 1870 the railhead was pushed into Emporia, a cow town 62 miles south of Topeka. Soon Abilene became the first major cattle town in Kansas, but within months it was eclipsed by Newton, where a huge yard was opened for the shipment of herds from the Chisholm Trail.

Rails were light; the roadbed lacked ballast. The job was done hastily and at minimum cost to meet the deadline with dwindling funds. The laborers lived mostly on beans, salt pork, sorghum, rotgut whiskey, and some buffalo meat. Their women cooked dried fruits for Sunday dinner. Generally the laborers slept in tents or crude shacks. A pay car cruising up and down the line dispensed their $2-a-day wages. Fort Dodge troops guarded them from Indian raids but not from individual thefts. Adding to their woes, a shipload of English-made rails sank at sea, rustlers stole cattle from the yards, and the Kansas River, which they had to bridge, was flooded. *See* PAY CAR.

Toiling like galley slaves, Robinson's tracklayers completed 3 miles plus 400 feet in a single day. Finally, on December 28, 1872, they reached the Colorado state line 2 months ahead of schedule, with a noisy, drunken celebration. The company's first annual report, dated March 1871, showed 497 miles of track. But 1873 was a panic year, and the ATSF had run out of money. Except for the surveying of a route to Pueblo, Colorado, construction was virtually at a standstill.

Laying rails as far as Colorado permitted the Santa Fe to cut into the Kansas Pacific's cattle traffic. By 1875 the millions of prairie-roaming buffalo had been wiped out, pauperizing the Indians; and the cattlemen moved in. Arrogant cowboys with six-shooters rode their horses into saloons, used engine headlights as targets, and killed more than a few railmen in arguments over booze, cards, and women. Meanwhile, ATSF was doing a lucrative business in the shipment of buffalo hides for robes and bones for fertilizer. In 1878 Fred Harvey and his famous girls began to revolutionize and glamorize eating houses on the Santa Fe system. *See* EXCURSION TRAINS; HARVEY, FREDERICK HENRY.

Colorado extension efforts put ATSF in head-on conflict with Brig. Gen. William J. Palmer's narrow-gauge Denver & Rio Grande (DR&G). When the armed clashes and litigation ended in 1880, DR&G had the sole right to build through the highly disputed Royal Gorge to Leadville, Colorado, but it paid its rival for the work it had already done on this project. Palmer canceled his plans to build a competing line to Santa Fe, New Mexico, while the Kansas-based road agreed to stay out of Rio Grande territory. Both antagonists shared the southwestern Colorado and Denver traffic. *See also* CANYON WAR.

The 1870s and 1880s saw the population of Kansas almost tripled and an even greater growth in the state's agriculture. ATSF was involved in this development by selling a considerable portion of its 3 million acres of land grants. (According to the Interstate Commerce Commission, the Santa Fe received nearly $12.5 million from such sales up to October 30, 1916.) Like other land-grant Western railroads, ATSF used its own agents, advertising, steamship lines, European land companies, etc., to encourage Scandinavian, German, British, and French farmers and artisans to emigrate to the American West, the Santa Fe especially promoting Kansas.

The ATSF cooperated with its land buyers by demonstrating modern techniques for making their farms pay. It also aided these people when drought, grasshoppers, and hailstorms ruined their crops and made them destitute. The railroad helped to form county relief societies which distributed free clothing, food, and seed grain—hard red Crimean wheat for next year's crops. It also cut freight rates on coal and other necessities, set a moratorium on land payments, and carried, without charge, over a million pounds of freight for its impoverished land buyers.

Besides creating goodwill for the Santa Fe, this colonization policy enabled vast numbers of settlers to stay on the prairie. Others, broke and discouraged, abandoned their farms and went back East. Every family living in a railroad's territory is, of course, a potential source of freight business. ATSF was looking to the future.

Thrusting southward from Raton, New Mexico, Robinson's men reached Las Vegas in 1879, conquered Glorietta Pass, 7453 feet above sea level, followed gorges and creek beds, and dropped the line more than 2000 feet in 40 miles. They cut through Apache Pass to the Rio Grande Valley, reaching Albuquerque and San Marcial in 1880. The Santa Fe's trail now extended 860 miles from Kansas City.

The main stem had bypassed the name city, Santa Fe, but an 18-mile branch to that point from Lamy had its last spike driven by Lew Wallace, author of *Ben Hur* and governor of New Mexico Territory. Another branch, from San Marcial to Deming, New Mexico, connecting with the Southern Pacific (SP), permitted the ATSF to run the first through train from Kansas City to California in 1881. A year later, after taking over the Sonora Rail-

The Santa Fe's Hi-Level streamliner* El Capitan *rounding a curve in Cajun Pass in the 1960s. The Santa Fe was making a vain attempt to upgrade passenger service, but finally had to turn it over to Amtrak in 1971. [Don Erb, Santa Fe Railway]

way south of the border, Santa Fe announced the opening of its 1700-mile mainline from Kansas City to Guaymas, Mexico, the world's longest rail route under one management. But the Sonora proved to be a financial disaster and was eventually traded to the SP for its Needles-Mojave property.

Early in 1881 the drive toward Los Angeles, which had begun near Albuquerque, completed its first 100 miles. The railroad's subcontractors in mountainous forested Arizona included a son of Brigham Young. Irish, Mexicans, Mormons, and Indians laid rail at the rate of a mile a day. Diablo Canyon, with sheer rock walls towering 250 feet above a creek, was bridged. Collis P. Huntington, SP tycoon, did all he could to block ATSF progress through California. He refused to let the line cross SP tracks at Colton, California, but backed down in the face of a court order. Jay Gould also tried to check the Santa Fe's westward thrust, but Robinson's crews soon reached San Bernardino. *See* GOULD, JAY; HUNTINGTON, COLLIS POTTER.

In 1884 ATSF bought a new line, the California Western, which was then incomplete but would take the railroad to San Diego. By closing a gap through the Mojave Desert and the difficult Cajon Pass, ATSF entered Needles, California, and thus in late 1885 had a through route from Kansas City to the West Coast. Shortly afterward, by leasing a stretch of SP line westward from Colton, ATSF reached Los Angeles, which was then a small town; but on May 11, 1887, it began running trains into Los Angeles on its own tracks.

In 1890 Kansas had the second-largest rail mileage of any state in the Union (mostly ATSF, Missouri Pacific, and Rock Island) and produced the lion's share of Santa Fe profits. The Santa Fe built new branches there and reached out from Indian Territory to Galveston, Texas, on the Gulf of Mexico, and to Chicago. In 1880 it bought the 1442-mile Frisco and the 327-mile Colorado Midland, but later it dropped both lines as unprofitable.

This metal and bamboo device, known as the golden peacock, was adopted by the Santa Fe to make sure that poles, wires, and other objects are not too close to the tracks. [R. B. Henderson, Santa Fe Railway]

This overexpansion plus the panic of 1893 threw the system into a receivership. In 1895 it was reorganized under the same name except that the word *Railway* was substituted for *Railroad.* The directors, including Cyrus K. Holliday, elected Edward P. Ripley president and ushered in an era of further expansion, modernization, and prosperity.

In 1900 the ATSF acquired a new railway linking San Francisco to Bakersfield, California, and from there to Mojave, California, by trackage rights over the SP through the rugged Tehachapi Pass, a route that is both an engineering marvel and a railroad bottleneck. In 2 miles of that pass (later simplified somewhat) were 15 tunnels, 2.5 percent grades, fifty 10-degree curves, and a 4025-foot summit elevation. Tehachapi Loop was built so that one end of a long freight train winding around it runs on tracks directly above the other end of the same train while climbing 2734 feet in 16 miles.

By 1912 the Santa Fe's total mileage was 10,627. In 1928 the system bought the Kansas City, Mexico & Orient. In 1941 ATSF mileage totaled 13,627 even after the shedding of unprofitable branch lines. It has been shrinking gradually ever since because of minor abandonments. In 1905 the steam-powered *Death Valley Coyote* special train made the Santa Fe's most spectacular speed record. The system is now fully dieselized, beginning in 1934 when Electro-Motive Corp. tested a nonarticulated 1800-horsepower diesel-electric loco on the Santa Fe. This test led first to dieselization of the crack train *Super Chief.* By 1953 diesels were making over 70 percent of Santa Fe runs. *See* DEATH VALLEY SCOTTY; STILWELL, ARTHUR EDWARD.

Automobiles had long been making passenger trains unprofitable, but ATSF was slow to admit defeat. In 1964, while other big roads were cutting service and selling their diners and Pullmans, it bought new passenger rolling stock, including 24 more Hi-Level chair cars (double-deckers), which it used on the *San Francisco Chief, Super Chief,* and *El Capitan.* To cut costs, *doodlebugs* (self-operating single cars) replaced regular trains between the name cities Atchison and Topeka. But neither new equipment nor thrift could stop ATSF from turning over its entire passenger service to Amtrak on May 1, 1971. *See* AMTRAK.

BIBLIOGRAPHY: Keith L. Bryant, Jr., *History of the Atchison, Topeka and Santa Fe Railway,* Macmillan, New York, 1974; Donald Duke and Stan Kistler, *Santa Fe: Steel Rails through California,* Golden West Books, San Marino, Calif., 1963; William S. Greever, *Arid Domain: The Santa Fe Railway and Its Western Land Grant,* Stanford University Press, Stanford, Calif., 1954; *Jane's World Railways and Rapid Transit Systems,* F. Watts, New York, 1977; Joe McMillan, *Santa Fe's Diesel Fleet,* Chatham Pub. Co., Burlingame, Calif., 1974; E. Dale Worley, *Iron Horses of the Santa Fe Trail,* Southwest Railroad Historical Society, Dallas, 1965.

SCL *See* SEABOARD COAST LINE RAILROAD.

Scott, Walter *See* DEATH VALLEY SCOTTY.

Seaboard Coast Line Railroad (SCL) Anchor line of the Family Lines System. It was a consolidation, effected July 1, 1967, of two Class I roads, the Seaboard Air Line Railroad (SAL) and the Atlantic Coast Line Railroad (ACL). Each company had roots more than a century and a quarter old in the soil of Virginia and North Carolina. At one time the world's longest single railroad was in North Carolina, and today the longest stretch of perfectly straight track in the United States, 78.8 miles, is SCL's line between Hamlet and Wilmington, North Carolina.

SCL history began at Weldon, North Carolina, on the Roanoke River near the Virginia state line. Its nucleus was the Petersburg Railroad, chartered by the state of Virginia in 1836. The original track consisted of strap-iron rails fastened to yellow-pine stringers, supported by crossties of hand-hewn oak. In 1833 the line was completed to Blakely, just across the river from Weldon; it comprised the first road of what eventually became the Atlantic Coast Line.

SAL's forerunner, the Seaboard Air Line Railway, was chartered on May 8, 1832. Its first train chugged into Weldon on December 1, 1836. To the south, the Wilmington & Weldon was slowly extending its track across eastern North Carolina. The final spike on this 161-mile line, the world's longest continuous track at that time, was driven on March 7, 1840, near Tar River Bridge at Rocky Mount, North Carolina.

One of ACL's ancestors, the Richmond & Petersburg Railroad (R&P), was chartered in 1836. Two years later it completed 22 miles of track between Richmond and Pocahontas on the north bank of the Appomattox River opposite Petersburg, but it was not connected physically with the Petersburg Railroad until after the Civil War. For more than 25 years passengers and freight were transferred across the river over a wagon bridge. Years later, R&P's original 1836 charter became ACL's basic charter.

In 1836, the second branch in SAL's family tree began to take shape as ground was broken at Gaston, North Carolina, for the Raleigh & Gaston Railroad (R&G). Despite the opposition of farmers with shotguns, the R&G reached Raleigh, the state capital, in 1840. The name Seaboard first appeared in 1846 when the R&P became the Seaboard & Roanoke. Seven years later this line was connected with the R&G for through rail service between Portsmouth and Raleigh, the first of many links which would eventually make up the Seaboard system.

In 1869–1870, Baltimore capitalists acquired an interest in the Wilmington & Weldon and four other railroads in that area, bringing unified management to them for the first time. In 1871 the group adopted the name Atlantic Coast Line because the track closely paralleled the ocean. Each of the affiliated companies retained its corporate identity, but all locomotives began carrying the ACL circle as well as the name of the individual line.

Consolidation of operations between Richmond, Virginia, and Tampa, Florida, began in 1900 when the SAL took over the 944-mile Florida Central & Peninsular Railroad. In 1915 the SAL merged with the Carolina, Atlantic & Western Railroad, which ran between Hamlet, North Carolina, and Charleston, South Carolina. The consolidated company became the Seaboard Air Line Railway, with almost 4000 miles of track.

The opening of the Fayetteville cutoff from Contentnea, near Wilson, North Carolina, to Pee Dee, South Carolina, in 1893 was a major step in ACL growth. A merger in 1900 extended the system from Richmond to Charleston and brought the Atlantic Coast Line into official existence. Two years later, acquisition of the Plant System in Florida, Georgia, and other Southern states gave the ACL nearly the form it had prior to the SAL merger.

That merger created a company with assets of $1.2 billion and 9629 route miles in Virginia, North Carolina, South Carolina, Georgia, Florida, and Alabama that ranked eighth in mileage among the nation's railroads and ninth in assets and revenue. On July 1, 1967, the SCL reached its present form by merging the Piedmont & Northern Railway into its system. Seaboard maintains general offices at Richmond and Jacksonville, Florida. In 1977 it owned 2288 road locomotives, 407 switchers, and 140,000 freight cars. Its passenger traffic was turned over to Amtrak in 1971.

On September 24, 1980, Seaboard Coast Line Industries, holding company of the SCL Railroad, was authorized by the Interstate Commerce Commission to merge with the Chessie System, the resultant company being CSX Corp. *See* CSX CORP.

BIBLIOGRAPHY: *Jane's World Railways and Rapid Transit Systems*, E. Watts, New York, 1977.

A Seaboard Coast Line phosphate train. [Seaboard Coast Line Industries, Inc.]

Shay, Matthew H. ***(1843–1915)*** Native of Watkins, New York, who went firing on the Erie in 1860 and was promoted to engineer in 1865. Shay was so strict a church member that he never worked on Sundays. For this reason he gave up a fast passenger run for a coal run, but he returned to the passenger run later when the management assigned another man to handle it on Sundays. Shay became national secretary of the Brotherhood of Locomotive Engineers. The Erie gave his name, *Matt H. Shay,* to its famous triplex Mallet, then the world's largest locomotive.

BIBLIOGRAPHY: Edward Harold Mott, *Between the Ocean and the Lakes: The Story of Erie,* J. S. Collins, New York, 1899.

Sheds *See* TRAINSHEDS.

Shelley, Kate ***(1860–1912)*** Only widely known railroad heroine. She lived at Boone, Iowa, in a small farmhouse facing the Chicago & North Western (C&NW) mainline and Honey Creek, a tributary of the Des Moines River. During the stormy night of July 6–7, 1881, when she was 15, a flood swept away 11 of the valley's 21 wooden bridges. Shortly after 11 p.m. Kate and her widowed mother saw a lone helper engine begin to cross the creek and heard a terrific crash, splash, and hiss of steam as the engine fell into the water with the collapsing bridge.

Because her father had been a C&NW section man, the girl knew what to do. Grabbing his old lantern, she rushed out into the rainy darkness to rescue, if possible, the men who had ridden the lost engine and to flag the passenger train due at midnight in Moingona, a mile away, before it could reach the now-bridgeless Honey Creek.

Four men had been on the engine. Two were gone. Kate saw the other two clinging to trees that overhung the swollen creek and shouted that she was going to Moingona for help and to flag the train. To do so she would have to cross the rain-swept wooden railroad bridge with no footwalk for pedestrians and now so gorged by the flooded river that water almost lapped the ties.

Kate did not *run* across that bridge. She crawled in the darkness, the gale having blown out her lantern, terrified lest the headlight of the eastbound limited suddenly shine in her face. Her hands and knees were bruised, cut, and splintered. But she made it and warned the Moingona agent. The train and the two engine survivors were saved. Grateful passengers gave her a hatful of money.

Next morning she awoke to fame. From far and wide came letters, gifts, ballads, and even offers of marriage. The Iowa State Legislature awarded her $200 in cash and a gold medal. The Order of Railway Conductors gave her a gold watch and chain. Named in her honor were a drinking fountain, a new iron bridge, a Brotherhood of Railroad Trainmen lodge, and a passenger train.

The C&NW management gave her a gold medal, half a barrel of flour, a load of coal, and for the last eight years of her life a job as Moingona station agent. Whenever Kate traveled by rail, even for shopping, the train would make an unscheduled stop at her trackside home. And when she died on January 21, 1912, the railroad sent a special train to her home for the funeral.

BIBLIOGRAPHY: Freeman Hubbard, *Railroad Avenue,* McGraw-Hill, New York, 1945.

Kate Shelley, who saved the 200-passenger Chicago & North Western (C&NW) express from disaster in 1881. She is shown here at the turn of the century on the platform of the C&NW station in Moingona, Iowa, scene of her heroism. [Chicago & North Western Railroad]

Shopmen's Strike of 1922 *See* STRIKES, MAJOR RAILROAD.

Shortest Rail Freight Haul Possibly the haul made in 1953 when a Chesapeake and Ohio four-car train pulled by a diesel switcher moved the total equipment of an electrical appliances plant through Richmond, Virginia, from its old quarters to a new location four blocks away.

Siamese Twins The twins Daisy and Violet Hilton perplexed Northern Pacific (NP) passenger conductors until the line's auditor, E. J. Johnson, decided: "They are so joined together, competent medical authorities have ruled, that when one dies the other must die, wherever one goes the other must go. Therefore, one fare is valid for their transportation." The NP Law Department concurred.

Signals Strange as it seems, wayside signals are not indispensable to safe railroad operation. Only about half of America's rail mileage has them, mostly on branch lines over which only one train may run. The first railway signals, smoke and bells, did not guide engineers. Before a train was due, the station agent would shinny up a high mast that stood beside the depot, perch himself on a crow's nest, and watch for locomotive smoke. When he spied it, he quickly got down and tolled a station bell to call travelers and shippers from their homes, shops, and farms. *See* STATION BELLS.

It is not true, as one story alleges, that a farmer waving his red shirt before an early-day train originated the red flag as a danger signal. That color has been a danger indication since Roman legions first bore the red banner of their war god, Mars, into battle more than 20 centuries ago.

The earliest common-carrier railways, like many miles today, were single-tracked, with turnouts or sidings to let traffic run in both directions on the same track; but in that bygone era the crews had no way of knowing the whereabouts of other trains. So center posts were set up midway between one siding and the next. Whichever train reached the landmark first had the right of way. A train running in the opposite direction on that track was required to back up and into the siding to let it pass.

One reckless procedure, never officially sanctioned but employed occasionally, consisted of an engineer without train orders running on "smoke orders," i.e., keeping a sharp lookout while he drove until he caught sight of smoke from a train ahead, hoping the other engineer was sufficiently far away and going slowly enough to avoid a head-on collision, and then beginning to reverse his own train. That hope was not always realized.

Much safer was the staff method, which, like the modern block signal system with interlocking, was designed to keep more than one train from using any section of track at the same time. That practice preceded the use of train orders. When starting a run, the engineer was handed a short staff or its equivalent, giving him the right-of-way on a single-tracked line. When two opposing trains met at a siding or a station, they were not allowed to proceed until they exchanged staffs. Another device, before the invention of semaphore signals, was a tall pole with a crossbar and lanyards whereby two different-colored flags were hoisted or struck.

Ball signals, from which was derived the rail-slang word *highball,* were used for many years, mostly in New England, one or two of them until the late 1960s. Today they are museum pieces. *Highball* means "Go ahead," "Keep going," or "Make a fast run." But when the ball was high, being lifted by a pulley to the top of a cross-barred staff standing beside a station or switch, it warned the engineer that another train occupied the same track just ahead. Lowering the ball, like lowering a semaphore arm or flashing a green light, indicated a clear track.

Originally green was a caution signal, "Go slow," while white signified "All clear." The change was made in about 1914 because a red roundel in a switch signal had fallen out, giving an engineer the impression that the signal was set for clear, which caused a disastrous wreck. *See* WARMAN, CYRUS.

The manually operated block system, introduced in England in 1839 but not adopted in the United States (near Philadelphia) until 1863, was created to maintain a safe headway between trains running on the same track. It was basically unlike the system it replaced in that it set up a time interval, rather than a space interval, between the trains. The towerman must be alert in clearing the block, making sure that a train is complete, with no cars dropped en route owing to broken couplers. Every train, even a locomotive running light (without cars), must display marker lights or flags on its front and rear ends.

Meanwhile, in 1851, Superintendent Charles Minot of the New York & Erie had taken advantage of his recently installed telegraph line to issue the world's first telegraphed train order. It changed the meeting point of two trains, but Minot himself had to get into the engine cab of one of them and run the train because the engineer refused to disobey the timetable. This started a system of operating trains by a combination of train orders and timetables, which includes spacing the trains and

***Early Philadelphia & Reading signal tower in Phoenixville, Pennsylvania.* [Scribner's Magazine]**

flag protection to guard against rear-end collisions. *See* TORPEDOES AND FUSEES.

The form of automatic block whereby trains themselves control the signaling, invented by Dr. William Robinson in 1872, is most efficient in increasing line capacity. The track circuit determines the presence or absence of trains. In case of a broken rail or failure of a battery or wire connection a clear signal cannot be displayed. The old-time mechanical interlocking machine that kept a train from moving into an occupied block has long since been replaced by the electrical type, a combination of interconnected relays.

Centralized traffic control is a system whereby switches are thrown and trains are given clear signal indications by means of a machine located in the dispatcher's office. This is the culmination of the interlocking of mainline tracks with branch lines extending from them, which began to be developed in 1857. It permits the dispatching of trains without telegraphy or train orders. Guided by a track chart with its tiny flashing lights, one man can now dispatch and control each train over a distance of 100 or more miles. *See also* CENTRALIZED TRAFFIC CONTROL.

After the color-light-position signal had replaced the flailing semaphore arms, the Pennsylvania Railroad began to experiment with—and was the first road to adopt, in the early 1920s—the color-light signal panel in the engine cab. This device receives and amplifies messages transmitted continuously through the rails. The Pennsy was in a preferred position to make such experiments because much of its mainline is electrified. *See also* AUTOMATIC TRAIN CONTROL.

The main advantage of this cab mechanism is that the engine crew can see and hear signal instructions even in stormy or foggy weather. In addition to many other modern developments such as radiotelephone communication between engine cab and caboose and dispatchers at distant points and the walkie-talkie, it is helping to decrease the number of trackside signal installations on North American rails.

See also SIGNALS, BLOCK; SIGNALS, DWARF; SIGNALS, HAND; SIGNALS, WHISTLE.

BIBLIOGRAPHY: John H. Armstrong, *The Railroad—What It Is, What It Does,* Simmons-Boardman, New York, 1978; Thomas C. Clarke and others, *The American Railway: Its Construction, Development, Management, and Appliances,* Scribner, New York, 1897; Robert S. Henry, *This Fascinating Railroad Business,* 3d ed., rev., Bobbs-Merrill, Indianapolis, 1946.

An intricate set of hand-operated interlocking switches filled the signal tower of the 1890s.

Signals, Block Fixed or wayside signals along the track that divide the railroad into sections, or blocks. They are so spaced that trains will run at safe distances from each other. The basis of today's block system is an electric current flowing through the rails. When all switches are closed and no train or other obstruction is in the block, the signal shows clear. When a train enters the block, its wheels and axles short-circuit the current, and the signal changes to indicate the necessity for stopping. Usually, the signal circuits are so arranged that a "Caution" signal shows when a train is in the second block ahead.

Block signals give their messages to the engineer through semaphores, which have movable blades, or arms, position-light signals, or color-light signals. Position-light signals have rows of yellow lights instead of semaphore blades. Color-light signals—green, yellow, and red—are visible by day as well as by night. Some railroads use a combination of signals.

Far right: Dwarf semaphore from around 1880. [Collection of Freeman Hubbard]

BIBLIOGRAPHY: C. Miles Burpee (ed.), *Railway Engineering and Maintenance Cyclopedia,* Simmons-Boardman, New York, 1942; Robert

S. Henry, *This Fascinating Railroad Business,* 3d ed., rev., Bobbs-Merrill, Indianapolis, 1946.

Signals, Dwarf Signals erected close to the ground and sometimes covered by metal hoods. They are used mostly in large yard and terminal areas where the overhead flashes of regular block signals cannot easily be seen. Dwarf signals were especially important during World War II because their extra-long hoods kept lights from the possibility of being spotted by enemy aircraft.

Signals, Hand While some hand signals are printed in the standard *Book of Rules,* many others in common use never appeared there, especially in the days before automated classification yards. Some unofficial signals had different meanings on various railroads; but with boomers circulating from one road to another, experienced switchmen and trainmen understood most of them. *See* BOOMERS.

Here are a few samples that were not in the rule book. One arm with clenched fist thrust straight up and held briefly motionless means "Track 1"; both arms held that way, "Track 2"; both arms up, half lowered, with one arm continuing down while the other is again thrust up, "Track 3." One arm up, with fingers spread but thumb clasped in the fist of the other hand, means "Track 4"; one arm up with fingers and thumb spread apart and hand given a slight forward motion, "Track 5." One arm up, fingers spread, suddenly closed in the fist and with left thumb extended and turned up, means "Track 6." A motion with the hand like shaking dice means "Track 7" (or use the sign for Track 5, followed by two pats on the palm of the extended hand with the other hand). Both arms akimbo means "Track 8"; a movement parallel to the hat brim and with fingers pointing toward it, "Track 9" (or a combination of signals for Tracks 4 and 5); two circles with hand at a right angle in the line of vision, "Track 10." Local usage varies for tracks above 10.

There are also unofficial hand signals for main track, siding or passing track, house track, corral or stock track, scale (weighing) track, rip (repair) track, caboose, etc. Among the innumerable others, some of them still in use, are the following:

Hotbox (overheated journal bearing on a passing train or on your own train): nose held with fingers.
Coupling (before the days of automatic coupling): Clenched fist of one hand inserted in the other half-open hand.
Take water (for steam locomotives): One fist raised to lips as if holding a glass of water and drinking.
Time to eat: Both hands clenched, thumbs extended, moved alternately toward lips.
Wait or take a break: Same as *eat,* but with thumbs down.
Load or unload freight: Pat shoulder with hand.
Drop or flying switch (outlawed long ago): Usually both arms at elbow, and movement with arms as if flying.
Back in: Back of one hand tapped by other hand or small of back patted with hand.

BIBLIOGRAPHY: *Model Railroader,* December 1948, September 1964; *Railroad Magazine,* November 1941.

Signals, Whistle A standard code of whistle signals is used on all kinds of locomotives to expedite train operation. Basically, it is a form of communication from the engineman to other trainmen and fellow railroaders like station agents, towermen, switchmen, and track workers. It also serves to warn pedestrians, cyclists, drivers of highway vehicles, and animals on the track that a train is coming and to sound an alarm when, for example, an engine crew sees a passing farmhouse burst into flame or livestock break down a fence. (Back in steam days, many an engineer and fireman whistled a greeting to his wife or girl friend from a locomotive approaching or passing through her hometown.) Anyone familiarizing himself or herself with this code can understand "whistle talk."

One short "Apply brakes. Stop." This signal has two meanings and ordinarily is used in emergencies. An engineer who sees some other train movement that is in danger will whistle one short sound, meaning "Stop." Or an engineer may whistle one short to a brakeman or switchman, meaning "Set hand brakes on cars."

Two short "Answer to a signal." This whistle the engineer uses to acknowledge hearing or seeing a signal that affects the train movement.

Three short "Back up." An engineer who wants to make a reverse movement or receives a signal to do so gives three short whistles. Or, when running, the engineer answers the signal to stop at the next passenger station.

Four short "Call for signals." This signal is used when an engineer wants a station agent, signal-tower operator, dispatcher, or someone else to give a signal so that the engineer will know what move to make. Usually the engineer hates to be kept waiting.

One long "Approaching station." This signal notifies employees there that the train is coming. It is used also when a train approaches a junction or a railroad crossing at grade.

Two long "Release brakes. Proceed." This signal notifies members of the train crew that the engineer is ready to move ahead and to release any brake that they may have applied.

Two long, one short, and one long "Approaching highway or street crossing." This signal is prolonged or repeated until the crossing is reached.

One long and two shorts (single track) The attention of engine and train crews of the same class, inferior trains, or yard engines and of trains at train-order meeting points is called to signals displayed for a following section. If these are not answered by a train, the train displaying the signals must stop and ascertain the cause.

(Two or more tracks) The attention of engine and train crews of train of the same class, of inferior trains moving in the same direction, and of yard engines is called to signals displayed for a following section.

One long and three short "Flagman protect rear of train." When the train stops, this signal reminds the flagman at the rear of the train to go back with a red signal, torpedoes, and fusees to stop any following train.

Two long "Approaching a meeting or waiting point."

One short and one long "Inspect train line for a leak or for brakes sticking."

Four or five long "Recall flagman." When again ready to proceed, the engineer whistles either four or five long sounds, depending on the direction the flagman has gone, calling the flagman back to the train. When there are more than two tracks, that signal is followed by one, two, or even three shorts, depending on the direction and the number of tracks.

Succession of short sounds "Alarm, especially for persons or livestock on the track."

BIBLIOGRAPHY: *Model Railroader,* February 1937, April 1957; *Railroad Magazine,* December 1942, May 1945; *Trains Magazine,* March 1945.

Silk Trains Trains that because they hauled material for the silk industry had priority over all other trains. They ran in Canada and the United States, on the Great Northern (GN), Milwaukee Road, Northern Pacific (NP), Santa Fe, Southern Pacific (SP), and all railroads in the Midwest and the East that helped to whisk across North America the cocoons of live Asiatic silkworms (fed on mulberry leaves) and manufactured silk goods.

Silk shipments ran into big money, even up to $10 million apiece in preinflation funds. Some were spread out over three trains for one cargo. Always, there was danger of the valuable stuff being hijacked, although no silk train was ever hijacked.

Another reason for speeding the silk cocoons was the danger of spoilage. A more urgent reason was the sharp fluctuations in price, for silk was usually consigned on order to a bank or brokerage house, not to a silk mill, and like other commodities was traded on commodity exchanges. A few hours' delay could wipe out a fortune. Even more important was the high cost of insuring silk in transit, 6 percent, on an hourly basis. Carriers wanted to get such costly items off their hands as soon as possible.

The various railroads competed keenly for the lucrative silk business, each doing its best to prove it could deliver the rich stuff faster than its rivals. Every man involved in a silk shipment was expected to be on his toes. It was an honor to handle such a train. *Harper's Weekly*'s description of a silk special as "dull-painted and windowless, yet the emperor of trains" on November 27, 1909, may have been the first journalistic mention of *all-silk* trains, although a Council Bluffs newspaper of November 24, 1870, had noted the passage of "49 railroad cars of tea and two of silk." The first through train from Vancouver to Montreal, after completion of the Canadian Pacific mainline in 1885, had silk cars in its consist.

Raw silk was shipped in bales tightly wrapped in straw matting, each weighing from 133 to 220 pounds. Baggage and express cars which carried it were kept as nearly moisture- and dust-proof as possible. No steam was allowed to pass through the coils of such cars, but for the crew's use a standard coach (with heaters) was coupled onto the end of the train. The Southern Pacific and CP were the only roads to use cars especially designed for the silk trade. An unusual feature of SP silk trains is that many included heavy shipments of tea.

Like the CP, the Union Pacific (UP) and SP jointly had their own mercantile line, the Occidental & Oriental Steamship Co., founded in 1876. It operated nine transpacific ships. All carried a good deal of silk in addition to tea, rice, sugar, and other commodities (even opium), much of which moved eastward from San Francisco by rail. Other cargoes for shipment by rail were landed at Vancouver, Tacoma, Seattle, and Portland.

In modern times the diesel-powered *Canadian,* queen of the CP's transcontinental rails, averaged 41 miles per hour from coast to coast. Any steam engineer who couldn't have beaten that time with a silk special would have been demoted to yard service. Jack Davidson at the throttle of a D-10 coalburner in the rugged days before oilburners and mechanical stokers wheeled the silk for 110 miles in 77 minutes.

The average Canadian Pacific silk train had 10 or 12 cars, occasionally 15, made up and standing on the Vancouver docks hours before an *Empress* liner was due. All of the train was loaded at the same time, 470 bales to the car, each car being filled and sealed in less than 8 minutes. Some trains were routed from Vancouver to Prescott, Ontario, and ferried over the St. Lawrence River to Ogdensburg, New York, to complete their long run on New York Central rails.

Canadian National (CN) operated more than 100 silk specials between 1925 and 1932 from Vancouver to New York via Toronto and Buffalo in conjunction with the New York Central. As a rule, CN change of motive power at divisional points took only about 2 minutes. Railway police were alerted all along the line, and at every stop armed guards patrolled the right-of-way. From Seattle to Chicago the UP's 60-hour silk schedule improved by 12 hours the fastest passenger run between those two points. The trip to New York via the Pennsy, the New York Central, or the Baltimore & Ohio took 15 more hours.

Beginning in January 1929, silk movement on Western roads became even faster. One $1,440,000 trainload of raw silk was highballed from San Francisco to

Chicago, 2259 miles, via SP, UP, and Chicago & North Western in the almost incredible time of 49 hours. There were green lights all the way. This record beat the UP's *Overland Limited*'s time by 9 hours.

The Great Northern scheduled 307 silk runs between 1925 and 1932, its peak period for that commodity, but made other runs, as early as 1922 and as late as November 25, 1933. On September 27, 1923, GN set a global record for long-distance travel, with mammoth oilburning loco No. 2517 hauling $5 million worth of silk from Seattle to St. Paul in 52 hours and 35 minutes—5 hours faster than the schedule of the *Oriental Limited.* Then, instead of putting the 2517 to bed in a roundhouse, General Manager C. O. Jenks sent her right back to Seattle coupled onto another GN train, the *White Flyer,* at that time the nations's fastest long-distance mail train, for another great performance.

This was a continuous run of 3700 miles with no stop except the St. Paul turnaround to take on engine crews, fuel oil, and water. Ordinarily, engines were changed 13 times between the two cities, which are about 1850 miles apart. The feat included a total of 24 changes of engine crews on the round trip, but with nearly all the men riding the train and taking their turns so as not to delay it.

Silk trains had relatively few mishaps. The only major wreck occurred on the CP between Haig and Yale, British Columbia, when the fifth car jumped the track while rounding a curve and fell into the Fraser River; three or four other cars followed but stopped short of the river. One broke on the water's edge. Bales of the precious silk, both raw and manufactured, went floating downstream. After much delay, the other cars were rerailed, and the train proceeded The final fast silk train in North America was operated in September 1941. The colorful era was ended by the introduction of silk substitutes such as nylon and rayon, the all-water route through the Panama Canal, the effects of the Depression of the 1930s, and the wage demands of the engine and train crews.

BIBLIOGRAPHY: *Railroad Magazine,* April 1965.

Silver Creek Wreck Just 10 miles west of Angola, New York, and 90 miles east of Ashtabula, Ohio, scenes of two of America's most frightful train wrecks, an eastbound excursion train heading from Erie, Pennsylvania, to Niagara Falls plowed head-on into a westbound local freight on a single-track line near the village of Silver Creek on September 14, 1886, killing 19 persons and seriously injuring 14 others. Pilot against pilot the locomotives struck and were battered into steel junk. Flues of one boiler jammed into flues of the other. This is said to have been the most disastrous wreck in the history of the Nickel Plate Road (New York, Chicago & St. Louis).

In keeping with practices of the time, the excursion train was made up of unevenly matched cars, the baggage-car coupler being higher than that of the smoker just behind. For that reason, the sudden impact lifted the baggage car and drove it backward into the smoker mowing down the seats and crushing their occupants. Lewis Brewer, the engineer, disappeared after the wreck. He wrote that he'd had orders to pass the freight at Silver Creek, but as that village had no sidetrack and as he had never before been instructed to meet a train there, he proceeded "cautiously" at 8 miles per hour, "which was all that any man could do."

BIBLIOGRAPHY: Wesley S. Griswold, *Train Wreck!* Stephen Greene, Brattleboro, Vt., 1969; Robert C. Reed, *Train Wrecks,* Superior Publishing, Seattle, 1968; Robert B. Shaw, *A History of Railroad Accidents, Safety Precautions, and Operating Procedures,* Northern Press, Potsdam, N.Y., 1978.

Single-Tracking Removing one set of rails on a stretch of mainline where two tracks have run before. This has been done on many North American railroads to save money on operations, taxes, etc. It is practicable in modern railroading, especially when switches, and thus trains, are controlled electronically from a central location. This control enables about the same amount of traffic to move over a single track that previously needed twin or multiple tracks, and much material is saved for reuse.

Skagit River Railway One of America's few city-owned railways, aside from subway and elevated systems, the others including the Cincinnati Southern and the City of Prineville Railway. The municipality of Seattle, Washington, owns this 31-mile mountain line through the Seattle Municipal Light and Power System. The line runs alongside the Skagit River, mostly through Mount Baker National Forest, from Rockport, Washington, where it connects with the Burlington Northern, to Diablo in the towering Cascades. In summertime, with open observation cars, it offers picnickers a package deal consisting of the 62-mile round trip and overnight accommodations in a Diablo hotel, the only place on the line where smoking is permitted because of the danger of forest fires. Built in 1918 to haul supplies from Rockport to the large dams and powerhouse at Diablo, the line passes through such superb scenery that it soon also became an excursion route. Part of the line is electrified.

Slack Give in couplers and draft gears. Too much or too little slack in freight trains can be dangerous. Slack allows cars to be coupled at low speeds without transmitting damaging forces to interior lading. It also permits long freight trains to be started. A 100-car freight, for example, may have over 100 feet of slack, the equivalent of two car lengths. Railmen know that slack running out, or stretching, can separate a train. Running in, or bunching up, can damage cars and contents and even cause derailments.

Preventing slack's damaging effects isn't simply a

matter of keeping your train stretched out. In hilly terrain you have to avoid both run-in and run-out at the same time. Various parts of the train may be going uphill and downhill concurrently, which creates both draw (pulling) and buff (compression) forces. If either force becomes excessive, there is likely to be trouble.

Now, with the aid of a Freight Master Train Dynamics Analyzer, such as the one on the Family Lines railroads, enginemen can sit before a stationary diesel locomotive control board, notch out the throttle, and see the drawbar forces being applied at every point of their train. They can see not only which parts of the train are traveling on grades but also exactly what effects those grades can have on their operation. And if they make mistakes, they can freeze time, analyze what they did wrong, and walk away without having to worry about damaged equipment. What they are running in this case, of course, is not an actual train but a computer simulation. The analyzer's computer is programmed so that for every throttle and brake action taken at the full-size control stand, the train represented on the screen reacts just as a real one would on the identical line.

Sleeping Cars The history of sleeping cars began in 1829, years before any railroad was long enough for overnight travel, when railroad surveyor R. F. Morgan of Stockbridge, Massachusetts, displayed the first-known design for such a car in Faneuil Hall, Boston, under the auspices of the new, locally organized Rail Road Association. Morgan's Rail Road Carriage was a double-decker so bulky that *The Boston Traveler* called it a "land barge." The lower level had five berths. An awning covered the upper deck, which had benches, a rear cupola topped by an American flag, and, in Morgan's words, a "captain's office." There is no record of this car having been built or even patented.

In 1836 the first sleeping car, possibly built from a plan patented that year by Charles McGraw, was put into service on the Cumberland Valley Railroad (later part of the Pennsylvania) between Baltimore and Philadelphia. *The Baltimore Chronicle* stated euphemistically that you could "go to rest in a pleasant berth, sleep as soundly as in your own bed at home, and on awakening next morning find yourself at the end of your journey." Actually, the bunks were crude and uncomfortable, with no pillows or bedding. Passengers usually slept in them without even taking off their boots or shoes. The car was discontinued in 1848.

Meanwhile, in 1843, the Erie tried out two sleepers, named *Erie* and *Ontario,* built in England by John Stephenson after models made by Thomas Brown. They were called diamond cars because their frames were constructed with diamond-shaped windows. Instead of bedding and pillows they had loose cushions covered with black haircloth, which only thick clothing could resist. Each car was 11 feet wide, with six seats on each side placed back to back. After a short time these cars were discontinued as too heavy for the light rails of their day, and they served as dormitories for trackmen.

As early as 1850 the Baltimore & Ohio began operating sleepers built with three tiers of bunks, into which travelers were sandwiched at night. As this road had sharp curves, it was not unusual for someone to fall from the top tier into the aisle, awaking his or her neighbors with groans or curses.

The three outstanding pioneers in the development of sleeping and parlor cars were Webster Wagner, Theodore T. Woodruff, and George M. Pullman. In 1870, when the Pullman Co. sued the Wagner Sleeping Car Co. on charges of infringement of patents, evidence showed that the Erie's diamond cars of 1843 had so much in common with Pullman and Wagner sleepers that both litigants agreed to drop the suit rather than have the court determine the extent of their rights.

While Wagner was getting under way, G. B. Gates, general manager of the Lake Shore & Michigan Southern (LS&MS), began building sleepers for that road. In 1869, however, the New York Central took over the LS&MS, and Wagner's company, a protégé of the Central, absorbed the Gates Sleeping Car Co. Still another builder was the Flower Sleeping Car Co., founded in Maine in 1882. Its cars had berths in the middle, with aisles to the right and left, an extravagant waste of space. But they had the advantage of a much freer circulation of air than in the other cars, and any two berths side by side could be made into a double bed if desired.

There was also the Mann Boudoir Car Co., incorporated in 1883 by Col. William D'Alton Mann, a New York celebrity of the gaslight era, designer and builder of elite railroad cars, and purveyor of gossip and scandal through his spicy magazine, *Town Topics.* The Mann cars were divided into compartments (Mann called them boudoirs). Each contained four seats that could be made into beds at night. At first they were built only for the European trade, but later for American lines also. Mann's cars were made in Belgium by the Société Anonyme des Wagons-Lits, a European rival of the Pullman Co. In 1883 his cars went into service between Boston and New York. Long before that year, Pullman cars were running on half a dozen British roads.

Mann cars were quite elegant but had a smaller passenger capacity than other sleepers, so the cost of riding in them was higher. The colonel really introduced sleepers to Europe and organized the Compagnie Internationale des Wagons-Lits to supply the demand for them.

In 1899 the Woodruff and Mann companies merged into the Union Palace Car Co., which the Pullman interests later absorbed, leaving only the Monarch Sleeping Car Co., which served part of New England and one road in Ohio, plus Wagner's Drawing Room Car Co., which had a monopoly on the Vanderbilt lines. Pullman Co. took over these last two competitors after both Pullman and Wagner had died.

In the 1940s the Pennsy and New York Central introduced overnight "budget" sleeper-coach trains between New York and Chicago, with reclining seats that let travelers lie back and sleep, fully clothed except for shoes. Car lights were dimmed; no trainman checked up on tickets during the night. As rail travel continued to decline, conventional sleeping cars dwindled in number and lost their elegance. In 1971, when Amtrak took over nearly all of America's intercity passenger service, they dropped still further, and sharply. The Brotherhood of Sleeping Car Porters went out of existence in 1978. During World War II, discarded Pullman cars were converted to sleepers for troop and hospital trains, many being given three-tier berths as on circus trains.

See also BROTHERHOOD OF SLEEPING CAR PORTERS AND REDCAPS; PULLMAN, GEORGE MORTIMER; WAGNER, WEBSTER; WOODRUFF, THEODORE T.

BIBLIOGRAPHY: Lucius Beebe, *Mansions on Rails,* Howell-North, Berkeley, Calif., 1959; August Mencken, *The Railroad Passenger Car: An Illustrated History of the First Hundred Years,* Johns Hopkins, Baltimore, 1957; Roy V. Wright, (ed.), *Car Builders' Cyclopedia of American Practice,* 15th ed., Simmons-Boardman, Chicago, 1940; reprinted, Kalmbach, Milwaukee, 1973.

Slip Switch (Slip-Switch Crossing) Arrangement installed in yards wherever one track crosses another and trains go from the first track to the second within close limits. It is like an ordinary crossing with the addition of one or two curved tracks. Normally, one track is always open. The other track, usually the diagonal, is not.

Smokestack Oddities A patented smoke consumer and spark arrester was incorporated into the 4-4-0 locomotive *Anson S. Marshall,* built in 1873 in the Concord, New Hampshire, shops of the Concord Railroad under the direction of the road's master mechanic, F. M. Stevens. Smoke was blown out of a large opening, only to go forward into a big separator. The sparks fell through a slender throat into the front end of the firebox, while the smoke escaped through screened slits.

Another New England road, the Boston & Lowell (B&L), made two unique experiments with spark arresters. Its *Eagle,* built by Rhode Island Works in 1870, had a smokestack resembling a large French horn, bent backward and then up and widened at the top. A spark arrester returned live sparks to the firebox through a pipe.

The B&L, which took over the Salem & Lowell in 1877, rebuilt into a 4-4-0 type a 4-6-0 that the Boston Locomotive Works (later Hinkley Locomotive Works) had constructed for the B&L in 1850. The rebuilding included an odd arrangement that looked like a normal smokestack but had on top a huge flat pan, with two pipes leading from it to another flat container on the cab roof. This device suggested a gigantic corn popper set on the smokestack with its handle connected to the cab roof. Whether or not the stack was open at the top is unknown, but evidently the sparks were passed through pipes to the top of the cab.

BIBLIOGRAPHY: Henry B. Comstock, *The Iron Horse,* Crowell, New York, 1971; *Railroad Magazine,* March 1937, February 1945; Angus Sinclair, *Development of the Locomotive Engine,* annotated ed. by John H. White, Jr., M.I.T., Cambridge, Mass., 1970; *Trains Magazine,* August 1956.

Snow Fighting A new Severe Storm Standby Plan, designed to keep winter freight traffic moving by rail, went into effect in December 1979 under the auspices of the Car Service Division (CSD) of the Association of American Railroads (AAR). It grew out of the previous

The Central Pacific needed eight woodburning engines to push this wedge plow through heavy snowdrifts in Nevada in 1874. [Southern Pacific Railroad]

winter's cooperative effort involving the AAR and the Interstate Commerce Commission (ICC). It aims to avoid critical buildups of cars stalled by heavy storms such as those in the Midwest during the winter of 1978–1979.

The new program, based on suggestions made by carriers and shippers, puts greater emphasis on operational aspects. On weekday mornings from mid-December through mid-March, CSD offices in Newark, Chicago, Minneapolis, St. Louis, and Washington poll 27 railroads operating in the Northern states, except on days when weather conditions obviously would not affect a railroad's operation. They seek information on terminal problems, embargoes contemplated, lines closed, reroute orders anticipated, and predicted recovery. Each district office telexes these data to AAR headquarters in Washington by noon so that a summary report can be sent to all major railroads and to the ICC by 2 p.m. each weekday.

In emergencies, the new plan gives special attention to freight cars without waybills. Central offices locate their intended destinations so that the cars can be transported without wasting time on a yard's "hold" track. Also, all roads are asked to give AAR a daily list of their freight cars and, conversely, waybills without cars, so that AAR matchmaking can let the cars be run with memo bills.

In the old days it was routine during a blizzard to classify all rail freight as perishable or nonperishable and to push the nonperishables, the great bulk of the traffic, onto the nearest sidings, perhaps to be snowed under and lie there for a week or a month, depending upon the weather. Every effort was concentrated on passenger trains, perishable freight, and snowplows. Prior to the rotary plow, railroaders used the push plow, or wedge plow, which simply replaced the locomotive pilot. There was also the wing plow, tall and graceful, that tossed up snow like a ship's prow throwing aside the water.

On January 9 and 10, 1890, in the Sierra snow belt, the white stuff fell continuously for 48 hours, at times at the rate of 5 inches an hour. Snowslides carrying rocks, trees, and earth were common. In canyons the snow piled up from 60 to 70 feet deep. Then, on January 12, a sudden warm spell dumped 5 inches of snow onto an average depth of 12 feet of snow, after which an abrupt freeze converted the entire landscape into a great ice field. Snowplows were useless. Only picks and shovels could even partially clear the rails. One broken rail ditched five locomotives and a wedge plow. Elsewhere, a plow engine and two others plunged down a 50-foot embankment. That year the Central (Southern) Pacific's whole San Francisco–Portland line was closed by ice and snow from January 20 to March 24. *It was the longest such blockade on record in the United States.*

Sometimes in the old Dakota Territory frozen cascades 20 to 30 feet high covered the Great Northern

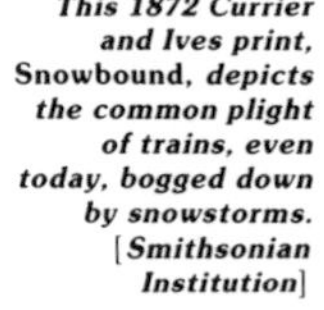

This 1872 Currier and Ives print, **Snowbound*****, depicts the common plight of trains, even today, bogged down by snowstorms. [Smithsonian Institution]***

track. Explosives had to be used to clear it. Preventive measures there and elsewhere in the West and Northwest included the installation of snow fences, heaters, and snowsheds. Snowsheds were used mostly in the Sierra Nevada, where, for example, 13 miles of them protected the SP roadbed, but over the years they were gradually eliminated, partly because they were fire hazards.

Canadian Pacific's famous Connaught Tunnel, bored 5 miles under the mountains, replaced many old-fashioned snowsheds. The earliest snowsheds had peaked roofs and vertical sides. Later ones were given heavy flat roofs and sides slanting outward at the top, with a ceiling wider than the inside floor. This construction kept in balance the accumulated snow on top without a wedging effect against the sides.

Snowsheds, originally continuous for miles, were eventually reduced to 2000 feet in length and located 50 feet apart to prevent the spread of fire in summer and early fall. In late autumn the intervals were closed by telescopic sections that moved on rails into and out of the various sheds. At some places in the Sierras, snowsheds often were buried under 150 to 200 feet of snow. Gangs of carpenters had to be sent out to prevent them from collapsing, while other forces busily shoveled off the snow.

At that time, rotary plows had been newly invented and were still rather primitive. The Central Pacific then had only one rotary, but it worked wonders. At Cascade that plow threw snow a distance of 150 feet from the track until it had worked itself into the drift to a depth of 40 feet, where it could no longer lift the snow out. A rotary that the Central Pacific borrowed from the Union Pacific did as much work in 6 hours, one official boasted, as 500 men could have done in a week.

The spreader is a device to widen the snow from the track after a plow has been through. Another device, the flanger, drops down and rides the rail tops on shoes, thereby gouging out the flange of the rails.

The Terminal Railroad Association of St. Louis adopted kerosine pans that burned for 6 hours, without refilling, to keep snow melted in the yards. A track superintendent invented this device. On the association track 4000 of these heaters were ignited before every expected blizzard. During that time, even in the coldest weather, not a single switch froze.

Natural gas and steam also have been used effectively for that purpose. So have electric heaters set in the ballast between ties. One such heater consists of a rod-shaped element, which may be cut to any desired length, clasped firmly to the rail. Snowblowers use a blast, sometimes from surplus military jet engines, to melt and blow away snow and ice from the track. Generally, they are operated in yards to clean switches but not for mainline service because of signal lines and ballast. The machine is ordinarily handled by a two-person crew, consisting of an operator and a ground person familiar with the location where it is used. It directs the heat and blast from the jet engine via a movable, hydraulically powered nozzle that tapers down to a flared opening about the width of a track gauge. The hot air clears snow from the cribs in turnouts, from under switch rods and connecting rods, and from frogs and guardrails. The snow is blasted away in less than a minute, leaving a fully clean switch mechanism.

Central Pacific rotary plow on the Cascade Bridge in 1890. It threw snow 150 feet from the track. [*Southern Pacific Railroad*]

The New York Central reputedly used the first snowblowers. Early models attached to a flatcar were moved around the yards by locomotives. Maintenance personnel found that by reducing fuel pressure to get a smaller blast, the machine could be mounted on a self-propelled unit. Railway Maintenance Corp. makes such blowers at Pittsburgh.

BIBLIOGRAPHY: Gerald M. Best, *Snowplow,* Howell-North, Berkeley, Calif., 1966; Roberty S. Henry, *This Fascinating Railroad Business,* 3d ed., rev., Bobbs-Merrill, Indianapolis, 1946.

SOO

Soo Line Rail line headquartered in Minneapolis, Minnesota, and named for the pronunciation of "Sault" in Sault Ste. Marie, Minnesota, terminus of its main predecessor, the Minneapolis, St. Paul & Sault Ste. Marie. It is a merger (in 1961) of that road, completed in 1888, with the Wisconsin Central (1871) and the Duluth, South Shore & Atlantic (1886). Its oldest antecedent, the Iron Mountain Railroad, dates back to 1855.

Founded primarily as a Minnesota grain hauler, the Soo is now controlled by the Canadian Pacific and operates 4589 miles of line in seven states of the United States. It handles about 10 billion ton-miles of freight a year, mostly farm products and supplies, manufactured goods, fuels, raw materials, and forest and mine products. In 1978 it had 4500 employees, 15 classification yards, 2 major shops, 226 locomotives, and 12,000 freight cars but no longer any passenger service.

According to an industrywide audit of energy use conducted by the Association of American Railroads in 1978, the Soo Line moved 65 percent more freight per gallon of fuel oil than the industry average and was the "best typical railroad" and overall "fuel-economy champion" of the Class I roads it surveyed. Among the many factors in Soo's fuel performance are maximizing horsepower-to-tonnage ratios, speed, shutting down engines when they are not needed, fuel-economy improvements by locomotive builders, careful handling of fuel to avoid waste from spills, scheduling work assignments to optimize locomotive use, and achieving a better ratio of net ton-miles to gross ton-miles. (Net ton-miles per gallon of fuel reflects the amount of fuel used to move the contents of freight cars only. Gross ton-miles per gallon reflects the amount of fuel used to move the contents of freight cars as well as the weight of the cars themselves, the locomotives, and the caboose.)

BIBLIOGRAPHY: John A. Gjevre, *A Saga of the Soo*, Molzahn Press, La Crosse, Wis., 1973; Leslie V. Suprey, *Steam Trains of the Soo*, 2d rev. ed., B&W Printers and Publishers, Mora, Minn., 1962.

South Carolina Railroad Line built in 1830, largely by slave labor hired from trackside plantations. It had a gross income of $1.5 million in 1860, before Fort Sumter was fired on. The first three Civil War years were years of illusive prosperity. Receipts for 1864 reached the unprecedented total of over $6 million, with 16 percent dividends paid to stockholders but in Confederate money. Nobody got permanently rich from it; the company itself didn't.

So thoroughly was the railroad destroyed on General Sherman's march to the sea that on June 19, 1865, when company officials again took control, the rolling stock was reduced to 4 locomotives, 5 passenger and baggage cars, and 36 freight cars, all needing repairs. The itemized list of losses included: "Negroes, 111, emancipated, $190,973." Cost of slaves ranged from $400 for a man named Jack to $907.12 for Hard-Times Gadsden. The list does not explain the 12 cents.

Directors of the South Carolina Railroad, at their president's suggestion, went on record in favor of "running freight trains with black engineers, under the management and control of white conductors . . . as soon as practicable." It is the only mention the author has seen of a Southern railroad's authorizing the use of black engineers, although there were many black firemen, including Casey Jones's. Even so, there is no evidence that the line actually employed Negroes in that capacity.

BIBLIOGRAPHY: Samuel M. Derrick, *Centennial History of the South Carolina Railroad,* Columbia, S.C., 1930.

Southern Pacific Lines (SP) Rail system that echoes the title of a cowboy song, "There's a Lot of Texas in Me." Its chronicle starts in the Lone Star State in 1851 with its oldest link, the Buffalo Bayou, Brazos & Colorado, laying wrought-iron rails 80 miles westward from what is now Houston to Alleyton. Next year the New Orleans, Opelousas & Great Western began building westward from New Orleans to the present Morgan City, Louisiana. During part of the Civil War, Union troops operated one end of this line and Confederates the other end. Reorganized after the war as the Louisiana & Texas, it joined the Buffalo Bayou road and eventually the Southern Pacific. In 1932 SP acquired its major subsidiary, the 1441-mile St. Louis Southwestern Railway, which reaches down into Texas and Louisiana through Illinois, Missouri, Tennessee, and Arkansas. Another segment is the 500-mile Texas & New Orleans, which the gigantic system absorbed in 1961 after having controlled and operated it for years. *See also* ST. LOUIS SOUTHWESTERN RAILWAY.

There's also a lot of California in the SP: a vast mileage network as well as headquarters in San Francisco. Its oldest Western component, the 23-mile Sacramento Valley Railroad (SV), was the West's first steam railroad. Theodore D. Judah built the SV line in 1855–1856 and later searched for and found a suitable eastward route over the Sierra Nevada range for the first transcontinental railroad. *See* JUDAH, THEODORE D.

At the end of 1978 the Southern Pacific had 13,290 miles of main track, 6611 of those miles welded rail, plus 6641 miles of yard and siding steel, and owned or leased 2422 diesel locos and 84,580 freight cars. Its circular trademark has been emblazoned on countless thousands of freight cars and tons of stationery, timetables, posters, calendars, advertisements, etc. With the words *Southern Pacific Lines,* it pictures a stretch of track pointed into the setting sun to symbolize the West and the Sunset Route of its former deluxe passenger train *Sunset Limited,* which Amtrak has been operating between New Orleans and Los Angeles since 1971.

Maps show the SP rail network as roughly semicircular, dipping down from northwest Oregon to swing around a very wide arc up into Illinois. It serves 12 states in the West and Southwest, including the Pacific and Gulf Coasts, totaling 1,200,000 square miles with a population of over 66 million. Known as the Golden Empire, this vast area supplies America with the lion's share of such commodities as copper, cotton, rice, oil, natural gas, etc., and a large percentage of the nation's farm crops, forest products, and manufactured goods. As for international trade, particularly with Pacific Basin countries and Mexico, SP serves 35 points of entry, more than any other United States railroad. The Golden Empire's economic wealth and growth reward SP's transportation system with a diverse traffic mix.

But Southern Pacific Transportation Company is much more than people operating flanged wheels over steel rails. Since 1969 it has been a holding company which now has assets of almost $5 billion. Its integrated transportation includes the railroad itself, which is the country's second largest (Burlington Northern tops the list) in terms of assets and freight revenue, as well as trucking operations, pipelines for both refined petroleum products and coal slurry, and an expanding intermodal service. Since 1969 Southern Pacific Marine Transport has been handling cargo between the United States and foreign ports in chartered shipping space. A subsidiary, Southern Pacific International, offers total transportation between inland locations anywhere in the United States and ports around the world. All this effectively combines rail, truck, and marine transport with highway trailers and piggyback. *See* PIGGYBACKING.

The conglomerate deals too in land development and management, leasing computer and consulting services, and a far-flung communications network. In 1979 Ticor, a leading financial-services holding company with nationwide operations in title insurance, private mortgage insurance, etc., joined SP's family of subsidiaries. SP's 1978 operating revenues set a record $2,280 million; its net income was $116,200,000. The company's 1979 capital investment program of $550,000,000 almost doubled that of any previous year. About $406,000,000 of this sum was spent on the railroad for purchasing new cars and locomotives, rebuilding older equipment, improving track, roadbed, signals, etc.

California's dynamic Big Four—Collis P. Huntington, Charles Crocker, Leland Stanford, and Mark Hopkins—were Sacramento merchants who, with considerable help, materialized Judah's dream of a transcontinental line. With the approval of Congress and President Lincoln, they formed the Central (later Southern) Pacific Railroad Company (CP), broke ground on January 8, 1862, at Sacramento, and started laying track eastward over the forbidding Sierra Nevada and across deserts to meet the Union Pacific's westward thrust at Promontory, Utah, in 1869. *See* GOLDEN SPIKE CEREMONY; UNION PACIFIC RAILROAD.

Chinese laborers did most of the hard physical toil of building the CP and were paid $30 to $40 a month in gold, the same as their Caucasian co-workers, except that an American or Chinese agent subtracted their food and supply costs monthly. (The white men were given free food and board.) Many of the Chinese used by Crocker had already been lured to California, as had many other men, by the gold rush of 1849 and were still living in the Far West. *See also* CHINESE LABOR.

The Big Four parlayed their risks, skill, and energy into huge personal fortunes. But unlike such speculators as Jay Gould, Jim Fisk, and Daniel Drew, who drove many early railroads to ruin, they kept building both the SP and the West, pushing not only eastward but also up into Oregon and down into Mexico. With wide empty spaces on the new rail maps, there was urgent need for additional settlers, crops, towns, and products to provide traffic. So SP and its Central Pacific predecessor, like other pioneer Western rail systems, advertised widely and set up promotional campaigns to bring more people, particularly farmers and artisans, into their territory.

Lured by promises, settlers crowded into slow, uncomfortable emigrant trains of wooden cars with their families, livestock, and farm equipment and inhaled the soot-filled air blown back from steam engines rolling westward. Special low fares for "land seekers' tickets" could be applied against the purchase of railway land at bargain prices of $1 to $10 an acre, payable in installments. Colonists traveling and settling together got group rates. Homesteaders endured endless hardships, but SP agricultural advisers helped the farmers to develop new crops and irrigating methods, and somehow most of them muddled through. *See* ZULU CARS.

In time, ice-cooled wooden refrigerator cars put their fruits and vegetables into distant markets. Exhibit trains, one called *California on Wheels,* promoted Western products and opportunities. SP lantern-slide lecturers went as far as Europe to extol the sunshine, oranges, and scenic wonders of prairies, tall redwood forests, and deep canyons. People came to settle or just to see. *See* REFRIGERATOR CARS.

Like the officials of the Canadian Pacific and Great Northern, the Big Four went into the Pacific steamship business to develop Oriental trade but gave it up years later. In 1879 the SP tried out oil fuel for some steam locomotives and after 1900 adopted it for general motive-power use. In 1882 the rail line was completed from Los Angeles to Tucson, Arizona. Next year the first train reached El Paso. Then SP connected with the Santa Fe at Deming, New Mexico, thus forming a second transcontinental rail route, and ran the first through train from New Orleans to Houston. Another last spike was driven near the Pecos River in Texas in 1883, linking Los Angeles with New Orleans on the southern transcontinental route.

In 1884 the Southern Pacific Company was incorporated in Kentucky, bringing numerous pioneer rail lines under its aegis and leasing the Central Pacific in 1885. Two years later it acquired and completed the California & Oregon Railroad, but it engaged with the Santa Fe in a costly and short-lived rate war which cut to $1 the colonist fare from the Missouri River to the West

A steam locomotive moves along a dirt highway without rails, under its own power, assisted by men and horses, en route to a Southern Pacific relocation job near Auburn, California, in 1911. [Gilbert H. Kneiss]

Coast. In 1898 SP bought the Sonora Railway in Guaymas, Mexico. In 1900 it founded the Southern Pacific Railroad Co. of Mexico and extended the line down Mexico's west coast to Guadalajara, by 1927 completing 117 miles, which it sold to the Mexican government's nationalized system in 1951.

In 1901 Edward H. Harriman, by gaining control of 45 percent of SP stock, became chairman and president of SP. In 1904 he made the original Golden Spike mainline route around Great Salt Lake a mere branch line by opening Lucin Cutoff across the lake. In 1942 Promontory was taken off the railroad map altogether as the last rails of that branch became scrap metal for wartime use. *See* HARRIMAN, EDWARD HENRY; LUCIN CUTOFF.

In 1905 disastrous Colorado River floods almost washed California's fertile and prosperous Imperial Valley out of existence, but Harriman's energetic management restored it. Fighting to rechannel the turbulent river, SP moved its rails many times as the Salton Sink literally became an inland sea.

In 1906 San Francisco's earthquake and fire destroyed SP's general offices and other railroad property. The company rushed medical personnel and supplies to the stricken city and evacuated 224,000 homeless refugees. In that year, too, SP and Union Pacific jointly incorporated Pacific Fruit Express. In 1907, with the SP and Santa Fe as joint owners, the Northwestern Pacific Railroad was formed from 41 small predecessor companies. SP bought its complete ownership in 1929.

San Francisco's Panama-Pacific International Exposition of 1915 boosted SP passenger traffic by 65 percent. The road's first diesel-powered train, the streamlined *City of San Francisco,* went into service in 1936 between Chicago and San Francisco. In 1952 high-Sierra blizzards marooned it for 3 days near the point where 106 years before, the 79-member Donner emigrant party had been stranded for the winter and 36 of them perished. But in 1952 all *City of San Francisco* passengers and crew were rescued.

Meanwhile, SP had introduced additional gleaming streamliners on various routes, some in conjunction with other roads: the *Coast Daylight, Sunset Limited, Californian, '49er, Golden State, Shasta Daylight, Starlight,* and *Challenger.* Their glory vanished in 1971 when Amtrak took over most of the nation's intercity rail passenger services. *See* AMTRAK; SUNSET LIMITED.

In 1910 SP began using the first of its many cab-ahead Mallets, built in its Sacramento shops. Over a 63-year period those shops turned out more than 200 new steam locomotives, completing the final one in 1937. The last new SP steam locos went into service in 1944, the road's peak year of wartime freight and passenger traffic. In 1950 its first mainline diesel locos began hauling freight. *See* MALLET.

In 1939 the road's first radio installation began functioning in the Sierra range to fill in for wire-line emergencies. In 1951 SP started piggyback service and began using welded ribbon rail. In 1955, aided by a research institute, it developed the Hydra-Cushion freight car for improved protection of shipments. Many other roads also use it now. In 1960 SP's new bi- and tri-level freight cars began hauling automobiles.

In 1965 Pacific Electric Railway, radiating out of Los Angeles, was merged into the parent company. Two years later, completion of the 78-mile Palmdale-Colton Cutoff, the largest new rail line built in the United States in 25 years, permitted SP trains to bypass congested New Orleans. In 1968 the first units of the $22 million Total Operations Processing System (TOPS) were placed in SP service. A great computer system, TOPS

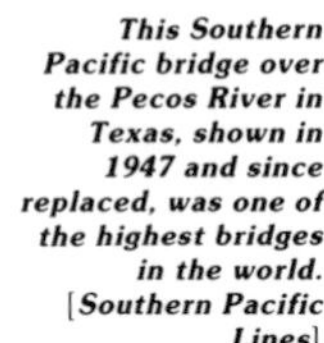

This Southern Pacific bridge over the Pecos River in Texas, shown in 1947 and since replaced, was one of the highest bridges in the world. [Southern Pacific Lines]

performs more than 400 functions. Among them is providing up-to-the-minute data on any one of the many freight cars on SP tracks.

In 1980 the Interstate Commerce Commission authorized SP to buy for $57 million the Rock Island's 965-mile line extending from Santa Rosa, New Mexico, to St. Louis via Kansas City.

BIBLIOGRAPHY: Lucius Beebe, *The Central Pacific and the Southern Pacific Railroads,* Howell-North, Berkeley, Calif., 1963; Donald Duke, *Southern Pacific Steam Locomotives,* Golden West Books, San Marino, Calif., 1962; *Jane's World Railways and Rapid Transit Systems,* F. Watts, New York, 1977; Oscar Lewis, *The Big Four: The Story of Huntington, Stanford, Hopkins, and Crocker,* Knopf, New York, 1938; Neill C. Wilson and Frank J. Taylor, *Southern Pacific: The Roaring Story of a Fighting Railroad,* McGraw-Hill, New York, 1952.

Southern Railway System Network of what was once more than 125 roads. It operates 10,248 route miles and a total track length of 17,031 miles, its northern limits being St. Louis, Cincinnati, and Washington, D.C., its headquarters. Its tracks are mostly in Kentucky, Tennessee, Virginia, North Carolina, South Carolina, Alabama, and Georgia.

The system comprises 3 Class I roads—the Alabama Great Southern; Central of Georgia; and Cincinnati, New Orleans & Texas Pacific; 2 Class II roads—the Georgia Southern & Florida; and the Norfolk Southern; and 14 Class III roads—the Atlantic & East Carolina; Birmingham Terminal; Camp Lejeune; Chattanooga Station; Georgia Northern; Interstate; Live Oak, Perry & South Georgia; Louisiana Southern; New Orleans Terminal; St. James River Terminal; State University; Tennessee, Alabama & Georgia; and Tennessee; plus 36 other companies, including many railroads, all but 6 of which the Southern wholly controls.

The Southern was organized to take over and strengthen the faltering Richmond & Danville System (R&D), which included some of the earliest United States railroads and which, incidentally, gave birth to a folk song. *See* "WRECK OF THE OLD 97, THE."

The Southern was the last major railroad to paint the names of steam locomotive engineers on the sides of its cabs, a practice it dropped in the 1930s. Today, although otherwise fully dieselized, it is almost the only big system operating occasional steam excursions (Union Pacific and Chessie also do it).

Its earliest antecedent, the South Carolina Canal & Railroad (SCC&RR) Company, was chartered in 1827–1828 to save Charleston's seaport trade from its rival, Savannah, Georgia. The idea was to build a rail or water route between Charleston and some point upstream on the Savannah River to divert freight and passenger traffic to Charleston. The terminal point chosen was Hamburg, South Carolina, just across the river from Augusta, Georgia.

The line was built by Horatio Allen, a young engineer just back from an intensive study of English railways, who probably knew more about railroading than any other American of his time. The road's first locomotive, *Best Friend of Charleston,* was appropriately named, considering the goal of the new line. The engine was a four-wheeler, all wheels being drivers, with a vertical boiler and iron-hubbed, wooden-spoked wheels, and no cab. She weighed about 4½ tons. Built by West Point Foundry in New York, she was delivered to Charleston by ship and put to work hauling construction material in November 1830.

The SCC&RR was then about 7 miles long. On Christmas Day, 1830, the *Best Friend,* with Allen at the throttle, became America's first engine to pull a regularly scheduled train. She rolled over wooden crossties and iron-capped timbered rails, pulling four or five cars with maybe 40 passengers.

Within 3 years, the South Carolina line, with 136 miles, became the world's longest railway. Its other distinctions include being the first railroad to use lighting for night operation and the first to carry United States mail.

Another early predecessor of the Southern was the 12-mile Chesterfield Railroad, chartered in 1828. It ran downhill from coalpits near Midlothian, Virginia, not far from Richmond. Gravity sent the loaded coal cars down the iron-capped wooden rails. Each train carried two mules, which pulled the empties back upgrade to the mines. The profits made by this line encouraged the Richmond & Danville to build a steam-powered road almost parallel to it. Before the R&D was completed in

The South Carolina Canal & Railroad Co. built and used wind-powered rail passenger trains (like this model) in 1830 before acquiring steam power.

1856, the Chesterfield was abandoned and part of its line was sold to its competitor. Still another Southern antecedent was the Central Railroad & Canal Co., chartered in 1833.

By 1843 the SCC&RR linked Savannah to East Macon, Georgia, but it had to wait 8 years for permission to cross the Ocmulgee River into Macon because some Macon citizens regarded railroads as a threat to local drayage, hotel, and warehouse business. Meanwhile, it had joined with the Louisville, Cincinnati & Charleston Railroad and built a branch to the South Carolina capital, Columbia.

Prior to the Civil War many other Southern predecessors sprang up in Virginia, North Carolina, Tennessee, Mississippi, and Alabama, linking the principal cities of the South. By 1856 the Richmond & Danville was completed to Danville. But before that, a shipload of iron rails it had ordered from England sank in mid-ocean, a head-on collision badly damaged two of its engines, a warehouse fire damaged two others, and the road's new Richmond station collapsed.

Another carrier, the Memphis & Charleston (M&C) chartered in 1848, reached from the Atlantic Ocean at Charleston to the Mississippi River at Memphis in 1857. Ocean water was sprayed into the river to symbolize the new railroad link. At that time the 760-mile M&C was the world's longest system of connected rail lines.

The Civil War was the first war in which railroads had a leading strategic role. The South became a battlefield in which all forms of transportation suffered heavily. The first big battle, Bull Run, was fought over a railroad junction. Confederate reinforcements rushed to the scene by train brought a secessionist victory. But the loss of a key railroad, the Memphis & Charleston, after the Battle of Shiloh a few months later gave the South a blow from which its military effort never fully recovered. The M&C was part of the vital Richmond-Memphis trunk line of the Confederacy. *See* CIVIL WAR.

Central of Georgia and other rail lines were deliberately wrecked in General Sherman's march to the sea and from Savannah northward through the Carolinas. In early April 1865, as Federal troops converged on Richmond, President Jefferson Davis called on Col. Lewis Harvie, president of the R&D, to get the Confederate government to safety. The R&D was the only rail route out of the city then still in secessionists' hands, but no one knew for how long. Special trains left the panicky capital with people, records, much gold, and other property. Davis's train carried 200 picked men and horses for escape in case it was captured. For 18 hours, until that train rolled into Danville, it was the seat of the Confederate government.

After the war, getting the South's railroads back into their owners' hands was a long-drawn-out problem, in addition to which destruction had been enormous. But eventually the South had a strong rail system without the excess trackage that was later to plague roads of the Northeast and Midwest.

In 1893, a year of financial panic, nearly every railroad in the Richmond & Danville–Richmond Terminal Co. complex was in receivership. To remedy this condition the Southern Railway System was formed in 1894. The new corporation owned outright two-thirds of the 4400 or so miles of line it operated. The rest it held through leases, operating agreements, and stock ownership. The Southern also controlled such lines as the Alabama Great Southern and the Georgia Southern & Florida, which were separately operated, and had less than a controlling interest in other lines like the Central of Georgia.

Samuel Spencer, the new system's first president, did much to weld it together, enlarge it, and make it profitable. In its modernization program the Southern bought and operated the first diesel-electric freight hauler built in America: a four-unit General Motors product previously tested on other roads. It also streamlined and dieselized two fine new passenger trains, the *Southerner* and the *Tennessean.* The management's creation of electronic freight yards with closed-circuit television, computerization, instant radio communication radar speed meters, and other devices added enormously to the Southern's operating efficiency.

The Southern even began using energy from the sun. This phase advanced beyond the experimental stage with the line's first solar-power installation to operate crossing signals at Rex, Georgia. Additional solar-energy installations have been made on other lines, and still others are in the planning stage.

In 1973 Southern unveiled a revolutionary new freight car capable of carrying more automobiles than the largest one previously in use. Named *Autogard,* it is designed both to maintain the lowest possible unit cost of transporting automobiles and to solve the main loss and damage problems that have troubled auto manufacturers and railroads alike since the early 1950s, when development of the hi-level and tri-level rack cars enabled railroads to recover much business from the highways.

Autogard provides protection from the weather, vandalism, and theft. Its sides and roof are built of high-tensile-strength steel, and the ends consist of infolding sliding doors. During the loading and unloading, the doors fold easily against the car sides, allowing ready access to all levels of the car simultaneously. The car can carry 18 full-size automobiles.

The Southern and the Norfolk & Western in mid-1980 announced a preliminary agreement to merge into a single company by exchanging stock, subject to approval by both roads' boards of directors and stockholders and by the Interstate Commerce Commission. The proposed new system would have 17,500 miles of track and $5.7 billion in assets. The systems' combined 1979 earnings were nearly $100 million.

BIBLIOGRAPHY: Much of this article's material has been taken from Albert S. Eggerton, Jr., *The Bicentennial Story of the Southern Railway,* Southern Railway System, Washington. See also *Jane's World*

Railways and Rapid Transit Systems, F. Watts, New York, 1977; David P. Morgan, *Locomotive 4501,* Kalmbach, Milwaukee, 1968; Angus Sinclair, *Development of the Locomotive Engine,* annotated ed. by John H. White, Jr., M.I.T., Cambridge, Mass., 1970.

SP *See* SOUTHERN PACIFIC LINES.

Speed Records *See* DEATH VALLEY SCOTTY; JARRETT AND PALMER SPECIAL; SPEED WAR.

Speed War On June 8, 1905, when its fastest New York-Chicago run took 23 hours, the Pennsylvania Railroad advertised a new extra-fare train, the *Pennsylvania Limited,* that had cut the time to 18 hours. The highly competitive New York Central quickly reduced the time of its *20th Century Limited* between the same two cities from 20 to 18 hours, effective June 18. The Pennsy route was then 905 miles; the Central's 965. The new Pennsy train on its initial run with a steam engine and four cars averaged a mile in 69 seconds. Its top speed, near Ada, Ohio, was a record-breaking 3 miles in 85 seconds at 127.3 miles per hour.

Even before it cut the *Century*'s time, the Central set new speed records. An inspection trip with a locomotive and three business cars from Buffalo to Chicago on June 12 covered 526 miles in 470 minutes. If the run had been made at that speed all the way from New York to Chicago, it would have taken only 14 hours and 25 minutes. Next day a Central train of four Pullmans made the Chicago-Buffalo run in 443 minutes. *The New York Daily Tribune* asked editorially, "Is Chicago to become a suburb of New York?"

On the night of June 21, 1905, the *Century* on its fourth 18-hour schedule from Chicago ran into an open switch at Mentor, Ohio, killing 21 people and injuring many others. The wreck cost about $1 million including insurance claims; and the Central restored the running time to 20 hours but soon put it back to 18 when the Pennsy refused to follow suit.

In 1912 the Pennsy flier was renamed the *Broadway Limited,* not for the famed theatrical street but to honor the broad right-of-way over which it operated, generally four tracks, with six between New York and Philadelphia. Celebrities of stage, screen, and politics made the passenger lists of both flagship trains a virtual *Who's Who.* It was a glory era of rosebuds for lady passengers, afterdinner mints, whisk brooms wielded lavishly, hair singed by the barber on board, and gilt-braided conductors with silver watches and a regal air. But when intercity rail travel declined, many frills of the great trains were dropped.

Meanwhile, as one railroad cut or raised its travel time, the other usually did likewise. New York-Chicago schedules seesawed to 19½ hours, 18, 20, and 17 hours and 45 minutes. The fastest time was in the late 1940s, when a spanking new *Broadway* made the outbound trip in 16 hours and returned in 15½.

In 1967 the *Century* was discontinued. The *Broadway* was still running on May 1, 1971, when Amtrak took over the nation's intercity passenger service. In 1972 the film star Gloria Swanson christened a refurbished *Broadway Limited.* And on the train's 75th birthday in 1977 its passengers were given free cake and champagne.

BIBLIOGRAPHY: Lucius Beebe, *20th Century: "The Greatest Train in the World,"* Howell-North, Berkeley, Calif., 1962; Lucius Beebe and Charles Clegg, *The Trains We Road,* 2 vols., Howell-North, Berkeley, California, 1965-1966; Freeman Hubbard, *Great Trains of All Time,* Grosset & Dunlap, New York, 1962.

Spikes Various types of spikes were used on early railroads to fasten rails to crossties, but the hook-headed spike is now standard all over the world. Robert L. Stevens (1787-1850) designed this spike in 1831 when he was chief engineer of the Camden & Amboy, a predecessor of the Pennsylvania Railroad.

Driving five spikes into a railroad tie in 87 seconds and pulling them out in 11 seconds set a world record at the 1975 National Gandy Dancer Contest, according to the *Guinness Book of World Records.* It was done by Burlington Northern's entrant in that contest, Mike Bonacci, then 24, a machine operator in the track department.

New York Central's fast 20th Century Limited began running on June 15, 1902. It is shown here with engine No. 604, three Pullman sleepers, a dining car, and a buffet-library-smoking-barber-mail car. [New York Central Railroad]

Spring Switch Switch that can be thrown automatically by the wheels of a locomotive or car passing over the track, without manual assistance.

Stamps, Postage A 1-cent stamp showing a 4-4-0 type of engine then in use on the European & North American Railway was issued in 1869 by New Brunswick, Canada, which before the Confederation printed its own postage. The Confederation's fiftieth-anniversary 20-cent stamp has a train in its design. In 1928 Newfoundland issued a stamp picturing an express train.

Left: One of the few train stamps ever issued by the U.S. Postal Service, this 3-center from 1876 pictured a locomotive and a coach. Right: A 3-cent stamp issued in 1952 commemorated the 125th anniversary of the Baltimore & Ohio Railroad. It shows a modern diesel train as well as a horse-drawn railroad car racing the engine Tom Thumb.

The first United States railroad stamp, in 1869, was a blue 3-center depicting a 4-4-0. In 1876 two envelope stamps had a locomotive and a coach in the design. Then came the 8-center of 1898, with soldiers guarding a train, and in 1901 a two-color 2-center picturing the *Empire State Limited* speeding on a four-track system. In 1912–1913 came a pretty 5-cent parcel post stamp picturing a mail train about to take a mailbag from a trackside rack. Others in that series were the 3-center depicting part of a mail car and the 26-center with railroad cars. A popular stamp was the one issued on April 30, 1950, the fiftieth anniversary of Casey Jones's death, picturing Casey himself. And there have been others of railroad interest in both the United States and Canada.

Standard Time A railroad innovation, standard time was adopted on October 11, 1883, at a General Time Convention held in Chicago's Grand Pacific Hotel. Prior to that date, clocks and watches varied wildly across the continent. According to train schedules, 12:00 noon in Washington, D.C. was 12:34 in Boston, 12:12 in New York, 12:08 in Philadelphia and New Orleans, 12:02 in Baltimore, 11:58 in Richmond, 12:31 in Pittsburgh, 12:07 in Indianapolis, 11:50 in St. Louis, and 12:14 in Montreal, to mention only a few.

The *Chicago Tribune* listed 27 different local times in Michigan, 38 in Wisconsin, 27 in Illinois, and 23 in Indiana. No one knows how many different local times were authorized in the United States prior to standard time; the railroads alone used about 100. Travelers from Maine to California had to change their watches on 20 occasions during the journey to have correct train time.

All this caused endless confusion. The railroad movement to standardize time began in May 1872, when a group of railroad superintendents, a forerunner of the Association of American Railroads (AAR), met in St. Louis to arrange summer passenger-train schedules. The group formed a permanent organization which became successively the Time-Table Convention, the General Time Convention (GTC), the American Railway Association, and finally the AAR. For many years William F. Allen, secretary of the GTC and managing editor of the *Official Guide of the Railways,* spearheaded the drive for standard time. The plan finally adopted had five zones, intercolonial time in eastern Canada and four in the United States: eastern, central, mountain, and Pacific times. These four were based on mean sun time on the 75th, 90th, 105th, and 120th meridians west of Greenwich, England.

After the plan had been adopted overwhelmingly, Secretary Allen, on behalf of the convention, directed that all railway clocks governing train operation be set to the new standard at exactly 12:00 noon on Sunday, November 18, 1883, which thus became "the day of two noons." Though accepted and used also by the federal government and by states, cities, and towns throughout the country, it is interesting to note that standard time went into effect with no federal legislation. Congress finally passed a Standard Time Act on March 19, 1918, embodying daylight saving time.

BIBLIOGRAPHY: John S. Allen, *Standard Time in America,* New York, 1951.

Standard Transportation Code (STC) Dictionary of sorts for the transportation industry, listing all shippable products from A to Z, from *abalone shells* to *zithers.* It identifies, each by a different seven-digit number, more than 14,000 commodities that move in transportation. STC numbers must appear on all waybills made at the point of origin and accompanying freight to its destination. The numbers must be used also when railroads and other carriers regulated by the Interstate Commerce Commission report to the ICC. The U.S. Department of Transportation, too, uses them. Mingled with well-known commodities like coal and grain are such items as sheet music, thistle seeds, manhole covers, totem poles, swords, kangaroo hides, Japanese-beetle traps, taximeters, lightning rods, and caskets. The list was developed in the early 1960s. A new section on dangerous items, especially explosives, was added to the STC on January 1, 1976.

Stanford, Leland ***(1824–1893)*** If his law office and library at Port Washington, Wisconsin, had not burned to the ground in 1852, Leland Stanford might never have become one of the Big Four team of rich merchants who founded and operated the Central Pacific Railroad (CP) and its successor, the Southern Pacific (SP), and who founded Stanford University.

He was born at Watervliet, New York, in the same farmhouse in which his future mother-in-law had been born. His father, Josiah Stanford, built roads and bridges and helped to build the Albany & Schenectady link in the future New York Central System. Leland decided to become an attorney. He moved to Wisconsin in 1848 to practice law, married Jane Lathrop in 1850, quit law because of the fire, and in 1852 crossed the Great Plains to California to seek his fortune in the wake of the gold rush. He sold supplies to miners, ran a store in San Francisco, then another one in Sacramento, where he met the future fellow members of the Big Four: Collis P. Huntington, Charles Crocker, and Mark Hopkins, and the construction engineer Theodore D. Judah. These men got him interested in eventually promoting and building the western end of the nation's first transcontinental railway.

Stanford did much for the CP and SP through his political influence as governor of California and later as United States senator (1885-1893). During his governorship (1861-1863), he approved land grants that got tracklaying started over the Sierra Nevada at Truckee and used his prestige to induce the state and several counties to make big contributions to the project. For many years he devoted full time to the railroad.

Besides being a major stockholder in construction companies that built the line, he was president of the Central Pacific from its inception until his death and of the Southern Pacific from 1885 to 1890. Stanford owned vast vineyards and bred fine horses. His personal fortune exceeded $50 million. He gave $20 million to found and endow the coeducational Leland Stanford Junior University [(LSJU) still its official name], commonly called Stanford University, in memory of his son, who died at 15. LSJU was opened in 1891 near Stanford's Palo Alto ranch and later acquired important departments in other cities. The railroad tycoon's widow gave it an additional $18 million after his death.

According to Stephen Birmingham's *California Rich* (Simon & Schuster, 1980), Mrs. Leland Stanford possessed one of the world's largest jewelry collections, and at one fasionable party she wore it all, including 60 diamond earrings. Birmingham says also that old Central Pacific maps of California showed 25 miles of nonexistent mountains, the better to defraud the state for the work of tracklaying.

See also CROCKER, CHARLES; HOPKINS, MARK; HUNTINGTON, COLLIS POTTER; SOUTHERN PACIFIC LINES.

BIBLIOGRAPHY: Hubert H. Bancroft, *History of the Life of Leland Stanford,* Biobooks, Oakland, Calif., 1952; George T. Clark, *Leland Stanford,* Stanford University Press, Stanford, Calif., 1931; Matthew Josephson, *The Robber Barons: The Great American Capitalists,* Harcourt, Brace, New York, 1934; Neill C. Wilson and Frank J. Taylor, *Southern Pacific: The Roaring Story of a Fighting Railroad,* McGraw-Hill, New York, 1952.

Station Bells In early railroading, bell ringing marked the arrival and departure of many trains, especially in New England and Canada. Bells perched on station roofs were quite common.

At Wilmington, North Carolina, the Atlantic Coast Line (now part of CSX Corp.) has been dingdonging a station bell since 1856. Cast in Philadelphia in 1855, it is (or was) rung 5 minutes before every train leaves and then a few seconds before the wheels start turning. The custom began in the days when Wilmington was a sleepy village. Villagers enjoyed visiting the depot at train time; their long adieus to their folks often delayed train departures. So in 1856 the bell was installed as a polite reminder that steam cars ran by schedule. Fifty-seven years later, the original building was remodeled and enlarged. Architect's plans banished the historic bell, but citizens protested so much that the railway management let it stay.

Mississippi boasts at least two station bells, each serving a different purpose. One is perched atop the Osyka depot, the first stop north of the Louisiana state line on the Illinois Central Gulf main stem out of New Orleans. It is rung every day at 11 a.m. as a time signal to the community. The other, in Avalon, stands on an upright post beside the old station and is sounded every Sunday as a call to worship. For nearly 10 years that structure served as both a railway station and a church and was said to be the only one in America at that time used for both purposes. Now it is only a church edifice.

John Bruce, first president of the Winchester & Potomac (which became part of the Baltimore & Ohio, or B&O) wrote in his 1836 annual report:

> No disappointment has occurred in the regularity of our transportation. . . . The depot bell has failed on but one or two occasions—when incessant rains have drenched our fuel—to sound a cheering note of the expected hour of arrival [of trains]; not one trip, however, has been lost . . .

The earliest-recorded American depot bell was hung in the station at Ellicott's Mills (now Ellicott City), 12.8 miles out of Baltimore, Maryland, on the original B&O mainline. As early as 1830 the arrival and departure of horse-drawn trains was marked by its pealing. That bell is now on display in the Baltimore & Ohio Railroad Museum in Baltimore, together with a bell from the Mount Clare shops, which is said to have been rung originally at train time at the Mount Clare Depot.

Those time-honored artifacts began to disappear when they ceased to fill a public need, when watches became cheap and plentiful and travelers no longer required a bell to tell the time. Another factor was the increasing number of trains, which caused considerable bell ringing, which must have confused railroad employees as well as passengers. The growth of cities also helped to silence the old metallic train announcers. Long ago, when towns were small, most of the residents could hear the station bell.

BIBLIOGRAPHY: Edwin P. Alexander, *Down at the Depot: American Railroad Stations from 1831 to 1920,* Crown, New York, 1970.

Station Chapel The old Pennsylvania Railroad's 30th Street Station, completed in March 1933, which has in its main lobby a beautifully sculptured war memorial of an angel bearing aloft the figure of a soldier presumably killed in battle, is believed to be the only American railroad depot built with a chapel. Elisha Lee, a Pennsy vice president, conceived the idea while seated in an ocean liner's chapel and died shortly after seeing it carried into effect. A cloistered second-floor suite was set apart as a sanctuary, funeral parlor, mortuary chamber, and retiring room for newlyweds and other travelers desiring privacy and peace. But it was used so seldom that it is no longer available for such purposes.

Station Hotels In early 1830s the railways often used inns as stations. Between 1850 and 1880 they built many fine station hotels and some resort hotels (those of the Canadian Pacific are still flourishing), either detached or unified with the depots. Travelers rode day coaches, stopped off to eat meals, and often stayed overnight. The hostelries were lavish, were well landscaped, and had big dining rooms. Mostly they were in the East, although the West and Southwest had the famous Harvey Houses. *See* HARVEY, FREDERICK HENRY.

But in 1880 sleeping and dining cars, advertised as "hotels on wheels," outmoded them. Most such buildings eventually burned or more modern depots replaced them; very few lasted into the 1960s. The National Trust for Historic Preservation, 1785 Massachusetts Avenue, N.W., Washington, D.C. 20036, and local groups fought a losing battle to save them. The Erie's Starrucca House, built about 1865 at Susquehanna, Pennsylvania, with a cathedral-like dining hall, is today a unique architectural survival.

See also BOARDING HOUSES.

BIBLIOGRAPHY: Edwin P. Alexander, *Down at the Depot: American Railroad Stations from 1831 to 1920,* Crown, New York, 1970; Archibald T. Robertson, *Slow Train to Yesterday,* Houghton Mifflin, Boston, 1945.

Stations, Railroad Passenger There are five kinds of stations: (1) *through station,* built beside tracks or under them in such a way that trains pass through it directly in either direction, a setup which eliminates a lot of switching; (2) *way station,* usually built to straddle the tracks, often consisting of buildings on both sides of the tracks and connected by a tunnel or an overpass; (3) *stub station,* one in which the tracks stop abruptly, so that trains must head in, back in, or depart in reverse; (4) *loop station,* one having an oval-shaped track connecting with the mainline so that trains proceeding via the loop head directly into their tracks beside the depot platform; and (5) *terminal station,* built at the end of a railroad line, usually at the end of the mainline. A *depot* is any kind of railroad station, particularly an old-time rural way station; the term "down by the depot" is nostalgic. *See also* articles on individual stations; UNION STATIONS.

STC *See* STANDARD TRANSPORTATION CODE.

Steam Locomotive Endurance Tests Canadian Pacific engine No. 2808 set a world record for steam power in 1930 by hauling the transcontinental passenger train *The Dominion* from Fort William, Ontario, to Calgary, Alberta, 1252 miles over 11 divisions without a change. Normally, a train was given a fresh steam engine at each division point. The day after the 2808 reached Calgary, she took another train all the way back to Fort William, pounding 2500 miles of rails in 38 hours.

Another steam-power triumph in 1930 was a nonstop mileage record set by the Frisco Lines (St. Louis–San Francisco Railway) No. 4213, a Baldwin-built Mikado weighing 608,000 pounds, covering 9700 miles in about 700 hours without servicing or having her fires dumped. The run took every available hour of a month and could have lasted longer but for the legal need for federal inspection. It used 80 crews, handling full tonnage at all times. The largest train the 4213 drew consisted of 115 freight cars (5025 tons) between Fort Scott, Kansas, and Kansas City, Missouri.

This test proved that a freight locomotive could be run for an entire calendar month without (1) stopped-up flues impairing her steaming ability or (2) having her firebox emptied or her boiler washed out from one government inspection point to the next. The test also proved that she could steam as well at the month's end as at the beginning.

Examination after the long endurance run showed the firebox, grates, cylinders, and valve packing in good shape; no cinders; and the brick arch in fair condition, burned thin in some places but with all bricks still in. The boiler's condition was good, with less than 25 percent of its flues stopped up. There were no air or steam links in the front. The wear on rod brass was below $\frac{1}{16}$ inch.

Steam Locomotives For nearly 125 years the railroads' main source of motive power, steam locomotives have been replaced in the North American continent and elsewhere by diesel-electrics, virtually the only exception in the United States being most of the seasonal tourist short lines, although Asian countries and South Africa still use many steamers. America's last all-steam nontourist railroad, the Edgemoor & Manetta, a short industrial road in South Carolina, used an old Porter-built steam switcher for many years between its company's mills at Leeds and a Seaboard Air Line connection at Edgemoor; but on July 9, 1975, the engine failed an Interstate Commerce Commission Safety test and had to be supplanted by a diesel.

The modern steam locomotives (the relatively few which are left in service) are completely self-contained units that pull or push freight or passenger cars. Basically, the steam-generating apparatus is a horizontal fire-tube type of boiler with fuel and water facilities. A throttle controls the quantity of steam which valves admit to the cylinders. The reverse lever is known colloquially as the Johnson bar. Piston pressure is sent through the main rod to the driving wheels, which are variable in number and are connected by side rods. Steam drawn off from the cylinders is emitted through the smokestack, thus forcing a draft in the firebox which aids the combustion of either coal or fuel oil. (Before the Civil War, most United States locomotives were wood-burners.) *See* JOHNSON BAR.

Tractive force is determined by the size of the driving wheels and the weight distribution upon them. For this reason, the drivers of freight engines are smaller than those of passenger engines, which as a rule have fewer wheels that support less weight. The leading and trailing trucks of passenger engines carry the large, heavy boilers.

Steam locos are classified by their axle or wheel arrangement. The system most widely used was devised by F. H. Whyte, whose personality, like that of the Johnson of the Johnson bar, is lost in history. Digits represent the number of wheels in each category, beginning at the front end just behind the pilot (cowcatcher): first the number of wheels in the leading truck, if any; then the number of driving wheels; and finally the trailing-truck wheels, if any. Hyphens separate the numbers.

American Locomotive Co. (Alco) had its own system, based on Whyte's but without hyphens. It used the letter C after the classification figure to denote "compound"

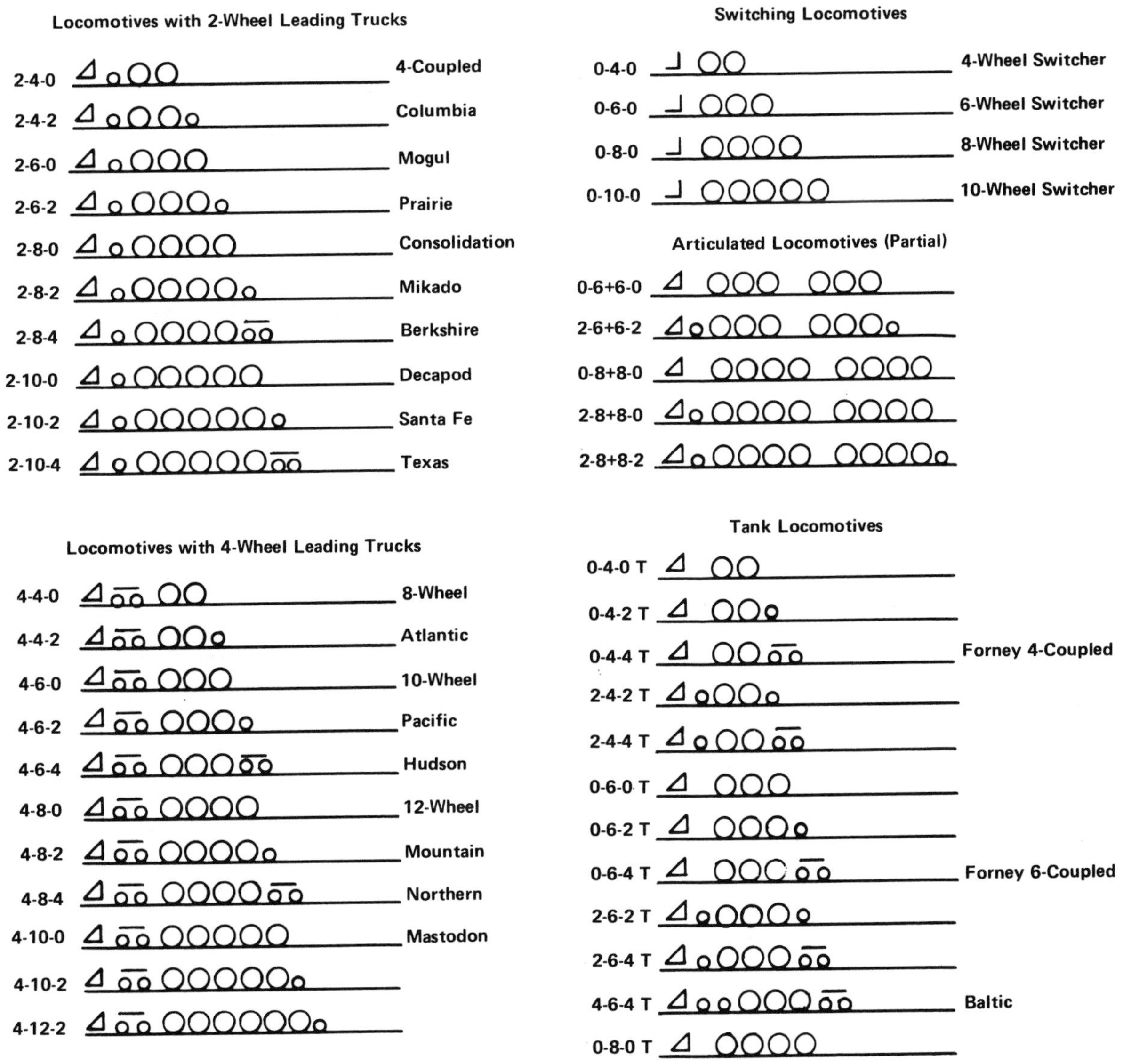

Locomotives with 2-Wheel Leading Trucks

Class	Name
2-4-0	4-Coupled
2-4-2	Columbia
2-6-0	Mogul
2-6-2	Prairie
2-8-0	Consolidation
2-8-2	Mikado
2-8-4	Berkshire
2-10-0	Decapod
2-10-2	Santa Fe
2-10-4	Texas

Locomotives with 4-Wheel Leading Trucks

Class	Name
4-4-0	8-Wheel
4-4-2	Atlantic
4-6-0	10-Wheel
4-6-2	Pacific
4-6-4	Hudson
4-8-0	12-Wheel
4-8-2	Mountain
4-8-4	Northern
4-10-0	Mastodon
4-10-2	
4-12-2	

Switching Locomotives

Class	Name
0-4-0	4-Wheel Switcher
0-6-0	6-Wheel Switcher
0-8-0	8-Wheel Switcher
0-10-0	10-Wheel Switcher

Articulated Locomotives (Partial)

Class
0-6+6-0
2-6+6-2
0-8+8-0
2-8+8-0
2-8+8-2

Tank Locomotives

Class	Name
0-4-0 T	
0-4-2 T	
0-4-4 T	Forney 4-Coupled
2-4-2 T	
2-4-4 T	
0-6-0 T	
0-6-2 T	
0-6-4 T	Forney 6-Coupled
2-6-2 T	
2-6-4 T	
4-6-4 T	Baltic
0-8-0 T	

The Whyte classification system was devised to classify steam locomotives according to their axle or wheel arrangements.

and S for "superheated" and T to denote "a connected tank" instead of a separate tender. A second row of figures was added for the weight in the nearest number of thousands of pounds. Thus, 282 S 241 told you that the engine was a 241,991-pound superheated Mikado. (Because of World War II some roads, like the Union Pacific, substituted the word *MacArthur* for *Mikado* for this wheel arrangement.)

Lima Locomotive Works adopted the Alco system but with hyphens. Baldwin Locomotive Works, the world's largest builder of steam power in its heyday, had its own classification system that preceded Whyte's. Included was a figure denoting the total number of engine wheels, followed by a fraction such as ½ to indicate a trailing truck, if any, or ⅓ for a trailing truck without a leading truck, if any, and a letter for the number of driving wheels. For example, 12½D stood for a 4-6-2 (Pacific) type. Usually inserted was a figure for the diameter of the cylinder, found by subtracting 3 from the size of the cylinder and multiplying the result by 2. Thus, 32 denoted the Pacific's 19-inch cylinder, the complete symbol being 12-32-½D. Most locomotive historians and steam railfans prefer Whyte's classification, which is less complicated than the Baldwin system.

In 1825 Col. John Stevens, inventor, steamboat builder, and railroad promoter, designed and built North America's first locomotive, a cabless, upright-boilered four-wheeler. He ran it experimentally on a circular track with strap-iron rails on his Hoboken, New Jersey estate.

Robert Stephenson & Co., in England, built the world's first practical locomotives for railways and shipped one of them, the *Stourbridge Lion,* to the Delaware and Hudson Canal Co. (now Delaware and Hudson Railway, or D&H) for hauling coal from the company's mines to a Honesdale, Pennsylvania, canal connection. Tried out in August 1829 with Horatio Allen as engineer, she was the first engine in North America to pull cars for a commercial railway. Too heavy for the D&H's flimsy trestles, she was soon retired and later disassembled. In 1905 her boiler and other parts were reassembled into a complete unit at the Smithsonian Institution in Washington.

In 1830 Peter Cooper, Baltimore merchant and later a New York philanthropist, designed and supervised the building of a very small engine, about 1½ horsepower and named *Tom Thumb,* for the originally horse-drawn Baltimore & Ohio. It had an upright boiler, upright cylinders, and tubes made from gun barrels. Cooper himself was its first engineer-fireman. The *Tom Thumb* was America's first native-built locomotive to do useful work.

The B&O then offered a $4000 premium for an engine built in the United States that would draw 15 tons gross weight at 15 miles an hour. Of the five entrants in this contest, the management accepted Ezekiel Childs's engine for yard operation and the *York,* designed by Phineas Davis and built by Davis & Gartner, for road service. The *York* was the first locomotive designed specifically for use on an anthracite-burning line.

Davis was put in charge of B&O's Mount Clare shops in Baltimore but met an accidental death shortly afterward on his own engine. The B&O went on with an innovative engine-building program that featured many famous iron horses, including Grasshopper and Camel types, eight-wheel connected units known as Mud Diggers, a double-ended Mallet and the first duplex (four-cylindered, rigid-framed) as well as such outstanding builders as Ross Winans and James Millholland. *See* WINANS, ROSS.

In 1828 the South Carolina Canal & Railroad Company (now part of the Southern Railway System) was chartered. For years it was the world's longest railroad. It was the first line which the directors decided from the start to operate with steam power. Horatio Allen of D&H fame, its chief engineer, was responsible for this decision.

The company's first engine, affectionately named the *Best Friend of Charleston,* was built at the West Point Foundry in New York City. She was a four-wheeler, all wheels being drivers, had two inclined cylinders and a vertical boiler, and weighed about 4½ tons. When she arrived by ship at Charleston, 7 miles of the road had been finished and she was put to work hauling construction material. Later, she pulled four or five cars holding 40 or 50 passengers at speeds up to 35 miles an hour, performing well. But one day her fireman fastened down her safety valve to keep it quiet. The resultant boiler explosion killed him and wrecked the engine. Julius D. Petsch rebuilt her and became the road's master mechanic, the first railroad man to hold a title that later was widely used in the railroad industry.

For the same company E. L. Miller designed a double-ended eight-wheeler, the *South Carolina,* and supervised her construction at the West Point Foundry in 1831. She looked somewhat like two very tall stacked engines backed up to each other, with an engineer working midway, not in a cab. Her big advantage was an ability to run in either direction without being reversed on a turntable or wye. Like most motive-power freaks, she spent too much time in the repair shops. Years later, other builders created efficient double-ended articulated engines. *See* LOCOMOTIVES, DOUBLE-ENDED.

The company's fourth iron horse, named *E. L. Miller,* was built in Philadelphia by Matthias W. Baldwin, who had already produced *Old Ironsides* for a Reading Railroad predecessor, the Philadelphia, Germantown & Norristown. *Old Ironsides* ran a mile in 58 seconds and 2¼ miles in 182 seconds, which seemed miraculous in those days.

In 1831 the Camden & Amboy (C&A), an early antecedent of the Pennsylvania Railroad (PRR), began operating in New Jersey with the Stephenson-built, 11-ton *John Bull,* which had four driving wheels and two tiny wheels on the world's first cowcatcher. The disassembled *John Bull* was shipped from England to Philadelphia. The C&A master mechanic, Isaac Dripps, who had never before seen a locomotive, took this one's parts in a sloop up the Delaware River to Bordentown, New Jersey, and patiently assembled them. He also made a small car into a wood-carrying tender and bought a whiskey cask to hold water for the *John Bull*.

Dripps and C&A President Robert L. Stevens, son of Col. John Stevens, built engines for the Camden & Amboy at Hoboken, starting a pattern which eventually gave the Pennsy the distinction of making a greater contribution to steam locomotive development than any other road. PRR outshopped a great many engines (including some that made history) for itself at Juniata and Altoona, besides buying numerous others of its own design from outside builders.

The biggest driving wheels of any American engine, 96 inches in diameter, were those of a Stevens type, the first of which Norris Bros. built for the Camden & Amboy at Lancaster, Pennsylvania, in about 1847. She had a very tall, barrel-like stack and a cab set higher than the boiler top and accessible only in front, and she weighed 47,000 pounds. Drivers and truck wheels were made of wrought iron, with wood filling the spaces between the spokes. The engine's 13- by 18-inch cylinders proved to be too big for her boiler.

Canadian-built locomotives date back to 1851, when James Good of Toronto constructed the Dominion's first, the 4-4-0 *Toronto,* for the Ontario, Simcoe & Huron Union Railroad. Several small loco works flourished in Canada in the nineteenth century. The two big ones were the Canadian Locomotive Co. and the Montreal Locomotive Works, in Kingston and Montreal, respectively. Both built units for export as well as domestic use.

A few individual railways in Canada, as in the United States, produced many of their own steam locos. The Grand Trunk Railway of Canada turned out its first engine in 1858 at its Point St-Charles shops in Montreal. The Canadian Pacific (CP) shops in Montreal built a total of 1056 locos, all steam, over a 61-year period, besides rebuilding 63 units of outside builders and handling countless repair jobs.

In 1877 Francis R. F. Brown became Grand Trunk works manager and in 1883 was appointed mechanical superintendent of the Canadian Pacific. Five months later his first CP engine, 4-4-0 No. 285, rolled off the transfer table for her official photographs. Unlike most engines, she had the steam dome set midway on the boiler, ahead of the sand dome. Three of Brown's 4-4-0s have been preserved, two in Montreal and one in Vancouver.

In 1904, H. H. Vaughan was appointed CP superintendent of motive power. He took charge of the new Angus shops in Montreal, which had just replaced the original works. In 1909 Angus built the first of its six Mallets, No. 1950, a compound 0-6-6-0. The road's peak year for loco production was 1911, when it built 96 engines of various wheel arrangements. Like United States heavy industry, the Angus shops concentrated on armament during both world wars. The final CP-built engine, 4-6-2 No. 1301, constructed in June 1944, has been preserved.

But the road continued to buy steam locos from outside builders, including 100 4-6-2s from Montreal Locomotive Works. The last steam loco was a powerful 2-10-4, No. 5935, the final standard-gauge steam engine built for any Canadian railway, delivered in March 1940 and now preserved. Three months later Canadian Pacific received its first batch of diesel-electrics.

In 1866 Baldwin built a 2-8-0 for the Lehigh Valley that was named the *Consolidation* because the LV had just been merged with other roads. Although 2-8-0s had been constructed previously, all of the many examples of that wheel arrangement which were turned out later for various carriers were designated Consolidation types.

The fantail type, usually a switcher, was so nicknamed because her tender sloped downward at the rear to improve the visibility of enginemen looking back for hand signals. Another type designed to give the engineer better visibility, but of the track ahead, was the once-popular Camelback, or Mother Hubbard type, the names being derived from the dromedary's hump and the Mother Goose character's hood. (It should not be confused with Ross Winans's Camel type.) The Camelback had two engine cabs. The main one, for the engineer, was located midway on the engine. The other was a shelter at the rear for the fireman. Camelbacks were widely used on the Reading, the Jersey Central, and numerous other roads. *See* FANTAIL ENGINE.

Another type with improved visibility of the track ahead was built with the cab (only one cab) in front. The Southern Pacific used many such engines successfully for years. America's largest and most powerful steam locomotives were the Mallets, especially those on the Union Pacific, the Virginian, the Norfolk & Western, and the Duluth, Missabe and Iron Range.

Steam locomotive efficiency, or thermal efficiency, is a physics problem solved by figuring the percentage of ingoing energy turned into useful work. Drawbar pull is expressed in terms of foot-pounds (the energy needed to move 1 pound 1 foot). This is compared with the number of like units contained in the fuel when burned in the firebox. Rarely has a steam locomotive had more than 6 or 7 percent efficiency when measured in this fashion. Cost, reliability, and capacity determine the rate. For example, compound locos were theoretically more efficient than single steamers, yet were discarded sooner, largely because of factors other than thermal efficiency.

See also AMERICAN LOCOMOTIVE CO.; BALDWIN LOCOMOTIVE WORKS; BELLS, LOCOMOTIVE; BOILERS, LOCO-

MOTIVE; BROOKS LOCOMOTIVE WORKS; CABS, LOCOMOTIVE; CINCINNATI LOCOMOTIVE BUILDERS; DIESEL VERSUS STEAM; HEAD-END ENGINES; HINKLEY LOCOMOTIVE WORKS; LIMA LOCOMOTIVE WORKS; LOCOMOTIVE DRIFTING; LOCOMOTIVES, DECORATED; LOCOMOTIVES, EXPERIMENTAL; MALLET; MASON, WILLIAM; SUPERHEATERS, LOCOMOTIVE; TAUNTON LOCOMOTIVE WORKS; TRACK PANS; TWELVE-WHEELERS; WHISTLES, LOCOMOTIVE; articles on large railroad systems.

BIBLIOGRAPHY: Henry B. Comstock, *The Iron Horse,* Crowell, New York, 1971; George L. Flower (ed.), *Locomotive Dictionary,* Newton K. Gregg, Novato, Calif., 1972; Angus Sinclair, *Development of the Locomotive Engine,* annotated ed. by John H. White, Jr., M.I.T., Cambridge, Mass., 1970; William A. Tuplin, *The Steam Locomotive,* Scribner, New York, 1975; John H. White, Jr., *American Locomotives,* John Hopkins, Baltimore, 1968; Roy V. Wright (ed.), *The Locomotive Cyclopedia of American Practice,* Simmons-Boardman, New York, 1941.

Stevens Hedges *See* TUMBLEWEED FENCES.

Stilwell, Arthur Edward (1859–1928) Native of Rochester, New York, who was largely responsible for creating two rail empires, the Kansas City Southern (KCS) and the Kansas City, Mexico & Orient. "My goal was to build railroads," he said, "to save the Midwestern farmers from unjust freight rates. . . . I achieved this ambition with approximately 2,300 miles of rail lines—more railroad mileage than the total laid by any other living man."

In 1880, when 93,270 route miles of railroads were in operation in the United States, Stillwell printed 5000 timetables for the Atlantic, Mississippi & Ohio Railroad, which until then had been operating without public schedules. In 1881 he married and moved to Kansas City, Kansas, where in 1887 he helped to promote a belt switching railway and then the Kansas City, Pittsburg & Gulf (KCP&G), which reached down into Louisiana, Arkansas, Oklahoma, and Texas.

This road is said to have constructed one-fourth of all American rail mileage built in 1895. George M. Pullman of sleeping-car fame aided Stilwell with funds and equipment. But the KCP&G went bankrupt. John W. ("Bet-You-a-Million") Gates took it over, renamed it Kansas City Southern, and dropped Stilwell. Profiting from an oil boom, the KCS was extended to Port Arthur, Texas, a town named for Arthur Stilwell. Its first diesel locomotive pulled a new passenger train, the *Flying Crow,* for which the road was called the "Route of the *Flying Crow*" (straight as the crow flies).

Stilwell, undaunted, turned to a long-envisioned project: a railroad to link Kansas City with its nearest Pacific port, Topolobampo, Mexico, on the Gulf of California. "I have designed a railroad 1,600 miles long," Stilwell announced, "which will bring the Pacific Ocean 400 miles nearer to Kansas City than any other present route. Not only that, but it will be 1,600 miles nearer to Central and South America than San Francisco is."

This railway, the Kansas City, Mexico & Orient (Stilwell hoped that it would haul shipments from Asia), was to run southwest through Oklahoma Territory and Texas and cross the Rio Grande, terminating at the Gulf of California. Stilwell built most of this fantastic route, with gaps between San Angelo, Texas, and El Oro, Mexico, and between Arapanapochic and Laguna, Mexico. A revolution south of the border plus lack of funds threw the road into bankruptcy in 1912.

A receiver extended the road only a few miles to Alpine, Texas, operating 735 miles of track in the United States and 320 in Mexico. In 1925 the Santa Fe bought the entire line for $14 million but sold its Mexican mileage to a sugar planter, from whom the Mexican government took it over and operated it.

BIBLIOGRAPHY: John Leeds Kerr and Frank P. Donovan, *Destination Topolobampo,* Golden West Books, San Marino, Calif., 1968.

Stone Creek Wreck On the night of February 29, 1890, two young hillbillies, Thomas Shaw and Warren Creswell, secretly removed a rail from the Southern Railway line on the bridge over the marshy Stone Creek in Twiggs County, Georgia, and dropped it into the water. This act wrecked a crack passenger train and a freight, killing three railroad men and injuring many people. Among the passengers aboard were the wives of the two saboteurs and Thomas's father, Richard Shaw.

Later, it turned out that the two Shaws and Creswell had plotted the crime. Mrs. Creswell testified that a few days before February 29 she had heard Richard Shaw boast, "We'll wreck the train and kill all the people so we can get a lot of money." The elder Shaw left the train, with the two young women still aboard, when it stopped at a drawbridge before reaching Stone Creek. Mrs. Creswell collected $350 for minor injuries, but her husband kept that sum himself, giving her only 25 cents in cash and a half dollar's worth of snuff. The three plotters were arrested. Richard Shaw was inexplicably freed, but the other two were given life terms in a convict labor camp.

Strasburg Rail Road Oldest common-carrier short line (4½ miles) in the United States, operating between Strasburg and Paradise, Pennsylvania. It was chartered on January 9, 1832, a few months after the world's first T rail had been laid on ties of the Camden & Amboy, the Pennsylvania Railroad's (PRR's) first predecessor. The Strasburg has always used T rail. If the Mauch Chunk switchback, also in Pennsylvania, had not been dismantled in the early 1940s, it, rather than the Strasburg, would now be America's oldest short line.

The road serves a prosperous, thrifty farming section, mostly Pennsylvania German, with more than a sprinkling of Amish, Mennonites, Quakers, and descendants of French Huguenots; many families have occupied the same homesteads for at least 8 or 10 generations. The stability of this population undoubtedly has had a lot to do with the railroad's long life. In 1861, when the Civil War broke out, it was sold at a sheriff's sale to a syndicate of 23 men, who kept it running. And in the national panic of 1873 it was sold again, that time to Thomas and Henry Baumgardner, descendants of a Hessian soldier who had deserted his command upon landing in the New World and joined George Washington's ragged Continentals.

For many years the short line bought outmoded steam locomotives from the PRR to meet its needs. Today, the line is mostly dieselized, hauling principally freight, but it operates steam excursions for tourists and railfans and maintains a souvenir shop and picnic faciities. As an added attraction, the Pennsylvania State Railroad Museum, housing historic locomotives, railroad cars, etc., was purposely built near the old short line.

Streamlining The streamlining of locomotives and cars in rail passenger service was designed during the Depression of the early 1930s to create a modern and more pleasing popular image in addition to serving the major purpose of speeding up trains at the lowest possible cost in energy. The principle is that of a falling drop of water, which is not round but elongated because it follows the line of least resistance in adapting its shape to air friction.

In 1865 the Rev. Samuel Calthrop of Rochester, New York, patented a design for a very smooth train with some resemblance to an earthworm, but, like the very first design for a sleeping car (nonstreamlined), it was never built. Three years later, Alfred E. Beach built and demonstrated a full-size cylindrical subway car, the "grandfather" of all railway streamliners, that was operated by wind pressure and actually carried passengers for a very short distance and a brief period of time beneath Broadway in New York. *See also* SUBWAY AND ELEVATED RAILWAYS.

In 1892 Frederick U. Adams wrote a book which said: "A train properly designed for minimizing the air resistance due to speed can be made to travel 100 miles an hour with less expenditure of power than is now required to move a train of equal weight and capacity at a rate of 50 miles an hour." Most passenger trains then had open platforms. Walking across them, especially while rounding curves at speed, was hazardous for small children and infirm travelers. Adams designed a train with closed coaches, thus becoming the father of the vestibule car. In 1900 he raised $8000 to streamline a Baltimore & Ohio train, known as the Adams Wind-Splitter. Although it could make 40 miles per hour in 37½ minutes, B&O officials were not favorably impressed, and the train went down in history as a freak.

In 1931 Dr. Oscar Tietjens, A German-born aerodynamic engineer at Westinghouse Research Laboratories in Pittsburgh, and his associate, K. C. Ripley, experimented with various kinds of railway equipment in a wind tunnel. To minimize wind resistance they recommended streamlining of passenger trains comparable to the design of the Graf Zeppelin and other aircraft.

Three notable pioneers in railway streamlining were Otto Kuhler, Raymond Loewy, and Henry Dreyfuss. In 1931 Kuhler patented a streamlined hood for steam locomotives with stainless-steel sheets that could be lifted up when necessary for work to be done on the locomotives' operating parts. As consulting engineer of American Locomotive Co., he was largely responsible for Alco's streamlining. *See* DREYFUSS, HENRY; KUHLER, OTTO; LOEWY, RAYMOND.

During 1932, before loco streamlining, many gasoline-powered railcars, or *doodlebugs,* were built with some form of streamlining. Other streamlined railcars were imported from French builders.

The first Pullman streamlined train, Union Pacific's (UP's) *M-1000,* a stainless-steel job, had a 12-cylinder distillate burner of 6000 horsepower. It just about set the style for streamlined trains in the United States. The second UP streamliner, *M-10001,* aluminum-sheathed, had less horsepower per pound of weight. It was powered by a diesel, weighed over 4000 pounds, and made 120 miles per hour on test runs. Like the first one, it had a 38-inch center of gravity and was not quite as wide as a standard train. Subsequent streamliners were somewhat wider and heavier.

Illinois Central's Pullman-built streamliner, consisting of five coaches with a Winton diesel of about 1200 horsepower, was strictly a lounging and eating train, with a buffet in every car. The Burlington *Zephyr,* inaugurated in 1934, was the first big sensation of the Budd type. New York Central's most famous modern steam locomotive, the *Commodore Vanderbilt,* was equipped with roller bearings, sheathed all over with stainless steel except around the driving wheels, and painted battleship gray with white striping. *See* BUDD COMPANY.

We have mentioned just a few of the many streamlined American engines, trains, and railcars. In time, the originally eye-catching streamliners were taken for granted and attracted less and less attention.

Streetcars North America's street railway service began in 1832 with New York and Harlem Railway (NY&H) operation of horse-drawn cars along the Bowery and Fourth Avenue in New York City. When NY&H adopted steam power, it ran local horsecars on the same tracks for a while, then rerouted them to Madison Avenue, north of 42d Street, while through steam trains continued to run on Fourth Avenue. Gradually the use of horsecars on iron rails spread to other cities, New Orleans being the second. At first, such cars were unheated in winter, but straw piled on the floor helped to keep the passengers' feet from freezing.

A team of horses (or mules, sometimes a single animal) could draw a larger, more heavily laden vehicle on rails than on the rough mud or gravel roads and streets of those days. But while cars could be used almost continuously, the horses in that exhausting job could be worked only 3 or 4 hours a day; and extra horses, like helper engines, had to be hitched on for steep hills. An average car required at least 8, sometimes 10, horses for each day's service. All had to be fed, watered, groomed, and otherwise cared for whether they were toiling or not. The manure problem was self-evident.

In the 1870s and 1880s many streetcars were towed by little boxlike "dummy" steam locomotives, often disguised with streetcar bodies to avoid frightening horses. Some experimental cars were self-propelled by internal-combustion engines, compressed air, stored steam, chemical reaction, or powerful spring motors. The two forms which eventually won out were the cable system and, especially, electric traction.

Electric propulsion was still in the early experimental stages when Andrew Hallidie, a wire-rope manufacturer, observing the drawbacks of trying to use horsecars on San Francisco's steep hills, devised a cable-car system. His Clay Street line, opened in 1873, was operated by a cable running in a conduit laid between the rails and below street level. A slot along the top of the conduit permitted a grip mechanism to be suspended from the car, hang down in the conduit, and engage the cable, which was propelled by a stationary engine in a fixed powerhouse. Releasing the grip stopped the car independently of other cars.

Though costly to install, this system was cheaper to operate than horsecars and far more satisfactory for heavily traveled lines. It was soon expanded in San Francisco, where its advantages overcame the hills. Other cities, with or without steep hills, also adopted it. In the 1880s and 1890s, New York had a lengthy cable-car system. So had Seattle, Cincinnati, Philadelphia, Washington, and many other big cities. Chicago's was the most extensive of all.

America's first street railway, the New York & Harlem Railway, operated horse-drawn cars patterned after stagecoaches of the period. In this painting, the horses are partly hidden by well-wishers in the right foreground. [Historical Paintings Collection, Continental Insurance Companies]

But this era was relatively short. Electric traction was being developed even while the large cable systems were being built. Cable cars would remain in use only where unusually steep grades precluded electric-car operation or made it less reliable or less safe. Nowadays, the only cable cars operated anywhere are in San Francisco, where they originated, except for a few funiculars, counterbalances, and other cable-operated mountain-climbing lines or aerial tramways. *See* LOOKOUT MOUNTAIN INCLINE RAILWAY.

Various men had been trying electric propulsion for railway cars since as early as the 1840s, but the crude motors and storage batteries prior to the late 19th century were unsuited to regular railroad service. Development of the electric generator in the 1870s led to renewed interest in the projects. Where to mount the motors on the cars, which at first were usually converted horsecars, was a dilemma. Some motors were mounted in the car body; others, under the floor, in the truck, or on the front platform. *See* ELECTRIFICATION.

Transmitting power to the wheels was another problem: gears, chains, belts, shafts, and connecting rods were tried out. How to supply electricity to the cars, and at what voltage, was the most controversial question of all. Some experimenters used the two running rails for positive and negative current; others put a third rail between the running rails or just outside one of them. Overhead wires, strung either over or alongside the tracks, were tried.

Collecting current from overhead wires posed another question. A two- or four-wheel troller, towed along the single or double wires by a rope attached to the car, came to be called a trolley; and a pole with a grooved wheel pressing upward against the overhead wire to collect the current was designated a trolley pole. In time, the cars themselves were named trolley cars, or trolleys.

Of the trolley systems tried out in the 1880s, Frank J. Sprague's was the most successful. Sprague was called the father of trolley cars. His experiments led to the development of motors best suited to electric traction. They were mounted with one side attached to the truck frame and the other to the axle on bearings. Sprague developed controls for his motors and used a single central overhead wire and a spring-loaded trolley pole. His first major installation of a "juice" streetcar system opened in Richmond, Virginia, in 1888.

Other cities had experimental lines in revenue service before then, notably a Montgomery, Alabama, line engineered by Charles van Depoele in 1886, but Sprague's Richmond trolley system preceded nearly all electric street railways. Leo Daft, who ran an experimental third-rail line between Saratoga and Mount McGregor, New York, used a locomotive named *Ampere,* equipped with electromagnetic wheel brakes. Until 1890 practically all electric-power plants in the United States were of his design.

Satisfied that the cost of Sprague's system was justified by its dependability, capacity, and ratio of expense to revenue, street railway managements far and wide adopted electric traction. The 1890s saw trolley lines based on his methods built in most major American cities and a great many smaller communities. Four-wheel trolleys could be built with twice the passenger capacity of the horsecars they supplanted.

Originally, most trolley cars were operated by a two-man crew, the motorman and the conductor. But as cars became larger and more crowded, the conductor missed collecting many fares, especially on open (summer) cars, where it was hard for him to make his way along a narrow running board often congested with standees. Pay-as-you-enter cars appeared in about 1905; the conductor took fares (usually a nickel or a transfer slip) on the rear platform, where passengers entered. Another fare-collection method, developed by Peter Witt, Cleveland transit commissioner, had a front-door entrance for passengers and a center door for exit, with fares being collected at the exits.

Many trolleys were chartered for tours, picnics, weddings, etc. There were cars for specialized uses such as work cars, freight cars, street sweepers, water sprinklers, snowplows, mail cars, luxury cars for elite riders, and hearses in which the mourners rode with the coffined body to the cemetery.

New York's last horsecar in regular service passed out in 1917, and America's last, at Pittsburgh, in 1921. Private automobiles, buses, and taxis (some known as jitneys) were then offering serious competition to rail transit lines. Some trolley companies used highway motor buses themselves, either as feeders to their own routes or as replacements on lightly traveled lines.

Some streetcar lines eliminated the cost of maintaining both open and enclosed cars for summer and winter use by acquiring enclosed trolleys whose sides could be replaced in hot weather with open-mesh wire screens or grilles. But open trolleys had a romantic appeal, especially for night riding.

In 1916, just 4 years after orders for new trolleys in the United States and Canada had reached an all-time annual peak of 5228, Charles O. Birney, a design and operation company engineer, combined in one design two significant economies: light weight and one-man operation. The Birney safety car was four-wheeler built to a standard design, with various door arrangements, intended for fare collection by the motorman as passengers boarded at the front, thus eliminating the conductor. Interlocking door controls and airbrakes kept the door from opening before the car was braked to a stop and required it to be closed before the car could be started.

While not notably fast or comfortable, Birney cars were easy on the rails and frugal of electricity as compared with the cars they usually supplanted. Their adoption permitted many a trolley line to stay in operation long after it would otherwise have been given up. Later, a double-truck Birney, similar to the four-wheeler but longer, appeared for use when greater capacity was needed.

In Denver, Colorado, a horse rode the Cherrelyn streetcar downhill and then pulled it back uphill. This trolley dates from the late 1800s.

Other lightweight designs arose in the 1920s as transit companies sought new ideas to remain in business, but the Depression of the 1930s hit streetcar riding hard. To offset automotive competition, a group of traction executives, the Electric Railway Presidents' Conference, designed a new type of high-capacity car which was fast, comfortable, quiet, and economical. The first 100 of these cars, known as PCCs, went into service in Brooklyn, New York, in 1936 and were well liked. They, too, were responsible for the continuation and popularity of numerous streetcar lines that otherwise might have been converted to buses sooner than they did. In the late 1970s most of North America's few surviving trolley systems were still using PCCs, although the last ones built for use on this continent (for San Francisco) date from 1952.

Despite all efforts to modernize streetcar lines, city after city saw its trolleys give way to buses and privately owned automobiles. Some dedicated groups of trolley-car enthusiasts began to set up operating trolley museums to save a few examples of the equipment they had grown up with but might never see again.

In the early 1970s, after being banished from most

The Munsie Street Railway in Vermont had an open-bench car pulled by a steam "dummy" named Vermonter.

This open car on the old California Street Line in San Francisco was the only piece of rolling stock to escape the fire and earthquake of 1906.

cities for about three decades, the trolley began showing some signs of a comeback. Increasing public awareness of air pollution and traffic congestion due to motor vehicles is supporting the trolley enthusiasts' view that the widespread replacement of streetcars by buses was a serious mistake.

In the mid-1970s, the first American streetcar design since the PCC was sponsored by the federal government's Urban Mass Transportation Administration. The new car is articulated, having two distinct bodies on three trucks, their inner sides sharing the center truck. Articulated cars had been built previously, but the new design uses the latest technology for safety, comfort, speed, and ease of transportation. Although dubbed "light rail vehicles," they were built for the heaviest kind of street and interurban use. Boeing-Vertol built the first order of them in 1976 for service in Boston, with San Francisco next on the list. Also, a single-body car similar to the PCC but with new technological features was designed by Canada's Urban Transportion Development Corporation for service in Toronto, where subways have replaced some trolley routes.

ROGER ARCARA

San Francisco cable cars have been especially efficient on hills since 1873. Special steel sections suspended from the cars grip a constantly moving cable 18 inches below street level. [Republic Steel Corporation]

Among the manufacturers of street and interurban electric railway cars were four in St. Louis: American Car Co., St. Louis Car Co., Laclede Car Co., and Brownell Car Co.; two in Chicago: Pullman and McGuire-Cummings; two in the Pittsburgh area: Standard Steel and American Car & Foundry; two in Massachusetts: Osgood Bradley, Worcester, and Briggs Carriage Co., Amesbury; and four in Ohio: Barney & Smith, Dayton; Cincinnati Car Co.; Niles Car Co, Niles; and Jewett Car Co., Newark. Others were J. G. Brill, Philadelphia; Jackson & Sharp, Wilmington, Delaware; Holman Car Co., San Francisco; Woeber Carriage Co., Denver; Perley A. Thomas (Southern Car Co.), High Point, North Carolina; and three in Ontario: Hawker-Siddeley, Ottawa Car & Mfg. Co., and Preston Car & Coach Co.

BIBLIOGRAPHY: George W. Hilton, *The Cable Car in America,* Howell-North, Berkeley, Calif., 1971; *Jane's World Railways and Rapid Transit Systems,* F. Watts, New York, 1977; William D. Middleton, *The Time of the Trolley,* Kalmbach, Milwaukee, 1967; John A. Miller, *Fares, Please!* Dover, New York, 1960; Frank Rowsome, Jr., *Trolley Car Treasury,* McGraw-Hill, New York, 1956.

Strike of March 15, 1855 First organized railroad labor walkout in America and possibly the first anywhere. On that date all 13 coaches of the 61-mile Boston & Thompson (B&T) Railroad were coupled to a woodburning locomotive, making what was then the longest train ever seen in New England. Pulling out of the Thompson depot in northeastern Connecticut with hundreds of workers aboard, it picked up more employees as it rolled along. Trainmen collected about $16 from the freeloading riders, enough money to buy cordwood for the trip to the road's business office in Boston.

Speaking for the employees, Conductor Bill Floyd said, in effect, to millowner and B&T president Welcome Farnum: "There are 1200 of us here, including 500 laborers who built the line to Thompson, and you promised to pay us today. This is the last train to run over your rails until we are paid in full for the past 6 months of our work."

Sympathetic Bostonians set up tables in the freighthouse adjoining the depot, fed the strikers, and provided sleeping accommodations for them. For 3 weeks no train ran between Boston and Thompson, and the strikers did what they could to sabotage the railroad. But after the third week, with the company's treasury empty and its credit gone, public sympathy for the strike waned. The 1200 men scattered, seeking work elsewhere.

In one sense, the strikers lost, for they never got the pay they had rightly earned and lost their old jobs. But for the first time railroad workers had shown that they could organize for a common cause. They tied up the road so tightly that not a wheel turned for 6 months.

BIBLIOGRAPHY: *Railroad Magazine,* August 1946.

Strike of 1877 First major American railroad strike and the bloodiest and most violent. The strikers themselves were mostly well-organized and orderly, but their sympathizers became unruly mobs that destroyed millions of dollars worth of railroad property, including Pittsburgh's four-story Union Depot, which was burned down. Military intervention brought about the deaths of at least 100 rioters and the wounding of an uncounted number of others.

Trouble started on July 16 when the Baltimore & Ohio (B&O), among other roads, cut the wages of freight train and engine men by 10 percent. This led to a walkout which tied up most of the railroads in 14 states from the Hudson River to the Mississippi and from Canada to Virginia.

Beside wage cuts, the men complained of irregular employment, many being laid off away from home for 3 or 4 days at a time, and slow pay; sometimes wages were held up for as long as 3 or 4 months in a row. Furthermore, the railroad employees had already suffered a 10 percent pay cut in the panic of 1873—a cut which had not been restored.

The main reason for the wage reductions of 1877 was the extreme competition by roads running between New York and Chicago. This cutthroat scramble for freight and passenger business had brought rates down to ridiculously low levels, often far below actual cost. For instance, livestock were carried between the two cities, more than 900 miles, at $1 a head, and passengers for as little as $2.50 a round trip. Someone had to pay for these losses; the burden was passed on to the employees.

The strike began in Baltimore and soon spread to Martinsburg, West Virginia, location of large B&O shops, where strikers forcibly prevented scabs, or newly hired men, from operating the trains. A special train rushed a company of 75 militiamen to Martinsburg. One soldier shot a striker in the head, hips, and arms. President Rutherford B. Hayes denounced the strikers in a proclamation and sent 400 regular Army troops to the city.

Inflamed by military interference, the strike spread over the whole B&O system. Trains were halted, and telegraph wires cut. On July 19 the Pennsylvania Railroad (PRR) freight men at Pittsburgh struck, immobilizing a dozen cattle trains at the East Liberty yards. By midnight 1500 cars were held on sidings there, 200 of them loaded with perishable goods. At Baltimore, a mob surrounded the armory, protesting the presence of troops. A shower of missiles destroyed windows and doors, injuring several soldiers. A mass concentration of police was powerless to quell the riot. At night 150 militia, with rifles loaded, marched from the armory to Camden Station, forcing back the angry demonstrators and dodging stones. Opening fire, they killed at least nine civilians and wounded many more.

At Pittsburgh, the situation was growing desperate. State militia increased the tension. Strikers and their sympathizers still refused to let freight cars move. The walkout spread to other railroads. No freight train was allowed to leave Hornellsville (now Hornell), where the Erie Railroad shops were located. Governors of five states (West Virginia, Maryland, Pennsylvania, New York, and Illinois) called for federal military aid. All New York State regiments of the National Guard (16,000 men) assembled in their armories. One regiment headed for Hornellsville on a special train. Strike sympathizers blocked the mainline by overturning a baggage car and damaging several locomotives. The train's fireman deserted and helped tear up the track at several places. More cars were overturned. Troops finally reached Hornellsville and started the operation of some trains out of that village.

On the night of July 22 several cars were burned at Reading, Pennsylvania, where soldiers killed 13 rioters and wounded nearly 50. The Lebanon Valley Railroad bridge over the Schuylkill River was burned. In Philadelphia, the mob set fire to an oil train. By this time men from the New York Central, Lackawanna, Jersey Central, Morris & Essex, and Lehigh & Susquehanna had walked out in support of the other strikers. At Indianapolis, labor sympathizers seized the Union Depot and refused to let any trains except mail cars run (mail cars were not interfered with at any point during the strike). At Chicago, the walkout involved the B&O, Michigan Central (a New York Central affiliate), Rock Island, Illinois Central, Chicago & Alton, and Burlington.

A large crowd broke into Johnson's Gun Works in Pittsburgh and seized 200 rifles and some small arms. Others rioters confiscated 300 additional rifles. Philadelphia troops in Pittsburgh, numbering over 800, with two Gatling guns and other battery pieces, retreated into the large PRR roundhouse at night and barricaded themselves against the uncontrollable mob. Rioters seized a cannon, loaded it, and planted it within 100 feet of the roundhouse. Before they could open fire, marksmen picked them off one by one. At dawn 13 bodies were found beside the cannon.

Unable to dislodge the troops in any other way, the mob decided to burn them out. An oil train set afire was run down the track; it burned the nearby sandhouse. The besieged soldiers saved the roundhouse with fire hydrants, but at seven o'clock next morning the penetrating smoke drove them out. The soldiers forced their way through the mob to Sharpsburg, killing and being killed.

At Pittsburgh, the rioters destroyed 1600 freight and

passenger cars, many loaded with valuable merchandise, and 128 locomotives, together with all railroad offices and machine shops in the area. They placed the cannon in nearby streets and threatened to blow the city fire fighters to pieces if they tried to quench the flames. The firemen fled.

While torches were being applied, thousands of men, women, and children pillaged the cars. Hundreds of wagons hauled off the loot. Fire gutted Union Depot. Hundreds of spectators climbed City Hall tower to get a clear view of leaping flames and billowing smoke that reddened the sky for miles. A huge grain elevator, not railroad property, also was reduced to ashes. The Panhandle Railroad depot and locomotive shop met the same fate. Before the sun went down that night of July 23, not a railroad building or car of the Pennsy and Panhandle in Pittsburgh was left unburned. At least 53 rioters in that city alone had been killed and 110 injured. All Pennsy trains were annulled until the military could assure their safety.

Throughout Pennsylvania during the second week in July there were riots, bloodshed, and railroad property burned. At Scranton, miners joined the rail walkout. More deaths resulted. In Chicago on July 26, soldiers fired into a crowd of labor sympathizers, killing 10 and wounding 64. As troops occupied the great rail centers, one after another, they quelled the rioting without mercy. Labor leaders had no wish to fight the Army. The strike gradually petered out.

William H. Vanderbilt, New York Central president, claiming that fewer than 500 of his employees had been involved in the strike, showed his appreciation by distributing $200,000 among his loyal operating employees. Thus ended the strike of 1877. Although wage cuts were not restored that year, the strikers had demonstrated a power that the officials never forgot. They had shown, too, the need for greater organization. As the unions grew in strength, railroad wages and working conditions improved. In that sense, the strike of 1877 was a long-range victory for labor.

BIBLIOGRAPHY: Ohio D. Boyle, *History of Railroad Strikes,* Brotherhood Pub. Co., Washington, 1935; Robert V. Bruce, *1877: Year of Violence,* Bobbs-Merrill, Indianapolis, 1959; David T. Burbank, *Reign of the Rabble: The St. Louis General Strike of 1877,* A. M. Kelley Publishers, New York, 1966; George H. Burgess and Miles C. Kennedy, *Centennial History of the Pennsylvania Railroad Company,* Pennsylvania Railroad, Philadelphia, 1949.

Strikebreaking Czar Pearl L. Bergoff could never have won a union labor popularity contest. His strike-prevention and strikebreaking business was established in 1900. The author, as editor of *Railroad Magazine,* visited his Fifth Avenue office in New York in 1935 to learn what kind of man he was. His specialty was transportation strikes, including those on 33 steam railroads and 28 electric lines. The Erie seems to have been his favorite railroad. Among the Erie strikes he handled were those of the boilermakers in 1907, barge captains in 1908, and tugboat masters, pilots, etc., in 1910, two Erie strikes in 1912, and the big walkout of Erie switchmen in 1920. The last-named, Bergoff told me, was his biggest money-maker. He supplied the company with 6000 to 7000 strikebreakers for 4½ months, for which Erie paid him about $2 million.

Bergoff was born in Detroit in 1882. His mother had expected a girl, hence the name Pearl. He was short and stocky, with a strong, fighting face and auburn hair. He had built a powerful machine for crushing strikes and admitted it. Associated in his business were a son and three brothers.

Bergoff did not deny that strikes were often bloody. In fact, he told me that more than once he himself had taken part in the fray. The bloodiest strike he dealt with was that of Pressed Steel Car Co. in 1909, in which at least 10 men were killed. In 1910 he fought a big strike of motormen and conductors on the Philadelphia Rapid Transit Co. Within 24 hours he had 1500 strikebreakers in Philadelphia. He housed them in three huge circus tents, with commissary and sleeping equipment. "The first day of that strike," Bergoff told me "2 of our men were killed. I buried one at my own expense. Before it was over, 3 or 4 had been killed and 50 wounded."

Bergoff handled four Baltimore & Ohio strikes. He told me that in 1910 the Delaware and Hudson had paid him about $35,000 for breaking a track workers' strike. But in 1918 he was badly defeated when he sent 3000 men to fight a Kansas City Street Railway strike. Police and irate citizens drove them out of the city. And 150 of his men were jailed at Milwaukee in connection with a walkout of electric railway light and power employees. He said, though, that then, in 1935, he was giving much more attention to preventing strikes than to breaking them. "Our technique has undergone a change," he added.

Strikes, Major Railroad The first major strike, or rather series of strikes coupled with destructive rioting and bloodshed, occurred in 1877, a depression year characterized by violence. It was caused by repeated wage cuts, the latest being 10 percent. The Pennsylvania Railroad (PRR) not only cut wages but ordered the double-heading of all trains on an important affiliate, the Fort Wayne & Chicago (FW&C), using twice as many cars on each train with a single crew. This action threw many men out of work.

On June 27 a newly organized FW&C trainmen's union declared a strike which was intended to precipitate a nationwide walkout of trainmen, but for some reason the Fort Wayne men hesitated. The strike actually started on July 16 on the Baltimore & Ohio at Martinsburg, West Virginia, a great coal-producing center, where it tied up train service for several days. Local militia sided with labor; so President Rutherford B.

Hayes sent 400 regular troops to the scene to restore order.

On July 17 strike sympathizers at Baltimore, Maryland, stormed and tried to burn the state armory. Soldiers fired on them; bloodshed resulted. Pittsburgh also was dominated by anti-railroad management feeling. On July 19 PRR crews there refused to move trains. Rioters attacked the Pennsy's 28th Street roundhouse, huge and solidly built. Here, too, local militia supported the strikers. A division of National Guard was rushed from Philadelphia to Pittsburgh by special train, arriving on July 22. They fired on the stone-throwing crowd, killing several people. Rioters set immensely destructive fires.

Claims filed against Allegheny County (Pittsburgh) for riot damage totaled $4,000,000; those of the PRR alone, $2,312,000. Eventually, settlement was made for a total of $2,772,000, of which the railroad company recieved $1,000,000. Meanwhile, on July 25, the PRR management met with a strikers' committee, and 3 days later traffic began to roll again in the devastated area. Before that time, the strike had spread northward to Albany, New York, on the Vanderbilt lines, where most employees remained loyal to the management, and as far west as Missouri and Kansas; but military forces finally brought it under control.

But this peace did not last long. The Knights of Labor, founded by Philadelphia garment workers in 1869, soon expanded into a national union for all branches of labor, with a peak membership between 600,000 and 700,000. Flushed with triumph after winning four of five fairly important railroad strikes, it struck the Gould system, principally the Texas & Pacific, demanding union recognition and a minimum daily wage of $1.50. Led by Martin Irons, a walkout of 900 men tied up 5000 miles of railroad in the Midwest. Jay Gould refused to arbitrate or reinstate discharged strikers. The use of federal troops accentuated occasional acts of violence. Collapse of the strike led to gradual disintegration of the once-powerful order a few years later. *See* GOULD, JAY.

Another "one big union," this one an all-railroad organization, American Railway Union (ARU), was organized in Chicago in 1893 under the energetic leadership of Eugene V. Debs. The following spring, Debs, as president of the ARU, called a strike to protest Great Northern wage cuts. The ARU tied up 4000 miles of that road, except for mail trains, and won its strike a week later. *See* DEBS, EUGENE VICTOR.

In June 1894 the Pullman plant workers in Illinois struck on the issue of wage cuts without a corresponding reduction in the rental of employees' homes owned by the Pullman Co. The ARU supported them with a walkout of 125,000 employees of Midwestern roads. Because of Debs's insistence, there was relatively little violence by the strikers, but a sweeping court injunction and United States troops called out by President Grover Cleveland broke the strike. Most of the railroad managements involved blacklisted the strikers afterward. *See* "CRANE WITH A BROKEN NECK"; PULLMAN, GEORGE MORTIMER.

The shopmen's strike of July 1922 was America's first nationwide railroad walkout. Conducted by the American Federation of Labor Railway Employees Department, representing 400,000 members, it was nonviolent. The Transportation Act of 1920 had created the U.S. Railroad Labor Board to set wages and working conditions but without authority to enforce them. The shopmen struck against a Board's wage-cutting decision as a violation of the Transportation Act.

President Warren G. Harding warned the striking shopmen not to interfere with the mails, tried vainly to mediate, and had Attorney General Harry M. Daugherty intervene on behalf of the carriers with a court injunction. The strike ended on October 27, 1922, in a settlement largely favoring railroad management, but both sides claimed victory. Its aftereffects included the Railway Labor Act of 1926, which unions and management accept, abolishing the Board.

See also STRIKE OF MARCH 15, 1855; STRIKE OF 1877; STRIKEBREAKING CZAR; UNIONS, RAILROAD LABOR.

BIBLIOGRAPHY: Ohio D. Boyle, *History of Railroad Strikes*, Brotherhood Pub. Co., Washington, 1935; Gerald G. Eggert, *Railroad Labor Disputes: The Beginnings of Federal Strike Policy*, University of Michigan Press, Ann Arbor, 1967.

Subway and Elevated Railways Lines that provide local passenger service (in many cases, express service also) in large cities. This is *rapid transit* because the lines are separated from street-level traffic. Their location, almost invariably in tunnels or open cuts or on viaducts above the streets, enables them to maintain speeds and schedules unhindered by motor and horse-drawn vehicles, pedestrians, pushcarts, animals, strollers, or bicycles.

The need for rapid transit arose in the mid-nineteenth century as urban population, business, industry, and housing increased. As cities grew, existing horsecar lines could not cope with the demands of more passengers traveling more often and greater distances in the face of those lines' limited capacity and traffic jams. Some form of off-street urban mass transportation was called for. Proposals for faster rail service above or below street level had been advanced since the 1830s, but not until 1863 was the world's first underground city transit line opened, in London, England.

The idea spread to New York. In 1867, Charles T. Harvey built and demonstrated a short, single-track elevated railroad above one curbline of Greenwich Street. Experimental operation for public use began in 1868. Cars were propelled by gripping or releasing an endless sprocket chain (later a cable) moving between the rails and powered by stationary steam engines. This method proved unsatisfactory, so small steam locomotives were acquired to pull the cars. The public quickly accepted elevated railway service despite objections to the inevitable smoke, embers, ashes, and clattering noise from overhead. America's first rapid transit network arose, literally, over New York City streets, four lines and several branches being in operation by the end of the 1870s.

Brooklyn, then a separate city across the East River from New York, saw its first elevated lines built during the 1880s; some extended via ramps at their outer ends to connect with suburban steam railways on ground-level rights-of-way in sparsely populated areas. By the turn of the century, Brooklyn had an extensive network of "el" lines.

About this time, Chicago began building an elevated system. It eventually focused on a loop encompassing many business blocks, serving several mainline railway terminals and giving the area its name, the Loop, which is still used. As in New York and Brooklyn, steam locomotives, mostly Forney types, drew the trains; passenger access was facilitated by station platforms built up to car-floor level. The drawbacks to steam operation in such service included limited train lengths and poor grade-climbing ability.

During the 1880s, experiments were made with electric traction, but the early "juice" locomotives suffered from some of the same disadvantages as the steamers. In the 1890s, Frank J. Sprague, who had already developed practical electric propulsion for streetcars, invented the then-revolutionary multiple-unit system of electric-train operation. By this method, traction motors in the trucks of several cars in a train could be controlled simultaneously by one motorman at the head end. This made possible the running of longer, faster trains that could negotiate steeper grades. It also permitted train operation in continuous tunnels and led to the development of the subway systems now extant in many big cities and still growing.

While horse-drawn streetcars were still being run, New York's Third Avenue Elevated Railroad had begun to provide faster, off-the-street, mass urban transportation. A train of the el is shown passing Cooper Union at Eighth Street. [Collection of Freeman Hubbard]

Meanwhile, in 1868, inventor Alfred E. Beach had demonstrated the Broadway Pneumatic Underground, bored under Broadway, near Murray Street, New York, for a bit more than 300 feet. A cylindrical passenger car running on rails and fitting closely into the tube was pushed by air pressure. When the operator released the brakes, the car, seating 22 people, rolled down a slight grade past a big wind tube, and the gale was turned on. The car moved underneath Broadway at about 6 miles per hour for one block. Beach said that a full-scale passenger subway, if built, ought to run trains at about 50 miles per hour. But the New York City government, then under the sway of Boss Tweed, refused to finance it. So the project was dropped.

Even so, the need for underground travel kept increasing. In 1897, the nation's first subway, the product of bold engineering genius, was opened under Tremont Street in Boston. At first trolley cars operated it. Various streetcar lines were routed into this tube beneath the congested downtown area. Service sped up because stops were made only at stations spaced several blocks apart instead of at every street corner. Later, multiple-unit trains from one of Boston's elevated lines, built after the advent of electric traction, used the tunnel. Other cities adopted the trolley subways, with surface cars from outlying areas rendering rapid transit service in central business districts. Among these cities were Rochester, New York; Philadelphia; Cleveland; and Newark, New Jersey.

As previously with els, New York City led the way to developing high-capacity subways. In March 1900, ground was broken for America's first multiple-unit rapid transit underground line, that of Interborough Rapid Transit Co. (IRT), the first 9 miles being opened on October 27, 1904. Expansion soon followed. The IRT system became a subway network with elevated extensions in four of the city's five boroughs and was operated in conjunction with Manhattan's el system, which it leased.

In 1908, the Hudson & Manhattan Railroad opened its subway under the Hudson River, a Herculean conquest of nature, achieved by engineers and by laborers called *sandhogs.* It used multiple-unit trains to connect several lower New York stations under Sixth Avenue with various steam railway terminals in New Jersey. At about that time, Philadelphia completed its Market Street subway from 69th Street into the downtown shopping area, with elevated extensions on each end.

A Brooklyn Rapid Transit system subsidiary built subways to connect Brooklyn, then an independent city but now a New York City borough, with Manhattan Island. This evolved into the vast Brooklyn-Manhattan system (BMT), using longer and wider cars for greater capacity.

New York's subway-el network became the world's

largest and most heavily used, the only one to operate 24 hours a day, 7 days a week. In 1979 it was carrying about 3,500,000 passengers a day over 710 miles of track and had more than 460 stations and 6600 passenger cars, as well as hundreds of work cars. It operates a nostalgic city transit museum.

But there are valid objections to els over city streets. They darken the area below them, their supporting steel pillars are street-level traffic hazards, they interfere with the privacy of people living or working in the second stories of adjacent buildings, the noisy trains upset sleeping habits, and they depreciate real estate values. Many elevated railway structures have been razed, in some cases being replaced by new underground routes.

Among the latter was New York's municipal Independent Subway, begun in 1925. Its first section, the Eighth Avenue line, was opened in 1932, mainly to supplant the old Ninth Avenue El, which was done away with in 1940. Elsewhere in the 1940s, other subway construction included Philadelphia's Broad Street and Ridge Avenue lines, Newark's trolley subway, and Chicago's first subway, opened in 1943.

Among the cities which have built subways since the end of World War II but not having had them previously are Cleveland, San Francisco (Bay Area, BART), and Washington; and, in Canada, Toronto, Montreal, and Edmonton. Mexico City and many cities in other countries have followed suit. Other subways are being built in Atlanta and Buffalo.

San Francisco's BART, a modern high-speed system, includes a tunnel 7 miles long under San Francisco Bay (the world's longest continuous underwater tube) and elevated extensions to suburban Fremont, Richmond, and Concord. BART trains run automatically at speeds up to 80 miles per hour, with electronic devices that control starting, stopping, and door operation, although a human attendant rides at the front of each train to override, when necessary, the automatic controls.

ROGER ARCARA

BIBLIOGRAPHY: Rodney Hitt, *The Car-Builder's Dictionary*, Railroad Gazette, Chicago, 1906; *Jane's World Railways and Rapid Transit Systems*, F. Watts, New York, 1977; John A. Miller, *Fares, Please!* Dover, New York, 1960; Frank Rowsome, Jr., *Trolley Car Treasury*, McGraw-Hill, New York, 1956; James B. Walker, *Fifty Years of Rapid Transit*, Law Printing Company, New York, 1918.

Summits Nearly all United States rail altitude records, past and present, are in Colorado. The highest standard-gauge summit still used on a *through line* is the Denver & Rio Grande Western's (D&RGW's) 10,238 feet at Tennessee Pass, north of Leadville. The highest adhesion-worked standard-gauge line, the Denver & Salt Lake (Moffat Road), reached 11,660 feet over Rollins or Corona Pass. Opened in 1907, this was a rail route until Moffat Tunnel was completed in 1928; it is now a highway. The D&RGW branch from Leadville to Ibex held the standard-gauge altitude record at 11,522 feet from 1928 until its abandonment in 1944.

The Forty-second Street Station of the Third Avenue El about 1928. The el was razed after World War II. [Etching by Otto Kuhler]

North America's highest narrow-gauge (3-foot) summit was on the Denver, South Park & Pacific (later Colorado & Southern, or C&S, a Burlington subsidiary). This line reached 11,596 feet at Alpine Tunnel, on the Como-Gunnison route, and 11,330 feet at Fremont Pass, north of Leadville. Opened in 1844, it was abandoned in 1937. The 600-yard Alpine Tunnel was built in 1881 and closed in 1917. A standard-gauge line from Leadville to Climax, 11,319 feet, was laid in 1911.

Other 3-foot-gauge summits include Marshall Pass, Colorado, 10,856 feet, on the D&RGW line through Gunnison; Lizard Head Peak, Colorado, 10,848 feet, on the Rio Grande Southern; the C&S Leadville line, 10,-207 feet; Monarch, Colorado, on the D&RGW, 10,028 feet (now standard-gauge), and Cumbres Pass, on the D&RGW, 10,015 feet. For the highest railways, *see* LOOKOUT MOUNTAIN INCLINE RAILWAY; MANITOU & PIKE'S PEAK RAILWAY.

The highest United States rail altitudes, in feet (* means "abandoned"); are Pikes Peak, on the Manitou & Pike's Peak (cog railway), 14,147; Corona, on the Denver & Salt Lake, *11,660; Red Mountain, on the Silverton, *11,650; Alpine Tunnel, on the C&S, *11,-596; Hagerman Pass, on the Colorado Midland (CM), *11,528; Boreas Pass, on the C&S, *11,494; Busk-Ivanhoe Tunnel, on the CM, *10,948; Marshall Pass, on the D&RGW, 10,856; and Tennessee Pass, on the D&RGW, 10,238.

The lowest point on any American railroad is California's Salton Sea on the Southern Pacific. According to W. H. Kirkenbride, former SP chief engineer, the lowest stretch is between Mileposts 625 and 626.1, being 1.1 miles of level grade 205.4 feet below sea level, just east of the switch at Mecca siding. Here are some figures: Salton, Milepost 637.8, is 201.5 feet below sea level; Pope, Milepost 651.1, is 207 feet below; and Wister, Milepost 660.1, is 203.1 feet below. There is no station at Mecca siding, Pope, or Wister; so Salton is America's lowest railroad depot.

SUNA *See* SWITCHMEN'S UNION OF NORTH AMERICA.

Sunday Trains Some early railroads, especially in New England, did not run trains on Sundays. Others did so with reservations. Printed on an 1850 timetable of an antecedent of the Boston & Maine were these words: "Persons purchasing tickets will be required to sign a pledge that they will use the tickets for no other purpose than attending church." Such tickets, however, could not be bought on the Sabbath.

Another New England road, the St. Johnsbury & Lake Champlain, chartered in 1880, had a strict rule not to run trains on Sunday while scale manufacturer Erastus Fairbanks of St. Johnsbury, Vermont, was president and chief stockholder of the road. Now and then his operating officials would surreptitiously disregard this rule in what they considered an emergency, such as sending out a snowplow on a Sunday to keep the line open in winter, shifting a few cars, or dispatching a work train for urgent track repairs. This they would do very early in the morning, while the pious Fairbanks was still asleep, and/or as quietly as possible lest he see or hear what was going on. Engineers were cautioned not to blow the usual crossing whistles, ring bells, or blow off steam. The penalty for being caught in a violation of the "blue Sunday" rule was a sharp rebuke and a threat of being fired if the offense were repeated.

Sunday passenger trains on the Lake Shore & Michigan Southern (New York Central) were unknown in the 1880s. If a train left Buffalo, New York, on a Saturday en route to Chicago and arrived at a large station near midnight, it would tie up there until Monday morning, then proceed to its destination. Crew members and some passengers usually took advantage of this layover to attend church.

BIBLIOGRAPHY: Benjamin A. Botkin and Alvin F. Harlow, *A Treasury of Railroad Folklore*, Crown, New York, 1953.

Sunflower Seeds Now the world's most important source of vegetable oil except for soybeans, sunflower seeds are becoming a bonanza for the railroads serving North and South Dakota, Minnesota, and Texas, where most sunflowers are grown. Thousands of covered-hopper cars a year are loaded with hundreds of thousands of tons of the seed for domestic and export markets. Sunflowers are not a new crop, but only since 1977 have they been moving by rail in significant quantities. The largest growing area is the Red River Valley of North Dakota and Minnesota, where the Burlington Northern is the key railroad, hauling most of the seed to the Head of the Lakes for export and to Minnesota for crushing. The biggest foreign market for American sunflower seed is Western Europe.

Sunset Limited Famous train named for the Southern Pacific slogan "Sunset Route." It made its first run on November 25, 1894, as "the last word in elegance," with wooden, open-vestibuled cars decorated in rococo style and illuminated at night with Pintsch gas chandeliers attached to the ceiling. Its ornate potbellied stoves had isinglass windows through which passengers could see the flames dancing within. There were wicker chairs and potted palms. Gleaming brass cuspidors littered the edges of the aisles. The diner served costly food and French wines. No effort was spared to simulate a first-class hotel. The "ladies' compartment car," attended by a maid, included a dainty parlor, seven sleeping rooms, and a library stocked with the works of Laura Jean Libbey, Bret Harte, Ouida, and other best-sellers of the day.

The *Sunset* linked New Orleans with San Francisco until 1912, when its Western terminal was changed to Los Angeles. Originally it had a weekly schedule, then ran twice a week, and later daily, including Sunday. Before being placed on a year-round basis, the train did not run in summer because it was routed through a hot desert, with no air conditioning then available.

Many stories and legends cling to this rolling hotel. One tells of Patty Moorhead, a Texas rancher's daughter, brashly riding her pony alone across the spidery Pecos River Bridge, 321 feet above the canyon in which she lived, one day in the mid-1890s, to save herself from going 20 miles downstream to ford the river in order to get home. Patty guided her mount along the narrow, steel-covered pathway beside the rails. Halfway across, the pony caught a foot between the ties. The girl heard the oncoming *Sunset Limited* whistle, but managed to free the hoof and reach the other side of the bridge in advance of the train. She never tried that feat again.

Patty was a favorite of early *Sunset* crews. They would toss out a daily newspaper as they passed her home far below. Her father never let the railroad use water from a large spring on his property, although engine crews repeatedly asked for such permission. After he died, however, Patty signed a contract giving them access to it for the rest of her life.

In 1950 the five *Sunset* trains in daily service were dieselized and given complete sets of new stainless-steel Budd cars. Today, under Amtrak auspices, the *Sunset Limited* is still burnishing the 2032 miles of rail between Los Angeles and New Orleans, but this is only part of its current transcontinental run, which includes 1378 additional miles between New Orleans and New York.

BIBLIOGRAPHY: Freeman Hubbard, *Great Trains of All Time,* Grosset & Dunlap, New York, 1962; *Southern Pacific Company, Pioneers of Western Progress,* Strassburger & Co., 1929; Neill C. Wilson and Frank J. Taylor, *Southern Pacific: The Roaring Story of a Fighting Railroad,* McGraw-Hill, New York, 1952.

Superheaters, Locomotive Prior to the use of superheaters, the only direct way to boost a steam locomotive's power was to increase its size. "Of all the improvements to the locomotive during the early 1900s," Angus Sinclair wrote in his authoritative *Development of the Locomotive Engine* in 1907, "none ranks higher than the superheater. Its remarkable effect on locomotive efficiency and power provided a reprieve when further development seemed at an end."

The superheater boosts power and reduces radiation loss in the cylinders, both substantially, without materially adding to the locomotive's cost or weight. Its small-diameter tubes convey saturated steam back through the fire tubes to the boiler for reheating. This raises the steam's temperature and energy but not its pressure.

From the first, engine builders were interested in the possibilities of a superheater, recognizing the need for compacting the utmost power into a given bulk of machinery. For many years all locomotive superheaters were placed not in the boiler flues but in the area ahead of them. The builders in those days did not utilize the higher temperatures available in the tubes because lubricants to withstand the high degree of superheat produced by that method had not yet been invented.

An early type, the smokebox superheater, was a compromise which furnished only a small degree of temperature rise; it blocked the front end, thus impeding the draft. Around 1860, Henry Tyson, the Baltimore & Ohio's master of machinery, fitted up a locomotive with a row of boiler tubes curving upward into the steam space above the water level, which was perhaps the first American step toward the modern superheater. A few years later, the Burlington tried out a superheater of the smokebox drum design. Located just behind the front flue sheet, it was honeycombed with fire tubes and had partitions directing steam through a long and tortuous path. Like all other early smokebox heaters, however, it did not raise the temperature enough to justify its initial cost and maintenance.

Then, in 1895, a German, Dr. Wilhelm Schmidt, known as the father of the modern locomotive superheater, began experimenting with this device. Schmidt was convinced that superheaters would never be successful until some means was found for creating a previously unknown height of steam temperature. His first attempt was a smokebox type which, unlike previous models, did not depend upon waste gases to heat the steam. Instead, he tapped the firebox itself to supply hot furnace gases directly to the steam. His fire-tube superheater, introduced in 1902, established the basic pattern for all subsequent designs.

In 1901 Canadian Pacific (CP) applied a previous Schmidt fire-tube design to one of its 4-6-0s, the first engine in North America so equipped. Then a heavier 10-wheeler compound, built by Schenectady Locomotive Co. for CP, became the initial installation of the perfected Schmidt superheater on the continent. In 1903 a variety of other fire-tube superheaters, all based on the original Schmidt arrangement, began appearing on the market. They included the Vaughn-Horsey, first installed on the CP; the Cole, used primarily by the Chicago & North Western and the New York Central; the Buck-Jacob, a Santa Fe favorite; and the later popular Elesco types built by Superheater Co. After about 1910 all new steam-road engines, and later switchers and industrial locomotives as well, were equipped with superheaters.

BIBLIOGRAPHY: Henry B. Comstock, *The Iron Horse,* Crowell, New York, 1971; Richard J. Cook, *Super Power Steam Locomotives,* Golden West Books, San Marino, Calif., 1966; Roy. V. Wright (ed.), *The Locomotive Cyclopedia of American Practice,* Simmons-Boardman, New York, 1941.

Switch Keys Keys which railroaders use to unlock and throw or "line" switches. They are also collectors' items. As a rule, each key is stamped with the initials of the road which owns it and issues it to an operating employee on a long-term loan. Nearly all keys are brass; some are iron. Employees terminating their jobs for any reason should turn in their keys to the company. With relatively few exceptions, they have no legal or moral right to keep the keys, sell them, or give them away. Many (but not all) switch keys held by hobbyists are technically stolen property. Among the few exceptions are those donated by railroad companies.

One key honestly obtained is the 14-karat-gold copy

Switch lock and key of the Frankfort & Kokomo Railroad (note the initials F&KRR on the key), now part of the Norfolk & Western Railway.

of a Pittsburgh & Lake Erie switch key which John W. Barriger held as president of the P&LE. Barriger turned in the original when he retired from that road at 65. Lucius Beebe had the replica made for him as a lasting memento. Before the Atchison, Topeka and Santa Fe *Railroad* was incorporated as a *Railway* it used a wax casting of a switch key to make six silver replicas, initialed AT&SFRR, and distributed them to six of its top executives.

Most of the keys were made by Adams & Westlake, which began manufacturing keys, lanterns, etc., in the 1870s. Some collectors acquired such items in the 1930s by having requests printed in weekly newspapers and small magazines, by purchase, and by writing to railroad public relations departments. As the hobby grew in popularity, many fakes were made by people who bought nonrailroad keys from local locksmiths and had them die-stamped with railroad initials. Possibly the world's largest collection consisted of 1200 switch keys owned by a Chesapeake and Ohio engineer.

Switchmen's Union of North America (SUNA) The Switchmen's Association was founded in Chicago in 1877 because the switchmen in that area were working 12 hours a day, every day in the month, for $50 a month, and an individual was helpless in trying to bargain with his railroad employer. The movement spread. In 1888 it was called the Switchmen's Mutual Aid Association of the United States of America, but a lockout on the Chicago & North Western and a disastrous strike on the Burlington killed it in July 1894. Three months later, the Switchmen's Union of North America was organized in Kansas City, Missouri. For almost 50 years it was the only operating rail labor union affililated with the American Federation of Labor. Since 1935 it has also been affiliated with the Canadian Labor Congress. Just before it merged into the United Transportation Union in 1968, the SUNA had 12,000 members, international headquarters in Buffalo, New York, and 273 locals in 35 states and 3 Canadian provinces.

Switchmobile Stubby, 208-horsepower, four-wheeled, diesel-powered switch engine (resembling a jeep) which climbs across tracks, travels on city streets, and pulls freight cars. It equals in power a 50-ton switch engine but weighs less than 36,000 pounds. Even so, it has sufficient tractive effort to pull a gross weight of over 1000 tons from a starting point. It never has to back up, being equipped with a special four-speed transmission enabling it to push or pull with equal power and speed in either direction. Coupling cars to this unit is standard procedure, since it is fitted with standard couplers and airbrake lines, front and rear. Compressed air is used in braking and steering. *See also* GEEP.

T

T Rail Rail devised by Robert L. Stevens, a wiry little railroad man in his mid-forties. Seated in the cabin of a sailing ship in the summer of 1830, he whittled models of various rail designs with a jackknife until he had one shaped like a broad-based letter T and decided it was what he wanted for the Camden & Amboy Railroad (C&A), of which he was president and chief engineer. In 1830 the C&A was being built in New Jersey and would eventually become a major part of the Pennsylvania Railroad (now Conrail).

When Stevens hit upon the T-rail concept, he was bound for England to buy a locomotive similar to the *Stourbridge Lion*, which had inaugurated American railroading the year before. He was not satisfied with the strap-iron rails of his day, laid on wooden sleepers (ties). They were too light and often worked loose, causing accidents. The broad-based high T, he concluded, would best stand the steady pound of locomotive driving wheels in all kinds of weather.

Stevens persuaded a reluctant family friend in Wales to roll T rails in his foundry. On May 16, 1831, the first delivery reached the C&A at Camden, New Jersey. Stevens bought stone blocks from a prison quarry at Ossining, New York, and had the new rails clamped to them by hook-headed spikes of his own design. The *John Bull*, which had been built for him in England and became the world's first locomotive to have a cowcatcher, or pilot, was also the first to run on T rails, in the fall of 1832. At that time the entire country had only 40 miles of railroad. Another 2800 miles were built before 1840.

Stevens abandoned the high T in 1845, adopting instead a heavier pear-shaped type; but in 1858 the Pennsy redesigned the rail back to a high T, which gradually became standard on all roads, as it is today. Meanwhile, in 1844, the rolling of heavy iron rails had been started in the United States by the Mount Savage Rolling Mills in Maryland, which manufactured inverted-U, or Evans-type, rails as well as the Stevens type.

In 1856 Henry Bessemer, an English metallurgical chemist, discovered a revolutionary new steelmaking process. His first steel rails were delivered in New York in 1863. Two years later a Chicago rolling mill rolled the first American-made steel rails, from ingots produced by an experimental steel works at Wyandotte, Wisconsin.

By 1880 the United States had 93,296 miles of railroad. By 1912 the manufacture of open-hearth steel rails had surpassed that of Bessemer rails. New steel alloys were being blended and tested. More than 73 different high-T designs were created to meet the needs of mainlines, yards, switches, and crossovers. The high T has been made with greater and greater strength and hardness to keep pace with the increasing speed, weight, length, and frequency of trains, the present maximum weight being 119 pounds to the yard.

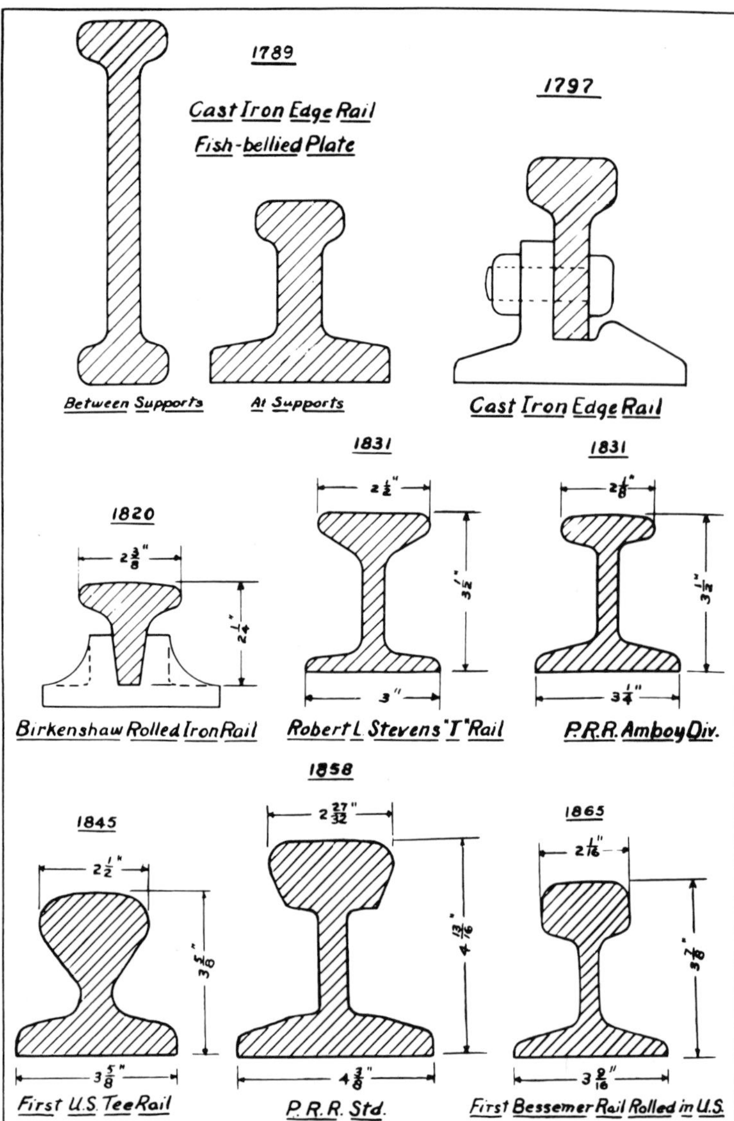

Stepping-stones in the development of the modern T rail. [**Railroad Magazine**]

Taunton Locomotive Works Firm in Taunton, Massachusetts, founded by W. W. Fairbanks, that built nearly 1000 engines, most of them noted for their trim lines, speed, good valve travel, boiler capacity, and smooth running, although some were criticized as being loose-jointed. The earliest ones were inside-connected 4-4-0 woodburners for New England roads. The first, named *Rough and Ready*, was completed on May 29, 1847, for the Eastern Railroad (now part of the Boston & Maine).

Another, the *Mount Holly*, of the vintage of 1849, inaugurated passenger service on the Rutland & Harrison. Later sold to the Burlington & Lamoille, it was renamed *William Hale*, was converted to a coalburner in 1881, and worked 51 years before being scrapped. The less fortunate *Oneida*, built in 1851, figured in several accidents and lawsuits. In 1856, while pulling the night express from Poughkeepsie, New York, she fell into the Hudson River, killing the crew and many passengers. She was scrapped about 1870.

A lucky Taunton iron horse was the *St. Albans*, which the Central Vermont Railroad renamed *Shelbourne*. Completed in 1869, she was converted to burning coal around 1880. Later rebuilt and sold in turn to two other roads, she continued working until 1915 without ever having had an accident, it is said, and always returning to the enginehouse under her own steam.

The *Daniel Webster*, which Taunton built for the Philadelphia, Baltimore & Washington, was America's first successful coalburning engine.

The plant's heaviest power consisted of Consolidation types. Its best customers were the Union Pacific (153 locomotives), Santa Fe (71), and Jersey Central (about 40). Taunton's proudest year was 1881, with 60 engines constructed. Several Taunton locos built for the Alabama & Chattanooga had handsome Russia-iron boilers with shiny brass bands, fancy painting, and upholstered walnut cabs with glass plates fitted over the engine names on their sides. In 1890 the last iron horse rolled out of the plant's erecting shop and was delivered to the narrow-gauge Boston, Revere Beach & Lynn.

BIBLIOGRAPHY: Angus Sinclair, *Development of the Locomotive Engine*, annotated ed. by John H. White, Jr., M.I.T., Cambridge, Mass., 1970.

Telegraphic Codes for Train Control In the early 1900s such codes included the following:

1. Display stop signal.
2. Block clear.
3. Block wanted for other than passenger train.
4. Train other than passenger has entered the block.
5. Block is not clear of train other than passenger.
7. Train following.
8. Opening block station (answer by record of trains in the extended block).
9. Closing block station (answer by No. 13).
12. Correct.
13. I understand (or, Understand?).
17. Display stop signal; train following.
18. What is the trouble?
19. Train order.
21 or 25. Busy on another wire.
31. Train order requiring signature of engineman and/or conductor.
36. Block wanted for passenger train.
46. Passenger train has entered block.
47. Display signals.
48. Signals are displayed.
55. Important.
56. Block is not clear of passenger train.
73. Compliments.
92. Deliver.
Com. Complete.

OS. Train report.
TM. Trainmaster
X. Acknowledgment of train order.

Television Television was used for the first time aboard a train when the Baltimore & Ohio teamed up with Bendix Radio for a practical demonstration of TV reception on October 7, 1948, bringing in the second game of World Series baseball (Cleveland Indians versus Boston Braves) in Boston. The test was conducted in a car attached to the *Marylander*, a train which left Washington, D.C., at 1:30 p.m. and was running about 80 miles per hour, with a special antenna for high-speed reception.

Thiehoff Family The seven railroading sons of Philip and Rose Thiehoff, who settled at Hunnewell, Missouri, in the 1880s, must have set a record. All seven learned telegraphy. They were W. F. Thiehoff, general manager, Burlington's eastern lines; Richard, conductor, Spokane, Portland & Seattle; Joseph, locomotive engineer, Burlington; Sam, station agent, Santa Fe; Yancey, telegraph operator, Burlington; Bert, chief dispatcher, Santa Fe; and Charles, conductor, Santa Fe. The same couple had three daughters, all married to railroaders, and many grandchildren and great-grandchildren who are or were either railroaders or the wives of railroaders.

Tie Plates Flanged plates between rails and ties that ensure a uniformly firm foundation, help hold the track gauge, and prevent rails from cutting into ties under the heavy impact of trains. That part of the rail resting on the tie plates is called the *base*. The top part, on which the wheels roll, is the *head*. The part between the base and the head of the rail is the *web*.

Although each tie plate has four square holes into which spikes are driven, ordinarily only two holes are used at a time, because ties don't need replacement as often as rails. Average tie life is 3 times that of rail life. When you replace a rail, you use the tie plate's alternate set of holes to let the new spikes gain an equally firm grip on another part of the wooden tie.

The S-shaped metal at the end of many ties is a *check iron,* designed to prevent the tie end from splitting apart. Each one is 6 inches long and an inch wide. One edge is sharpened and hammered into the tie end before installation in the track. At least one and sometimes more irons are used at both ends of the tie. Other shapes are the letters G and Z.

Ties (Crossties) Ties were first laid on the Camden & Amboy (C&A), which was built between 1831 and 1835 from Camden to South Amboy, New Jersey. Their use came about by chance. Stone blocks, a few of which are still extant, were being used to support the wrought-iron rails, as on all other United States and English railways at that time. When a stone shipment was delayed, Robert L. Stevens, president and chief engineer of the road, ordered wooden slabs to be laid temporarily crosswise to the track, to be replaced later. Surprisingly, the slabs proved so superior to stone that all the stone blocks were replaced with wooden ties, instead of the reverse.

The C&A also pioneered in three other basics of track construction: the T rail, the hook-headed spike, and the forerunner of the modern rail joint, all three invented by Stevens. Leased to the Pennsylvania Railroad in 1871, the line is now part of Conrail. *See* T RAIL.

Ties are the largest expense item in track maintenance. Although experiments have been and are being made with a wide variety of other materials such as stone, concrete, metals, and plastics, no single material surpasses wood in low initial cost, comparatively light weight, and relatively long life when treated with preservatives. Besides, wood is a natural insulator for track-signal circuits and is resilient enough to absorb impacts.

At least 30 different kinds of wood have served or are serving for crossties, particularly oak, southern pine, gum, Douglas fir, beech, and maple. Timber-preserving experiments by railroads and the lumber industry have prolonged tie life for more than 30 years, or at least 400 percent longer than the life of untreated ties, and it is being lengthened still further as time goes on. This helps to conserve the nation's timber supply. Wood preserving by pressure was introduced by the Louisville & Nashville at Pascagoula, Mississippi, in 1875.

A green tie contains about two gallons of water; the drying process may take from 6 to 18 months. The most common treating fluids are creosote solutions of coal tar or petroleum. Zinc chloride also is used. A Class I road may have several tie and lumber-processing plants scattered over its system.

Crossties are standardized in lengths of 8, 8½, and 9 feet. They also come in seven sizes according to width and length. Mainline tracks where traffic is heavy are usually supported by ties spaced more closely together than on branch and short lines. In the average mile of track, about 3000 crossties are spaced about 21 inches apart from center to center. Tie plates of proper size and design are important in protecting ties against mechanical wear on wood. *See* DATE NAILS.

The tie machine invented by R. H. Abbott, a Chesapeake and Ohio division engineer, and associates, removes and replaces wooden ties automatically without disturbing the adjacent roadbed. Unlike other automatic tie-removal machines, this one does not straddle the track but permits trains to run without delays.

BIBLIOGRAPHY: *Maintenance of Way Cyclopedia*, Simmons-Boardman, New York, 1921——.

Tigrett, Isaac Burton *See* GULF, MOBILE, & OHIO RAILROAD.

Timetables, Earliest United States and Canadian The first railroad timetable issued in North America is believed to have been the Baltimore & Ohio notice that appeared in the Baltimore *American and Commercial Advertiser* of Friday, May 21, 1830, stating:

> The Railroad between Baltimore and Ellicotts' Mills will be opened for the transportation of passengers, on MONDAY, the 24th instant. A brigade, or train of coaches, will leave the Company's Depot on Pratt-street, and return, making three trips each day—starting at the following hours precisely, viz:
>
> Leave Baltimore at 7 A.M. and Ellicotts' at 9 A.M.
> Leave Baltimore at 11 A.M. and Ellicotts' at 1 P.M.
> Leave Baltimore at 4 P.M. and Ellicotts' at 6 P.M.
>
> The price for the trip of twenty-six miles, will be seventy-five cents for each person. Tickets may be had at the Depot. . . .

On September 22, 1831, the Mohawk & Hudson (New York Central's first predecessor), publicized this timetable, which named the engine but no arrival time:

> Carriages will leave the head of the inclined plane ¾ of a mile from the city of Schenectady, at the following times: ½ past 4 in the morning, 8 o'clock A.M., 12 do noon, 2 do P.M., 4 do P.M. [*do* means "ditto."]
>
> Leave Albany at the head of Lydius street 2 miles from the Hudson river, at the following times: ½ past 6 o'clock A.M., 10 do A.M., ¼ past 4 do P.M.
>
> The Locomotive Engine De Witt Clinton will depart in the following order: Leave head of plane at Schenectady at 8 o'clock A.M. and 4 o'clock P.M. Head of Lydia street, Albany, at 10 o'clock A.M. and ¼ past 4 P.M.

Canada's first rail schedule was advertised in the *Montreal Gazette* of July 23, 1836, by a road officially opened 2 days before:

> The Champlain and St Lawrence Railroad Company, in connection with the Steamer Princess Victoria, will be prepared to convey Passengers between Montreal and St. Johns, on Monday, the 25th instant, as follows:—
>
> Steamer, from Montreal, 8 o'clock A.M., 2 do P.M., 4 do P.M. From La Prairie, 6 o'clock, A.M., 9 do A.M., 3 do P.M.
>
> Locomotive, from St. Johns, 8 o'clock, A.M., 2 do P.M. From La Prairie, 9 o'clock, A.M. 5 do P.M.

Torpedoes and Fusees Devices that are often used by flagmen, in addition to flags and lanterns, to protect the rear of a standing or overdue train. Clamped to rail tops, thin turtle-necked torpedoes known as *guns* or *caps* explode as wheels roll over them, thus warning a following train crew to be on the lookout for a train ahead. The fusee, or flare, is a rod-shaped cylinder containing a mixture of wood pulp or similar material and sodium or potassium nitrate impregnated with strontium, lithium, or calcium, depending upon the shade of red desired.

There have been various kinds of torpedoes. Early ones were explosives crudely wrapped in paper and sealing wax, with no way to attach them to the rail unless you could slap a little soft mud on one, hoping to make it stick. Other torpedoes of long ago were tar-dipped and had a tiny wooden peg to push into a rail-joint crevice. Then came a round, tin-box kind with lead straps to clamp to the rail. Still others had steel springs, often clamped into place with the aid of a small fork. Finally the modern fiber-cased torpedo was developed.

Prior to World War I, when green signified "caution" and white meant "clear," trainmen used a kind of fusee that burned for 15 minutes, first red, then green, and lastly white, 5 minutes each. Later fusees burned only red for 5 minutes. Another kind had a cap on its head; you banged it head down on the rail to ignite it. This was fine unless the rail was wet and you had to light it with a match.

BIBLIOGRAPHY: William F. Knapke and Freeman Hubbard, *The Railroad Caboose*, Golden West Books, San Marino, Calif., 1968.

Towns Named for Railroad Presidents At least 200 cities and towns all over the United States must fit into this category. A partial survey made by Frank P. Donovan, Jr., lists 162, Minnesota topping the list with 20, followed by Iowa with 19 and Texas with 17. Such nomenclature is almost unknown in New England, most of whose communities were laid out and built before the railroad era. But the iron horse was responsible for countless settlements in the Midwest and Far West. Grateful pioneers named their towns for the heads of companies which had brought them there. In some cases, rail officials themselves christened the new stations.

The railroad president for whom the most communities were named was John I. Blair, head of the Sioux City & Pacific (now Chicago & North Western) and other roads, who lived to be 97 and is credited with having laid more miles of steel than anyone else. But the

Fusee on the track and torpedo on the rail. These two devices are commonly used by rear brakemen on trains stopped unexpectedly for any reason between stations. This equipment guards against rear-end collisions. [Canadian Pacific Railway]

Northern Pacific, with 22 names, heads the roll of railroads with on-line communities named for its presidents. A comparable nomenclature exists in Canada.

Track, Straight and Curved America's longest stretch of straight track is the Seaboard Coast Line's (CSX's) 78.66 miles of line between Wilmington and Hamlet, North Carolina, which does not have even a slight curve. The nation's longest stretch of curved track is the Pontchartrain curve on the Illinois Central Gulf's line between Ruddock and Trinity, Louisiana. This curve skirts the western shore of Lake Pontchartrain and extends for 9.45 miles. The longest perfectly uniform curve is believed to be on the Missouri Pacific between Alexandria and Cheyneyville, Louisiana, 5.7 miles.

Track Geometry Car The most advanced unit of its kind, this car helps the Southern Pacific (SP) Engineering Department to get a much clearer picture of track conditions than is possible with visual inspection, the usual method. Underneath the bright orange self-propelled car are 12 measuring wheels. As the car moves along the track, these wheels determine such factors as whether or not the rails are properly aligned, level, smooth, in gauge (to 0.1 inch), and surfaced to the extent required for the particular class of track and whether one rail is higher than the other over a set distance.

The 80,000-pound car collects data at operating speeds up to 70 miles per hour and under the pressure and other conditions that a loaded train would create. These dynamic measurements indicate what changes take place underneath a train moving over a specified section of track. Measurements are taken about every 2 feet (they could be taken at 6-inch intervals) while the car is running. Locations are pinpointed so precisely on paper printouts that a roadmaster can, for instance, know that 280 feet from Milepost 99 an area of track 10 feet long is 0.6 inch out of gauge, or 0.1 inch over Federal Railway Administration (FRA) standards. The car is powered by a 48-horsepower diesel engine and can be operated from either end. Several other roads and the FRA have track geometry cars, but SP's unit has the latest, most advanced features.

Track Pans Water-filled troughs that enabled steam locomotives to take on water without stopping, mostly on large Eastern roads, especially the Pennsylvania and New York Central, from the 1880s until the early 1900s. They were about 1000 feet long, about 20 inches wide, and deep enough to receive a water scoop lowered from a suspended position directly under the middle of the tender. Many gallons of water could be scooped up in 12 to 15 seconds while train speed was 40 or 45 miles per hour. Firemen operated the scoop with a lever in the cab.

The scoop mechanism on some steam locomotives, seen here from underneath, that took water from track pans while the train was moving. [New York Central Railroad]

Track Scales Scales used to weigh cars and their contents and to charge accordingly. A ticket is stamped showing the gross weight (car and its freight) and the tare (empty car), which is subtracted from the gross to give net weight, the basis on which the shipper is charged.

Track Structures Dynamic Test Facility New operation at the Chicago Technical Center of the Association of American Railroads. From the outside it resembles a corrugated-iron-sided warehouse. Inside is a microcosm of the nation's 300,000-plus miles of railroad track, all under one roof. Included is a 150-foot segment of track curving skyward at each end, somewhat like a roller coaster. At its center a 45-foot section can be transformed to represent any track in the country. This section accommodates any combination of track components and any type of subsoil down to a 12-foot depth. The facility helps rail researchers to find out what happens to track structure subjected to continuous pounding by freight trains. It bridges the gap between laboratory testing and field evaluations. Tests made here cost less than full-scale field tests and do not interfere with railroad operations.

To simulate freight traffic over the experimental track a special vehicle was designed. Loaded with scrap metal, it weighs 263,000 pounds, equal to a 100-ton car's weight. It is only 25 feet long, but its truck spacing is 12.5 feet, which simulates the end truck spacing of two coupled 100-ton cars, from which prototype track structures get the greatest strains. Hydraulic motors propel the test vehicle on one truck powered by an overhead catenary, in much the same way as a streetcar. Ramps at each end slow its forward momentum and reverse its direction. On five 8-hour days a week the vehicle rocks back and forth, subjecting the track to 30,000 gross tons per hour. Every 5 days it puts on the track the equivalent of the weight of 200 freight trains.

Train Dynamics Analyzer In-depth computerized training device for enginemen in train-handling methods, giving them a close look at the stresses and strains in their trains. It simulates the forces that a train builds up in moving over a segment of track. By watching a video display the enginemen know at a glance the milepost locations, upcoming grades and curves, and what happens to each car as the airbrake is applied or released. With a flick of a switch an operator can back up a computer program and repeat the movements to test different control procedures. The analyzer also can be used to duplicate conditions on an actual run involving a problem or derailment to help determine its cause. Packaged like a 20-foot container, the unit is portable but needs electric power to operate.

Train-Order Hoops and Forks "In 1896, before the Pennsylvania Railroad began using telephones," writes Ernest E. Miller, "I worked at RK tower as a boy operator. We could not contact station agents directly but would send them messages and train orders by using a stock 6 or 7 inches long, splitting the ends, securing the tissues with rubber bands, and handing them up to the first train going in the direction of the agency, to be thrown off at the station. One day I tried a better method. I made a hoop with a grapevine. The crew man accepting it could insert an arm through it and thus the train would not have to slow down for handing up orders. The agent I worked for was so pleased that he had me make a bundle of hoops at one cent each. Years later, the Pennsy officially adopted train-order hoops."

In 1896, the Maine Central began using barrel hoops to deliver orders, tieing the tissue to a crosswise string. In 1904, long before they became standard equipment for operators, the Rock Island adopted large lightweight train-order hoops shaped somewhat like tennis rackets without the webbing, which later came into general use on other roads. A more sophisticated development was the train-order fork, Y-shaped; the order was attached to the middle of a tough cord connecting both upper ends of the Y. Usually the trainman quickly removed the tissue and tossed the hoop or fork back to the operator as the train sped by. Sometimes he kept the hoop or fork in the caboose and threw out an extra in place of the one he retained. Today, nearly all train orders are delivered by radio telephone. *See also* DOGS.

BIBLIOGRAPHY: William F. Knapke and Freeman Hubbard, *The Railroad Caboose*, Golden West Books, San Marino, Calif., 1968.

Train Orders Fewer and fewer trains today are being operated by train orders, but the hobby of collecting such orders is growing. Railroad men called them *flimsies* because they were originally handwritten (more recently typed) on tissue-paper forms, usually 7 by 7¼ inches, green, but sometimes white, yellow, or pink, with carbon copies to be handed to the head and rear ends of trains and to be kept on file in the office. Basically, they govern train movements not covered by current operating timetables, including extra and special trains, speed restrictions, rights over certain trains, unusual circumstances, and emergencies such as wrecks, fires, snowslides, landslides, other obstacles on the track, and washouts. *See* TRAIN-ORDER HOOPS AND FORKS.

The first telegraphed train order—which revolutionized dispatching—was issued on September 27, 1851, by large and portly Charles Minot, general superintendent of the Erie Railroad, while the westbound day express he was riding waited at Turner's Station (now Harriman), New York, for a meet with a delayed eastbound train. It stated:

> To Agent & Operator Goshen [New York]: Hold eastbound train till further orders Charles Minot, Supt Erie

Then he wrote and signed another order and handed it to his train conductor:

> To Conductor & Engineer, Day Express: Run to Goshen regardless of opposing train

His engineer refused to obey such an order even though it came from the boss, saying, in effect: "I'll be damned if I run by that thing." Minot took him out of the cab and ran the train himself. By doing so, the superintendent saved an hour or more of the westbound's time and started a practice that eventually became general on railroads all over North America.

Train dispatchers issue these orders in accordance with the Standard Code of Operating Rules, Block Rules, and Interlocking Rules. In 1889 the General Time Convention adopted the first standard code, designated Uniform Train Rules and Rules for the Movement of Trains by Telegraphic Orders. Since then, the code has often been modified to meet changing conditions. For instance, in the late 1880s and the 1890s extra and special trains were instructed to "run wild." Prior to that, some even ran on a single track on *smoke orders*, with no train orders at all but proceeding until a crew member saw the distant smoke of an approaching train, whereupon the train nearest a siding would head forward or backward into it. Modern orders instruct extra and special trains to "run extra." Certain trains which in the old days were instructed to "run regardless" of other trains are now "given rights" over other trains between certain points. But no two roads have identical train-order codes.

The basic difference between a 19 and a 31 order is that the latter requires the train to stop for the signature of the man to whom it is addressed, while the 19 form is delivered to the crew on the fly, although the train must slow down to facilitate delivery. In 1932 a new book of rules made the 31 form obsolete on most Canadian trackage. A clearance form issued in connection with train orders everywhere shows, among other data, the numbers of all orders to be delivered to a train.

In 1959 railfan Carroll Sanders of Harrisburg, Pennsylvania, organized the National Association of Train Order Collectors. Most members are railfans; others are railroad men, especially active or retired dispatchers, operators, and station agents. They buy, sell, and trade specimens and get others from engine and train crews and station employees.

Trainbox Box about 2 feet long by 10 inches wide, commonly used by a passenger train conductor many years ago to hold his official reports and uniform peaked cap. The train porter usually carried the trainbox to the train and placed it opposite his seat. When opened up, it served as a desk.

Trainsheds The type of trainshed invented by Lincoln Bush, chief engineer of the Delaware, Lackawanna & Western, was first installed in 1905 when that road built its Hoboken, New Jersey, terminal. His design differed essentially from the umbrella- and butterfly-type sheds in being continuous except for the slot or gutter through which locomotive smoke and steam escaped. The Bush shed and, to a lesser extent, each of two other designs offered major protection from the weather. Furthermore, the space within the trainshed was much freer from smoke and dirt and was well-ventilated. Construction cost only about half the price of the old type of arched sheds which preceded the Bush design.

Maintenance also was much cheaper. In the decade following 1905 other large stations were erected with Bush sheds, including Lackawanna's impressive depot in Scranton, Pennsylvania, the Chicago & North Western edifice in Chicago, the Michigan Central station in Detroit, the Jersey Central terminal in Jersey City, and Canadian Pacific's Windsor Station in Montreal.

Trainsheet Dispatcher's record of his trains. At the close of his shift he signs the sheet and states the hours during which he was on duty. The trainsheet has official and legal value in settling arguments and in explaining situations or problems involving train movements.

Down its center are listed names of stations and other data, varying on different railroads, such as the mileage between depots, their office calls, and the capacities of sidings. Some trainsheets do not show blind sidings (those not having a telegraph office nearby) but only the telegraph offices. One side of this column lists the trains running in one direction; the other side, opposing trains. On roads where westbound or northbound trains are superior to eastbounds or southbounds, the superior ones are listed on the right side of the sheet.

Passenger trains head the list on either side, followed by freight movements. Information on crews, time on duty, etc., varies somewhat on different roads. Many companies require the names of the entire crew; others specify only the engineer and the conductor. The time of a train's departure from a terminal is recorded; so is the amount of equipment handled: the number of passenger cars or freight loads, empties, and tonnage. Most roads figure tonnage in terms of 2000 pounds. Some use 1000 pounds, called an M. For example, a 3500-ton train has the equivalent of 7000 M.

Station agents or operators report to the dispatcher (DS) each train that passes. The DS records on his sheet its arrival and departure time, or at least the time at which it goes by, when and if he is fortunate enough to get one by without stopping it for orders. When cars are to be set out or picked up, the dispatcher's entry on the sheet is, respectively, a minus or a plus sign. Since the radiotelephone was adapted to train operation, the use of written train orders has largely been discontinued.

See also TRAIN-ORDER HOOPS AND FORKS.

Tramway, North America's First An inclined plane was laid with wooden rails, over which merchandise was hauled up and down the Niagara escarpment near the present border between New York State and Canada. Its motive power was the muscular effort of men winding and unwinding a giant spool to which a cable was attached. Built in 1762 by Major Wiggins, the English cammander at Niagara, with military sappers and volunteer labor, it followed an old Indian train down the bluff. Writing to his superior, Gen. Jeffrey Amherst, he said that supplies could be loaded on a trunk or carriage equipped with runners and dragged uphill by two or three men working a large windlass. The "rails" were two sets of parallel wooden planks down the face of the cliff, held in place with hefty wooden pegs hammered deeply into the soil.

In 1764 Capt. John Montressor, an engineer, improved on this device by having both sledges, one on each side of the track, joined to the same cable after passing through the windlass so that a descending car would help to pull the other car up. According to some historians, wheels replaced runners in the latter years of the tramway.

Trummer, Frank (Monk) Robber of boxcars and railroad loading platforms of merchandise which he estimated to be worth about $1 million, mostly during the 1920s. Trummer operated between Denver and Chicago. He reputedly invented the rope-ladder system of entering moving railroad cars, a device copied by other outlaws. Besides serving three prison terms, he had several bullet scars. *See* PERRY, OLIVER CURTIS.

Late in life, while going straight, Trummer told his life story. "I never worked for any railroad," he said, "but for a while I was on the payroll of the Chicago, Burlington & Quincy. They paid me to lay off their freight, although technically I was hired to aid in tracing boxcar thieves."

Tumbleweed Fences (Stevens Hedges) Barriers that keep sand from covering the Texas & Pacific (T&P) tracks between El Paso and Big Spring, Texas. Known as Stevens hedges from the T&P general roadmaster L. R. Stevens, who originated them in 1953, they consist of pipes 1 inch in diameter driven into the earth with two strands of barbed wire strung between them. Tumbleweeds piled up against the barrier filter out the sand, eliminating the work of clearing tracks. Stevens hedges cost only one-fifth as much as replacing rock ballast fouled with sand.

Tunnels America's first railroad tunnel, 300 yards long, was opened in 1834 at Staple Bend, near Johnstown, Pennsylvania, on the Allegheny Portage, a Pennsylvania Railroad antecedent linking canals between Hollidaysburg and Johnstown.

The world's only railroad tunnel not built by human power is said to be the Southern Railway System's Natural Bridge in southwestern Virginia. Soil erosion gradually created it eons ago. In 1890 builders of the Virginia & Southwestern Railroad (which the Southern leased a few years later) laid a track through it.

Cascade Tunnel is the longest railroad bore in the Western Hemisphere. The 9 next longest tunnels in the United States are listed in the table below with their locations, railroads, lengths, numbers of tracks, and ruling grades. *See* CASCADE TUNNEL.

Prior to completion of the Cascade, the Hoosac in the Hoosac Range of Massachusetts was America's longest railroad bore. Begun in 1851, it was completed after 24 years of fighting great obstacles. At first, its drilling was done by hand with the aid of primitive black powder. Later, nitroglycerin was used. Very few machines in those days could gnaw hard rock. For ventilation, a central shaft was driven down more than 1000 feet, and corridors were pushed outward in both directions toward the end headings.

Three times in 9 years lack of funds halted the project. In 1869, after little progress had been made, a contractor from Montreal took over and revitalized the job, drilling, blasting, and clearing the area at several points simultaneously. By driving the discouraged workers and improving equipment and techniques, the tunnel builders in November 1874 heard the last deafening blast from both portals and saw daylight stream through a ragged connecting gap.

On October 13, 1875, the first train rolled through. The big bore had been completed at a cost exceeding $17 million and a loss of lives estimated at up to 196. More than 1 million tons of rock had been removed, half a million pounds of nitroglycerin exploded, and 20 million bricks troweled together to form a firm sleeve at the western end, where the rock was so soft and moisture-saturated that tunnelers called it porridge.

Steam, gas, and smoke hung so thickly in the tunnel that after a train ran through, following trains had a long wait for clear air before they could proceed. For this reason, in 1911 the Hoosac was electrified with single-catenary construction. All steam trains kept their power shut off while inside the bore, and electric motors towed them.

Name	Location	Railroad	Length (feet)	Number of tracks	Ruling grade
Moffat	East Portal, Colorado	Denver and Rio Grande Western	32,798	1	0.90
Hoosac	North Adams, Massachusetts	Boston & Maine	25,081	2	0.50
Hudson River	Penn Station, New York, New York	Amtrak	15,600	4	1.90
East River	Penn Station, New York, New York	Amtrak	14,172	4	1.50
Snoqualmie	Hyak, Washington	Milwaukee Road	11,890	1	0.41
Park Avenue	Grand Central Terminal, New York, New York	Conrail	10,440	4	1.02
No. 41	Norden, California	Southern Pacific	10,326	1	1.47
St. Paul Pass	East Portal, Montana	Milwaukee Road	8,774	1	0.02
Detroit River	Detroit, Michigan	Conrail	8,390	2	2.00

On February 20, 1912, 14 years before the Hoosac was enlarged and double-tracked, an eastbound passenger train crashed into the rear of an eastbound freight in mid-tunnel because of a misreading of automatic electric block signals. Fire broke out, dislodging hundreds of tons of rock from above the tunnel roof, which tumbled down onto the wreckage. Four trainmen were killed, and 17 freight cars were destroyed. A much more tragic disaster was avoided only by the fact that the deadheading passenger engine crew quickly got up steam and backed their train out to the fresh air before the heat became unbearable. Two days passed before the tunnel interior had cooled enough to let wrecking crews reach the collision scene.

The nation's worst tunnel disaster occurred in a Brooklyn Rapid Transit Co. subway on November 1, 1918. That morning, members of the Brotherhood of Locomotive Engineers, including many New York City subway motormen, went on a wildcat strike, taking advantage of the wartime labor shortage. That evening in Brooklyn a Brighton Beach train was operated by a man recently promoted to the job of motorman and unfamiliar with the line. He should have turned down Franklin Avenue but didn't. After some delay, a towerman switched the train back onto its right course.

The new motorman, instead of decelerating to 6 miles per hour, as speed-limit signs indicated he should have done while rounding the rather sharp Malbone Street curve just inside the tunnel entrance, increased his speed to make up for lost time. His train jumped the track and rammed into a concrete wall, killing an undetermined number of people (possibly 97) and causing the city to change Malbone Street's name to Empire Boulevard.

Tunnel building's folk hero is the "steel-drivin' man," John Henry. *See* JOHN HENRY.

In railway construction, when the line meets a rock barrier, it is often best to cut directly through. If the grade is not too far below the rock surface, the cut is made with a steep-sided trench. But rain brings down upon the slopes the softer material from above, and frost detaches bits of rock which, in falling, may cause serious accidents to trains. Snow lodging in deep cuts could stop traffic.

Therefore, a tunnel, usually costing more than a moderately deep cut, is often the most economical expedient. The difficulties involved in tunnel construction usually depend upon the kind of material found as the work advances. As a rule, solid rock presents the fewest difficulties, but sometimes huge portions of rock, where the tunnel roof is to be, press downward with enormous weight, being detached from the adjacent mass owing to natural seams. Elsewhere, soft material is found, and temporary supports, usually timber of great strength, often must be used at every foot of progress to prevent the material from forcing its way into the excavation already made.

Canadian Tunnels The Dominion's two longest railway bores, both double-tracked, are the Canadian Pacific's (CP's) Connaught Tunnel, 5.02 miles, built between 1913 and 1916 in British Columbia, with a ruling grade of 0.96, and the Canadian National's (CN's) Mount Royal Tunnel, 3.09 miles, built between 1912 and 1914 in Montreal by the Canadian Northern, which later became part of the CN, with a ruling grade of 0.50.

Until 1916 the Canadian Pacific mainline twisted around the base of Mount MacDonald in the Selkirks, making the equivalent of seven circles in its route through Rogers Pass, named for the pioneer surveyor who discovered it. Snowsheds and track patrols could not ward off the thunderous snowslides, such as the fatal one in 1910 that razed the station buildings there and held up traffic for days.

Construction of the tunnel—20 feet wide, cement-lined, and named for the Duke of Connaught, then Governor General of Canada—eliminated 200 degrees of curvature, lowered by 552 feet the railway's highest point, clipped 4.52 miles off the transcontinental mileage, scrapped nearly 5 miles of snowsheds, and reduced the operational hazards due to 30-foot average yearly snowfalls.

Canada also has some remarkable spiral tunnels built by CP in Kicking Horse Pass, British Columbia, where

America's only natural railroad tunnel, located on the Southern Railway System near Bristol, Virginia, was created by soil erosion. This is a view from within Little Tunnel.

the railway doubles back on itself roughly like a figure 8. From the east the track enters the first tunnel, 3200 feet long, under Cathedral Mountain, and after turning almost in a circle it passes under itself, emerging 48 feet lower. The track then crosses a river and enters the second tunnel, 2900 feet long, under Mount Ogden. After circling again and once more passing beneath itself, it comes out 45 feet lower and continues westward. These spiral bores were driven through crystalline limestone. Variations in the rock's hardness, water seepage, and severe winter weather added to the difficulties of constructing them.

Much of Montreal's business center stretches narrowly between Mount Royal and the St. Lawrence River. Canadian Northern engineers building toward it in 1911 had no way of getting their railway into the city except by tunneling through the mountain, which they did. Another Canadian Northern-built tunnel extends through 7 miles of ridges between Fraser Valley and Vancouver, British Columbia. It is double-tracked and electrically operated.

The power of men and horses was a major factor in the construction of the Hoosac Tunnel through the Hoosac Range of Massachusetts between 1851 and 1875. [The American Railway, Scribner, New York, 1897]

Two rail-roadway tunnels cross the Canadian-United States border. One is the Canadian National bore 1000 feet beneath the St. Clair River, built by the Grand Trunk Railway. Completed in 1890, when the shields from both sides of the river met in exact alignment, it links Sarnia, Ontario, with Port Huron, Michigan. This tunnel, with a capacity of 2000 motor vehicles a day, cut 30 minutes from the running time of through trains and saved a heavy cost of ferry fees. The other underwater border crossing is the Detroit-Windsor bore which the New York Central put into service in 1910.

See also CASCADE TUNNEL.

BIBLIOGRAPHY: Thomas C. Clarke and others, *The American Railway*, Scribner, New York, 1897; Robert S. Henry, *This Fascinating Railroad Business*, 3d ed., rev., Bobbs-Merrill, Indianapolis, 1946; Robert B. Shaw, *A History of Railroad Accidents, Safety Precautions, and Operating Practices*, Northern Press, Potsdam, N.Y., 1978.

Turntables and Wyes A locomotive ending its run or about to start a new run may be turned around on a wye, a simple track loop, or on a (more complicated) turntable. Wyes are preferred where space is available and traffic does not call for a quick turnaround. They are relatively cheap to build, need no mechanical care, and do not break down. You can find them mostly on small railroads, branches of industrial roads, military lines, and minor spurs of big systems. But for heavy traffic at engine terminals or in areas where compactness is necessary there must be a turntable, colloquially known as a merry-go-round.

The world's first recorded railway turntable was used in France to turn a single rococo open car that uniformed lackeys pushed on a short amusement railway built in 1714 by King Louis XIV for the hoop-skirted ladies and periwigged gentlemen of his Versailles court. Oddly enough, the United States also had a turntable before it had a locomotive. Engineer Gridley Bryant devised it for the horse-drawn Granite Railway, which was opened on October 7, 1826, to haul huge granite blocks from a quarry in Quincy, Massachusetts, in building a monument to mark the site of the Battle of Bunker Hill. It was a circular granite block, like an oversize stone found in a gristmill, pivoted in the center and delicately balanced.

Nearly all American turntables were wooden truss "armstrong" types, now almost completely obsolete, vastly different from the electrically propelled giants that move the mighty diesels. Locomotive development over the years created problems in turntable design beyond mere strength and massiveness. A report from a Philadelphia & Columbia Railroad official dated November 30, 1855, said that the turntable at the Philadelphia enginehouse "was not large enough to turn an engine and tank together, rendering the operation of turning laborious and tedious," and had to be replaced by a 50-foot table. He added: "The [new] table is made of cast-iron and manufactured by William Sellers & Co., of Philadelphia, with Parry's anti-friction box, or pivot, of which I cannot speak too highly. No gearing is required, and two men can turn the heaviest locomotive in one-third the time that half a dozen men could with the old arrangement."

That table was basically a type widely used today. Two heavy cast-iron bridge girders supported the engine and tender. It was held up in the middle on a pivot. On each end, two cast-iron wheels ran on a circular rail on a stone or brick shelf at the side of the pit. A sliding bar used as a lock kept the table from slipping when an engine was entering or leaving the table.

The chief improvements in turntables since then have been in more delicate balancing, reduction of friction, and application of either electricity, a gasoline engine, or compressed air. Cast-iron girders have given way to steel. Today, electrically driven tables can turn the largest road locos or the smallest switchers with a flick of the operator's controller.

Of three main types of tables, the cantilever, or center-balanced, type is still in use on some short lines and branches. They are made in either the *through* or the *deck* pattern. Another is the articulated, or center-hinged, type. A third is the continuous-girder type, supported at three points. This is a modern adaptation of the old balanced table. The two last-mentioned varieties are known as nontipping tables.

There is also a Mundt type, developed by Engineer Mundt on the Dutch State Railways and now used in North America. Mundt improved the articulated type by distributing the load more efficiently, without the disadvantages of using a hinged girder and a crosshead pivot in the center. The Mundt table has a continuous girder reinforced from the outside ends to within a certain distance from the center. When it is under a load, deflection takes place at the section not reinforced. Thus the carrying wheels at both ends share the weight of the center pivot.

Most of the really large turntables in the United States and Canada, some 135 feet long, are of the continuous-girder type. Now and then a locomotive creates a relatively minor problem by falling off an approaching track into the pit. But the mechanical failure of a turntable itself has serious consequences. It could tie up a big terminal as well as all the motive-power services in the enginehouse. In at least one case, at Londonderry, Vermont, a locomotive was delayed for 2 days on a nonfunctioning table. So turntable construction is given careful consideration by some of the best brains in the railroad industry.

BIBLIOGRAPHY: C. Miles Burpee (ed.), *Railway Engineering and Maintenance Cyclopedia*, Simmons-Boardman, New York, 1942; Robert S. Henry, *This Fascinating Railroad Business*, 3d ed., rev., Bobbs-Merrill, Indianapolis, 1946.

Twelve-Wheelers (Mastodons)

Twelve-Wheelers (Mastodons) Steam locomotives of the 4-8-0 type. The first of this type, named the *Centipede* because of her many wheels, was built by Ross

Top: The armstrong hand-operated type of turntable, shown here at Greenville Junction, Maine, in 1963, is practically obsolete. [David Plowden] Center: The roundhouse and turntable of the Philadelphia & Reading Railroad is typical of modern electrically driven operations. [William M. Rittase] Bottom: Sometimes a locomotive creates problems by falling off an approaching track into the pit. [David L. Joslyn]

Winans at Baltimore, Maryland, in 1856 and sold to the Baltimore & Ohio in 1863. She had 43-inch drivers and 22- by 22-inch cylinders and weighed about 20 tons. Baldwin built 120 12-wheelers for the Norfolk & Western (NW) from 1906 to 1910. Richmond and the road's own Roanoke shops produced still others for the NW. Brooks built 4-8-0s for the Jersey Central, the Lackawanna, the Great Northern, the Union Pacific, the Buffalo, Rochester & Pittsburgh, and the Illinois Central (IC). When one of the IC's 12-wheelers was completed in 1899, with 23- by 30-inch cylinders, 57-inch drivers, and a weight of 232,200 pounds, she was the world's heaviest freight locomotive. She was designed to haul a train weighing 2045 tons, exclusive of engine, tender, and caboose, up a grade of 38 feet per mile, combined with 3-degree curves, at 15 miles per hour.

Two-Way Radio Means of providing an instant link between dispatchers or supervisors at division headquarters and train crews, maintenance-of-way gangs, and other personnel traveling in the field. It surpasses the trackside telephone system because (1) train or track defects can be reported more promptly, thus preventing delays or potential mishaps; (2) switching instructions can be issued to trains en route; and (3) train location information for track maintenance crews can be continuously updated. The radio system also provides a backup for conventional dispatching practice.

U

Uintah Railway Three-foot-gauge line that was one of the world's crookedest rail lines and one of the most difficult to operate. Completed in 1904, it ran through Utah's Uintah Basin for 63 miles between Watson, Utah, and Mack, Colorado, where it connected with the Denver and Rio Grande. Barber Asphalt Co. built it to haul a black, brittle asphalt for use in making paint, varnish, insulation, and roofing. Because a Salt Lake City man named S. H. Gilson first promoted this mineral, it still bears his name, Gilsonite.

The Uintah's most distinguishing characteristics were its many sharp curves and steep grades. One section 6 miles long as the crow flies was so twisted that it had 26 miles of track. From Mack, 4540 feet above sea level, it ran for 28 miles north to Atchee on a grade of about 2 percent, meaning a 2-foot rise in every 100 feet of track.

Just before entering Atchee, where the railway's shops and roundhouse were located, the grade was 5 percent. Between that point and Baxter Pass, the line's highest point, 8437 feet above sea level, it was a rugged 7½ percent. From there for 7 miles to Wendella it eased down to 3, 2, and 1½ percent. Two short branches had grades as high as 5 percent. The steepest section, Atchee–Wendella, had 233 curves (reverse, hairpin, etc.), many of them 66 degrees. The Uintah ran a daily passenger train through scenic grandeur. One of its locomotives was the world's largest narrow-gauge Mallet, a 2-6-6-2 type built by Baldwin in 1926. *See* MALLET.

BIBLIOGRAPHY: Henry E. Bender, Jr., *Uintah Railway: The Gilsonite Route,* Howell-North, Berkeley, Calif., 1970; Herbert F. Kretchma, *The Story of Gilsonite,* American Gilsonite Co., Salt Lake City, 1957; *Railroad Magazine,* July 1940.

UMLER *See* UNIVERSAL MACHINE LANGUAGE EQUIPMENT REGISTER.

Union Pacific Railroad (UP) "Away, away, I'm bound away/Across the wide Missouri," from an old song, was a bold venture into the unknown before the West had a single railroad. It also typifies the pioneering, adventurous spirit that built the Union Pacific in the late 1860s. Routinely today, its special trains on fast schedules thunder from shore to shore of the wide Missouri with container-freight hauls as bridge movements between Pacific ports and the Missouri River gateways for exporters and importers at Chicago and Western points. Union Pacific's market area is even greater than its immediate operating territory because its run-through trains use the tracks of more than one other railroad without changing locomotives. Thus they deliver many commodities to customers located far from UP trackage.

This is America's fifth largest rail system in terms of revenue. Its 9315 route miles in 13 states spread from Council Bluffs, Iowa, and Kansas City, Missouri, westward across prairies and mountains to Portland, Oregon, and Vancouver, Longview, Tacoma, and Seattle, Washington, and southward to Los Angeles Harbor and Long Beach, California. Since 1969, centenary of the golden spike ceremony at Promontory, Utah, the railroad has been owned by a holding company, Union Pacific Corp., that embraces also Champlin Petroleum Co. (oil and gas), Upland Industries Corp. (land), and Rocky Mountain Energy Co. (coal and other minerals). Union Pacific has announced plans to acquire the Missouri Pacific and Western Pacific, which, if consummated, would preserve UP's status as the nation's largest railroad holding company.

In 1859, oxen-drawn covered wagons took 3 months or more to bump over virgin soil from the Missouri River to the West Coast. Pony Express riders, with relays of fresh horses, carrying tissue-paper mail at $1 per ounce but no freight, took 8 days to gallop between St. Joseph, Missouri, and Placerville, California. A transcontinental railway was needed. On July 1, 1862, President Lincoln signed the Pacific Railroad Act, which gave birth to both the Union Pacific and the Central (now Southern) Pacific. Major General Grenville M. Dodge was appointed chief engineer in charge of UP construction. Dr. Thomas Clark Durant (1820-1885), who had abandoned a medical career to help build the railroad, became UP vice president and general manager. He promised to finish 247 miles of line into Nebraska Territory at the 100th parallel as soon as possible. Until he did so, the charter to build and operate the eastern part of the transcontinental railroad westward would not become official and the UP could not realize on the company and federal bonds. *See* DODGE, GRENVILLE MELLEN.

The route lay through desert and unexplored country teeming with hostile Indians and over three mountain ranges. UP's base was on the frontier side of the unbridged wide Missouri. Every bit of equipment, food, and rolling stock had to be brought to Omaha by freight wagon or river steam packet from St. Joseph, Missouri, or St. Louis. Crossties were worth almost their weight in silver because of the cost of hauling them hundreds of miles over the mountains and virtually treeless plains. Milepost 191, Fort Kearney, Nebraska Territory, was the prairie's westernmost outpost of civilization, if a ramshackle military stockade and a collection of shanties could be called civilization.

For this job General Dodge had about 10,000 specialists and laborers, mostly Irish, many of them Civil War veterans from both North and South who knew how to obey orders. The line advanced at the rate of a mile and a half a day, then 2 miles, with sometimes even 4 or 5 miles of new track being laid between sunup and sunset in all kinds of weather. Steam trains bringing supplies, food, mail, the payroll, and newspapers kept arriving at the railhead as it moved on. Upon reaching his first major goal in October 1866, Dodge brought to the scene a gala excursion trainload of governmental dignitaries, military officers, newspaper reporters, and potential stockholders.

The Sioux captured a party of UP engineers in Wyoming's Black Hills and sent them to Dodge with a warning: "We do not want you here. You are scaring away our buffalo. Turn back or we make war." William F. (Buffalo Bill) Cody (1846-1917), who had been hired to provide the track gangs with buffalo meat, told Dodge that the white men were doing much more than scaring away buffalo. "We're wiping out the herd mighty fast," he said, "and the Indian sees it. If we were killing for food alone, he probably wouldn't care so much; but it's the slaughter of hundreds of thousands of bison, yes, and millions, for the hides alone, and leaving the carcases rot where they lie—that's what makes the Indians determined to fight." *See also* EXCURSION TRAINS.

Dodge's men pushed on furiously to reach Ogden, Utah Territory, before the eastward-advancing Central Pacific railroad builders. For every mile of distance gained on the Central, the UP would draw $64,000 in bonds and 12,600 acres of public land.

In May 1866, some 15,000 tons of government freight lay piled up on the prairie at North Platte for transportation. There were 1200 wagons, with 800 teamsters, about 5000 other men, and a few women, camped in tents and shacks. Six weeks later, the busy railhead moved on. The big, flashy saloon-gambling house, taken down piece by piece in numbered sections, was hauled away. Fewer than 500 people lingered on the site. Next stop was Julesburg, known as "the wickedest city in America," the scene of gunfights over cards, liquor, and loose women. From this point the show moved on to Cheyenne, repeating the same story with variations; then to Laramie, Benton, Green City, Bryan, and Wasatch, where it is recorded that only 5 occupants of the 43 graves in Boot Hill died natural deaths. The last of the moving towns was Corinne, at the north end of Great Salt Lake.

Charles Crocker, a merchant who had become one of the Central Pacific's Big Four, boasted that his road could lay 10 miles of track in a single day. UP's Dr. Durant wired him: "Ten thousand dollars you can't do it before witnesses." Durant lost the bet. The extraordinary feat was set for April 28, 1869. As for witnesses, the UP men stopped work that day and trooped by thousands along the Central's right-of-way like spectators in the bleachers. *See* CROCKER, CHARLES.

Crocker planned for the test far in advance. Everything was ready. Eight of his huskiest Irish tracklayers laid crossties and iron rails and spiked them down at the amazing rate of 144 feet a second, the gait of a walking horse. Toiling from 7 A.M. to 7 P.M., with an hour off for lunch, they completed the 10 miles, with 1800 feet over for good measure. During 11 grueling hours those men had handled almost 2 million pounds of dead weight. For details on the wedding of the rails at Promontory 12 days later, *see* GOLDEN SPIKE CEREMONY.

Among those actively involved in the early UP management and making considerable money from it were Oakes Ames (1804-1873) and his brother Oliver (1807-1877), Massachusetts shovel makers whose business was so successful that on the Western frontier an Ames shovel was regarded as legal tender. In 1867, seven influential UP stockholders, led by Oakes Ames and Dr. Durant, got control of an obscure construction company, Crédit Mobilier (CM), which had been chartered in Pennsylvania for another purpose. They made a deal for this company to build the remaining 667 miles of UP for a total cost of nearly $48 million, of which $20 million, it is estimated, would be divided as profit among the very few CM stockholders. This left the road, when completed, badly in debt, although the government's generous gifts to it had been expected to put UP on a firm financial basis.

In an effort to head off an investigation by Congress, Oakes Ames, who had ousted Dr. Durant from the control of Crédit Mobilier, offered blocks of valuable CM stock to leading congressmen at par. His methods were typical of those of other railroad builders of his day. In 1872 Charles Dana, editor of the New York *Sun*, published the details of this scheme, which rocked the nation in the midst of a presidential campaign; and Congress publicly censured Oakes Ames.

In 1893 the Union Pacific Co. passed into a receivership. E. H. Harriman and his associates reorganized the property. The present railroad company, incorporated on July 1, 1897, began operation on February 1, 1898. *See* HARRIMAN, EDWARD HENRY.

With its birth pangs and receivership far in the past, the Union Pacific today is one of America's great and prosperous corporations. In 1975, for its second consecutive year, it invested about $200 million in new and improved equipment, rights-of-way, and facilities. The bulk of this sum was spent on 3872 freight cars, nearly half of them built in UP's own shops. In that year, too, it completed a massive $14 million improvement program on its route between North Platte and Kansas City. During 1977 the road's earnings from normal operations reached $116.3 million, topping $100 million for the first time.

Containerized freight accounts for much of the road's import-export traffic. The East Lost Angeles yard boasts two huge straddle cranes. The trailer-container yards at Seattle, Denver, Portland, Salt Lake City, and Hinkle, Oregon, have 45-ton (piggybacker) side loaders capable of top- or bottom-lifting trailers 20 to 40 feet long.

Union Pacific's locomotive history dates from 1865, when locomotive No. 1, a Danforth & Cooke product from Paterson, New Jersey, was unloaded from a Missouri River steamboat, reassembled, and set up on UP rails. It was named *General Sherman* and put to work on the westward construction. This basic type, a 4-4-0, had four driving wheels preceded by a four-wheel truck. In 1868 a much larger engine with eight driving wheels, built by Baldwin, was introduced in UP freight service, and a bit later came the 4-6-0 for passenger work.

While the UP used 4-4-0s until after the turn of the century, it operated 4-6-0s on local and branch-line runs until as late as 1928 and one of them on the Saratoga and Encampment run in Wyoming in 1955. The UP began using the Mogul, or 2-6-0, in 1890, the two-wheel pony truck enabling additional weight to be placed on the six drivers, creating greater tractive effort. It used Moguls only in freight service, and they were not very successful.

Next came the Consolidation type, or 2-8-0. UP used some of these for over 50 years. The 4-8-0 freight haulers were first built in 1899, but UP had relatively few of them. In 1911 the popular Mikado (later, MacArthur) type was developed with a 2-8-2 wheel arrangement. A later version had larger cylinders and larger driving wheels and was the first engine equipped with the mechanical coal stoker. UP used these on passenger runs between Cheyenne and Laramie to maintain schedules over Sherman Hill between 1917 and 1922, when Mountain types, or 4-8-2s, replaced them.

Between 1904 and 1911 UP operated the Atlantic type, 4-4-2, and the Pacific type, with a four-wheel pony truck, six driving wheels, and two trailing wheels, in passenger service. The Atlantics were very satisfactory in hauling trains of light wooden passenger cars across the plains but were unsuitable for Wyoming's steep grades, to which the Pacifics were then assigned. With the advent of heavy steel passenger cars, the Pacifics were required in Nebraska, and the 4-8-2 Mountain type was designed for the Wyoming hills.

Later, UP began using 2-10-2 Sante Fe types for fast freight, primarily on level runs and easy grades. For handling comparable tonnage in mountain territory, the

***Rural depot of the Union Pacific at Valley, Nebraska, in 1948.** [Myron B. Hochstetler, Jr.; Graflex photo contest]*

railroad developed the 2-8-8-0 Mallet compound-type locomotive. This was really two engines under one boiler with an articulated arrangement. Later, such units were rebuilt as the simple articulated type.

UP's next step was the 4-10-2 Overland three-cylinder type. Then came the three-cylinder type with a 4-12-2 wheel arrangement. These engines were very heavy and costly to maintain but were used extensively east of Cheyenne nearly up to the end of UP's steam era. In 1937 the Northern-type (4-8-4) passenger engine produced amazing speeds of over 100 miles per hour at very low operating costs. On the freight side, the giant 4-6-6-4 Challenger type and the 4-8-8-4 Big Boy freight haulers of 1941, the world's largest steam locos, capped the UP steam-power story. *See* NEUHART, DAVID E.

The greatest number of steam units owned by Union Pacific at one time was 1953, in 1924. The last full year that UP operated steam was 1957, but steam was used for supplemental power on the mainline during the fall seasons of 1958 and 1959. The last miles made by the Big Boys in regular service were in July 1959. The only steam loco maintained operable today is the 4-8-4 Northern 8444, which was extensively overhauled in the fall of 1971 and is stored at Cheyenne for occasional fan excursions in the Denver-Laramie-Cheyenne territory. (However, in 1979 work was begun to restore Challenger 3985 to operating condition.) But 46 steam locos donated by the UP are on display at various points throughout the United States, nearly all of them in UP territory.

In 1949 UP started experimenting with 4500-horsepower gas-turbine-electric locos, of which it added a significant number. Later innovations produced an 8500-horsepower model (two units coupled together) and an experimental model to burn powdered coal for fuel. Diesel manufacturers soon met the turbine challenges with superhorsepower units. The largest turbocharged engines develop 6600 horsepower. When used in a combination of three, they produce 19,800 horsepower. In addition, the three-unit combination overcomes the hazard of having all the pulling energy in one unit. For the moment, the diesel engine still reigns supreme, but few observers in this energy-deficient age would venture a guess on what form standard railroad power will take in the years to come.

In January 1980 the Union Pacific and Missouri Pacific announced a preliminary agreement for a merger, valued at about $900 million, that would form the nation's third-largest transportation-based conglomerate, with revenue exceeding $5 billion and 21,200 miles of track. The proposed merger is subject to approval by both companies' stockholders and the Interstate Commerce Commission. For more details *see* MISSOURI PACIFIC RAILROAD.

See also AMES MONUMENT PLOT; LOCOMOTIVES, GAS-TURBINE-ELECTRIC; MALLET.

BIBLIOGRAPHY: Charles E. Ames, *Pioneering the Union Pacific: A Reappraisal of the Builders of the Railroad,* Appleton-Century-Crofts, New York, 1969; Robert G. Athearn, *Union Pacific Country,* Rand McNally, Chicago, 1971; Lucius Beebe, *The Overland Limited,* Howell-North, Berkeley, Calif., 1963; Gerald M. Best, *Iron Horses to Promontory,* Golden West Books, San Marino, Calif., 1969; Wesley S. Griswold, *A Work of Giants: Building the First Transcontinental Railroad,* McGraw-Hill, New York, 1962; *Jane's World Railways and Rapid Transit Systems,* F. Watts, New York, 1977; William W. Kratville, *Union Pacific Locomotives,* Kratville Publications, Omaha, 1967.

Union Stations In bygone days union stations abounded in drama. There were special trains for big conventions, Derby races, and other major events. There were misty-eyed farewells; glad reunions; receptions for celebrities; shopping and dining; lost children; Salvation Army lassies shaking tambourines; unwanted babies deserted; sudden deaths; soldiers leaving for foreign battlefields; elderly couples losing their tickets; lovers hugging, kissing, and quarreling; coffins loaded inconspicuously into baggage cars; Easter splendor; gaily decorated Christmas trees and Yuletide carols; and pickpockets, beggars. bums, and prostitutes. All these are part of union-station history. The great terminals are kept clean and well-policed, but on very rare occasions they have seen murders and riots. For an account of rioters burning Pittsburgh Union Depot, *see* STRIKE OF 1877.

On June 18, 1933, Frank Nash, an Oklahoma desperado, got off a train at Kansas City Union Station, handcuffed and guarded by four FBI agents, two detectives, and a police chief. They walked briskly through the station out to the plaza. Before they could board a waiting automobile, four gangsters opened fire with machine guns, killing Nash and three other men, and sped away in a fast car.

One President of the United States, James A. Garfield, was shot down by an assassin in a Washington railroad depot, but not a union station. Ordinarily, union stations are busy and cheerful. The dedication of almost every one of them was colorful, with a vast crowd filling the big new edifice. Nashville Union Station was dedicated in 1908 with festivities lasting 3 days and 3 nights.

Louisville's old Central Station, built by the Louisville & Nashville Railroad in 1891 and described by the *Louisville Times* as "the largest and finest south of the Ohio River," did not become a union station until Chesapeake and Ohio trains began using it in 1963. One July night in 1905 much of the Louisville depot was burned down despite the convergence of nearly every piece of city fire apparatus, each horse-drawn. Trains standing under the big shed were switched quickly to safety. As the gutted building's masonry was still intact, the edifice was rebuilt in time for Yuletide travel.

St. Louis Union Station, unique because its architecture is like a medieval wall and gateway, with even a watchtower, and because of the large number of railroads it served, was the nation's largest union station when completed in 1894. In its heyday in the 1940s it had 42 tracks, all on the street level (no other station could match that exact record), as compared with 49, but on two levels, at Grand Central Terminal, 33 on two levels at the once-great Washington Union Station, now remodeled into mostly a visitors' bureau, and 31 on one level at the now sadly depreciated New Orleans Union Terminal.

In those days St. Louis Union Station averaged 200 to 220 trains from midnight to midnight, as compared with New York's original Penn Station (since razed and replaced by a smaller depot), with 900, and Grand Central Terminal, with between 400 and 450. It served 17 different railroads. The nearest rival in that respect, Kansas City Union Station, mustered only 12 roads; St. Paul Union Station, 9; Dallas Union Terminal, 8; Chicago's Dearborn Station and New Orleans Union Terminal, 7 roads each; and Denver Union Station, 6 roads.

A terminal exists for the purpose of making and breaking up trains and sending them out. The St. Louis facility was called a *pocket terminal* because, with but one exception, a Missouri Pacific commuter local, all regularly scheduled passenger trains entered it backward. At a time when the station was involved in interchanging about 1900 passenger cars in a 24-hour period, it was doing the same for some 12,500 freight cars, for even then, while the rail passenger business was flourishing, the Terminal Railroad Association of St. Louis, which owned and operated the vast setup, derived the lion's share of its revenue from freight traffic.

Cincinnati Union Terminal, possibly America's most beautifully sited passenger depot, erected by the city in 1933, was one of the last architecturally great railroad stations built anywhere. No train has utilized it since since 1972, when the final few passenger trains still serving Cincinnati were shifted to a modest jerry-built station outside town. Several times on the verge of being razed, the handsome edifice was saved in 1980, when the city leased it for $2 a year to a real estate developer for nonrail use as a shopping mall and entertainment area.

BIBLIOGRAPHY: Edwin P. Alexander, *Down at the Depot: American Railroad Stations from 1831 to 1920,* Crown, New York, 1970; John A. Droege, *Passenger Terminals and Trains,* McGraw-Hill, New York, 1916.

Unions, Railroad Labor The Knights of Labor, while not a railroad union, had a great many railroad men among nearly 700,000 members and sponsored several important railroad strikes. Organized by Philadelphia garment workers in 1869, it was an ambitious effort to unify all American workers, both skilled and unskilled. In 1893 Eugene V. Debs organized the American Railway Union, which aimed to create a solid labor front among railroaders, but without the support of conservative rail labor unions the ARU lost its Pullman

The St. Louis Union Station was designed to resemble a gateway in a medieval city, complete with a watchtower. In 1894, date of its completion, it was the largest union station in the United States.

strike and soon disintegrated. *See* "CRANE WITH A BROKEN NECK"; DEBS, EUGENE VICTOR; PULLMAN, GEORGE MORTIMER; STRIKES, MAJOR RAILROAD.

The Industrial Workers of the World (IWW), founded in 1905 to hasten the overthrow of capitalism, had relatively little impact on the rail labor movement, although it had many railroad members and its red membership cards were often used to get free freight-train rides, meals, and overnight lodging from "worthy brothers" who recognized them.

The American Federation of Labor (AFL), comprising United States and Canadian autonomous craft and industrial unions, chiefly the former, was founded in 1886. Its strong Railway Employees Department called the shopmen's strike of 1922, America's first nationwide railroad walkout. The Congress of Industrial Organizations (CIO), an expelled offshoot of AFL but later merged into AFL-CIO, also played a leading role in the railroad labor movement.

The chief unions to which railroaders belong today—those which bargain nationally, representing about 98 percent of the organized work force on United States railroads—are the International Brotherhood of Boilermakers and Blacksmiths; Brotherhood of Railway Carmen; Brotherhood of Railway, Airline and Steamship Clerks; American Train Dispatchers Association; International Brotherhood of Electrical Workers; Brotherhood of Locomotive Engineers (BLE); International Brotherhood of Firemen & Oilers; International Association of Machinists and Aerospace Workers; Brotherhood of Maintenance of Way Employees; Sheet Metal Workers International Association; Brotherhood of Railroad Signalmen; Railway Yardmasters of America; and United Transportation Union (UTU). *See* BROTHERHOOD OF LOCOMOTIVE ENGINEERS.

The UTU made its debut on January 1, 1969, as an amalgamation of four big operating unions: the Brotherhood of Railroad Trainmen (BRT), the Brotherhood of Locomotive Firemen and Enginemen [(BLF&E) not affiliated with the Brotherhood of Locomotive Engineers], the Order of Railway Conductors and Brakemen (ORC&B), and the Switchmen's Union of North America (SUNA). Exploratory talks leading to the amalgamation were begun in January 1968 by chiefs of four separate unions: Charles Luna of the BRT and C. F. Lane of the ORC&B, both of whom began their rail careers on the Santa Fe; H. E. Gilbert of the BLF&E, formerly on the Chicago & Alton; and Neil P. Speirs of SUNA, a former Southern Pacific switchman, the only Canadian among them.

The four unions' memberships voted nearly 7 to 1 for the merger. The BLE, which had refused to support the ARU in 1893–1894, also declined to join the UTU. Luna became UTU's first president, with Lane, Gilbert, and Speirs as assistant presidents. UTU international headquarters is at 14600 Detroit Ave., Cleveland, Ohio 44107. Outside of the UTU and the independent BLE are other rail labor unions, mostly affiliated with the AFL-CIO and including clerks, etc., in both rail and non-rail labor. The Brotherhood of Sleeping Car Porters, organized in 1925, lost its identity in 1978 by affiliating with the Brotherhood of Railway and Airline Clerks.

Meanwhile, in 1929, the standard rail unions formed the Railway Labor Executives Association (RLEA), which handled management-employee relations. After the U.S. Supreme Court declared unconstitutional the Railroad Retirement Act of 1934, a New Deal measure, the RLEA and the Association of American Railroads jointly supported legislation setting up the retirement and unemployment system for railroad employees which is in effect today.

On national issues, bargaining is done by the National Railway Labor Conference (NRLC) and the National Carriers Conference Committee (NCCC). The latter, headquartered in Washington, is a permanent staff body that provides information relating to rail labor matters on a day-to-day basis. The NCCC consists of representatives of 10 major railroads and the NRLC chairman. In each set of negotiations it has the power of attorney to negotiate for participating railroads.

BIBLIOGRAPHY: Carroll R. Daugherty, *Labor Problems in American Industry,* Houghton Mifflin, Boston, 1933; Gerald G. Eggert, *Railroad Labor Disputes: The Beginnings of Federal Strike Policy,* University of Michigan Press, Ann Arbor, 1967; Herbert Harris, *American Labor,* Yale, New Haven, 1939.

Unit Trains These trains are mass producers in transportation. They save money through a more intensive use of equipment, cutting time spent at terminals, and eliminating the need for classification, weighing of cars, and other yard costs. This modern concept means the expeditious movement of freight with the lowest possible out-of-pocket expense and a minimum investment in railroad equipment through a high rate of use.

Some roads handling huge volumes of coal, grain, ore, bulk consumer goods, etc., offer unit-train service wherein cars are assigned and kept in shuttle operation between large originating and destination areas. Many such trains are scheduled well in advance so that motive power can be reserved more or less for this purpose. In most cases, these trains are limited to a few gathering points and not more than two destinations. Equipment use is much higher than in ordinary service despite excessive detention time occasionally at origin and/or destination.

A major user of this concept, the Southern Railway, first applied it between an electric-generating company's mines and power plant in Alabama in early 1960. The Southern designed and had built a fleet of 100-ton aluminum Silversides gondolas for unit trains but did not begin using them on a broad scale until 1962, when Congress provided the right-of-domain for coal pipeline construction. Within months after that, most coal-hauling roads were operating unit trains, which offset the new legislation and closed the coal pipelines then in operation

United Transportation Union *See* UNIONS, RAILROAD LABOR.

Universal Machine Language Equipment Register (UMLER) Detailed description of every freight car in North America, stored on three computer discs equivalent to 6000 feet of tape. Three discs may seem a small number for data on 2,249,000 freight cars (the 1978 figure), but UMLER is, indeed, an enormous computer file. If the average keypuncher working a 40-hour week were to transfer the whole file onto computer cards, the job would require 50 years and about 6,250,000 cards. If those cards were stacked up, they would reach the height of a 400-story building, and if placed end to end they would reach from Washington to St. Louis, or 800 miles.

UMLER is as vital to the railroad industry as it is big. It permits the analyzing of the entire freight-car fleet by any one of its mechanical or cost units or combination of those units. UMLER data for each car include ownership, dimensions, capacity, weight, chief components, cost, and hourly and mileage rates.

The railroads use UMLER primarily in fixing charges. A road incurs set fees when a "foreign" car (one it does not own) moves over its tracks. The carrier pays the car's owner a flat hourly fee (prior to July 1978 it was a daily rate), plus a fee per mile. But if the owner is a private-car company, it pays only a mileage fee.

Car hire and trailer rules of the Association of American Railroads (AAR) require that all railroad-owned freight cars in interchange service be registered in the UMLER file, and a railroad tariff obliges private-car owners to do the same. A car not in UMLER technically does not exist, and no hourly or mileage rates have to be paid on it.

UMLER serves also to help trace cars and their locations. It is used additionally in computer models of trains to help railroads determine ideal car placements, and it probably would be consulted in any study involving the freight-car fleet. Basically, anyone who has anything to do with freight cars is likely to rely on UMLER information.

This system serves increasingly for car-distribution data, particularly for identifying cars assigned to *pools* (fleets of specially equipped cars assigned by a railroad for a specific purpose). The most common pools are those assigned to a shipper or a commodity. In 1978 North America had about 5000 such pools with a total capacity of some 300,000 cars.

UMLER data are constantly changing with changes in car ownerships, car weights (slightly, owing to usage), new components added to cars, cars put into and taken out of pools, etc. AAR maintains UMLER in its Washington headquarters. In addition to AAR, 20 carriers maintain parallel UMLER files with all data in the original file except age and cost of cars (confidential data known only by AAR and car owners).

UP *See* UNION PACIFIC RAILROAD.

Vanderbilt, Cornelius ***(1794-1877)*** Known as Commodore Vanderbilt from his early maritime career, he did not become a railroad man until his seventieth year, but then made himself the mightiest rail baron of his era. By looking at the northeastern entrance to Grand Central Terminal in New York City you can see, just above the marquee, a reminder of his nautical interests: three iron-sculptured rats climbing up iron ship's hawsers but kept off the deck by cone-shaped rat guards. *See* GRAND CENTRAL TERMINAL.

C. Van Derbilt, as he always signed himself, was born on a Staten Island farm in New York Harbor on May 27, 1794. The future commodore's father, also named Cornelius, was a Tory who ran farm produce across the Narrows from Staten Island to a British Army garrison in New York during the Revolutionary War and later started the first ferry service over that route. C. Van Derbilt's mother had been a clergyman's house servant named Phoebe Hand. The fourth of her nine children, Cornelius, nicknamed Cornele, had no schooling at all after his twelfth birthday. It is said that the only book he ever read through was Bunyan's *Pilgrim's Progress,* on his deathbed, when he also read parts of the Bible. On his thirteenth birthday he bought a little sailing boat, which he said 60 years later gave him more satisfaction than he got out of cornering the market and buying the New York & Harlem Railroad.

During the War of 1812 the commissary of troops defending the port of New York openly accused him of working with a ring of smugglers as a war profiteer. But no one ever accused Vanderbilt of laziness, dullness, or lack of ambition.

At first Cornele laughed at Robert Fulton's steamboats, which were cutting travel time between New York and Albany from 36 hours to 18; but early in 1818 he decided that "steam's bound to beat sail" and sold his ferry business and bought three steamers and put them into service. Although shrewd and creative, he was no pioneer. In operating steamboats on the Hudson River he heralded himself as the people's champion against the Fulton-Livingston monopoly. He opposed every monopoly except his own. In 1825 Cornele began operating a joint trip by steamboat and stagecoach between New York and Philadelphia; and he kept building more and more steamboats, combining speed with comfort.

At 52, when Vanderbilt lived in a mansion on New York's Washington Square, he was a tall, commanding figure in a plug hat, topcoat, and broadcloth, with gray hair and sideburns, his handsome face showing conscious power and ruthlessness. In those days there was no transcontinental railroad or Panama Canal. Vanderbilt saw the need for such a canal and tried to induce British capital to cut a waterway across Nicaragua. Failing in this, he built the *Prometheus,* the first oceangoing steamship financed by only one man's money, and followed her with seven more huge luxury liners. With that superb fleet he set up a combined steamship and mule-stage service between New York and the newly opened California gold-mine fields. This paid him $1 million a year. When fur trader John Jacob Astor died in 1848, leaving $18 million, his son William became America's richest man, Vanderbilt being the second richest.

On March 2, 1836, Cornele rode a passenger train on the Camden & Amboy Railroad (later part of the Pennsy) in New Jersey. That date marked the country's, if not the world's, first head-on train collision, and it delayed for years Vanderbilt's sensational plunge into the railroad industry. C. Van Derbilt had his lungs punctured by two broken ribs. As a steamboat magnate then he had little use for railroads, but especially now that he had become a train casualty. After his recovery, friends urged him to invest in the Hudson River Railroad, then being built. Vanderbilt bluntly refused. "No, siree," he said. "I'd be a damn fool to compete with steamboats."

Meanwhile, he had built the world's largest and most luxurious steam yacht, the *North Star,* in which he toured the coasts of Europe with a chaplain as well as the surgeon who had treated him after the train wreck. During the Civil War he sold the U.S. Navy Department some of his obsolete ships that were later found unfit for service. At a congressional inquiry, planks from one of them were found to be too rotten to hold a nail. So Vanderbilt was accused of being a war profiteer, as his father had been in the Revolutionary War and as he himself had been in the War of 1812. To offset these charges, the commodore *loaned* his *North Star* to the Navy for the duration of the war. He was angry when the government accepted her as a permanent gift and gave him a gold medal.

His first dabble in railroading was a brief and dubious alliance with Daniel (Uncle Dan'l) Drew, known as the Great Bear of Wall Street. Vanderbilt biographer A. D. N. Smith describes Drew as "a shambling, mealy-mouthed coward, saved from mediocrity by the almost insane cunning of his weasel mind." The two men jointly bought control of the Boston & Stonington Railroad (later part of the New Haven system) for a direct connection between Boston and New York for their rival steamboat lines. At that time no railroad linked the two cities.

Vanderbilt's son, William (Billy) H. Vanderbilt, with the old man's backing, had been appointed receiver for the 13-mile Staten Island Railroad, a horse-operated line bankrupted in the 1857 panic, and he did a good job of reviving it. The commodore was proud because his son was clever enough to sell manure from the company's horses for use as fertilizer. Billy's success kindled his father's interest in railroading. Although Cornele was nearing his seventieth birthday—an age at which most men retire, if indeed they are still living—he sold his steamship business and began life anew as a railroad man. And in his last 12 years he multiplied his fortune tenfold.

A powerful figure, he looked youthful despite his white hair and sideburns. In the fall of 1862 he noted that the Erie (New York, Lake Erie & Western) and New York Central were fighting each other. The Erie, in the clutches of Drew, a tobacco-chewing hypocrite, was being sacked. It was hopelessly in debt, with equipment badly worn, frequent train wrecks, and its stock a plaything for Drew.

The commodore was disgusted. He felt that industrial properties should, above all, give big incomes to their owners, and he said so. He knew that the best way to get revenue was to improve service and equipment before raising rates. He studied the New York Central, too. That trunk line (five small roads recently merged) ran across the state but ended at Albany, about 142 miles north of New York City. It was partly at Drew's mercy, depending upon his riverboats for access to the big city except in winter, when the Hudson was frozen over. Two small railroads, the Hudson River line and the New York & Harlem, neither of which was strong enough to pay dividends, provided uncertain north-south service.

Acting on his own motto, "Never tell what you're goin' to do till you've done it," Vanderbilt secretly began buying Harlem stock in the fall of 1862. It was then quoted at $9. The next April, after he had taken control, it shot up to $50. He then persuaded the New York City Council to extend its horse-operated right-of-way down Broadway to the southern tip of Manhattan, where he had often beached his little ferryboat many years before. This he did by a liberal distribution of gifts to politicians. Through the influence of Boss William M. Tweed, whose rule set a new low in misgovernment, he also induced the Governor to veto a similar franchise which the New York Legislature had granted to a rival carrier.

Harlem stock jumped to $100. Then Drew pushed his whole fist into the pie. The City Council rescinded Vanderbilt's franchise, and a court injunction forbade him to lay tracks in the street. Drew's group dumped all its Harlem shares into the market, even selling more shares than it owned, forcing the price down to $72. Uncle Dan'l rubbed his hands in glee. The old rooster, Cornele, was ready to be plucked.

But Cornele was not naive. He had deliberately bought not only all of Harlem's real shares but also many thousands of imaginary shares which brokers sold him with the expectation of buying them back later, cheap. In short, he had cornered the market. When time came to deliver the extra shares, none could be had except on Vanderbilt's terms. It was a sad day for Drew and the other bears. The winner finally compromised at $170. It is said that if he had held out much longer, he would have wrecked nearly every big broker on Wall Street and caused a national panic.

In the fall of 1863, during the Civil War's darkest hours, New York Central & Hudson River stock was selling at $25. Vanderbilt bought a controlling interest in that road. Then, again prodded by Boss Tweed, the Legislature approved a merger of it with the Harlem road. Thereupon Hudson River rail stock soared to $150. A Drew raid cut it down to $90, but once more the shrewd commodore cornered the market.

By December 11, 1867, Vanderbilt had cornered $16 million of New York Central securities. He took over that east-west road, made himself president and his son Billy vice president. Beyond all doubt, he was one of the world's strong men. Though ignorant in book learning, he sensed that the hour had struck for railroad expansion. Just as he had improved steamboats to an amazing degree, he now undertook to better his railroads. To do this, he advanced $2 million of his own money to buy new equipment. Within a few months the Central, like the Harlem and Hudson River roads, was pouring a golden stream of dividends into his coffers.

In 1869, after his wife's death, he wed a young aristocratic Southerner, Frances A. Crawford, and got legislative permission to unite his three railroads. Thus he formed a great system extending from New York to Buffalo via Albany. His city horsecar line continued jogging its way from the steam cars' terminus to southern Manhattan. (Part of this horsecar service lasted until 1917).

He watered his rail stock, of course, raising its valuation from $44 million to $85 million. Said historian Charles F. Adams, a descendant of two Presidents: "$50,000 of absolute water was poured over every mile of track between New York and Buffalo." From this the commodore is said to have added $6 million in cash and $20 million in stock to his personal treasury. But although he raised freight and passenger rates to new heights, he improved his railroads. According to *The New York Tribune,* he did more than any other man of his time to restore public confidence in the railroads. The old sea dog from Staten Island was now the wealthiest American.

In 1866 he said he had bought enough Erie stock to warrant adding that road to his own system. Joining the owners of another road, the Boston, Hartford & Erie, gave him partial control of the Erie. Then Vanderbilt made his biggest mistake: he permitted his old enemy, Drew, to remain on the Erie Board of Directors and at the same time added Jay Gould and James Fisk to the directorate.

See DREW, DANIEL; FISK, JAMES; GOULD, JAY.

Firmly entrenched in the Erie again, the Great Bear authorized a bond issue of $10 million ostensibly to pay for replacing worn-out rails and laying a third rail to let standard-gauge trains run on the Erie's 6-foot-gauge tracks. All the directors, including the usually astute Vanderbilt, voted with Drew for these improvements.

But Drew, Gould, and Fisk converted the $10 million bonds into stock to unload on Vanderbilt, who was still buying as much Erie as he could so as to gain full control. They watered the securities to that extent without increasing the company's real estate, rolling stock, or other physical assets. In other words, they multiplied the amount of certificates on which dividends must be paid without adding to the means of earning money to pay the additional dividends.

The conspirators kept printing new stock as fast as Vanderbilt could buy it. Soon the victim had all of his ready cash, about $7 million, tied up in almost worthless Erie holdings. For a while the fabulous Vanderbilt tottered on the brink of ruin. At length he steadied himself by threatening to flood the market with his own New York Central stock, which could have caused a major panic, and the banks soon loaned him the money he needed. Later, the commodore got back most of his $7 million and retired from the Erie.

Thereafter, he concentrated on expanding and maintaining his own system. He acquired three connecting roads: Canada Southern, Michigan Central, and Lake Shore & Michigan Southern. The last-named was $7 million in debt, but in 2 years he put it on a paying basis. The old mariner rejoiced when his rails finally entered Chicago.

The national panic of 1873, due partly to Gould, forced many carriers into receiverships; but the storm left Vanderbilt unmoved. He answered calamity howlers by declaring a New York Central dividend of $3 million. A contemporary cartoonist, impressed by his titanic sturdiness, pictured Vanderbilt as "The Colossus of Roads," towering above the earth like the ancient bronze figure on the Greek island of Rhodes, one of the Seven Wonders of the World.

In his final years the old man fought disastrous rate wars with the Pennsylvania, the Erie, and the Baltimore & Ohio, reducing freight and passenger rates between New York and Chicago to money-losing levels. To recoup their losses, the managements cut wages sharply. This precipitated in July 1877 the first major railroad strike. *See* STRIKE OF 1877.

But the aged and ailing tycoon did not live to see it. He died on January 4, 1877, in the mansion he had built for himself, leaving 63 descendants. Symbolically, as Vanderbilt passed away, heavy snow caved in the roof of his Grand Central Station (predecessor of the present Grand Central Terminal).

BIBLIOGRAPHY: William A. Croffut, *The Story of the Vanderbilts and Their Fortune,* Belford, Clarke & Company, New York, 1886; C. C. Fitzmorris, Jr., *Commodore Vanderbilt and the Railroads,* Princeton University Press, Princeton, N.J., 1933; Edward Hungerford, *Men and Iron: The History of New York Central,* Crowell, New York, 1958; Matthew Josephson, *The Robber Barons,* Harcourt, Brace, New York, 1934; Gustavus Myers, *History of the Great American Fortunes,* 3 vols., Charles H. Kerr & Company, Chicago, 1910.

Van Horne, William Cornelius (1843–1915)

Railroad official who arrived in Winnipeg in January 1882 as general manager of the Canadian Pacific Railway (CP) under contract to build the transcontinental line that the Dominion government had promised to British Columbia if that province would join the eastern provinces in the federation. This railway had been talked about for nearly half a century, and almost $4 million had been spent on surveys; but little progress had been made toward building it.

Van Horne was born on February 3, 1843, near Joliet, Illinois, son of the city's first mayor. At 13 he had mastered telegraphy and was given a job in the office of Michigan Central's master mechanic in Chicago. At 27 he was made superintendent of transportation on the Chicago & Alton.

Next he became general superintendent of the bankrupt St. Louis, Kansas City & Northern (later Wabash). After putting that road on its feet, he did the same for the Southern Minnesota, also bankrupt, as president and general manager. Then, in 1880, he was made president of the Chicago, Milwaukee & St. Paul and stayed with it until he got the CP offer.

In Canada, he assembled material and supplies for railway building and hired a St. Paul firm to build 900 miles westward from Winnipeg. The day after the contract was signed, the firm advertised for 3000 men and 4000 horses. Subcontracts were let for the grading. All season long, graders trod on the heels of locating engineers; tracklayers crowded graders off the dump. When bridge building lagged, night crews were put on. The number of employees was stepped up to 10,000.

At Winnipeg Van Horne saw that materials and supplies moved to the front as fast as they could be used. Each supply train carried enough material for 1 mile of track. No tracklaying machines were available. Everything had to be done by hand when the Canadian Pacific was creeping across the prairie at the rate of 2 or 3 miles a day.

When freezing ground ended the season, the score was 508 miles of railway and 32 stations built, 807 miles of telegraph line set up, and 620 miles of rail line located. Two tough sections remained. One was through 600 miles of mountains at the west end. By agreement, a contractor named Onderdonk was building eastward from Port Moody, British Columbia, for the government. When completed, the line was to be turned over to the CP. *See* CANADIAN PACIFIC RAILWAY.

The other difficult section was along the north shore of Lake Superior, an unbroken wilderness of granite alternating with bottomless muskeg. During 1882 CP had bought a line to Collingwood on Georgian Bay. Van Horne arranged steamship service from that point to Lake Superior to distribute materials and supplies at points 100 miles apart. Portage roads were built for dogsleds to distribute supplies over the ice in winter. Stone quarries were opened. Three dynamite factories were built. These saved time, expense, and some transportation problems. Even so, a single north-shore mile cost half as much again as other miles.

CP mainline and branches built in 1883 brought the total mileage up to 1552. Van Horne canceled the choice of Port Moody as the western terminus, picked a new site, and named it Vancouver. Favoring the shortest practical commercial route, he abandoned Yellowhead Pass, originally chosen by the chief engineer, and designated instead Kicking Horse Pass, much farther south. But the grade westward from the Continental Divide was far more than the 2 percent maximum allowed by government contract. The best that CP engineers could do was 4½ percent, 237 feet to the mile, for the dozen miles from Hector to Field. Not until the famous spiral tunnels were constructed, much later, was the grade cut to 2 percent. *See* TUNNELS.

At Van Horne's suggestion, the Canadian Pacific, instead of following the American custom of giving away revenue-producing sidelines such as express, sleeping cars, hotels, etc., retained everything that could possibly earn a dollar. Even so, his greatest achievement was to keep things going while the treasury was bare. Directors pledged their personal fortunes to push the railway through. Canadian businessmen had such faith in Van Horne and advanced so much credit and supplies that if CP had blown up, the national economy might have gone bankrupt. Construction forces went without pay for months.

But the government finally came across with a substantial loan, and the line was completed. On November 11, 1885, the last spike was driven by Donald A. Smith, afterward Lord Strathcona, at Craigellachie, 251 miles east of Vancouver and 2534 miles west of Montreal, just 46 months after Van Horne had taken over the job of building 500 miles a year.

Van Horne never gave up his American citizenship. In 1885, at 45, he was made president of the Canadian Pacific. He announced that when its stock rose to par and its mileage reached 10,000 he would resign. Both goals were reached in 1899, and Van Horne kept his word. Afterward, he built Cuba's first railroad. He died on September 11, 1915, as Canada's and Cuba's greatest railway builder.

BIBLIOGRAPHY: Pierre Berton, *The Impossible Railway: The Building of the Canadian Pacific,* Knopf, New York, 1972; Stewart H. Holbrook, *The Story of American Railroads,* Crown, New York, 1947; Roderick G. MacBeth, *The Romance of the Canadian Pacific Railway,* Ryerson Press, Toronto, 1934; Glenn C. Quiett, *They Built the West,* Appleton-Century, New York, 1934; Walter Vaughan, *The Life and Work of Sir William Van Horne,* Century, New York, 1920.

VIA Rail Canada, Inc. Canadian equivalent of Amtrak in the United States. It became a crown corporation independent of the Canadian National and CP Rail systems on April 1, 1978, and gradually assumed full responsibility for managing all the Dominion's rail passenger services except commuter lines. With national headquarters in Montreal, VIA has regional headquarters at Montreal, Moncton, Toronto, and Winnipeg, each in the charge of a vice president.

As in the United States, Canada's early railways were primarily a factor in developing the nation, helping to link together a widely scattered population. Trains had advantages over other methods of travel and held a top-rated position as the popular way of getting from one place to another until after World War II, when the automobile and the airplane became appealing alternatives. As rail passenger service slumped, less money was spent on new equipment and much existing rolling stock became outdated, with service becoming inefficient and costly.

Trains are not cheap transportation. Canada's railways were spending more than $20 million a year to keep the rail passenger system running. Taxpayers paid most of this loss. With a projected cost of up to $400 million by 1980, Transport Canada decided it was time for action. Today's rail passenger policy aims to provide efficient and attractive service in areas where rail is an appropriate form of passenger transportation and to cut the level of government subsidies paid for this service.

VIA is responsible to Parliament and responsive to public demands. It plans, markets, and performs onboard customer services. It permits economies not possible when the two great companies operated independent passenger services. The VIA system emphasizes style and comfort with new LRC (light, rapid, comfortable) equipment in an effort to bring back to the rails as many motorists and plane riders as possible.

Nearly 4000 former CN and CP Rail employees joined VIA Rail Canada, which acquired ownership of all CN and CP Rail passenger locomotives. But locomotive engineers, conductors, and brakemen remain employees of those two companies. As of now, VIA does not own any track, although it operates 14,324 route miles of main track with regular passenger service and 1065 route miles with mixed (partly freight) trains. It serves about 750 individual points, large and small, and carries an estimated 5 million people a year. The federal government compensates CN and CP Rail for the cost of operating VIA trains over their lines.

Video Display Terminals These terminals, linked to computers with an occasional telephone connected to a computer, are replacing most phones in such business offices as those of the Association of American Railroads (AAR) headquarters in Washington, D.C. The AAR is one of the system's first users in that area and in the rail industry. The modern concept of data communication is transmission from one computer to another. For many years this was done via standard telephone lines. Although some such linkings are still being used, direct computer-to-computer contact through high-speed circuits is increasingly coming into style.

Because the railroads need constantly changing information in their day-to-day operations, it is only natural for them to lead in the rapidly developing field of data communication. Through its Technical Control Center (TCC), the AAR currently acts as a central coordinator for 96 railroads. Besides being able to input facts and figures or retrieve them from AAR computers, a railroad can use the TCC to exchange information with other roads connected to the system. A pilot project is under way to give the carriers the same capability with their shippers.

According to AAR officials, the next step in data communications will be electronic mail. Since the AAR installed the Wang word-processing system, this eventuality is closer than ever before. In fact, the association plans to install a Wang key station to transmit data anywhere in the country. With this capability, a person at the AAR could send instantly a memo, letter, or report to any railroad equipped to receive it, thus avoiding long postal delays. The AAR also foresees the development of computers that can simulate speech, say, by 1990, to provide people with information over the phone by talking computers.

Villard, Henry (1835-1900) Villard, who landed in New York as a penniless German immigrant unable to speak a word of English at age 18, eventually became president of the Northern Pacific (NP), America's first northern transcontinental railway, and by completing that road linked the head of the Great Lakes with the Columbia River and Puget Sound and thus opened a vast northwestern wilderness to settlement.

A lawyer's son, he was born on April 10, 1835, in Bavaria and baptized Ferdinand Heinrich Gustav Hilgard. Because of his father's threat to put him into the army, he changed his name to Henry Villard and emigrated to America. Hampered by language difficulties but working his way westward, he had his first railroad job in the crew of a wood train on the Indiana & Madison Railroad. He started a brilliant career in journalism by writing for the *Belleville* (Ohio) *Zeitung*.

Hired by the New York *Staats-Zeitung* as a correspondent in the Midwest, Villard reported on the Lincoln-Douglas debates and met Abraham Lincoln, who years later signed a charter creating the Northern Pacific Railroad Co. He covered the Pikes Peak gold rush, wrote a Pikes Peak book, and covered Lincoln's nomination and presidential campaign for *The New York Herald* and the Associated Press. Later he wrote eyewitness accounts of major Civil War battles for the *Herald, The New York Tribune,* and a Washington news agency of his own.

He married Helen F. Garrison, the only daughter of the abolitionist champion William Lloyd Garrison, and long afterward bought *The Nation,* a magazine which his son, Oswald Garrison Villard, edited for many years. Because of poor health, he returned to Germany for medical treatment. There he became interested in the plight of Germans who held stock in mismanaged railways in the northwestern United States. On their behalf, he visited Oregon in 1874 and was fired with enthusiasm for the potential development of that region.

In 1876 he was elected president of the Oregon & California Railroad and the Oregon Steamship Co., and later was appointed one of two receivers of the Kansas Pacific Railroad. He organized and headed the Oregon Railway & Navigation Co., created the Oregon Improvement Co. and the Oregon & Transcontinental Co., and started building a railroad along the Columbia River's south branch.

Finding his potential rail empire threatened by the Northern Pacific, pushing slowly eastward across the Dakotas and Montana, he formed a company, known colloquially as Villard's Blind Pool, that bought stock control of the NP in 1881 and elected him president of it. With 25,000 laborers, including 15,000 Chinese, his management advanced NP construction more rapidly, completed the mainline, and built nearly 500 miles of branch lines. On September 8, 1883, watched by 500 invited guests, Villard and ex-President Ulysses S. Grant drove the NP's last spike at Gold Creek, Montana.

To help settle the Northwest, Villard set up 955 local immigration agents in Great Britain and continental Europe. Six years after the spike ceremony, the Dakotas, Montana, Washington, and Idaho had enough population to join the Union as states. But construction costs had far exceeded estimates; the NP ran out of money. Villard had to resign from the presidency of the Northern Pacific but remained a leading figure in the financial world. In 1887 he was elected to the NP Board of Directors as financial chairman and later as chairman. He left the railroad scene after the panic of 1893 had thrown the NP and many other roads into bankruptcy.

Villard was still a force to be reckoned with. While completing his two-volume *Memoirs,* he helped to organize Edison General Electric Co., served 2 years as its president, gained control of Milwaukee's street railway lines, which he electrified, and bought *The New York Evening Post.* He died on November 12, 1900, at Dobbs Ferry, New York.

BIBLIOGRAPHY: *The Northern Pacific Railroad,* Jay Cooke & Co., Philadelphia, 1873; James B. Hedges, *Henry Villard and the Railways of the Northwest,* Yale, New Haven, Conn., 1930; Robert S. Macfarlane, *Henry Villard and the Northern Pacific,* Newcomen Society in North America, New York, 1954; Charles R. Wood, *The Northern Pacific: The Main Street of the Northwest,* Superior Publishing, Seattle, 1967.

Wagner, Webster *(1817-1882)*

***Wagner, Webster** (1817-1882)* Parlor-car inventor. Born on October 2, 1817, at Palatine Bridge, New York, he was apprenticed to his wagon-building brother James but decided there was more money in railroading. He resigned and worked for 17 years as a railroad station agent in his hometown. During that time he watched through trains of comfortless cars go by his depot. Then he had a bright idea. He applied to William H. Vanderbilt for permission to use an old coach to develop his idea of what a sleeping car should be. It took him months to fit up that car. One day in 1868 the two Vanderbilts, William and his father, inspected it; and the old commodore asked, "How many of these things have you got?" Wagner said, "Only one." The old man encouraged him. "Go ahead! Build more! It's a devilish good thing, and you can't have too many of them."

That started Wagner on the road to fame and fortune. With his brother's help, he built four cars, and they began running on the rails on September 1, 1868. The first car had a single tier of berths. Later, he added upper berths. Thus the modern sleeper was born. To ventilate the upper berths beneath a flat roof he devised and applied the pitched roof, much higher than that of the old cars. This roof was so useful that it was applied to day coaches also. Meanwhile, Wagner had put into operation his first drawing-room car for day travel.

Neither Wagner nor George M. Pullman invented the first sleeping car. *See* SLEEPING CARS.

On January 13, 1882, while riding in a parlor car built and owned by his company, Wagner and seven other passengers were burned to death in a rear-end collision at Spuyten Duyvil, just outside New York City.

BIBLIOGRAPHY: Wesley S. Griswold, *Train Wreck!* Stephen Greene, Brattleboro, Vt., 1968; August Mencken, *The Railroad Passenger Car,* Johns Hopkins, Baltimore, 1957; Robert C. Reed, *Train Wrecks,* Superior Publishing, Seattle, 1968; Robert B. Shaw, *A History of Railroad Accidents, Safety Precautions, and Operating Practices,* Northern Press, Potsdam, N.Y., 1978.

***Warman, Cyrus** (1855-1914)* Born on June 25, 1855, at Greenup, Illinois, the boy who later won fame as Cy Warman, poet and prose writer, drifted to Colorado and worked as an engine wiper, then as a fireman and engineer, on the Denver and Rio Grande. He quit railroading to devote full time to writing, but he eventually went back to it and was assistant to the president of the Grand Trunk when he died at Chicago on April 7, 1914.

His most famous story, "A Thousand Miles in a

***One of the luxury cars that Webster Wagner built for the Vanderbilts' New York Central Railroad between 1868 and 1878. Wagner died in one of these cars in a train wreck in 1882.** [Collection of Freeman Hubbard]*

Night," tells of a trip from Chicago to New York in an engine cab. In his day, white was the clear signal on railroads, while green meant "caution." Warman's best-loved poem, "Will the Lights Be White?" ends with these words:

Swift toward life's terminal I trend;
The run seems short tonight.
God only knows what's at the end;
I hope the lamps are white.

Water Tanks; Water Towers (Landmarks) Nostalgic symbols of the steam age, water tanks are vanishing landmarks. In 1951, when diesel power was gradually taking over, some 26,000 of them, ranging in capacity from 35,000 to 500,000 gallons, were in daily use on American railroads. Today there are probably none left in year-round daily service, although some are still available for rare or occasional steam-train excursions on 8 or 10 common carriers and nearly 100 railfan-operated steam tourist short lines, many of them very short, in the United States and Canada.

Numerous water tanks were made of creosoted pine held together by adjustable circular steel bands; others were of steel construction. Homer Croy's novel *West of the Water Tower* recalls this long-gone way of life. Many a passenger waiting for a train under a blazing sun would stroll over to the dripping water tank and find shelter in its shade.

Hoboes would wait there, too, to board freights and ride the "side-door Pullman." Hobo jungles often grew up in such areas. Those tanks served as bulletin boards for hoboes. It was not unusual to see messages chalked on the tanks, telling about trains, routes, places to get handouts, and towns or railroads to avoid because of hostile police. More than one gang of robbers hid in the shadow of a water tower on a dark night before holding up an express train. The derogatory term *tank town,* which a theatrical troupe is said to have coined to describe a small or backward community, implied that the place had little else besides a water tower.

The long-gone era of water tanks and steam engines is still remembered on the Cass Scenic Railroad in West Virginia, where this Shay engine was photographed in 1979. [Dan Fink]

The steam locomotive was thirsty. Most road engines near the end of the steam era needed some 10,000 gallons of water at a filling. Louisville & Nashville's big M-1s, however, had tenders that each held 22,000 gallons.

A fireman would climb out of the cab, stand on the end of the tender, and deftly pull a chain that lowered the water tower's big spout to release a torrent of water into the locomotive tank, which sometimes overflowed into a tiny flood. Then he'd shut off and return the spout to an upright position. In large cities and towns where standpipes were attached to community water systems, elevated water towers were not necessary; but in smaller inhabited areas there was not sufficient pressure in the mains to lift water directly into the tender, and elevated tanks were needed.

Faster passenger and freight schedules demanded fewer water stops. Even while railroads were still operating under 100 percent steam power, some in the Southwest were able to start retiring water towers and their adjacent facilities through the use of larger tender tanks and a water car coupled behind the locomotive. Water cars were filled with water and connected with the tender by a hose. *See* TRACK PANS.

The modern diesel uses a negligible quantity of water as compared with the old-time steamer, and much of this water is recirculated for additional use.

BIBLIOGRAPHY: S. Kip Farrington, Jr., *Railroading from the Head End,* Doubleday, Doran, New York, 1943.

Waycars *See* CABOOSES.

Welded Rail Consisting of twin strands of continuous ribbon steel, welded rail is far stronger than jointed track. It is heavier, weighing some 132 pounds per yard versus the 100-pound rail previously standard on, for example, the Southern mainline between New Orleans and Birmingham. Also it has no joints, which in ordinary rail occur every 39 feet and are the track structure's weakest part. Furthermore, it eliminates the old familiar clickety-clack of train wheels passing over rail joints and thus gives passengers and freight a smoother ride. More important, it is far less likely to fail under the increasingly heavy and varied loads of today's trains. And by avoiding the pounding of rail ends by wheels passing over joints, it dramatically lowers the cost of track maintenance.

Installing welded rail is a far cry from the days of muscular gandy dancers (trackmen). Modern machines do most of the work. The rails are welded into ¼-mile lengths at a central location. Then they are hauled in special trains of usually 33 cars to the point of installation. Each train carries 54 ribbons of rail, enough for 6¾ miles of new track. As preliminary steps in rail laying, new crossties are unloaded along the track at locations where old ties have been marked for replacement.

New ballast is then distributed. Tie plates and spikes, rail anchors, tie plugs, and creosote are unloaded. As the train moves into position and the replacement actually begins, two strands of rail are threaded onto a rail pusher and fed out over a roller car (used to steady and guide the rail) between the old rails. The new ribbon rail is then guided into place and spiked to gauge. The old steel is taken to shops to be processed for other use or scrapped.

Wellington Avalanche On February 22, 1910, a very cold Tuesday night, local passenger train No. 25, with seven cars pulled by 12-wheeled engine No. 1413, steamed out of the Great Northern terminal at Spokane, Washington, for the long run to Seattle through the snow-covered wheat belt, across the frozen Columbia River, and over the high Cascade Range. Spokane newspapers reported excessive snowfall along the route, with minor slides and a few casualties, and some of the train's 70-odd passengers were uneasy. Brakeman Ross Phillips and Conductor J. L. Pettit, collecting fares, tried to reassure them. The fear was not unreasonable. Each year the Cascades' upper ridges got about 45 feet of snow and thousands of avalanches, big and little.

Most avalanches occur in areas previously burned over by forest fires, since timber anchors huge snow masses but stumps do not. On No. 25's route, the bald mountaintop nearly 3000 feet above Wellington, Washington, with its blackened stumps and scraggly second-growth timber, was a natural breeding place for slides. Only the rocky shelf, ranging from 1000 to less than 100 feet wide, which held a small wooden village, with its tracks, offered any break in the slope that dropped rather sharply to the Tye River, about 150 feet below.

The first Cascade Tunnel, completed in 1900 and electrified to avoid the suffocating fumes of locomotive smoke, was an engineering marvel. Construction engineers located this bore too high above the slope. They knew, of course, that a longer tunnel built at a lower elevation would have been safer and more efficient, but at that time laying steel through the Cascades cost so much that the Great Northern could not afford the more expensive project. Because of that, both the tunnel and train No. 25 would be involved in America's deadliest snowslide.

Early Wednesday morning the train reached Leavenworth, Washington, where the slow climb into the Cascades began. At that spot all westbound trains were assigned helper engines to boost them over the big hump. As No. 25 pulled up to the snow-covered depot, its slanted roof hung thickly with icicles, another train was already there: No. 27, the fast mail which had left Spokane hours before the local. Pettit went into the station to find out what was wrong. Snow had begun to fall. He learned that a slide nearby had closed the track.

For 10 hours after 25's arrival at Leavenworth, the two Spokane-Seattle trains waited there. At length the track was reopened, the two locomotive stacks barked, and mighty driving wheels gripped the snowy rails. But they were stopped again, at Cascade, a mountain hamlet at the east portal of Cascade Tunnel, where a gale had piled up the swirling snow and cut off the electric current. Both trains were delayed outside the tunnel.

Inside the cars, time dragged by on leaden feet. The marooned people grew more and more impatient. Finally, on Thursday night, February 24, the electric power was restored. One of the "juice" locomotives used in tunnel service took the two trains, in turn, through the chilling, dark bore.

The trains rolled ¼ mile past the far end of the tunnel to the little Wellington depot and stopped about 400 yards beyond it. Both occupied sidings on a ledge, less than 100 feet wide, that jutted out of the slope.

Friday morning, cold, gray, and snowy, found Superintendent Jim O'Neill, a broad-shouldered fighting Irishman, on the scene, personally taking charge of the bottleneck. At Wellington, on three parallel tracks, Death had planned a grisly carnival. The mail train stood highest up on the slope, beside the passenger train, while O'Neill's business car shared the lowest track with a live steam engine, two boxcars, and three electric locomotives. Beyond this outermost track, a steep, winding trail led down the mountainside to the iced-over Tye River in a gorge 150 feet below. Four railroad men bunked in O'Neill's car: the superintendent himself, his cook, his secretary, and Trainmaster A. R. Blackburn. A gang of 30 track laborers was assigned to sleep on the baggage-car floor.

Despite the storm, which had become a blizzard, a large group of bored passengers left the train Friday morning to explore Wellington, which lay buried almost to roof level under 11 feet of snow. Local residents had burrowed like moles through the glistening whiteness, honeycombing it with passageways reinforced by timbers that let them move around town without snowshoes.

On Saturday morning, the ominous roar of occasional snowslides, muffled by distance and the storm, made the travelers jumpy. Some passengers urged Superintendent O'Neill to back their train into the tunnel. "At least," they argued, "we'd be safe from avalanches." But the women seemed terrified by the very thought that huge masses of snow might "lock up" the tunnel while they were inside. Besides, that tunnel was bitterly cold, and cars couldn't be heated in it because coal smoke would foul the air to the point of suffocation. So O'Neill decided to let the trains stay where they were.

They stood there 4 days. The news butcher's meager food supply had been sold out even before the train reached Wellington; so the snowbound men, women, and children were fed from the local restaurant at the Great Northern's expense. Snow kept falling, sometimes at the rate of a foot an hour.

Fear was increasing. The telegraph wires went dead. The frightened passengers turned to religion for solace, holding a prayer meeting in the observation car. They spent the rest of Saturday aimlessly. Some wandered through the cars and into the isolated village without knowing what to do. Others played cards. A dozen women with about six children told stories and played games.

On Saturday night, it seems, Death got tired of waiting. A howling wind blew down a frame shack, killing two railway men who had been sleeping in it. O'Neill kept sending urgent telegrams, ordering and begging the outside world to send aid.

On Sunday morning O'Neill announced a way of escape for passengers who wanted to leave the train. He said guides would lead them down a steep incline through 3 miles of deep snow to the vacation resort of Scenic Hot Springs (now called Scenic). They'd be tied to one another by ropes, like those which mountain climbers used in the Alps, to keep them from tumbling off the slippery trail. That was too desperate a gamble for most of the passengers, who felt that staying with their comfortably heated train would be less hazardous than sliding down a mountain. But a few bold men stepped forward as Conductor Pettit led the way down the unmarked trail. Jim O'Neill followed later. The energetic superintendent was eager to reach the far end of the snow barricade so that he could personally speed the efforts to break through.

At Wellington, the short winter day drew to a close. A sleet storm was followed at about midnight by a treacherous chinook—a warm, moist southwest wind. Then came a gale accompanied by thunder and lightning. About one o'clock on the fatal morning of March 1 a locomotive engineer, Charles Andrews, was awakened in the bunkhouse by a nightmare and what he described as "an occult warning." He dressed and left the building.

The whole mountainside appeared to be sliding. About 10 or 20 acres of solidly packed snow had broken loose from the summit, unchecked by tall timber which a forest fire had burned years before, and was rushing down at faster than express-train speed into Tye River Canyon, sweeping everything in its path—the two trains, three steam engines, four electric locomotives, a rotary snowplow, the engine shed and water tower, part of another frame building, and telegraph poles and wires. O'Neill's car did not leave the rails, but like a wicked giant playing with scissors the avalanche sheared off its roof. Tons of snow engulfed the car, killing Trainmaster Blackburn and the superintendent's secretary and his cook.

The slide had cut a deep swath ½ mile wide. Up the slope at Wellington, the startled railroaders quickly assembled lanterns, axes, picks, shovels, crowbars, rope, and other equipment, and they hit the snowy trail down to the dark gorge. All was desolation. Misty rain slanted across the wreckage. Thunderclaps added to the horror, but stabs of forked lightning helped the rescuers to grope their way. At first they could see only dim, gleaming whiteness and steam engines from whose stacks the wind beat thin wisps of smoke, a partly covered juice locomotive, and a dismantled rotary plow. The coaches were entirely buried.

The most lethal of all avalanches occurred at 1:20 a.m. on Tuesday, March 1, the exact time being determined by the stopped watches on the bodies of victims. Only 17 of the estimated 115 human beings hurled into the canyon with the trains came out alive; 3 men died in the superintendent's car, making the total death list from the big slide at least 101. Almost miraculously, 4 survivors found in the gorge were not even hurt. Among them was an 18-month-old baby, discovered alone in the snow, crying. Both of its parents had perished.

No mail was reported lost in the Wellington disaster. A man sent to the scene took charge of the delayed mail and the personal belongings of dead employees. Not until late Tuesday evening did a doctor and a nurse with medical supplies arrive at Scenic by a special train from Everett. Guides assisted them up the slippery mountain trail to the emergency hospital.

Superintendent O'Neill reached the spot the following day. He had been toiling heroically with rotary-plow crews farther down the line in a futile effort to break through the snow barricade before disaster struck. He promptly set a force of about 300 men to digging. One big problem was how to dispose of so much snow. Cuts 12 feet deep were dug and blasted into the slide. The hum of giant power and the boom of dynamite echoed from crag to crag in the lofty Cascades, starting new slides.

O'Neill had the mainline reopened 10 days after the monstrous slide. Wellington, renamed Tye and then abandoned years later, is today not even a ghost town. The lonely, bleak ledge on which it stood is bereft of all signs of human habitation. They say that even the timber wolves shun it. The once-famous old Cascade Tunnel has long since been closed. A new, better, and safer one, almost 8 miles long, was built by the Great Northern farther down the slope. *See* CASCADE TUNNEL.

Western Maryland Railway (WM) Rail line that since 1972 had been part of the Chessie System through the Chesapeake and Ohio's ownership of majority stock but is now part of CSX Corp. Extending westward from Baltimore, it forks at Cumberland, Maryland, to termini at Connellsville, Pennsylvania, and Webster Springs, West Virginia, in the coalfields. This road was nicknamed the Mason and Dixon Line because it nearly parallels the Pennsylvania-Maryland boundary that before the Civil War popularly separated the North from the South, or the free states from the slave states (although slaveholding Maryland never seceded).

The road was chartered on May 27, 1852; construction began 10 years later. In 1863 the Union Army took over the WM for 5 days as a supply line for the Battle of Gettysburg. Afterward, its trains carried the wounded, the dead, and Confederate prisoners to Baltimore. Five months later, President Lincoln rode over lines that subsequently became part of the WM to deliver his Gettsyburg Address. After the war, the WM, developed from 30 railroads by mergers and reorganizations, was expanded and modernized.

The WM climbs the Allegheny Mountains, including Black Fork grade, an operating challenge virtually unequaled in the East, with 10 miles of unrelieved 3.05 percent grade that in some places reaches a maximum of 3.85. In steam days, 2-8-0 type engines could handle only 10 loads (mostly coal) up this steep hill, which often necessitated the use of as many as 8 or 10 engines on a single train, half the number being cut into mid-train and the rest divided between front and rear. Although largely a freight line, the WM for years operated crack passenger trains between Baltimore and Chicago.

See also CHESSIE SYSTEM.

BIBLIOGRAPHY: Harold A. Williams, *The Western Maryland Railway Story,* Western Maryland Railway Company, Baltimore, 1952.

Western North Carolina Railroad (WNC) Rail line, now forming about 130 miles of Southern Railway mainline, that was incorporated in 1855 to cross the Blue Ridge between Asheville and Salisbury, North Carolina. Built by convict labor over a route as tortuous as any ever undertaken in the South, it was completed in 1879. The Civil War halted construction. Afterward, it was halted again by the disappearance of two WNC executives in the face of charges that they had diverted $4 million in state-endorsed bonds to their own use. After a reorganization in 1877, tracklaying was resumed.

Two armies of railroad builders had started at opposite ends of the line. They met in 1879 in the center of Swannanoa Tunnel, the grades and centers joining exactly, after the eastern group had toiled painfully up 1092 feet from the site of an old Indian fort. So roundabout was the corkscrew route that between Mileposts 115 and 120 the tracks were never much more than ½ mile apart. Many tales are told of runaway trains which caused very expensive and often fatal accidents.

For a long time after the joining of the eastern and western ends of rail, the state continued leasing convicts to the company, mostly to clean out cuts and replace fills. Though the WNC had cost North Carolina taxpayers a lot of money, it opened up a prosperous lumber industry, huge furniture factories, and cotton and hosiery mills. Shortly after its completion, the WNC was leased to the 140-mile Richmond & Danville (R&D).

In 1894 the Southern took over the R&D, bought the WNC outright, and popularized the latter's western terminus, Asheville, as an elite vacation resort in the "Land of the Sky."

BIBLIOGRAPHY: Grady Jefferys and John Gilbert, *Crossties through Carolina: The Story of North Carolina's Early Day Railroads,* Helios Press, New York. 1969.

Western Pacific Railroad (WP) While Arthur W. Keddie, a young Scottish surveyor, was exploring for a new California wagon road through the valley of the Feather River (named for floating feathers of wild pigeons), he found the mountains via Beckwourth Pass more than 2000 feet lower than Donner Pass to the south, which the Southern (originally Central) Pacific (SP) eventually used. Keddie unsuccessfully sought financial help from Collis P. Huntington, future SP president, for the building of a railroad through Beckwourth Pass.

Undaunted, Keddie got Brig. Gen. William S. Rosecrans of Civil War fame and others interested in his project. In 1869 construction was started over that route, but it never got far. Not until 1903 was the Western Pacific Railway incorporated to build up the river's North Fork and across the Sierra Nevada via Beckwourth Pass. George Jay Gould, who controlled a rail empire inherited from his father, guaranteed WP's $50 million bond issue only if the road's grades did not exceed 1 percent or its curves 10 degrees. These restrictions meant costly construction but gave WP a superior line that it would not have had otherwise.

Feather River Canyon offers one of America's most intricate train-dispatching jobs because it consists of three forks, a branch, and two creeks. The WP has 41 steel bridges and 44 tunnels on its entire route from Sacramento across California and Nevada to Salt Lake City, Utah, where it connects with the Union Pacific and the Denver and Rio Grande Western—a total of 1246 miles of mainline track and 472 miles of branch lines and sidings.

Trains enter the canyon on the river's Middle Fork about 5 miles east of Portola at Milepost 326. After winding along this fork for about 27 miles, they go through a tunnel into the North Fork area but are still many miles from the fork itself. Then they traverse a rather high plateau through which Spanish Creek flows, roll along the East Branch to the North Fork, follow that fork through a series of tunnels, and eventually cross the Feather River into nonrugged terrain.

WP tracklaying began in 1905. California's mountains and Nevada's hot deserts compounded the problem of locating and constructing the line in a remote region where labor was scarce. But it was built. The eastbound and westbound track gangs met on November 1, 1909, on Spanish Creek bridge near the town named after Keddie. A new transcontinental rail route through the Sierra Nevada had been achieved. Arthur Keddie, then 68, wept with joy.

The road's general offices are in San Francisco. Through freight service was inaugurated in 1909; through passenger service, in 1910. Traffic agreements with steamship lines and the Santa Fe gave the new railroad access to all Pacific coastal cities and the Orient. But the WP's high construction cost and inadequacy of traffic in its early years brought financial hardship to the Gould rail empire, which was helping to support the new road. *See* GOULD, GEORGE JAY.

In 1906 the WP Railway was sold at foreclosure and reorganized as the Western Pacific Railroad Company. Under new management, freight and passenger service was improved and branch lines were bought or built, among them being the Tidewater Southern, the interurban electric Sacramento Northern, and the Alameda Belt Line, a switching operation. In 1926 Arthur Curtiss James, one of the last major rail financiers, acquired control of the WP. He forged a 200-mile link with the Great Northern, driving a gold spike at Bieber, California, in 1931. But in 1935 the Depression threw WP into a receivership from which it did not emerge until 1944.

The *California Zephyr,* one of America's best passenger trains, jointly owned and operated by the WP, Rio Grande, and Burlington Route, was put into service in 1949 and made its final run on March 22, 1970.

WP's first diesel, a 600-horsepower switcher, was bought from Electro-Motive Corp. in 1939. But the road's first nonsteam motive power consisted of two gas-powered Budd motor cars placed in service on its San Diego branch in 1922 and sold in 1939 to the Georgia Car & Locomotive Co. The last steam locos WP acquired were four big 2-8-8-2s from Baldwin and seven 4-6-6-4s from Alco in 1938.

In 1945 the road received its first freight diesels, and in 1947 its first passenger diesels.

Aside from railfan excursions, 0-6-0 switcher No. 164, running light, was probably the last WP steam loco to operate on her own power. Today, the 164 is displayed in a station park at Oroville, California.

Union Pacific has announced plans to acquire the Missouri Pacific and Western Pacific, which, if consummated, would preserve UP's status as the nation's largest railroad holding company.

The difficult Feather River Canyon, in California, was finally crossed by the Western Pacific. A WP freight train is pictured here. The three forks, two creeks, and one branch of the canyon crossing create a challenging dispatching job. [Elmer Treloar]

BIBLIOGRAPHY: Spencer Crump, *Western Pacific: The Railroad That Was Built Too Late,* Trans-Anglo Books, Los Angeles, 1963; Guy L. Dunscomb, *Locomotives of the Western Pacific,* 1963; Gilbert H. Kneiss, *Fifty Candles for Western Pacific,* Western Pacific Railroad, San Francisco, 1953.

Westinghouse, George (1846–1941) Westinghouse was known as "the man who stopped the trains" by his greatest invention, the automatic airbrake. This device revolutionized transportation worldwide, making it safer, more dependable, and more economical. It conferred on trains, electric railway cars, and even heavy-duty trucks and buses the power to stop quickly, thus contributing mightily to civilization as we know it, saving lives, time, and property, especially railroad property.

Born near Schenectady, New York, one of three brothers, Westinghouse must have inherited mechanical skill from his father, also named George, who manufactured primitive farm and mill machinery and small stationary steam engines and patented seven simple devices of his own. In 1865, after returning home from Civil War service, the future airbrake genius happened to watch the clumsy efforts of a train crew to rerail cars that had jumped the track. So he invented a rerailing frog by means of which a locomotive could drag cars back onto the rails. He also invented railway signaling devices.

His major career resulted from his being delayed on a trip from Troy to Schenectady by the head-on collision of two freight trains on a straight, smooth, level stretch of track in sunlight. "The engineers saw each other and tried to stop," Westinghouse was told, "but there wasn't time." Quick emergency stopping in that era was impossible because each car had to be braked individually. When an engineer whistled for brakes, the trainmen would rush from car to car to "tie 'em down" with clubs like pick handles.

Westinghouse began working to design a brake that would make railroading safer. By 1870 the United States had already granted 305 patents for continuous train brakes, in addition to 650 issued in England, but none of them solved the problem. Westinghouse studied these and other kinds and knew why each one didn't work. He tried and discarded steam and electricity as power sources. Then he got the idea he needed by reading a magazine article that told how engineers building Mont Cenis Tunnel in the French-Italian Alps pumped compressed air through a 3000-foot pipeline to power the rock drills. Using that principle, he devised a straight airbrake, which he patented on April 13, 1869. A Pittsburgh industrialist financed the equipment needed for a test. Westinghouse offered his brake to the New York Central and the Erie. Neither road was interested.

Then he talked the general superintendent of the Panhandle Railroad (later part of the Pennsylvania) into letting him use his equipment on the Steubenville, Ohio, accommodation train—an engine and four coaches. As the train testing the new airbrake emerged from Grant's Hill in Pittsburgh, Pennsylvania, at 30 miles per hour, the engineer, Dan Tait, was horrified to see a huckster's cart on the track only two city blocks ahead. The driver applied his whip, but his team reared and stalled the cart directly in front of the fast-moving train. Tait yanked the brake valve. To his amazement, he stopped with the point of his pilot 10 feet from the cart. This was the first successful emergency stop in railroad history.

In 1869 the inventor established the Westinghouse Air Brake Co., whose plant at Wilmerding, Pennsylvania, was completed in 1870. This business boomed from the start. The first airbrake order came from the Michigan Central, and the second from the Chicago North Western. In 1873 Westinghouse, a handsome, well-built man with a handlebar mustache, produced a more efficient version of his brake, in which an accident to it would set the brakes and stop the train. In case of a break in two, both parts of the train would stop immediately.

Besides his own inventions, Westinghouse controlled 2700 patents of other inventors. He became president of 30 corporations totally capitalized at $200 million and employing 50,000 men. His personal fortune at death was estimated at $50 million.

BIBLIOGRAPHY: Frank Crane, *George Westinghouse: His Life and Achievements,* Wise, New York, 1925; Henry G. Prout, *A Life of George Westinghouse,* American Society of Mechanical Engineers, New York, 1921.

Wheels A car having flanged oaken wheels with conical treads was built in about 1525 for a Transylvanian mine and centuries later was placed on exhibition at the Berlin (Germany) Transport Museum. In 1754 the *Dictionary of Arts and Sciences* pictured a "wagonways" cart which may well have been the first use of cast-iron wheels. It hauled stones from an English quarry. In 1816, also in England, George Stephenson and W. Losch patented an assembly having a cast-iron chilled rim plus wrought spokes molded solid with the center.

In 1850, with a variety of cast-iron wheels already in use, Nathan Washburn of Worcester, Massachusetts, patented and began building a double-plate wheel. Made of two disks united near the rim, it had curved brackets or reinforcements on the back and served its purpose so well that, with few changes, it remained the standard design for American freight cars until 1928, when the single-plate wheel superseded it.

The chief claim offered in favor of the carbon white iron rim is a coefficient of friction between it and the brakeshoe which materially exceeds that of a steel tread subjected to the same pressure. Too, the easily machined hubs of a cast-iron wheel ensure correct wheel fits and lower machine-shop costs. Passenger coaches, however, need a "quieter" disk. In the 1880s the Allen paper wheel reached the height of its popularity. Formed from rough strawboard pressed hydraulically under a great weight, the core of this job was bound with steel wire. Two thin plates of the same substance locked the tire to the web. Paper wheels were finally eliminated when rolling-stock weight became too heavy for them. Wood, too, has served as a material for wheel cores, but it never found much favor. An arrangement with a pneumatic disk between the core and the rim also was tried out for some time. Rubber-insert wheels came into use on streetcar equipment and on subway cars such as some of those operated today on the Paris Métro.

But steel has been found to be the most practical substance for heavy-duty car wheels. Charles T. Schoen of Pittsburgh was the first to develop the solid forged and rolled steel wheel for railroads. An early advocate of large-capacity cars, he brought out all-steel coal hoppers of 50-ton capacity in 1897 for the Bessemer & Lake Erie Railroad. But the cast-iron wheels of that period could not withstand the strain of such heavy loads. By 1903 Schoen had devised machinery for shaping solid forged and rolled steel disks and began the first manufacture of what became known as the wrought-steel wheel. Other car builders followed suit.

BIBLIOGRAPHY: Robert S. Henry, *This Fascinating Railroad Business,* 3d ed., rev., Bobbs-Merrill, Indianapolis, 1946.

Whistle-Stop *See* CAMPAIGN TRAINS.

Whistler, George Washington ***(1800–1849)*** Distinguished engineer and pioneer builder of railroads and locomotives. His achievements were obscured by the fame of his son, the painter James Abbott McNeill Whistler, whose *Portrait of the Artist's Mother,* showing an old lady seated on a chair, is a picture of the major's wife.

Casey Jones's homemade locomotive whistle, now on display in the Casey Jones Museum in Jackson, Tennessee. His locomotive could always be identified, miles before coming into view, by this whistle's unique plaintive moans.

Major Whistler supervised tracklaying over the Baltimore & Ohio's first mile of track and laid out routes for several New England lines and part of the Erie. He also built locomotives in his native Lowell, Massachusetts, including the first two known to have been equipped with whistles: the Long Island's *Hicksville* and the Wilmington & Susquehanna's *Susquehanna.* He laid rails through the twisting Berkshire valleys in western Massachusetts in such a manner as to win the engineering world's praise.

Czar Nicholas I of Russia invited him to build a 420-mile railroad from St. Petersburg (now Leningrad) to Moscow. Whistler took his family to Russia and set to work. On his advice, the Czar adopted a 5-foot gauge. Whistler was appalled by the wholesale corruption he observed on this project.

After 3 years in Russia, Whistler wanted to return to his homeland with his family. "America is the only country worth living in," he wrote to a friend. But he died of cholera in Russia a few months before the railroad was completed. His grave is in Stonington, Connecticut.

BIBLIOGRAPHY: Albert Parry, *Whistler's Father,* Bobbs-Merrill, Indianapolis, 1939.

Whistles, Locomotive The first two American locos definitely known to have been equipped with whistles were two woodburners, the Long Island Rail Road's *Hicksville* and the *Susquehanna* of the Wilmington & Susquehanna (later part of the Pennsylvania Railroad). Both engines were built at Lowell, Massachusetts, in 1836 under the supervision of George Washington Whistler. Another early engine having a whistle was the *Sandusky,* built at Paterson, New Jersey, in 1837 for the Mad River & Lake Erie (later New York Central). *See* WHISTLER, GEORGE WASHINGTON.

Possibly no one sound was more comforting to early Western settlers than the plaintive wail of woodburning engines, which told them that they were not alone. It linked them with the folks back East.

By "valving," or changing the pressure of steam admitted into the quill, engineers could change the tones and even play tunes. "Dutch" Elford, a Cincinnati Southern engineer, won local fame by playing *Oh, How I Love Jesus!* on his whistle. Casey Jones had a homemade six-chime whistle with six slender tubes bound together, the shortest being exactly half the length of the longest. With its interpretive tone, the "ballast scorcher" could make the quill say its prayers or scream like a banshee. This whistle is preserved today in the Casey Jones Museum at Jackson, Tennessee. *See* CASEY JONES.

With the advent of superheated steam power, the whistle was moved forward on the locomotive boiler to a place where audibility was increased and the engineer's vision less obstructed by steam clouds. Around 1890 some roads began mounting their whistles ahead of the smokestacks and using parabolic amplifiers. This move paid dividends in reducing the number of grade-crossing accidents. Some carriers used the so-called headlight type of whistle with its barrel top set nearly parallel to the boiler top.

Most whistles were of brass, often alloyed with nickel or iron. The metal had to be tempered to withstand extremely high temperature and about 275 pounds of steam pressure. A chamber had between three and six divisions, evoking a multinoted harmonious pitch. This gave the whistle popular appeal.

Air horns were developed around 1918, long before diesel motive power, for use on early gas-electric self-propelled rail cars. Later they were applied to electric locomotives and then to diesel-electrics. They vary from single-noted instruments to ones with five chiming pitches. Many steam locomotives, too, were equipped with air-pressure horns. Today, numerous air horns simulate, but never quite attain, the nostalgia-inducing wail of the old-time steam locomotive.

BIBLIOGRAPHY: Henry B. Comstock, *The Iron Horse,* Crowell, New York, 1971; Lawrence W. Sagle, *What Makes the Locomotives Go?* Penn Craft Books, 1950.

White Pass & Yukon Route (WP&Y) Consisting of 110.7 miles of superb scenery and fading memories of death by cold, hunger, and hurtling down mountainsides, the WP&Y was originally a by-product of the gold rush in the late 1890s into Yukon Territory in northwestern Canada and part of Alaska.

Today, as a modern railway, one of the few narrow-gauge lines left in North America, it plays a vital role in the Yukon's economy, keeping the area's mineral resources competitive in world markets and helping to assure a secondary source of income, tourism. Passengers comfortably riding diesel-powered trains during the May–October season cross a cantilever steel bridge spanning a 250-foot chasm, Dead Horse Gulch, near the summit of White Pass, and can look down upon the old pack trail where thousands of horses and mules, overworked beyond endurance to tote supplies to Dawson, lost their footing on the slippery trail and plunged to death far below.

Aside from cruelty to animals, the saga woven around the WP&Y includes lust for gold, raw courage, heroism and endurance, death, crime, and engineering genius. The railway was built on mountainsides so steep that men had to be suspended on ropes to prevent their falling while they were cutting and leveling the grade.

So many thousands of gold seekers, mostly men, entered the territory during the gold rush of 1898 and so unexpectedly that food became scarce and had to be rationed. With tons of supplies from the United States piled up on the Skagway and Dyea beaches and an army of prospectors eager to get going, George A. Brackett of Minneapolis started a wagon road to relieve the situation; but so many people and animals continued to perish on the trail that the need for a railway became increasingly urgent.

Michael J. Heaney, an Irish contractor who had been involved in pushing the Canadian Pacific Railway

A mixed train of the White Pass & Yukon Route crossing the 215-foot-high bridge over Dead Horse Gulch, Alaska. [Nicholas Morant, CP Rail]

through the Rockies, set about building an Alaska-Yukon railway backed by the British financier Thomas Tancred. It took 26 months of blasting solid rock, chipping, shoveling, laying rails, and tamping ties to complete this project. Within 21 miles of Skagway, determined men endangering their lives built a roadbed on the side of tall and forbidding cliffs, 2885 feet above sea level, despite high winds, 40-foot snowdrifts, and bone-chilling rain and fog. They also bridged the nightmare of Dead Horse Gulch.

On July 21, 1898, the first locomotive seen in Alaska, the most northerly engine in North America, chuffed down Skagway's main street, Broadway. Many men worked on the rail line during the winter, leaving for the Midas lure when springtime navigation opened. An estimated 35,000 men from a long list of various trades and professions helped to build the WP&Y.

A location was made along Lewis Lake shore, but the line was so irregular that to improve the grade the water's surface had to be lowered about 14 feet. An outlet channel was excavated, whereupon the water cut its way through the sandy hill there, creating a huge canyon. This reduced the lake level by more than 70 feet, necessitating construction of two large trestles above the canyon.

The railway's last spike was driven on July 29, 1900, at Carcross (caribou crossing), where vast caribou herds swim the river. The line's northern terminal, however, is Whitehorse, the Yukon capital, where it meets the United States-built Alaska Highway. Its southern terminal is Skagway, from which the railway cuts across a corner of British Columbia before entering Yukon Territory.

After the gold rush petered out, the territory's population dwindled sharply. During the Depression of the 1930s the trains ran but once a week, still with steam power (diesels were to come later), while rotary plows kept the line open during the long winters.

Since World War II, WP&Y has been hauling lead, zinc, coal, copper concentrate, silver, and asbestos to Skagway en route to world markets but has a financial struggle to keep operating. In 1978 the railway carried 75,000 passengers in parlor cars, many being tourists and campers with their autos and camping material on flatcars. The Skagway-Whitehorse trip takes about 8 hours either way through spectacular scenery including a moss-filled path worn into rocky cliffs by thousands of men of the gold rush.

BIBLIOGRAPHY: Tuppan Adney, *The Klondike Stampede,* Harper, New York, 1900; S. H. Graves, *On the "White Pass" Pay-Roll,* Paladin Press, New York, 1970; Cy Martin, *Gold Rush Narrow Gauge,* Trans-Anglo Books, Corona del Mar, Calif., 1974.

White Train *See* GHOST TRAIN.

Whitney, Asa Two notable railroad figures with this name lived during years that almost completely overlapped. The first man (1791-1874) was an inventor and manufacturer. Born in Townsend, Massachusetts, he learned the blacksmith's trade as a boy and set up a machinist's shop at Brownville, New York, and another in Vermont. Hiring out to the Mohawk & Hudson Railroad, first antecedent of the New York Central System, he served as its master mechanic (1830-1833) and superintendent (1833-1839). For the next 2 years he was a New York State canal commissioner. In 1842 he went into partnership with Matthias W. Baldwin, whose steam locomotive works in Philadelphia eventually became the world's largest. He got rich by manufacturing car wheels from an annealing process he invented, became president of the Reading Railroad, and bequeathed $50,000 to the University of Pennsylvania.

The second Asa Whitney (1797-1872), known as the father of Pacific railroads, was born in North Groton, Connecticut, and spent years as a New York merchant and importer. In 1845 he began urging Congress to build a railroad from Lake Michigan to the West Coast via the South Pass in the Rockies. He toured the country, addressing state legislatures and public meetings, getting in touch with politicians, and writing pamphlets and newspaper articles in an effort to prod Congress into action on this project. Although he did much to create public support for a Pacific railroad, sectional differences of opinion on its route delayed congressional authorization of the first United States transcontinental line until 1862. A third A. Whitney—Alexander H.—became president of the 175,000-member Brotherhood of Railroad Trainmen in the late 1920s.

Whyte Classification System *See* STEAM LOCOMOTIVES.

Winans, Ross (1796-1887) Locomotive builder, best known for his iron Camels. Winans kept a stable in Baltimore and lent horses to the newly formed Baltimore & Ohio Railroad (B&O), among other customers, to haul their early horse-drawn trains. At 34 he went to work for the B&O and soon became its assistant master of machinery, his immediate superior being George Gillingham, master of machinery.

In 1833 the two men went into business for themselves. The B&O allowed them to manage its Mount Clare shops, without salaries, and to use its employees and machinery, in return for which they would build locomotives and sell them to the B&O at special low prices and at the same time build and sell locomotives to other railroads. Thus the firm of Gillingham & Winans became one of the 20-odd locomotive builders in America at that time.

Winans's first production under this setup was an upright-boilered four-wheeler with horizontal cylinders. Her main rods connected her gears to the driving rods, which thus operated in the opposite direction, in an ungainly motion that gave the engine her unflattering name *Crab.* But she functioned satisfactorily. Some machines of this design were sold to the Western Railroad of Massachusetts.

Winans also created the Mud Digger, another unflattering name for a type with an eight-connected driving-wheel arrangement and a coalburning horizontal boiler. She, too, performed well. His chief claim to fame, however, was his Camel type (not to be confused with Camelbacks). He completed the first one in 1848, and turned out scores of them for the B&O and many other lines. The Camel's cylinders measured 12 by 22 (later, 19) inches. With her two middle pairs of drivers, she could take curves easily. But her most characteristic feature was an enormous cab, set squarely atop her boiler like a camel's hump—hence the name.

Winans also designed and built railroad cars. As early as 1834 he patented the first passenger car to use double trucks. He also designed the B&O's hopper cars, the first railroad cars in American history to carry loads exceeding their own weight. Over a 40-year period, more than 3000 such cars were built for the B&O alone, plus many for other railroads. His basic design was so sound that it became the prototype for the modern drop-bottom hoppers.

BIBLIOGRAPHY: Carroll Bateman, *The Baltimore and Ohio: The Story of the Railroad That Grew Up with the United States,* Baltimore & Ohio Print. Plant, Baltimore, 1951; Lawrence W. Sagle, *A Picture History of B&O Motive Power,* Simmons-Boardman, New York, 1953; Angus Sinclair, *Development of the Locomotive Engine,* annotated ed. by John H. White, Jr., M.I.T., Cambridge, Mass., 1970.

WM *See* WESTERN MARYLAND RAILWAY.

WNC *See* WESTERN NORTH CAROLINA RAILROAD.

Women Women have not been prominent in North American railroading, an enterprise traditionally identified with "iron men." Among the exceptions have been these women, who recorded firsts:

Susan Morningstar was the first woman known to have been employed by any American railroad. She began clerking for the Baltimore & Ohio in 1855, in the days when people were aghast at the idea of women going into business. Later in the 1800s, Mrs. Abbie C. Vaughan, who worked on the B&O's Pittsburgh division, is said to have been the first woman telegrapher anywhere to learn the Morse code. She taught it to her railroading husband and their four children. Their home was a B&O office. Whenever a call came, the member of the family nearest to the key took over. After her husband died, Mrs. Vaughan moved to Mexico and worked as a railroad telegrapher there.

Annabelle Cooper is said to have been the only American woman ever hired to run an overhead traveling crane that could lift anything from boiler plates to steam locomotives. Looking more like a college student than a machinist, she got the job in the Grand Trunk Western repair shops in Battle Creek, Michigan at age 25 in 1918 because so many men were leaving to fight in World War I. She rode in a little carriage, throwing levers, 50 feet above the floor. After making an estimated 1 million lifts without an accident, she retired in 1961.

Ann Livingston at 19 became Canadian National's (and possibly Canada's) first switchwoman in 1974, being assigned to Vancouver, British Columbia, one of CN's relatively few yards with bunkhouse facilities for women. A year later CN hired P. E. Darss as probably the first female redcap on any North American railroad.

Evelyn Newell was 26 years old in 1975 when she became the first dues-paying woman engineer member of the Brotherhood of Locomotive Engineers. Born and raised in the Bavarian Alps, she came to the United States in 1967. Her first railroading jobs consisted of clerical and station work on the Chicago & North Western in Wisconsin. In 1972, after 3 weeks of intensive training with a locomotive simulator that cost the Southern Pacific $1 million, she became a locomotive fireman on the SP's Western division. A year later she was promoted to engineer, first in yard and hostling jobs and then in mainline freight service, with a 5-year wait to qualify for passenger runs, possibly in Amtrak service. Her eventual ambition, she said, is to be a road foreman of engines.

For an account of the best-known heroine in railroad history, *see* SHELLEY, KATE. *See also* BOARDING HOUSES; HARVEY, FREDERICK HENRY; WOMEN, TRAINS NAMED FOR.

Women, Trains Named for More than 1000 American intercity passenger trains had names, most of them indicating rank, importance, speed, geographical places, or famous men. Other names were purely romantic or designated birds, animals, flowers, and even an insect (the Frisco's *Firefly*). But history records only four named for specific women: the *Pocahontas* (Norfolk & Western), the *Ann Rutledge* (Alton; Gulf, Mobile, & Ohio), the *Kate Shelley* (Chicago & North Western; *see* SHELLEY, KATE); and the *Nellie Bly* (Pennsylvania).

Pocahontas, an Indian chief's daughter, reputedly saved Capt. John Smith's life; Ann Rutledge was Abraham Lincoln's first sweetheart; Kate Shelley saved a train; and newspaper reporter Nellie Bly set a globe-girdling record of 72½ days in 1889.

The (Central of) Georgia's *Nancy Hanks* was not named for Lincoln's mother but for a racehorse bearing her name. The very few other trains with feminine names included *Queen of the Valley, Miss Lou* [isiana], *The Sun Queen, The Southern Belle,* the *Phoebe Snow,* and *The Mermaid.*

BIBLIOGRAPHY: Freeman Hubbard, *Great Trains of Time,* New York, Grosset & Dunlap, 1962; *Railroad Magazine,* July 1946.

Woodruff, Theodore T. (d. 1892) Pioneer builder of sleeping cars. Born at Watertown, New York, he worked as a master car builder for the Terre Haute & Alton Railroad in 1856-1857. He invented possibly the first practical sleeping car, patented it on December 2, 1856, nearly 3 years before George M. Pullman's first patent, and built it at Springfield, Massachusetts. It had 12 sections, 6 on each side, with upper and lower berths.

In 1872 he organized the car-building Central Traction Co., capitalized at $100,000, and put 20 of his sleepers in service on Eastern and Midwestern railroads. After developing a prosperous business, he was nearly ruined by bitter litigation with the Pullman Co. and was accidentally killed by an express train on May 2, 1892, at Gloucester, New Jersey. Seven years later his company merged with the car-building organization of Col. William D'Alton Mann, forming the Union Palace Car Co. Eventually the Pullman Co. absorbed all its competitors, including the Union Palace Car Co. *See* PULLMAN, GEORGE MORTIMER.

BIBLIOGRAPHY: Lucius Beebe, *Mansions on Rails,* Howell-North, Berkeley, Calif., 1957; August Mencken, *The Railroad Passenger Car: An Illustrated History of the First Hundred Years,* Johns Hopkins, Baltimore, 1957.

World War I In this war, the nation apparently forgot a hard-won lesson of the Civil War, namely, the need for a unified command in railroad operations with military objectives. Early in the war two glaring errors cut efficiency: failure to unload freight cars promptly and an unorganized system of priorities for government freight.

In April 1917 company executives organized a Railroad War Board to coordinate the rail network. It achieved some pooling of cars and coal supplies but was hampered by an inchoate priority system. Bundles of preference tags distributed to thousands of federal agents were used indiscriminately and often allotted to shippers as personal favors. On Eastern roads some 180,000 loaded cars were piled up with no place to go, while a shortage of 158,000 cars was reported. The Pennsylvania Railroad complained near the end of 1917 that 85 percent of its vital Pittsburgh division was moving under priority orders.

A great new shipyard was being built on South Philadelphia's Hog Island as a wartime measure. Weeks before the site had a track laid or an unloading facility built, thousands of carloads of lumber, structural steel, and other building materials were rushed there by priority orders and stood near the island backed up for miles, unloaded. Newspapers called this situation a national scandal.

Meanwhile, on August 29, 1916, Congress authorized the creation of a U.S. Railroad Administration (USRA) to control and operate the nation's rail lines in wartime. In December 1917 President Woodrow Wilson set up such an administration and appointed his son-in-law, William G. McAdoo, Director General of Railroads.

McAdoo was a construction engineer, financier, and politician. He had built the first Hudson River tubes, had assisted in Wilson's election to the Presidency, and had been Secretary of the Treasury. During the war, besides his rail post, he directed large Liberty Loan issues and served as chairman of the Federal Reserve Board, the Federal Farm Loan Board, and the very important War Finance Corporation. Branding the freight priority system "devoid of all common sense," he ordered that freight-car loadings be held up until shippers authorized them.

Most of the top supervision was done by the capable Assistant Director General of Railroads, Walker D. Hines (1870-1934), a railroad lawyer. Hines succeeded McAdoo as Director General in January 1919 and held that post until the Interstate Commerce Commission handed the roads back to private ownership on March 1, 1920. Later he wrote an excellent book on the USRA.

The takeover (i.e., the technical leasing of railroad facilities to the government) eventually involved 532 properties with 366,000 miles of track having a paper value of $18 billion. It included terminal companies, a major express service, and some coastal and inland waterways and piers, but no city transit system, interurban line, or industrial railroad. Corporate structures were left intact. For the most part, the federal managers operating each unit were company officials. Regional directors, subject to the central administration in Washington, coordinated their efforts. The stockholders and bondholders were paid dividends and interest based on net operating income during the 3 preceding years, 1914-1917.

Centralization and standardization cut down sharply on competitive waste. Engines and rolling stock were standardized, with fewer types and no frills, which limited the scope of individual builders. Unified terminals were organized; the buying of supplies and equipment was centralized, with priority given to items needed most urgently. Repair shops and maintenance were pooled. These steps reduced expenses and the overlapping of duties performed by labor.

Besides being curtailed, passenger service for nonwar personnel was pooled and standardized, with consolidated ticket offices, mileage books good on all roads, universal ticket forms and baggage rules, etc. Advertising of passenger trains was eliminated.

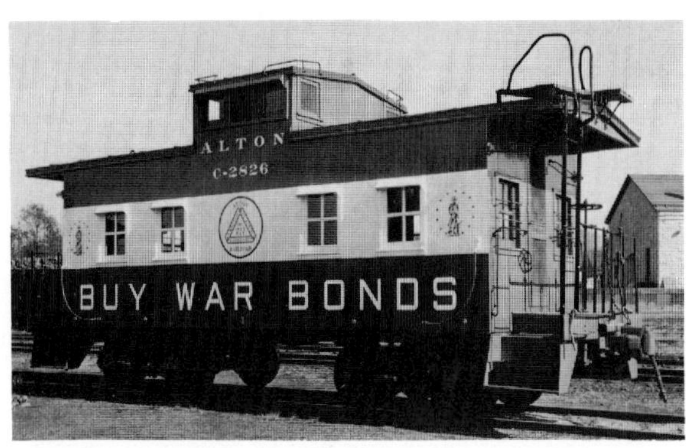

This Alton Railroad caboose helped sell war bonds in a Liberty Loan drive during World War I.

The government spent $4120 million on the roads during the war, largely for new equipment and improvements. It also raised wages and formally recognized the 8-hour day for some 2 million railroad employees.

The railroad executives' support of the USRA was mixed. Some opposed it and even secretly sabotaged its programs, fearing that the experiment might lead eventually to nationalization. But in general the roads worked closely with the USRA. They brought about a more efficient movement of raw materials to factories, of finished goods to the places where they were needed, and of military personnel to training centers, then to embarkation points, and finally back home.

While the railroads were busy on the home front, the rolling stock, operating battalions, etc., that were shipped overseas enabled commanders to carry out offensives and make quick changes in strategy. In the European war zone, American standard-gauge operation, except for camouflaged artillery spurs, stopped just beyond artillery range of the front line. The trains' motive power consisted mostly of American-built coal-burning locos and gasoline rail tractors.

The Americans also used many small European railroad cars without airbrakes in the same trains with their own airbrake-equipped cars. This created a difficult situation. Derailments were frequent. The field roads handled ammunition, all manner of supplies, and hospital trains. Three-car artillery units were shifted from place to place, usually at night, for short stands, in camouflaged positions.

While the USRA succeeded as a wartime effort, it failed financially from the company management viewpoint. It cost the American rail industry an estimated loss of nearly $2 million a day during its 26-month period. This loss was due mostly to higher wages for employees as well as price rises not offset by increased freight rates.

BIBLIOGRAPHY: S. Kip Farrington, *Railroads at War,* Coward-McCann, New York, 1946; Walker D. Hines, *War History of American Railroads,* Yale, New Haven, Conn., 1928; James A. Van Fleet, *Rail Transport and the Winning of Wars,* Association of American Railroads, Washington, 1956.

World War II More than 350,000 American railroad men, approximately 1 in 5, were called into military service in World War II, mostly to go overseas. Their skill, courage, patriotism, and teamwork did much to ensure the final victory, but more than 10,000 of them never came back alive.

Germany's conquest of much of Europe, with Great Britain tottering, stepped up America's defense policy in 1940 and set in motion the building of tens of thousands of locomotives, both steam and diesel, and considerably more rolling stock. The new equipment was needed first to take countless tons of munitions, food, clothing, and other goods to ports for shipment overseas, particularly to England.

After the United States declared war, the rail equipment was needed more urgently to move enlisted men and draftees to training camps, to Army, Navy, Marine, and Coast Guard posts, and to points of embarkation and to ensure a continuous flow of military and other supplies for America and its allies. Not only that, but seemingly endless numbers of locomotives and rolling stock, tons of rails, and other transportation ingredients were highballed to docks and wharves for loading onto merchant ships.

Railroad managements had to train many new workers, including women, to fill the jobs of employees siphoned into combat. Highway vehicles played a relatively minor role on America's home front during World War II as compared with the railroads, which carried 90 percent of all freight and 97 percent of the military personnel involved in the war effort.

The railroad companies discarded their time-tested advertising policies for the duration. They wrote a new chapter in transportation history by discouraging public rail travel, especially during the peak periods of weekends, Christmas, Thanksgiving Day, and the summer vacation season, with posters, magazine and newspaper ads, radio announcements, window and car cards, leaflets, blotters, etc.

Not only had transportation become limited by military needs, but the sharp rationing of highway travel threw onto the railroads more passengers than they could carry. In peacetime this would have been the realization of a traffic official's fondest dreams. With a war on, no company could buy a locomotive or a club car whenever it needed one, and trains weren't big enough to hold all the people who wanted to ride.

Among the problems faced by civilians in wartime were frequently late trains, busy telephone wires in stations, overcrowded cars, meals in the diner (if available) below standard, and observation cars and roomettes no longer available, having been converted for troop movements. The ad copywriters and artists blamed such conditions on Adolf Hitler and Emperor Hirohito so that people would damn the warlords instead of the railroads. They also pointed out what the carriers were doing to bring about victory. "The Canadian National," said a CN advertisement, "is Canada's greatest single war industry."

Brigadier General Carl R. Gray, general manager of the U.S. Military Railway Service (MRS) during the war, was the operating vice president of the Omaha Railway system in 1941 when Gen. John L. Kingman persuaded him to revitalize the Service. He did so, redesigning it almost identically along the lines of a large privately owned rail system.

Within 3 weeks after the bombing of Pearl Harbor, members of the 502d Paratroop Battalion at Fort Benning, Georgia, were being taught how to operate a locomotive for use in the event that they should seize enemy motive power. The first railway operating battalion activated for World War II, the 711th, was sent to Fort Belvoir, Virginia, for basic training. Shipped down to the cypress swamps of Louisiana, it built a 50-mile military railroad between Camps Claiborne and Polk.

Gray organized the Transportation Corps by combining the former railway functions of the Corps of Engineers and the Quartermaster Corps, to which he added highway and even some water transport. The Engineering Headquarters, Railway, corresponded to the office of an operating vice president of a privately owned rail system. Gray made grand division headquarters, of which there were 10, the equivalent of a general superintendent's offices.

Each of the 42 MRS operating battalions compared in structure with a division superintendent's organization, and there were six shop battalions to maintain motive power and rolling stock. Heading the MRS's Transportation, Engineering, Equipment, and Stores Departments were assistant general managers. The colonels in charge of division headquarters were entrusted with the duties of general superintendents.

Ten railway grand divisions supervised the battalions. Lieutenant colonels, as superintendents, commanded the operating and shop battalions. The MRS personnel from "brass collars" down to privates were drawn almost entirely from privately owned railroads. Each railway operating division was divided into four units. A Company, which had two track platoons and one bridge platoon, was responsible for building and maintaining the right-of-way. B Company's duty was to keep the rolling equipment operable. This unit had two platoons, each being a complete roundhouse and engine terminal, plus a third platoon for shop repairs of motive power. The railway operating battalion's largest company, C, kept the train crews supplied with whatever they needed to operate the trains.

Even more important was the headquarters service company, which provided the railway troops with telegraphers, dispatchers, and linemen as well as with food, housing, and other essentials. Besides all these units, the MRS was supported by shop battalions and could call on the Army Corps of Engineers whenever a bridge, section of railroad, etc., had to be built. These men had the necessary technical training, experience, and equipment to handle such jobs. Before the war ended, there were 38 active railway operating battalions, some of them having as many as 24 officers and 800 enlisted men.

Most of the United States war effort was eventually moved by rail from mines, oil fields, farms, and factories to embarkation ports for shipment to Europe, Africa, and other foreign lands. Soviet Russia alone received over 1900 steam and 50 diesel locomotives plus thousands of tons of other equipment. Among the items sent to the U.S.S.R. were a dozen mobile steam-power plants to furnish electricity to recaptured cities. American Car and Foundry Co. at Berwick, Pennsylvania, turned over the first of them to the Soviet government in 1944.

The Seabees effectively handled such railroading as there was on the Pacific front in World War II. In the Philippines, Corregidor, with a short military railroad of its own, had a heroic role. The U.S. Navy did not take over Hawaii's Oahu Railway until 5 years after the war ended, but armed forces assigned to Schofield Barracks were constantly on the alert in guarding the island. During the war, the Japanese occupied Guam and operated a small tramway on that island. Also during the war, uniformed railroaders of the MRS kept traffic rolling on the White Pass & Yukon Route in Alaska and Canada.

BIBLIOGRAPHY: Carl H. Gray, *Railways in Eighteen Countries,* Scribner, New York, 1955; James A. Van Fleet, *Rail Transport and the Winning of Wars,* Association of American Railroads, Washington, 1956; Chester Wardlow, *U.S. Army in World War II,* U.S. Army, Office of the Chief of Military History, 1951; Ron Ziel, *Steel Rails to Victory,* Hawthorn, New York, 1970.

World's Slowest Train Term applied to the mixed train of the 300-mile Alberta & Great Waterways (AG&W) before that railway joined the Canadian National system. It ran once a week at an average speed of about 4 miles an hour between Edmonton, Alberta, and Fort McMurray in the far north. The trip usually took from 3 days to 1 week, depending upon the extent of the repairs the little engine needed in the makeshift roundhouse at Lac-la-Biche, a French-Indian settlement midway on the journey, where the train stayed overnight.

The slow pace allowed plenty of time for crew and passengers alike to play solitaire, poker, or checkers and to sleep. Now and then they would stop to let the passengers pick berries or build little fires along the right-of-way to steep their tea or guzzle beer at each tiny station. Sometimes a lone, shabby trapper or gold prospector halted the train to ask hopefully if it had a letter for him. The crew carried a large stock of candy and tobacco, not only for themselves and the bored passengers but also to sell to Indians met along the way.

The A&GW was the gateway to the northland via the Athabasca and Slave Rivers. It hauled gold prospectors, traders, and pioneers heading for the Northwest Territories.

WP *See* WESTERN PACIFIC RAILROAD.

WP&Y *See* WHITE PASS AND YUKON ROUTE.

"Wreck of the Old 97, The" Like most rail songs, this one is based on tragedy. Number 97 was a real Southern Railway train carrying fast mail and express between Washington, D.C., and Atlanta, Georgia. Her career began late in 1902, only about a year before the wreck, and ended early in 1907, when Congress refused to renew funds for this special service. The word *Old* signifies endearment, not age. Her average speed, 37½ miles per hour, was good, considering the single trackage, mediocre roadbed, sharp curves, rather steep grades, and wooden trestles. Keeping her on schedule was almost a religion with the crews. The ballad states, "This is not 38 but it's Old 97. . . ."

Crews were changed at each division point on the long run. The trip was like a relay foot race: if one runner makes a poor showing, his teammates try to offset it. On the fatal September 27, 1903, delays en route had caused the Southern's pet train, southbound, to reach Monroe, Virginia, 165 miles south of Washington, an hour behind schedule. Engineer Joseph A. Broady, tall and slim, took it over with 10-wheeled engine No. 1102 at Monroe. He was nicknamed Steve for the much-publicized Steve Brodie, who had won a bet a few years before by a spectacular dive off Brooklyn Bridge into the East River.

According to the ditty, Steve was told to "get 'er in Spencer on time." The 166-mile run from Monroe to Spencer, North Carolina, normally averaged 4¼ hours. Even if Old 97 had not been wrecked, operating conditions being what they were, Joe could not have cut the time by as much as an hour.

But with two firemen on the job, one passing coal from the tender and the other scooping it into the firebox, he tried to get the train back on schedule. Danger lurked on the outskirts of Danville, Virginia, where the wooden Stillhouse Trestle on White Oak Mountain carried the track over Cherrystone Creek, 75 feet below. Joe had to round a curve and descend a grade to reach Danville.

At 3 p.m. he blasted his whistle and is said to have taken the curve at full speed. The song says, "He was going downhill at ninety miles an hour," likely an exaggeration. At any rate, the 10-wheeler jumped the rails, hurtled into the gully, and buried her nose in a marshy cow pasture, pulling down all of the train's five cars and tearing off the corner of a cotton mill in the mad plunge.

Engineer Broady, the song says, "was found in the wreck with his hand on the throttle/And a-scalded to death with the steam." The death list also included both firemen, the conductor, the flagman, five postal clerks, possibly the 12-year-old son of one of them, who may have gone along for the ride, and a Southeastern Express Co. employee. Seven other postal clerks were injured. The express messenger escaped without a scratch. Flames from the firebox set the broken wooden cars afire.

Part of the mail was saved. Later, engine 1102 was lifted out of the mire, rebuilt, and gave additional service until mid-1932. Meanwhile, among the hillbillies who gathered beside the wreckage to gape or to help in the rescue work was David Graves George, who is said to have been a telegraph operator at the time of the wreck. George testified later in court that he had arrived on the scene while canaries that had escaped from a crate in the express car were still warbling, did all he could to help, and was inspired to write the ballad "The Wreck of the Old 97," which is sung to the tune of "The Ship That Never Returned."

Gradually that song spread over the country, bidding fair to rival "Casey Jones" in popularity. Victor Talking Machine Co. began recording it in 1924, having obtained the words and music from Prof. R. W. Gordon of Harvard University, who had been collecting American folk songs. Gordon said he had bought the rights to it from George W. Noah and Fred Lewy, both of whom claimed to have written the ballad. Victor paid royalties to those two men and to Henry Whitter, whose by-line appeared on a piece of sheet music entitled "The Wreck of the Southern Old 97."

David George took the case to court. In 1933 a judge ruled that he was the original author of the disputed ballad, granted an injunction against Victor, and ordered the company to pay him $65,295 in royalties on the 5 million records of that song which it had issued. A federal circuit court of appeals reversed that judgment. The case then went to the U.S. Supreme Court, which in 1934 reversed the appellate court. But litigation arose over the accounting. In 1939 the case went again to the nation's highest tribunal. This time the Court firmly declined to review it.

BIBLIOGRAPHY: Freeman Hubbard, *Railroad Avenue,* McGraw-Hill, New York, 1945; Robert B. Shaw, *A History of Railroad Accidents, Safety Precautions, and Operating Practices,* Northern Press, Potsdam, N.Y., 1978.

Wreckdozer Modern efficient machine that combines the characteristics of a bulldozer and a wrecking crane (big hook). It can push, pull, and lift almost anything. It can be moved aboard a flatcar at speeds up to 70 miles per hour to the scene of a derailment or other accident. The crane, because of its ungainly weight distribution, can be moved at only 30 miles per hour and, unlike the wreckdozer, cannot move ahead when rails are missing.

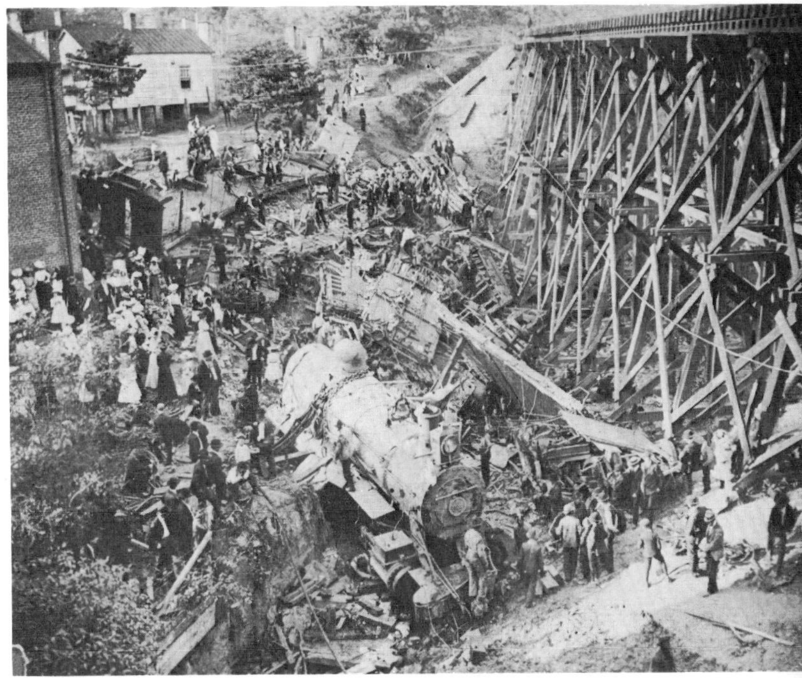

The Southern Railway fast mail train No. 97 plunged off a trestle near Danville, Virginia, in 1903. This catastrophe inspired the ballad, "The Wreck of the Old 97."

Wrecks Accounts of train wrecks are found, for the most part, under place names. Examples are ASHTABULA WRECK; CHATSWORTH WRECK; EDEN WRECK; HALIFAX EXPLOSION; MEADOW BROOK DISASTER; NASHVILLE WRECK; PROSPECT WRECK; ST. THOMAS WRECK; WELLINGTON AVALANCHE. Exceptions include AMBLER, PENNSYLVANIA; FOUR-TRAIN WRECK; WAGNER, WEBSTER.

"Wrong Side of the Railroad Track, The" Once-common expression that dates back to the days when street-level tracks bisected cities and towns in the industrial Northeast. Mill and factory workers and railroad shopmen usually lived near their places of employment on one side of town while their more affluent neighbors had homes, often on higher ground, on the other side. The distinction between these groups was a recognized part of community life, lines being drawn even in schools and churches. In Boston, for instance, studies showed that many adults and children living in the South Bend House neighborhood almost never crossed the tracks and knew nothing about the Back Bay section. The term fell into disuse after New Deal measures of the 1930s and later desegregation.

Wyes *See* TURNTABLES AND WYES.

Y, Z

Yards, Railroad The standard *Book of Rules* defines *yard* as "a system of tracks within defined limits, provided for the making up of trains, storing of cars, and other purposes, over which movements not authorized by timetable or train order may be made subject to prescribed signals and rules, or special instructions." Between yard-limit signs, often miles apart, you find many tracks in the "other purposes" category, such as industry tracks, team tracks, transfer tracks for interchanging cars with connecting lines, repair (rip) tracks, and tracks on which motive power moves to and from trains.

For nearly a century, yards were bottlenecks in freight traffic. Then the electronic age, by creating the modern, automated classified yard, expedited the movement of loaded and empty cars enormously. Speeding up freight service, it brought greater revenue to shippers and consignees as well as to the railroads themselves.

A vast area is devoted to receiving yards, departure yards, and storage yards for cars to be loaded or unloaded. The old yards had tracks to ice docks for icing perishable shipments, but modern *reefers* are self-refrigerating. The classification yard's main purpose is to assemble freight cars from various sources into *blocks* of cars (this is not to be confused with the block signal system on mainline tracks) and head them toward their individual destinations by combining them into trains for line haul. This is done in one of two principal ways: flat and gravity, the former being in a fairly level area and the latter including a hump, or artificially built knoll, down which the cars roll. Most large railroads use both methods.

Many years ago, switchmen rode the cars down the hump and manually braked them to a stop. (Today, the hump rider is as rare as a buffalo nickel.) Freight cars for delivery to industries must be lined up so as to avoid unnecessary switching later on in congested areas: i.e., the head car is set out on the first industry track, and so on. Furthermore, trains must be *blocked* (lined up for station order). Most freight originates as LCL (less-than-carload lots). A modern trend is toward solid unit trains for shipment over long distances, which simplifies railroad operation, but until recent years such trains were rare. *See* UNIT TRAINS.

Very few yards today are truly flat. Nearly all of them were in the early days of railroading. In flat yards, switch engines shunt the cars into various tracks, sometimes over slight grades. The success or failure of old-style flat-yard switching depended upon the switchmen's judgment in passing signals to engineers and the latter's interpretation of them. *See* SIGNALS, HAND.

Setouts and pickups are made by freight crews handling trains for intermediate points. Sometimes the cars become so scrambled that they must be reblocked at a yard. The hump technique was greatly improved by the development of retarders to control the speed of cars entering the classification tracks. Retarders are comparable to the *snubbers* used by circuses to ease their gaily painted wagons, chariots, and cages on wheels down a ramp from flatcars to the ground in the unloading of old-time circus trains. Retarders cut labor costs by eliminating hump riders, but hand-operated retarders did relatively little to reduce collision damage.

The Union Pacific and the Reeves Instrument Corp., after a year's research and experiment, jointly developed the *electronic yardmaster,* the first full train application of automatic switching and car-retarding control ever used in any freight classification yard. It was the outgrowth of wartime electronic expertise used by the U.S. Army in guided missiles.

Ordinarily, when long strings of freight cars were dispersed, sorted, and reassembled into trains, the cars were uncoupled one by one, nudged over the hump, and allowed to coast freely down the fan-shaped spreading tracks of the classification yard. The cars' speed depended upon the steepness of the incline and the amount of pressure that the retarder operator decided to apply to them in the retarders to set the cars on the spots where they belonged. If the operator guessed wrong, the cars might stop short of their designated spots or even crash into trains already made up, thus damaging both cars and contents badly. A large part of the many millions of dollars which railroads pay in freight loss and damage has resulted from such errors in judgment.

The electronic yardmaster eliminates such errors. With lightning speed and complete accuracy it calculates the speed of the moving cars and applies the retarder brakes, gently bringing each car to a stop at the right place. This system takes control as soon as the cars are pushed over the hump. As they roll down the slope toward the retarder, their individual speeds are fed to an electronic brain. At the same time, another electronic device, similar to those used on range-finder equipment in World War II, computes the distance the car has to travel in order to couple with other cars standing on the classification tracks, a distance ranging from a few hundred feet to two-thirds of a mile.

Retarders beside the rails in a hump yard. Cylinders actuate the inner and outer brake shoes to exert pressure on both sides of wheels and so reduce the speed of cars. [Atlas Copco, Inc.]

When a car first enters the series of electropneumatic car retarders, a radar speed meter, similar to meters used in many communities to apprehend automobile speed-limit violators, measures its velocity and decides at what speed the car must be released to reach its coupling point.

Using these data, the electronic brain figures the exact braking pressure needed to let the car roll free and couple at no more than 3 miles an hour. The retarder control automatically takes care of this as soon as it gets word from the brain. The brain can retain routing instructions for 100 cars at the same time.

The device shortens its range as the retarder track fills up with coupled cars and releases cars accordingly to compensate for the shortened distance. All that the control operator has to do now is select the track for which the cars are destined. This the operator does by pushing the proper button before the freight train is pushed over the hump.

Each classification yard has a receiving, or arrival, yard with enough tracks to accommodate trains coming in from various lines over several hours. Upon the arrival of a train at the yard, power units and the caboose are uncoupled. Then the humping engine, often a six-axle unit with a slug attached, couples up to the rear of the incoming cars on one track.

An inspection pit is part of each major yard. Here, each car's running gear can be examined for possible defects and can be given any necessary in-train or rip-track attention. In some cases car inspection is done from small utility vehicles operated on specially built runways. Before a car is shoved over the hump, its air must be bled from its brake cylinders so that it will roll freely. A *pin puller* stands at the right side of the hump with a switch list showing where the cars are to be uncoupled.

For the most part, American yards built in the days of steam power and relatively short trains changed little prior to the adoption of automation. Cities growing up around them had kept the railroads from expanding their antiquated yard facilities. Also, the fast-rising tide of highway motor vehicles had to be routed over, around, or above them.

Then the push-button idea took hold and spread rapidly. Every railroad journalist is familiar with the frequency of press releases telling about new automated yards with more advanced technology that either are on the drawing boards or are actually being built or opened in outlying areas that are not very densely populated. The future of push-button yards holds many undreamed-of devices for moving freight cars more quickly and efficiently and at relatively less cost. Even now, yards built to handle up to 4000 cars a day are not unusual.

BIBLIOGRAPHY: John H. Armstrong, *The Railroad—What It Is, What It Does,* Simmons-Boardman, New York, 1978; Robert S. Henry, *This Fascinating Railroad Business,* 3d ed., rev., Bobbs-Merrill, Indianapolis, 1946.

YMCAs, Railroad At their peak, nearly 180 such establishments—homes away from home for train and engine crews laying over at remote places between runs—were located on American railroads. Henry W. Stager, a Lake Shore line dispatcher who later became a division superintendent, was largely instrumental in starting this movement. He had seen the body of a man killed in the performance of duty carried through a Cleveland station and heard a curious bystander ask, "Who is it?" and the callous reply, "Only a railroad man."

In the middle and late 1800s, particularly before the unions had been founded or grown strong, life on the rails was cheap. Relatively little thought was given to the welfare of the men who kept the wheels rolling. After long and hard hours on the high iron, often 12 hours of continuous work, exhausted and famished crews reached isolated division points where the grub served in beaneries was unfit to eat and where the beds, infested with vermin, were seldom empty long enough for the linen to be changed.

There were too many gin mills with back-room pool tables and dives. Vice was prevalent. Many of the frequent train wrecks could be laid directly to excessive periods of duty and unhealthy "rest" periods when booze, gambling, wenching, and brawling were favorite pastimes. Thousands of railroaders were killed or maimed.

One day the evangelist George Myers held religious services in the same depot where Stager had witnessed the aforementioned incident. Stager attended the meeting, recalled the scene, and took advantage of the opportunity to launch a movement to provide decent meals and lodgings for railroad men far from home. Thus, in Cleveland, the first Railroad Y was organized on April 14, 1872, in the days of the Vanderbilts and Goulds and before the invention of the automatic coupler.

Possibly the most colorful of all Railroad Y's grew out of the old Babahatchie Inn, a sprawling, three-story frame building at Oakdale, Tennessee, 84 miles north of Chattanooga. If faced the Southern (then Cincinnati Southern, or CS) Railway tracks, with the turbulent Emory River at its back. Each winter the river froze over. The CS erected it in 1880 to feed and lodge weary railroaders and as an eating place for passengers. Few old Western frontier towns could boast of more hell raising than Oakdale, walled in by the Cumberland Mountains.

In 1902 trainmaster Morgan Crane quit the railway to run Babahatchie Inn under private management, charging 25 cents each for meals and a dime for beds that were seldom made up. By 1906 conditions had gotten so far out of hand at Babahatchie and Oakdale that the railroad management persuaded the national YMCA to run the inn and tendered it free use of the property. Thereupon the old building was cleaned and renovated from cellar to garret. New equipment replaced shabby furniture, utensils, and other supplies.

Like the other Railroad Y's, the one at Oakdale had a wholesome effect on the well-being of railroaders and on the industry; but all of them were gradually phased out as living conditions in general improved. The Santa Fe's equivalent of Railroad Y's was its Fred Harvey system of hotels and restaurants, mostly in the Southwest, for railroaders and the public alike. Several carriers, under union pressure, built crew quarters for layovers between runs. The last Railroad Y was closed in about 1970. *See* BOARDING HOUSES; HARVEY, FREDERICK HENRY.

BIBLIOGRAPHY: John F. Moore, *The Story of the Railroad "Y,"* Association Press, New York, 1930.

Zulu Cars Freight cars in which farmers' families migrating westward rode with their household goods and farm implements—and often livestock as well. Edward Mahoney, who was a Santa Fe rate clerk in Denver in the 1920s, recalled seeing a steady stream of emigrants go by rail to California, often referred to as the Promised Land. He said:

> Our regular tariff rate on household goods covered used furniture. We also had a special cut rate on "emigrant movables" to encourage farm treks, and we separated the two categories by specifying that the latter must include such items as a plow. A shrewd moving company in Denver bought an old plow, which they often shipped by rail with customers' household goods—afterward bring it back to Denver again and again—to take advantage of the lower rate. That same plow took many a ride to and from California.

For the origin of this term and other details see LINGO OF THE RAILS—*Zulu Cars.*

Index

A-No. 1 (hobo), 156
A-1, Lima (locomotive), 182
AAR-100 (lab-on-wheels), 179
Abbott, R. H., 223
Active (locomotive), 217
Adams, Charles Francis, 118, 132
Adams, Frederick U., 309
Air conditioning, 1, 312, 334
Akron, Canton and Youngstown Railroad (AC&Y), 238
Alabama Great Southern Railway (AGS), 299
Alaska Railroad (AAR), 1–2, 261
Alco Products, Inc. (*see* American Locomotive Co.)
Algoma (trainferry), 137
Algoma Central Railway (AC), 155
Algoma Eastern Railway (AE), 2
Allegheny Portage Railway (AP), 2–3
Allen, Horatio, 200, 216, 299
Allen, William F., 202
Alton Railroad (*see* Chicago & Alton Railroad)
Altoona shops, Pennsylvania Railroad, 253
Ambler, Mary Benjamin, 3
Ambler (Pa.) wreck, 3
America (silver engine), 248, 277
American Car and Foundry Co. (ACF), 177, 360
American Electric Headlight Co., 145
American Express (train), 255
American Federation of Labor (AFL), 245, 338
American Flyer (toy trains), 224
American Freedom Train (AFT), 100, 121–122, 199
American Locomotive Co. (Alco), 3–5, 18, 26, 38, 121, 122, 177, 182, 199, 203, 216, 248
American Railway Union (ARU), 89, 90, 315, 337
American Short Line Railroad Association (ASLRA), 5
American Train Dispatchers Association (ATDA), 338
American Union Telegraph Co. (AUT), 115
Ames, Oakes, 5, 334–335
Ames, Oliver, 5, 128, 334–335
Ames Monument plot, 5–6
Ampere (locomotive), 310
Amtrak (National Railroad Passenger Corp; NRPC), 6–7
Anderson, Gertie, 145
Andover (locomotive), 33
Andover & Haverhill Railroad (formerly Andover & Wilmington Railroad), 33
Andrews, James J., railroad raid attempted by, 7–9, 101, 208
Androscoggin & Kennebec Railroad (A&K), 214
Angola (N.Y.), wreck, 9–10
Angus shops, Canadian Pacific Railway, 56, 307
Animals, wild, 2, 10–11, 24–25, 113–114, 158, 356
Animas Forks (parlor car), 219
Ann Arbor No. 1 (trainferry), 137
Ann Arbor Railroad (AA), 137
Antelope (locomotive), 150
Arcara, Roger, 312, 317
Arcata & Mad River Railroad (A&MR), 11
Ariel (locomotive), 205
Armored cars, 11–12, 183, 209, 249
Arms, Harrison, 267
Armstrong, George R., 213, 214
"Armstrong" turntables, 330, 331
Aroostook Valley Railroad (AV), 167
Articulated locomotives (*see* Mallet)
Ashley, James R., 137
Ashpan Act, 279
Ashtabula (trainferry), 138
Ashtabula (Ohio) wreck, 12
Association of American Railroads (AAR), 12–13, 19, 52, 58, 78, 93, 123, 124, 179, 223, 224, 259, 263, 268, 270, 277, 320, 325, 326, 329, 345
Association of Colored Railway Trainmen and Locomotive Firemen (ACRT&LF), 233
Atchison, Topeka and Santa Fe Railway (*see* Santa Fe Railway)
Atlanta & St. Andrews Bay Railway (Bay Line), 13
Atlanta & West Point Railway (West Point Route), 72, 128, 226
Atlantic (locomotive), 23
Atlantic, Missouri & Ohio Railway (AM&O), 239
Atlantic & Great Western Railroad (A&GW), 112, 227, 237
Atlantic & Gulf Railroad, 224
Atlantic Coast Line (ACL), 153, 226, 285
Atlantic Highlands, Red Bank & Long Branch Electric Railway (AHRD&LBE), 168
Auburn & Syracuse Railway, 47, 48
Augusta (locomotive), 259
AuRoRa (dome train), 2, 231, 232
Aurora Branch Railroad (AB), 65
Auto-Train Corp., 13
Automatic block signals, 288–289
Automatic fare collection, 13
Automatic Firedoor Act, 280
Automatic train control (ATC), 13–14
Automatic train-recording system (ATRS), 14–15
Automobile-train crash, first, 15
Avalanches:
  in Alaska, 2
  in Cascade Tunnel in Washington, 60
  in Wellington, Washington, 349–350
Averell, William J., 142

Babahatchie Inn in Oakdale, Tennessee, 365
Bacon & Derious Circus, 68
Bailey, James A., 69
Baldwin, Matthias William, 17–19
Baldwin-Fairbanks-Morse, 95, 96
Baldwin-Lima-Hamilton Corp., 18, 19
Baldwin Locomotive Works, 12, 17–19, 26, 27, 68, 93–96, 109, 110, 216, 217, 257, 271, 306, 307
Ball, Edward, 121
Ball, Webb C., 19
Ball Railway Time Service, 19
Ballads, 19–21, 27, 49, 90, 156, 174, 177, 347–348
  "The Big Rock Candy Mountain," 20, 156, 211–212
  "Casey Jones" (Saunders), 61–62
  "The Dying Hobo," 156
  "The Grave of a Section Hand" (Barrett), 220
  "The Wreck of the Old 97," 360–361
Ballast, 21
Balloon cars, 21
Baltimore & Ohio Railroad (B&O), 1, 2, 4, 21–24, 31, 50, 82, 84, 93, 98, 99, 117–118, 143, 152, 177, 196, 216–218, 228, 257, 302, 303

Baltimore & Ohio Union Terminal Railroad (B&OUT), 64
Bangor & Aroostook Railroad (BAR), 24
Bangor & Old Town Railroad (B&OT), 214
Bangor & Piscataquis Canal & Railroad, 214
Bangs, George S., 214
Barnard, Bill, 229, 230
Barnes, J. L., 264
Barnsville (Ga.) wreck, 72, 73
Barnum, Phineas Taylor, 68, 69
Barnum & Bailey circus, 69
Barrett, Lawrence, 123
Barriger, John W., III, 19, 225, 320
Barry, Ed, 149, 150
Bartholomew, Johnny, 146
Bass, Sam, 24
Bay Line (Atlanta & St. Andrews Bay Railway), 13
Beach, Alfred E., 309, 316
Beach, Charles L., 246
Beatty, Clyde, 69
Beauregard, Gen. Pierre G. T., 8, 163
Beaver control, 24–25
Beaver Meadow Railroad, 50
Beck, Samuel, 169
Bedford & Billerica Railroad, 215
Bedwell, Harry, 25, 117
Beebe, Lucius, 25, 30, 340
Beggs, Eugene, 25–26
Belfast & Moosehead Lake Railroad (B&ML), 26
Bells:
  locomotive, 26–28, 280
  station, 303–304
Belmont, August, 142, 221
Beloeil wreck (near Montreal), 275–276
Bergoff, Pearl L. (strikebreaking czar), 314
Bessemer & Lake Erie Railroad (BLE), 28–29
Best Friend of Charleston (locomotive), 152, 299, 306
Bible racks and Bibles, 29
Bicycle Railway, 29–30
Bidding in on a run, 30
Big Boys (locomotives), 4, 216, 217, 336
Big Four (rail lingo), 186
"Big Rock Candy Mountain, The" (ballad), 20, 156, 211–212
Big Shop (*see* American Locomotive Co.)
Birmingham & Northwestern Railroad (B&NW), 139
Birmingham Southern Railroad (BS), 169
Birney, Charles O., 311
Black Diamond (train), 30
Black Friday, 119, 132
Black Hills Central Railroad, 271
Blacks (*see* Negroes)
Blackstone, Timothy V., 139
Blair, John I., 324
Bliss, Charles P., 12
Block signals, 14, 288, 289
Blue Goose (locomotive), 65
Boarding houses, 30–31, 50, 144, 280, 304, 365
Boiler Inspection Act, 280
Boilers, locomotive, 31
Book of Rules, 32
Boomers, 25, 32–33, 39, 68, 113, 116, 117, 155, 185, 186, 211, 212
Boston, Revere Beach & Lynn Railroad, 14, 232
Boston & Albany Railroad (B&A), 152, 269, 274
Boston & Maine Railroad (B&M), 33, 145, 152, 199, 215, 274, 275, 322
Boston & Portland Railroad, 33
Boston & Providence Railroad, 50, 200, 218
Boston & Thompson Railroad, 312, 313
Boynton, Eben H., 29, 322
Brace, Charles Lorenz, 246
Bradley, Col. William H., 128
Brady, James (Diamond Jim), 40
Brady, Jane, 30
Brady, Matthew B., 27
Brady, William A., 238
Brake-test record, 33
Brakes, 14, 33, 42, 237, 279, 353
Breese, Knowland & Co., 237
Bridges, 11, 24, 33–36, 58, 67, 74, 112, 113, 120, 130–131, 147, 151, 167, 207
  battles and raids on, 7, 9, 21, 23, 71–72, 102
  fires and wrecks on, 12, 107–108, 146, 149–150, 235, 262, 275–276, 361
  flood signal devices for, 119
  floods and, 175–176, 286
  Hell Gate Bridge in New York, 35, 253
  Lucin Cutoff in Idaho, 143, 208
  Pecos River Bridge in Texas, 36, 249, 298, 318
  Portage Bridge in New York, 34, 259
Bridgton & Harrison Railway, 215
Brill Magazine, 254
British Columbia Railway (BC Rail; Pacific Great Eastern), 36–37
Broad Street Station in Philadelphia, 37, 109, 252
Broadway Limited (train), 109, 203, 251, 254, 301
Broady, Joseph A. (Steve), 361
Brooklyn Rapid Transit Co., 329
Brooks, C. E., 54
Brooks, Horatio G., 37–38
Brooks Locomotive Works, 3, 37–38
Brotherhood of Locomotive Engineers (BLE), 38–39
Brotherhood of Locomotive Firemen and Enginemen (BLF&E), 39, 51, 89, 230
Brotherhood of Railroad Trainmen (BRT), 39–40
Brotherhood of Sleeping Car Porters and Redcaps (BSCP&R), 40–42
  (*See also* Randolph, A. Philip)
Brown, Ashbel S., 275
Brown, K. A., 270
Brunterm Ltd., 54
Bryan, William Jennings, 52
Bryant, Gridley, 330
Buchanan, James, 128, 184
Buchanan, William, 236
Buda Company (section cars), 59
Budd, Edward G., 42
Budd Company, 42–43
Buffalo, Corry & Pittsburgh Railroad, 262
Buffalo Bayou, Brazos & Colorado Railroad, 296
Buffalo Bill (Col. William Frederick Cody), 113, 114, 334
Buffalo-hunting excursions, 113–114
Bunker Hill Monument tramway, 58, 59, 150, 330, 331
Burleigh, Albert, 24
Burlington Northern Inc. (BN), 43–44, 158, 166, 219
Burlington Route (*see* Chicago, Burlington & Quincy Railroad)
Burlington *Zephyr* (train), 309
  (*See also* Zephyr trains)
Burney, Bill, 275
Burnside, Maj. Gen. Ambrose E., 282
Burroughs, John, 45
Buses operated by railroads, 24, 52, 140, 215
Bush, Lincoln, 327
Butte, Anaconda & Pacific Railway, 111
Buttons, uniform, 45, 253

Cab Curtain Act, 280
Cab-in-fronters (locomotive type), 51, 307
Cable cars, 157, 307, 310, 312
Cabooses, 28, 47–50, 262
Cabs, locomotive, 13, 14, 28, 38, 50–51, 96, 97, 279, 280, 306, 307
Cachet collecting, 51
Cajon Pass in California, 88, 283
Calais Street Railway, 167, 214
Caledon (double-ended locomotive), 200
California & Oregon Railroad, 297
California State Narrow-Gauge Railroad Museum, 228
California Zephyr (train), 352
Calthrop, Rev. Samuel, 309
Camden & Amboy Railroad, 26, 152, 213, 253, 306, 307, 321, 323, 342
Camelbacks (double-cabbed locomotives), 50, 91, 281, 307, 359
Camels (locomotive type), 50, 307, 357
Campaign trains, 51–52
Campbell, John, 91
Canada:
  earliest railways in, 151, 154
  first diesel (Canadian National 9000), 98
  Urban Transportation Development Corp., 312
Canada Southern Railway, 166, 343
Canadian, The (train), 56
Canadian Locomotive Co., 97, 98, 306
Canadian National Railways (CN), 52–56, 97, 135, 138, 154, 158, 164, 166, 199, 226
Canadian Northern Railway, 154
Canadian Pacific Railway (CP Rail), 2, 28, 29, 49, 54–56, 97, 124, 125, 138, 146, 147, 154, 155, 166, 199, 215, 216, 343, 345

Canadian Pacific Railway (CP Rail)(*Cont.*):
largest bridge in 1885, 35
Canadian Railroad Historical Society (CRHS), 269
Canadian railways, history of, 154–155 (*see also specific railway*)
Cannon Ball (Long Island Rail Road train), 56–57
Cannonball (Illinois Central train), 61
Cañon City & San Juan Railroad (CC&SJ), 57, 58
Canyon War, 57–58, 283
Car and Locomotive Cyclopedia, 254
Car identification labels, 58
Carlisle & Finch train models, 224
Carnegie, Andrew, 131, 169, 258
Carroll, Charles, 21
Carrollton Viaduct at Gwynn's Falls, Baltimore, Maryland, 34
Cars (*see specific car*)
Carson & Colorado Railroad (C&C), 59–60
Carter, Jimmy, 42, 75, 93, 271
Cascade Tunnel in Washington State, 60, 328, 349, 350
Cascadin, Charles, 10
Casement, Daniel T., 129
Casement, Jack, 129
Casey Jones (John Luther Jones), 25, 30, 60–62, 164, 233, 354
"Casey Jones" (Saunders), 61–62
Cass Scenic Railroad, 348
Cassatt, Alexander Johnston, 130, 131, 173, 250, 251
Cassin, Dennis, 62
Cat-cracked fuel, 62
Catawissa Railroad, 243
Catskill Mountain Railway, 246
Centennial DD-40X (diesel locomotive), 234
Centennial Narrow-Gauge Railway, 62
Central American railways, 155
Central Electric Railfans Association (CERA), 269
Central Pacific Railroad (*see* Southern Pacific Lines)
Central Rail Road & Banking Co. of Georgia, 54
Central Railroad of New Jersey (Jersey Central; CNJ), 4, 78, 94, 181, 202, 281
Central Railway of Georgia, 157, 174, 231, 299, 300, 357
Central Vermont Railway, 166
Centralized traffic control (CTC), 62–63
Chains on cabooses, 49
Challenger (train), 298
Chambers, Bill, 136
Champlain & St. Lawrence Railway, 84, 181, 324
Chandler, W. A., 273
Chapel cars, 63
Chapman, John K., 63
Chatsworth (Ill.) wreck, 63–64
Cherokee Strip, 64, 221
Chesapeake and Ohio Railway (C&O; Chessie System), 52, 64–65, 82, 137, 138, 216–217
Chessie System, 64, 65 (*see* Chesapeake and Ohio Railway; CSX Corp.)
Chesterfield Railroad, 299
Chicago, Burlington & Quincy Railroad (Burlington Route; CBQ; Q), 65–66, 76, 95, 143, 144, 162, 172, 245
Chicago, Cincinnati & St. Louis Railroad (CC&SL), 145
Chicago, Indianapolis & Louisville Railroad (Monon Route), 207, 225
Chicago, Madison & Northern Railroad, 142
Chicago, Milwaukee, St. Paul & Pacific Railroad (*see* Milwaukee Road)
Chicago, New Albany & Louisville Railroad, 225
Chicago, North Shore & Milwaukee Railway, 257
Chicago, Rock Island & Pacific Railroad (*see* Rock Island Railroad)
Chicago & Alton Railroad (Alton; C&A), 100, 139, 140, 142, 162, 172, 184, 212, 264, 358
Chicago & Eastern Illinois Railroad (C&EI), 181, 207, 222
Chicago & Galena Railroad, 162
Chicago & Gulf Railroad, 136
Chicago & North Western Transportation Co. (C&NW), 48, 66, 87, 102, 136, 173, 213, 214, 286, 353
Chicago conflagration, 163–164
Chicago Elevated Railroad, 199
Chicago Great Western Railroad (CGW), 87
Chicago Museum of Science and Industry, 228, 229
Chicago South Shore & South Bend Railroad, 64, 168
Chinese labor, 66–67, 136, 297
Cincinnati, New Orleans & Pacific Railway (Queen and Crescent Route), 67–68, 299
Cincinnati locomotive builders, 67
Cincinnati Southern Railway (CS), 67–68
Rat-Hole Division, 67
Cinder arresters, 68
CIO (Congress of Industrial Organizations), 233, 338
Circus trains, 68–71, 158
City of Iron Horses (Paterson, N.J.), 247–248
City of Kansas City (train), 238
City of New Orleans (train), 164
City of Saginaw II (trainferry), 137
City of St. Louis (train), 238
City of San Francisco (train), 298
Civil War, 11–12, 71–73, 102, 163, 171–173, 207, 211, 238, 296, 351
Andrews railroad raid during, 7–9
hospital trains during, 157
Class I railroads, 73–74
Clergue, Francis H., 2
Cleveland, Grover, 52, 90, 148, 199
Cleveland & Pittsburgh Railroad, 131, 252
Climax locomotives, 204
Clinchfield Railroad, 74, 82, 115
Coal, 28, 44, 64, 65, 74–76, 82, 90–92,
Coal (*Cont.*):
130, 137, 164, 181, 207, 208, 218, 238, 239, 253, 254, 272
Coddington, E. E., 225
Cody, Col. William Frederick (Buffalo Bill), 113, 114, 334
Coffin, Lorenzo, 76
Cole, Francis J., 4
Cole, W. W., Circus, 68
Colonist cars, 76
(*See also* Zulu cars)
Colorado & Southern Railway (C&S), 76–77
Colorado Midland Railroad (CM), 77
Colorado Springs & Cripple Creek District Railway, 119
Columbia River gorge in Washington and Oregon, 43
Columbus & Indiana Central Railroad, 201
Commodore Vanderbilt (*see* Vanderbilt, Cornelius)
Commodore Vanderbilt (locomotive), 4, 309
Common carrier, 77, 308–309
Commuter trains, 17, 18, 33, 56, 77–78, 199, 205, 206
Computer systems, 56, 78, 158
video display terminals, 345
Conductors, Order of Railway, 245
Conductors' punch designs, 245
Congress of Industrial Organizations (CIO), 233, 338
Connaught Tunnel in British Columbia, 295, 329
Conneaut (funeral train), 261
Connecticut & Passumpsic River Railway, 54
Connecticut Co. (transit system), 125
Conrail, 78–79, 250, 252
Consolidated Railroad Corporation (*see* Conrail)
Consolidation (locomotive and locomotive type), 307
Conventions, regional railroad, 79–80
Convict labor, 103, 246, 351
Cook, Harry E., 228
Cooke, John, 247, 248
Cooke Locomotive Works, 3, 25, 247, 248
Coolidge, Calvin, 52
Cooper, Annabelle, 357
Cooper, Peter, 22, 80, 306
Cooper, William, 108
Copper ore, 80
Copper River & North Western Railroad (CR&NW), 80
Cornfield meet (head-on collision), 187
Corning, Erastus, 236
Costa Rican railways, 155
Cottage City Electric Railway, 217
Cotton Belt (*see* St. Louis Southwestern Railway)
Countess of Dufferin (locomotive), 55
Coup, William, 68, 69
Couplers, 76, 80–81, 173, 279
Cowcatchers (pilots), 81, 257–258
CP Rail (*see* Canadian Pacific Railway)
"Crane with a broken neck," 81

Crédit Mobilier scandal, 132, 335
Creswell, Warren, 308
Crewless freight trains, 169, 171
Cripple Creek Central Railway, 119
Crocker, Charles, 66, 81–82, 334
Crocker, E. B., 66, 67, 81–82
Crossing frogs, 124, 125
Crownsheet (part of steam locomotive), 82
CSX Corp., 82, 83, 272
(*See also* Chessie System; Seaboard Coast Line)
Cuban railways, 103, 158, 344
Cumberland Valley Railroad, 292
Currency issued by railroads, 82–85
Currier & Ives print, 294
Curves, longest, 85
Cyrus K. Holliday (locomotive), 282

Daft, Leo, 310
Dan Patch Line, 87–88, 94, 157, 267
Danforth, Charles, 247, 248
Daniels, George H., 41, 235
Date nails, 88
Davenport, Joseph, 50
Davenport, Thomas, 108
Davis, Clyde W., 219
Davis, D. W., 273
Davis, Gussie L., 20
Davis, Jefferson, 260, 300
Davis, Phineas, 22, 23
Dawson, Henry, 26
Daylight Special (train), 164
Dead Horse Gulch in Yukon Territory, Canada, 355
Death Valley Railroad, 88
Death Valley Scotty (Walter Scott), 88
De Autremont brothers (train robbers), 89
Debs, Eugene Victor, 39, 52, 89–90, 315
Decorated locomotives, 39, 77, 148, 199, 260, 261
Delano, Pennsylvania, 90–91
Delaware, Lackawanna & Western Railroad (*see* Erie Lackawanna Railway)
Delaware, Lehigh, Schuylkill & Susquehanna Railroad (DLS&S), 181
Delaware & Bound Brook Railroad, 124
Delaware and Hudson Railway (D&H), 39, 49, 84, 91–92, 166, 238
Delaware & Northern Railroad, 238
Delmonico (dining car), 100
Demurrage, 92
Densmore, Amos, 244
Denver and Rio Grande Western Railroad (D&RGW), 31, 57, 58, 92, 107, 108, 130,149, 347, 348
Denver & Southwestern Railroad, 119
Denver Pacific Railroad, 132, 133
Depoele, Charles van, 310
Depots (*see* Stations)
Derail and derailer, 93
Deregulation of railroads, 93
D'Erlanger, Baron Frederic, 67, 68
Des Jardines Canal wreck (near Montreal), 275–276
Detroit United Railways, 167
Dewey, Comdr. George, 199
De Witt Clinton (locomotive), 152, 235, 236, 324
Diamond Special (train), 164
Diesel, Rudolf, 94
Diesel-electric locomotives, 54, 93–99, 157, 201, 254, 285
  developments: of the 1920s and 1930s, 94–96
    of the 1950s and 1960s, 96–97
    recent, 97
  effect of World War I, 93–94
  effect of World War II, 96
  operation of, 99
  versus steam, 99
Diesel-hydraulic locomotives, 98–99
Diesel operation, 99
Dietzel, Oscar, 205
Dietzel, Mrs. Oscar, 205
Dining cars, 99–100
  all-electric, 99
Discovery Train, 100–101
Disney, Walt, 101–102
Dixie Flagler (train), 207
Dodge, Grenville Mellen, 102–103, 129, 277, 334
Dodge City, Kansas, 57, 88, 114, 144
Dogs, 89, 103–104, 259
Dominican Republic railways, 155
Dominion Atlantic Railway (DA), 141
Dorchester (locomotive), 181
Double-ended locomotives, 164, 199-201, 306
Douglas, Stephen A., 51
Drake, Edwin L., 242
Draney, John, 261
Drew, Daniel (Uncle Dan'l), 104, 118, 131, 132, 242, 243
Dreyfuss, Henry, 4, 104
Drifting locomotive, 198
Drinking cups, individual, 104–105
Dripps, Isaac L., 81, 257
Drummer, 30
Dubuque & Iowa City Railroad, 142, 163, 201
Dudley, Plimmon Henry, 105
Duluth, Missabe & Iron Range Railroad (DMIR), 169
Duluth, Mississippi & Northern Railroad, 145
Duluth, South Shore & Atlantic Railroad DSS&A), 137, 295
Duluth, Winnipeg & Pacific Railway, 166
Duluth Limited (train), 150
Dunn, Tom, 150
Durant, Thomas Clark, 128, 324, 325
Dwarf signals, 288
Dynamometer car, 105

E. L. Miller (locomotive), 18, 26
Eads, James Buchanan, 35
Earp, James W., 117
East Boston Locomotive Co., 237
East Erie Commercial Railroad, 198
Eastern Minnesota Railway, 149
Eastern Railroad (of Massachusetts), 274, 275
Eastman, Joseph Bartlett, 107, 180
Eddystone plant, Baldwin Locomotive Works, 17
Eden (Colo.) wreck, 107–108
Edgemoor & Manetta Railroad, 304–305
Edison, Thomas Alva, 108, 237
Edmonston, James R., 98, 99, 234
Edwards, Edgar A., 145
Eisenhower, Dwight David, 51
El Capitan (train), 283
Electric Headlight Act, 279–280
Electric Railroaders' Association (ERA), 269
Electric Railway Presidents' Conference (ERPC), 311
Electrification, 108–111, 205, 206, 251, 254
Electro-Motive Corp., 95
Electronic yardmaster, 364
Elevated railways and subways, 133, 199–200, 315–317
Elgin, Joliet & Eastern Railroad (EJ&E), 169
Ellet, Charles, Jr., 35
Elliott, Daniel, 345
Ellis, John, 4
El Salvador, National Railways of, 155
Ely, Herman, 169
Ely, Sam, 169
Empire Builder (train), 111
Empire State Express (train), 62, 105, 236
Empire Transportation Co., 243
Enthusiast, The (magazine), 269
Erie & Kalamazoo Railroad (E&K), 84, 111, 236
Erie & Ontario Railway (E&O), 151
Erie Lackawanna Railway (EL), 78, 111–113, 238
Erie Railroad (ER), 13, 14, 34, 38, 63, 72, 78, 104, 111–113, 118, 119, 131, 132, 143, 152, 237, 242, 243, 259, 343
Erie Railroad war, 112, 113
Esquimalt & Nanaimo Railway, 55
Evans & Sontag (play), 113
Excursion trains, 23, 113–114
Expo Limited (train), 56

Fairbanks, Erastus, 318
Fairbanks, W. W., 322
Fairbanks-Morse Co., 95–97, 203, 234
Family Lines System, 115, 207, 292
Fant, David, 199
Fantail engines, 115, 207
Fare collection, automatic, 13
Farm trains, 24, 254, 273
Farnum, Henry, 276
Fast freight lines, 115–116
Fast Mail (train), 214
Father of high-speed trains (Plimmon Henry Dudley), 105

Feather River Canyon in California, 352
Featherbedding (make-work), 116
Featherstonehaugh, George W., 235, 249
Ferdinand Magellan (presidential car), 51, 52, 261
Ferries (*see* Great Lakes trainferries)
Fiction, railroad, 116–117
Field, Cyrus West, 80, 133
Fillmore, Millard, 38, 112
Fire fighters, 117–118, 149, 150, 163, 164
Firemen, locomotive, 39, 89, 90
Fish, Stuyvesant, 142
Fisher, Charles E., 201, 202, 218, 269
Fisk, James (Jubilee Jim; Prince of Erie), 104, 118–119, 131, 132, 342, 343
Flagler, Henry Morrison, 25, 120, 228
Flannery, Patrick, 118
Flood signal devices, 119
Floods, 175–176, 218, 286
Florence & Cripple Creek Railway (F&CC), 118, 119
Florida East Coast Railway (FEC), 119–121
Flower Sleeping Car Co., 292
Fluorescent lighting, 30, 121, 178
Flying Dutchman (sail train), 22
Folger, William H., 232
Fontaine, Eugene, 201, 202
Forbes, E. G., 5
Ford, Gerald, 122
Ford, Henry, Museum, 228
Forney, Matthias N., 18, 51
Fort Worth, Denver & Gulf Railroad, 226
Four-train wreck, 121
Frankfort & Kokomo Railroad, 319
Franklin Institute, Philadelphia, 228
Freak locomotives (*see* Locomotives, experimental)
Freak wreck, 205
Freedom Train, American (AFT), 100, 121–122, 199
Freight:
  coal (*see* Coal)
  copper ore, 80
  grain (*see* Grain traffic)
  iron ore (*see* Iron ore)
  livestock (*see* Livestock)
  loss and damage to, 123–124
  lumber, 203–205
  minibridge, 221
  oil shipments, 242–244
  oversize shipments, 246
  piggybacking (*see* Piggybacking)
  potato shipments, 24, 260
  silk trains, 290–291
  sunflower seeds, 318
Freight cars, 122–123, 363–364
  markings for, 122
  privately owned, 123
  railvan, 270
Freight lines, fast, 115–116
Freight Master Train Dynamics Analyzer, 292
Freight rates, 93, 136, 147, 167, 343
Frémont, Gen. John Charles, 280
Frick, Henry Clay, 142
Frisco Lines (St. Louis–San Francisco Railway), 43, 280
Frog wars, 124–125
FT (diesel locomotive set), 95
Full-crew laws, 116
Fuller, William A., 8
Funeral trains, 183–184, 260–261, 264
Fusees and torpedoes, 324
FYI (fastest Canadian train), 56

Gaines, Maj. Gen. Edmund R., 71
Galloway, Samuel, 3
Garfield, James Abram, 260, 336
Gas-electric railroad, first, 87
Gas-turbine-electric locomotives, 95, 202, 234, 336
Gates, John W., 366
GATX (General American Transportation Corp.), 122, 123
Gauge (track width), 68, 87, 112, 113, 127, 202, 207, 215
Geep (locomotive), 127–128
General (locomotive), 8, 9, 208
General American Transportation Corp. (GATX), 122, 123
General Burnside (locomotive), 282
General Electric Co., 4, 93, 94, 108–110, 202, 226, 234
General Motors Corp., 95–97, 121, 127, 128, 203
General Time Convention, 326
George VI (king of Great Britain), 277
George, David Graves, 361
George C. Whitcomb Co., 14
Georgetown Loop in Colorado, 76
Georgia & Southern Florida Railroad, 299
Georgia Railroad, 115, 128, 233
GG-1 (electric locomotive type), 109, 110, 203, 254
Ghost Train (White Train), 128
Golden peacock (for tunnel clearance), 284
Golden spike ceremony, 103, 128–130, 334
Good, James, 307
Gordon, David, 53
Gould, Encrease P., 237
Gould, George Jay, 130–131, 351
Gould, Jay, 65, 104, 118, 131–133, 147, 148, 222, 244, 343
Gould, William, 218
Grab irons, 279
Grain traffic, 53, 123, 133–134, 137, 138, 147
Grand Central Terminal in New York City, 108, 134–135, 343
Grand Trunk Pacific Railway, 154
Grand Trunk Railway, 117
Grand Trunk Railway of Canada, 135, 154, 237, 259
Grand Trunk Western Railway, 138, 166
Granger laws, 136
Granite Railway (Bunker Hill monument), 150, 151, 330
Grant, Davis B., 248
Grant, Oliver D. F., 248
Grant, Ulysses S., 52, 102, 130, 132, 148, 183, 199, 260, 346
Grant Locomotive Works, 148, 201, 202
Grasshopper-type locomotives, 23, 50
Graves, trackside, 136
Gravity cars, 136–137
Gray, Aylmer, 150
Gray, Brig. Gen. Carl R., 359
Great Central Passenger Station in Chicago, 163
Great Express Robbery, The (book and play), 117
Great Lakes trainferries, 103, 137–138, 166
Great Northern Railway (GN; Big G), 43, 44, 60, 90, 125, 138, 139, 146–149, 154, 166, 349, 350
Great Slave Lake Railway (GSL), 138, 154
Great Train Robbery, The (first railroad motion-picture story), 226
Great Western (trainferry), 137
Great Western Railway, 154, 184
Greater Winnipeg Water District Railway, 155
Green Diamond (train), 164
Green Lines (fast freight), 115
Green Mountain (Iowa) wreck, 277
Guatemalan railways, 155
Gulf, Mobile & Northern Railroad (GM&N), 139
Gulf, Mobile, & Ohio Railroad (GM&O), 138–140
Gulf Transport Co., 140
Gwynn's Falls Bridge (Carrollton Viaduct) in Baltimore, Maryland, 34

H. H. Paine (locomotive), 38
Hagenbeck & Wallace circus train wreck, 70
Haire, Joe, 266
Halifax, Nova Scotia, explosion in, 141
Halifax-Truro Railway, 257
Hallidie, Andrew, 310
Hand signals, 289
Handcars, 54, 58
Hannibal & St. Joseph Railroad, 65, 143, 215, 217, 222
Harding, Warren Gamaliel, 2, 52, 261, 315
Harper's Ferry, 21, 23
Harkness, Anthony, 67
Harriman, Edward Henry, 23, 131, 139, 141–143, 174, 208, 212, 298, 335
Harrington, S. H., 13–14
Harrison, Benjamin, 52, 76, 173, 199
Harris's, W. H., Nickel Plate circus, 68
Hart, George, 50
Harvey, Charles T., 315
Harvey, Frederick Henry, 143–144, 213, 246
Haswell, Amelia, 255, 256
Haupt, Col. Herman, 72
Hawaii, Oahu Railway in, 241–242, 360
Hayes, Rutherford Birchard, 52, 313, 314
Haywire Mac (*see* McClintock, Harry Kirby)
Head-end engines, 145

Headlights, electric, 145, 279, 280
Heaney, Michael J., 80, 355, 356
Heisler locomotives, 204
Hell Gate Bridge in New York, 35, 253
"Hell of a way to run a railroad," 145
Hen-cooped locomotive pilots, 251
Henry, John, 20, 174, 233
Hercules (locomotive), 217
Heroes and heroines, 3, 34, 145–146, 149, 150, 177, 286
Hiawatha (locomotive), 4, 177
High Bridge (first railway cantilever), 35
Highball trackside signal, 190, 237
Highest and lowest rail altitudes in the United States, 317–318
Hill, James Jerome, 43, 55, 90, 125, 143, 146–149
Hill, John, 149
Hill, Louis W., 149
Hinckley (Minn.) holocaust, 40, 149–150
Hines, Walker Downer, 158
Hinkley, Isaac, 150
Hinkley Locomotive Works, 150
History of North American railroading, 150–155
Hobby, railroad (*see* Model railroading; Railfans)
Hoboes, 53, 57, 155–156
Hog law, 188, 279
Hogan, Charles H., 236
Holliday, Cyrus K., 282, 284
Holman, W. J., 202
Holman absurdity, the (engine), 202
Honduras railways, 155
Honeymoon express (*Black Diamond*), 30
Honneger, Arthur, 247
Hood, William, 208
Hoosac Tunnel at North Adams, Massachusetts, 33, 328–330
Hopkins, Mark, 81, 156–157, 159, 297, 303
Horse-drawn cars, 2, 21, 22, 151, 185, 217, 222, 259, 302, 309, 310, 316, 342, 356
Horse names on locomotives, 157
Horseshoe Curve in western Pennsylvania, 253
Hospital trains, 157–158
Hostesses, train, 139
Hotchkiss, William, 29
Houston Belt & Terminal Railway (HB&T), 158
Howe truss bridges, 34
Howe's London Circus, 68
Hoyt, Rev. Wayland, 63
Hudson & Manhattan Railroad, 251, 316
Hudson Bay Line, 53, 154, 158, 251
Huey Long Bridge at New Orleans, 36
Hull-Rust-Mahoning Mine (largest open-pit operation), 169
Huntington, Collis Potter, 42, 65, 81, 156, 157, 159, 176, 208, 284, 297, 303
Huron Bay & Iron Range Railway, 169
Hurricanes, 120

Icebreakers (trainferries), 137, 138
Icing machine, 274
Illinois Central Gulf Railroad (ICG), 36, 164
Illinois Central Railroad (IC), 13, 99, 142, 153, 160–164
Imperial Limited (train), 55
"In the Baggage-Coach Ahead" (song), 20
Inclined planes, 2, 150, 206, 246, 272, 327, 328
Independent Subway, New York City, 317
Indianapolis interurban terminal, 168
Industrial Workers of the World (Wobblies), 156, 338
Insects, 164–165, 281
Inspection cars, 59, 165
Interboro Rapid Transit Co. (IRT), New York City, 316
Intercolonial Railway, 54, 141, 154
Interlocking (trackage, signals), 164, 165, 288
International boundary line, 165
International Great Northern Railway (IGN), 222
International railroading, 166–167
Interstate Commerce Commission (ICC), 14, 73, 74, 93, 133, 134, 136, 142, 167, 219, 220, 233, 258, 271, 272, 305
Interurban electric railways, 167–169
Iron Mountain Railroad (IM), 172, 222, 295
Iron ore, 2, 28, 111, 149, 169, 207
Irons, Martin, 315
Ivanhoe (Ind.) wreck, 70

Jackass & Western railway (J&W), 49, 171
Jackson, Andrew, 50, 113, 151, 157
Jackson, Tom, 171
Jamaican railways, 155
James, Arthur Curtiss, 352
James, Jesse Woodson, 157, 171–173, 277
James Guthrie (locomotive), 217
Janney, Charles J., 145
Janney, Eli Hamilton, 80, 81, 173
Janus (double-ended locomotive), 200
Jarrett and Palmer special train, 173–174
Jay Gould (locomotive), 38
Jersey Central Railroad (*see* Central Railroad of New Jersey)
Jersey City Locomotive Works, 237
Jim Crow cars, 233
John Bull (locomotive), 26, 257, 306, 307
John H. Murray's Railroad Circus, 68
"John Henry," 20, 174, 233
John Wilkes (train), 178
Johnson, Andrew, 52, 183
Johnson, Lyndon Baines, 271
Johnson bar, 174–175, 305
Johnstown flood in Pennsylvania, 175–176
Jones, John Luther (*see* Casey Jones)
Josserand, Peter, 32
Judah, Theodore Dehone, 157, 159, 176, 296, 303
Jumbo (famous elephant), 69
Jupiter (locomotive), 3, 130

K-4 (locomotive type), 252
Kansas & Missouri Railway bridge, 34
Kansas City, Mexico & Orient Railway (KCM&O), 284, 308
Kansas City Southern Railroad, 142, 308
Katy (*see* Missouri-Kansas-Texas Railroad)
Keddie, Arthur W., 351
Kelley, Father Francis C., 63
Kennar, Edward, 177
Kennebec Central Railroad, 215
Kettle Valley Railway, 125
Keystone Road (*see* Pennsylvania Railroad)
Kirkwood, James F., 34
Kitson, Norman W., 147
Knight, William, 7–9
Knights of Labor, 133, 315, 337
Kreicher, Charles S., 145, 146
Kuhler, Otto, 23, 51, 177–178
  etching by, 317
Kuhn, Loeb & Co., 142, 143, 149

Lab-on-wheels (AAR-100), 179
Labor unions (see Unions, railroad labor)
Lackawanna Road (*see* Erie Lackawanna Railway)
Lacombe, Father, 55
LaCrosse & Milwaukee Railroad, 220
Laird, John P., 253
Lake Shore & Michigan Southern Railway (Lake Shore Road), 10, 12, 181, 236, 242, 244
Lake Superior Museum of Transportation, 110
La Mothe iron car, 184, 254
Land grants, 128, 160, 179–180, 221, 282
Lanterns, trainmen's and switchmen's, 180
Lap order, 180
La Salle Street Station in Chicago, 181
Lathrop, Gilbert A., 31
Lauder, James, 26
Lawrence, Lewis, 26
Laws affecting railroads, 76, 167, 198, 213, 233, 234
  deregulation of railroads, 93
  featherbedding, 116
  Granger laws, 136
  mergers, 219–220
  safety laws (*see* Safety laws)
  (*See also* Interstate Commerce Commission)
Leach, Joshua, 39
Lebanon (locomotive), 33
Lee, Elisha, 304
Lee, Gen. Robert E., 71, 157, 173
Lee, Vernon, 118
Lehigh & New England Railroad (L&NE), 253
Lehigh Valley Railroad (LV), 30, 51, 75, 78, 90, 91, 177, 178, 181, 200, 227, 228, 253
Leiper, Thomas, 181
Leitzel, Lillian, 70
Lentz, L. B., circus train, 68
Liberty Bell, 130, 181–182, 184

Light rail vehicles (LVR), 312
Lightning (locomotive), 4
Lightning Express (train), 163
Lima Locomotive Works, 182–183, 216, 307
Lincoln, Abraham, 51, 52, 72, 102, 128, 151, 157, 163, 211, 225, 228, 260, 334, 345, 351
funeral train for, 183-184, 264
trip to inauguration, 184–185
Lindenthal, Gustav, 35
Lingo of the rails, 185–197
Link-and-pin couplers, 80–83
Lintner, Fred, 146
Lionel toy trains, 224
Little Schuylkill Navigation Railroad & Canal Co., 272
Livestock, 104, 163, 197–198, 283
Livingston, Ann, 357
Locomotive drifting, 198
Locomotive Firemen's Magazine, 89
Locomotive obstacle course, 198
Locomotives:
bicentennial-painted, 198–199
decorated (*see* Decorated locomotives)
diesel-electric (*see* Diesel-electric locomotives)
diesel-hydraulic, 98–99
double-ended, 164, 199–201, 306
electric, 108–111, 251
(*See also* Interurban electric railways; Streetcars; Subway and elevated railways)
experimental, 201–202
gas-turbine-electric, 95, 202, 234, 336
manufacture of, 202
military, 202–203
steam (*see* Steam locomotives)
(*See also* Cabs)
Loewy, Raymond, 96, 110, 203, 225
Logging railroads, 203–205
Long Island & Eastern Express (train), 121
Long Island Rail Road (LIRR), 205–206, 251
Longest railroad receivership, 272–273
Lookout Mountain Incline Railway, 206–207
Louise Railroad, 64, 65
Louisiana & Texas Railroad, 296
Louisville, New Orleans & Texas Railway, 163
Louisville & Nashville Railroad (L&N), 7, 9, 82, 115, 118, 165, 207–208, 217, 219, 225, 249, 260
Louisville (Ky.) Central Station, 336
Lowest point on railroads in the United States, 317–318
Lucas, Walter Arndt, 26, 210, 248
Lucin (Utah) Cutoff, 143, 208
Ludlow & Southern Railway (L&S), 208–209
Lumber railroads (*see* Logging railroads)
Luna, Charles, 338
Lynde, Francis, 117

M-10000 earthworm (locomotive), 234
McAdam, Ernest, 146
McAdoo, William Gibbs, 153, 250, 358
McCallum, Daniel Craig, 71, 211
McClellan, Gen. George Brinton, 163, 244
McClintock, Harry Kirby (Haywire Mac), 20, 49, 211–212
McCloud River Railroad, 201, 204
McCoy, Elijah, 212
McCrea, James, 251, 253
McDonald, A. R., 49
McGraw, Charles, 292
McGraw, James H., Sr., 149
McGraw-Hill Book Company, 149
McGuire, Dan, 12
McInerny, Daniel T., 255
McIntosh & Seymour locomotive plant, 94
McKay & Aldus Iron & Locomotive Works, 237
McKeen, William Riley, Jr., 93, 212–213
McKinley, William, 261
McQueen, Walter, 4
Mad River & Lake Erie Railroad, 112, 247
Mail, 57, 104, 140, 143, 213–214, 360, 361
Maine, two-foot-gauge railroads in, 215
Maine Central Railroad (MEC), 214–215
Make-work (featherbedding), 116
Malbone Street subway wreck in Brooklyn, New York, 329
Mallet (locomotive type), 4, 31, 93, 201, 215–217, 306, 307
Mammoth Cave Railroad, 217
Manassas Gap Railroad, 71, 72
Manitou & Pike's Peak Railway, 217
Mann, Col. William D'Alton, 292
Maritana (first parlor car), 265
Martha's Vineyard Railroad, 217
Martinez-Benicia Bridge over San Francisco Bay inlet, 36
Mason, Col. Roswell B., 160, 162
Mason, William, 51, 201, 217–218, 257, 261
Master Car Builders Association (MCBA), 81, 173
Masterson, Bat, 57–58, 258
Maternity special trains, 90, 218
Mauch Chunk Railroad, 218
Meadow Brook disaster in Rhode Island, 218
Mears, Otto, 218–219
Memphis & Charleston Railroad, 124
Mergers, 219–220
Merritt, Leonidas, 169
Merritt family, 169
Metroliners, 251
Metropolitan Transportation Authority (New York), 206
Mexican railways, 57, 68, 92, 103, 143, 155, 165, 199, 201, 220, 282, 284, 296, 298, 308
Michigan Central Railroad, 38, 70, 137, 152, 162, 212
Michigan Southern Railroad, 152
Midland Terminal Railway, 77
Mifflin (locomotive), 252
Miles of railroad track, 220
Milholland, John, 51, 216, 306
Military locomotives, 202
Miller, E. L., 306
(See also *E. L. Miller*)
Miller platform, 264, 274, 275
Milwaukee & St. Paul Railroad (*see* Milwaukee Road)
Milwaukee Road (Chicago, Milwaukee, St. Paul & Pacific Railroad; CMStP&P), 27, 51, 65, 110, 111, 177, 220–221
Mineral Range Railroad, 80
Minibridge freight shipments, 221
Minneapolis, Northfield & Southern Railway, 88, 165
Minneapolis, St. Paul, Rochester & Dubuque Electric Traction Co. (Dan Patch Line), 87
Minneapolis, St. Paul & Sault Ste. Marie Railway (Soo Line), 295
Minneapolis & St. Louis Railway (longest receivership), 221, 272–273
Minnesota Southern Railway, 165
Minnesota Valley Railroad, 201
Minot, Charles, 287, 326
Mississippi (locomotive), 160
Mississippi Central Railroad, 27, 163
Mississippi Railroad, 142
Missouri-Kansas-Texas Railroad (Katy), 103, 119, 221
Missouri Pacific Eagle (train), 30, 222
Missouri Pacific Railroad (MP), 30, 107, 130, 132, 133, 153, 158, 164, 192, 220–222
Mitchell, Alexander A., 90, 91
Mobile & Ohio Railway, 7, 61, 139
Model railroading, 26, 222–225
Modern Railroads Rail Transit (magazine), 254
Moffat Tunnel in Colorado, 225, 328
Mohawk & Hudson Railroad, 152, 235, 249, 324
Monon Route, 207, 225
Monorails, 29, 225–226
Monson Railroad, 215
Montreal Locomotive Works, 56, 98, 307
Moore, E. A., 255
Morgan, R. E., 142, 143, 292
Morningstar, Susan, 357
Mother Hubbard locomotives (*see* Camelbacks)
Motion pictures, 19, 23, 226–227
Mount Clare (Md.) station and shops, 22, 306
Mount Royal Tunnel in Montreal, 330
Mountaineer (locomotive), 200
Mud diggers (locomotive types), 306
Mud Run (Pa.) collision, 227–228
Muhlfield, James E., 216
Mule-drawn car, 204
Murphy, Anthony, 8
Murray's John H., Railroad Circus, 68
Museum of Science and Industry in Chicago, 228, 229
Museums, 98, 228–229
Muskeg on right-of-way, 145, 158
Mystery of the 13 (train robbery), 229–230

Name trains, passenger, 164, 231–232, 357
Nancy Hanks (train), 357
Nantucket Railroad, 232
Naperville Junction Railway, 166
NARP News (periodical), 269
Nash, Frank, 336
Nashville, Chattanooga & St. Louis Railway (NC&StL), 207, 232, 233
Nashville (Tenn.) wreck, 232–233
Nast, Thomas, 119, 127
National Association of Railroad Passengers (NARP), 254
National Association of Train Order Collectors (NATOC), 327
National Button Society (NBC), 45
National Carriers Conference Committee (NCCC), 338
National Livestock Loss Prevention Board (NLLPB), 198
National Model Railroad Association (NMRA), 224
National Museum of Transport, 229, 238
National Railroad Passenger Corp. (Amtrak), 6, 7
National Railway Historical Society (NRHS), 203, 235, 269
National Railway Labor Conference (NRLC), 338
National Steel Car Corp. (NSC), 98
National Transcontinental Railway, 53, 154
Natural railroad tunnel, America's only, 329
Near Creek Railroad, 28
Negroes (blacks), 61, 174, 212, 233–234, 270, 271, 296
Nettleton, George H., 280
Neuhart, David E., 234
New Albany & Salem Railroad (NA&S), 225
New Brunswick Railway, 55
New England Limited (ghost train), 128
New Hamburg (N.Y.) wreck, 234–235
New Jersey Locomotive & Machinery Co., 247
New Jersey Railroad & Transportation Co., 150
New Orleans, Jackson & Great Northern Railroad, 163
New Orleans & Pacific Railroad, 103
New York, Chicago & St. Louis Railroad (Nickel Plate Road; NKP), 182, 239
New York, Lake Erie & Western Railroad (NYLE&W), 112
New York, New Haven & Hartford Railroad (New Haven Road), 108, 121, 125, 128, 134, 152, 253
New York, Ontario & Western Railroad (NYO&W), 235
New York & Harlem Railway, 42, 236, 309
New York & Hudson River Railroad (NY&HR), 234, 236
New York & New England Railroad (NY&NE), 121
New York & Oswego Midland Railway (NY&OM), 325
New York Central System (NYC), 4, 5, 62, 94, 95, 105, 108, 109, 134, 135, 146,
New York Central System (NYC) (*Cont.*): 166, 181, 182, 235–237, 249, 250, 252, 255, 260, 301, 347
New York Circus, 68
New York City's first train wreck, 342
New York Express (train), 10
New York Locomotive Works, 237
Newburyport (locomotive), 275
Newell, Evelyn, 357
Newfoundland Railway, 53, 154
News butchers (train peddlers), 101, 237–238
Niagara, St. Catherines & Toronto Railway, 167
Niagara tramway, 327
Nicaragua's Pacific Railway, 155
Nickel Plate Road (New York, Chicago & St. Louis Railroad; NKP), 182, 239
Nicknames of railroads, 238
999 (speed-record locomotive), 236
Norfolk & Western Railway (NW), 27, 74–76, 91, 136, 216, 217, 238–239, 253
Norfolk Southern Railway, 299
Norris, Edward, 4
Norris, Frank, 117
Norris, Septimus, 4
North America Car Corp., 239
North American railroading, history of, 150–155
North Coast Limited (train), 231, 247
North Missouri Railroad, 71, 238
North Pacific Coast Railroad, 51
North Pennsylvania Railroad, 3
Northern Alberta Railways, 55, 155
Northern Cross Railroad, 238
Northern Pacific Railway (NP), 142, 143, 147, 166, 199, 216, 247, 259, 345, 346
(*See also* Burlington Northern Inc.)
Northern Railroad of New Jersey, 13
Northern Securities Corp., 143
Nova Scotia Railway, 151

Oahu Railway (Hawaii), 241–242, 360
O'Connell, Dan, 89, 155, 156
Official Intermodel Equipment Register, The, 242
Official Railway Equipment Register, The, 242
Official Railway Guide, The, 242
Ogdensburg & Lake Champlain Railroad (O&LC), 142
Oil Creek Railroad, 243
Oil shipments, 146, 242–244
Old Colony Railroad, 26, 269
Old Ironsides (locomotive), 17, 18, 152
Old Reliable, The (*see* Louisville & Nashville Railroad)
Oldest common-carrier short line, Strasburg Rail Road, 308–309
Oldest railroad man (John K. Chapman), 63
Oneida Community of Perfectionists, 235
O'Neill, James, 349, 350
Ontario Northland Railway (ON), 155
Operating ratio, 245
Opposition to early railroads, 136, 151, 152
Orange & Alexandria Railroad, 157
Order of Railway Conductors (ORC), 245
Order of Sleeping Car Conductors, 245
Oregon, California & Eastern Railroad, 205
Oregon & Northwestern Railroad, 205
Oregon Railway & Navigation Co., 142, 346
Oregon Short Line (OSL), 142
Orphan trains, 246
Osborn, Prime F., III, 82
Osborn, William H., 163
Osborne, Richard R., 34
Otis Railway, 246
Overland Limited (train), 258, 261
Overseas extension of Florida East Coast Railway, 120
Oversize freight shipments, 246
Owney (Railway Post Office dog), 104

Pacific Electric Railroad, 168, 298
Pacific Express (train), 12, 55, 235
Pacific Great Eastern Railway (British Columbia Railway; PGE), 36–37
Pacific Railroad, 153, 221
Pacific 231 (Honneger symphony), 247
Packard, Frank L., 116, 117
Packard, Joe, 245
Paine, Harry H., 38
Palmer, Gen. William Jackson, 57, 92, 139, 283
Pan-American (train), 207
Panama Limited (train), 164
Panama Railroad, 155, 259
Parrott, George, 228
Passenger Train Journal (magazine), 229, 254
Paterson, New Jersey, locomotive builders in, 17, 25, 26, 247–248
Paterson Horse Railroad, 247
Pay car (pay train), 248–249
PCCs (modern streetcars), 311, 312
Peabody, George, 163
Pecos River Bridge in Texas, 36, 249, 298, 318
Peddlers, train (news butchers), 101, 237–238
Pegleg Railroad (Bradford & Foster Brook Railway), 225
Penn Central Transportation Company (PC), 156, 181, 249–250
Penn Station in New York City, 250–251, 304
Pennington, Rev. James W. C., 234
Pennsylvania Limited (train), 301
Pennsylvania Public Works System, 2
Pennsylvania Railroad (Keystone Road; Pennsy; PRR; Standard Railroad of the World), 2, 14, 35, 37, 68, 100, 109, 124, 130, 143, 146, 151, 154, 165, 173, 206, 228, 252–254, 257, 260, 301, 351

Peoria & Pekin Union Railroad, 164
Pere Marquette Railway, 166
Periodicals, 254–255
Perlman, Alfred E., 230, 236
Perry, Oliver Curtis, 255–256
Petsch, Julius D., 306
Philadelphia, Baltimore & Washington Railroad (PB&W), 157, 322
Philadelphia, Germantown & Norristown Railroad, 18
Philadelphia, Newtown & New York Railroad, 84
Philadelphia, Wilmington & Baltimore Railroad (PW&B), 12, 80, 184, 213, 219
Philadelphia & Columbia Railroad, 3, 252, 330
Philadelphia & Erie Railroad, 243
Philadelphia & Reading Railroad (*see* Reading Railroad)
Phoebe Snow (train), 75, 357
Pierce, Franklin, 128
Pierce, Robert B. F., 145
Piggybacking (make work), 53, 164, 221, 256–257
Pilots (cowcatchers), 81, 257–258
Pinkerton, Allan, 117, 184, 185, 255, 258, 274
Pioneer (locomotive), 214
Pioneer (Pullman car), 184
Pioneer Zephyr (train), 42, 66, 229
Pipelines, 243, 244
Pitkin, Albert J., 4, 236
Pittenger, Sgt. William, 8
Pittsburg Locomotive Works, 3
Pittsburgh, Chicago & St. Louis Railroad, 252
Pittsburgh, Fort Wayne & Chicago Railroad, 172, 252
Pittsburgh, McKeesport & Youghiogheny Railroad (PM&Y), 258
Pittsburgh & Lake Erie Railroad (P&LE), 258
Pittsburgh & West Virginia Railroad, 238
Plant, Henry B., 162, 285
Pneumatic subway in New York City, 316
Pocket List of Railroad Officials, The, 242
Poell, George H., 258
Police, railroad, 258–259
Ponce & Guayama Railway, 155
Pontchartrain Railroad, 85, 259
Pony Express, 65, 128, 213, 302, 334
Poor, John Alfred, 259
Poor's Manual of Railroads, 259
Portage Allegheny Railway, 2, 3
Portage Bridge in New York, 34, 259
Porters, sleeping car and station, 40–42, 233, 270–271, 293
Portland, Saco & Portsmouth Co., 259
Portland Company, 259
Post Boy (locomotive), 205
Post Office, Railway (*see* Mail)
Potato shipments, 24, 260
Preamble Express (train), 122
President (Pullman car), 265
Presidential funeral trains, 183–184, 260–261, 264
Presidential rail travel, 51–52, 112, 184–185
Prince Edward Island Railway, 154
Prineville, City of, Railway, 261–262
Privately owned freight cars, 123
Progressive Railroading (magazine), 254
Prospect (Pa.) wreck, 262–263
Pruyn, John V. L., 236
Public relations and advertising, 70, 235, 359
Public Service of New Jersey, 168
Pueblo Test Center in Colorado, 263
Puerto Rican railways, 155
Pullman, George Mortimer, 40, 90, 184, 263–266, 308
Pushcar, 8, 58, 59
Pyle, George C., 145

Quebec, Montreal & Southern Railway, 166
Queen and Crescent Route, 68
Quebec bridge, 36
Quebec North Shore and Labrador Railway, 49, 155, 169

Racehorses, special cars for, 87–88, 157, 267
Racial segregation on trains, 233
Rail, welded, 348–349
Rail altitudes in the United States, highest and lowest, 317–318
Rail Classics (magazine), 255
Rail cross-sections, 268, 322
Rail detector cars, 267–268
Rail Passenger Act, 6
Rail shrinkage, 268
Rail Travel News Letter, 255
Railfan & Railroad (magazine), 116, 254
Railfans, 45, 51, 222, 254, 268–269
Railroad and railway, definitions of, 270
Railroad Enthusiast, The (magazine), 269
Railroad Magazine (originally *Railroad Man's Magazine*), 25, 116, 211, 254
Railroad Operations Modular Processing System (ROMPS), 277
Railroad presidents, towns named for, 324–325
Railroad Town (Delano, Pa.), 90–91
Railroad War Board, 258
Railroads Illustrated (magazine), 255
Railvan, 270
Railway Age (magazine), 254
Railway and Locomotive Historical Society, 229, 269
Railway Express Agency (REA), 10, 11
Railway Labor Act of 1926, 245
Railway Labor Executives Association (RLEA), 245, 338
Railway Mail Association, 214
Railway Mail Service, 213
Railway Tracks and Structures (magazine), 254
Railway Yardmasters of America, 338
Randolph, A. Philip, 41, 42, 234, 270–271
Rapid City, Black Hills & Western Railroad, 271
Rat-Hole Division (Cincinnati Southern Railway), 67
Rate bureaus (rate fixing), 93, 167, 244, 271
Rate wars, rebates and, 243, 244, 272
Raton Mountain switchback, 271, 283
Raub, Christian, 201
Raub Central Power locomotive, 201
Reading Railroad (RDG), 4, 17, 18, 23, 75, 124, 152, 257, 272, 281, 287, 331
Reagan, Ronald, 67, 79, 231
Rebates and rate wars, 243, 244, 272
Rebel, The (train), 139
Receivership, longest, in the United States, 272–273
Red River Valley Railway, 125
Redcaps, 40–42, 181, 273, 293
Refrigerator cars, 24, 164, 273–274
Reid, John, 274
Reitman, Ben L., 155
Relay (Md.) viaduct, 34
Remote control, 274
Reno brothers (outlaws), 153, 274
Rent-a-train, 164
Retarders in hump yard, 338, 364
Retirement Act, 153, 277–278
Revere (Mass.) wreck, 274–275
Rhode Island Locomotive Works, 4
Richelieu River wreck (near Montreal), 275–276
Richmond, Fredericksburg & Potomac Railroad (RFP), 72, 152
Richmond & Allegheny Railroad, 64
Richmond & Danville Railway, 249, 261, 299
Richmond Locomotive Works, 3, 4
Ridenour, Mark, 176
Ridgely, Nicholas N., 238
Riding the rods, 194
Right-of-way, 276, 328
  muskeg on, 145, 158
Ringling Brothers, 69
Rio Grande Southern Railroad, 131
Robberies, train, 24, 89, 153, 255–256, 274, 276, 328
  Jesse James gang, 157, 171–173, 277
  Mystery of the 13, 229–230
Robinson, Albert A., 57, 282, 283
Robinson, William, 288
Rock Island Railroad (Chicago, Rock Island & Pacific Railroad; CRIP; RI; The Rock), 64, 74, 81, 116, 145, 165, 172, 181, 219, 248, 276–277
Rockefeller, John D., 63, 120, 123, 131, 142, 169, 221, 239, 243, 272
Roebling, John A., 35
Roger (locomotive), 238
Rogers, Henry H., 239
Rogers, Jacob, 247
Rogers, Thomas A., 4, 247
Rogers Locomotive and Machine Works, 4, 238, 247–248
Romans, W., 201

ROMPS (Railroad Operations Modular Processing System), 277
Roosevelt, Franklin Delano, 52, 90, 107, 153, 261
Roosevelt, Theodore, 52, 88, 142, 244, 261
Root, James, 150
Rosenburg, Charles, 182
Rosoff, Samuel R., 237–238
Rotary snowplow, 295
Roundhouse, 58, 72, 95, 224, 313, 315, 331
Royal train, 277
Royster, William Wallace, 277–288
Run-through trains, 278
Rutland & Washington Railroad, 131
Rutland Railway, 166

Sacramento (Calif.) shops, 298
Sacramento Valley Railroad, 176, 296
Safety Appliance Act, 76, 173, 279
Safety laws, 76, 173, 245, 279–280
Sage, Russell, 103, 131–133
Sail-operated railcars, 151, 299
St. Andrews & Quebec Railway, 54
St. Christopher (Island), St. Kitts Sugar Railway on, 155
St-Hilaire (Que.) drawbridge wreck, 36
St. Johnsbury & Lake Champlain Railway, 318
St. Louis & Iron Mountain Railway, 222
St. Louis–San Francisco Railway (Frisco Lines), 43, 280
St. Louis Southwestern Railway (Cotton Belt; SLSW), 280–281, 296
St. Louis Union Station, 337
St-Luc yard at Montreal, Canadian Pacific Railway, 56
St. Paul, Minneapolis & Manitoba Railroad, 147
St. Paul & Duluth Railroad, 149
St. Paul & Pacific Railroad, 147
St. Thomas (Ont.) wreck, 69, 281
San Francisco cable cars, 310, 312
Sanding the rails, 281–282
Sandusky (locomotive), 248
Sandy River & Rangeley Lakes Railroad, 215
Santa Fe Railway (Atchison, Topeka and Santa Fe Railway; ATSF), 64, 88, 100, 142–144, 208, 209, 216, 282–284
  steam locomotive cab, 50
Saratoga & Schenectady Railroad, 213
Saunders, Stuart, 250
Saunders, Wallace, 61
Savage, Marion W., 87
Schaumburg, William C., 225
Schenectady Locomotive Engine Manufactory, 3, 4
Schiff, Jacob Henry, 142
Schmidt, Wilhelm, 319
Schoen, Charles T., 354
Schuylkill East Side Terminal Railway, 23
Scott, Thomas B., 103, 184
Scott, Walter (Death Valley Scotty), 88
Scranton, George, 112
Seaboard Air Line, 95, 306
Seaboard Coast Line Railroad (SCL), 82, 115, 128, 208, 285
Section cars, 58–59
Sexton, Pat, 146
Seymour, Winfred W., 42
Shakopee (experimental locomotive), 201
Shaw, Henry F., 201
Shaw, Thomas, 308
Shay, Ephraim, 182
Shay, Matthew H., 286
Shay locomotives, 182
Sheffield, George, 59
Shelley, Kate, 180, 286, 357
Sherman, Gen. William Tecumseh, 72, 73, 128, 296, 300
Shohola (Pa.) train wreck, 72–73
Shortest rail freight haul, 286
Siamese twins as passengers, 286
Sieg, Joseph, 146
Sierra Railway, 227
Signals, 68, 109, 165, 286–290
  block, 288–289
  dwarf, 289
  flood, 119
  hand, 289
  highball trackside, 190, 237
  whistle, 289–290
Silk trains, 290–291
Silver Creek (N.Y.) wreck, 291
Silverton, Gladstone, and Northerly Railroad, 219
Silverton Northen Railroad, 219
Silverton Railroad, 218–219
Simmons-Boardman Publishing Corporation, 254
Sinclair, Angus, 50
Single-tracking, 291
Skagit River Railway, 291
Skelly, Billy, 237
Slack, 291–292
Sleeping car porters (*see* Porters)
Sleeping cars, 292–293, 347, 357, 358
Slip switch, 293
Smeed, E. C., 72
Smith, Alfred Emanuel, 52
Smith, Rev. Boston W., 63
Smith, C. Shaler, 35, 58
Smith, Donald Alexander (Lord Strathcona), 55, 147, 344
Smithsonian Institution, 34, 228, 306
"Smoke orders," 287, 307
Smokestack oddities, 293
"Snake heads," 111, 225, 236
"Snow, Phoebe," 75, 357
Snow fighting, 2, 99, 293–295
Snowsheds, 295
Socrates (locomotive), 12
Sodus Point & Southern Railroad, 142
Solar energy, 56, 300
Songs (*see* Ballads)
Sonora Railway, 298
Sontag, John, 113
Soo Line, 116, 295–296
South Carolina (double-ended locomotive), 306
South Carolina Canal and Railroad Co. (SCC&R), 22, 152, 200, 213, 216, 299, 300, 306
South Carolina Railroad, 296
South Eastern Railway, 55
South Improvement Co., 244
South Wind (train), 207, 208
Southern Pacific Lines (SP), 36, 81, 117, 128–130, 142, 168, 174, 176, 216, 227, 296–299
Southern Railway System, 35, 68, 133, 165, 199, 290, 299–301, 329, 360
Spark arresters, 68, 90
Spaulding, Edwin A., 14, 15
Spaulding, William A., 68
Spaulding & Rogers (S&R) show, 68
Spearman, Frank H., 118
Special trains:
  campaign, 51–52
  circus, 68–71, 158
  excursion, 23, 113–114
  funeral (*see* Funeral trains)
  Jarrett and Palmer, 173–174
  for racehorses, 87–88, 157, 267
  royal, 277
Speed records, 42, 55, 56, 66, 68, 88, 110, 117, 118, 301, 306
Speed war, 301
Sperry rail service, 105, 268
Spikes, 128, 130, 301
Spokane International Railway, 167
Sprague, Frank J., 310, 311
Sprague, Julian C., 273
Spring switch, 302
SPV-2000 (Budd railcar), 42
Stager, Henry W., 365
Stamps, postage, 302
Standard Oil Company, 244, 272
"Standard Railroad of the World, The" (*see* Pennsylvania Railroad)
Standard time, 19, 302
Standard Transportation Code (STC), 302
Stanford, Leland, 66, 67, 81, 129, 130, 159, 302–303
Starrucca Viaduct in New York, 34
State Works in Pennsylvania, 252
Station bells, 303–304
Station hotels, 30, 32, 144, 304, 365
Stations, passenger, 22, 37, 134, 135, 181, 250, 303, 304, 336
Steam locomotives, 3, 5, 17, 19, 28, 37, 54, 55, 62, 67, 80, 81, 145, 202, 215, 219, 304–308, 325, 334–336
  boilers for, 31
  builders of, 150, 182–183, 212, 217–218, 247–248, 306–307, 322
  cabs for, 38, 50–51, 306, 307
  crownsheet for, 82
  versus diesel, 99
  direct steaming, 100
  endurance tests for, 304
  fantail engines, 115, 207
  miniature, 26

Steam locomotives (*Cont.*):
pilots, 257–258
twelve-wheelers, 331–332
Steam Passenger Service Directory, 229
Stephen, George (Lord Mount Stephen), 147
Stephenson, Robert, 306
Stevens, Col. John, 150, 249, 306
Stevens, John F., 60
Stevens, L. R., 328
Stevens, Robert Livingston, 307, 321, 323
Stevens hedges, 328
Stillhouse trestle (Va.) wreck, 360–361
Stilwell, Arthur Edward, 308
Stollman, Howard, 216
Stone Creek (Ga.) wreck, 308
Stourbridge Lion (locomotive), 91, 152, 306
Straight and curved track, 85, 325
Strasburg Rail Road, 228, 308–309
Streamlining, 4, 51, 104, 177, 178, 309
Street Railway Journal (magazine), 149
Streetcars, 51, 309–312, 314
segregation on, 234
Stremmatograph, 105
Strikebreaking czar (Pearl L. Bergoff), 314
Strikes, 81, 90, 119, 121, 312–315, 337–338
first major strike (1877), 313–314
first organized strike (1855), 312–313
during World War II, 153
(*See also* Unions)
Strobridge, J. H., 66, 81
Strong, William R., 57
Subway and elevated railways, 133, 199–200, 315–317
Sullivan, Katherine, 139
Summits and lowest points of rail altitudes in the United States, 317–318
Sunday trains, 318
Sunflower seeds, 318
Sunset Limited (train), 318–319
Superheaters, locomotive, 219, 234, 306
Superpower steam, 182, 183
Sutherland, J. B., 273
Swift, Gustavus, 273
Swinburne, William, 247, 248
Switch keys, 319–320
Switchback, Raton Mountain, 271, 283
Switchmen's Union of North America (SUNA), 320
Switchmobile, 320

T rail, 105, 253, 321–322
Taft, William Howard, 52
Tait, Dan, 353
Tank cars, 122, 123, 243, 244
Taunton Locomotive Works, 322
Telegraphic codes for train control, 322–323
Telegraphy, 23, 25, 53, 130, 133, 322, 326
Teletype, 66
Television, first railroad, 323
Tennessee Central Railway, 207
Tennessee Coal, Iron & Railroad Co., 169
Terminology, railroad, 185–197
Terre Haute & Indianapolis Railroad, 2
Texas (locomotive), 9
Texas & Pacific Railway, 24, 103, 130, 132, 182, 222, 223, 328
Thermal efficiency, 307
Thiehoff family, 323
Third Avenue Elevated Railroad in New York City, 316, 317
Thomas, Evan, 22
Thomas, Lou, 218
Thomas, Phillip E., 218
Thomas, William J., 51
Thomas viaduct in Maryland, 23
Thompson, Clyde S., 235
Thompson, Jared (Yankee), 38
Thompson, Myrtle, 30, 31
Thomson, John, 181
Thomson, John E., 128
Thomson, John Edgar, 128, 181, 252
Ties (crossties; tie plates), 102, 128–130, 323
Tietjens, Oscar, 309
Tiffany summer and winter car, 273
Tigrett, Isaac Burton, 139, 140
Time, standard, 19, 302
Timetables, earliest North American, 56, 324
Tinplate model trains, 224
Toland, Ralph, 146
Toledo, Peoria & Western Railroad, 63, 64
Tom Thumb (locomotive), 22, 80, 228, 302, 306
Tonopah & Tidewater Railroad, 88
Toronto, Grey & Bruce Railway, 200
Toronto, Hamilton & Buffalo Railway, 167
Toronto Locomotive Works, 151, 152
Torpedoes and fusees, 324
Towns named for railroad presidents, 324–325
Track:
miles of, 220
straight and curved, 85, 325
Track geometry car, 325
Track pans, 173, 325
Track scales, 325
Track structures dynamic test facility, 325–326
Traffic control,
centralized, 62–63
Train Collectors Association (TCA), 224
Train control:
automatic, 13–14
telegraphic codes for, 322–323
Train dynamics analyzer, 326
Train-order hoops and forks, 103, 326
Train orders, 103, 180, 326–327
Train robbers (*see* Robberies, train)
Trainbox, conductor's, 327
Trainferries, Great Lakes, 103, 137–138, 166
Trains Magazine, 254
Trainsheds, 327
Trainsheet, 134, 327
Tramps, 155
(*See also* Hoboes)
Tramway, North America's first, 150, 327–328
Trans Canada Limited (train), 55
Transportation Act of 1920, 315
Traveler (locomotive), 23
Traveling Post Office, 214
Trilevel automobile car, 257
Trolley car museums, 228, 229
Truman, Harry S, 32, 39, 42, 52, 153
Trummer, Frank (Monk), 328
Tumbleweed fences (Stevens hedges), 328
Tunnels, 3, 23, 33, 74, 89, 93, 146, 167, 174, 206, 235, 250, 251, 349–351
Canadian, 329–330
Cascade Tunnel, 60, 328, 349, 350
Moffat Tunnel, 225
Summit Tunnel, 67
Turbine trains, 8, 53
Turntables and wyes, 165, 217, 218, 224, 330–331
Tweed, William Marcy (Boss), 119, 132, 316, 342
Twelve-wheelers (Mastodons), 331–332
20th Century Limited (train), 104, 135
Two-foot-gauge railroads in Maine, 215
Two-way freight hauls, 28
Two-way radio for trainmen and dispatchers, 332
Tyler Tap Railway, 281
Tyson, Henry, 319

Uintah Railroad, 333
Uncle Dick (locomotive), 271
Uniform buttons, 45, 253
Union Pacific Railroad (UP), 5, 6, 66, 67, 95, 102, 103, 116, 117, 132, 133, 142, 143, 174, 212, 213, 220, 226, 228, 229, 234, 258, 260, 333–336
golden spike ceremony, 103, 128–130, 334
Union Palace Car Co., 265
Union Railroad, 28, 169
Union stations, 55, 92, 336–337
(*See also* Grand Central Terminal in New York City; Penn Station in New York City)
Union Switch & Signal Co., 14, 99
Union Tank Line, 123
Unions, railroad labor, 337–338
(*See also* Debs, Eugene Victor; Strikes)
Unit trains, 53, 75, 133, 134, 338–339
United Railroad & Canal Co. of New Jersey, 173, 250, 252
U.S. Army Corps of Engineers, 94, 360
U.S. Army Transportation Corps, 360
U.S. Military Railway Service (MRS), 359, 360
U.S. Railroad Administration (USRA), 14, 358
(*See also* Diesel-electric locomotives, effect of World War II)
U.S. Railroad Labor Board (RLB), 315
United States Steel Corp., 28, 169
United Transportation Union (UTU), 338
Universal Machine Language Equipment Register (UMLER), 339

Urban Mass Transit Administration (UMTA), 312
Utica & Schenectady Railroad, 249

Van, brake (*see* Cabooses)
Vandalia Railroad, 212
Van Depoele, Charles, 310
Vanderbilt, Cornelius, 104, 115, 119, 131–133, 141, 341–343
Vanderbilt, William Henry, 130–132, 155, 213, 214, 239, 253, 314, 342
Van Horne, William Cornelius, 155, 343–344
Van Rensselaer, Stephen, 235
Van Sweringen, Mantis J., 239
Van Sweringen, Oris P., 239
Vauclain, Samuel M., 18–19, 201
Vaughan, Abbie G., 357
Vaughan, H. H., 307
Velocipedes (section cars), 58–59
VIA Rail Canada, Inc. (VRC), 344–345
Video display terminals, 345
Vilas, Royal C., 145
Villard, Henry, 67, 345–346
Vincennes (locomotive), 248
Virginia & Truckee Railroad, 143, 146, 227, 229
Virginia Central Railway, 65
Virginian Railway, 97, 216, 238, 239, 253, 307
Vixen (locomotive), 201

Wabash, St. Louis & Pacific Railroad, 142
"Wabash Cannonball, The," 20, 156
Wabash Railway (Wab), 130–132, 166, 239
Wages, 38–40, 89, 90, 121, 133, 237, 265, 312, 313, 359
Wagner, Webster, 265, 347
Wallace, Lew, 255, 283
War Production Board (WPB), 96
Warman, Cyrus, 347–348
Warren, Earl, 52
Washburn, Nathan, 353
Washington, George, 64, 65, 121, 309
Watches, 18, 19, 22, 32, 159, 309
(*See also* Standard time)
Water tanks and water towers (landmarks), 348
Watered stock, origin of term, 104
Waterloo Railroad, 164
Waters, Don, 117
Watkins, Hays T., 82
Watson, T. B., 48
Watt, Thomas E., 252
Webb, Simeon T. (Sim), 61, 233
Welded rail, 348–349
Welland Railway, 167
Wellington (Wash.) avalanche, 60, 349–350
Wells Fargo & Co., 113, 230
West Albany (N.Y.) shops, 236
West Point Foundry, 200, 237
West Point Route of the Atlanta & West Point Railway, 72, 128, 226, 260
Western & Atlantic Railway, 7, 8
Western Maryland Railway, (WM), 64, 65, 130, 350–351
Western North Carolina Railroad (WNC), 351
Western Pacific Railroad (WP), 130, 216, 351–353
Western Railroader, The (magazine), 255
Western Railway of Alabama, 128, 226, 261
Western Union Telegraph Co., 133
Westinghouse, George, 66, 274, 279, 353
Westinghouse Electric Co., 95, 96, 246
Westminster Southern Railway, 125
Weyerhaeuser Co., 204, 205, 221
Wheat in hopper cars, 123
Wheeler, Charles T., 258
Wheeling & Lake Erie Railroad, 130
Wheels, 23, 353–354
Whistle stop (*see* Campaign trains)
Whistler, George Washington, 21, 354
Whistles, locomotive, 136, 354–355
Whitcomb locomotives, 19
White, Stanford, 251
White Pass & Yukon Route (WP&Y), 155, 166, 355–356, 360
Whitney, Alexander H., 356
Whitney, Asa, 356
Whitney, Silas, 181
Who's Who in Railroading and Rail Transit, 264
Whyte, William, 125
Whyte locomotive classification, 305, 306
Wild animals (*see* Animals, wild)
Wilder, Rufus A., 273
Wilgus, William J., 134
Willamette Iron & Steel Co., 204
Willard, Daniel, 23
William R. Smith (locomotive), 9
Williams, Nat, 48
Willkie, Wendell, 52
Wilmington, Baltimore & Washington Railroad, 23
Wilson, Col. A. I., 225
Wilson, John (Alf), 8
Wilson, Woodrow, 42, 153, 358
Winans, Ross, 50, 356–357
Windsor (trainferry), 133
Wiscasset, Waterville & Farmington Railway, 215
Wisconsin Central Railroad, 295
Witt, Peter, 311
Wolley, Leonide, 145
Wellover Oil Co., 243
Women, 357
trains named for, 357
(*See also* Heroes and heroines)
Woodard, William E., 182
Woodruff, Theodore T., 265, 357–358
Woodstock Railroad, last run of, 38
Woodworth, Charles J., 39
Wootten, John E., 50
Work rules (featherbedding), 116
World War I, 93–94, 358–359
World War II, 53, 96, 158, 180, 203, 356, 359–360
World's slowest train, 360
"Wreck of the Old 97, The,", 360–361
Wreckdozer, 361
Wrecks, train, 362
four-train wreck, 121
freak wreck, 205
(*See also specific location of wreck*)
Wright, Thomas J., 245
"Wrong side of the railroad track," 362
Wurtz, Maurice, 91
Wurtz, William, 91
Wyes and turntables (*see* Turntables and wyes)

Yards, railroad, 363–364
freight classification, 56
Yazoo & Mississippi Valley Railroad, 163
YMCAs, railroad, 365
Yoakum, Benjamin Franklin, 280
Yonah (locomotive), 8, 9
York (locomotive), 22
Young, Brigham, 284
Young, Robert R., 236
Younger brothers (train robbers), 172

Zephyr trains, 42, 66, 95, 229, 309, 352
Zulu cars, 197, 297, 365
(*See also* Colonist cars)

Freeman Hubbard qualifies as an authority on railroading with his 36 years as editor in chief of *Railroad Men's Magazine* (founded in 1906) and its successor, *Railroad Magazine,* plus 6 additional years on its staff, and currently as editor emeritus of the merged *Railfan & Railroad.* Hundreds of his articles on railroading have appeared in magazines and newspapers. He has also written seven books, including *Railroad Avenue* (McGraw-Hill, 1945; history and lore), *Great Trains of All Time,* and *Great Days of the Circus,* coauthored *Pennsylvania Songs and Legends* and *The Railroad Caboose,* reviewed railroad books for *The New York Times,* and helped to compile an album of railroad songs. The Railway and Locomotive Historical Society awarded him the only two medals it ever issued for two successive years of distinctive achievement.

Hubbard's literary heritage was the Hubbard Bros. (book) Publishing Company, founded in 1868 by his grandfather and a great-uncle and still functioning when he was a small boy. He became interested in railroading through his father, Walter W. Hubbard, a Pennsylvania Railroad employee for 43 years, and an uncle who was confidential secretary to a president of that system. His wife, the former Naomi Critchett, was the daughter of Charles Critchett, who for many years operated a railroad car that took federal government supplies to Indian reservations.